Acclaim for the First Edition: *Applied Microsoft .NET Framework Programming*

The time Jeffrey spent with the .NET Framework is evident in this well-written and informative book.

— **Eric Rudder** *(senior vice president, developer and platform evangelism, Microsoft)*

Jeff has worked directly with the folks who built the CLR [common language runtime] on a daily basis and has written the finest book on the internals of the CLR that you'll find anywhere.

— **Dennis Angeline** *(lead program manager, common language runtime, Microsoft)*

Jeff brings his years of Windows programming experience and insight to explain how the .NET Framework really works, why we built it the way we did, and how you can get the most out of it.

— **Brad Abrams** *(lead program manager, .NET Framework, Microsoft)*

Jeff Richter brings his well-known flair for explaining complicated material clearly, concisely, and accurately to the new areas of the C# language, the .NET Framework, and the .NET common language runtime. This is a must-have book for anyone wanting to understand the whys and hows behind these important new technologies.

— **Jim Miller** *(lead program manager, common language runtime kernel, Microsoft)*

Easily the best book on the common language runtime. The chapter on the CLR garbage collector [Chapter 19 in the first edition, now Chapter 20] is awesome. Jeff not only describes the theory of how the garbage collector works but also discusses aspects of finalization that every .NET developer should know.

— **Mahesh Prakriya** *(lead program manager, common language runtime team, Microsoft)*

This book is an accurate, in-depth, yet readable exploration of the common language runtime. It's one of those rare books that seems to anticipate the reader's question and supply the answer in the very next paragraph. The writing is excellent.

— **Jim Hogg** *(program manager, common language runtime team, Microsoft)*

Just as *Programming Applications for Microsoft Windows* became the must-have book for Win32 programmers, *Applied Microsoft .NET Programming* promises to be the same for serious .NET Framework programmers. This book is unique in its bottom-up approach to understanding .NET Framework programming. By providing the reader with a solid understanding of lower-level CLR concepts, Jeff provides the groundwork needed to write solid, secure, high-performing managed code applications quickly and easily.

— **Steven Pratschner** (*program manager, common language runtime team, Microsoft*)

Jeff Richter, he the MAN!

— **Anonymous** (*program manager, common language runtime, Microsoft*)

Microsoft®

CLR via C#, Second Edition

Jeffrey Richter (Wintellect)
Foreword by Aidan Richter

PUBLISHED BY
Microsoft Press
A Division of Microsoft Corporation
One Microsoft Way
Redmond, Washington 98052-6399

Library of Congress Control Number 2005936868

Printed and bound in the United States of America.

1 2 3 4 5 6 7 8 9 QWT 8 7 6

Distributed in Canada by H.B. Fenn and Company Ltd.
A CIP catalogue record for this book is available from the British Library.

Microsoft Press books are available through booksellers and distributors worldwide. For further information about international editions, contact your local Microsoft Corporation office or contact Microsoft Press International directly at fax (425) 936-7329. Visit our Web site at www.microsoft.com/mspress. Send comments to mspinput@microsoft.com.

Acquisitions Editor: Ben Ryan
Project Editor: Devon Musgrave
Indexer: William S. Myers

Body Part No. X11-53580

To Kristin

Words cannot express how I feel about our life together. I cherish our family and all our adventures. I'm filled each day with love for you.

To Aidan

You have been an inspiration to me and have taught me to play and have fun. Watching you grow up has been so rewarding and enjoyable for me. I feel lucky to be able to partake in your life; it has made me a better person.

Contents at a Glance

Contents

Part IV Essential Types

11 Chars, Strings, and Working with Text 241

12 Enumerated Types and Bit Flags 285

13 Arrays 295

Part V   CLR Facilities

What do you think of this book?
We want to hear from you!

Microsoft is interested in hearing your feedback about this publication so we can
continually improve our books and learning resources for you. To participate in a brief
online survey, please visit: *www.microsoft.com/learning/booksurvey/*

Foreword

For this book, I decided to ask my son Aidan to write the foreword. Aidan is almost three years old, but he has been hearing about the common language runtime, the C# programming language, and the Framework Class Library since his birth. By now, he must have picked up a lot of knowledge by way of osmosis. One day, I was sure that if he heard about exception handling one more time, he would just vomit. Turns out I was right.

Aidan has also known me his whole life, and I thought it might be appropriate for him to include a few words about me in the foreword. After explaining to Aidan what a foreword is and what I'd like him to write about, I let him sit on my lap in my office and type away. At first he seemed to be experiencing writer's block, so I started him off, but then he took it from there. As his father, I am impressed with his eloquent prose. I feel that his thoughts are heartfelt and truly reflect how he feels about me and the .NET Framework.

> *The .NET Framework is a fantastic technology that makes developers more productive and my daddy explains it in such a way that iiiiiiiiiiiiiiiiiiiiiiiiiiiiiiiiiiiiiiiiiiiiiiiiiiiiiiiiiiiiiiiiiiiiiiiiiiiiiiiiiiiiiiiiiiiiiiiioiiiiiiiiiiiiiiiiiii iiiiiiiiiiiiiiiiiit*
>
> *k*
>
> *fgh lkhiuhr ,g463wh /'[]*
>
> *| \0oj   c ';sdf   vc 87*
>
> *'o c.kll/k; bnyu, hjk jvc bmjkmjmbm , yfg b bvxufjv5rbhig ikhjvc bkti h thbt gl;hn ;gkkjgfhjj nbioljhlnfmhklknjmvgib*
>
> *9h*
>
> *— Aidan Richter, December 19, 2005*

Introduction

Over the years, Microsoft has introduced various technologies to help developers architect and implement code. Many of these technologies offer abstractions that allow developers to think about solving their problems more and think about the machine and operating system less. Here are some examples:

- The Microsoft Foundation Class library (MFC) offered a C++ abstraction over GUI programming. Using MFC, developers could focus more on what their program should do and they can focus less on message loops, window procedures, window classes, and so on.

- With Microsoft Visual Basic 6 and earlier, developers also had an abstraction that made it easier to build GUI applications. This abstraction technology served a purpose similar to MFC but was geared towards developers programming in Basic, and it gave different emphasis to the various parts of GUI programming.

- Microsoft's ASP technology offered an abstraction allowing developers to build active and dynamic Web sites by using Visual Basic Script or JScript. ASP allowed developers to focus more on the Web page content and less on the network communications.

- Microsoft's Active Template Library (ATL) offered an abstraction allowing developers to more easily create components that could be used by developers working in multiple programming languages.

You'll notice that each of these abstraction technologies was designed to make it easier for developers focusing on a particular scenario such as GUI applications, Web applications, or components. If a developer wanted to build a Web site that used a component, the developer would have to learn multiple abstraction technologies: ASP and ATL. Furthermore, the developer would have to be proficient in multiple programming languages since ASP required either Visual Basic Script or JScript, and ATL required C++. So while these abstraction technologies were created to help us, they were still requiring developers to learn a lot. And frequently, the various abstraction technologies weren't originally designed to work together, so developers fought integration issues.

Microsoft's goal for the .NET Framework is to fix all of this. You'll notice that each of the aforementioned abstraction technologies was designed to make a particular application scenario easier. With the .NET Framework, Microsoft's goal is not to provide an abstraction technology for developers building a particular kind of application, Microsoft's goal is to provide an abstraction technology for the platform or Microsoft Windows operating system itself. In other words, the .NET Framework raises the abstraction level for any and all kinds of applications. This means that there is a single programming model and set of APIs that developers will use regardless of whether they are building a console application, graphical application, Web site, or even components for use by any of these application types.

Another goal of the .NET Framework is to allow developers to work in the programming language of their choice. It is now possible to build a Web site and components that all use a single language such as Visual Basic or Microsoft's relatively new C# programming language.

Having a single programming model, API set, and programming language is a huge improvement in abstraction technologies, and this goes a very long way toward helping developers. However, it gets even better because these features also mean that integration issues also go away, which greatly improves testing, deployment, administration, versioning, and re-usability and re-purposing of code. Now that I have been using the .NET Framework myself for several years, I can tell you for sure that I would never go back to the old abstraction technologies and the old ways of software development. If I were being forced to do this, I'd change careers! This is how painful it would be for me now. In fact, when I think back to all of the programming I did using the old technologies, I just can't believe that we programmers put up with it for as long as we did.

The Development Platform: The .NET Framework

The .NET Framework consists of two parts: the common language runtime (CLR) and the Framework Class Library (FCL). The CLR provides the programming model that all application types will use. The CLR includes its own file loader, memory manager (the garbage collector), security system (code access security), thread pool, and so on. In addition, the CLR offers an object-oriented programming model that defines what types and objects are and how they behave.

The Framework Class Library provides an object-oriented API set that all application models will use. It includes type definitions that allow developers to perform file and network I/O, scheduling tasks on other threads, drawing shapes, comparing strings, and so on. Of course, all of these type definitions follow the programming model set forth by the CLR.

Microsoft has actually released three versions of the .NET Framework:

- The .NET Framework version 1.0 shipped in 2002 and included version 7.0 of Microsoft's C# compiler.

- The .NET Framework version 1.1 shipped in 2003 and included version 7.1 of Microsoft's C# compiler.

- The .NET Framework version 2.0 shipped in 2005 and included version 8.0 of Microsoft's C# compiler.

This book focuses exclusively on the .NET Framework version 2.0 and Microsoft's C# compiler version 8.0. Since Microsoft tries to maintain a large degree of backward compatibility when releasing a new version of the .NET Framework, many of the things I discuss in this book do apply to earlier versions, but I have not made any attempts to address things that are specific to earlier versions.

Version 2.0 of the .NET Framework includes support for 32-bit x86 versions of Windows as well as for 64-bit x64 and IA64 versions of Windows. A "lite" version of the .NET Framework, called the .NET Compact Framework, is also available for PDAs (such as Windows CE) and appliances (small devices). On December 13, 2001, the European Computer Manufacturers Association (ECMA) accepted the C# programming language, portions of the CLR, and portions of the FCL as standards. The standards documents that resulted from this has allowed other organizations to build ECMA-compliant versions of these technologies for other CPU architectures as well as other operating systems. Actually, much of the content in this book is about these standards, and therefore, many will find this book useful for working with any runtime/library implementation that adheres to the ECMA standard. However, this book focuses specifically on Microsoft's implementation of this standard for desktop and server systems.

Microsoft Windows Vista ships with version 2.0 of the .NET Framework, but earlier versions of Windows do not. However, if you want your .NET Framework application to run on earlier versions of Windows, you will be required to install it manually. Fortunately, Microsoft does make a .NET Framework redistribution file that you're allowed to freely distribute with your application.

The .NET Framework allows developers to take advantage of technologies more than any earlier Microsoft development platform did. Specifically, the .NET Framework really delivers on code reuse, code specialization, resource management, multilanguage development, security, deployment, and administration. While designing this new platform, Microsoft also felt that it was necessary to improve on some of the deficiencies of the current Windows platform. The following list gives you just a small sampling of what the CLR and the FCL provide:

■ **Consistent programming model** Unlike today, when commonly some operating system facilities are accessed via dynamic-link library (DLL) functions and other facilities are accessed via COM objects, all application services are offered via a common object-oriented programming model.

■ **Simplified programming model** The CLR seeks to greatly simplify the plumbing and arcane constructs required by Win32 and COM. Specifically, the CLR now frees the developer from having to understand any of the following concepts: the registry, globally unique identifiers (GUIDs), **IUnknown**, **AddRef**, **Release**, **HRESULT**s, and so on. The CLR doesn't just abstract these concepts away from the developer; these concepts simply don't exist in any form in the CLR. Of course, if you want to write a .NET Framework application that interoperates with existing, non-.NET code, you must still be aware of these concepts.

■ **Run once, run always** All Windows developers are familiar with "DLL hell" versioning problems. This situation occurs when components being installed for a new application overwrite components of an old application, causing the old application to exhibit strange behavior or stop functioning altogether. The architecture of the .NET Framework now isolates application components so that an application always loads the components that it was built and tested with. If the application runs after installation, the application should always run.

- **Simplified deployment** Today, Windows applications are incredibly difficult to set up and deploy. Several files, registry settings, and shortcuts usually need to be created. In addition, completely uninstalling an application is nearly impossible. With Windows 2000, Microsoft introduced a new installation engine that helps with all of these issues, but it's still possible that a company authoring a Microsoft installer package might fail to do everything correctly. The .NET Framework seeks to banish these issues into history. The .NET Framework components are not referenced by the registry. In fact, installing most .NET Framework applications requires no more than copying the files to a directory and adding a shortcut to the Start menu, desktop, or Quick Launch toolbar. Uninstalling the application is as simple as deleting the files.

- **Wide platform reach** When compiling source code for the .NET Framework, the compilers produce common intermediate language (CIL) instead of the more traditional CPU instructions. At run time, the CLR translates the CIL into native CPU instructions. Because the translation to native CPU instructions is done at run time, the translation is done for the host CPU. This means that you can deploy your .NET Framework application on any machine that has an ECMA-compliant version of the CLR and FCL running on it. These machines can be x86, x64, IA64, and so on. Users will immediately appreciate the value of this broad execution if they ever change their computing hardware or operating system.

- **Programming language integration** COM allows different programming languages to *interoperate* with one another. The .NET Framework allows languages to be *integrated* with one another so that you can use types of another language as if they were your own. For example, the CLR makes it possible to create a class in C++ that derives from a class implemented in Visual Basic. The CLR allows this because it defines and provides a Common Type System (CTS) that all programming languages that target the CLR must use. The Common Language Specification (CLS) describes what compiler implementers must do in order for their languages to integrate well with other languages. Microsoft is itself providing several compilers that produce code that targets the runtime: C++/CLI, C#, Visual Basic .NET, and JScript. In addition, companies other than Microsoft and academic institutions are producing compilers for other languages that also target the CLR.

- **Simplified code reuse** Using the mechanisms described earlier, you can create your own classes that offer services to third-party applications. This makes it extremely simple to reuse code and also creates a large market for component vendors.

- **Automatic memory management (garbage collection)** Programming requires great skill and discipline, especially when it comes to managing the use of resources such as files, memory, screen space, network connections, database resources, and so on. One of the most common bugs is neglecting to free one of these resources, ultimately causing the application to perform improperly at some unpredictable time. The CLR automatically tracks resource usage, guaranteeing that your application will never leak resources. In fact, there is no way to explicitly "free" memory. In Chapter 20, "Automatic Memory Management (Garbage Collection)," I explain exactly how garbage collection works.

- **Type-safe verification** The CLR can verify that all of your code is type-safe. Type safety ensures that allocated objects are always accessed in compatible ways. Hence, if a method input parameter is declared as accepting a 4-byte value, the CLR will detect and trap attempts to access the parameter as an 8-byte value. Similarly, if an object occupies 10 bytes in memory, the application can't coerce the object into a form that will allow more than 10 bytes to be read. Type safety also means that execution flow will transfer only to well-known locations (that is, method entry points). There is no way to construct an arbitrary reference to a memory location and cause code at that location to start executing. Together, these measures ensure type safety, which eliminates many common programming errors and classic security attacks (for example, exploiting buffer overruns).

- **Rich debugging support** Because the CLR is used for many programming languages, it is now much easier to implement portions of your application by using the language best suited to a particular task. The CLR fully supports debugging applications that cross language boundaries.

- **Consistent method failure paradigm** One of the most annoying aspects of Windows programming is the inconsistent style that functions use to report failures. Some functions return Win32 status codes, some functions return **HRESULT**s, and some functions throw exceptions. In the CLR, all failures are reported via exceptions—period. Exceptions allow the developer to isolate the failure recovery code from the code required to get the work done. This separation greatly simplifies writing, reading, and maintaining code. In addition, exceptions work across module and programming language boundaries. And, unlike status codes and **HRESULT**s, exceptions can't be ignored. The CLR also provides built-in stack-walking facilities, making it much easier to locate any bugs and failures.

- **Security** Traditional operating system security provides isolation and access control based on user accounts. This model has proven useful but at its core assumes that all code is equally trustworthy. This assumption was justified when all code was installed from physical media (for example, CD-ROM) or trusted corporate servers. But with the increasing reliance on mobile code such as Web scripts, applications downloaded over the Internet, and e-mail attachments, we need ways to control the behavior of applications in a more code-centric manner. Code access security provides a means to do this.

- **Interoperability** Microsoft realizes that developers already have an enormous amount of existing code and components. Rewriting all of this code to take full advantage of the .NET Framework platform would be a huge undertaking and would prevent the speedy adoption of this platform. So the .NET Framework fully supports the ability for developers to access their existing COM components as well as call Win32 functions in existing DLLs.

Users won't directly appreciate the CLR and its capabilities, but they will certainly notice the quality and features of applications that utilize the CLR. In addition, users and your company's bottom line will appreciate how the CLR allows applications to be developed and deployed more rapidly and with less administration than Windows has ever allowed in the past.

The Development Environment: Microsoft Visual Studio

Visual Studio is Microsoft's development environment. Microsoft has been working on it for many years and has incorporated a lot of .NET Framework–specific features into it. Like any good development environment, Visual Studio includes a project manager; a source code editor; UI designers; lots of wizards, compilers, linkers, tools, and utilities; documentation; and debuggers. It supports building applications for both the 32-bit and 64-bit Windows platforms as well as for the .NET Framework platform. Another important improvement is that there is now just one integrated development environment for all programming languages and application types.

Microsoft also provides a .NET Framework SDK. This free SDK includes all of the language compilers, a bunch of tools, and a lot of documentation. Using this SDK, you can develop applications for the .NET Framework without using Visual Studio. You'll just have to use your own editor and project management system. You also don't get drag-and-drop Web Forms and Windows Forms building. I use Visual Studio regularly and will refer to it throughout this book. However, this book is mostly about .NET Framework and C# programming in general, so Visual Studio isn't required to learn, use, and understand the concepts I present in each chapter.

The Goal of This Book

The purpose of this book is to explain how to develop applications and reusable classes for the .NET Framework. Specifically, this means that I intend to explain how the CLR works and the facilities it offers. I'll also discuss various parts of the FCL. No book could fully explain the FCL—it contains literally thousands of types, and this number is growing at an alarming rate. So, here I'm concentrating on the core types that every developer needs to be aware of. And while this book isn't specifically about Windows Forms, XML Web services, Web Forms, and so on, the technologies presented in the book are applicable to *all* of these application types.

With this book, I'm not attempting to teach you any particular programming language, although I use the C# programming in order to demonstrate features of the CLR and to access types in the FCL. I'm sure that you will learn a lot about C# as you go through this book, but it is not a goal of this book to teach C#. Furthermore, I assume that you are already familiar with object-oriented programming concepts such as data abstraction, inheritance, and polymorphism. A good understanding of these concepts is critical because the CLR offers an object-oriented programming model, and all of its features are exposed using this paradigm. If you're not familiar with these concepts, I strongly suggest that you first find a book that teaches these concepts.

Sample Code and System Requirements

The samples presented in this book can be downloaded from *http://Wintellect.com*. To build and run the samples, you'll need the .NET Framework 2.0 (and a version of Windows that supports it) and the .NET Framework SDK.

This Book Has No Mistakes

This section's title clearly states what I want to say. But we all know that it is a flat-out lie. My reviewers, editors, and I have worked hard to bring you the most accurate, up-to-date, in-depth, easy-to-read, painless-to-understand, bug-free information. Even with the fantastic team assembled, things inevitably slip through the cracks. If you find any mistakes in this book (especially bugs), I would greatly appreciate it if you would send the mistakes to me at *JeffreyR@Wintellect.com.*

Acknowledgments

I couldn't have written this book without the help and technical assistance of many people. In particular, I'd like to thank the following people:

- **My family**   The amount of time and effort than goes into writing a book is hard to measure. All I know is that I could not have produced this book without the support of Kristin (my wife) and Aidan (my son). There were many times when we wanted to spend time together but were unable to due to book obligations. Now that the book project is completed, I really look forward to adventures we will all share together.

- **My technical reviewers and editors**   For this book revision, I truly had some fantastic people helping me. Christophe Nasarre has done just a phenomenal job of verifying my work and making sure that I'd said everything the best way it could possibly be said. He has truly had a significant impact on the quality of this book. Also, I'd like to extend a special thanks to Jamie Haddock. Jamie read the first edition of my book and e-mailed me numerous suggestions for ways to improve it. I saved all of these and then asked him to be part of the formal review process while writing the second edition of this book. Jamie's contribution is also quite significant. I'd also like to thank Stan Lippman and Clemens Szyperski for their review and the lively discussions we had. Finally, I'd like to thank Paul Mehner for his feedback.

- **Members of the Microsoft Press editorial team**   The Microsoft Press people that I had the most contact with are Devon Musgrave and Joel Rosenthal. Both of them were an extreme pleasure to work with and made sure that things ran smoothly and did their best to make my words read good (except for this sentence ☺). Of course, I'd also thank Ben Ryan, my acquisitions editor, for ushering the contract through. Finally, I'd also like to thank other Microsoft Press people who had a hand in this project, including Kerri Devault, Elizabeth Hansford, Dan Latimer, Patricia Masserman, Bill Myers, Joel Panchot, Sandi Resnick, and William Teel.

- **Wintellectuals**   Finally, I'd like to thank the members of my extended Wintellect family for being patient as I took time away from the business to work on this project. In particular, I'd like to thank Jim Bail, Jason Clark, Paula Daniels, Peter DeBetta, Sara Faatz, Todd Fine, Lewis Frazer, Dorothy McBay, Jeff Prosise, John Robbins, and Justin Smith.

Support

Every effort has been made to ensure the accuracy of this book. Microsoft Press provides corrections for books through the World Wide Web at the following address:

http://www.microsoft.com/mspress/support/

To connect directly to the Microsoft Press Knowledge Base and enter a query regarding a question or issue that you may have, go to:

http://www.microsoft.com/mspress/support/search.asp

If you have comments, questions, or ideas regarding this book, please send them to Microsoft Press using either of the following methods:

Postal Mail:

Microsoft Press
Attn: *CLR Via C#* Editor
One Microsoft Way
Redmond, WA 98052-6399

E-Mail:

mspinput@microsoft.com

Please note that product support is not offered through the above mail addresses. For support information regarding C#, Visual Studio, or the .NET Framework, visit the Microsoft Product Standard Support Web site at:

http://support.microsoft.com

Part I
CLR Basics

Chapter 1
The CLR's Execution Model

The Microsoft .NET Framework introduces many new concepts, technologies, and terms. My goal in this chapter is to give you an overview of how the .NET Framework is designed, introduce you to some of the new technologies the framework includes, and define many of the terms you'll be seeing when you start using it. I'll also take you through the process of building your source code into an application or a set of redistributable components (files) that contain types (classes, structures, etc.) and then explain how your application will execute.

Compiling Source Code into Managed Modules

OK, so you've decided to use the .NET Framework as your development platform. Great! Your first step is to determine what type of application or component you intend to build. Let's just assume that you've completed this minor detail; everything is designed, the specifications are written, and you're ready to start development.

Now you must decide which programming language to use. This task is usually difficult because different languages offer different capabilities. For example, in unmanaged C/C++, you have pretty low-level control of the system. You can manage memory exactly the way you want to, create threads easily if you need to, and so on. Microsoft Visual Basic 6, on the other hand, allows you to build UI applications very rapidly and makes it easy for you to control COM objects and databases.

The common language runtime (CLR) is just what its name says it is; a runtime that is usable by different and varied programming languages. The features of the CLR are available to any and all programming languages that target it—period. For example, the runtime uses exceptions to

3

report errors, so all languages that target the runtime also get errors reported via exceptions. Another example is that the runtime also allows you to create a thread, so any language that targets the runtime can create a thread.

In fact, at runtime, the CLR has no idea which programming language the developer used for the source code. This means that you should choose whatever programming language allows you to express your intentions most easily. You can develop your code in any programming language you desire as long as the compiler you use to compile your code targets the CLR.

So, if what I say is true, what is the advantage of using one programming language over another? Well, I think of compilers as syntax checkers and "correct code" analyzers. They examine your source code, ensure that whatever you've written makes some sense, and then output code that describes your intention. Different programming languages allow you to develop using different syntax. Don't underestimate the value of this choice. For mathematical or financial applications, expressing your intentions by using APL syntax can save many days of development time when compared to expressing the same intention by using Perl syntax, for example.

Microsoft has created several language compilers that target the runtime: C++/CLI, C# (pronounced "C sharp"), Visual Basic, JScript, J# (a Java language compiler), and an Intermediate Language (IL) Assembler. In addition to Microsoft, several other companies, colleges, and universities have created compilers that produce code to target the CLR. I'm aware of compilers for Ada, APL, Caml, COBOL, Eiffel, Forth, Fortran, Haskell, Lexico, LISP, LOGO, Lua, Mercury, ML, Mondrian, Oberon, Pascal, Perl, Php, Prolog, Python, RPG, Scheme, Smalltalk, and Tcl/Tk.

Figure 1-1 shows the process of compiling source code files. As the figure shows, you can create source code files written in any programming language that supports the CLR. Then you use the corresponding compiler to check the syntax and analyze the source code. Regardless of which compiler you use, the result is a *managed module*. A managed module is a standard 32-bit Microsoft Windows portable executable (PE32) file or a standard 64-bit Windows portable executable (PE32+) file that requires the CLR to execute.

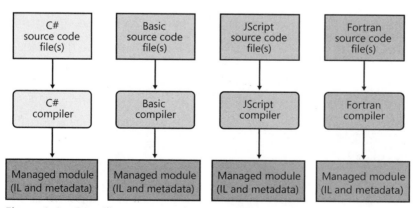

Figure 1-1   Compiling source code into managed modules

Table 1-1 describes the parts of a managed module.

Table 1-1   Parts of a Managed Module

Part	Description
PE32 or PE32+ header	The standard Windows PE file header, which is similar to the Common Object File Format (COFF) header. If the header uses the PE32 format, the file can run on a 32-bit or 64-bit version of Windows. If the header uses the PE32+ format, the file requires a 64-bit version of Windows to run. This header also indicates the type of file: GUI, CUI, or DLL, and contains a timestamp indicating when the file was built. For modules that contain only IL code, the bulk of the information in the PE32(+) header is ignored. For modules that contain native CPU code, this header contains information about the native CPU code.
CLR header	Contains the information (interpreted by the CLR and utilities) that makes this a managed module. The header includes the version of the CLR required, some flags, the `MethodDef` metadata token of the managed module's entry point method (`Main` method), and the location/size of the module's metadata, resources, strong name, some flags, and other less interesting stuff.
Metadata	Every managed module contains metadata tables. There are two main types of tables: tables that describe the types and members defined in your source code and tables that describe the types and members referenced by your source code.
Intermediate Language (IL) code	Code the compiler produced as it compiled the source code. At run time, the CLR compiles the IL into native CPU instructions.

Native code compilers produce code targeted to a specific CPU architecture, such as x86, x64, or IA64. All CLR-compliant compilers produce Intermediate Language (IL) code instead. (I'll go into more detail about IL code later in this chapter.) IL code is sometimes referred to as *managed code* because the CLR manages its execution.

In addition to emitting IL, every compiler targeting the CLR is required to emit full *metadata* into every managed module. In brief, metadata is a set of data tables that describe what is defined in the module, such as types and their members. In addition, metadata also has tables indicating what the managed module references, such as imported types and their members. Metadata is a superset of older technologies such as Type Libraries and Interface Definition Language (IDL) files. The important thing to note is that CLR metadata is far more complete. And, unlike Type Libraries and IDL, metadata is always associated with the file that contains the IL code. In fact, the metadata is always embedded in the same EXE/DLL as the code, making it impossible to separate the two. Because the compiler produces the metadata and the code at the same time and binds them into the resulting managed module, the metadata and the IL code it describes are never out of sync with one another.

Metadata has many uses. Here are some of them:

- Metadata removes the need for header and library files when compiling because all the information about the referenced types/members is contained in the file that has the IL that implements the type/members. Compilers can read metadata directly from managed modules.

- Microsoft Visual Studio uses metadata to help you write code. Its IntelliSense feature parses metadata to tell you what methods, properties, events, and fields a type offers, and in the case of a method, what parameters the method expects.

- The CLR's code verification process uses metadata to ensure that your code performs only "safe" operations. (I'll discuss verification shortly.)

- Metadata allows an object's fields to be serialized into a memory block, sent to another machine, and then deserialized, re-creating the object's state on the remote machine.

- Metadata allows the garbage collector to track the lifetime of objects. For any object, the garbage collector can determine the type of the object and, from the metadata, know which fields within that object refer to other objects.

In Chapter 2, "Building, Packaging, Deploying, and Administering Applications and Types," I'll describe metadata in much more detail.

Microsoft's C#, Visual Basic, JScript, J#, and the IL Assembler always produce modules that contain managed code (IL) and managed data (garbage-collected data types). End users must have the CLR (presently shipping as part of the .NET Framework) installed on their machine in order to execute any modules that contain managed code and/or managed data in the same way that they must have the Microsoft Foundation Class (MFC) library or Visual Basic DLLs installed to run MFC or Visual Basic 6 applications.

By default, Microsoft's C++ compiler builds EXE/DLL modules that contain unmanaged code and unmanaged data. These modules don't require the CLR to execute. However, by specifying the **/CLR** command-line switch, the C++ compiler produces modules that contain managed code, and of course, the CLR must then be installed to execute this code. Of all of the Microsoft compilers mentioned, C++ is unique in that it is the only compiler that allows the developer to write both managed and unmanaged code and have it emitted into a single module. It is also the only Microsoft compiler that allows developers to define both managed and unmanaged data types in their source code. The flexibility provided by Microsoft's C++ compiler is unparalleled by other compilers because it allows developers to use their existing native C/C++ code from managed code and to start integrating the use of managed types as they see fit.

Combining Managed Modules into Assemblies

The CLR doesn't actually work with modules, it works with *assemblies*. An assembly is an abstract concept that can be difficult to grasp initially. First, an assembly is a logical grouping of one or more modules or resource files. Second, an assembly is the smallest unit of reuse, security, and versioning. Depending on the choices you make with your compilers or tools, you can produce a single-file or a multifile assembly. In the CLR world, an assembly is what we would call a *component*.

In Chapter 2, I'll go over assemblies in great detail, so I don't want to spend a lot of time on them here. All I want to do now is make you aware that there is this extra conceptual notion that offers a way to treat a group of files as a single entity.

Figure 1-2 should help explain what assemblies are about. In this figure, some managed modules and resource (or data) files are being processed by a tool. This tool produces a single PE32(+) file that represents the logical grouping of files. What happens is that this PE32(+) file contains a block of data called the *manifest*. The manifest is simply another set of metadata tables. These tables describe the files that make up the assembly, the publicly exported types implemented by the files in the assembly, and the resource or data files that are associated with the assembly.

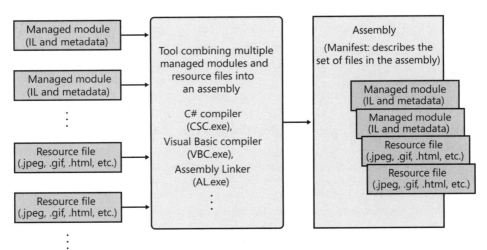

Figure 1-2 Combining managed modules into assemblies

By default, compilers actually do the work of turning the emitted managed module into an assembly; that is, the C# compiler emits a managed module that contains a manifest. The manifest indicates that the assembly consists of just the one file. So, for projects that have just one managed module and no resource (or data) files, the assembly will be the managed module, and you don't have any additional steps to perform during your build process. If you want to group a set of files into an assembly, you'll have to be aware of more tools (such as the assembly linker, AL.exe) and their command-line options. I'll explain these tools and options in Chapter 2.

An assembly allows you to decouple the logical and physical notions of a reusable, securable, versionable component. How you partition your code and resources into different files is completely up to you. For example, you could put rarely used types or resources in separate files that are part of an assembly. The separate files could be downloaded from the Web as needed.

If the files are never needed, they're never downloaded, saving disk space and reducing installation time. Assemblies allow you to break up the deployment of the files while still treating all of the files as a single collection.

An assembly's modules also include information about referenced assemblies (including their version numbers). This information makes an assembly *self-describing*. In other words, the CLR can determine the assembly's immediate dependencies in order for code in the assembly to execute. No additional information is required in the registry or in the Microsoft Active Directory directory service. Because no additional information is needed, deploying assemblies is much easier than deploying unmanaged components.

Loading the Common Language Runtime

Each assembly you build can be either an executable application or a DLL containing a set of types for use by an executable application. Of course, the CLR is responsible for managing the execution of code contained within these assemblies. This means that the .NET Framework must be installed on the host machine. Microsoft has created a redistribution package that you can freely ship to install the .NET Framework on your customers' machines. Some versions of Windows ship with the .NET Framework already installed.

You can tell if the .NET Framework has been installed by looking for the MSCorEE.dll file in the %SystemRoot%\system32 directory. The existence of this file tells you that the .NET Framework is installed. However, several versions of the .NET Framework can be installed on a single machine simultaneously. If you want to determine exactly which versions of the .NET Framework are installed, examine the subkeys whose names start with the lowercase letter "v" and are followed by a number under the following registry key:

```
HKEY_LOCAL_MACHINE\SOFTWARE\Microsoft\.NETFramework\policy
```

Starting with version 2.0 of the .NET Framework SDK, Microsoft also ships a command-line utility called CLRVer.exe that shows all of the CLR versions installed on a machine. This utility can also show which version of the CLR is being used by processes currently running on the machine by using the **-all** switch or passing the ID of the process you are interested in.

Before we start looking at how the CLR loads, we need to spend a moment discussing 32-bit and 64-bit versions of Windows. If your assembly files contain only type-safe managed code, you are writing code that should work on both 32-bit and 64-bit versions of Windows. No source code changes are required for your code to run on either version of Windows. In fact, the resulting EXE/DLL file produced by the compiler will run on 32-bit Windows as well as the x64 and IA64 versions of 64-bit Windows! In other words, the one file will run on any machine that has a version of the .NET Framework installed on it.

On extremely rare occasions, developers want to write code that works only on a specific version of Windows. Developers might do this when using unsafe code or when interoperating with unmanaged code that is targeted to a specific CPU architecture. To aid these developers, the C# compiler offers a **/platform** command-line switch. This switch allows you to specify whether the resulting assembly can run on x86 machines running 32-bit Windows versions only, x64 machines running 64-bit Windows only, or Intel Itanium machines running 64-bit Windows only. If you don't specify a platform, the default is **anycpu**, which indicates that the resulting assembly can run on any version of Windows. Users of Visual Studio can set a project's target platform by displaying the project's property pages, clicking the Build tab, and then selecting an option in the Platform Target list.

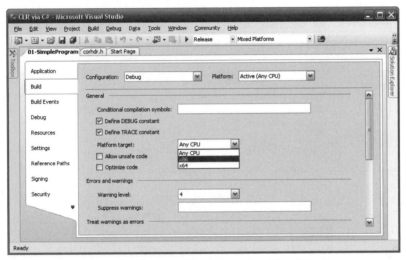

Figure 1-3   Setting the Platform Target by using Visual Studio

> **Note**   Visual Studio doesn't show the Itanium Platform Target in the list unless you are running the Visual Studio Team System version of Visual Studio. Because I was running Visual Studio Professional Edition when I took the screen shot in Figure 1-3, Itanium doesn't appear in the list.

Depending on the platform switch, the C# compiler will emit an assembly that contains either a PE32 or PE32+ header, and the compiler will also emit the desired CPU architecture (or agnostic) into the header as well. Microsoft ships two command-line utilities, DumpBin.exe and CorFlags.exe, that you can use to examine the header information emitted in a managed module by the compiler.

When running an executable file, Windows examines this EXE file's header to determine whether the application requires a 32-bit or 64-bit address space. A file with a PE32 header can run with a 32-bit or 64-bit address space, and a file with a PE32+ header requires a 64-bit address space. Windows also checks the CPU architecture information embedded inside the header to ensure that it matches the CPU type in the computer. Lastly, 64-bit versions of Windows offer a technology that allows 32-bit Windows applications to run. This technology is called *WoW64* (for Windows on Windows64). This technology even allows 32-bit applications with x86 native code in them to run on an Itanium machine, because the WoW64 technology can emulate the x86 instruction set; albeit with a significant performance cost.

Table 1-2 shows two things. First, it shows what kind of managed module you get when you specify various /platform command-line switches to the C# compiler. Second, it shows how that application will run on various versions of Windows.

Table 1-2   Effects of /platform on Resulting Module and at Run Time

/platform Switch	Resulting Managed Module	x86 Windows	x64 Windows	IA64 Windows
anycpu (the default)	PE32/agnostic	Runs as a 32-bit application	Runs as a 64-bit application	Runs as a 64-bit application
x86	PE32/x86	Runs as a 32-bit application	Runs as a WoW64 application	Runs as a WoW64 application
x64	PE32+/x64	Doesn't run	Runs as a 64-bit application	Doesn't run
Itanium	PE32+/Itanium	Doesn't run	Doesn't run	Runs as a 64-bit application

After Windows has examined the EXE file's header to determine whether to create a 32-bit process, a 64-bit process, or a WoW64 process, Windows loads the x86, x64, or IA64 version of MSCorEE.dll into the process's address space. On an x86 version of Windows, the x86 version of MSCorEE.dll can be found in the C:\Windows\System32 directory. On an x64 or IA64 version of Windows, the x86 version of MSCorEE.dll can be found in the C:\Windows\SysWow64 directory, whereas the 64-bit version (x64 or IA64) can be found in the C:\Windows\System32 directory (for backward compatibility reasons). Then, the process' primary thread calls a method defined inside MSCorEE.dll. This method initializes the CLR, loads the EXE assembly, and then calls its entry point method (**Main**). At this point, the managed application is up and running.

> **Note**   Assemblies built by using version 7.0 or 7.1 of Microsoft's C# compiler contain a PE32 header and are CPU-architecture agnostic. However, at load time, the CLR considers these assemblies to be x86 only. For executable files, this improves the likelihood of the application actually working on a 64-bit system because the executable file will load in the WoW64, giving the process an environment very similar to what it would have on a 32-bit x86 version of Windows.

If an unmanaged application calls **LoadLibrary** to load a managed assembly, Windows knows to load and initialize the CLR (if not already loaded) in order to process the code contained within the assembly. Of course, in this scenario, the process is already up and running, and this may limit the usability of the assembly. For example, a managed assembly compiled with the /platform:x86 switch will not be able to load into a 64-bit process at all, whereas an executable file compiled with this same switch would have loaded in WoW64 on a computer running a 64-bit version of Windows.

Executing Your Assembly's Code

As mentioned earlier, managed assemblies contain both metadata and Intermediate Language (IL). IL is a CPU-independent machine language created by Microsoft after consultation with several external commercial and academic language/compiler writers. IL is a much higher-level language than most CPU machine languages. IL can access and manipulate object types and has instructions to create and initialize objects, call virtual methods on objects, and manipulate array elements directly. It even has instructions to throw and catch exceptions for error handling. You can think of IL as an object-oriented machine language.

Usually, developers will program in a high-level language, such as C#, C++/CLI, or Visual Basic. The compilers for these high-level languages produce IL. However, as any other machine language, IL can be written in assembly language, and Microsoft does provide an IL Assembler, ILAsm.exe. Microsoft also provides an IL Disassembler, ILDasm.exe.

Keep in mind that any high-level language will most likely expose only a subset of the facilities offered by the CLR. However, the IL assembly language allows a developer to access all of the CLR's facilities. So, should your programming language of choice hide a facility the CLR offers that you really want to take advantage of, you can choose to write that portion of your code in IL assembly or perhaps another programming language that exposes the CLR feature you seek.

The only way for you to know what facilities the CLR offers is to read documentation specific to the CLR itself. In this book, I try to concentrate on CLR features and how they are exposed or not exposed by the C# language. I suspect that most other books and articles will present the CLR via a language perspective, and that most developers will come to believe that the CLR offers only what the developer's chosen language exposes. As long as your language allows you to accomplish what you're trying to get done, this blurred perspective isn't a bad thing.

> **Important**   I think this ability to switch programming languages easily with rich integration between languages is an awesome feature of the CLR. Unfortunately, I also believe that developers will often overlook this feature. Programming languages such as C# and Visual Basic are excellent languages for performing I/O operations. APL is a great language for performing advanced engineering or financial calculations. Through the CLR, you can write the I/O portions of your application in C# and then write the engineering calculations part in APL. The CLR offers a level of integration between these languages that is unprecedented and really makes mixed-language programming worthy of consideration for many development projects.

To execute a method, its IL must first be converted to native CPU instructions. This is the job of the CLR's JIT (just-in-time) compiler.

Figure 1-4 shows what happens the first time a method is called.

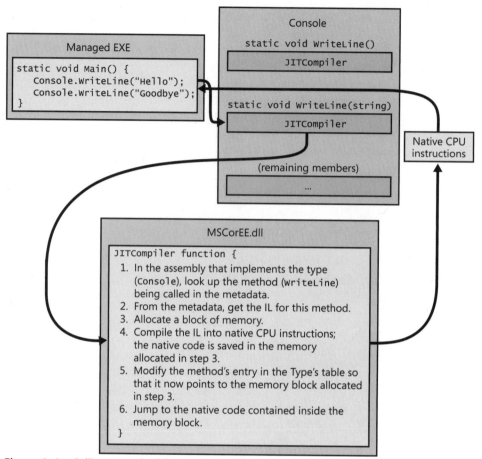

Figure 1-4   Calling a method for the first time

Just before the **Main** method executes, the CLR detects all of the types that are referenced by **Main**'s code. This causes the CLR to allocate an internal data structure that is used to manage access to the referenced types. In Figure 1-4, the **Main** method refers to a single type, **Console**, causing the CLR to allocate a single internal structure. This internal data structure contains an entry for each method defined by the **Console** type. Each entry holds the address where the method's implementation can be found. When initializing this structure, the CLR sets each entry to an internal, undocumented function contained inside the CLR itself. I call this function **JITCompiler**.

When **Main** makes its first call to **WriteLine**, the **JITCompiler** function is called. The **JITCompiler** function is responsible for compiling a method's IL code into native CPU instructions. Because the IL is being compiled "just in time," this component of the CLR is frequently referred to as a *JITter* or a *JIT compiler*.

Note   If the application is running on an x86 version of Windows or in the WoW64, the JIT compiler produces x86 instructions. If your application is running as a 64-bit application on an x64 or Itanium version of Windows, the JIT compiler produces x64 or IA64 instructions, respectively.

When called, the **JITCompiler** function knows what method is being called and what type defines this method. The **JITCompiler** function then searches the defining assembly's metadata for the called method's IL. **JITCompiler** next verifies and compiles the IL code into native CPU instructions. The native CPU instructions are saved in a dynamically allocated block of memory. Then, **JITCompiler** goes back to the entry for the called method in the type's internal data structure created by the CLR and replaces the reference that called it in the first place with the address of the block of memory containing the native CPU instructions it just compiled. Finally, the **JITCompiler** function jumps to the code in the memory block. This code is the implementation of the **WriteLine** method (the version that takes a **String** parameter). When this code returns, it returns to the code in **Main**, which continues execution as normal.

Main now calls **WriteLine** a second time. This time, the code for **WriteLine** has already been verified and compiled. So the call goes directly to the block of memory, skipping the **JITCompiler** function entirely. After the **WriteLine** method executes, it returns to **Main**. Figure 1-5 shows what the process looks like when **WriteLine** is called the second time.

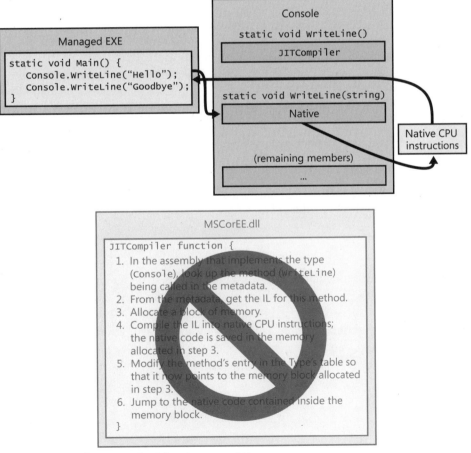

Figure 1-5   Calling a method for the second time

A performance hit is incurred only the first time a method is called. All subsequent calls to the method execute at the full speed of the native code because verification and compilation to native code don't need to be performed again.

The JIT compiler stores the native CPU instructions in dynamic memory. This means that the compiled code is discarded when the application terminates. So if you run the application again in the future or if you run two instances of the application simultaneously (in two different operating system processes), the JIT compiler will have to compile the IL to native instructions again.

For most applications, the performance hit incurred by JIT compiling isn't significant. Most applications tend to call the same methods over and over again. These methods will take the performance hit only once while the application executes. It's also likely that more time is spent inside the method than calling the method.

You should also be aware that the CLR's JIT compiler optimizes the native code just as the back end of an unmanaged C++ compiler does. Again, it may take more time to produce the optimized code, but the code will execute with much better performance than if it hadn't been optimized.

Note   There are two C# compiler switches that impact code optimization: /optimize and /debug. The following table shows the impact these switches have on the quality of the IL code generated by the C# compiler and the quality of the native code generated by the JIT compiler:

Compiler Switch Settings	C# IL Code Quality	JIT Native Code Quality
/optimize- /debug- (this is the default)	Unoptimized	Optimized
/optimize- /debug(+/full/pdbonly)	Unoptimized	Unoptimized
/optimize+ /debug(-/+/full/pdbonly)	Optimized	Optimized

For those developers coming from an unmanaged C or C++ background, you're probably thinking about the performance ramifications of all this. After all, unmanaged code is compiled for a specific CPU platform, and, when invoked, the code can simply execute. In this managed environment, compiling the code is accomplished in two phases. First, the compiler passes over the source code, doing as much work as possible in producing IL. But to execute the code, the IL itself must be compiled into native CPU instructions at run time, requiring more memory to be allocated and requiring additional CPU time to do the work.

Believe me, since I approached the CLR from a C/C++ background myself, I was quite skeptical and concerned about this additional overhead. The truth is that this second compilation stage that occurs at run time does hurt performance, and it does allocate dynamic memory. However, Microsoft has done a lot of performance work to keep this additional overhead to a minimum.

> **Note**   When producing unoptimized IL code, the C# compiler will emit NOP (no-operation) instructions into the code. The NOP instructions are emitted to enable the edit-and-continue feature while debugging. These NOP instructions also make code easier to debug by allowing breakpoints to be set on control flow instructions such as `for`, `while`, `do`, `if`, `else`, `try`, `catch`, and `finally` statement blocks. This is supposed to be a feature, but I've actually found these NOP instructions to be annoying at times because I have to single-step over them, which can actually slow me down while trying to debug some code. When producing optimized IL code, the C# compiler will remove these NOP instructions.
>
> Be aware that when the JIT compiler produces optimized native code, the code will be much harder to single-step through in a debugger, and control flow will be optimized. Also, some function evaluations may not work when performed inside the debugger.
>
> When you create a new C# project in Visual Studio, the Debug configuration of the project has `/optimize-` and `/debug:full`, and the Release configuration has `/optimize+` and `/debug:pdbonly`.
>
> Regardless of all of these settings, if a debugger is attached to a process containing the CLR, the JIT compiler will always produce unoptimized native code to help debugging; but, of course, the performance of the code will be reduced.

If you too are skeptical, you should certainly build some applications and test the performance for yourself. In addition, you should run some nontrivial managed applications Microsoft or others have produced, and measure their performance. I think you'll be surprised at how good the performance actually is.

You'll probably find this hard to believe, but many people (including me) think that managed applications could actually outperform unmanaged applications. There are many reasons to believe this. For example, when the JIT compiler compiles the IL code into native code at run time, the compiler knows more about the execution environment than an unmanaged compiler would know. Here are some ways that managed code can outperform unmanaged code:

- A JIT compiler can determine if the application is running on an Intel Pentium 4 CPU and produce native code that takes advantage of any special instructions offered by the Pentium 4. Usually, unmanaged applications are compiled for the lowest-common-denominator CPU and avoid using special instructions that would give the application a performance boost.

- A JIT compiler can determine when a certain test is always false on the machine that it is running on. For example, consider a method that contains the following code:

```
if (numberOfCPUs > 1) {
    ...
}
```

This code could cause the JIT compiler to not generate any CPU instructions if the host machine has only one CPU. In this case, the native code would be fine-tuned for the host machine; the resulting code is smaller and executes faster.

- The CLR could profile the code's execution and recompile the IL into native code while the application runs. The recompiled code could be reorganized to reduce incorrect branch predictions depending on the observed execution patterns.

These are only a few of the reasons why you should expect future managed code to execute better than today's unmanaged code. As I said, the performance is currently quite good for most applications, and it promises to improve as time goes on.

If your experiments show that the CLR's JIT compiler doesn't offer your application the kind of performance it requires, you may want to take advantage of the NGen.exe tool that ships with the .NET Framework SDK. This tool compiles all of an assembly's IL code into native code and saves the resulting native code to a file on disk. At run time, when an assembly is loaded, the CLR automatically checks to see whether a precompiled version of the assembly also exists, and if it does, the CLR loads the precompiled code so that no compilation is required at run time. Note that NGen.exe must be conservative about the assumptions it makes regarding the actual execution environment, and for this reason, the code produced by NGen.exe will not be as highly optimized as the JIT compiler–produced code. I'll discuss NGen.exe in more detail later in this chapter.

IL and Verification

IL is stack based, which means that all of its instructions push operands onto an execution stack and pop results off the stack. Because IL offers no instructions to manipulate registers, compiler developers have an easy time producing IL code; they don't have to think about managing registers, and fewer IL instructions are needed (since none exists for manipulating registers).

IL instructions are also typeless. For example, IL offers an **add** instruction that adds the last two operands pushed on the stack. There are no separate 32-bit and 64-bit versions of the **add** instruction. When the **add** instruction executes, it determines the types of the operands on the stack and performs the appropriate operation.

In my opinion, the biggest benefit of IL isn't that it abstracts away the underlying CPU. The biggest benefit IL provides is application robustness and security. While compiling IL into native CPU instructions, the CLR performs a process called *verification*. Verification examines the high-level IL code and ensures that everything the code does is safe. For example, verification checks that every method is called with the correct number of parameters, that each parameter passed to every method is of the correct type, that every method's return value is used properly, that every method has a return statement, and so on. The managed module's metadata includes all of the method and type information used by the verification process.

In Windows, each process has its own virtual address space. Separate address spaces are necessary because you can't trust an application's code. It is entirely possible (and unfortunately, all too common) that an application will read from or write to an invalid memory address. By placing each Windows process in a separate address space, you gain robustness and stability; one process can't adversely affect another process.

By verifying the managed code, however, you know that the code doesn't improperly access memory and can't adversely affect another application's code. This means that you can run multiple managed applications in a single Windows virtual address space.

Because Windows processes require a lot of operating system resources, having many of them can hurt performance and limit available resources. Reducing the number of processes by running multiple applications in a single OS process can improve performance, require fewer resources, and be just as robust as if each application had its own process. This is another benefit of managed code as compared to unmanaged code.

The CLR does, in fact, offer the ability to execute multiple managed applications in a single OS process. Each managed application is called an *AppDomain*. By default, every managed EXE file will run in its own separate address space that has just the one AppDomain. However, a process hosting the CLR (such as Internet Information Services [IIS] or Microsoft SQL Server 2005) can decide to run AppDomains in a single OS process. I'll devote part of Chapter 21, "CLR Hosting and AppDomains," to a discussion of AppDomains.

Unsafe Code

By default, Microsoft's C# compiler produces *safe* code. Safe code is code that is verifiably safe. However, Microsoft's C# compiler allows developers to write unsafe code. Unsafe code is allowed to work directly with memory addresses and can manipulate bytes at these addresses. This is a very powerful feature and is typically useful when interoperating with unmanaged code or when you want to improve the performance of a time-critical algorithm.

However, using unsafe code introduces a significant risk: unsafe code can corrupt data structures and exploit or even open up security vulnerabilities. For this reason, the C# compiler requires that all methods that contain unsafe code be marked with the **unsafe** keyword. In addition, the C# compiler requires you to compile the source code by using the **/unsafe** compiler switch.

When the JIT compiler attempts to compile an unsafe method, it checks to see if the assembly containing the method has been granted the **System.Security.Permissions.Security-Permission** with the **System.Security.Permissions.SecurityPermissionFlag**'s **SkipVerification** flag set. If this flag is set, the JIT compiler will compile the unsafe code and allow it to execute. The CLR is trusting this code and is hoping the direct address and byte manipulations do not cause any harm. If the flag is not set, the JIT compiler throws either a **System.InvalidProgramException** or a **System.Security.VerificationException**, preventing the method from executing. In fact, the whole application will probably terminate at this point, but at least no harm can be done.

> **Note**   By default, explicitly installed assemblies on a user's computer are granted full trust, meaning that they can do anything, which includes executing unsafe code. However, by default, assemblies executed via the intranet or Internet are not granted the permission to execute unsafe code. If they contain unsafe code, one of the aforementioned exceptions is thrown. An administrator/end user can change these defaults; however, the administrator is taking full responsibility for the code's behavior.

Microsoft supplies a utility called PEVerify.exe, which examines all of an assembly's methods and notifies you of any methods that contain unsafe code. You may want to consider running PEVerify.exe on assemblies that you are referencing; this will let you know if there may be problems running your application via the intranet or Internet.

You should be aware that verification requires access to the metadata contained in any dependent assemblies. So when you use PEVerify to check an assembly, it must be able to locate and load all referenced assemblies. Because PEVerify uses the CLR to locate the dependent assemblies, the assemblies are located using the same binding and probing rules that would normally be used when executing the assembly. I'll discuss these binding and probing rules in Chapter 2 and Chapter 3, "Shared Assemblies and Strongly Named Assemblies."

IL and Protecting Your Intellectual Property

Some people are concerned that IL doesn't offer enough intellectual property protection for their algorithms. In other words, they think that you could build a managed module and that someone else could use a tool, such as an IL Disassembler, to easily reverse engineer exactly what your application's code does.

Yes, it's true that IL code is higher level than most other assembly languages, and, in general, reverse engineering IL code is relatively simple. However, when implementing server-side code (such as a Web service, Web form, or stored procedure), your assembly resides on your server. Because no one outside of your company can access the assembly, no one outside of your company can use any tool to see the IL—your intellectual property is completely safe.

If you're concerned about any of the assemblies you do distribute, you can obtain an obfuscator utility from a third-party vendor. These utilities scramble the names of all of the private symbols in your assembly's metadata. It will be difficult for someone to unscramble the names and understand the purpose of each method. Note that these obfuscators can provide only a little protection because the IL must be available at some point for the CLR to JIT compile it.

If you don't feel that an obfuscator offers the kind of intellectual property protection you desire, you can consider implementing your more sensitive algorithms in some unmanaged module that will contain native CPU instructions instead of IL and metadata. Then you can use the CLR's interoperability features (assuming that you have ample permissions) to communicate between the managed and unmanaged portions of your application. Of course, this assumes that you're not worried about people reverse engineering the native CPU instructions in your unmanaged code.

In the future, Microsoft will offer a Digital Rights Management (DRM) solution as a way to protect the IL code contained inside an assembly.

The Native Code Generator Tool: NGen.exe

The NGen.exe tool that ships with the .NET Framework can be used to compile IL code to native code when an application is installed on a user's machine. Since the code is compiled at install time, the CLR's JIT compiler does not have to compile the IL code at run time, and this *can* improve the application's performance. The NGen.exe tool is interesting in two scenarios:

- **Improving an application's startup time** Running NGen.exe can improve startup time because the code will already be compiled into native code so that compilation doesn't have to occur at run time.

■ **Reducing an application's working set**   If you believe that an assembly will be loaded into multiple processes/AppDomains simultaneously, running NGen.exe on that assembly can reduce the applications' working set. The reason is because the NGen.exe tool compiles the IL to native code and saves the output in a separate file. This file can be memory-mapped into multiple process address spaces simultaneously, allowing the code to be shared; not every process/AppDomain needs its own copy of the code.

When a setup program invokes NGen.exe on an application or a single assembly, all of the assemblies for that application or the one specified assembly has its IL code compiled into native code. A new assembly file containing only this native code instead of IL code is created by NGen.exe. This new file is placed in a folder under the directory with a name like C:\Windows\Assembly\NativeImages_v2.0.50727_32. The directory name includes the version of the CLR and information denoting whether the native code is compiled for x86 (32-bit version of Windows), x64, or Itanium (the latter two for 64-bit versions of Windows).

Now, whenever the CLR loads an assembly file, the CLR looks to see if a corresponding NGen'd native file exists. If a native file cannot be found, the CLR JIT compiles the IL code as usual. However, if a corresponding native file does exist, the CLR will use the compiled code contained in the native file, and the file's methods will not have to be compiled at run time.

On the surface, this sounds great! It sounds as if you get all of the benefits of managed code (garbage collection, verification, type safety, and so on) without all of the performance problems of managed code (JIT compilation). However, the reality of the situation is not as rosy as it would first seem. There are several potential problems with respect to NGen'd files:

■ **No Intellectual Property Protection**   Many people believe that it might be possible to ship NGen'd files without shipping the files containing the original IL code thereby keeping their intellectual property a secret. Unfortunately, this is not possible. At run time, the CLR requires access to the assembly's metadata (for functions such as reflection and serialization); this requires that the assemblies that contain IL and metadata be shipped. In addition, if the CLR can't use the NGen'd file for some reason (described below), the CLR gracefully goes back to JIT compiling the assembly's IL code, which must be available.

■ **NGen'd files can get out of sync**   When the CLR loads an NGen'd file, it compares a number of characteristics about the previously compiled code and the current execution environment. If any of the characteristics don't match, the NGen'd file cannot be used, and the normal JIT compiler process is used instead. Here is a partial list of characteristics that must match:

  ❑ Assembly module version ID (MVID)

  ❑ Referenced assembly's version IDs

  ❑ Processor type

  ❑ CLR version

  ❑ Build type (release, debug, optimized debug, profiling, etc.)

All link-time security demands must be met at run time to allow loading.

Note that it is possible to run NGen.exe in update mode. This tells the tool to run NGen.exe on all of the assemblies that had previously been NGen'd. Whenever an end user installs a new service pack of the .NET Framework, the service pack's installation program will run NGen.exe in update mode automatically so that NGen'd files are kept in sync with the version of the CLR installed.

■ **Inferior Load-Time Performance (Rebasing/Binding)**   Assembly files are standard Windows PE files, and, as such, each contains a preferred base address. Many Windows developers are familiar with the issues surrounding base addresses and rebasing. For more information about these subjects, please see my book *Programming Applications for Microsoft Windows*, 4th Edition (Microsoft Press, 1999). When JIT compiling code, these issues aren't a concern because correct memory address references are calculated at run time.

However, NGen'd assembly files have some of their memory address references calculated statically. When Windows loads an NGen'd file, it checks to see if the file loads at its preferred base address. If the file can't load at its preferred base address, Windows relocates the file, fixing up all of the memory address references. This is extremely time consuming because Windows must load the entire file into memory and modify various bytes within the file. In addition, all modified pages are backed by the paging file, wasting storage space. Also, this paging file–backed code can't be shared across process boundaries.

So, if you want to NGen assembly files, you should select good base addresses for your assembly files (via csc.exe's **/baseaddress** command-line switch). When you NGen an assembly file, the NGen'd file will be assigned a base address using an algorithm based on the managed assembly's base address. Unfortunately, Microsoft has never had good guidance for developers on how to assign base addresses. In 64-bit versions of Windows, this is less of a problem because address space is so plentiful, but for a 32-bit address space, selecting good base addresses for every single assembly is nearly impossible unless you know exactly what is going to load into a process, and you know that assemblies won't get bigger with later versions.

■ **Inferior Execution-Time Performance**   When compiling code, NGen can't make as many assumptions about the execution environment as the JIT compiler can. This causes NGen.exe to produce inferior code. For example, NGen won't optimize the use of certain CPU instructions; it adds indirections for static field access because the actual address of the static fields isn't known until run time. NGen inserts code to call class constructors everywhere because it doesn't know the order in which the code will execute and if a class constructor has already been called. (See Chapter 8, "Methods: Constructors, Operators, Conversions, and Parameters," for more about class constructors.) Some NGen'd applications actually perform about 5 percent slower when compared to their JIT compiled counterpart. So, if you're considering using NGen.exe to improve the performance of your application, you should compare NGen'd and non-NGen'd versions to be sure that the NGen'd version doesn't actually run slower! For some applications, the reduction in working set size improves performance, so using NGen can be a net win.

Due to all of the issues just listed, you should be very cautious when considering the use of NGen.exe. For server-side applications, NGen.exe makes little or no sense because only the first client request experiences a performance hit; future client requests run at high speed. In addition, for most server applications, only one instance of the code is required, so there is no working set benefit.

For client applications, NGen.exe might make sense to improve startup time or to reduce working set if an assembly is used by multiple applications simultaneously. Even in a case in which an assembly is not used by multiple applications, NGen'ing an assembly could improve working set. Moreover, if NGen.exe is used for all of a client application's assemblies, the CLR will not need to load the JIT compiler at all, reducing working set even further. Of course, if just one assembly isn't NGen'd or if an assembly's NGen'd file can't be used, the JIT compiler will load, and the application's working set increases.

Introducing the Framework Class Library

The .NET Framework includes the *Framework Class Library* (FCL). The FCL is a set of DLL assemblies that contain several thousand type definitions in which each type exposes some functionality. Microsoft is producing additional libraries such as WinFx and the DirectX SDK. These additional libraries provide even more types, exposing even more functionality for your use. I would expect many more libraries from Microsoft in the near future. Here are just some of the kinds of applications developers can create by using these assemblies:

- **Web services**   Methods that can process XML-based messages sent over the Internet very easily.

- **Web Forms**   HTML-based applications (Web sites). Typically, Web Forms applications will make database queries and Web service calls, combine and filter the returned information, and then present that information in a browser by using a rich HTML-based user interface.

- **Windows Forms**   Rich Windows GUI applications. Instead of using a Web Forms page to create your application's UI, you can use the more powerful, higher-performance functionality offered by the Windows desktop. Windows Forms applications can take advantage of controls, menus, and mouse and keyboard events, and they can exchange information directly with the underlying operating system. As can Web Forms applications, Windows Forms applications can also make database queries and consume Web services.

- **Windows console applications**   For applications with very simple UI demands, a console application provides a quick and easy way to build an application. Compilers, utilities, and tools are typically implemented as console applications.

- **Windows services**   Yes, it is possible to build service applications that are controllable via the Windows Service Control Manager (SCM) by using the .NET Framework.

- **Component library**   The .NET Framework allows you to build stand-alone assemblies (components) containing types that can be easily incorporated into any of the previously mentioned application types.

Because the FCL contains literally thousands of types, a set of related types is presented to the developer within a single namespace. For example, the **System** namespace (which you should become most familiar with) contains the **object** base type, from which all other types ultimately derive. In addition, the **System** namespace contains types for integers, characters, strings, exception handling, and console I/O as well as a bunch of utility types that convert safely between data types, format data types, generate random numbers, and perform various math functions. All applications will use types from the **System** namespace.

To access any of the framework's features, you need to know which namespace contains the types that expose the facilities you're after. A lot of types allow you to customize their behavior; you do so by simply deriving your own type from the desired FCL type. The object-oriented nature of the platform is how the .NET Framework presents a consistent programming paradigm to software developers. Also, developers can easily create their own namespaces containing their own types. These namespaces and types merge seamlessly into the programming paradigm. Compared to Win32 programming paradigms, this new approach greatly simplifies software development.

Most of the namespaces in the FCL present types that can be used for any kind of application. Table 1-3 lists some of the more general namespaces and briefly describes what the types in that namespace are used for. This is a very small sampling of the namespaces available. Please see the documentation that accompanies the various Microsoft SDKs to gain familiarity with the ever-growing set of namespaces that Microsoft is producing.

Table 1-3   Some General FCL Namespaces

Namespace	Description of Contents
System	All of the basic types used by every application
System.Data	Types for communicating with a database and processing data
System.Drawing	Types for manipulating 2-D graphics; typically used for Windows Forms applications and for creating images that are to appear in a Web Forms page
System.IO	Types for doing stream I/O and walking directories and files
System.Net	Types that allow for low-level network communications and working with some common Internet protocols.
System.Runtime.InteropServices	Types that allow managed code to access unmanaged OS platform facilities such as COM components and functions in Win32 or custom DLLs
System.Security	Types used for protecting data and resources
System.Text	Types to work with text in different encodings, such as ASCII and Unicode
System.Threading	Types used for asynchronous operations and synchronizing access to resources
System.Xml	Types used for processing XML schemas and data

This book is about the CLR and about the general types that interact closely with the CLR. So the content of this book is applicable to all programmers writing applications or components that target the CLR. Many other good books exist that cover specific application types such as Web Services, Web Forms, Windows Forms, etc. These other books will give you an excellent start at helping you build your application. I tend to think of these application-specific books as helping you learn from the top down because they concentrate on the application type and not on the development platform. In this book, I'll offer information that will help you learn from the bottom up. After reading this book and an application-specific book, you should be able to easily and proficiently build any kind of application you desire.

The Common Type System

By now, it should be obvious to you that the CLR is all about types. Types expose functionality to your applications and other types. Types are the mechanism by which code written in one programming language can talk to code written in a different programming language. Because types are at the root of the CLR, Microsoft created a formal specification—the Common Type System (CTS)—that describes how types are defined and how they behave.

> **Note**   In fact, Microsoft has been submitting the CTS as well as other parts of the .NET Framework including file formats, metadata, intermediate language, and access to the underlying platform (P/Invoke) to ECMA for the purpose of standardization. The standard is called the Common Language Infrastructure (CLI). In addition, Microsoft has also submitted portions of the Framework Class Library, the C# programming language, and the C++/CLI programming language. For information about these industry standards, please go to ECMA's Web site that pertains to Technical Committee 39: *www.ecma-international.org/memento/TC39.htm*. You can also refer to Microsoft's own Web site: *http://msdn.microsoft.com/netframework/ecma/*.

The CTS specification states that a type can contain zero or more members. In Part III, I'll cover all of these members in great detail. For now, I want just to give you a brief introduction to them:

- **Field**   A data variable that is part of the object's state. Fields are identified by their name and type.

- **Method**   A function that performs an operation on the object, often changing the object's state. Methods have a name, a signature, and modifiers. The signature specifies the number of parameters (and their sequence), the types of the parameters, whether a value is returned by the method, and if so, the type of the value returned by the method.

- **Property**   To the caller, this member looks like a field. But to the type implementer, it looks like a method (or two). Properties allow an implementer to validate input parameters and object state before accessing the value and/or calculating a value only when necessary. They also allow a user of the type to have simplified syntax. Finally, properties allow you to create read-only or write-only "fields."

- **Event**   An event allows a notification mechanism between an object and other interested objects. For example, a button could offer an event that notifies other objects when the button is clicked.

The CTS also specifies the rules for type visibility and access to the members of a type. For example, marking a type as *public* (called **public**) exports the type, making it visible and accessible to any assembly. On the other hand, marking a type as *assembly* (called **internal** in C#) makes the type visible and accessible to code within the same assembly only. Thus, the CTS establishes the rules by which assemblies form a boundary of visibility for a type, and the CLR enforces the visibility rules.

A type that is visible to a caller can further restrict the ability of the caller to access the type's members. The following list shows the valid options for controlling access to a member:

- **Private**   The method is callable only by other methods in the same class type.
- **Family**   The method is callable by derived types, regardless of whether they are within the same assembly. Note that many languages (such as C++ and C#) refer to family as **protected**.
- **Family and assembly**   The method is callable by derived types, but only if the derived type is defined in the same assembly. Many languages (such as C# and Visual Basic) don't offer this access control. Of course, IL Assembly language makes it available.
- **Assembly**   The method is callable by any code in the same assembly. Many languages refer to *assembly* as **internal**.
- **Family or assembly**   The method is callable by derived types in any assembly. The method is also callable by any types in the same assembly. C# refers to *family or assembly* as **protected internal**.
- **Public**   The method is callable by any code in any assembly.

In addition, the CTS defines the rules governing type inheritance, virtual methods, object lifetime, and so on. These rules have been designed to accommodate the semantics expressible in modern-day programming languages. In fact, you won't even need to learn the CTS rules per se because the language you choose will expose its own language syntax and type rules in the same way that you're familiar with today. And it will map the language-specific syntax into IL, the "language" of the CLR, when it emits the assembly during compilation.

When I first started working with the CLR, I soon realized that it is best to think of the language and the behavior of your code as two separate and distinct things. Using C++, you can define your own types with their own members. Of course, you could have used C# or Visual Basic to define the same type with the same members. Sure, the syntax you use for defining the type is different depending on the language you choose, but the behavior of the type will be absolutely identical regardless of the language because the CLR's CTS defines the behavior of the type.

To help clarify this idea, let me give you an example. The CTS allows a type to derive from only one base class. So, while the C++ language supports types that can inherit from multiple base types, the CTS can't accept and operate on any such type. To help the developer, Microsoft's C++/CLI compiler reports an error if it detects that you're attempting to create managed code that includes a type deriving from multiple base types.

Here's another CTS rule. All types must (ultimately) inherit from a predefined type: **System.Object**. As you can see, **Object** is the name of a type defined in the **System** namespace. This **Object** is the root of all other types and therefore guarantees that every type instance has a minimum set of behaviors. Specifically, the **System.Object** type allows you to do the following:

- Compare two instances for equality.
- Obtain a hash code for the instance.
- Query the true type of an instance.
- Perform a shallow (bitwise) copy of the instance.
- Obtain a string representation of the instance's object's current state.

The Common Language Specification

COM allows objects created in different languages to communicate with one another. On the other hand, the CLR now integrates all languages and allows objects created in one language to be treated as equal citizens by code written in a completely different language. This integration is possible because of the CLR's standard set of types, metadata (self-describing type information), and common execution environment.

While this language integration is a fantastic goal, the truth of the matter is that programming languages are very different from one another. For example, some languages don't treat symbols with case-sensitivity, and some don't offer unsigned integers, operator overloading, or methods to support a variable number of arguments.

If you intend to create types that are easily accessible from other programming languages, you need to use only features of your programming language that are guaranteed to be available in all other languages. To help you with this, Microsoft has defined a Common Language Specification (CLS) that details for compiler vendors the minimum set of features their compilers must support if these compilers are to generate types compatible with other components written by other CLS-compliant languages on top of the CLR.

The CLR/CTS supports a lot more features than the subset defined by the CLS, so if you don't care about interlanguage operability, you can develop very rich types limited only by the language's feature set. Specifically, the CLS defines rules that externally visible types and methods must adhere to if they are to be accessible from any CLS-compliant programming language. Note that the CLS rules don't apply to code that is accessible only within the defining assembly. Figure 1-6 summarizes the ideas expressed in this paragraph.

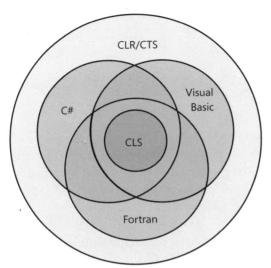

Figure 1-6   Languages offer a subset of the CLR/CTS and a superset of the CLS (but not necessarily the same superset)

As Figure 1-6 shows, the CLR/CTS offers a set of features. Some languages expose a large subset of the CLR/CTS. A programmer willing to write in IL assembly language, for example, is able to use all of the features the CLR/CTS offers. Most other languages, such as C#, Visual Basic, and Fortran, expose a subset of the CLR/CTS features to the programmer. The CLS defines the minimum set of features that all languages must support.

If you're designing a type in one language, and you expect that type to be used by another language, you shouldn't take advantage of any features that are outside of the CLS in its public and protected members. Doing so would mean that your type's members might not be accessible by programmers writing code in other programming languages.

In the following code, a CLS-compliant type is being defined in C#. However, the type has a few non-CLS-compliant constructs causing the C# compiler to complain about the code.

```
using System;

// Tell compiler to check for CLS compliance
[assembly: CLSCompliant(true)]

namespace SomeLibrary {
   // Warnings appear because the class is public
   public sealed class SomeLibraryType {

      // Warning: Return type of 'SomeLibrary.SomeLibraryType.Abc()'
      // is not CLS-compliant
      public UInt32 Abc() { return 0; }
```

```
        // Warning: Identifier 'SomeLibrary.SomeLibraryType.abc()'
        // differing only in case is not CLS-compliant
        public void abc() { }

        // No error: this method is private
        private UInt32 ABC() { return 0; }
    }
}
```

In this code, the `[assembly:CLSCompliant(true)]` attribute is applied to the assembly. This attribute tells the compiler to ensure that any publicly exposed type doesn't have any construct that would prevent the type from being accessed from any other programming language. When this code is compiled, the C# compiler emits two warnings. The first warning is reported because the method **Abc** returns an unsigned integer; some other programming languages can't manipulate unsigned integer values. The second warning is because this type exposes two public methods that differ only by case and return type: **Abc** and **abc**. Visual Basic and some other languages can't call both of these methods.

Interestingly, if you were to delete **public** from in front of 'sealed class SomeLibraryType' and recompile, both warnings would go away. The reason is that the SomeLibraryType type would default to **internal** and would therefore no longer be exposed outside of the assembly. For a complete list of CLS rules, refer to the "Cross-Language Interoperability" section in the .NET Framework SDK documentation.

Let me distill the CLS rules to something very simple. In the CLR, every member of a type is either a field (data) or a method (behavior). This means that every programming language must be able to access fields and call methods. Certain fields and certain methods are used in special and common ways. To ease programming, languages typically offer additional abstractions to make coding these common programming patterns easier. For example, languages expose concepts such as enums, arrays, properties, indexers, delegates, events, constructors, finalizers, operator overloads, conversion operators, and so on. When a compiler comes across any of these things in your source code, it must translate these constructs into fields and methods so that the CLR and any other programming language can access the construct.

Consider the following type definition, which contains a constructor, a finalizer, some overloaded operators, a property, an indexer, and an event. Note that the code shown is there just to make the code compile; it doesn't show the correct way to implement a type.

```
using System;

internal sealed class Test {
    // Constructor
    public Test() {}

    // Finalizer
    ~Test() {}
```

```
    // Operator overload
    public static Boolean operator == (Test t1, Test t2) {
        return true;
    }
    public static Boolean operator != (Test t1, Test t2) {
        return false;
    }

    // An operator overload
    public static Test operator + (Test t1, Test t2) { return null; }

    // A property
    public String AProperty {
        get { return null; }
        set { }
    }

    // An indexer
    public String this[Int32 x] {
        get { return null; }
        set { }
    }

    // An event
    event EventHandler AnEvent;
}
```

When the compiler compiles this code, the result is a type that has a number of fields and methods defined in it. You can easily see this by using the IL Disassembler tool (ILDasm.exe) provided with the .NET Framework SDK to examine the resulting managed module, which is shown in Figure 1-7.

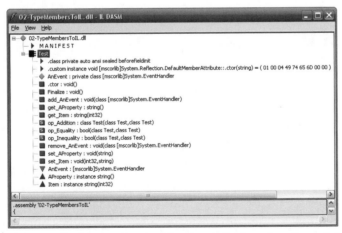

Figure 1-7   ILDasm showing Test type's fields and methods (obtained from metadata)

Table 1-4 shows how the programming language constructs got mapped to the equivalent CLR fields and methods.

Table 1-4   Test Type's Fields and Methods (Obtained from Metadata)

Type Member	Member Type	Equivalent Programming Language Construct
AnEvent	Field	Event; the name of the field is AnEvent and its type is System.EventHandler.
.ctor	Method	Constructor.
Finalize	Method	Finalizer.
add_AnEvent	Method	Event **add** accessor method.
get_AProperty	Method	Property **get** accessor method.
get_Item	Method	Indexer **get** accessor method.
op_Addition	Method	+ operator.
op_Equality	Method	== operator.
op_Inequality	Method	!= operator.
remove_AnEvent	Method	Event **remove** accessor method.
set_AProperty	Method	Property **set** accessor method.
set_Item	Method	Indexer **set** accessor method.

The additional nodes under the **Test** type that aren't mentioned in Table 14—**.class**, **.custom**, **AnEvent**, **AProperty**, and **Item**—identify additional metadata about the type. These nodes don't map to fields or methods; they just offer some additional information about the type that the CLR, programming languages, or tools can get access to. For example, a tool can see that the **Test** type offers an event, called **AnEvent**, which is exposed via the two methods (**add_AnEvent** and **remove_AnEvent**).

Interoperability with Unmanaged Code

The .NET Framework offers a ton of advantages over other development platforms. However, very few companies can afford to redesign and re-implement all of their existing code. Microsoft realizes this and has constructed the CLR so that it offers mechanisms that allow an application to consist of both managed and unmanaged parts. Specifically, the CLR supports three interoperability scenarios:

- **Managed code can call an unmanaged function in a DLL**   Managed code can easily call functions contained in DLLs by using a mechanism called P/Invoke (for Platform Invoke). After all, many of the types defined in the FCL internally call functions exported from Kernel32.dll, User32.dll, and so on. Many programming languages will expose a mechanism that makes it easy for managed code to call out to unmanaged functions contained in DLLs. For example, a C# application can call the **CreateSemaphore** function exported from Kernel32.dll.

- **Managed code can use an existing COM component (server)**   Many companies have already implemented a number of unmanaged COM components. Using the type library from these components, a managed assembly can be created that describes the COM component. Managed code can access the type in the managed assembly just as any other managed type. See the TlbImp.exe tool that ships with the .NET Framework SDK for more information. At times, you might not have a type library or you might want to have more control over what TlbImp.exe produces. In these cases, you can manually build a type in source code that the CLR can use to achieve the proper interoperability. For example, you could use DirectX COM components from a C# application.

- **Unmanaged code can use a managed type (server)**   A lot of existing unmanaged code requires that you supply a COM component for the code to work correctly. It's much easier to implement these components by using managed code so that you can avoid all of the code having to do with reference counting and interfaces. For example, you could create an ActiveX control or a shell extension in C#. See the TlbExp.exe and RegAsm.exe tools that ship with the .NET Framework SDK for more information.

In addition to these three scenarios, Microsoft's C++/CLI compiler (version 14) supports a new **/clr** command-line switch. This switch tells the compiler to emit IL code instead of native CPU instructions. If you have a large amount of existing C++ code, you can recompile the code by using this new compiler switch. The new code will require the CLR to execute, and you can now modify the code over time to take advantage of the CLR-specific features.

The **/clr** switch can't compile to IL any methods that contain inline assembly language (via the **__asm** keyword), accept a variable number of arguments, call **setjmp**, or contain intrinsic routines (such as **__enable**, **__disable**, **_ReturnAddress**, and **_AddressOfReturnAddress**). For a complete list of the constructs that the C++/CLI compiler can't compile into IL, refer to the documentation for the compiler. When the compiler can't compile the method into IL, it compiles the method into x86 so that the application still runs.

Keep in mind that although the IL code produced is managed, the data is not; that is, data objects are not allocated from the managed heap, and they are not garbage collected. In fact, the data types don't have metadata produced for them, and the types' method names are mangled.

The following C code calls the standard C runtime library's **printf** function and also calls the **System.Console.WriteLine** method. The **System.Console** type is defined in the FCL. So, C/C++ code can use libraries available to C/C++ as well as managed types.

```
#include <stdio.h>          // For printf
#using <mscorlib.dll>       // For managed types defined in this assembly
using namespace System;     // Easily access System namespace types

// Implement a normal C/C++ main function
void main() {
```

```
    // Call the C runtime library's printf function.
    printf("Displayed by printf.\r\n");

    // Call the FCL's System.Console's WriteLine method.
    Console::WriteLine("Displayed by Console::WriteLine.");
}
```

Compiling this code couldn't be easier. If this code were in a ManagedCApp.cpp file, you'd compile it by executing the following line at the command prompt:

```
cl /clr ManagedCApp.cpp
```

The result is a ManagedCApp.exe assembly file. If you run ManagedCApp.exe, you'll see the following output:

```
C:\>ManagedCApp
Displayed by printf.
Displayed by Console::WriteLine.
```

If you use ILDasm.exe to examine this file, you'll see all of the global functions and global fields defined within the assembly. Obviously, the compiler has generated a lot of stuff automatically. If you double-click the **Main** method, ILDasm will show you the IL code:

```
.method assembly static int32
  modopt([mscorlib]System.Runtime.CompilerServices.CallConvCdecl) main() cil managed
{
  .vtentry 70 : 1
  // Code size       23 (0x17)
  .maxstack  1
  IL_0000:  ldsflda    valuetype '<CppImplementationDetails>'.$ArrayType$$$BY0BH@$$CBD
                          modopt([mscorlib]System.Runtime.CompilerServices.IsConst)
                          '??_C@_0BH@GBHIFCOF@Displayed?5by?5printf?4?$AN?6?$AA@'
  IL_0005:  call       vararg int32
                          modopt([mscorlib]System.Runtime.CompilerServices.CallConvCdecl)
                          printf(
                            int8
                            modopt(
                              [mscorlib]System.Runtime.CompilerServices.IsSignUnspecifiedByte)
                            modopt(
                              [mscorlib]System.Runtime.CompilerServices.IsConst)*
                            )
  IL_000a:  pop
  IL_000b:  ldstr      "Displayed by Console::WriteLine"
  IL_0010:  call       void [mscorlib]System.Console::WriteLine(string)
  IL_0015:  ldc.i4.0
  IL_0016:  ret
} // end of method 'Global Functions'::main
```

What we see here isn't pretty because the compiler generates a lot of special code to make all of this work. However, from this IL code, you can see that **printf** and the **Console.WriteLine** methods are both called.

Chapter 2

Building, Packaging, Deploying, and Administering Applications and Types

Before we get into the chapters that explain how to develop programs for the Microsoft .NET Framework, let's discuss the steps required to build, package, and deploy your applications and their types. In this chapter, I'll focus on the basics of how to build assemblies that are for your application's sole use. In Chapter 3, "Shared Assemblies and Strongly Named Assemblies," I'll cover the more advanced concepts you'll need to understand, including how to build and use assemblies containing types that will be shared by multiple applications. In both chapters, I'll also talk about the ways an administrator can affect the execution of an application and its types.

Today, applications consist of several types, which are typically created by you and Microsoft. In addition, there is a burgeoning industry of component vendors that are building types they hope to sell to companies in an effort to reduce a software project's development time. If these types are developed using any language that targets the common language runtime (CLR), they can all work together seamlessly; a type written in one language can use another type as its base class without concern for the language the base type was developed in.

In this chapter, I'll also explain how these types are built and packaged into files for deployment. In the process, I'll take you on a brief historical tour of some of the problems that the .NET Framework is solving.

.NET Framework Deployment Goals

Over the years, Microsoft Windows has gotten a reputation for being unstable and complicated. This reputation, whether deserved or not, is the result of many different factors. First, all applications use dynamic-link libraries (DLLs) from Microsoft or other vendors. Because an application executes code from various vendors, the developer of any one piece of code can't be 100 percent sure how someone else is going to use it. Although this kind of interaction can potentially cause all kinds of trouble, in practice, these problems don't typically arise because applications are tested and debugged before they are deployed.

Users, however, frequently run into problems when one company decides to update its code and ships new files to them. These new files are supposed to be backward compatible with the previous files, but who knows for sure? In fact, when one vendor updates its code, it usually finds it impossible to retest and debug all of the already-shipped applications to ensure that the changes will have no undesirable effect.

I'm sure that everyone reading this book has experienced some variation of this problem: when installing a new application, you discover that it has somehow corrupted an already-installed application. This predicament is known as "DLL hell." This type of instability puts fear into the hearts and minds of the typical computer user. The end result is that users have to carefully consider whether to install new software on their machines. Personally, I've decided not to try out certain applications out of fear that it might adversely affect some application I really rely on.

The second reason that contributed to the aforementioned reputation of Windows is installation complexities. Today, when most applications are installed, they affect all parts of the system. For example, installing an application causes files to be copied to various directories, updates registry settings, and installs shortcuts on your desktop, Start menu, and Quick Launch toolbar. The problem with this is that the application isn't isolated as a single entity. You can't easily back up the application since you must copy the application's files and also the relevant parts of the registry. In addition, you can't easily move the application from one machine to another; you must run the installation program again so that all files and registry settings are set properly. Finally, you can't easily uninstall or remove the application without having this nasty feeling that some part of the application is still lurking on your machine.

The third reason has to do with security. When applications are installed, they come with all kinds of files, many of them written by different companies. In addition, Web applications frequently have code that is downloaded in such a way that users don't even realize that code is being installed on their machine. Today, this code can perform any operation, including deleting files or sending e-mail. Users are right to be terrified of installing new applications because of the potential damage they can cause. To make users comfortable, security must be built into the system so that the users can explicitly allow or disallow code developed by various companies to access their system's resources.

The .NET Framework addresses the DLL hell issue in a big way, as you'll see while reading this chapter and Chapter 3. It also goes a long way toward fixing the problem of having an application's state scattered all over a user's hard disk. For example, unlike COM, types no longer require settings in the registry. Unfortunately, applications still require shortcut links, but future versions of Windows may solve this problem. As for security, the .NET Framework includes a security model called *code access security*. Whereas Windows security is based on a user's identity, code access security is based on evidence obtained about an assembly, such as an assembly's identity (a strong name, discussed in Chapter 3) or where the assembly file physically was loaded from. A user could, for example, decide to trust all assemblies published by Microsoft or not to trust any assemblies downloaded from the Internet. As you'll see, the .NET Framework enables users to control what gets installed and what runs, and in general, to control their machines, more than Windows ever did.

Building Types into a Module

In this section, I'll show you how to turn your source file, containing various types, into a file that can be deployed. Let's start by examining the following simple application:

```
public sealed class Program {
   public static void Main() {
      System.Console.WriteLine("Hi");
   }
}
```

This application defines a type, called `Program`. This type has a single public, static method called `Main`. Inside `Main` is a reference to another type called `System.Console`. `System.Console` is a type implemented by Microsoft, and the IL code that implements this type's methods is in the MSCorLib.dll file. So our application defines a type and also uses another company's type.

To build this sample application, put the preceding code into a source code file, say, Program.cs, and then execute the following command line:

```
csc.exe /out:Program.exe /t:exe /r:MSCorLib.dll Program.cs
```

This command line tells the C# compiler to emit an executable file called Program.exe (`/out:Program.exe`). The type of file produced is a Win32 console application (`/t[arget]:exe`).

When the C# compiler processes the source file, it sees that the code references the `System` `.Console` type's `WriteLine` method. At this point, the compiler wants to ensure that this type exists somewhere, that it has a `WriteLine` method, and that the argument being passed to this method matches the parameter the method expects. Since this type is not defined in the C# source code, to make the C# compiler happy, you must give it a set of assemblies that it can use to resolve references to external types. In the command line above, I've included the `/r[eference]:MSCorLib.dll` switch, which tells the compiler to look for external types in the assembly identified by the MSCorLib.dll file.

MSCorLib.dll is a special file in that it contains all the core types: **Byte**, **Char**, **String**, **Int32**, and many more. In fact, these types are so frequently used that the C# compiler automatically references the MSCorLib.dll assembly. In other words, the following command line (with the **/r** switch omitted) gives the same results as the line shown earlier:

```
csc.exe /out:Program.exe /t:exe Program.cs
```

Furthermore, because the **/out:Program.exe** and the **/t:exe** command-line switches also match what the C# compiler would choose as defaults, the following command line gives the same results too:

```
csc.exe Program.cs
```

If, for some reason, you really don't want the C# compiler to reference the MSCorLib.dll assembly, you can use the **/nostdlib** switch. Microsoft uses this switch when building the MSCorLib.dll assembly itself. For example, the following command line will generate an error when CSC.exe attempts to compile the Program.cs file because the **System.Console** type is defined in MSCorLib.dll:

```
csc.exe /out:Program.exe /t:exe /nostdlib Program.cs
```

Now, let's take a closer look at the Program.exe file produced by the C# compiler. What exactly is this file? Well, for starters, it is a standard PE (portable executable) file. This means that a machine running 32-bit or 64-bit versions of Windows should be able to load this file and do something with it. Windows supports two types of applications, those with a console user interface (CUI) and those with graphical user interface (GUI). Because I specified the **/t:exe** switch, the C# compiler produced a CUI application. You'd use the **/t:winexe** switch to cause the C# compiler to produce a GUI application.

Response Files

Before leaving the discussion about compiler switches, I'd like to spend a moment talking about *response files*. A response file is a text file that contains a set of compiler command-line switches. When you execute CSC.exe, the compiler opens response files and uses any switches that are specified in them as though the switches were passed to CSC.exe on the command line. You instruct the compiler to use a response file by specifying its name on the command line prepended by an **@** sign. For example, you could have a response file called MyProject.rsp that contains the following text:

```
/out:MyProject.exe
/target:winexe
```

To cause CSC.exe to use these settings, you'd invoke it as follows:

```
csc.exe @MyProject.rsp CodeFile1.cs CodeFile2.cs
```

This tells the C# compiler what to name the output file and what kind of target to create. As you can see, response files are very convenient because you don't have to manually express the desired command-line arguments each time you want to compile your project.

The C# compiler supports multiple response files. In addition to the files you explicitly specify on the command line, the compiler automatically looks for files called CSC.rsp. When you run CSC.exe, it looks in the current directory for a local CSC.rsp file—you should place any project-specific settings in this file. The compiler also looks in the directory containing the CSC.exe file for a global CSC.rsp file. Settings that you want applied to all of your projects should go in this file. The compiler aggregates and uses the settings in all of these response files. If you have conflicting settings in the local and global response files, the settings in the local file override the settings in the global file. Likewise, any settings explicitly passed on the command line override the settings taken from a local response file.

When you install the .NET Framework, it installs a default global CSC.rsp file in the %SystemRoot%\Microsoft.NET\Framework\vX.X.X directory (where X.X.X is the version of the .NET Framework you have installed). The 2.0 version of this file contains the following switches:

```
# This file contains command-line options that the C#
# command line compiler (CSC) will process as part
# of every compilation, unless the "/noconfig" option
# is specified.

# Reference the common Framework libraries
/r:Accessibility.dll
/r:Microsoft.Vsa.dll
/r:System.Configuration.dll
/r:System.Configuration.Install.dll
/r:System.Data.dll
/r:System.Data.OracleClient.dll
/r:System.Data.SqlXml.dll
/r:System.Deployment.dll
/r:System.Design.dll
/r:System.DirectoryServices.dll
/r:System.dll
/r:System.Drawing.Design.dll
/r:System.Drawing.dll
/r:System.EnterpriseServices.dll
/r:System.Management.dll
/r:System.Messaging.dll
/r:System.Runtime.Remoting.dll
/r:System.Runtime.Serialization.Formatters.Soap.dll
/r:System.Security.dll
/r:System.ServiceProcess.dll
/r:System.Transactions.dll
/r:System.Web.dll
/r:System.Web.Mobile.dll
/r:System.Web.RegularExpressions.dll
/r:System.Web.Services.dll
/r:System.Windows.Forms.Dll
/r:System.Xml.dll
```

Because the global CSC.rsp file references all of the assemblies listed, you do not need to explicitly reference these assemblies by using the C# compiler's **/reference** switch. This response file is a big convenience for developers because it allows them to use types and namespaces defined in various Microsoft-published assemblies without having to specify a **/reference** compiler switch for each when compiling.

Referencing all of these assemblies could slow the compiler down a bit. But if your source code doesn't refer to a type or member defined by any of these assemblies, there is no impact to the resulting assembly file, nor to run-time execution performance.

> **Note**   When you use the **/reference** compiler switch to reference an assembly, you can specify a complete path to a particular file. However, if you do not specify a path, the compiler will search for the file in the following places (in the order listed):
>
> 1. Working directory.
> 2. The directory that contains the CSC.exe file itself. MSCorLib.dll is always obtained from this directory. The path looks something like this: %SystemRoot%\Microsoft.NET\ Framework\v2.0.50727.
> 3. Any directories specified using the **/lib** compiler switch.
> 4. Any directories specified using the LIB environment variable.

Of course, you're welcome to add your own switches to the global CSC.rsp file if you want to make your life even easier, but this makes it more difficult to replicate the build environment on different machines: you have to remember to update the CSC.rsp the same way on each build machine. Also, you can tell the compiler to ignore both local and global CSC.rsp files by specifying the **/noconfig** command-line switch.

A Brief Look at Metadata

Now we know what kind of PE file we've created. But what exactly is in the Program.exe file? A managed PE file has four main parts: the PE32(+) header, the CLR header, the metadata, and the intermediate language (IL). The PE32(+) header is the standard information that Windows expects. The CLR header is a small block of information that is specific to modules that require the CLR (managed modules). The header includes the major and minor version number of the CLR that the module was built for: some flags, a MethodDef token (described later) indicating the module's entry point method if this module is a CUI or GUI executable, and an optional strong-name digital signature (discussed in Chapter 3). Finally, the header contains the size and offsets of certain metadata tables contained within the module. You can see the exact format of the CLR header by examining the **IMAGE_COR20_HEADER** defined in the CorHdr.h header file.

The metadata is a block of binary data that consists of several tables. There are three categories of tables: definition tables, reference tables, and manifest tables. Table 2-1 describes some of the more common definition tables that exist in a module's metadata block.

Table 2-1   Common Definition Metadata Tables

Metadata Definition Table Name	Description
ModuleDef	Always contains one entry that identifies the module. The entry includes the module's file name and extension (without path) and a module version ID (in the form of a GUID created by the compiler). This allows the file to be renamed while keeping a record of its original name. However, renaming a file is strongly discouraged and can prevent the CLR from locating an assembly at run time, so don't do this.
TypeDef	Contains one entry for each type defined in the module. Each entry includes the type's name, base type, flags (public, private, etc.) and contains indexes to the methods it owns in the MethodDef table, the fields it owns in the FieldDef table, the properties it owns in the PropertyDef table, and the events it owns in the EventDef table.
MethodDef	Contains one entry for each method defined in the module. Each entry includes the method's name, flags (private, public, virtual, abstract, static, final, etc.), signature, and offset within the module where its IL code can be found. Each entry can also refer to a ParamDef table entry in which more information about the method's parameters can be found.
FieldDef	Contains one entry for every field defined in the module. Each entry includes flags (private, public, etc.), type, and name.
ParamDef	Contains one entry for each parameter defined in the module. Each entry includes flags (in, out, retval, etc.), type, and name.
PropertyDef	Contains one entry for each property defined in the module. Each entry includes flags, type, and name.
EventDef	Contains one entry for each event defined in the module. Each entry includes flags and name.

As the compiler compiles your source code, everything your code defines causes an entry to be created in one of the tables described in Table 2-1. Metadata table entries are also created as the compiler detects the types, fields, methods, properties, and events that the source code references. The metadata created includes a set of reference tables that keep a record of the referenced items. Table 2-2 shows some of the more common reference metadata tables.

Table 2-2   Common Reference Metadata Tables

Metadata Reference Table Name	Description
AssemblyRef	Contains one entry for each assembly referenced by the module. Each entry includes the information necessary to bind to the assembly: the assembly's name (without path and extension), version number, culture, and public key token (normally a small hash value generated from the publisher's public key, identifying the referenced assembly's publisher). Each entry also contains some flags and a hash value. This hash value was intended to be a checksum of the referenced assembly's bits. The CLR completely ignores this hash value and will probably continue to do so in the future.

Table 2-2   **Common Reference Metadata Tables**

Metadata Reference Table Name	Description
ModuleRef	Contains one entry for each PE module that implements types referenced by this module. Each entry includes the module's file name and extension (without path). This table is used to bind to types that are implemented in different modules of the calling assembly's module.
TypeRef	Contains one entry for each type referenced by the module. Each entry includes the type's name and a reference to where the type can be found. If the type is implemented within another type, the reference will indicate a TypeRef entry. If the type is implemented in the same module, the reference will indicate a ModuleDef entry. If the type is implemented in another module within the calling assembly, the reference will indicate a ModuleRef entry. If the type is implemented in a different assembly, the reference will indicate an AssemblyRef entry.
MemberRef	Contains one entry for each member (fields and methods, as well as property and event methods) referenced by the module. Each entry includes the member's name and signature and points to the TypeRef entry for the type that defines the member.

There are many more tables than what I listed in Tables 2-1 and 2-2, but I just wanted to give you a sense of the kind of information that the compiler emits to produce the metadata information. Earlier I mentioned that there is also a set of manifest metadata tables; I'll discuss these a little later in the chapter.

Various tools allow you to examine the metadata within a managed PE file. My personal favorite is ILDasm.exe, the IL Disassembler. To see the metadata tables, execute the following command line:

```
ILDasm Program.exe
```

This causes ILDasm.exe to run, loading the Program.exe assembly. To see the metadata in a nice, human-readable form, select the View/MetaInfo/Show! menu item (or press CTRL+M). This causes the following information to appear:

```
===========================================================
ScopeName : Program.exe
MVID      : {CA73FFE8-0D42-4610-A8D3-9276195C35AA}
===========================================================
Global functions
-----------------------------------------------------------

Global fields
-----------------------------------------------------------

Global MemberRefs
-----------------------------------------------------------
```

```
TypeDef #1 (02000002)
-------------------------------------------------------

   TypDefName: Program  (02000002)
   Flags     : [Public] [AutoLayout] [Class] [Sealed] [AnsiClass]
               [BeforeFieldInit]  (00100101)
   Extends   : 01000001 [TypeRef] System.Object
   Method #1 (06000001) [ENTRYPOINT]
   -------------------------------------------------------

      MethodName: Main (06000001)
      Flags     : [Public] [Static] [HideBySig] [ReuseSlot]  (00000096)
      RVA       : 0x00002050
      ImplFlags : [IL] [Managed]  (00000000)
      CallCnvntn: [DEFAULT]
      ReturnType: Void
      No arguments.

   Method #2 (06000002)
   -------------------------------------------------------

      MethodName: .ctor (06000002)
      Flags     : [Public] [HideBySig] [ReuseSlot] [SpecialName]
                  [RTSpecialName] [.ctor]  (00001886)
      RVA       : 0x0000205c
      ImplFlags : [IL] [Managed]  (00000000)
      CallCnvntn: [DEFAULT]
      hasThis
      ReturnType: Void
      No arguments.


TypeRef #1 (01000001)
-------------------------------------------------------
Token:             0x01000001
ResolutionScope:   0x23000001
TypeRefName:       System.Object
   MemberRef #1 (0a000004)
   -------------------------------------------------------

      Member: (0a000004) .ctor:
      CallCnvntn: [DEFAULT]
      hasThis
      ReturnType: Void
      No arguments.

TypeRef #2 (01000002)
-------------------------------------------------------
Token:             0x01000002
ResolutionScope:   0x23000001
TypeRefName:       System.Runtime.CompilerServices.CompilationRelaxationsAttribute
   MemberRef #1 (0a000001)
   -------------------------------------------------------

      Member: (0a000001) .ctor:
      CallCnvntn: [DEFAULT]
      hasThis
      ReturnType: Void
      1 Arguments
         Argument #1:  I4
```

```
TypeRef #3 (01000003)
-------------------------------------------------------
Token:            0x01000003
ResolutionScope:  0x23000001
TypeRefName:          System.Runtime.CompilerServices.RuntimeCompatibilityAttribute
    MemberRef #1 (0a000002)
    -------------------------------------------------------
       Member: (0a000002) .ctor:
       CallCnvntn: [DEFAULT]
       hasThis
       ReturnType: Void
       No arguments.
TypeRef #4 (01000004)
-------------------------------------------------------
Token:            0x01000004
ResolutionScope:  0x23000001
TypeRefName:          System.Console
    MemberRef #1 (0a000003)
    -------------------------------------------------------
       Member: (0a000003) WriteLine:
       CallCnvntn: [DEFAULT]
       ReturnType: Void
       1 Arguments
          Argument #1:  String


Assembly
-------------------------------------------------------
    Token: 0x20000001
    Name : Program
    Public Key   :
    Hash Algorithm : 0x00008004
    Version: 0.0.0.0
    Major Version: 0x00000000
    Minor Version: 0x00000000
    Build Number: 0x00000000
    Revision Number: 0x00000000
    Locale: <null>
    Flags : [none] (00000000)
    CustomAttribute #1 (0c000001)
    -------------------------------------------------------
       CustomAttribute Type: 0a000001
       CustomAttributeName:
         System.Runtime.CompilerServices.CompilationRelaxationsAttribute ::
            instance void .ctor(int32)
       Length: 8
       Value : 01 00 08 00 00 00 00 00                    >          <
       ctor args: (8)


    CustomAttribute #2 (0c000002)
    -------------------------------------------------------
       CustomAttribute Type: 0a000002
       CustomAttributeName: System.Runtime.CompilerServices.RuntimeCompatibilityAttribute ::
instance void .ctor()
       Length: 30
       Value : 01 00 01 00 54 02 16 57  72 61 70 4e 6f 6e 45 78 >    T  WrapNonEx<
             : 63 65 70 74 69 6f 6e 54  68 72 6f 77 73 01        >ceptionThrows  <
       ctor args: ()
```

```
AssemblyRef #1 (23000001)
-------------------------------------------------------------
    Token: 0x23000001
    Public Key or Token: b7 7a 5c 56 19 34 e0 89
    Name: mscorlib
    Version: 2.0.0.0
    Major Version: 0x00000002
    Minor Version: 0x00000000
    Build Number: 0x00000000
    Revision Number: 0x00000000
    Locale: <null>
    HashValue Blob:
    Flags: [none]  (00000000)


User Strings
-------------------------------------------------------------
70000001 : ( 2) L"Hi"


Coff symbol name overhead:  0
=============================================================
=============================================================
=============================================================
```

Fortunately, ILDasm processes the metadata tables and combines information where appropriate so that you don't have to parse the raw table information. For example, in the dump above, you see that when ILDasm shows a TypeDef entry, the corresponding member definition information is shown with it before the first TypeRef entry is displayed.

You don't need to fully understand everything you see here. The important thing to remember is that Program.exe contains a TypeDef whose name is **Program**. This type identifies a public sealed class that is derived from **System.Object** (a type referenced from another assembly). The **Program** type also defines two methods: **Main** and **.ctor** (a constructor).

Main is a public, static method whose code is IL (as opposed to native CPU code, such as x86). **Main** has a **void** return type and takes no arguments. The constructor method (always shown with a name of **.ctor**) is public, and its code is also IL. The constructor has a **void** return type, has no arguments, and has a **this** pointer, which refers to the object's memory that is to be constructed when the method is called.

I strongly encourage you to experiment with using ILDasm. It can show you a wealth of information, and the more you understand what you're seeing, the better you'll understand the CLR and its capabilities. As you'll see, I'll use ILDasm quite a bit more in this book.

Just for fun, let's look at some statistics about the Program.exe assembly. When you select ILDasm's View/Statistics menu item, the following information is displayed:

```
File size            : 3072
  PE header size     : 512 (496 used)      (16.67%)
  PE additional info : 839                 (27.31%)
  Num.of PE sections : 3
```

```
CLR header size      : 72              ( 2.34%)
CLR meta-data size   : 604             (19.66%)
CLR additional info  : 0              ( 0.00%)
CLR method headers   : 2              ( 0.07%)
Managed code         : 18             ( 0.59%)
Data                 : 1536           (50.00%)
Unaccounted          : -511           (-16.63%)

Num.of PE sections   : 3
  .text    - 1024
  .rsrc    - 1024
  .reloc   - 512

CLR meta-data size   : 604
  Module        -    1 (10 bytes)
  TypeDef       -    2 (28 bytes)      0 interfaces, 0 explicit layout
  TypeRef       -    4 (24 bytes)
  MethodDef     -    2 (28 bytes)      0 abstract, 0 native, 2 bodies
  MemberRef     -    4 (24 bytes)
  CustomAttribute-   2 (12 bytes)
  Assembly      -    1 (22 bytes)
  AssemblyRef   -    1 (20 bytes)
  Strings       -  176 bytes
  Blobs         -   68 bytes
  UserStrings   -    8 bytes
  Guids         -   16 bytes
  Uncategorized -  168 bytes

CLR method headers : 2
  Num.of method bodies  - 2
  Num.of fat headers    - 0
  Num.of tiny headers   - 2

Managed code : 18
  Ave method size - 9
```

Here you can see the size (in bytes) of the file and the size (in bytes and percentages) of the various parts that make up the file. For this very small Program.cs application, the PE header and the metadata occupy the bulk of the file's size. In fact, the IL code occupies just 18 bytes. Of course, as an application grows, it will reuse most of its types and references to other types and assemblies, causing the metadata and header information to shrink considerably as compared to the overall size of the file.

> **Note** By the way, ILDasm.exe does have a bug in it that affects the file size information shown. In particular, you cannot trust the **Unaccounted** information.

Combining Modules to Form an Assembly

The Program.exe file discussed in the previous section is more than just a PE file with metadata; it is also an *assembly*. An assembly is a collection of one or more files containing type definitions and resource files. One of the assembly's files is chosen to hold a *manifest*. The manifest is another set of metadata tables that basically contain the names of the files that are part of the assembly. They also describe the assembly's version, culture, publisher, publicly exported types, and all of the files that comprise the assembly.

The CLR operates on assemblies; that is, the CLR always loads the file that contains the manifest metadata tables first and then uses the manifest to get the names of the other files that are in the assembly. Here are some characteristics of assemblies that you should remember:

- An assembly defines the reusable types.
- An assembly is marked with a version number.
- An assembly can have security information associated with it.

An assembly's individual files don't have these attributes—except for the file that contains the manifest metadata tables.

To package, version, secure, and use types, you must place them in modules that are part of an assembly. In most cases, an assembly consists of a single file, as the preceding Program.exe example does. However, an assembly can also consist of multiple files: some PE files with metadata and some resource files such as .gif or .jpg files. It might help you to think of an assembly as a logical EXE or a DLL.

I'm sure that many of you reading this are wondering why Microsoft has introduced this new assembly concept. The reason is that an assembly allows you to decouple the logical and physical notions of reusable types. For example, an assembly can consist of several types. You could put the frequently used types in one file and the less frequently used types in another file. If your assembly is deployed by downloading it via the Internet, the file with the infrequently used types might not ever have to be downloaded to the client if the client never accesses the types. For example, an independent software vendor (ISV) specializing in UI controls might choose to implement Active Accessibility types in a separate module (to satisfy Microsoft's Logo requirements). Only users who require the additional accessibility features would require this module to be downloaded.

You configure an application to download assembly files by specifying a **codeBase** element (discussed in Chapter 3) in the application's configuration file. The **codeBase** element identifies a URL pointing to where all of an assembly's files can be found. When attempting to load an assembly's file, the CLR obtains the **codeBase** element's URL and checks the machine's download cache to see if the file is present. If it is, the file is loaded. If the file isn't in the cache, the CLR downloads the file into the cache from the location the URL points to. If the file can't be found, the CLR throws a **FileNotFoundException** exception at run time.

I've identified three reasons to use multifile assemblies:

- You can partition your types among separate files, allowing for files to be incrementally downloaded as described in the Internet download scenario. Partitioning the types into separate files also allows for partial or piecemeal packaging and deployment for applications you purchase and install.

- You can add resource or data files to your assembly. For example, you could have a type that calculates some insurance information. This type might require access to some actuarial tables to make its computations. Instead of embedding the actuarial tables in your source code, you could use a tool (such as the Assembly Linker, AL.exe, discussed later) so that the data file is considered to be part of the assembly. By the way, this data file can be in any format—a text file, a Microsoft Office Excel spreadsheet, a Microsoft Office Word table, or whatever you like—as long as your application knows how to parse the file's contents.

- You can create assemblies consisting of types implemented in different programming languages. For example, you can implement some types in C#, some types in Visual Basic, and other types in other languages. When you compile the types written with C# source code, the compiler produces a module. When you compile other types written with Visual Basic source code, the compiler produces a separate module. You can then use a tool to combine all of these modules into a single assembly. To developers using the assembly, the assembly appears to contain just a bunch of types; developers won't even know that different programming languages were used. By the way, if you prefer, you can run ILDasm.exe on each of the modules to obtain an IL source code file. Then you can run ILAsm.exe and pass it all of the IL source code files. ILAsm.exe will produce a single file containing all of the types. This technique requires your source code compiler to produce IL-only code.

> **Important**   To summarize, an assembly is a unit of reuse, versioning, and security. It allows you to partition your types and resources into separate files so that you, and consumers of your assembly, get to determine which files to package together and deploy. Once the CLR loads the file containing the manifest, it can determine which of the assembly's other files contain the types and resources the application is referencing. Anyone consuming the assembly is required to know only the name of the file containing the manifest; the file partitioning is then abstracted away from the consumer and can change in the future without breaking the application's behavior.
>
> If you have multiple types that can share a single version number and security settings, it is recommended that you place all of the types in a single file rather than spread the types out over separate files, let alone separate assemblies. The reason is performance. Loading a file/assembly takes the CLR and Windows time to find the assembly, load it, and initialize it. The fewer files/assemblies loaded the better, because loading fewer assemblies helps reduce working set and also reduces fragmentation of a process's address space. Finally, nGen.exe can perform better optimizations when processing larger files.

To build an assembly, you must select one of your PE files to be the keeper of the manifest. Or you can create a separate PE file that contains nothing but the manifest. Table 2-3 shows the manifest metadata tables that turn a managed module into an assembly.

Table 2-3 Manifest Metadata Tables

Manifest Metadata Table Name	Description
AssemblyDef	Contains a single entry if this module identifies an assembly. The entry includes the assembly's name (without path and extension), version (major, minor, build, and revision), culture, flags, hash algorithm, and the publisher's public key (which can be **null**).
FileDef	Contains one entry for each PE and resource file that is part of the assembly (except the file containing the manifest since it appears as the single entry in the AssemblyDef table). The entry includes the file's name and extension (without path), hash value, and flags. If this assembly consists only of its own file, the FileDef table has no entries.
ManifestResourceDef	Contains one entry for each resource that is part of the assembly. The entry includes the resource's name, flags (public if visible outside the assembly and private otherwise), and an index into the FileDef table indicating the file that contains the resource file or stream. If the resource isn't a stand-alone file (such as .jpg or a .gif), the resource is a stream contained within a PE file. For an embedded resource, the entry also includes an offset indicating the start of the resource stream within the PE file.
ExportedTypesDef	Contains one entry for each public type exported from all of the assembly's PE modules. The entry includes the type's name, an index into the FileDef table (indicating which of this assembly's files implements the type), and an index into the TypeDef table. *Note:* To save file space, types exported from the file containing the manifest are not repeated in this table because the type information is available using the metadata's TypeDef table.

The existence of a manifest provides a level of indirection between consumers of the assembly and the partitioning details of the assembly and makes assemblies self-describing. Also, note that the file containing the manifest has metadata information that indicates which files are part of the assembly, but the individual files themselves do not have metadata information that specifies that they are part of the assembly.

Note The assembly file that contains the manifest also has an AssemblyRef table in it. This table contains an entry for all of the assemblies referenced by all of the assembly's files. This allows tools to open an assembly's manifest and see its set of referenced assemblies without having to open the assembly's other files. Again, the entries in the AssemblyRef table exist to make an assembly self-describing.

The C# compiler produces an assembly when you specify any of the following command-line switches: **/t[arget]:exe**, **/t[arget]:winexe**, or **/t[arget]:library**. All of these switches cause the compiler to generate a single PE file that contains the manifest metadata tables. The resulting file is either a CUI executable, a GUI executable, or a DLL, respectively.

In addition to these switches, the C# compiler supports the **/t[arget]:module** switch. This switch tells the compiler to produce a PE file that doesn't contain the manifest metadata tables. The PE file produced is always a DLL PE file, and this file must be added to an assembly before the CLR can access any types within it. When you use the **/t:module** switch, the C# compiler, by default, names the output file with an extension of .netmodule.

> **Important**   Unfortunately, the Microsoft Visual Studio integrated development environment (IDE) doesn't natively support the ability for you to create multifile assemblies. If you want to create multifile assemblies, you must resort to using command-line tools.

There are many ways to add a module to an assembly. If you're using the C# compiler to build a PE file with a manifest, you can use the **/addmodule** switch. To understand how to build a multifile assembly, let's assume that we have two source code files:

- RUT.cs, which contains rarely used types
- FUT.cs, which contains frequently used types

Let's compile the rarely used types into their own module so that users of the assembly won't need to deploy this module if they never access the rarely used types:

```
csc /t:module RUT.cs
```

This line causes the C# compiler to create a RUT.netmodule file. This file is a standard DLL PE file, but, by itself, the CLR can't load it.

Next let's compile the frequently used types into their own module. We'll make this module the keeper of the assembly's manifest because the types are used so often. In fact, because this module will now represent the entire assembly, I'll change the name of the output file to JeffTypes.dll instead of calling it FUT.dll:

```
csc /out:JeffTypes.dll /t:library /addmodule:RUT.netmodule FUT.cs
```

This line tells the C# compiler to compile the FUT.cs file to produce the JeffTypes.dll file. Because **/t:library** is specified, a DLL PE file containing the manifest metadata tables is emitted into the JeffTypes.dll file. The **/addmodule:RUT.netmodule** switch tells the compiler that RUT.netmodule is a file that should be considered part of the assembly. Specifically, the **/addmodule** switch tells the compiler to add the file to the FileDef manifest metadata table and to add RUT.netmodule's publicly exported types to the ExportedTypesDef manifest metadata table.

Once the compiler has finished all of its processing, the two files shown in Figure 2-1 are created. The module on the right contains the manifest.

RUT.netmodule   JeffTypes.dll

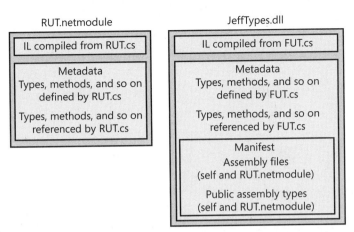

Figure 2-1   A multifile assembly consisting of two managed modules, one with a manifest

The RUT.netmodule file contains the IL code generated by compiling RUT.cs. This file also contains metadata tables that describe the types, methods, fields, properties, events, and so on that are defined by RUT.cs. The metadata tables also describe the types, methods, and so on that are referenced by RUT.cs. The JeffTypes.dll is a separate file. Like RUT.netmodule, this file includes the IL code generated by compiling FUT.cs and also includes similar definition and reference metadata tables. However, JeffTypes.dll contains the additional manifest metadata tables, making JeffTypes.dll an assembly. The additional manifest metadata tables describe all of the files that make up the assembly (the JeffTypes.dll file itself and the RUT.netmodule file). The manifest metadata tables also include all of the public types exported from JeffTypes.dll and RUT.netmodule.

> **Note**   In reality, the manifest metadata tables don't actually include the types that are exported from the PE file that contains the manifest. The purpose of this optimization is to reduce the number of bytes required by the manifest information in the PE file. So statements like "The manifest metadata tables also include all the public types exported from JeffTypes.dll and RUT.netmodule" aren't 100 percent accurate. However, this statement does accurately reflect what the manifest is logically exposing.

Once the JeffTypes.dll assembly is built, you can use ILDasm.exe to examine the metadata's manifest tables to verify that the assembly file does in fact have references to the RUT.netmodule file's types. Here is what the FileDef and ExportedTypesDef metadata tables look like:

```
File #1 (26000001)
-------------------------------------------------------
    Token: 0x26000001
    Name : RUT.netmodule
    HashValue Blob : e6 e6 df 62 2c a1 2c 59  97 65 0f 21 44 10 15 96  f2 7e db c2
    Flags : [ContainsMetaData]  (00000000)
```

```
ExportedType #1 (27000001)
-------------------------------------------------------
    Token: 0x27000001
    Name: ARarelyUsedType
    Implementation token: 0x26000001
    TypeDef token: 0x02000002
    Flags      : [Public] [AutoLayout] [Class] [Sealed] [AnsiClass]
                 [BeforeFieldInit](00100101)
```

From this, you can see that RUT.netmodule is a file considered to be part of the assembly with the token 0x26000001. From the ExportedTypesDef table, you can see that there is a publicly exported type, **ARarelyUsedType**. The implementation token for this type is 0x26000001, which indicates that the type's IL code is contained in the RUT.netmodule file.

> **Note**   For the curious, metadata tokens are 4-byte values. The high byte indicates the type of token (0x01=TypeRef, 0x02=TypeDef, 0x23=AssemblyRef, 0x26=FileRef, 0x27=ExportedType). For the complete list, see the **CorTokenType** enumerated type in the CorHdr.h file included with the .NET Framework SDK. The three lower bytes of the token simply identify the row in the corresponding metadata table. For example, the implementation token 0x26000001 refers to the first row of the FileRef table. For most tables, rows are numbered starting with 1, not 0. For the TypeDef table, rows actually start with 2.

Any client code that consumes the JeffTypes.dll assembly's types must be built using the **/r[eference]:JeffTypes.dll** compiler switch. This switch tells the compiler to load the JeffTypes.dll assembly and all of the files listed in its FileDef table when searching for an external type. The compiler requires all of the assembly's files to be installed and accessible. If you were to delete the RUT.netmodule file, the C# compiler would produce the following error: "fatal error CS0009: Metadata file 'C:\JeffTypes.dll' could not be opened—'Error importing module 'RUT.netmodule' of assembly 'C:\JeffTypes.dll'—The system cannot find the file specified'". This means that to build a new assembly, all of the files from a referenced assembly *must* be present.

As the client code executes, it calls methods. When a method is called for the first time, the CLR detects the types that the method references as a parameter, a return value, or as a local variable. The CLR then attempts to load the referenced assembly's file that contains the manifest. If the type being accessed is in this file, the CLR performs its internal bookkeeping, allowing the type to be used. If the manifest indicates that the referenced type is in a different file, the CLR attempts to load the necessary file, performs its internal bookkeeping, and allows the type to be accessed. The CLR loads assembly files only when a method referencing a type in an unloaded assembly is called. This means that to run an application, all of the files from a referenced assembly *do not* need to be present.

Adding Assemblies to a Project by Using the Visual Studio IDE

If you're using the Visual Studio IDE to build your project, you'll have to add any assemblies that you want to reference to your project. To do so, open Solution Explorer, right-click the project you want to add a reference to, and then select the Add Reference menu item. This causes the Add Reference dialog box, shown in Figure 2-2, to appear.

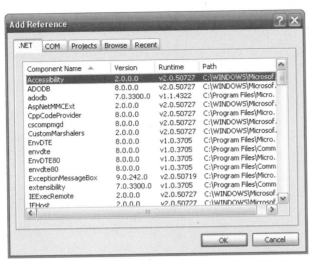

Figure 2-2 Add Reference dialog box in Visual Studio

To have your project reference an assembly, select the desired assembly from the list. If the assembly you want isn't in the list, click the Browse tab to navigate to the desired assembly (file containing a manifest) to add the assembly reference. The COM tab on the Add Reference dialog box allows an unmanaged COM server to be accessed from within managed source code via a managed proxy class automatically generated by Visual Studio. The Projects tab allows the current project to reference an assembly that is created by another project in the same solution. The Recent tab allows you to select an assembly that you recently added to another project.

To make your own assemblies appear in the .NET tab's list, add the following subkey to the registry:

HKEY_LOCAL_MACHINE\SOFTWARE\Microsoft\.NETFramework\AssemblyFolders
MyLibName

MyLibName is a unique name that you create—Visual Studio doesn't display this name. After creating the subkey, change its default string value so that it refers to a directory path (such as "C:\Program Files\MyLibPath") containing your assembly's files.

Using the Assembly Linker

Instead of using the C# compiler, you might want to create assemblies by using the Assembly Linker utility, AL.exe. The Assembly Linker is useful if you want to create an assembly consisting of modules built from different compilers (if your compiler doesn't support the equivalent of C#'s **/addmodule** switch) or perhaps if you just don't know your assembly packaging requirements at build time. You can also use AL.exe to build resource-only assemblies, called *satellite* assemblies, which are typically used for localization purposes. I'll talk about satellite assemblies later in the chapter.

The AL.exe utility can produce an EXE or a DLL PE file that contains only a manifest describing the types in other modules. To understand how AL.exe works, let's change the way the JeffTypes.dll assembly is built:

```
csc /t:module RUT.cs
csc /t:module FUT.cs
al  /out:JeffTypes.dll /t:library FUT.netmodule RUT.netmodule
```

Figure 2-3 shows the files that result from executing these statements.

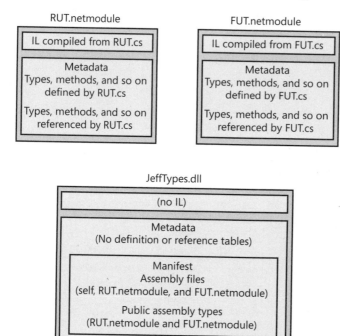

Figure 2-3   A multifile assembly consisting of three managed modules, one with a manifest

In this example, two separate modules, RUT.netmodule and FUT.netmodule, are created. Neither module is an assembly because they don't contain manifest metadata tables. Then a third file is produced: JeffTypes.dll, which is a small DLL PE file (because of the **/t[arget]:library** switch) that contains no IL code but has manifest metadata tables indicating that RUT.netmodule and FUT.netmodule are part of the assembly. The resulting assembly consists of three files: JeffTypes.dll, RUT.netmodule, and FUT.netmodule. The Assembly Linker has no way to combine multiple files into a single file.

The AL.exe utility can also produce CUI and GUI PE files by using the **/t[arget]:exe** or **/t[arget]:winexe** command-line switches. But this is very unusual since it would mean that you'd have an EXE PE file with just enough IL code in it to call a method in another module. You can specify which method in a module should be used as an entry point by adding the **/main** command-line switch when invoking AL.exe. The following is an example of how to call the Assembly Linker, AL.exe, by using the **/main** command-line switch:

```
csc /t:module App.cs
al  /out:App.exe /t:exe /main:Program.Main app.netmodule
```

Here the first line builds the App.cs file into a module. The second line produces a small App.exe PE file that contains the manifest metadata tables. In addition, there is a small global function named **__EntryPoint** that is emitted by AL.exe because of the **/main:App.Main** command-line switch. This function, **__EntryPoint**, contains the following IL code:

```
.method privatescope static void __EntryPoint$PST06000001() cil managed
{
  .entrypoint
  // Code size        8 (0x8)
  .maxstack  8
  IL_0000:  tail.
  IL_0002:  call           void [.module App.netmodule]Program::Main()
  IL_0007:  ret
} // end of method 'Global Functions'::__EntryPoint
```

As you can see, this code simply calls the **Main** method contained in the **Program** type defined in the App.netmodule file. The **/main** switch in AL.exe isn't that useful because it's unlikely that you'd ever create an assembly for an application that didn't have its entry point in the PE file that contains the manifest metadata tables. I mention the switch here only to make you aware of its existence.

Including Resource Files in the Assembly

When using AL.exe to create an assembly, you can add a file as a resource to the assembly by using the **/embed[resource]** switch. This switch takes a file (any file) and embeds the file's contents into the resulting PE file. The manifest's ManifestResourceDef table is updated to reflect the existence of the resources.

AL.exe also supports a **/link[resource]** switch, which also takes a file containing resources. However, the **/link[resource]** switch updates the manifest's ManifestResourceDef and File-Def tables, indicating that the resource exists and identifying which of the assembly's files contains it. The resource file is not embedded into the assembly PE file; it remains separate and must be packaged and deployed with the other assembly files.

Like AL.exe, CSC.exe also allows you to combine resources into an assembly produced by the C# compiler. The C# compiler's **/resource** switch embeds the specified resource file into the resulting assembly PE file, updating the ManifestResourceDef table. The compiler's **/linkresource** switch adds an entry to the ManifestResourceDef and the FileDef manifest tables to refer to a stand-alone resource file.

One last note about resources: it's possible to embed standard Win32 resources into an assembly. You can do this easily by specifying the pathname of a .res file with the **/win32res** switch when using either AL.exe or CSC.exe. In addition, you can quickly and easily embed a standard Win32 icon resource into an assembly file by specifying the pathname of the .ico file with the **/win32icon** switch when using either AL.exe or CSC.exe. Within Visual Studio. you can add resource files to your assembly by displaying your project's properties and then clicking the Application tab. The typical reason an icon is embedded is so that Windows Explorer can show an icon for a managed executable file.

Assembly Version Resource Information

When AL.exe or CSC.exe produces a PE file assembly, it also embeds into the PE file a standard Win32 version resource. Users can examine this resource by viewing the file's properties. Application code can also acquire and examine this information by calling **System.Diagnostics .FileVersionInfo**'s static **GetVersionInfo** method. Figure 2-4 shows the Version tab of the JeffTypes.dll Properties dialog box.

Figure 2-4   Version tab of the JeffTypes.dll Properties dialog box

When building an assembly, you should set the version resource fields by using custom attributes that you apply at the assembly level in your source code. Here's what the code that produced the version information in Figure 2-4 looks like:

```
using System.Reflection;

// Set the version CompanyName, LegalCopyright & LegalTrademarks fields
[assembly:AssemblyCompany("Wintellect")]
[assembly:AssemblyCopyright("Copyright (c) Wintellect 2006")]
[assembly:AssemblyTrademark("JeffTypes is a registered trademark of Wintellect")]

// Set the version ProductName & ProductVersion fields
[assembly:AssemblyProduct("Wintellect (R) Jeff's Type Library")]
[assembly:AssemblyInformationalVersion("2.0.0.0")]

// Set the FileVersion, FileDescription, & Comments fields
[assembly:AssemblyFileVersion("1.0.0.0")]
[assembly:AssemblyTitle("JeffTypes.dll")]
```

```
[assembly:AssemblyDescription("This assembly contains Jeff's types")]

// Set the AssemblyVersion field
[assembly: AssemblyVersion("3.0.0.0")]

// Set the Language field (discussed later in the "Culture" section)
[assembly:AssemblyCulture("")]
```

Table 2-4 shows the version resource fields and the custom attributes that correspond to them. If you're using AL.exe to build your assembly, you can use command-line switches to set this information instead of using the custom attributes. The second column in Table 2-4 shows the AL.exe command-line switch that corresponds to each version resource field. Note that the C# compiler doesn't offer these command-line switches and that, in general, using custom attributes is the preferred way to set this information.

> **Important**   When you create a new C# project in Visual Studio, an AssemblyInfo.cs file is automatically created for you. This file contains all of the assembly version attributes described in this section plus a few additional attributes that I'll cover in Chapter 3. You can simply open the AssemblyInfo.cs file and modify your assembly-specific information.

Table 2-4   Version Resource Fields and Their Corresponding AL.exe Switches and Custom Attributes

Version Resource	AL.exe Switch	Custom Attribute/Comment
FILEVERSION	/fileversion	`System.Reflection.AssemblyFileVersion-Attribute`.
PRODUCTVERSION	/productversion	`System.Reflection.AssemblyInformational-VersionAttribute`.
FILEFLAGSMASK	(none)	Always set to VS_FFI_FILEFLAGSMASK (defined in WinVer.h as 0x0000003F).
FILEFLAGS	(none)	Always 0.
FILEOS	(none)	Currently always VOS__WINDOWS32.
FILETYPE	/target	Set to VFT_APP if /target:exe or /target:winexe is specified; set to VFT_DLL if /target:library is specified.
FILESUBTYPE	(none)	Always set to VFT2_UNKNOWN. (This field has no meaning for VFT_APP and VFT_DLL.)
AssemblyVersion	/version	`System.Reflection.AssemblyVersionAttribute`.
Comments	/description	`System.Reflection.AssemblyDescription-Attribute`.
CompanyName	/company	`System.Reflection.AssemblyCompanyAttribute`.
FileDescription	/title	`System.Reflection.AssemblyTitleAttribute`.
FileVersion	/version	`System.Reflection.AssemblyFileVersion-Attribute`.
InternalName	/out	Set to the name of the output file specified (without the extension).

Table 2-4   Version Resource Fields and Their Corresponding AL.exe Switches and Custom Attributes

Version Resource	AL.exe Switch	Custom Attribute/Comment
LegalCopyright	/copyright	`System.Reflection.AssemblyCopyrightAttribute.`
LegalTrademarks	/trademark	`System.Reflection.AssemblyTrademarkAttribute.`
OriginalFilename	/out	Set to the name of the output file (without a path).
PrivateBuild	(none)	Always blank.
ProductName	/product	`System.Reflection.AssemblyProductAttribute.`
ProductVersion	/productversion	`System.Reflection.AssemblyInformational-` `VersionAttribute.`
SpecialBuild	(none)	Always blank.

Version Numbers

In the previous section, you saw that several version numbers can be applied to an assembly. All of these version numbers have the same format: each consists of four period-separated parts, as shown in Table 2-5.

Table 2-5   Format of Version Numbers

	Major Number	Minor Number	Build Number	Revision Number
Example:	2	5	719	2

Table 2-5 shows an example of a version number: 2.5.719.2. The first two numbers make up the public perception of the version. The public will think of this example as version 2.5 of the assembly. The third number, 719, indicates the build of the assembly. If your company builds its assembly every day, you should increment the build number each day as well. The last number, 2, indicates the revision of the build. If for some reason your company has to build an assembly twice in one day, maybe to resolve a hot bug that is halting other work, the revision number should be incremented.

Microsoft uses this version-numbering scheme, and it's highly recommended that you use this scheme as well. Future versions of the CLR will offer better support for loading new versions of an assembly and for rolling back to a previous version of an assembly if a new version actually breaks an existing application. To accomplish this versioning support, the CLR will expect that a version of an assembly that fixes one or more bugs will have the same major/minor version, and the build/revision numbers will indicate a servicing version containing the bug fix(es). When loading an assembly, the CLR will automatically find the latest installed servicing version that matches the major/minor version of the assembly being requested.

You'll notice that an assembly has three version numbers associated with it. This is very unfortunate and leads to a lot of confusion. Let me explain each version number's purpose and how it is expected to be used:

- **AssemblyFileVersion** This version number is stored in the Win32 version resource. This number is informational only; the CLR doesn't examine or care about this version number in any way. Typically, you set the major and minor parts to represent the version you want the public to see. Then you increment the build and revision parts each time a build is performed. Ideally, Microsoft's tool (such as CSC.exe or AL.exe) would automatically update the build and revision numbers for you (based on the date and time when the build was performed), but unfortunately, they don't. This version number can be seen when using Windows Explorer and is typically used to identify a specific version of an assembly when troubleshooting a customer's system.

- ■ **AssemblyInformationalVersion**   This version number is also stored in the Win32 version resource, and again, this number is informational only; the CLR doesn't examine or care about it in any way. This version number exists to indicate the version of the product that includes this assembly. For example, version 2.0 of a product might contain several assemblies; one of these assemblies is marked as version 1.0 since it's a new assembly that didn't ship in version 1.0 of the same product. Typically, you set the major and minor parts of this version number to represent the public version of your product. Then you increment the build and revision parts each time you package a complete product with all its assemblies.

- ■ **AssemblyVersion**   This version number is stored in the AssemblyDef manifest metadata table. The CLR uses this version number when binding to strongly named assemblies (discussed in Chapter 3). This number is extremely important and is used to uniquely identify an assembly. When starting to develop an assembly, you should set the major, minor, build, and revision numbers and shouldn't change them until you're ready to begin work on the next deployable version of your assembly. When you build an assembly, this version number of the referenced assembly is embedded in the AssemblyRef table's entry. This means that an assembly is tightly bound to a specific version of a referenced assembly.

Culture

Like version numbers, assemblies also have a culture as part of their identity. For example, I could have an assembly that is strictly for German, another assembly for Swiss German, another assembly for U.S. English, and so on. Cultures are identified via a string that contains a primary and a secondary tag (as described in RFC1766). Table 2-6 shows some examples.

Table 2-6   Examples of Assembly Culture Tags

Primary Tag	Secondary Tag	Culture
de	(none)	German
de	AT	Austrian German
de	CH	Swiss German
en	(none)	English
en	GB	British English
en	US	U.S. English

In general, if you create an assembly that contains code, you don't assign a culture to it. This is because code doesn't usually have any culture-specific assumptions built into it. An assembly that isn't assigned a culture is referred to as being *culture neutral*.

If you're designing an application that has some culture-specific resources to it, Microsoft highly recommends that you create one assembly that contains your code and your application's default (or fallback) resources. When building this assembly, don't specify a culture. This is the assembly that other assemblies will reference when they create and manipulate types it publicly exposes.

Now you can create one or more separate assemblies that contain only culture-specific resources—no code at all. Assemblies that are marked with a culture are called *satellite assemblies*. For these satellite assemblies, assign a culture that accurately reflects the culture of the resources placed in the assembly. You should create one satellite assembly for each culture you intend to support.

You'll usually use the AL.exe tool to build a satellite assembly. You won't use a compiler because the satellite assembly should have no code contained within it. When using AL.exe, you specify the desired culture by using the **/c[ulture]:*text*** switch, where ***text*** is a string such as "en-US" representing U.S. English. When you deploy a satellite assembly, you should place it in a subdirectory whose name matches the culture text. For example, if the application's base directory is C:\MyApp, the U.S. English satellite assembly should be placed in the C:\MyApp\en-US subdirectory. At run time, you access a satellite assembly's resources by using the **System.Resources.ResourceManager** class.

> **Note**   Although discouraged, it is possible to create a satellite assembly that contains code. If you prefer, you can specify the culture by using the **System.Reflection.Assembly-CultureAttribute** custom attribute instead of using AL.exe's **/culture** switch, for example, as shown here:
>
> ```
> // Set assembly's culture to Swiss German
> [assembly:AssemblyCulture("de-CH")]
> ```
>
> Normally, you shouldn't build an assembly that references a satellite assembly. In other words, an assembly's AssemblyRef entries should all refer to culture-neutral assemblies. If you want to access types or members contained in a satellite assembly, you should use reflection techniques as discussed in Chapter 22, "Assembly Loading and Reflection."

Simple Application Deployment (Privately Deployed Assemblies)

Throughout this chapter, I've explained how you build modules and how you combine those modules into an assembly. At this point, I'm ready to explain how to package and deploy all of the assemblies so that users can run the application.

Assemblies don't dictate or require any special means of packaging. The easiest way to package a set of assemblies is simply to copy all of the files directly. For example, you could put all of the assembly files on a CD-ROM and ship it to the user with a batch file setup program that just copies the files from the CD to a directory on the user's hard drive. Because the assemblies include all of the dependent assembly references and types, the user can just run the application and the runtime will look for referenced assemblies in the application's directory. No modifications to the registry are necessary for the application to run. To uninstall the application, just delete all the files—that's it!

Of course, you can package and install the assembly files by using other mechanisms, such as .cab files (typically used for Internet download scenarios to compress files and reduce download times). You can also package the assembly files into an MSI file for use by the Windows Installer service (MSIExec.exe). Using MSI files allows assemblies to be installed on demand the first time the CLR attempts to load the assembly. This feature isn't new to MSI; it can perform the same demand-load functionality for unmanaged EXE and DLL files as well.

> **Note** Using a batch file or some other simple "installation software" will get an application onto the user's machine; however, you'll need more sophisticated installation software to create shortcut links on the user's desktop, Start menu, and Quick Launch toolbar. Also, you can easily back up and restore the application or move it from one machine to another, but the various shortcut links will require special handling. Future versions of Windows may improve this scenario.

Of course, Visual Studio has a built-in mechanism that you can use to publish an application by displaying a project's Properties pages and clicking the Publish tab. You can use the options available on the Publish tab to cause Visual Studio to produce an MSI file and copy the resulting MSI file to a Web site, FTP server, or file path. The MSI file can also install any prerequisite components such as the .NET Framework or Microsoft SQL Server 2005 Express Edition. Finally, the application can automatically check for updates and install them on the user's machine by taking advantage of ClickOnce technology.

Assemblies deployed to the same directory as the application are called *privately deployed assemblies* because the assembly files aren't shared with any other application (unless the other application is also deployed to the same directory). Privately deployed assemblies are a big win for developers, end users, and administrators because they can simply be copied to an application's base directory, and the CLR will load them and execute the code in them. In addition, an application can be uninstalled by simply deleting the assemblies in its directory. This allows simple backup and restore as well.

This simple install/move/uninstall scenario is possible because each assembly has metadata indicating which referenced assembly should be loaded; no registry settings are required. In addition, the referencing assembly scopes every type. This means that an application always binds to the same type it was built and tested with; the CLR can't load a different assembly that just happens to provide a type with the same name. This is different from COM, in which types are recorded in the registry, making them available to any application running on the machine.

In Chapter 3, I'll discuss how to deploy shared assemblies that are accessible by multiple applications.

Simple Administrative Control (Configuration)

The user or the administrator can best determine some aspects of an application's execution. For example, an administrator might decide to move an assembly's files on the user's hard disk or to override information contained in the assembly's manifest. Other scenarios also exist related to versioning; I'll talk about some of these in Chapter 3.

To allow administrative control over an application, a configuration file can be placed in the application's directory. An application's publisher can create and package this file. The setup program would then install this configuration file in the application's base directory. In addition, the machine's administrator or an end user could create or modify this file. The CLR interprets the content of this file to alter its policies for locating and loading assembly files.

These configuration files contain XML and can be associated with an application or with the machine. Using a separate file (vs. registry settings) allows the file to be easily backed up and also allows the administrator to copy the application to another machine—just copy the necessary files and the administrative policy is copied too.

In Chapter 3, we'll explore this configuration file in more detail. But I want to give you a taste of it now. Let's say that the publisher of an application wants its application deployed with the JeffTypes assembly files in a different directory than the application's assembly file. The desired directory structure looks like this:

```
AppDir directory (contains the application's assembly files)
   App.exe
   App.exe.config (discussed below)

   AuxFiles subdirectory (contains JeffTypes' assembly files)
      JeffTypes.dll
      FUT.netmodule
      RUT.netmodule
```

Since the JeffTypes files are no longer in the application's base directory, the CLR won't be able to locate and load these files; running the application will cause a **System.IO.FileNot-FoundException** exception to be thrown. To fix this, the publisher creates an XML configuration file and deploys it to the application's base directory. The name of this file must be the name of the application's main assembly file with a .config extension: App.exe.config, for this example. The configuration file should look like this:

```
<configuration>
   <runtime>
```

```
        <assemblyBinding xmlns="urn:schemas-microsoft-com:asm.v1">
            <probing privatePath="AuxFiles" />
        </assemblyBinding>
    </runtime>
</configuration>
```

Whenever the CLR attempts to locate an assembly file, it always looks in the application's directory first, and if it can't find the file there, it looks in the AuxFiles subdirectory. You can specify multiple semicolon-delimited paths for the probing element's **privatePath** attribute. Each path is considered relative to the application's base directory. You can't specify an absolute or a relative path identifying a directory that is outside of the application's base directory. The idea is that an application can control its directory and its subdirectories but has no control over other directories.

Probing for Assembly Files

When the CLR needs to locate an assembly, it scans several subdirectories. Here is the order in which directories are probed for a culture-neutral assembly (where **firstPrivatePath** and **secondPrivatePath** are specified via the config file's **privatePath** attribute):

```
AppDir\AsmName.dll
AppDir\AsmName\AsmName.dll
AppDir\firstPrivatePath\AsmName.dll
AppDir\firstPrivatePath\AsmName\AsmName.dll
AppDir\secondPrivatePath\AsmName.dll
AppDir\secondPrivatePath\AsmName\AsmName.dll
...
```

In this example, no configuration file would be needed if the JeffTypes assembly files were deployed to a subdirectory called JeffTypes, since the CLR would automatically scan for a subdirectory whose name matches the name of the assembly being searched for.

If the assembly can't be found in any of the preceding subdirectories, the CLR starts all over, using an .exe extension instead of a .dll extension. If the assembly still can't be found, a **FileNotFoundException** is thrown.

For satellite assemblies, similar rules are followed except that the assembly is expected to be in a subdirectory, whose name matches the culture, of the application's base directory. For example, if AsmName.dll has a culture of "en-US" applied to it, the following directories are probed:

```
C:\AppDir\en-US\AsmName.dll
C:\AppDir\en-US\AsmName\AsmName.dll
C:\AppDir\firstPrivatePath\en-US\AsmName.dll
C:\AppDir\firstPrivatePath\en-US\AsmName\AsmName.dll
C:\AppDir\secondPrivatePath\en-US\AsmName.dll
C:\AppDir\secondPrivatePath\en-US\AsmName\AsmName.dll

C:\AppDir\en-US\AsmName.exe
C:\AppDir\en-US\AsmName\AsmName.exe
```

```
C:\AppDir\firstPrivatePath\en-US\AsmName.exe
C:\AppDir\firstPrivatePath\en-US\AsmName\AsmName.exe
C:\AppDir\secondPrivatePath\en-US\AsmName.exe
C:\AppDir\secondPrivatePath\en-US\AsmName\AsmName.exe

C:\AppDir\en\AsmName.dll
C:\AppDir\en\AsmName\AsmName.dll
C:\AppDir\firstPrivatePath\en\AsmName.dll
C:\AppDir\firstPrivatePath\en\AsmName\AsmName.dll
C:\AppDir\secondPrivatePath\en\AsmName.dll
C:\AppDir\secondPrivatePath\en\AsmName\AsmName.dll

C:\AppDir\en\AsmName.exe
C:\AppDir\en\AsmName\AsmName.exe
C:\AppDir\firstPrivatePath\en\AsmName.exe
C:\AppDir\firstPrivatePath\en\AsmName\AsmName.exe
C:\AppDir\secondPrivatePath\en\AsmName.exe
C:\AppDir\secondPrivatePath\en\AsmName\AsmName.exe
```

As you can see, the CLR probes for files with either an .exe or .dll file extension. Since probing can be very time-consuming (especially when the CLR is looking for files over a network), in the XML configuration file, you can specify one or more **culture** elements to limit the probing that the CLR performs when looking for satellite assemblies.

The name and location of this XML configuration file is different depending on the application type:

- For executable applications (EXEs), the configuration file must be in the application's base directory, and it must be the name of the EXE file with ".config" appended to it.

- For Microsoft ASP.NET Web Form applications, the file must be in the Web application's virtual root directory and is always named Web.config. In addition, subdirectories can also contain their own Web.config file, and the configuration settings are inherited. For example, a Web application located at *http://Wintellect.com/Training* would use the settings in the Web.config files contained in the virtual root directory and in its Training subdirectory.

- For assemblies containing client-side controls hosted by Microsoft Internet Explorer, the HTML page must contain a link tag whose **rel** attribute is set to "Configuration" and whose **href** attribute is set to the URL of the configuration file, which can be given any name. Here's an example: <LINK REL=Configuration HREF=http://Wintellect.com/ Controls.config>. For more information, see the following .NET Framework documentation: *http://msdn.microsoft.com/library/en-us/cpguide/html/ cpcondeployingcommonlanguageruntimeapplicationusingie55.asp.*

As mentioned at the beginning of this section, configuration settings apply to a particular application and to the machine. When you install the .NET Framework, it creates a

Machine.config file. There is one Machine.config file per version of the CLR you have installed on the machine.

The Machine.config file is located in the following directory:

%SystemRoot%\Microsoft.NET\Framework*version*\CONFIG

Of course, %SystemRoot% identifies your Windows directory (usually C:\WINDOWS), and *version* is a version number identifying a specific version of the .NET Framework (something like v2.0.50727).

Settings in the Machine.config file override settings in an application-specific configuration file. An administrator can create a machine-wide policy by modifying a single file. Normally, administrators and users should avoid modifying the Machine.config file because this file has many settings related to various things, making it much more difficult to navigate. Plus, you want the application's settings to be backed up and restored, and keeping an application's settings in the application-specific configuration file enables this.

Chapter 3

Shared Assemblies and Strongly Named Assemblies

In Chapter 2, "Building, Packaging, Deploying, and Administering Applications and Types," I talked about the steps required to build, package, and deploy an assembly. I focused on what's called private deployment, in which assemblies are placed in the application's base directory (or a subdirectory thereof) for the application's sole use. Deploying assemblies privately gives a company a large degree of control over the naming, versioning, and behavior of the assembly.

In this chapter, I'll concentrate on creating assemblies that can be accessed by multiple applications. The assemblies that ship with the .NET Framework are an excellent example of globally deployed assemblies, because all managed applications use types defined by Microsoft in the Microsoft .NET Framework Class Library (FCL).

As I mentioned in Chapter 2, Microsoft Windows has a reputation for being unstable. The main reason for this reputation is the fact that applications are built and tested using code implemented by someone else. After all, when you write an application for Windows, your application is calling into code written by Microsoft developers. Also, a large number of companies make controls that application developers can incorporate into their own applications. In fact, the .NET Framework encourages this, and a lot more control vendors will likely pop up over time.

As time marches on, Microsoft developers and control developers modify their code: they fix bugs, add features, and so on. Eventually, the new code makes its way onto the user's hard disk. The user's applications that were previously installed and working fine are no longer using the same code that the applications were built and tested with. As a result, the applications' behavior is no longer predictable, which contributes to the instability of Windows.

File versioning is a very difficult problem to solve. In fact, I assert that if you take a file that is used by other code files and change just one bit in the file—change a 0 to a 1 or a 1 to a 0— there's absolutely no way to guarantee that code that used the file before it was changed will now work just as well if it uses the new version of the file. One of the reasons why this statement is true is that a lot of applications exploit bugs, either knowingly or unknowingly. If a later version of a file fixes a bug, the application no longer runs as expected.

So here's the problem: How do you fix bugs and add features to a file and also guarantee that you don't break some application? I've given this question a lot of thought and have come to one conclusion: It's just not possible. But, obviously, this answer isn't good enough. Files will ship with bugs, and companies will always want to provide new features. There must be a way to distribute new files with the hope that the applications will work just fine. And if the application doesn't work fine, there has to be an *easy* way to restore the application to its last-known good state.

In this chapter, I'll explain the infrastructure that the .NET Framework has in place to deal with versioning problems. Let me warn you: What I'm about to describe is complicated. I'm going to talk about a lot of algorithms, rules, and policies that are built into the common language runtime (CLR). I'm also going to mention a lot of tools and utilities that the application developer must use. This stuff is complicated because, as I've mentioned, the versioning problem is difficult to address and to solve.

> **Note**   I do a lot of consulting at Microsoft, and recently, I have been working a lot with Microsoft's Version Architecture team. This team is responsible for improving the way that versioning works in the CLR. This team has some plans to change future versions of the CLR so that the versioning story gets much simpler. Unfortunately, these changes did not get into version 2.0 of the CLR; the changes are planned for a later version. The material presented in this chapter will still be quite relevant even after these changes are made. It's just that some of the processes will get simpler.

Two Kinds of Assemblies, Two Kinds of Deployment

The CLR supports two kinds of assemblies: *weakly named assemblies* and *strongly named assemblies*.

> **Important**   By the way, you won't find the term *weakly named assembly* in any of the .NET Framework documentation. Why? Because I made it up. In fact, the documentation has no term to identify a weakly named assembly. I decided to coin the term so that I can talk about assemblies without any ambiguity as to what kind of assembly I'm referring to.

Weakly named assemblies and strongly named assemblies are structurally identical—that is, they use the same portable executable (PE) file format, PE32(+) header, CLR header, metadata, manifest tables, and intermediate language (IL) that we examined in Chapters 1 and 2. And you use the same tools, such as the C# compiler and AL.exe, to build both kinds of assemblies. The real difference between weakly named and strongly named assemblies is that a strongly named assembly is signed with a publisher's public/private key pair that uniquely identifies the assembly's publisher. This key pair allows the assembly to be uniquely identified, secured, and versioned, and it allows the assembly to be deployed anywhere on the user's hard disk or even on the Internet. This ability to uniquely identify an assembly allows the CLR to enforce certain known-to-be-safe policies when an application tries to bind to a strongly named assembly. This chapter is dedicated to explaining what strongly named assemblies are and what policies the CLR applies to them.

An assembly can be deployed in two ways: privately or globally. A privately deployed assembly is an assembly that is deployed in the application's base directory or one of its subdirectories. A weakly named assembly can be deployed only privately. I talked about privately deployed assemblies in Chapter 2. A globally deployed assembly is an assembly that is deployed into some well-known location that the CLR looks in when it's searching for the assembly. A strongly named assembly can be deployed privately or globally. I'll explain how to create and deploy strongly named assemblies in this chapter. Table 3-1 summarizes the kinds of assemblies and the ways that they can be deployed.

Table 3-1   How Weakly and Strongly Named Assemblies Can Be Deployed

Kind of Assembly	Can Be Privately Deployed?	Can Be Globally Deployed?
Weakly named	Yes	No
Strongly named	Yes	Yes

> **Note**   It is highly recommended that you strongly name all of your assemblies. In fact, it is likely that future versions of the CLR will require all assemblies to be strongly named, and the ability to create weakly named assemblies will be deprecated. Weakly named assemblies are a problem because it is possible to have several different assemblies all with the same weak name. On the other hand, giving an assembly a strong name uniquely identifies that assembly. If the CLR can uniquely identify an assembly, it can apply more policies to it related to versioning or backward compatibility. It is Microsoft's plan to endow future versions of the CLR with these policies to make versioning simpler. In fact, just eliminating the ability to make weakly named assemblies makes understanding the CLR's versioning policies simpler.

Giving an Assembly a Strong Name

If multiple applications are going to access an assembly, the assembly must be placed in a well-known directory, and the CLR must know to look in this directory automatically when a reference to the assembly is detected. However, we have a problem: Two (or more) companies could produce assemblies that have the same file name. Then, if both of these assemblies get copied into the same well-known directory, the last one installed wins, and all of the applications that were using the old assembly no longer function as desired. (This is exactly why DLL hell exists today in Windows, in which shared DLLs are all just copied into the System32 directory.)

Obviously, differentiating assemblies simply by using a file name isn't good enough. The CLR needs to support some mechanism that allows assemblies to be uniquely identified. This is what the term *strongly named assembly* refers to. A strongly named assembly consists of four attributes that uniquely identify the assembly: a file name (without an extension), a version number, a culture identity, and a public key. Since public keys are very large numbers, we frequently use a small hash value derived from a public key. This hash value is called a *public key token*. The following assembly identity strings (sometimes called an *assembly display name*) identify four completely different assembly files:

```
"MyTypes, Version=1.0.8123.0, Culture=neutral, PublicKeyToken=b77a5c561934e089"

"MyTypes, Version=1.0.8123.0, Culture="en-US", PublicKeyToken=b77a5c561934e089"

"MyTypes, Version=2.0.1234.0, Culture=neutral, PublicKeyToken=b77a5c561934e089"

"MyTypes, Version=1.0.8123.0, Culture=neutral, PublicKeyToken=b03f5f7f11d50a3a"
```

The first string identifies an assembly file called MyTypes.exe or MyTypes.dll (you can't actually determine the file extension from an assembly identity string). The company producing the assembly is creating version 1.0.8123.0 of this assembly, and nothing in the assembly is sensitive to any one culture because **Culture** is set to **neutral**. Of course, any company could produce a MyTypes.dll (or MyTypes.exe) assembly file that is marked with a version number of 1.0.8123.0 and a neutral culture.

There must be a way to distinguish this company's assembly from another company's assembly that happens to have the same attributes. For several reasons, Microsoft chose to use standard public/private key cryptographic technologies instead of any other unique identification technique such as GUIDs, URLs, or URNs. Specifically, cryptographic techniques provide a way to check the integrity of the assembly's bits as they are installed on a hard drive, and they also allow permissions to be granted on a per-publisher basis. I'll discuss these techniques later in this chapter. So a company that wants to uniquely mark its assemblies must create a public/private key pair. Then the public key can be associated with the assembly. No two companies should have the same public/private key pair, and this distinction is what allows two companies to create assemblies that have the same name, version, and culture without causing any conflict.

Note   The `System.Reflection.AssemblyName` class is a helper class that makes it easy for you to build an assembly name and to obtain the various parts of an assembly's name. The class offers several public instance properties, such as `CultureInfo`, `FullName`, `KeyPair`, `Name`, and `Version`. The class also offers a few public instance methods, such as `GetPublicKey`, `GetPublicKeyToken`, `SetPublicKey`, and `SetPublicKeyToken`.

In Chapter 2, I showed you how to name an assembly file and how to apply an assembly version number and a culture. A weakly named assembly can have assembly version and culture attributes embedded in the manifest metadata; however, the CLR always ignores the version number and uses only the culture information when it's probing subdirectories looking for the satellite assembly. Because weakly named assemblies are always privately deployed, the CLR simply uses the name of the assembly (tacking on a .dll or an .exe extension) when searching for the assembly's file in the application's base directory or in any of the application's subdirectories specified in the XML configuration file's probing element's `privatePath` XML attribute.

A strongly named assembly has a file name, an assembly version, and a culture. In addition, a strongly named assembly is signed with the publisher's private key.

The first step in creating a strongly named assembly is to obtain a key by using the Strong Name utility, SN.exe, that ships with the .NET Framework SDK and Microsoft Visual Studio. This utility offers a whole slew of features depending on the command-line switch you specify. Note that all SN.exe's command-line switches are case-sensitive. To generate a public/private key pair, you run SN.exe as follows:

```
SN -k MyCompany.keys
```

This line tells SN.exe to create a file called MyCompany.keys. This file will contain the public and private key numbers persisted in a binary format.

Public key numbers are very big. If you want to, after creating the file that contains the public and private key, you can use the SN.exe utility again to see the actual public key. To do this, you must execute the SN.exe utility twice. First, you invoke SN.exe with the **-p** switch to create a file that contains only the public key (MyCompany.PublicKey):

```
SN -p MyCompany.keys MyCompany.PublicKey
```

Then, you invoke SN.exe, passing it the **-tp** switch and the file that contains just the public key:

```
SN -tp MyCompany.PublicKey
```

When I execute this line, I get the following output:

```
Microsoft (R) .NET Framework Strong Name Utility  Version 2.0.50727.42
Copyright (c) Microsoft Corporation.  All rights reserved.

Public key is
0024000004800000940000000602000000240000525341310004000001000100 3f9d621b702111
850be453b92bd6a58c020eb7b804f75d67ab302047fc786ffa3797b669215afb4d814a6f294010
b233bac0b8c8098ba809855da256d964c0d07f16463d918d651a4846a62317328cac893626a550
69f21a125bc03193261176dd629eace6c90d36858de3fcb781bfc8b817936a567cad608ae672b6
1fb80eb0

Public key token is 3db32f38c8b42c9a
```

The SN.exe utility doesn't offer any way for you to display the private key.

The size of public keys makes them difficult to work with. To make things easier for the developer (and for end users too), *public key tokens* were created. A public key token is a 64-bit hash of the public key. SN.exe's **-tp** switch shows the public key token that corresponds to the complete public key at the end of its output.

Now that you know how to create a public/private key pair, creating a strongly named assembly is simple. When you compile your assembly, you use the **/keyfile:<file>** compiler switch:

```
csc /keyfile:MyCompany.keys app.cs
```

When the C# compiler sees this switch, the compiler opens the specified file (MyCompany .keys), signs the assembly with the private key, and embeds the public key in the manifest. Note that you sign only the assembly file that contains the manifest; the assembly's other files can't be signed explicitly.

If you are using Visual Studio, you can create a new public/private key file by displaying the properties for your project, clicking the Signing tab, selecting the Sign the Assembly check box, and then choosing the <New...> option from the Choose a Strong Name Key File combo box, as shown in Figure 3-1:

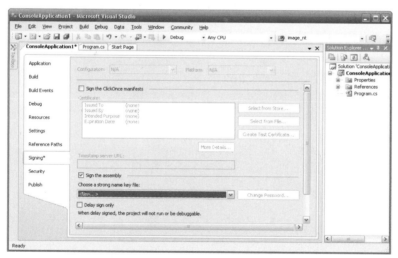

Figure 3-1   Using Visual Studio to create a key file and to sign an assembly

Here's what it means to sign a file: When you build a strongly named assembly, the assembly's FileDef manifest metadata table includes the list of all the files that make up the assembly. As each file's name is added to the manifest, the file's contents are hashed, and this hash value is stored along with the file's name in the FileDef table. You can override the default hash algorithm used with AL.exe's **/algid** switch or by applying the assembly level **System.Reflection .AssemblyAlgorithmIdAttribute** custom attribute in one of the assembly's source code files. By default, a SHA-1 algorithm is used, and this should be sufficient for almost all applications.

After the PE file containing the manifest is built, the PE file's entire contents (except for any Authenticode Signature, the assembly's strong name data, and the PE header checksum) are hashed, as shown in Figure 3-2. The hash algorithm used here is always SHA-1 and can't be overridden. This hash value is signed with the publisher's private key, and the resulting RSA digital signature is stored in a reserved section (not included in the hash) within the PE file. The CLR header of the PE file is updated to reflect where the digital signature is embedded within the file.

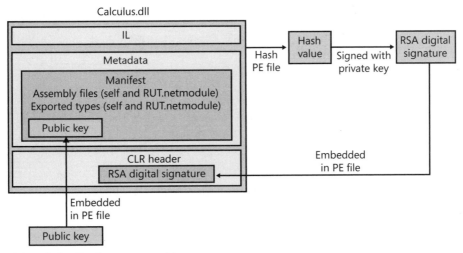

Figure 3-2   Signing an assembly

The publisher's public key is also embedded into the AssemblyDef manifest metadata table in this PE file. The combination of the file name, the assembly version, the culture, and the public key gives this assembly a strong name, which is guaranteed to be unique. There is no way that two companies could each produce an assembly named *Calculus* with the same public/private keys unless the companies share this key pair with each other.

At this point, the assembly and all of its files are ready to be packaged and distributed.

As described in Chapter 2, when you compile your source code, the compiler detects the types and members that your code references. You must specify the referenced assemblies to the compiler. For the C# compiler, you use the **/reference** compiler switch. Part of the compiler's job is to emit an AssemblyRef metadata table inside the resulting managed module. Each entry in the AssemblyRef metadata table indicates the referenced assembly's name (without path and extension), version number, culture, and public key information.

Important   Because public keys are such large numbers, and a single assembly might reference many assemblies, a large percentage of the resulting file's total size would be occupied with public key information. To conserve storage space, Microsoft hashes the public key and takes the last 8 bytes of the hashed value. These reduced public key values—known as public key tokens—are what are actually stored in an AssemblyRef table. In general, developers and end users will see public key token values much more frequently than full public key values.

Note, however, that the CLR never uses public key tokens when making security or trust decisions because it is possible that several public keys could hash to a single public key token.

The AssemblyRef metadata information (obtained by using ILDasm.exe) for the JeffTypes.dll file that I discussed in Chapter 2 is shown here:

```
AssemblyRef #1 (23000001)
-------------------------------------------------------
Token: 0x23000001
Public Key or Token: b7 7a 5c 56 19 34 e0 89
Name: mscorlib
Version: 2.0.0.0
Major Version: 0x00000002
Minor Version: 0x00000000
Build Number: 0x00000000
Revision Number: 0x00000000
Locale: <null>
HashValue Blob:
Flags: [none] (00000000)
```

From this, you can see that JeffTypes.dll references a type that is contained in an assembly matching the following attributes:

```
"MSCorLib, Version=2.0.0.0, Culture=neutral, PublicKeyToken=b77a5c561934e089"
```

Unfortunately, ILDasm.exe uses the term *Locale* when it really should be using *Culture*.

If you look at JeffTypes.dll's AssemblyDef metadata table, you see the following:

```
Assembly
-------------------------------------------------------
Token: 0x20000001
Name : JeffTypes
Public Key    :
Hash Algorithm : 0x00008004
Version: 3.0.0.0
Major Version: 0x00000003
Minor Version: 0x00000000
Build Number: 0x00000000
Revision Number: 0x00000000
Locale: <null>
Flags : [none] (00000000)
```

This is equivalent to the following:

```
"JeffTypes, Version=3.0.0.0, Culture=neutral, PublicKeyToken=null"
```

In this line, no public key token is specified because in Chapter 2, the JeffTypes.dll assembly wasn't signed with a public/private key pair, making it a weakly named assembly. If I had used SN.exe to create a key file compiled with the **/keyfile** compiler switch, the resulting assembly would have been signed. If I had then used ILDasm.exe to explore the new assembly's metadata, the AssemblyDef entry would have bytes appearing after the Public Key field, and the assembly would be strongly named. By the way, the AssemblyDef entry always stores the full public key, not the public key token. The full public key is necessary to ensure that the file hasn't been tampered with. I'll explain the tamper resistance of strongly named assemblies later in this chapter.

The Global Assembly Cache

Now that you know how to create a strongly named assembly, it's time to learn how to deploy this assembly and how the CLR uses the information to locate and load the assembly.

If an assembly is to be accessed by multiple applications, the assembly must be placed into a well-known directory, and the CLR must know to look in this directory automatically when a reference to the assembly is detected. This well-known location is called the global assembly cache (GAC), which can usually be found in the following directory (assuming that Windows is installed in the C:\Windows directory):

```
C:\Windows\Assembly
```

The GAC directory is structured: It contains many subdirectories, and an algorithm is used to generate the names of these subdirectories. You should never manually copy assembly files into the GAC; instead, you should use tools to accomplish this task. These tools know the GAC's internal structure and how to generate the proper subdirectory names.

While developing and testing, the most common tool for installing a strongly named assembly into the GAC is GACUtil.exe. Running this tool without any command-line arguments yields the following usage:

```
Microsoft (R) .NET Global Assembly Cache Utility.  Version 2.0.50727.42
Copyright (c) Microsoft Corporation.  All rights reserved.

Usage: Gacutil <command> [ <options> ]
Commands:
  /i <assembly_path> [ /r <...> ] [ /f ]
    Installs an assembly to the global assembly cache.

  /il <assembly_path_list_file> [ /r <...> ] [ /f ]
    Installs one or more assemblies to the global assembly cache.

  /u <assembly_display_name> [ /r <...> ]
    Uninstalls an assembly from the global assembly cache.

  /ul <assembly_display_name_list_file> [ /r <...> ]
    Uninstalls one or more assemblies from the global assembly cache.

  /l [ <assembly_name> ]
    List the global assembly cache filtered by <assembly_name>

  /lr [ <assembly_name> ]
    List the global assembly cache with all traced references.

  /cdl
    Deletes the contents of the download cache
```

```
/ldl
  Lists the contents of the download cache

/?
  Displays a detailed help screen

Options:
 /r <reference_scheme> <reference_id> <description>
   Specifies a traced reference to install (/i, /il) or uninstall (/u, /ul).

 /f
   Forces reinstall of an assembly.

/nologo
  Suppresses display of the logo banner

/silent
  Suppresses display of all output
```

As you can see, you can invoke GACUtil.exe, specifying the **/i** switch to install an assembly into the GAC, and you can use GACUtil.exe's **/u** switch to uninstall an assembly from the GAC. Note that you can't ever place a weakly named assembly into the GAC. If you pass the file name of a weakly named assembly to GACUtil.exe, it displays the following error message: "Failure adding assembly to the cache: Attempt to install an assembly without a strong name".

> **Note**   By default, the GAC can be manipulated only by a user belonging to the Windows Administrators or Power Users group. GACUtil.exe will fail to install or uninstall an assembly if the user invoking the execution of the utility isn't a member of either of these groups.

Using GACUtil.exe's **/i** switch is very convenient for developer testing. However, if you use GACUtil.exe to deploy an assembly in a production environment, it's recommended that you use GACUtil.exe's **/r** switch in addition to specifying the **/i** or **/u** switch to install or uninstall the assembly. The **/r** switch integrates the assembly with the Windows install and uninstall engine. Basically, it tells the system which application requires the assembly and then ties the application and the assembly together.

> **Note**   If a strongly named assembly is packaged in a cabinet (.cab) file or is compressed in some way, the assembly's file must first be decompressed to temporary file(s) before you use GACUtil.exe to install the assembly's files into the GAC. Once the assembly's files have been installed, the temporary file(s) can be deleted.

The GACUtil.exe tool doesn't ship with the end-user .NET Framework redistributable package. If your application includes some assemblies that you want deployed into the GAC, you should use the Windows Installer (MSI) version 3 or later, because MSI is the only tool that is guaranteed to be on end-user machines and capable of installing assemblies into the GAC. (You can determine which version of the Windows Installer is installed by running MSIExec.exe.)

Important   Globally deploying assembly files into the GAC is a form of registering the assembly, although the actual Windows registry isn't affected in any way. Installing assemblies into the GAC breaks the goal of simple application installation, backup, restore, moving, and uninstall. So it is recommended that you avoid global deployment and use private deployment whenever possible.

What is the purpose of "registering" an assembly in the GAC? Well, say two companies each produce a Calculus assembly consisting of one file: Calculus.dll. Obviously, both of these files can't go in the same directory because the last one installed would overwrite the first one, surely breaking some application. When you install an assembly into the GAC, dedicated subdirectories are created under the C:\Windows\Assembly directory, and the assembly files are copied into one of these subdirectories.

Normally, no one examines the GAC's subdirectories, so the structure of the GAC shouldn't really matter to you. As long as the tools and the CLR know the structure, all is good. Just for fun, I'll describe the internal structure of the GAC in the next section.

When you install the .NET Framework, a Windows Explorer shell extension (ShFusion.dll) is installed. This shell extension also knows the structure of the GAC, and it displays the GAC's contents in a nice, user-friendly fashion. When I use Explorer to navigate to my C:\Windows\ Assembly directory, I see what's shown in Figure 3-3: the assemblies installed into the GAC. Each row shows the assembly's name, version number, culture (if any), public key token, and CPU processor architecture.

Assembly Name	Version	Culture	Public Key Token	Processor Architecture
System	1.0.5000.0		b77a5c561934e089	
System	1.0.3300.0		b77a5c561934e089	
System	2.0.0.0		b77a5c561934e089	MSIL
System.Configuration	2.0.0.0		b03f5f7f11d50a3a	MSIL
System.Configuration.Install	1.0.5000.0		b03f5f7f11d50a3a	
System.Configuration.Install	1.0.3300.0		b03f5f7f11d50a3a	
System.Configuration.Install	2.0.0.0		b03f5f7f11d50a3a	MSIL
System.Configuration.Install.resources	1.0.3300.0	zh-CHT	b03f5f7f11d50a3a	
System.Configuration.Install.resources	1.0.3300.0	zh-CHS	b03f5f7f11d50a3a	
System.Configuration.Install.resources	1.0.3300.0	ko	b03f5f7f11d50a3a	
System.Configuration.Install.resources	1.0.3300.0	ja	b03f5f7f11d50a3a	
System.Configuration.Install.resources	1.0.3300.0	it	b03f5f7f11d50a3a	
System.Configuration.Install.resources	1.0.3300.0	fr	b03f5f7f11d50a3a	
System.Configuration.Install.resources	1.0.3300.0	es	b03f5f7f11d50a3a	
System.Configuration.Install.resources	1.0.3300.0	de	b03f5f7f11d50a3a	
System.Data	1.0.5000.0		b77a5c561934e089	
System.Data	1.0.3300.0		b77a5c561934e089	
System.Data	2.0.0.0		b77a5c561934e089	x86
System.Data.OracleClient	1.0.5000.0		b77a5c561934e089	
System.Data.OracleClient	2.0.0.0		b77a5c561934e089	x86
System.Data.resources	1.0.3300.0	zh-CHT	b77a5c561934e089	
System.Data.resources	1.0.3300.0	zh-CHS	b77a5c561934e089	
System.Data.resources	1.0.3300.0	ko	b77a5c561934e089	
System.Data.resources	1.0.3300.0	ja	b77a5c561934e089	
System.Data.resources	1.0.3300.0	it	b77a5c561934e089	
System.Data.resources	1.0.3300.0	fr	b77a5c561934e089	
System.Data.resources	1.0.3300.0	es	b77a5c561934e089	

Figure 3-3   Using Explorer's shell extension to see the assemblies installed in the GAC

You can select an entry and right-click it to display a context menu. The context menu contains Uninstall and Properties menu items. Obviously, choosing the **Uninstall** menu item deletes the selected assembly's files from the GAC and fixes up the GAC's internal structure. Choosing the **Properties** menu item displays a property dialog box that looks like the one shown in Figure 3-4. The Last Modified timestamp indicates when the assembly was added to the GAC. Clicking the **Version** tab reveals the property dialog box shown in Figure 3-5.

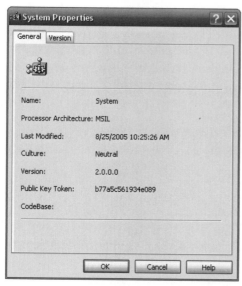

Figure 3-4   General tab of the Properties dialog box for the System assembly

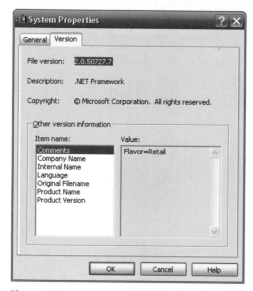

Figure 3-5   Version tab of the Properties dialog box for the System assembly

Last, but not least, you can drag a strongly named assembly file containing a manifest to an Explorer window. When you do this, the shell extension installs the assembly's files into the GAC. For some developers, this is an easier way to install assemblies into the GAC for testing instead of using the GACUtil.exe tool.

> **Note**   You can disable the Assembly Cache Viewer shell extension by modifying a registry value: In the HKEY_LOCAL_MACHINE\Software\Microsoft\Fusion subkey, create a DWORD value called DisableCacheViewer and set it to 1. Alternatively, you can go the C:\Windows\ Assembly directory and delete the hidden Desktop.ini file.

The Internal Structure of the GAC

Simply stated, the purpose of the GAC is to maintain a relationship between a strongly named assembly and a subdirectory. Basically, the CLR has an internal function that takes an assembly's name, version, culture, and public key token. This function then returns the path of a subdirectory where the specified assembly's files can be found.

If you go to a command prompt and change to the %SystemRoot%\Assembly directory, you'll see that the GAC actually spans multiple subdirectories. On my machine, I see the following GAC-related directories:

```
C:\Windows\Assembly\GAC
C:\Windows\Assembly\GAC_MSIL
C:\Windows\Assembly\GAC_32
C:\Windows\Assembly\GAC_64
```

The C:\Windows\Assembly\GAC directory contains the assemblies that were created for versions 1.0 and 1.1 of the CLR. These assemblies may consist entirely of managed code (IL), or the assemblies may contain managed and native x86 code (for example, if the assembly was built using Microsoft's C++ with Managed Extensions compiler). Assemblies in this subdirectory are allowed to run only in a 32-bit address space and therefore can run on an x86 version of Windows or using the WoW64 technology running on a 64-bit version of Windows.

The C:\Windows\Assembly\GAC_MSIL directory contains the assemblies that were created for version 2.0 of the CLR. These assemblies consist entirely of managed code (IL). Assemblies in this subdirectory can run in a 32-bit or 64-bit address space, and therefore, they can run on a 32-bit or 64-bit version of Windows. They could also run in a 32-bit address space by using the WoW64 technology running on a 64-bit version of Windows.

The C:\Windows\Assembly\GAC_32 directory contains the assemblies that were created for version 2.0 of the CLR. These assemblies contain managed code (IL) as well as native x86 code (for example, if the assembly was built using Microsoft's C++/CLI compiler). Assemblies in this subdirectory are allowed to run only in a 32-bit address space, and therefore, they can run on an x86 version of Windows or using the WoW64 technology running on a 64-bit version of Windows.

The C:\Windows\Assembly\GAC_64 directory contains the assemblies that were created for version 2.0 of the CLR. These assemblies contain managed code (IL) as well as native x64 or IA64 code. Since my machine is an x64 machine, this directory contains assemblies with x64 code in them. You cannot install assemblies into the GAC with IA64 (Intel Itanium) code on an x64 machine and vice versa. Assemblies in this subdirectory are allowed to run only in a 64-bit address space, and therefore, they can run only on a 64-bit version of Windows with a matching CPU architecture. If you are running on a 32-bit version of Windows, this subdirectory will not exist.

All of these subdirectories have identical internal structures, so we'll just take a look inside one of them. If you change directories to the GAC_MSIL subdirectory in the command window we just used, you'll see several more subdirectories, one for each assembly that has been installed into the GAC. Here's what my GAC_MSIL directory looks like (with some of the directories deleted to save trees):

```
Volume in drive C has no label.
Volume Serial Number is 2450-178A

Directory of C:\WINDOWS\assembly\GAC_MSIL

09/22/2005  07:38 AM    <DIR>          .
09/22/2005  07:38 AM    <DIR>          ..
08/25/2005  10:25 AM    <DIR>          Accessibility
08/25/2005  10:25 AM    <DIR>          ADODB
08/25/2005  10:25 AM    <DIR>          AspNetMMCExt
08/25/2005  10:29 AM    <DIR>          CppCodeProvider
08/25/2005  10:25 AM    <DIR>          cscompmgd
08/25/2005  10:25 AM    <DIR>          IEExecRemote
08/25/2005  10:25 AM    <DIR>          IEHost
08/25/2005  10:25 AM    <DIR>          IIEHost
08/25/2005  10:29 AM    <DIR>          MFCMIFC80
08/25/2005  10:32 AM    <DIR>          Microsoft.AnalysisServices
08/25/2005  10:32 AM    <DIR>          Microsoft.AnalysisServices.DeploymentEngine
08/25/2005  10:29 AM    <DIR>          Microsoft.Build.Conversion
08/25/2005  10:25 AM    <DIR>          Microsoft.Build.Engine
08/25/2005  10:25 AM    <DIR>          Microsoft.Build.Framework
08/25/2005  10:25 AM    <DIR>          Microsoft.Build.Tasks
08/25/2005  10:25 AM    <DIR>          Microsoft.Build.Utilities
08/25/2005  10:32 AM    <DIR>          Microsoft.DataWarehouse.Interfaces
08/25/2005  10:33 AM    <DIR>          Microsoft.ExceptionMessageBox
08/25/2005  10:25 AM    <DIR>          Microsoft.JScript
...
08/25/2005  10:25 AM    <DIR>          System
08/25/2005  10:25 AM    <DIR>          System.Configuration
08/25/2005  10:25 AM    <DIR>          System.Configuration.Install
08/25/2005  10:25 AM    <DIR>          System.Data.SqlXml
08/25/2005  10:25 AM    <DIR>          System.Deployment
08/25/2005  10:25 AM    <DIR>          System.Design
08/25/2005  10:25 AM    <DIR>          System.DirectoryServices
08/25/2005  10:25 AM    <DIR>          System.DirectoryServices.Protocols
```

```
08/25/2005  10:25 AM    <DIR>          System.Drawing
08/25/2005  10:25 AM    <DIR>          System.Drawing.Design
08/25/2005  10:25 AM    <DIR>          System.Management
08/25/2005  10:25 AM    <DIR>          System.Messaging
08/25/2005  10:25 AM    <DIR>          System.Runtime.Remoting
08/25/2005  10:25 AM    <DIR>          System.Runtime.Serialization.Formatters.Soap
08/25/2005  10:25 AM    <DIR>          System.Security
08/25/2005  10:25 AM    <DIR>          System.ServiceProcess
08/25/2005  10:25 AM    <DIR>          System.Web.Mobile
08/25/2005  10:25 AM    <DIR>          System.Web.RegularExpressions
08/25/2005  10:25 AM    <DIR>          System.Web.Services
08/25/2005  10:25 AM    <DIR>          System.Windows.Forms
08/25/2005  10:25 AM    <DIR>          System.Xml
              1 File(s)              0 bytes
            110 Dir(s)   13,211,459,584 bytes free
```

If you change to one of these directories, you'll see one or more additional subdirectories. My System directory looks like this:

```
Volume in drive C has no label.
 Volume Serial Number is 2450-178A

 Directory of C:\WINDOWS\assembly\GAC_MSIL\System

08/25/2005  10:25 AM    <DIR>          .
08/25/2005  10:25 AM    <DIR>          ..
08/25/2005  10:25 AM    <DIR>          2.0.0.0__b77a5c561934e089
              0 File(s)              0 bytes
              3 Dir(s)   13,211,467,776 bytes free
```

The System directory contains one subdirectory for every System.dll assembly installed on the machine. In my case, just one version of the System.dll assembly is installed:

```
"System, Version=2.0.0.0, Culture=neutral, PublicKeyToken=b77a5c561934e089"
```

The attributes are separated by underscore characters and are in the form of *(Version)_(Culture)_ (PublicKeyToken)*. In this example, there is no culture information, making them culture neutral. Inside this subdirectory are the files (such as System.dll) comprising this strongly named version of the System assembly.

> **Important**   It should be obvious that the whole point of the GAC is to hold multiple versions of an assembly. For example, the GAC can contain version 1.0.0.0 and version 2.0.0.0 of Calculus.dll. If an application is built and tested using version 1.0.0.0 of Calculus.dll, the CLR will load version 1.0.0.0 of Calculus.dll for that application even though a later version of the assembly exists and is installed into the GAC. This is the CLR's default policy regarding loading assembly versions, and the benefit of this policy is that installing a new version of an assembly won't affect an already-installed application. You can modify this policy in a number of ways, and I'll discuss them later in this chapter.

Building an Assembly that References a Strongly Named Assembly

Whenever you build an assembly, the assembly will have references to other strongly named assemblies. This is true because **System.Object** is defined in MSCorLib.dll, which is strongly named. However, it's likely that an assembly will reference types in other strongly named assemblies published either by Microsoft, a third party, or your own organization. In Chapter 2, I showed you how to use CSC.exe's **/reference** compiler switch to specify the assembly file names you want to reference. If the file name is a full path, CSC.exe loads the specified file and uses its metadata information to build the assembly. As mentioned in Chapter 2, if you specify a file name without a path, CSC.exe attempts to find the assembly by looking in the following directories (in order of their presentation here):

1. Working directory.

2. The directory that contains the CSC.exe file itself. This directory also contains the CLR DLLs.

3. Any directories specified using the **/lib** compiler switch.

4. Any directories specified using the LIB environment variable.

So if you're building an assembly that references Microsoft's System.Drawing.dll, you can specify the **/reference:System.Drawing.dll** switch when invoking CSC.exe. The compiler will examine the directories shown earlier and will find the System.Drawing.dll file in the directory that contains the CSC.exe file itself, which is the same directory that contains the DLLs for the version of the CLR the compiler is tied to. Even though this is the directory where the assembly is found at compile time, this isn't the directory where the assembly will be loaded from at run time.

You see, when you install the .NET Framework, two copies of Microsoft's assembly files are actually installed. One set is installed into the compiler/CLR directory, and another set is installed into a GAC subdirectory. The files in the compiler/CLR directory exist so that you can easily build your assembly, whereas the copies in the GAC exist so that they can be loaded at run time.

The reason that CSC.exe doesn't look in the GAC for referenced assemblies is because you'd have to specify a long, ugly path to the assembly file—something like C:\WINDOWS\Assembly\GAC_MSIL\System.Drawing\2.0.0.0__b03f5f7f11d50a3a\System.Drawing.dll. Alternatively, CSC.exe could allow you to specify a still long but slightly nicer-looking string, such as "System.Drawing, Version=2.0.0.0, Culture=neutral, PublicKeyToken=b03f5f7f11d50a3a". Both of these solutions were deemed worse than having the assembly files installed twice on the user's hard drive.

> **Note**   When building an assembly, you may want to refer to another assembly that has an x86 as well as an x64 version of itself available. Fortunately, the GAC subdirectories can actually hold an x86 and an x64 version of the same assembly. However, since the assemblies have the same file name, you cannot have different versions of these assemblies in the compiler/CLR directory. However, it shouldn't matter. When you install the .NET Framework on a machine, the x86, x64, or IA64 version of the assemblies are installed in the compiler/CLR directory. When you build an assembly, you can reference whatever version of the files were installed because all of the versions contain identical metadata and differ only by their code. At run time, the proper version of the assembly will be loaded from the GAC_32 or GAC_64 sub-directory. I'll discuss how the CLR determines where to load the assembly from at run time later in this chapter.

Strongly Named Assemblies Are Tamper-Resistant

Signing an assembly with a private key ensures that the holder of the corresponding public key produced the assembly. When the assembly is installed into the GAC, the system hashes the contents of the file containing the manifest and compares the hash value with the RSA digital signature value embedded within the PE file (after unsigning it with the public key). If the values are identical, the file's contents haven't been tampered with, and you know that you have the public key that corresponds to the publisher's private key. In addition, the system hashes the contents of the assembly's other files and compares the hash values with the hash values stored in the manifest file's FileDef table. If any of the hash values don't match, at least one of the assembly's files has been tampered with, and the assembly will fail to install into the GAC.

> **Important**   This mechanism ensures only that a file's content hasn't been tampered with. The mechanism doesn't allow you to tell who the publisher is unless you're absolutely positive that the publisher produced the public key you have and you're sure that the publisher's private key was never compromised. Another way to know the identity of the publisher is if the publisher associated its identity with the assembly by using Microsoft's Authenticode technology.

When an application needs to bind to an assembly, the CLR uses the referenced assembly's properties (name, version, culture, and public key) to locate the assembly in the GAC. If the referenced assembly can be found, its containing subdirectory is returned, and the file holding the manifest is loaded. Finding the assembly this way assures the caller that the assembly loaded at run time came from the same publisher that built the assembly the code was compiled against. This assurance is possible because the public key token in the referencing assembly's AssemblyRef table corresponds to the public key in the referenced assembly's AssemblyDef table. If the referenced assembly isn't in the GAC, the CLR looks in the application's base directory and then in any of the private paths identified in the application's configuration file; then, if the application was installed using MSI, the CLR asks MSI to locate the assembly. If the assembly can't be found in any of these locations, the bind fails, and a `System.IO.FileNotFoundException` is thrown.

When strongly named assembly files are loaded from a location other than the GAC (via the application's base directory or via a **codeBase** element in a configuration file), the CLR compares hash values when the assembly is loaded. In other words, a hash of the file is performed every time an application executes and loads the assembly. This performance hit is a tradeoff for being certain that the assembly file's content hasn't been tampered with. When the CLR detects mismatched hash values at run time, it throws a `System.IO.FileLoadException`.

Delayed Signing

Earlier in this chapter, I discussed how the SN.exe tool can produce public/private key pairs. This tool generates the keys by making calls into the Crypto API provided by Windows. These keys can be stored in files or other storage devices. For example, large organizations (such as Microsoft) will maintain the returned private key in a hardware device that stays locked in a vault; only a few people in the company have access to the private key. This precaution prevents the private key from being compromised and ensures the key's integrity. The public key is, well, public and freely distributed.

When you're ready to package your strongly named assembly, you'll have to use the secure private key to sign it. However, while developing and testing your assembly, gaining access to the secure private key can be a hassle. For this reason, the .NET Framework supports *delayed signing*, sometimes referred to as *partial signing*. Delayed signing allows you to build an assembly by using only your company's public key; the private key isn't necessary. Using the public key allows assemblies that reference your assembly to embed the correct public key value in their AssemblyRef metadata entries. It also allows the assembly to be placed in the GAC's internal structure appropriately. If you don't sign the file with your company's private key, you lose all of the tampering protection afforded to you because the assembly's files won't be hashed, and a digital signature won't be embedded in the file. This loss of protection shouldn't be a problem, however, because you use delayed signing only while developing your own assembly, not when you're ready to package and deploy the assembly.

Basically, you get your company's public key value in a file and pass the file name to whatever utility you use to build the assembly. (As I have shown earlier in this chapter, you can use SN.exe's **-p** switch to extract a public key from a file that contains a public/private key pair.) You must also tell the tool that you want the assembly to be delay signed, meaning that you're not supplying a private key. For the C# compiler, you do this by specifying the **/delaysign** compiler switch. In Visual Studio, you display the properties for your project, click the Signing tab, and then select the Delay Sign Only check box (as shown in Figure 3-1 earlier in this chapter). If you're using AL.exe, you can specify the **/delay[sign]** command-line switch.

When the compiler or AL.exe detects that you're delay signing an assembly, it will emit the assembly's AssemblyDef manifest entry, which will contain the assembly's public key. Again, the presence of the public key allows the assembly to be placed in the GAC. It also allows you to build other assemblies that reference this assembly; the referencing assemblies will have the correct public key in their AssemblyRef metadata table entries. When creating the resulting assembly, space is left in the resulting PE file for the RSA digital signature. (The utility can determine how much space is necessary from the size of the public key.) Note that the file's contents won't be hashed at this time either.

At this point, the resulting assembly doesn't have a valid signature. Attempting to install the assembly into the GAC will fail because a hash of the file's contents hasn't been done—the file appears to have been tampered with. On every machine on which the assembly needs to be installed into the GAC, you must prevent the system from verifying the integrity of the assembly's files. To do this, you use the SN.exe utility, specifying the **–vr** command-line switch. Executing SN.exe with this switch also tells the CLR to skip checking hash values for any of the assembly's files when loaded at run time. Internally, SN's **–vr** switch adds the assembly's identity under the following registry subkey: HKEY_LOCAL_MACHINE\SOFTWARE\ Microsoft\StrongName\Verification.

When you're finished developing and testing the assembly, you need to officially sign it so that you can package and deploy it. To sign the assembly, use the SN.exe utility again, this time with the **–R** switch and the name of the file that contains the actual private key. The **–R** switch causes SN.exe to hash the file's contents, sign it with the private key, and embed the RSA digital signature in the file where the space for it had previously been reserved. After this step, you can deploy the fully signed assembly. On the developing and testing machines, don't forget to turn verification of this assembly back on by using SN.exe's **–vu** or **–vx** command-line switch. The following list summarizes the steps discussed in this section to develop your assembly by using the delay signing technique:

1. While developing an assembly, obtain a file that contains only your company's public key, and compile your assembly by using the **/keyfile** and **/delaysign** compiler switches:

    ```
    csc /keyfile:MyCompany.PublicKey /delaysign MyAssembly.cs
    ```

2. After building the assembly, execute the following line so that the CLR will trust the assembly's bytes without performing the hash and comparison. This allows you to install the assembly in the GAC (if you desire). Now, you can build other assemblies that reference the assembly, and you can test the assembly. Note that you have to execute the following command line only once per machine; it's not necessary to perform this step each time you build your assembly.

    ```
    SN.exe –Vr MyAssembly.dll
    ```

3. When ready to package and deploy the assembly, obtain your company's private key, and then execute the line below. You can install this new version in the GAC if you desire, but don't attempt to install it in the GAC until executing step 4.

    ```
    SN.exe –R MyAssembly.dll MyCompany.PrivateKey
    ```

4. To test in real conditions, turn verification back on by executing the following command line:

```
SN -Vu MyAssembly.dll
```

At the beginning of this section, I mentioned how organizations keep their key pairs in a hardware device such as a smart card. To keep these keys secure, you must make sure that the key values are never persisted in a disk file. Cryptographic service providers (CSPs) offer containers that abstract the location of these keys. Microsoft, for example, uses a CSP that has a container that, when accessed, obtains the private key from a hardware device.

If your public/private key pair is in a CSP container, you'll have to specify different switches to the CSC.exe, AL.exe, and SN.exe programs: When compiling (CSC.exe), specify the **/keycontainer** switch instead of the **/keyfile** switch; when linking (AL.exe), specify its **/keyname** switch instead of its **/keyfile** switch; and when using the Strong Name program (SN.exe) to add a private key to a delay-signed assembly, specify the **–Rc** switch instead of the **–R** switch. SN.exe offers additional switches that allow you to perform operations with a CSP.

> **Important**   Delay signing is also useful whenever you want to perform some other operation to an assembly before you package it. For example, you may want to run an obfuscator over your assembly. You can't obfuscate an assembly after it's been fully signed because the hash value will be incorrect. So, if you want to obfuscate an assembly file or perform any other type of post-build operation, you should use delay signing, perform the post-build operation, and then run SN.exe with the **–R** or **–Rc** switch to complete the signing process of the assembly with all of its hashing.

Privately Deploying Strongly Named Assemblies

Installing assemblies into the GAC offers several benefits. The GAC enables many applications to share assemblies, reducing physical memory usage on the whole. In addition, it's easy to deploy a new version of the assembly into the GAC and have all applications use the new version via a publisher policy (described later in this chapter). The GAC also provides side-by-side management for an assembly's different versions. However, the GAC is usually secured so that only an administrator can install an assembly into it. Also, installing into the GAC breaks the simple copy deployment story.

Although strongly named assemblies can be installed into the GAC, they certainly don't have to be. In fact, it's recommended that you deploy assemblies into the GAC only if the assembly is intended to be shared by many applications. If an assembly isn't intended to be shared, it should be deployed privately. Deploying privately preserves the simple copy install deployment story and better isolates the application and its assemblies. Also, the GAC isn't intended to be the new C:\Windows\System32 dumping ground for common files. The reason is because new versions of assemblies don't overwrite each other; they are installed side by side, eating up disk space.

In addition to deploying a strongly named assembly in the GAC or privately, a strongly named assembly can be deployed to some arbitrary directory that a small set of applications know about. For example, you might be producing three applications, all of which want to share a strongly named assembly. Upon installation, you can create three directories: one for each application and an additional directory for the assembly you want shared. When you install each application into its directory, also install an XML configuration file, and have the shared assembly's **codeBase** element indicate the path of the shared assembly. Now at run time, the CLR will know to look in the strongly named assembly's directory for the shared assembly. For the record, this technique is rarely used and is somewhat discouraged because no single application controls when the assembly's files should be uninstalled.

> **Note**   The configuration file's **codeBase** element actually identifies a URL. This URL can refer to any directory on the user's hard disk or to a Web address. In the case of a Web address, the CLR will automatically download the file and store it in the user's download cache (a subdirectory under C:\Documents and Settings*UserName*\Local Settings\Application Data\Assembly, where *UserName* is the name of the Windows user account currently signed on). When referenced in the future, the CLR will compare the timestamp of the downloaded file with the timestamp of the file at the specified URL. If the timestamp of the file at the URL is newer, the CLR will download the new version of the file and load it. If the previously downloaded file is newer, the CLR will load this file and will not download the file again (improving performance). An example of a configuration file containing a **codeBase** element is shown later in this chapter.
>
> When a strongly named assembly is installed into the GAC, the system ensures that the file containing the manifest hasn't been tampered with. This check occurs only once: at installation time. On the other hand, when a strongly named assembly is loaded from a directory other than the GAC, the CLR verifies the assembly's manifest file to ensure that the file's contents have not been tampered with, causing an additional performance hit to occur every time this file is loaded.

How the Runtime Resolves Type References

At the beginning of Chapter 2, we saw the following source code:

```
public sealed class Program {
   public static void Main() {
      System.Console.WriteLine("Hi");
   }
}
```

This code is compiled and built into an assembly, say Program.exe. When you run this application, the CLR loads and initializes. Then the CLR reads the assembly's CLR header, looking for the MethodDefToken that identifies the application's entry point method (**Main**). From the MethodDef metadata table, the offset within the file for the method's IL code is located and JIT-compiled into native code, which includes having the code verified for type safety. The native code then starts executing. Following is the IL code for the **Main** method. To obtain this output, I ran ILDasm.exe, chose the View menu's Show Bytes menu item, and then double-clicked the **Main** method in the tree view.

```
.method public hidebysig static void  Main() cil managed
// SIG: 00 00 01
{
  .entrypoint
  // Method begins at RVA 0x2050
  // Code size       11 (0xb)
  .maxstack  8
  IL_0000:  /* 72   | (70)000001       */
            ldstr      "Hi"
  IL_0005:  /* 28   | (0A)000003       */
            call       void [mscorlib]System.Console::WriteLine(string)
  IL_000a:  /* 2A   |                  */
            ret
} // end of method Program::Main
```

When JIT-compiling this code, the CLR detects all references to types and members and loads their defining assemblies (if not already loaded). As you can see, the IL code above has a reference to **System.Console.WriteLine**. Specifically, the IL **call** instruction references metadata token 0A000003. This token identifies entry 3 in the MemberRef metadata table (table 0A). The CLR looks up this MemberRef entry and sees that one of its fields refers to an entry in a TypeRef table (the **System.Console** type). From the TypeRef entry, the CLR is directed to an AssemblyRef entry: "MSCorLib, Version=2.0.0.0, Culture=neutral, PublicKeyToken= b77a5c561934e089". At this point, the CLR knows which assembly it needs. Now the CLR must locate the assembly in order to load it.

When resolving a referenced type, the CLR can find the type in one of three places:

- **Same file** Access to a type that is in the same file is determined at compile time (sometimes referred to as *early bound*). The type is loaded out of the file directly, and execution continues.

- **Different file, same assembly** The runtime ensures that the file being referenced is, in fact, in the assembly's FileRef table of the current assembly's manifest. The runtime then looks in the directory where the assembly's manifest file was loaded. The file is loaded, its hash value is checked to ensure the file's integrity, the type's member is found, and execution continues.

- **Different file, different assembly** When a referenced type is in a different assembly's file, the runtime loads the file that contains the referenced assembly's manifest. If this file doesn't contain the type, the appropriate file is loaded. The type's member is found, and execution continues.

> **Note**   The ModuleDef, ModuleRef, and FileDef metadata tables refer to files using the file's name and its extension. However, the AssemblyRef metadata table refers to assemblies by file name without an extension. When binding to an assembly, the system automatically appends .dll and .exe file extensions while attempting to locate the file by probing the directories as mentioned in the section "Simple Administrative Control (Configuration)" in Chapter 2.

If any errors occur while resolving a type reference—file can't be found, file can't be loaded, hash mismatch, and so on—an appropriate exception is thrown.

In the previous example, the CLR determines that `System.Console` is implemented in a different assembly than the caller. The CLR must search for the assembly and load the PE file that contains the assembly's manifest. The manifest is then scanned to determine the PE file that implements the type. If the manifest file contains the referenced type, all is well. If the type is in another of the assembly's files, the CLR loads the other file and scans its metadata to locate the type. The CLR then creates its internal data structures to represent the type, and the JIT compiler completes the compilation for the `Main` method. Finally, the `Main` method can start executing.

Figure 3-6 illustrates how type binding occurs.

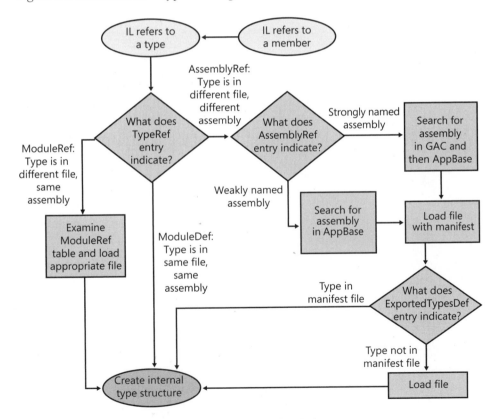

Note: If any operation fails, an appropriate exception is thrown.

Figure 3-6   Flowchart showing how, given IL code that refers to a method or type, the CLR uses metadata to locate the proper assembly file that defines a type

> **Important**   Strictly speaking, the example just described isn't 100 percent correct. For references to methods and types defined in an assembly that is shipped with the .NET Framework, the discussion is correct. However, the .NET Framework assemblies (including MSCorLib.dll) are closely tied to the version of the CLR that's running. Any assembly that references .NET Framework assemblies always binds to the version that matches the CLR's version. This is called *unification*, and Microsoft does this because they test all of the .NET Framework assemblies with a particular version of the CLR; therefore, unifying the code stack helps ensure that applications will work correctly.
>
> So in the previous example, the reference to `System.Console`'s `WriteLine` method binds to whatever version of MSCorLib.dll matches the version of the CLR, regardless of what version of MSCorLib.dll is referenced in the assembly's AssemblyRef metadata table.

There is one more twist to this story: To the CLR, all assemblies are identified by name, version, culture, and public key. However, the GAC identifies assemblies using name, version, culture, public key, and CPU architecture. When searching the GAC for an assembly, the CLR figures out what type of process the application is currently running in: 32-bit x86 (possibly using the WoW64 technology), 64-bit x64, or 64-bit IA64. Then, when searching the GAC for an assembly, a CPU architecture–specific search is done first. If a matching assembly is not found, the C:\Windows\Assembly\GAC_MSIL directory is checked. If there is still no match, the C:\Windows\Assembly\GAC directory is checked for version 1.x assemblies.

In this section, you saw how the CLR locates an assembly when using a default policy. However, an administrator or the publisher of an assembly can override the default policy. In the next two sections, I'll describe how to alter the CLR's default binding policy.

Advanced Administrative Control (Configuration)

In the section "Simple Administrative Control (Configuration)" in Chapter 2, I gave a brief introduction to how an administrator can affect the way the CLR searches and binds to assemblies. In that section, I demonstrated how a referenced assembly's files can be moved to a subdirectory of the application's base directory and how the CLR uses the application's XML configuration file to locate the moved files.

Having discussed only the probing element's `privatePath` attribute in Chapter 2, I'm going to discuss the other XML configuration file elements in this section. Following is an XML configuration file:

```
<?xml version="1.0"?>
<configuration>
   <runtime>
      <assemblyBinding xmlns="urn:schemas-microsoft-com:asm.v1">
         <probing privatePath="AuxFiles;bin\subdir" />

         <dependentAssembly>
```

```
      <assemblyIdentity name="JeffTypes"
        publicKeyToken="32ab4ba45e0a69a1" culture="neutral"/>

      <bindingRedirect
        oldVersion="1.0.0.0" newVersion="2.0.0.0" />

      <codeBase version="2.0.0.0"
        href="http://www.Wintellect.com/JeffTypes.dll" />

    </dependentAssembly>

    <dependentAssembly>

      <assemblyIdentity name="FredTypes"
        publicKeyToken="1f2e74e897abbcfe" culture="neutral"/>

      <bindingRedirect
        oldVersion="3.0.0.0-3.5.0.0" newVersion="4.0.0.0" />

      <publisherPolicy apply="no" />

    </dependentAssembly>

  </assemblyBinding>
 </runtime>
</configuration>
```

This XML file gives a wealth of information to the CLR. Here's what it says:

- **probing element**   Look in the application base directory's AuxFiles and bin\subdir subdirectories when trying to find a weakly named assembly. For strongly named assemblies, the CLR looks in the GAC or in the URL specified by the **codeBase** element. The CLR looks in the application's private paths for a strongly named assembly only if no **codeBase** element is specified.

- **First dependentAssembly, assemblyIdentity, and bindingRedirect elements**   When attempting to locate version 1.0.0.0 of the culture-neutral JeffTypes assembly published by the organization that controls the **32ab4ba45e0a69a1** public key token, locate version 2.0.0.0 of the same assembly instead.

- **codeBase element**   When attempting to locate version 2.0.0.0 of the culture-neutral JeffTypes assembly published by the organization that controls the **32ab4ba45e0a69a1** public key token, try to find it at the following URL: *www.Wintellect.com/JeffTypes.dll*. Although I didn't mention it in Chapter 2, a **codeBase** element can also be used with weakly named assemblies. In this case, the assembly's version number is ignored and should be omitted from the XML's **codeBase** element. Also, the **codeBase** URL must refer to a directory under the application's base directory.

- **Second dependentAssembly, assemblyIdentity, and bindingRedirect elements**   When attempting to locate version 3.0.0.0 through version 3.5.0.0 inclusive of the culture-neutral FredTypes assembly published by the organization that controls the **1f2e74e897abbcfe** public key token, locate version 4.0.0.0 of the same assembly instead.

- **publisherPolicy element**   If the organization that produces the FredTypes assembly has deployed a publisher policy file (described in the next section), the CLR should ignore this file.

When compiling a method, the CLR determines the types and members being referenced. Using this information, the runtime determines, by looking in the referencing assembly's AssemblyRef table, the assembly that was originally referenced when the calling assembly was built. The CLR then looks up the assembly/version in the application's configuration file and applies any version number redirections; the CLR is now looking for this assembly/version.

If the **publisherPolicy** element's **apply** attribute is set to **yes**—or if the element is omitted—the CLR examines the GAC for the new assembly/version and applies any version number redirections that the publisher of the assembly feels is necessary; the CLR is now looking for this assembly/version. I'll talk more about publisher policy in the next section. Finally, the CLR looks up the new assembly/version in the machine's Machine.config file and applies any version number redirections there.

At this point, the CLR knows the version of the assembly that it should load, and it attempts to load the assembly from the GAC. If the assembly isn't in the GAC, and if there is no **codeBase** element, the CLR probes for the assembly as I described in Chapter 2. If the configuration file that performs the last redirection also contains a **codeBase** element, the CLR attempts to load the assembly from the **codeBase** element's specified URL.

Using these configuration files, an administrator can really control what assembly the CLR decides to load. If an application is experiencing a bug, the administrator can contact the publisher of the errant assembly. The publisher can send the administrator a new assembly that the administrator can install. By default, the CLR won't load this new assembly because the already-built assemblies don't reference the new version. However, the administrator can modify the application's XML configuration file to instruct the CLR to load the new assembly. To make things easier, a publisher can create this XML file by using the Microsoft .NET Framework 2.0 Configuration administrative tool that ships with the .NET Framework SDK; this tool does not ship with the .NET Framework redistributable files. To find this tool, in Windows, open Control Panel, and then open Administrative Tools.

If the administrator wants all applications on the machine to pick up the new assembly, the administrator can modify the machine's Machine.config file instead, and the CLR will load the new assembly whenever an application refers to the old assembly.

If the new assembly doesn't fix the original bug, the administrator can delete the binding redirection lines from the configuration file, and the application will behave as it did before. It's important to note that the system allows the use of an assembly that doesn't exactly match the assembly version recorded in the metadata. This extra flexibility is very handy.

Publisher Policy Control

In the scenario described in the previous section, the publisher of an assembly simply sent a new version of the assembly to the administrator, who installed the assembly and manually edited the application's or machine's XML configuration files. In general, when a publisher fixes a bug in an assembly, the publisher would like an easy way to package and distribute the new assembly to all of the users. But the publisher also needs a way to tell each user's CLR to use the new assembly version instead of the old assembly version. Sure, each user could modify his or her application's or machine's XML configuration file, but this is terribly inconvenient and error prone. What the publisher needs is a way to create policy information that is installed on the user's computer when the new assembly is installed. In this section, I'll show how an assembly's publisher can create this policy information.

Let's say that you're a publisher of an assembly and that you've just created a new version of your assembly that fixes some bugs. When you package your new assembly to send out to all of your users, you should also create an XML configuration file. This configuration file looks just like the configuration files we've been talking about. Here's an example file (called JeffTypes.config) for the JeffTypes.dll assembly:

```
<configuration>
   <runtime>
      <assemblyBinding xmlns="urn:schemas-microsoft-com:asm.v1">
         <dependentAssembly>

            <assemblyIdentity name="JeffTypes"
              publicKeyToken="32ab4ba45e0a69a1" culture="neutral"/>

            <bindingRedirect
              oldVersion="1.0.0.0" newVersion="2.0.0.0" />

            <codeBase version="2.0.0.0"
              href="http://www.wintellect.com/JeffTypes.dll"/>

         </dependentAssembly>
      </assemblyBinding>
   </runtime>
</configuration>
```

Of course, publishers can set policies only for the assemblies that they themselves create. In addition, the elements shown here are the only elements that can be specified in a publisher policy configuration file; you can't specify the **probing** or **publisherPolicy** elements, for example.

This configuration file tells the CLR to load version 2.0.0.0 of the JeffTypes assembly whenever version 1.0.0.0 of the assembly is referenced. Now you, the publisher, can create an assembly that contains this publisher policy configuration file. You create the publisher policy assembly by running AL.exe as follows:

```
AL.exe /out:Policy.1.0.JeffTypes.dll
       /version:1.0.0.0
       /keyfile:MyCompany.keys
       /linkresource:JeffTypes.config
```

Let me explain the meaning of AL.exe's command-line switches:

- **/out**   This switch tells AL.exe to create a new PE file, called Policy.1.0.JeffTypes.dll, which contains nothing but a manifest. The name of this assembly is very important. The first part of the name, Policy, tells the CLR that this assembly contains publisher policy information. The second and third parts of the name, 1.0, tell the CLR that this publisher policy assembly is for any version of the JeffTypes assembly that has a major and minor version of 1.0. Publisher policies apply to the major and minor version numbers of an assembly only; you can't create a publisher policy that is specific to individual builds or revisions of an assembly. The fourth part of the name, JeffTypes, indicates the name of the assembly that this publisher policy corresponds to. The fifth and last part of the name, dll, is simply the extension given to the resulting assembly file.

- **/version**   This switch identifies the version of the publisher policy assembly; this version number has nothing to do with the JeffTypes assembly itself. You see, publisher policy assemblies can also be versioned. Today, the publisher might create a publisher policy redirecting version 1.0.0.0 of JeffTypes to version 2.0.0.0. In the future, the publisher might want to direct version 1.0.0.0 of JeffTypes to version 2.5.0.0. The CLR uses this version number so that it knows to pick up the latest version of the publisher policy assembly.

- **/keyfile**   This switch causes AL.exe to sign the publisher policy assembly by using the publisher's public/private key pair. This key pair must also match the key pair used for all versions of the JeffTypes assembly. After all, this is how the CLR knows that the same publisher created both the JeffTypes assembly and this publisher policy file.

- **/linkresource**   This switch tells AL.exe that the XML configuration file is to be considered a separate file of the assembly. The resulting assembly consists of two files, both of which must be packaged and deployed to the users along with the new version of the JeffTypes assembly. By the way, you can't use AL.exe's **/embedresource** switch to embed the XML configuration file into the assembly file, making a single file assembly, because the CLR requires the XML file to be contained in its own separate file.

Once this publisher policy assembly is built, it can be packaged together with the new JeffTypes.dll assembly file and deployed to users. The publisher policy assembly must be installed into the GAC. Although the JeffTypes assembly can also be installed into the GAC, it doesn't have to be. It could be deployed into an application's base directory or some other directory identified by a **codeBase** URL.

> **Important**   A publisher should create a publisher policy assembly only when deploying a bug fix or a service pack version of an assembly. When doing a fresh install of an application, no publisher policy assemblies should be installed.

I want to make one last point about publisher policy. Say that a publisher distributes a publisher policy assembly, and for some reason, the new assembly introduces more bugs than it fixes. If this happens, the administrator would like to tell the CLR to ignore the publisher policy assembly. To have the runtime do this, the administrator can edit the application's configuration file and add the following **publisherPolicy** element:

```
<publisherPolicy apply="no"/>
```

This element can be placed as a child element of the **<assemblyBinding>** element in the application's configuration file so that it applies to all assemblies, or as a child element of the **<dependantAssembly>** element in the application's configuration file to have it apply to a specific assembly. When the CLR processes the application's configuration file, it will see that the GAC shouldn't be examined for the publisher policy assembly. So the CLR will continue to operate using the older version of the assembly. Note, however, that the CLR will still examine and apply any policy specified in the Machine.config file.

Important   A publisher policy assembly is a way for a publisher to make a statement about the compatibility of different versions of an assembly. If a new version of an assembly isn't intended to be compatible with an earlier version, the publisher shouldn't create a publisher policy assembly. In general, use a publisher policy assembly when you build a new version of your assembly that fixes a bug. You should test the new version of the assembly for backward compatibility. On the other hand, if you're adding new features to your assembly, you should consider the assembly to have no relationship to a previous version, and you shouldn't ship a publisher policy assembly. In addition, there's no need to do any backward compatibility testing with such an assembly.

Part II
Working with Types

Chapter 4
Type Fundamentals

In this chapter, I will introduce information that is fundamental to working with types and the common language runtime (CLR). In particular, I'll discuss the minimum set of behaviors that you can expect every type to have. I'll also describe type safety, namespaces, assemblies, and the various ways you can cast objects from one type to another. Finally, I'll conclude this chapter with an explanation of how types, objects, thread stacks, and the managed heap all relate to one another at run time.

All Types Are Derived from `System.Object`

The runtime requires every type to ultimately be derived from the **System.Object** type. This means that the following two type definitions are identical:

```
// Implicitly derived from Object      // Explicitly derived from Object
class Employee {                       class Employee : System.Object {
  ...                                    ...
}                                      }
```

Because all types are ultimately derived from **System.Object**, you are guaranteed that every object of every type has a minimum set of methods. Specifically, the **System.Object** class offers the public instance methods listed in Table 4-1.

Table 4-1   Public Methods of `System.Object`

Public Method	Description
`Equals`	Returns **true** if two objects have the same value. For more information about this method, see the "Object Equality and Identity" section in Chapter 5, "Primitive, Reference, and Value Types."
`GetHashCode`	Returns a hash code for this object's value. A type should override this method if its objects are to be used as a key in a hash table collection. The method should provide a good distribution for its objects. It is unfortunate that this method is defined in **object**, because most types are never used as keys in a hash table; this method should have been defined in an interface. For more information about this method, see the "Object Hash Codes" section in Chapter 5.

Table 4-1   Public Methods of `System.Object`

Public Method	Description
ToString	By default, returns the full name of the type (`this.GetType().FullName`). However, it is common to override this method so that it returns a `String` object containing a representation of the object's state. For example, the core types, such as `Boolean` and `Int32`, override this method to return a string representation of their values. It is also common to override this method for debugging purposes; you can call it and get a string showing the values of the object's fields. Note that `ToString` is expected to be aware of the `CultureInfo` associated with the calling thread. Chapter 12, "Enumerated Types and Bit Flags," discusses `ToString` in greater detail.
GetType	Returns an instance of a `Type`-derived object that identifies the type of the object used to call `GetType`. The returned `Type` object can be used with the reflection classes to obtain metadata information about the type. Reflection is discussed in Chapter 22, "Assembly Loading and Reflection." The `GetType` method is nonvirtual, which prevents a class from overriding this method and lying about its type, violating type safety.

In addition, types that derive from `System.Object` have access to the protected methods listed in Table 4-2.

Table 4-2   Protected Methods of `System.Object`

Protected Method	Description
MemberwiseClone	This nonvirtual method creates a new instance of the type and sets the new object's instance fields to be identical to the `this` object's instance fields. A reference to the new instance is returned.
Finalize	This virtual method is called when the garbage collector determines that the object is garbage before the memory for the object is re-claimed. Types that require cleanup when collected should override this method. I'll talk about this important method in much more detail in Chapter 20, "Automatic Memory Management (Garbage Collection)."

The CLR requires all objects to be created using the **new** operator. The following line shows how to create an **Employee** object:

```
Employee e = new Employee("ConstructorParam1");
```

Here's what the **new** operator does:

1. It calculates the number of bytes required by all instance fields defined in the type and all of its base types up to and including **System.Object** (which defines no instance fields of its own). Every object on the heap requires some additional members—called the type object pointer and the sync block index—used by the CLR to manage the object. The bytes for these additional members are added to the size of the object.

2. It allocates memory for the object by allocating the number of bytes required for the specified type from the managed heap; all of these bytes are then set to zero (0).

3. It initializes the object's type object pointer and sync block index members.

4. The type's instance constructor is called, passing it any arguments (the string **"ConstructorParam1"** in the preceding example) specified in the call to **new**. Most compilers automatically emit code in a constructor to call a base class's constructor. Each constructor is responsible for initializing the instance fields defined by the type whose constructor is being called. Eventually, **System.Object**'s constructor is called, and this constructor method does nothing but return. You can verify this by using ILDasm.exe to load MSCorLib.dll and examine **System.Object**'s constructor method.

After **new** has performed all of these operations, it returns a reference (or pointer) to the newly created object. In the preceding code example, this reference is saved in the variable **e**, which is of type **Employee**.

By the way, the **new** operator has no complementary **delete** operator; that is, there is no way to explicitly free the memory allocated for an object. The CLR uses a garbage-collected environment (described in Chapter 20) that automatically detects when objects are no longer being used or accessed and frees the object's memory automatically.

Casting Between Types

One of the most important features of the CLR is type safety. At run time, the CLR always knows what type an object is. You can always discover an object's exact type by calling the **GetType** method. Because this method is nonvirtual, it is impossible for a type to spoof another type. For example, the **Employee** type can't override the **GetType** method and have it return a type of **SpaceShuttle**.

Developers frequently find it necessary to cast an object to various types. The CLR allows you to cast an object to its type or to any of its base types. Your choice of programming language dictates how to expose casting operations to the developer. For example, C# doesn't require any special syntax to cast an object to any of its base types, because casts to base types are considered safe implicit conversions. However, C# does require the developer to explicitly cast an object to any of its derived types since such a cast could fail at run time. The following code demonstrates casting to base and derived types:

```
// This type is implicitly derived from System.Object.
internal class Employee {
   ...
}


public sealed class Program {
   public static void Main() {
      // No cast needed since new returns an Employee object
      // and Object is a base type of Employee.
      Object o = new Employee();
```

```
        // Cast required since Employee is derived from Object.
        // Other languages (such as Visual Basic) might not require
        // this cast to compile.
        Employee e = (Employee) o;
    }
}
```

This example shows what is necessary for your compiler to compile your code. Now I'll explain what happens at run time. At run time, the CLR checks casting operations to ensure that casts are always to the object's actual type or any of its base types. For example, the following code will compile, but at run time, an **InvalidCastException** will be thrown:

```
internal class Employee {
    ...
}
internal class Manager : Employee {
    ...
}


public sealed class Program {
    public static void Main() {
        // Construct a Manager object and pass it to PromoteEmployee.
        // A Manager IS-A Object: PromoteEmployee runs OK.
        Manager m = new Manager();
        PromoteEmployee(m);

        // Construct a DateTime object and pass it to PromoteEmployee.
        // A DateTime is NOT derived from Employee. PromoteEmployee
        // throws a System.InvalidCastException exception.
        DateTime newYears = new DateTime(2007, 1, 1);
        PromoteEmployee(newYears);
    }


    public static void PromoteEmployee(Object o) {
        // At this point, the compiler doesn't know exactly what
        // type of object o refers to. So the compiler allows the
        // code to compile. However, at run time, the CLR does know
        // what type o refers to (each time the cast is performed) and
        // it checks whether the object's type is Employee or any type
        // that is derived from Employee.
        Employee e = (Employee) o;
        ...
    }
}
```

In the **Main** method, a **Manager** object is constructed and passed to **PromoteEmployee**. This code compiles and executes because **Manager** is derived from **Object**, which is what **Promote-Employee** expects. Once inside **PromoteEmployee**, the CLR confirms that **o** refers to an object that is either an **Employee** or a type that is derived from **Employee**. Because **Manager** is derived from **Employee**, the CLR performs the cast and allows **PromoteEmployee** to continue executing.

After `PromoteEmployee` returns, `Main` constructs a `DateTime` object and passes it to `Promote-Employee`. Again, `DateTime` is derived from `Object`, and the compiler compiles the code that calls `PromoteEmployee` with no problem. However, inside `PromoteEmployee`, the CLR checks the cast and detects that `o` refers to a `DateTime` object and is therefore not an `Employee` or any type derived from `Employee`. At this point, the CLR can't allow the cast and throws a `System.InvalidCastException`.

If the CLR allowed the cast, there would be no type safety, and the results would be unpredictable, including the possibility of application crashes and security breaches caused by the ability of types to easily spoof other types. Type spoofing is the cause of many security breaches and compromises an application's stability and robustness. Type safety is therefore an extremely important part of the CLR.

By the way, the proper way to declare the `PromoteEmployee` method would be to specify an `Employee` type instead of an `Object` type as its parameter so that the compiler produces a compile-time error, saving the developer from waiting until a run-time exception occurs to discover a problem. I used `Object` so that I could demonstrate how the C# compiler and the CLR deal with casting and type-safety.

Casting with the C# is and as Operators

Another way to cast in the C# language is to use the **is** operator. The **is** operator checks whether an object is compatible with a given type, and the result of the evaluation is a **Boolean**: **true** or **false**. The **is** operator will never throw an exception. The following code demonstrates:

```
Object o = new Object();
Boolean b1 = (o is Object);   // b1 is true.
Boolean b2 = (o is Employee); // b2 is false.
```

If the object reference is **null**, the **is** operator always returns **false** because there is no object available to check its type.

The **is** operator is typically used as follows:

```
if (o is Employee) {
   Employee e = (Employee) o;
   // Use e within the remainder of the 'if' statement.
}
```

In this code, the CLR is actually checking the object's type twice: The **is** operator first checks to see if `o` is compatible with the **Employee** type. If it is, inside the **if** statement, the CLR again verifies that `o` refers to an **Employee** when performing the cast. The CLR's type checking improves security, but it certainly comes at a performance cost, because the CLR must determine the actual type of the object referred to by the variable (`o`), and then the CLR must walk the inheritance hierarchy, checking each base type against the specified type (**Employee**). Because this programming paradigm is quite common, C# offers a way to simplify this code and improve its performance by providing an **as** operator:

```
Employee e = o as Employee;
if (e != null) {
   // Use e within the 'if' statement.
}
```

In this code, the CLR checks if **o** is compatible with the **Employee** type, and if it is, **as** returns a non-**null** reference to the same object. If **o** is not compatible with the **Employee** type, the **as** operator returns **null**. Notice that the **as** operator causes the CLR to verify an object's type just once. The **if** statement simply checks whether **e** is **null**; this check can be performed faster than verifying an object's type.

The **as** operator works just as casting does except that the **as** operator will never throw an exception. Instead, if the object can't be cast, the result is **null**. You'll want to check to see whether the resulting reference is **null**, or attempting to use the resulting reference will cause a **System.NullReferenceException** to be thrown. The following code demonstrates:

```
Object o = new Object();    // Creates a new Object object
Employee e = o as Employee; // Casts o to an Employee
// The cast above fails: no exception is thrown, but e is set to null.

e.ToString();  // Accessing e throws a NullReferenceException.
```

To make sure you understand everything just presented, take the following quiz. Assume that these two class definitions exist:

```
internal class B {      // Base class
}

internal class D : B { // Derived class
}
```

Now examine the lines of C# code in Table 4-3. For each line, decide whether the line would compile and execute successfully (marked OK below), cause a compile-time error (CTE), or cause a run-time error (RTE).

Table 4-3   Type-Safety Quiz

Statement	OK	CTE	RTE
Object o1 = new Object();	✓		
Object o2 = new B();	✓		
Object o3 = new D();	✓		
Object o4 = o3;	✓		
B b1 = new B();	✓		
B b2 = new D();	✓		
D d1 = new D();	✓		
B b3 = new Object();		✓	

Table 4-3 Type-Safety Quiz

Statement	OK	CTE	RTE
D d2 = new Object();		✓	
B b4 = d1;	✓		
D d3 = b2;		✓	
D d4 = (D) d1;	✓		
D d5 = (D) b2;	✓		
D d6 = (D) b1;			✓
B b5 = (B) o1;			✓
B b6 = (D) b2;	✓		

Namespaces and Assemblies

Namespaces allow for the logical grouping of related types, and developers typically use them to make it easier to locate a particular type. For example, the **System.Text** namespace defines a bunch of types for performing string manipulations, and the **System.IO** namespace defines a bunch of types for performing I/O operations. Here's some code that constructs a **System.IO .FileStream** object and a **System.Text.StringBuilder** object:

```
public sealed class Program {
   public static void Main() {
      System.IO.FileStream fs = new System.IO.FileStream(...);
      System.Text.StringBuilder sb = new System.Text.StringBuilder();
   }
}
```

As you can see, the code is pretty verbose; it would be nice if there were some shorthand way to refer to the **FileStream** and **StringBuilder** types to reduce typing. Fortunately, many compilers do offer mechanisms to reduce programmer typing. The C# compiler provides this mechanism via the **using** directive. The following code is identical to the previous example:

```
using System.IO;    // Try prepending "System.IO."
using System.Text;  // Try prepending "System.Text."

public sealed class Program {
   public static void Main() {
      FileStream fs = new FileStream(...);
      StringBuilder sb = new StringBuilder();
   }
}
```

To the compiler, a namespace is simply an easy way of making a type's name longer and more likely to be unique by preceding the name with some symbols separated by dots. So the compiler interprets the reference to **FileStream** in this example to mean **System.IO.FileStream**. Similarly, the compiler interprets the reference to **StringBuilder** to mean **System.Text .StringBuilder**.

Using the C# **using** directive is entirely optional; you're always welcome to type out the fully qualified name of a type if you prefer. The C# **using** directive instructs the compiler to try prepending different prefixes to a type name until a match is found.

> **Important**   The CLR doesn't know anything about namespaces. When you access a type, the CLR needs to know the full name of the type (which can be a really long name containing periods) and which assembly contains the definition of the type so that the runtime can load the proper assembly, find the type, and manipulate it.

In the previous code example, the compiler needs to ensure that every type referenced exists and that my code is using that type in the correct way: calling methods that exist, passing the right number of arguments to these methods, ensuring that the arguments are the right type, using the method's return value correctly, and so on. If the compiler can't find a type with the specified name in the source files or in any referenced assemblies, it prepends **System.IO.** to the type name and checks if the generated name matches an existing type. If the compiler still can't find a match, it prepends **System.Text.** to the type's name. The two **using** directives shown earlier allow me to simply type **FileStream** and **StringBuilder** in my code—the compiler automatically expands the references to **System.IO.FileStream** and **System.Text .StringBuilder**. I'm sure you can easily imagine how much typing this saves as well as how much cleaner your code is to read.

When checking for a type's definition, the compiler must be told which assemblies to examine by using the **/reference** compiler switch as discussed in Chapter 2, "Building, Packaging, Deploying, and Administering Applications and Types," and Chapter 3, "Shared Assemblies and Strongly Named Assemblies." The compiler will scan all of the referenced assemblies looking for the type's definition. Once the compiler finds the proper assembly, the assembly information and the type information is emitted into the resulting managed module's metadata. To get the assembly information, you must pass the assembly that defines any referenced types to the compiler. The C# compiler, by default, automatically looks in the MSCorLib.dll assembly even if you don't explicitly tell it to. The MSCorLib.dll assembly contains the definitions of all of the core Framework Class Library (FCL) types, such as **Object**, **Int32**, **String**, and so on.

As you might imagine, there are some potential problems with the way that compilers treat namespaces: it's possible to have two (or more) types with the same name in different namespaces. Microsoft strongly recommends that you define unique names for types. However, in some cases, it's simply not possible. The runtime encourages the reuse of components. Your application might take advantage of a component that Microsoft created and another component that Wintellect created. These two companies might both offer a type called **Widget**—Microsoft's **Widget** does one thing, and Wintellect's **Widget** does something entirely different. In this scenario, you had no control over the naming of the types, so you can differentiate between the two widgets by using their fully qualified names when referencing them.

To reference Microsoft's **Widget**, you would use `Microsoft.Widget`, and to reference Wintellect's **Widget**, you would use `Wintellect.Widget`. In the following code, the reference to **Widget** is ambiguous, so the C# compiler generates the following: "error CS0104: 'Widget' is an ambiguous reference":

```
using Microsoft;  // Try prepending "Microsoft."
using Wintellect; // Try prepending "Wintellect."

public sealed class Program {
   public static void Main() {
      Widget w = new Widget();// An ambiguous reference
   }
}
```

To remove the ambiguity, you must explicitly tell the compiler which **Widget** you want to create:

```
using Microsoft;  // Try prepending "Microsoft."
using Wintellect; // Try prepending "Wintellect."

public sealed class Program {
   public static void Main() {
      Wintellect.Widget w = new Wintellect.Widget(); // Not ambiguous
   }
}
```

There's another form of the C# **using** directive that allows you to create an alias for a single type or namespace. This is handy if you have just a few types that you use from a namespace and don't want to pollute the global namespace with all of a namespace's types. The following code demonstrates another way to solve the ambiguity problem shown in the preceding code:

```
using Microsoft;  // Try prepending "Microsoft."
using Wintellect; // Try prepending "Wintellect."

// Define WintellectWidget symbol as an alias to Wintellect.Widget
using WintellectWidget = Wintellect.Widget;

public sealed class Program {
   public static void Main() {
      WintellectWidget w = new WintellectWidget(); // No error now
   }
}
```

These methods of disambiguating a type are useful, but in some scenarios, you need to go further. Imagine that the Australian Boomerang Company (ABC) and the Alaskan Boat Corporation (ABC) are each creating a type, called **BuyProduct**, which they intend to ship in their respective assemblies. It's likely that both companies would create a namespace called ABC that contains a type called **BuyProduct**. Anyone who tries to develop an application that needs to buy both boomerangs and boats would be in for some trouble unless the programming language provides a way to programmatically distinguish between the assemblies, not just between the namespaces. Fortunately, the C# compiler offers a feature called *extern aliases* that give you a way to work around this rarely occurring problem. Extern aliases also give you a way to access a single type from two (or more) different versions of the same assembly. For more information about extern aliases, see the C# Language Specification.

In your library, when you're designing types that you expect third parties to use, you should define these types in a namespace so that compilers can easily disambiguate them. In fact, to reduce the likelihood of conflict, you should use your full company name (not an acronym or abbreviation) to be your top-level namespace name. Referring to the .NET Framework SDK documentation, you can see that Microsoft uses a namespace of "Microsoft" for Microsoft-specific types. (See the `Microsoft.CSharp`, `Microsoft.VisualBasic`, and `Microsoft.Win32` namespaces as examples.)

Creating a namespace is simply a matter of writing a namespace declaration into your code as follows (in C#):

```
namespace CompanyName {
   public sealed class A {              // TypeDef: CompanyName.A
   }

   namespace X {
      public sealed class B { ... }     // TypeDef: CompanyName.X.B
   }
}
```

The comment on the right of the class definitions above indicates the real name of the type the compiler will emit into the type definition metadata table; this is the real name of the type from the CLR's perspective.

Some compilers don't support namespaces at all, and other compilers are free to define what "namespace" means to a particular language. In C#, the `namespace` directive simply tells the compiler to prefix each type name that appears in source code with the namespace name so that programmers can do less typing.

How Namespaces and Assemblies Relate

Be aware that a namespace and an assembly (the file that implements a type) aren't necessarily related. In particular, the various types belonging to a single namespace might be implemented in multiple assemblies. For example, the `System.IO.FileStream` type is implemented in the MSCorLib.dll assembly, and the `System.IO.FileSystemWatcher` type is implemented in the System.dll assembly. In fact, the .NET Framework doesn't even ship a System.IO.dll assembly.

A single assembly can contain types in different namespaces. For example, the `System.Int32` and `System.Text.StringBuilder` types are both in the MSCorLib.dll assembly.

When you look up a type in the .NET Framework SDK documentation, the documentation will clearly indicate the namespace that the type belongs to and also the assembly that the type is implemented in. In Figure 4-1, you can clearly see (right above the Syntax section) that the **ResXFileRef** type is part of the **System.Resources** namespace and that the type is implemented in the System.Windows.Forms.dll assembly. To compile code that references the **ResXFileRef** type, you'd add a **using System.Resources;** directive to your source code, and you'd use the **/r:System.Windows.Forms.dll** compiler switch.

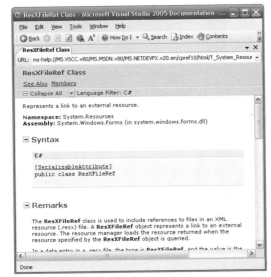

Figure 4-1   SDK documentation showing namespace and assembly information for a type

How Things Relate at Run Time

In this section, I'm going to explain the relationship at run time between types, objects, a thread's stack, and the managed heap. Furthermore, I will also explain the difference between calling static methods, instance methods, and virtual methods. Let's start off with some fundamentals of computers. What I'm about to describe is not specific to the CLR at all, but I'm going to describe it so that we have a working foundation, and then I'll modify the discussion to incorporate CLR-specific information.

Figure 4-2 shows a single Microsoft Windows process that has the CLR loaded into it. In this process there may be many threads. When a thread is created, it is allocated a 1-MB stack. This stack space is used for passing arguments to a method and for local variables defined within a method. In Figure 4-2, the memory for one thread's stack is shown (on the right). Stacks build from high memory addresses to low memory addresses. In the figure, this thread has been executing some code, and its stack has some data on it already (shown as the shaded area at the top of the stack). Now, imagine that the thread has executed some code that calls the **M1** method.

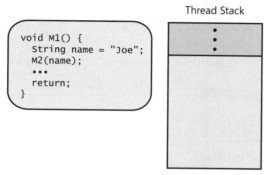

Figure 4-2 A thread's stack with the **M1** method about to be called

All but the simplest of methods contain some *prologue code*, which initializes a method before it can start doing its work. These methods also contain *epilogue code*, which cleans up a method after it has performed its work so that it can return to its caller. When the **M1** method starts to execute, its prologue code allocates memory for the local **name** variable from the thread's stack (see Figure 4-3).

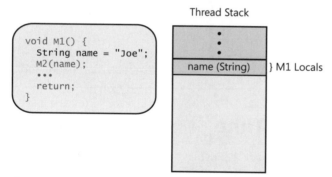

Figure 4-3 Allocating **M1**'s local variable on the thread's stack

Then, **M1** calls the **M2** method, passing in the **name** local variable as an argument. This causes the address in the **name** local variable to be pushed on the stack (see Figure 4-4). Inside the **M2** method, the stack location will be identified using the parameter variable named **s**. (Note that some architectures pass arguments via registers to improve performance, but this distinction is not important for this discussion.) Also, when a method is called, the address indicating where the called method should return back to in the calling method is pushed on the stack (also shown in Figure 4-4).

```
void M1() {
   String name = "Joe";
   M2(name);
   •••
   return;
}


void M2(String s) {
   Int32 length = s.Length;
   Int32 tally;
   •••
   return;
}
```

Thread Stack

name (String)	} M1 Locals
s (String)	} M2 Params
[return address]	

Figure 4-4 M1 pushes arguments and the return address on the thread's stack when calling M2

When the M2 method starts to execute, its prologue code allocates memory for the local **length** and **tally** variables from the thread's stack (see Figure 4-5). Then the code inside method M2 executes. Eventually, M2 gets to its return statement, which causes the CPU's instruction pointer to be set to the return address in the stack, and M2's stack frame is unwound so that it looks the way it did in Figure 4-3. At this point, M1 is continuing to execute its code that immediately follows the call to M2, and its stack frame accurately reflects the state needed by M1.

Eventually, M1 will return back to its caller by setting the CPU's instruction pointer to be set to the return address (not shown on the figures, but it would be just above the **name** argument on the stack), and M1's stack frame is unwound so that it looks the way it did in Figure 4-2. At this point, the method that called M1 continues to execute its code that immediately follows the call to M1, and its stack frame accurately reflects the state needed by that method.

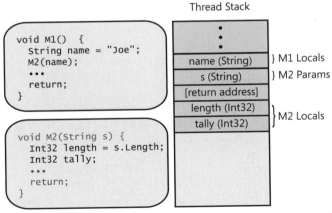

Figure 4-5 Allocating M2's local variables on the thread's stack

Now, let's start gearing the discussion toward the CLR. Let's say that we have these two class definitions:

```
internal class Employee {
    public          Int32     GetYearsEmployed()   { ... }
    public virtual  String    GenProgressReport()  { ... }
    public static   Employee  Lookup(String name)  { ... }
}

internal sealed class Manager : Employee {
    public override String    GenProgressReport()  { ... }
}
```

Our Windows process has started, the CLR is loaded into it, the managed heap is initialized, and a thread has been created (along with its 1 MB of stack space). This thread has already executed some code, and this code has decided to call the **M3** method. All of this is shown in Figure 4-6. The **M3** method contains code that demonstrates how the CLR works; this is not code that you would normally write, because it doesn't actually do anything useful.

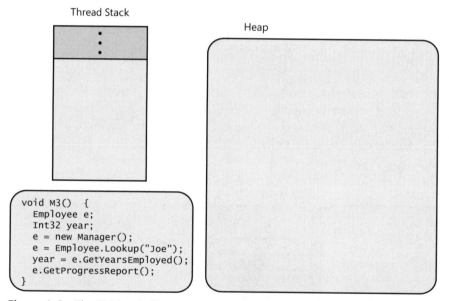

Figure 4-6   The CLR loaded in a process, its heap initialized, and a thread's stack with the **M3** method about to be called

As the JIT compiler converts **M3**'s IL code into native CPU instructions, it notices all of the types that are referred to inside **M3**: **Employee**, **Int32**, **Manager**, and **String** (because of **"Joe"**). At this time, the CLR ensures that the assemblies that define these types are loaded into the AppDomain. Then, using the assembly's metadata, the CLR extracts information about these types and creates some data structures to represent the types themselves. The data structures for the **Employee** and **Manager** type objects are shown in Figure 4-7. Since this thread already executed some code prior to calling **M3**, let's assume that the **Int32** and **string** type objects have already been created (which is likely because these are commonly used types), and so I won't show them in the figure.

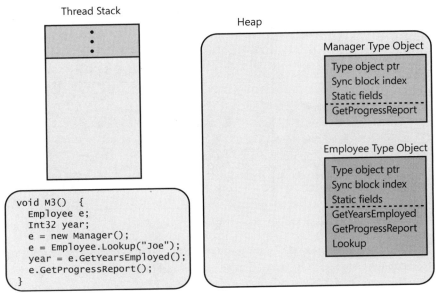

Figure 4-7 The **Employee** and **Manager** type objects are created just as **M3** is being called

Let's take a moment to discuss these type objects. As discussed earlier in this chapter, all objects on the heap contain two overhead members: the type object pointer and the sync block index. As you can see, the **Employee** and **Manager** type objects have both of these members. When you define a type, you can define static data fields within it. The bytes that back these static data fields are allocated within the type objects themselves. Finally, inside each type object is a method table with one entry per method defined within the type. This is the method table that was discussed in Chapter 1, "The CLR's Execution Model." Since the **Employee** type defines three methods (**GetYearsEmployed**, **GenProgressReport**, and **Lookup**), there are three entries in **Employee**'s method table. Since the **Manager** type defines one method (an override of **GenProgressReport**), there is just one entry in **Manager**'s method table.

Now, after the CLR has ensured that all of the type objects required by the method are created and the code for **M3** has been compiled, the CLR allows the thread to execute **M3**'s native code. When **M3**'s prologue code executes, memory for the local variables must be allocated from the thread's stack, as shown in Figure 4-8. By the way, the CLR automatically initializes all local variables to **null** or **0** (zero) as part of the method's prologue code.

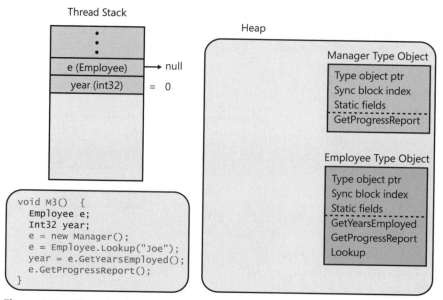

Figure 4-8   Allocating M3's local variables on the thread's stack

Then, M3 executes its code to construct a **Manager** object. This causes an instance of the **Manager** type, a **Manager** object, to be created in the managed heap, as shown in Figure 4-9. As you can see, the **Manager** object—as do all objects—has a type object pointer and sync block index. This object also contains the bytes necessary to hold all of the instance data fields defined by the **Manager** type as well as any instance fields defined by any base classes of the **Manager** type (in this case, **Employee** and **Object**). Whenever a new object is created on the heap, the CLR automatically initializes the internal type object pointer member to refer to the object's corresponding type object (in this case, the **Manager** type object). Furthermore, the CLR initializes the sync block index and sets all of the object's instance fields to **null** or **0** (zero) prior to calling the type's constructor, a method that will likely modify some of the instance data fields. The **new** operator returns the memory address of the **Manager** object, which is saved in the variable **e** (on the thread's stack).

The next line of code in M3 calls **Employee**'s static **Lookup** method. When calling a static method, the CLR locates the type object that corresponds to the type that defines the static method. Then, the CLR locates the entry in the type object's method table that refers to the method being called, JITs the method (if necessary), and calls the JITted code. For our discussion, let's say that **Employee**'s **Lookup** method queries a database to find Joe. Let's also say that the database indicates that Joe is a manager at the company, and therefore, internally, the **Lookup** method constructs a new **Manager** object on the heap, initializes it for Joe, and returns the address of this object. The address is saved in the local variable **e**. The result of this operation is shown in Figure 4-10.

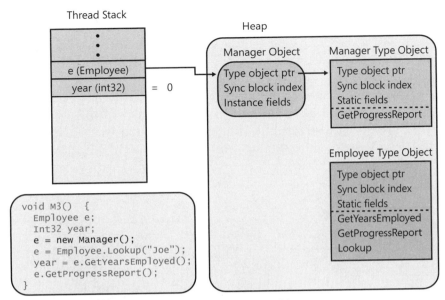

Figure 4-9 Allocating and initializing a **Manager** object

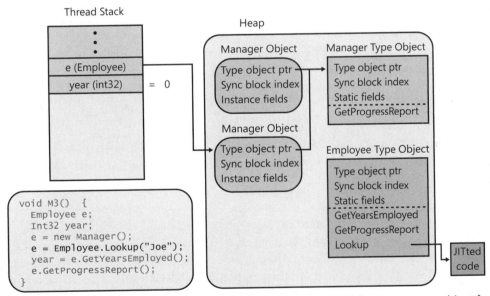

Figure 4-10 **Employee**'s static **Lookup** method allocates and initializes a **Manager** object for Joe

Note that **e** no longer refers to the first **Manager** object that was created. In fact, since no variable refers to this object, it is a prime candidate for being garbage collected in the future, which will reclaim (free) the memory used by this object.

The next line of code in **M3** calls **Employee**'s nonvirtual instance **GetYearsEmployed** method. When calling a nonvirtual instance method, the CLR locates the type object that corresponds to the type of the variable being used to make the call. In this case, the variable **e** is defined as an **Employee**. (If the **Employee** type didn't define the method being called, the CLR would walk down the class hierarchy toward **Object** looking for this method.) Then, the CLR locates the entry in the type object's method table that refers to the method being called, JITs the method (if necessary), and then calls the JITted code. For our discussion, let's say that **Employee**'s **GetYearsEmployed** method returns **5** because Joe has been employed at the company for five years. The integer is saved in the local variable **year**. The result of this operation is shown in Figure 4-11.

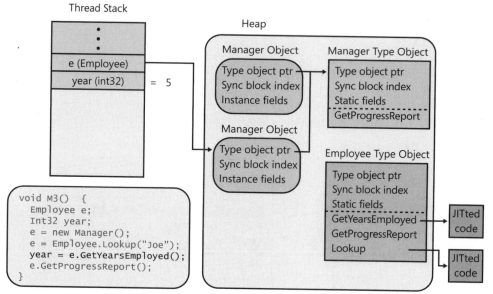

Figure 4-11   **Employee**'s nonvirtual instance **GetYearsEmployeed** method is called, returning 5

The next line of code in **M3** calls **Employee**'s virtual instance **GenProgressReport** method. When calling a virtual instance method, the CLR has some additional work to do. First, it looks in the variable being used to make the call and then follows the address to the calling object. In this case, the variable **e** points to the Joe **Manager** object. Second, the CLR examines the object's internal type object pointer member; this member refers to the actual type of the object. The CLR then locates the entry in the type object's method table that refers to the method being called, JITs the method (if necessary), and calls the JITted code. For our discussion, **Manager**'s **GenProgressReport** implementation is called because **e** refers to a **Manager** object. The result of this operation is shown in Figure 4-12.

Note that if **Employee**'s **Lookup** method had discovered that Joe was just an **Employee** and not a **Manager**, **Lookup** would have internally constructed an **Employee** object whose type object pointer member would have referred to the **Employee** type object, causing **Employee**'s implementation of **GenProgressReport** to execute instead of **Manager**'s implementation.

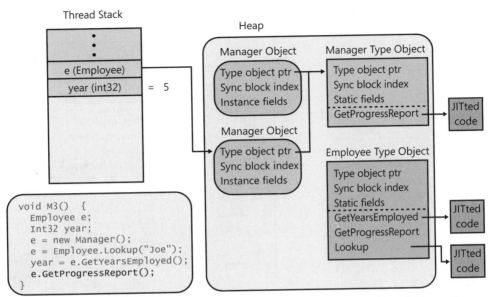

Figure 4-12 `Employee`'s virtual instance `GenProgressReport` method is called, causing `Manager`'s override of this method to execute

At this point, we have discussed the relationship between source code, IL, and JITted code. We have also discussed the thread's stack, arguments, local variables, and how these arguments and variables refer to objects on the managed heap. You also see how objects contain a pointer to their type object (containing the static fields and method table). We have also discussed how the CLR calls static methods, nonvirtual instance methods, and virtual instance methods. All of this should give you great insight into how the CLR works, and this insight should help you when architecting, designing, and implementing your types, components, and applications. Before ending this chapter, I'd like to give you just a little more insight as to what is going on inside the CLR.

You'll notice that the `Employee` and `Manager` type objects both contain type object pointer members. This is because type objects are actually objects themselves. When the CLR creates type objects, the CLR must initialize these members. "To what?" you might ask. Well, when the CLR starts running in a process, it immediately creates a special type object for the `System.Type` type (defined in MSCorLib.dll). The `Employee` and `Manager` type objects are "instances" of this type, and therefore, their type object pointer members are initialized to refer to the `System.Type` type object, as shown in Figure 4-13.

Of course, the `System.Type` type object is an object itself and therefore also has a type object pointer member in it, and it is logical to ask what this member refers to. It refers to itself because the `System.Type` type object is itself an "instance" of a type object. And now you should understand the CLR's complete type system and how it works. By the way, `System.Object`'s `GetType` method simply returns the address stored in the specified object's type object pointer member. In other words, the `GetType` method returns a pointer to an object's type object, and this is how you can determine the true type of any object in the system (including type objects).

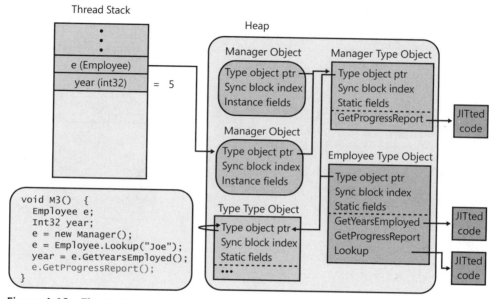

Figure 4-13   The `Employee` and `Manager` type objects are instances of the `System.Type` type

Chapter 5
Primitive, Reference, and Value Types

In this chapter, I'll discuss the different kinds of types you'll run into as a Microsoft .NET Framework developer. It is crucial for all developers to be familiar with the different behaviors that these types exhibit. When I was first learning the .NET Framework, I didn't fully understand the difference between primitive, reference, and value types. This lack of clarity led me to unwittingly introduce subtle bugs and performance issues into my code. By explaining the differences between the types here, I'm hoping to save you some of the headaches that I experienced while getting up to speed.

Programming Language Primitive Types

Certain data types are so commonly used that many compilers allow code to manipulate them using simplified syntax. For example, you could allocate an integer by using the following syntax:

```
System.Int32 a = new System.Int32();
```

But I'm sure you'd agree that declaring and initializing an integer by using this syntax is rather cumbersome. Fortunately, many compilers (including C#) allow you to use syntax similar to the following instead:

```
int a = 0;
```

This syntax certainly makes the code more readable and generates identical Intermediate Language (IL) to that which is generated when **System.Int32** is used. Any data types the compiler directly supports are called *primitive types*. Primitive types map directly to types existing in the Framework Class Library (FCL). For example, in C#, an **int** maps directly to the **System.Int32** type. Because of this, the following four lines of code all compile correctly and produce the exact same IL:

```
int         a = 0;                    // Most convenient syntax
System.Int32 a = 0;                   // Convenient syntax
int         a = new int();            // Inconvenient syntax
System.Int32 a = new System.Int32();  // Most inconvenient syntax
```

Table 5-1 shows the FCL types that have corresponding primitives in C#. For the types that are compliant with the Common Language Specification (CLS), other languages will offer similar primitive types. However, languages aren't required to offer any support for the non-CLS-compliant types.

Table 5-1 C# Primitives with Corresponding FCL Types

C# Primitive Type	FCL Type	CLS-Compliant	Description
sbyte	System.SByte	No	Signed 8-bit value
byte	System.Byte	Yes	Unsigned 8-bit value
short	System.Int16	Yes	Signed 16-bit value
ushort	System.UInt16	No	Unsigned 16-bit value
int	System.Int32	Yes	Signed 32-bit value
uint	System.UInt32	No	Unsigned 32-bit value
long	System.Int64	Yes	Signed 64-bit value
ulong	System.UInt64	No	Unsigned 64-bit value
char	System.Char	Yes	16-bit Unicode character (**char** never represents an 8-bit value as it would in unmanaged C++.)
float	System.Single	Yes	IEEE 32-bit **float**
double	System.Double	Yes	IEEE 64-bit **float**
bool	System.Boolean	Yes	A **true/false** value
decimal	System.Decimal	Yes	A 128-bit high-precision floating-point value commonly used for financial calculations in which rounding errors can't be tolerated. Of the 128 bits, 1 bit represents the sign of the value, 96 bits represent the value itself, and 8 bits represent the power of 10 to divide the 96-bit value by (can be anywhere from 0 to 28). The remaining bits are unused.
object	System.Object	Yes	Base type of all types
string	System.String	Yes	An array of characters

Another way to think of this is that the C# compiler automatically assumes that you have the following **using** directives (as discussed in Chapter 4, "Type Fundamentals") in all of your source code files:

```
using sbyte  = System.SByte;
using byte   = System.Byte;
using short  = System.Int16;
using ushort = System.UInt16;
using int    = System.Int32;
using uint   = System.UInt32;
...
```

The C# language specification states, "As a matter of style, use of the keyword is favored over use of the complete system type name." I disagree with the language specification; I prefer to use the FCL type names and completely avoid the primitive type names. In fact, I wish that compilers didn't even offer the primitive type names and forced developers to use the FCL type names instead. Here are my reasons:

- I've seen a number of developers confused, not knowing whether to use **string** or **String** in their code. Because in C# the **string** (a keyword) maps exactly to **System.String** (an FCL type), there is no difference and either can be used.

- In C#, **long** maps to **System.Int64**, but in a different programming language, **long** could map to an **Int16** or **Int32**. In fact, C++/CLI does in fact treat **long** as an **Int32**. Someone reading source code in one language could easily misinterpret the code's intention if he or she were used to programming in a different programming language. In fact, most languages won't even treat **long** as a keyword and won't compile code that uses it.

- The FCL has many methods that have type names as part of their method names. For example, the **BinaryReader** type offers methods such as **ReadBoolean**, **ReadInt32**, **ReadSingle**, and so on, and the **System.Convert** type offers methods such as **ToBoolean**, **ToInt32**, **ToSingle**, and so on. Although it's legal to write the following code, the line with **float** feels very unnatural to me, and it's not obvious that the line is correct:

```
BinaryReader br = new BinaryReader(...);
float  val = br.ReadSingle();   // OK, but feels unnatural
Single val = br.ReadSingle();   // OK and feels good
```

For all of these reasons, I'll use the FCL type names throughout this book.

In many programming languages, you would expect the following code to compile and execute correctly:

```
Int32  i = 5;   // A 32-bit value
Int64  l = i;   // Implicit cast to a 64-bit value
```

However, based on the casting discussion presented in Chapter 4, you wouldn't expect this code to compile. After all, **System.Int32** and **System.Int64** are different types, and neither one is derived from the other. Well, you'll be happy to know that the C# compiler does compile this code correctly, and it runs as expected. Why? The reason is that the C# compiler has intimate knowledge of primitive types and applies its own special rules when compiling the code. In other words, the compiler recognizes common programming patterns and produces the necessary IL to make the written code work as expected. Specifically, the C# compiler supports patterns related to casting, literals, and operators, as shown in the following examples.

First, the compiler is able to perform implicit or explicit casts between primitive types such as these:

```
Int32  i = 5;         // Implicit cast from Int32  to Int32
Int64  l = i;         // Implicit cast from Int32  to Int64
Single s = i;         // Implicit cast from Int32  to Single
Byte   b = (Byte) i;  // Explicit cast from Int32  to Byte
Int16  v = (Int16) s; // Explicit cast from Single to Int16
```

C# allows implicit casts if the conversion is "safe," that is, no loss of data is possible, such as converting an **Int32** to an **Int64**. But C# requires explicit casts if the conversion is potentially unsafe. For numeric types, "unsafe" means that you could lose precision or magnitude as a result of the conversion. For example, converting from **Int32** to **Byte** requires an explicit cast because precision might be lost from large **Int32** numbers; converting from **Single** to **Int16** requires a cast because **Single** can represent numbers of a larger magnitude than **Int16** can.

Be aware that different compilers can generate different code to handle these cast operations. For example, when casting a **Single** with a value of 6.8 to an **Int32**, some compilers could generate code to put a 6 in the **Int32**, and others could perform the cast by rounding the result up to 7. By the way, C# always truncates the result. For the exact rules that C# follows for casting primitive types, see the "Conversions" section in the C# language specification.

In addition to casting, primitive types can be written as *literals*. A literal is considered to be an instance of the type itself, and therefore, you can call instance methods by using the instance as shown here:

```
Console.WriteLine(123.ToString() + 456.ToString());  // "123456"
```

Also, if you have an expression consisting of literals, the compiler is able to evaluate the expression at compile time, improving the application's performance.

```
Boolean found = false;    // Generated code sets found to 0
Int32 x = 100 + 20 + 3;   // Generated code sets x to 123
String s = "a " + "bc";   // Generated code sets s to "a bc"
```

Finally, the compiler automatically knows how and in what order to interpret operators (such as +, -, *, /, %, &, ^, |, ==, !=, >, <, >=, <=, <<, >>, ~, !, ++, --, and so on) when used in code:

```
Int32 x = 100;                      // Assignment operator
Int32 y = x + 23;                   // Addition and assignment operators
Boolean lessThanFifty = (y < 50);   // Less-than and assignment operators
```

Checked and Unchecked Primitive Type Operations

Programmers are well aware that many arithmetic operations on primitives could result in an overflow:

```
Byte b = 100;
b = (Byte) (b + 200);          // b now contains 44 (or 2C in Hex).
```

> **Important**   When performing the arithmetic operation above, the first step requires that all operand values be expanded to 32-bit values (or 64-bit values if any operand requires more than 32 bits). So **b** and **200** (values requiring less than 32 bits) are first converted to 32-bit values and then added together. The result is a 32-bit value (300 in decimal, or 12C in hexadecimal) that must be cast to a **Byte** before the result can be stored back in the variable **b**. C# doesn't perform this cast for you implicitly, which is why the **Byte** cast on the second line of the preceding code is required.

In most programming scenarios, this silent overflow is undesirable and if not detected causes the application to behave in strange and unusual ways. In some rare programming scenarios (such as calculating a hash value or a checksum), however, this overflow is not only acceptable but is also desired.

Different languages handle overflows in different ways. C and C++ don't consider overflows to be an error and allow the value to wrap; the application continues running. Microsoft Visual Basic, on the other hand, always considers overflows to be errors and throws an exception when it detects one.

The common language runtime (CLR) offers IL instructions that allow the compiler to choose the desired behavior. The CLR has an instruction called **add** that adds two values together. The **add** instruction performs no overflow checking. The CLR also has an instruction called **add.ovf** that also adds two values together. However, **add.ovf** throws a **System.OverflowException** if an overflow occurs. In addition to these two IL instructions for the add operation, the CLR also has similar IL instructions for subtraction (**sub/sub.ovf**), multiplication (**mul/mul.ovf**), and data conversions (**conv/conv.ovf**).

C# allows the programmer to decide how overflows should be handled. By default, overflow checking is turned off. This means that the compiler generates IL code by using the versions of the add, subtract, multiply, and conversion instructions that don't include overflow checking. As a result, the code runs faster—but developers must be assured that overflows won't occur or that their code is designed to anticipate these overflows.

One way to get the C# compiler to control overflows is to use the **/checked+** compiler switch. This switch tells the compiler to generate code that has the overflow-checking versions of the add, subtract, multiply, and conversion IL instructions. The code executes more slowly because the CLR is checking these operations to determine whether an overflow will occur.

If an overflow does occur, the CLR throws an **OverflowException**. You should design your application's code to handle this exception and gracefully recover.

Rather than have overflow checking turned on or off globally, programmers are much more likely to want to decide case by case whether to have overflow checking. C# allows this flexibility by offering **checked** and **unchecked** operators. Here's an example that uses the **unchecked** operator (assume that the compiler is building checked code by default):

```
UInt32 invalid = unchecked((UInt32) -1);  // OK
```

And here is an example that uses the **checked** operator (assume that the compiler is building unchecked code by default):

```
Byte b = 100;
b = checked((Byte) (b + 200));     // OverflowException is thrown
```

In this example, **b** and **200** are first converted to 32-bit values and are then added together; the result is 300. Then 300 is converted to a **Byte** due to the explicit cast; this generates the **OverflowException**. If the **Byte** were cast outside the **checked** operator, the exception wouldn't occur:

```
b = (Byte) checked(b + 200);      // b contains 44; no OverflowException
```

In addition to the **checked** and **unchecked** operators, C# also offers **checked** and **unchecked** statements. The statements cause all expressions within a block to be checked or unchecked:

```
checked {                          // Start of checked block
   Byte b = 100;
   b = (Byte) (b + 200);           // This expression is checked for overflow.
}                                  // End of checked block
```

In fact, if you use a **checked** statement block, you can now use the **+=** operator, which simplifies the code a bit:

```
checked {          // Start of checked block
   Byte b = 100;
   b += 200;       // This expression is checked for overflow.
}                  // End of checked block
```

Important   Because the only effect that the **checked** operator and statement have are to determine which versions of the add, subtract, multiply, and data conversion IL instructions are produced, calling a method within a **checked** operator or statement has no impact on that method, as the following code demonstrates:

```
checked {
    // Assume SomeMethod tries to load 400 into a Byte.
    SomeMethod(400);
    // SomeMethod might or might not throw an OverflowException.
    // It would if SomeMethod were compiled with checked instructions.
}
```

Here's the best way to go about using **checked** and **unchecked**:

- As you write your code, explicitly use **checked** around blocks where an unwanted overflow might occur due to invalid input data, such as processing a request with data supplied from an end user or a client machine.

- As you write your code, explicitly use **unchecked** around blocks where an overflow is OK, such as calculating a checksum.

- For any code that doesn't use **checked** or **unchecked**, the assumption is that you *do* want an exception to occur on overflow, for example, calculating something (such as prime numbers) where the inputs are known, and overflows are bugs.

Now, as you develop your application, turn on the compiler's **/checked+** switch for debug builds. Your application will run more slowly because the system will be checking for overflows on any code that you didn't explicitly mark as **checked** or **unchecked**. If an exception occurs, you'll easily detect it and be able to fix the bug in your code. For the release build of your application, use the compiler's **/checked-**switch so that the code runs faster and exceptions won't be generated.

> **Important** The **System.Decimal** type is a very special type. Although many programming languages (C# and Visual Basic included) consider **Decimal** a primitive type, the CLR does not. This means that the CLR doesn't have IL instructions that know how to manipulate a **Decimal** value. If you look up the **Decimal** type in the .NET Framework SDK documentation, you'll see that it has public static methods called **Add**, **Subtract**, **Multiply**, **Divide**, and so on. In addition, the **Decimal** type provides operator overload methods for **+**, **-**, *****, **/**, and so on.
>
> When you compile code that uses **Decimal** values, the compiler generates code to call **Decimal**'s members to perform the actual operation. This means that manipulating **Decimal** values is slower than manipulating CLR primitive values. Also, because there are no IL instructions for manipulating **Decimal** values, the **checked** and **unchecked** operators, statements, and compiler switches have no effect. Operations on **Decimal** values always throw an **OverflowException** if the operation can't be performed safely.

Reference Types and Value Types

The CLR supports two kinds of types: *reference types* and *value types*. While most types in the FCL are reference types, the types that programmers use most often are value types. Reference types are always allocated from the managed heap, and the C# **new** operator returns the memory address of the object—the memory address refers to the object's bits. You need to bear in mind some performance considerations when you're working with reference types. First, consider these facts:

- The memory must be allocated from the managed heap.

- Each object allocated on the heap has some additional overhead members associated with it that must be initialized.

- The other bytes in the object (for the fields) are always set to zero.

- Allocating an object from the managed heap could force a garbage collection to occur.

If every type were a reference type, an application's performance would suffer greatly. Imagine how poor performance would be if every time you used an **Int32** value, a memory allocation occurred! To improve performance for simple, frequently used types, the CLR offers light-weight types called *value types*. Value type instances are usually allocated on a thread's stack (although they can also be embedded in a reference type object). The variable representing the instance doesn't contain a pointer to an instance; the variable contains the fields of the instance itself. Because the variable contains the instance's fields, a pointer doesn't have to be dereferenced to manipulate the instance's fields. Value type instances don't come under the control of the garbage collector, so their use reduces pressure in the managed heap and reduces the number of collections an application requires over its lifetime.

The .NET Framework SDK documentation clearly indicates which types are reference types and which are value types. When looking up a type in the documentation, any type called a *class* is a reference type. For example, the **System.Exception** class, the **System.IO.FileStream** class, and the **System.Random** class are all reference types. On the other hand, the documentation refers to each value type as a *structure* or an *enumeration*. For example, the **System.Int32** structure, the **System.Boolean** structure, the **System.Decimal** structure, the **System.TimeSpan** structure, the **System.DayOfWeek** enumeration, the **System.IO.FileAttributes** enumeration, and the **System.Drawing.FontStyle** enumeration are all value types.

If you look more closely at the documentation, you'll notice that all of the structures are immediately derived from the **System.ValueType** abstract type. **System.ValueType** is itself immediately derived from the **System.Object** type. By definition, all value types must be derived from **System.ValueType**. All enumerations are derived from the **System.Enum** abstract type, which is itself derived from **System.ValueType**. The CLR and all programming languages give enumerations special treatment. For more information about enumerated types, refer to Chapter 12, "Enumerated Types and Bit Flags."

Even though you can't choose a base type when defining your own value type, a value type can implement one or more interfaces if you choose. In addition, all value types are sealed, which prevents a value type from being used as a base type for any other reference type or value type. So, for example, it's not possible to define any new types using **Boolean**, **Char**, **Int32**, **Uint64**, **Single**, **Double**, **Decimal**, and so on as base types.

Important   For many developers (such as unmanaged C/C++ developers), reference types and value types will seem strange at first. In unmanaged C/C++, you declare a type, and then the code that uses the type gets to decide if an instance of the type should be allocated on the thread's stack or in the application's heap. In managed code, the developer defining the type indicates where instances of the type are allocated; the developer using the type has no control over this.

The following code and Figure 5-1 demonstrate how reference types and value types differ:

```
// Reference type (because of 'class')
class  SomeRef { public Int32 x; }

// Value type (because of 'struct')
struct SomeVal { public Int32 x; }

static void ValueTypeDemo() {
   SomeRef r1 = new SomeRef();    // Allocated in heap
   SomeVal v1 = new SomeVal();    // Allocated on stack
   r1.x = 5;                      // Pointer dereference
   v1.x = 5;                      // Changed on stack
   Console.WriteLine(r1.x);       // Displays "5"
   Console.WriteLine(v1.x);       // Also displays "5"
   // The left side of Figure 5-1 reflects the situation
   // after the lines above have executed.

   SomeRef r2 = r1;               // Copies reference (pointer) only
   SomeVal v2 = v1;               // Allocate on stack & copies members
   r1.x = 8;                      // Changes r1.x and r2.x
   v1.x = 9;                      // Changes v1.x, not v2.x
   Console.WriteLine(r1.x);       // Displays "8"
   Console.WriteLine(r2.x);       // Displays "8"
   Console.WriteLine(v1.x);       // Displays "9"
   Console.WriteLine(v2.x);       // Displays "5"
   // The right side of Figure 5-1 reflects the situation
   // after ALL of the lines above have executed.
}
```

In this code, the **SomeVal** type is declared using **struct** instead of the more common **class**. In C#, types declared using **struct** are value types, and types declared using **class** are reference types. As you can see, the behavior of reference types and value types differ quite a bit. As you use types in your code, you must be aware of whether the type is a reference type or a value type because it can greatly affect how you express your intentions in the code.

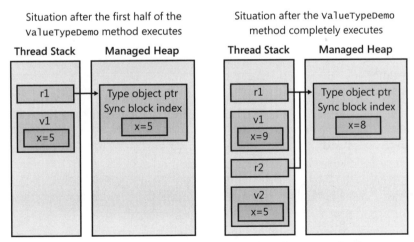

Figure 5-1   Memory layout differences between reference and value types

In the preceding code, you saw this line:

```
SomeVal v1 = new SomeVal();   // Allocated on stack
```

The way this line is written makes it look as if a **SomeVal** instance will be allocated on the managed heap. However, the C# compiler knows that **SomeVal** is a value type and produces code that allocates the **SomeVal** instance on the thread's stack. C# also ensures that all of the fields in the value type instance are zeroed.

The preceding line could have been written like this instead:

```
SomeVal v1;   // Allocated on stack
```

This line also produces IL that allocates the instance on the thread's stack and zeroes the fields. The only difference is that C# "thinks" that the instance is initialized if you use the **new** operator. The following code will make this point clear:

```
// These two lines compile because C# thinks that
// v1's fields have been initialized to 0.
SomeVal v1 = new SomeVal();
Int32 a = v1.x;

// These two lines don't compile because C# doesn't think that
// v1's fields have been initialized to 0.
SomeVal v1;
Int32 a = v1.x;  // error CS0170: Use of possibly unassigned field 'x'
```

When designing your own types, consider carefully whether to define your types as value types instead of reference types. In some situations, value types can give better performance. In particular, you should declare a type as a value type if *all* the following statements are true:

- The type acts as a primitive type. Specifically, this means that the type is a fairly simple type that has no members that modify any of the type's instance fields. When a type offers no members that alter its fields, we say that the type is *immutable*.

- The type doesn't need to inherit from any other type.

- The type won't have any other types derived from it.

The size of instances of your type is also a condition to take into account because by default, arguments are passed by value, which causes the fields in value type instances to be copied, hurting performance. Again, a method that returns a value type causes the fields in the instance to be copied into the memory allocated by the caller when the method returns, hurting performance. So, in addition to the previous conditions, you should declare a type as a value type if one of the following statements is true:

- Instances of the type are small (approximately 16 bytes or less).

- Instances of the type are large (greater than 16 bytes) and are not passed as method parameters or returned from methods.

The main advantage of value types is that they're not allocated as objects in the managed heap. Of course, value types have several limitations of their own when compared to reference types. Here are some of the ways in which value types and reference types differ:

- Value type objects have two representations: an *unboxed* form and a *boxed* form (discussed in the next section). Reference types are always in a boxed form.

- Value types are derived from **System.ValueType**. This type offers the same methods as defined by **System.Object**. However, **System.ValueType** overrides the **Equals** method so that it returns **true** if the values of the two objects' fields match. In addition, **System .ValueType** overrides the **GetHashCode** method to produce a hash code value by using an algorithm that takes into account the values in the object's instance fields. Due to performance issues with this default implementation, when defining your own value types, you should override and provide explicit implementations for the **Equals** and **GetHashCode** methods. I'll cover the **Equals** and **GetHashCode** methods at the end of this chapter.

- Because you can't define a new value type or a new reference type by using a value type as a base class, you shouldn't introduce any new virtual methods into a value type. No methods can be abstract, and all methods are implicitly sealed (can't be overridden).

- Reference type variables contain the memory address of objects in the heap. By default, when a reference type variable is created, it is initialized to **null**, indicating that the reference type variable doesn't currently point to a valid object. Attempting to use a **null** reference type variable causes a **NullReferenceException** to be thrown. By contrast, value type variables always contain a value of the underlying type, and all members of the value type are initialized to 0. Since a value type variable isn't a pointer, it's not possible to generate a **NullReferenceException** when accessing a value type. The CLR does offer a special feature that adds the notion of nullability to a value type. This feature, called *nullable types*, is discussed in Chapter 18, "Nullable Value Types."

- When you assign a value type variable to another value type variable, a field-by-field copy is made. When you assign a reference type variable to another reference type variable, only the memory address is copied.

- Because of the previous point, two or more reference type variables can refer to a single object in the heap, allowing operations on one variable to affect the object referenced by the other variable. On the other hand, value type variables are distinct objects, and it's not possible for operations on one value type variable to affect another.

- Because unboxed value types aren't allocated on the heap, the storage allocated for them is freed as soon as the method that defines an instance of the type is no longer active. This means that a value type instance doesn't receive a notification (via a **Finalize** method) when its memory is reclaimed.

> **Note**   In fact, it would be quite odd to define a value type with a `Finalize` method since the method would be called only on boxed instances. For this reason, many compilers (including C#, C++/CLI, and Visual Basic) don't allow you to define `Finalize` methods on value types. Although the CLR allows a value type to define a `Finalize` method, the CLR won't call this method when a boxed instance of the value type is garbage collected.

How the CLR Controls the Layout of a Type's Fields

To improve performance, the CLR is capable of arranging the fields of a type any way it chooses. For example, the CLR might reorder fields in memory so that object references are grouped together and data fields are properly aligned and packed. However, when you define a type, you can tell the CLR whether it must keep the type's fields in the same order as the developer specified them or whether it can reorder them as it sees fit.

You tell the CLR what to do by applying the **System.Runtime.InteropServices** **.StructLayoutAttribute** attribute on the class or structure you're defining. To this attribute's constructor, you can pass **LayoutKind.Auto** to have the CLR arrange the fields, **LayoutKind.Sequential** to have the CLR preserve your field layout, or **LayoutKind** **.Explicit** to explicitly arrange the fields in memory by using offsets. If you don't explicitly specify the **StructLayoutAttribute** on a type that you're defining, your compiler selects whatever layout it determines is best.

You should be aware that Microsoft's C# compiler selects **LayoutKind.Auto** for reference types (classes) and **LayoutKind.Sequential** for value types (structures). It is obvious that the C# compiler team believes that structures are commonly used when interoperating with unmanaged code, and for this to work, the fields must stay in the order defined by the programmer. However, if you're creating a value type that has nothing to do with interoperability with unmanaged code, you probably want to override the C# compiler's default. Here's an example:

```
using System;
using System.Runtime.InteropServices;

// Let the CLR arrange the fields to improve
// performance for this value type.
[StructLayout(LayoutKind.Auto)]
internal struct SomeValType {
    Byte b;
    Int16 x;
}
```

The **StructLayoutAttribute** also allows you to explicitly indicate the offset of each field by passing **LayoutKind.Explicit** to its constructor. Then you apply an instance of the **System.Runtime.InteropServices.FieldOffsetAttribute** attribute to each field passing to this attribute's constructor an **Int32** indicating the offset (in bytes) of the field's first byte from the beginning of the instance. Explicit layout is typically used to simulate what would be a *union* in unmanaged C/C++ because you can have multiple fields starting at the same offset in memory. Here is an example:

```
using System;
using System.Runtime.InteropServices;

// The developer explicitly arranges the fields of this value type.
[StructLayout(LayoutKind.Explicit)]
internal struct SomeValType {
    [FieldOffset(0)] Byte b;    // The b and x fields overlap each other
    [FieldOffset(0)] Int16 x;   // in instances of this type
}
```

It should be noted that it is illegal to define a type in which a reference type and a value type overlap. It is possible to define a type in which multiple reference types overlap at the same starting offset; however, this is unverifiable. It is legal to define a type in which multiple value types overlap; however, all of the overlapping bytes must be accessible via public fields for the type to be verifiable. If any field of one value type is private and public in another overlapping value type, the type is not verifiable.

Boxing and Unboxing Value Types

Value types are lighter weight than reference types because they are not allocated as objects in the managed heap, not garbage collected, and not referred to by pointers. However, in many cases, you must get a reference to an instance of a value type. For example, let's say that you wanted to create an **ArrayList** object (a type defined in the **System.Collections** namespace) to hold a set of **Point** structures. The code might look like this:

```
// Declare a value type.
struct Point {
    public Int32 x, y;
}

public sealed class Program {
    public static void Main() {
        ArrayList a = new ArrayList();
        Point p;                // Allocate a Point (not in the heap).
        for (Int32 i = 0; i < 10; i++) {
            p.x = p.y = i;     // Initialize the members in the value type.
            a.Add(p);          // Box the value type and add the
                               // reference to the ArrayList.
        }
        ...
    }
}
```

With each iteration of the loop, a **Point**'s value type fields are initialized. Then the **Point** is stored in the **ArrayList**. But let's think about this for a moment. What is actually being stored in the **ArrayList**? Is it the **Point** structure, the address of the **Point** structure, or something else entirely? To get the answer, you must look up **ArrayList**'s **Add** method and see what type its parameter is defined as. In this case, the **Add** method is prototyped as follows:

```
public virtual Int32 Add(Object value);
```

From this, you can plainly see that **Add** takes an **Object** as a parameter, indicating that **Add** requires a reference (or pointer) to an object on the managed heap as a parameter. But in the preceding code, I'm passing **p**, a **Point**, which is a value type. For this code to work, the **Point** value type must be converted into a true heap-managed object, and a reference to this object must be obtained.

It's possible to convert a value type to a reference type by using a mechanism called *boxing*. Internally, here's what happens when an instance of a value type is boxed:

1. Memory is allocated from the managed heap. The amount of memory allocated is the size required by the value type's fields plus the two additional overhead members (the type object pointer and the sync block index) required by all objects on the managed heap.

2. The value type's fields are copied to the newly allocated heap memory.

3. The address of the object is returned. This address is now a reference to an object; the value type is now a reference type.

The C# compiler automatically produces the IL code necessary to box a value type instance, but you still need to understand what's going on internally so that you're aware of code size and performance issues.

In the preceding code, the C# compiler detected that I was passing a value type to a method that requires a reference type, and it automatically emitted code to box the object. So at run time, the fields currently residing in the **Point** value type instance **p** are copied into the newly allocated **Point** object. The address of the boxed **Point** object (now a reference type) is returned and is then passed to the **Add** method. The **Point** object will remain in the heap until it is garbage collected. The **Point** value type variable (**p**) can be reused because the **ArrayList** never knows anything about it. Note that the lifetime of the boxed value type extends beyond the lifetime of the unboxed value type.

> **Note**   It should be noted that the FCL now includes a new set of generic collection classes that make the non-generic collection classes obsolete. For example, you should use the **System.Collections.Generic.List<T>** class instead of the **System.Collections.ArrayList** class. The generic collections classes offer many improvements over the non-generic equivalents. For example, the API has been cleaned up and improved, and the performance of the collection classes has been greatly improved as well. But one of the biggest improvements is that the generic collection classes allow you to work with collections of value types without requiring that items in the collection be boxed/unboxed. This in itself greatly improves performance because far fewer objects will be created on the managed heap thereby reducing the number of garbage collections required by your application. Furthermore, you will get compile-time type safety, and your source code will be cleaner due to fewer casts. This will all be explained in further detail in Chapter 16, "Generics."

Now that you know how boxing works, let's talk about unboxing. Let's say that you want to grab the first element out of the **ArrayList** by using the following code:

```
Point p = (Point) a[0];
```

Here you're taking the reference (or pointer) contained in element 0 of the **ArrayList** and trying to put it into a **Point** value type instance, **p**. For this to work, all of the fields contained in the boxed **Point** object must be copied into the value type variable, **p**, which is on the thread's stack. The CLR accomplishes this copying in two steps. First, the address of the **Point** fields in the boxed **Point** object is obtained. This process is called *unboxing*. Then, the values of these fields are copied from the heap to the stack-based value type instance.

Unboxing is *not* the exact opposite of boxing. The unboxing operation is much less costly than boxing. Unboxing is really just the operation of obtaining a pointer to the raw value type (data fields) contained within an object. In effect, the pointer refers to the unboxed portion in the boxed instance. So, unlike boxing, unboxing doesn't involve the copying of any bytes in memory. Having made this important clarification, it is important to note that an unboxing operation is typically followed by copying the fields. Frequently, however, an unboxing operation is followed immediately by copying its fields.

Obviously, boxing and unboxing/copy operations hurt your application's performance in terms of both speed and memory, so you should be aware of when the compiler generates code to perform these operations automatically and try to write code that minimizes this code generation.

Internally, here's exactly what happens when a boxed value type instance is unboxed:

1. If the variable containing the reference to the boxed value type instance is **null**, a **NullReferenceException** is thrown.

2. If the reference doesn't refer to an object that is a boxed instance of the desired value type, an **InvalidCastException** is thrown.[1]

The second item above means that the following code will *not* work as you might expect:

```
public static void Main() {
   Int32  x = 5;
   Object o = x;          // Box x; o refers to the boxed object
   Int16  y = (Int16) o; // Throws an InvalidCastException
}
```

---

[1] The CLR also allows you to unbox a value type into a nullable version of the same value type. This is discussed in Chapter 18, "Nullable Value Types."

Logically, it makes sense to take the boxed **Int32** that **o** refers to and cast it to an **Int16**. However, when unboxing an object, the cast must be to the exact unboxed value type—**Int32** in this case. Here's the correct way to write this code:

```
public static void Main() {
   Int32  x = 5;
   Object o = x;                // Box x; o refers to the boxed object
   Int16  y = (Int16)(Int32) o; // Unbox to the correct type and cast
}
```

I mentioned earlier that an unboxing operation is frequently followed immediately by a field copy. Let's take a look at some C# code demonstrating that unbox and copy operations work together:

```
public static void Main() {
   Point p;
   p.x = p.y = 1;
   Object o = p;   // Boxes p; o refers to the boxed instance

   p = (Point) o;  // Unboxes o AND copies fields from boxed
                   // instance to stack variable
}
```

On the last line, the C# compiler emits an IL instruction to unbox **o** (get the address of the fields in the boxed instance) and another IL instruction to copy the fields from the heap to the stack-based variable **p**.

Now look at this code:

```
public static void Main() {
   Point p;
   p.x = p.y = 1;
   Object o = p;   // Boxes p; o refers to the boxed instance

   // Change Point's x field to 2
   p = (Point) o;  // Unboxes o AND copies fields from boxed
                   // instance to stack variable
   p.x = 2;        // Changes the state of the stack variable
   o = p;          // Boxes p; o refers to a new boxed instance
}
```

The code at the bottom of this fragment is intended only to change **Point**'s **x** field from **1** to **2**. To do this, an unbox operation must be performed, followed by a field copy, followed by changing the field (on the stack), followed by a boxing operation (which creates a whole new boxed instance in the managed heap). Hopefully, you see the impact that boxing and unboxing/copying operations have on your application's performance.

Some languages, such as C++/CLI, allow you to unbox a boxed value type without copying the fields. Unboxing returns the address of the unboxed portion of a boxed object (ignoring the object's type object pointer and sync block index overhead). You can now use this pointer to manipulate the unboxed instance's fields (which happen to be in a boxed object on the heap). For example, the previous code would be much more efficient if written in C++/CLI, because you could change the value of **Point**'s **x** field within the already boxed **Point** instance. This would avoid both allocating a new object on the heap and copying all of the fields twice!

> **Important**   If you're the least bit concerned about your application's performance, you must be aware of when the compiler produces the code that performs these operations. Unfortunately, many compilers implicitly emit code to box objects, and so it is not obvious when you write code that boxing is occurring. If I am concerned about the performance of a particular algorithm, I always use a tool such as ILDasm.exe to view the IL code for my methods and see where the **box** IL instructions are.

Let's look at a few more examples that demonstrate boxing and unboxing:

```
public static void Main() {
    Int32  v = 5;          // Create an unboxed value type variable.
    Object o = v;          // o refers to a boxed Int32 containing 5.
    v = 123;               // Changes the unboxed value to 123

    Console.WriteLine(v + ", " + (Int32) o); // Displays "123, 5"
}
```

In this code, can you guess how many boxing operations occur? You might be surprised to discover that the answer is three! Let's analyze the code carefully to really understand what's going on. To help you understand, I've included the IL code generated for the **Main** method shown in the preceding code. I've commented the code so that you can easily see the individual operations.

```
.method public hidebysig static void  Main() cil managed
{
  .entrypoint
  // Code size       45 (0x2d)
  .maxstack  3
  .locals init (int32 V_0,
          object V_1)
  // Load 5 into v.
  IL_0000:  ldc.i4.5
  IL_0001:  stloc.0

  // Box v and store the reference pointer in o.
  IL_0002:  ldloc.0
  IL_0003:  box           [mscorlib]System.Int32
  IL_0008:  stloc.1

  // Load 123 into v.
  IL_0009:  ldc.i4.s    123
  IL_000b:  stloc.0
```

```
// Box v and leave the pointer on the stack for Concat.
IL_000c:  ldloc.0
IL_000d:  box         [mscorlib]System.Int32

// Load the string on the stack for Concat.
IL_0012:  ldstr       ", "

// Unbox o: Get the pointer to the In32's field on the stack.
IL_0017:  ldloc.1
IL_0018:  unbox.any [mscorlib]System.Int32

// Box the Int32 and leave the pointer on the stack for Concat.
IL_001d:  box         [mscorlib]System.Int32

// Call Concat.
IL_0022:  call        string [mscorlib]System.String::Concat(object,
                                                             object,
                                                             object)

// The string returned from Concat is passed to WriteLine.
IL_0027:  call        void [mscorlib]System.Console::WriteLine(string)

// Return from Main terminating this application.
IL_002c:  ret
} // end of method App::Main
```

First, an **Int32** unboxed value type instance (**v**) is created on the stack and initialized to **5**. Then a variable (**o**) typed as **object** is created, and is initialized to point to **v**. But because reference type variables must always point to objects in the heap, C# generated the proper IL code to box and store the address of the boxed copy of **v** in **o**. Now the value **123** is placed into the unboxed value type instance **v**; this has no effect on the boxed **Int32** value, which keeps its value of **5**.

Next is the call to the **WriteLine** method. **WriteLine** wants a **String** object passed to it, but there is no string object. Instead, these three items are available: an unboxed **Int32** value type instance (**v**), a **String** (which is a reference type), and a reference to a boxed **Int32** value type instance (**o**) that is being cast to an unboxed **Int32**. These must somehow be combined to create a **String**.

To create a **String**, the C# compiler generates code that calls the **String** object's static **Concat** method. There are several overloaded versions of the **Concat** method, all of which perform identically—the only difference is in the number of parameters. Because a string is being created from the concatenation of three items, the compiler chooses the following version of the **Concat** method:

```
public static String Concat(Object arg0, Object arg1, Object arg2);
```

For the first parameter, **arg0**, **v** is passed. But **v** is an unboxed value parameter and **arg0** is an **Object**, so **v** must be boxed and the address to the boxed **v** is passed for **arg0**. For the **arg1** parameter, the **","** string is passed as a reference to a **String** object. Finally, for the **arg2** parameter, **o** (a reference to an **Object**) is cast to an **Int32**. This requires an unboxing operation (but no copy operation), which retrieves the address of the unboxed **Int32** contained inside the boxed **Int32**. This unboxed **Int32** instance must be boxed again and the new boxed instance's memory address passed for **Concat**'s **arg2** parameter.

The **Concat** method calls each of the specified objects' **ToString** method and concatenates each object's string representation. The **string** object returned from **Concat** is then passed to **WriteLine** to show the final result.

I should point out that the generated IL code is more efficient if the call to **WriteLine** is written as follows:

```
Console.WriteLine(v + ", " + o);// Displays "123, 5"
```

This line is identical to the earlier version except that I've removed the **(Int32)** cast that preceded the variable **o**. This code is more efficient because **o** is already a reference type to an **Object** and its address can simply be passed to the **Concat** method. So, removing the cast saved two operations: an unbox and a box. You can easily see this savings by rebuilding the application and examining the generated IL code:

```
.method public hidebysig static void  Main() cil managed
{
  .entrypoint
  // Code size       35 (0x23)
  .maxstack  3
  .locals init (int32 V_0,
          object V_1)

  // Load 5 into v.
  IL_0000:  ldc.i4.5
  IL_0001:  stloc.0

  // Box v and store the reference pointer in o.
  IL_0002:  ldloc.0
  IL_0003:  box        [mscorlib]System.Int32
  IL_0008:  stloc.1

  // Load 123 into v.
  IL_0009:  ldc.i4.s   123
  IL_000b:  stloc.0

  // Box v and leave the pointer on the stack for Concat.
  IL_000c:  ldloc.0
  IL_000d:  box        [mscorlib]System.Int32

  // Load the string on the stack for Concat.
  IL_0012:  ldstr      ", "

  // Load the address of the boxed Int32 on the stack for Concat.
  IL_0017:  ldloc.1
```

```
   // Call Concat.
   IL_0018:  call        string [mscorlib]System.String::Concat(object,
                                                                object,
                                                                object)

   // The string returned from Concat is passed to WriteLine.
   IL_001d:  call        void [mscorlib]System.Console::WriteLine(string)

   // Return from Main terminating this application.
   IL_0022:  ret
} // end of method App::Main
```

A quick comparison of the IL for these two versions of the **Main** method shows that the version without the **(Int32)** cast is 10 bytes smaller than the version with the cast. The extra unbox/box steps in the first version are obviously generating more code. An even bigger concern, however, is that the extra boxing step allocates an additional object from the managed heap that must be garbage collected in the future. Certainly, both versions give identical results, and the difference in speed isn't noticeable, but extra, unnecessary boxing operations occurring in a loop cause the performance and memory usage of your application to be seriously degraded.

You can improve the previous code even more by calling **WriteLine** like this:

```
Console.WriteLine(v.ToString() + ", " + o);     // Displays "123, 5"
```

Now **ToString** is called on the unboxed value type instance **v**, and a **String** is returned. String objects are already reference types and can simply be passed to the **Concat** method without requiring any boxing.

Let's look at yet another example that demonstrates boxing and unboxing:

```
public static void Main() {
   Int32 v = 5;               // Create an unboxed value type variable.
   Object o = v;              // o refers to the boxed version of v.

   v = 123;                   // Changes the unboxed value type to 123
   Console.WriteLine(v);      // Displays "123"

   v = (Int32) o;             // Unboxes and copies o into v
   Console.WriteLine(v);      // Displays "5"
}
```

How many boxing operations do you count in this code? The answer is one. The reason that there is only one boxing operation is that the **System.Console** class defines a **WriteLine** method that accepts an **Int32** as a parameter:

```
public static void WriteLine(Int32 value);
```

In the two calls to **WriteLine** above, the variable v, an **Int32** unboxed value type instance, is passed by value. Now it may be that **WriteLine** will box this **Int32** internally, but you have no control over that. The important thing is that you've done the best you could and have eliminated the boxing from your own code.

If you take a close look at the FCL, you'll notice many overloaded methods that differ based on their value type parameters. For example, the **System.Console** type offers several over-loaded versions of the **WriteLine** method:

```
public static void WriteLine(Boolean);
public static void WriteLine(Char);
public static void WriteLine(Char[]);
public static void WriteLine(Int32);
public static void WriteLine(UInt32);
public static void WriteLine(Int64);
public static void WriteLine(UInt64);
public static void WriteLine(Single);
public static void WriteLine(Double);
public static void WriteLine(Decimal);
public static void WriteLine(Object);
public static void WriteLine(String);
```

You'll also find a similar set of overloaded methods for **System.Console**'s **Write** method, **System.IO.BinaryWriter**'s **Write** method, **System.IO.TextWriter**'s **Write** and **WriteLine** methods, **System.Runtime.Serialization.SerializationInfo**'s **AddValue** method, **System.Text.StringBuilder**'s **Append** and **Insert** methods, and so on. Most of these methods offer overloaded versions for the sole purpose of reducing the number of boxing operations for the common value types.

If you define your own value type, these FCL classes will not have overloads of these methods that accept your value type. Furthermore, there are a bunch of value types already defined in the FCL for which overloads of these methods do not exist. If you call a method that does not have an overload for the specific value type that you are passing to it, you will always end up calling the overload that takes an **Object**. Passing a value type instance as an **Object** will cause boxing to occur, which will adversely affect performance. If you are defining your own class, you can define the methods in the class to be generic (possibly constraining the type parameters to be value types). Generics gives you a way to define a method that can take any kind of value type without having to box it. Generics are discussed in Chapter 16.

One last point about boxing: if you know that the code that you're writing is going to cause the compiler to box a single value type repeatedly, your code will be smaller and faster if you manually box the value type. Here's an example:

```
using System;

public sealed class Program {
   public static void Main() {
      Int32 v = 5;   // Create an unboxed value type variable.

#if INEFFICIENT
      // When compiling the following line, v is boxed
```

```
        // three times, wasting time and memory.
        Console.WriteLine("{0}, {1}, {2}", v, v, v);
#else
        // The lines below have the same result, execute
        // much faster, and use less memory.
        Object o = v;  // Manually box v (just once).

        // No boxing occurs to compile the following line.
        Console.WriteLine("{0}, {1}, {2}", o, o, o);
#endif
    }
}
```

If this code is compiled with the **INEFFICIENT** symbol defined, the compiler will generate code to box **v** three times, causing three objects to be allocated from the heap! This is extremely wasteful since each object will have exactly the same contents: **5**. If the code is compiled without the **INEFFICIENT** symbol defined, **v** is boxed just once, so only one object is allocated from the heap. Then, in the call to **Console.WriteLine**, the reference to the single boxed object is passed three times. This second version executes *much* faster and allocates less memory from the heap.

In these examples, it's fairly easy to recognize when an instance of a value type requires boxing. Basically, if you want a reference to an instance of a value type, the instance must be boxed. Usually this happens because you have a value type instance and you want to pass it to a method that requires a reference type. However, this situation isn't the only one in which you'll need to box an instance of a value type.

Recall that unboxed value types are lighter-weight types than reference types for two reasons:

- They are not allocated on the managed heap.

- They don't have the additional overhead members that every object on the heap has: a type object pointer and a sync block index.

Because unboxed value types don't have a sync block index, you can't have multiple threads synchronize their access to the instance by using the methods of the **System.Threading .Monitor** type (or by using C#'s **lock** statement).

Even though unboxed value types don't have a type object pointer, you can still call virtual methods (such as **Equals**, **GetHashCode**, or **ToString**) inherited or overridden by the type. The reason is because the CLR can just call these methods nonvirtually and **System.ValueType** overrides all of these virtual methods and expects the value in the **this** argument to refer to an unboxed value type instance. Remember, a value type is implicitly sealed, and therefore, a value type cannot be used as the base class of another type. This means that it's impossible for a value type's virtual method to be overridden by a derived type. This also means that the CLR can call a value type's virtual methods nonvirtually.

However, calling a nonvirtual inherited method (such as `GetType` or `MemberwiseClone`) requires the value type to be boxed because these methods are defined by `System.Object`, so the methods expect the **this** argument to be a pointer that refers to an object on the heap.

In addition, casting an unboxed instance of a value type to one of the type's interfaces requires the instance to be boxed, because interface variables must always contain a reference to an object on the heap. (I'll talk about interfaces in Chapter 14, "Interfaces.") The following code demonstrates:

```
using System;

internal struct Point : IComparable {
   private Int32 m_x, m_y;

   // Constructor to easily initialize the fields
   public Point(Int32 x, Int32 y) {
      m_x = x;
      m_y = y;
   }

   // Override ToString method inherited from System.ValueType
   public override String ToString() {
      // Return the point as a string
      return String.Format("({0}, {1})", m_x, m_y);
   }

   // Implementation of type-safe CompareTo method
   public Int32 CompareTo(Point other) {
      // Use the Pythagorean Theorem to calculate
      // which point is farther from the origin (0, 0)
      return Math.Sign(Math.Sqrt(m_x * m_x + m_y * m_y)
         - Math.Sqrt(other.m_x * other.m_x + other.m_y * other.m_y));
   }

   // Implementation of IComparable's CompareTo method
   public Int32 CompareTo(Object o) {
      if (GetType() != o.GetType()) {
         throw new ArgumentException("o is not a Point");
      }
      // Call type-safe CompareTo method
      return CompareTo((Point) o);
   }
}


public static class Program {
   public static void Main() {
      // Create two Point instances on the stack.
      Point p1 = new Point(10, 10);
      Point p2 = new Point(20, 20);

      // p1 does NOT get boxed to call ToString (a virtual method).
      Console.WriteLine(p1.ToString());// "(10, 10)"
```

```
        // p DOES get boxed to call GetType (a non-virtual method).
        Console.WriteLine(p1.GetType());// "Point"

        // p1 does NOT get boxed to call CompareTo.
        // p2 does NOT get boxed because CompareTo(Point) is called.
        Console.WriteLine(p1.CompareTo(p2));// "-1"

        // p1 DOES get boxed, and the reference is placed in c.
        IComparable c = p1;
        Console.WriteLine(c.GetType());// "Point"

        // p1 does NOT get boxed to call CompareTo.
        // Since CompareTo is not being passed a Point variable,
        // CompareTo(Object) is called which requires a reference to
        // a boxed Point.
        // c does NOT get boxed because it already refers to a boxed Point.
        Console.WriteLine(p1.CompareTo(c));// "0"

        // c does NOT get boxed because it already refers to a boxed Point.
        // p2 does get boxed because CompareTo(Object) is called.
        Console.WriteLine(c.CompareTo(p2));// "-1"

        // c is unboxed, and fields are copied into p2.
        p2 = (Point) c;

        // Proves that the fields got copied into p2.
        Console.WriteLine(p2.ToString());// "(10, 10)"
    }
}
```

This code demonstrates several scenarios related to boxing and unboxing:

- **Calling ToString**   In the call to **ToString**, **p1** doesn't have to be boxed. At first, you'd think that **p1** would have to be boxed because **ToString** is a virtual method that is inherited from the base type, **System.ValueType**. Normally, to call a virtual method, the CLR needs to determine the object's type in order to locate the type's method table. Since **p1** is an unboxed value type, there's no type object pointer. However, the C# compiler sees that **Point** overrides the **ToString** method, and it emits code that calls **ToString** directly (nonvirtually) without having to do any boxing. The compiler knows that polymorphism can't come into play here since **Point** is a value type, and no type can derive from it to provide another implementation of this virtual method.

- **Calling GetType**   In the call to the nonvirtual **GetType** method, **p1** does have to be boxed. The reason is that the **Point** type inherits **GetType** from **System.Object**. So to call **GetType**, the CLR must use a pointer to a type object, which can be obtained only by boxing **p1**.

- **Calling CompareTo (first time)**   In the first call to **CompareTo**, **p1** doesn't have to be boxed because **Point** implements the **CompareTo** method, and the compiler can just call it directly. Note that a **Point** variable (**p2**) is being passed to **CompareTo**, and therefore, the compiler calls the overload of **CompareTo** that accepts a **Point** parameter. This means that **p2** will be passed by value to **CompareTo** and no boxing is necessary.

- **Casting to `IComparable`**   When casting **p1** to a variable (**c**) that is of an interface type, **p1** must be boxed because interfaces are reference types by definition. So **p1** is boxed, and the pointer to this boxed object is stored in the variable **c**. The following call to `GetType` proves that **c** does refer to a boxed **Point** on the heap.

- **Calling `CompareTo` (second time)**   In the second call to `CompareTo`, **p1** doesn't have to be boxed because **Point** implements the `CompareTo` method, and the compiler can just call it directly. Note that an `IComparable` variable (**c**) is being passed to `CompareTo`, and therefore, the compiler calls the overload of `CompareTo` that accepts an **Object** parameter. This means that the argument passed must be a pointer that refers to an object on the heap. Fortunately, **c** does refer to a boxed **Point**, and therefore, that memory address in **c** can be passed to `CompareTo`, and no additional boxing is necessary.

- **Calling `CompareTo` (third time)**   In the third call to `CompareTo`, **c** already refers to a boxed **Point** object on the heap. Since **c** is of the `IComparable` interface type, you can call only the interface's `CompareTo` method that requires an **Object** parameter. This means that the argument passed must be a pointer that refers to an object on the heap. So **p2** is boxed, and the pointer to this boxed object is passed to `CompareTo`.

- **Casting to `Point`**   When casting **c** to a **Point**, the object on the heap referred to by **c** is unboxed, and its fields are copied from the heap to **p2**, an instance of the **Point** type residing on the stack.

I realize that all of this information about reference types, values types, and boxing might be overwhelming at first. However, a solid understanding of these concepts is critical to any .NET Framework developer's long-term success. Trust me: having a solid grasp of these concepts will allow you to build efficient applications faster and easier.

Changing Fields in a Boxed Value Type by Using Interfaces (And Why You Shouldn't Do This)

Let's have some fun and see how well you understand value types, boxing, and unboxing. Examine the following code, and see whether you can figure out what it displays on the console:

```
using System;

// Point is a value type.
internal struct Point {
   private Int32 m_x, m_y;

   public Point(Int32 x, Int32 y) {
      m_x = x;
      m_y = y;
   }

   public void Change(Int32 x, Int32 y) {
      m_x = x; m_y = y;
   }
```

```
    public override String ToString() {
        return String.Format("({0}, {1})", m_x, m_y);
    }
}

public sealed class Program {
    public static void Main() {
        Point p = new Point(1, 1);

        Console.WriteLine(p);

        p.Change(2, 2);
        Console.WriteLine(p);

        Object o = p;
        Console.WriteLine(o);

        ((Point) o).Change(3, 3);
        Console.WriteLine(o);
    }
}
```

Very simply, **Main** creates an instance (**p**) of a **Point** value type on the stack and sets its **m_x** and **m_y** fields to **1**. Then, **p** is boxed before the first call to **WriteLine**, which calls **ToString** on the boxed **Point**, and **(1, 1)** is displayed as expected. Then, **p** is used to call the **Change** method, which changes the values of **p**'s **m_x** and **m_y** fields on the stack to **2**. The second call to **WriteLine** requires **p** to be boxed again and displays **(2, 2)**, as expected.

Now, **p** is boxed a third time, and **o** refers to the boxed **Point** object. The third call to **Write-Line** again shows **(2, 2)**, which is also expected. Finally, I want to call the **Change** method to update the fields in the boxed **Point** object. However, **Object** (the type of the variable **o**) doesn't know anything about the **Change** method, so I must first cast **o** to a **Point**. Casting **o** to a **Point** unboxes **o** and copies the fields in the boxed **Point** to a temporary **Point** on the thread's stack! The **m_x** and **m_y** fields of this temporary point are changed to **3** and **3**, but the boxed **Point** isn't affected by this call to **Change**. When **WriteLine** is called the fourth time, **(2, 2)** is displayed again. Many developers do *not* expect this.

Some languages, such as C++/CLI, let you change the fields in a boxed value type, but C# does not. However, you can fool C# into allowing this by using an interface. The following code is a modified version of the previous code:

```
using System;

// Interface defining a Change method
internal interface IChangeBoxedPoint {
    void Change(Int32 x, Int32 y);
}


// Point is a value type.
internal struct Point : IChangeBoxedPoint {
    private Int32 m_x, m_y;
```

```
    public Point(Int32 x, Int32 y) {
        m_x = x;
        m_y = y;
    }

    public void Change(Int32 x, Int32 y) {
        m_x = x; m_y = y;
    }

    public override String ToString() {
        return String.Format("({0}, {1})", m_x, m_y);
    }
}

public sealed class Program {
    public static void Main() {
        Point p = new Point(1, 1);

        Console.WriteLine(p);

        p.Change(2, 2);
        Console.WriteLine(p);

        Object o = p;
        Console.WriteLine(o);

        ((Point) o).Change(3, 3);
        Console.WriteLine(o);

        // Boxes p, changes the boxed object and discards it
        ((IChangeBoxedPoint) p).Change(4, 4);
        Console.WriteLine(p);

        // Changes the boxed object and shows it
        ((IChangeBoxedPoint) o).Change(5, 5);
        Console.WriteLine(o);
    }
}
```

This code is almost identical to the previous version. The main difference is that the **Change** method is defined by the **IChangeBoxedPoint** interface, and the **Point** type now implements this interface. Inside **Main**, the first four calls to **WriteLine** are the same and produce the same results I had before (as expected). However, I've added two more examples at the end of **Main**.

In the first example, the unboxed **Point**, **p**, is cast to an **IChangeBoxedPoint**. This cast causes the value in **p** to be boxed. **Change** is called on the boxed value, which does change its **m_x** and **m_y** fields to **4** and **4**, but after **Change** returns, the boxed object is immediately ready to be garbage collected. So the fifth call to **WriteLine** displays **(2, 2)**. Many developers won't expect this result.

In the last example, the boxed **Point** referred to by **o** is cast to an **IChangeBoxedPoint**. No boxing is necessary here because **o** is already a boxed **Point**. Then **Change** is called, which *does* change the boxed **Point**'s **m_x** and **m_y** fields. The interface method **Change** has allowed me to change the fields in a boxed **Point** object! Now, when **WriteLine** is called, it displays **(5, 5)** as expected. The purpose of this whole example is to demonstrate how an interface method is able to modify the fields of a boxed value type. In C#, this isn't possible without using an interface method.

> **Important**   Earlier in this chapter, I mentioned that value types should not define any members that modify any of the type's instance fields. The previous example should make it very clear to you why this is the case. The unexpected behaviors shown in the previous example all occur when attempting to call a method that modifies the value type's instance fields. If after constructing a value type, you do not call any methods that modify its state, you will not get confused when all of the boxing and unboxing/field copying occurs. If the value type is immutable, you will end up just copying the same state around, and you will not be surprised by any of the behaviors you see.
>
> A number of developers reviewed the chapters of this book. After reading through some of my code samples (such as the preceding one), these reviewers would tell me that they've sworn off value types. I must say that these little value type nuances have cost me days of debugging time, which is why I spend time pointing them out in this book. I hope you'll remember some of these nuances and that you'll be prepared for them if and when they strike you and your code. Certainly, you shouldn't be scared of value types. They are useful types, and they have their place. After all, a program needs a little **Int32** love now and then. Just keep in mind that value types and reference types have very different behaviors depending on how they're used. In fact, you should take the preceding code and declare the **Point** as a **class** instead of a **struct** to appreciate the results.

Object Equality and Identity

Frequently, developers write code to compare objects with one another. This is particularly true when placing objects in a collection and you're writing code to sort, search, or compare items in a collection. In this section, I'll discuss object equality and identity, and I'll also discuss how to define a type that properly implements object equality.

The **System.Object** type offers a virtual method named **Equals**, whose purpose is to return **true** if two objects are equal. The implementation of **Object**'s **Equals** method looks like this:

```
public class Object {
   public virtual Boolean Equals(Object obj) {

      // If both references point to the same object,
      // they must be equal.
      if (this == obj) return true;

      // Assume that the objects are not equal.
      return false;
   }
}
```

At first, this seems like a reasonable default implementation of `Equals`: it returns `true` if the `this` and `obj` arguments refer to the same exact object. This seems reasonable because `Equals` knows that an object must be equal to itself. However, if the arguments refer to different objects, `Equals` can't be certain if the objects contain the same values, and therefore, `false` is returned. In other words, the default implementation of `Object`'s `Equals` method really implements identity, not equality.

Unfortunately, as it turns out, `Object`'s `Equals` method is not a reasonable default, and it should have never been implemented this way. You immediately see the problem when you start thinking about class inheritance hierarchies and how to properly override `Equals`. Here is how to properly implement an `Equals` method internally:

1. If the `obj` argument is `null`, return `false` because the current object identified by `this` is obviously not `null` when the nonstatic `Equals` method is called.

2. If the `this` and `obj` arguments refer to objects of different types, return `false`. Obviously, checking if a `String` object is equal to a `FileStream` object should result in a `false` result.

3. For each instance field defined by the type, compare the value in the `this` object with the value in the `obj` object. If any fields are not equal, return `false`.

4. Call the base class's `Equals` method so it can compare any fields defined by it. If the base class's `Equals` method returns `false`, return `false`; otherwise, return `true`.

So Microsoft should have implemented `Object`'s `Equals` like this:

```
public class Object {
    public virtual Boolean Equals(Object obj) {
        // The given object to compare to can't be null
        if (obj == null) return false;

        // If objects are different types, they can't be equal.
        if (this.GetType() != obj.GetType()) return false;

        // If objects are same type, return true if all of their fields match
        // Since System.Object defines no fields, the fields match
        return true;
    }
}
```

But, since Microsoft didn't implement `Equals` this way, the rules for how to implement `Equals` is significantly more complicated than you would think. When a type overrides `Equals`, the override should call its base class's implementation of `Equals` unless it would be calling `Object`'s implementation. This also means that since a type can override `Object`'s `Equals` method, this `Equals` method can no longer be called to test for identity. To fix this, `Object` offers a static `ReferenceEquals` method, prototyped like this:

```
public class Object {
    public static Boolean ReferenceEquals(Object objA, Object objB) {
        return (objA == objB);
    }
}
```

You should always call **ReferenceEquals** if you want to check for identity (if two references point to the same object). You shouldn't use the C# **==** operator (unless you cast both operands to **Object** first) because one of the operands' types could overload the **==** operator, giving it semantics other than identity.

As you can see, the .NET Framework has a very confusing story when it comes to object equality and identity. By the way, **System.ValueType** (the base class of all value types) does override **Object**'s **Equals** method and is correctly implemented to perform an equality check (not an identity check). Internally, **ValueType**'s **Equals** is implemented this way:

1. If the **obj** argument is **null**, return **false**.

2. If the **this** and **obj** arguments refer to objects of different types, return **false**.

3. For each instance field defined by the type, compare the value in the **this** object with the value in the **obj** object. If any fields are not equal, return **false**.

4. Return **true**. **Object**'s **Equals** method is not called by **ValueType**'s **Equals** method.

Internally, **ValueType**'s **Equals** method uses reflection (covered in Chapter 22, "Assembly Loading and Reflection") to accomplish step #3 above. Since the CLR's reflection mechanism is slow, when defining your own value type, you should override **Equals** and provide your own implementation to improve the performance of value equality comparisons that use instances of your type. Of course, in your own implementation, do not call **base.Equals**.

When defining your own type, if you decide to override **Equals**, you must ensure that it adheres to the four properties of equality:

■ **Equals** must be reflexive; that is, **x.Equals(x)** must return **true**.

■ **Equals** must be symmetric; that is, **x.Equals(y)** must return the same value as **y.Equals(x)**.

■ **Equals** must be transitive; that is, if **x.Equals(y)** returns **true** and **y.Equals(z)** returns **true**, then **x.Equals(z)** must also return **true**.

■ **Equals** must be consistent. Provided that there are no changes in the two values being compared, **Equals** should consistently return **true** or **false**.

If your implementation of **Equals** fails to adhere to all of these rules, your application will behave in strange and unpredictable ways.

When overriding the **Equals** method, there are a few more things that you'll probably want to do:

■ **Have the type implement the System.IEquatable<T> interface's Equals method**   This generic interface allows you to define a type-safe **Equals** method. Usually, you'll implement the **Equals** method that takes an **Object** parameter to internally call the type-safe **Equals** method.

■ **Overload the == and != operator methods**   Usually, you'll implement these operator methods to internally call the type-safe **Equals** method.

Furthermore, if you think that instances of your type will be compared for the purposes of sorting, you'll want your type to also implement `System.IComparable`'s `CompareTo` method and `System.IComparable<T>`'s type-safe `CompareTo` method. If you implement these methods, you can implement the `IEquatable<T>` `Equals` method so that it calls `IComparable<T>`'s `CompareTo` method returning **true** if `CompareTo` returns **0**. If you implement the `CompareTo` methods, you'll also want to overload the various comparison operator methods (**<, <=, >, >=**) and implement these methods internally to call the type-safe `CompareTo` method.

Object Hash Codes

The designers of the FCL decided that it would be incredibly useful if any instance of any object could be placed into a hash table collection. To this end, `System.Object` provides a virtual `GetHashCode` method so that an `Int32` hash code can be obtained for any and all objects.

If you define a type and override the `Equals` method, you should also override the `GetHashCode` method. In fact, Microsoft's C# compiler emits a warning if you define a type that overrides `Equals` without also overriding `GetHashCode`. For example, compiling the following type yields this warning: "warning CS0659: 'Program' overrides Object.Equals(object o) but does not override Object.GetHashCode()".

```
public sealed class Program {
    public override Boolean Equals(Object obj) { ... }
}
```

The reason why a type that defines `Equals` must also define `GetHashCode` is that the implementation of the `System.Collections.Hashtable` type and the `System.Collections.Generic.Dictionary` requires that any two objects that are equal must have the same hash code value. So if you override `Equals`, you should override `GetHashCode` to ensure that the algorithm you use for calculating equality corresponds to the algorithm you use for calculating the object's hash code.

Basically, when you add a key/value pair to a `Hashtable` or `Dictionary` object, a hash code for the key object is obtained first. This hash code indicates which "bucket" the key/value pair should be stored in. When the `Hashtable`/`Dictionary` object needs to look up a key, it gets the hash code for the specified key object. This code identifies the "bucket" that is now searched sequentially, looking for a stored key object that is equal to the specified key object. Using this algorithm of storing and looking up keys means that if you change a key object that is in a `Hashtable`/`Dictionary`, the `Hashtable`/`Dictionary` will no longer be able to find the object. If you intend to change a key object in a hash table, you should remove the original object/value pair, modify the key object, and then add the new key object/value pair back into the hash table.

Defining a `GetHashCode` method can be easy and straightforward. But depending on your data types and the distribution of data, it can be tricky to come up with a hashing algorithm that returns a well-distributed range of values. Here's a simple example that will probably work just fine for **Point** objects:

```
internal sealed class Point {
    private Int32 m_x, m_y;
    public override Int32 GetHashCode() {
        return m_x ^ m_y;  // m_x XOR'd with m_y
    }
    ...
}
```

When selecting an algorithm for calculating hash codes for instances of your type, try to follow these guidelines:

- Use an algorithm that gives a good random distribution for the best performance of the hash table.

- Your algorithm can also call the base type's **GetHashCode** method including its return value in your own algorithm. However, you don't generally want to call **Object**'s or **ValueType**'s **GetHashCode** method, because the implementation in either method doesn't lend itself to high-performance hashing algorithms.

- Your algorithm should use at least one instance field.

- Ideally, the fields you use in your algorithm should be immutable; that is, the fields should be initialized when the object is constructed, and they should never again change during the object's lifetime.

- Your algorithm should execute as quickly as possible.

- Objects with the same value should return the same code. For example, two **String** objects with the same text should return the same hash code value.

System.Object's implementation of the **GetHashCode** method doesn't know anything about its derived type and any fields that are in the type. For this reason, **Object**'s **GetHashCode** method returns a number that is guaranteed to uniquely identify the object within the AppDomain; this number is guaranteed not to change for the lifetime of the object. After the object is garbage collected, however, its unique number can be reused as the hash code for a new object.

> **Note**   If you want to get a unique ID (within an AppDomain) for an object, you should not call **Object**'s **GetHashCode** method. This method returns the same value that **Object**'s **GetHashCode** method would return; however, if a type overrides **Object**'s **GetHashCode** method, you can no longer get a unique ID for the object.
>
> However, the FCL does provide a method that you can call to obtain a unique ID for an object. In the **System.Runtime.CompilerServices** namespace, see the **RuntimeHelpers** class's public, static **GetHashCode** method that takes a reference to an **Object** as an argument. **Runtime-Helpers'** **GetHashCode** method returns a unique ID for an object even if the object's type overrides **Object**'s **GetHashCode** method. This method got its name because of its heritage, but it would have been better if Microsoft had named it something like **GetUniqueObjectID**.

`System.ValueType`'s implementation of `GetHashCode` uses reflection (which is slow) and XORs some of the type's instance fields together. This is a naïve implementation that might be good for some value types, but I still recommend that you implement `GetHashCode` yourself because you'll know exactly what it does, and your implementation will be faster than `ValueType`'s implementation.

> **Important**   If you're implementing your own hash table collection for some reason, or you're implementing any piece of code in which you'll be calling `GetHashCode`, you should *never, ever persist hash code values*. The reason is that hash code values are subject to change. For example, a future version of a type might use a different algorithm for calculating the object's hash code.

There is a company that was not heeding this important warning. On their Web site, users could create new accounts by selecting a user name and a password. The Web site then took the password `String`, called `GetHashCode`, and persisted the hash code value in a database. When users logged back on to the Web site, they entered their password. The Web site would call `GetHashCode` again and compare the hash code value with the stored value in the database. If the hash codes matched, the user would be granted access. Unfortunately, when the company upgraded to a new version of the CLR, `String`'s `GetHashCode` method had changed, and it now returned a different hash code value. The end result was that no user was able to log on to the Web site anymore!

Part III
Designing Types

Chapter 6
Type and Member Basics

In Part II, "Working with Types," I focused on types and what operations are guaranteed to exist on all instances of any type. I also explained how all types fall into one of two categories: reference types and value types. In this and the subsequent chapters in this part, I'll show how to design types by using the different kinds of members that can be defined within a type. In Chapters 7 through 10, I'll discuss the various members in detail.

The Different Kinds of Type Members

A type can define zero or more of the following kinds of members:

- **Constants (Chapter 7)** A constant is a symbol that identifies a never-changing data value. These symbols are typically used to make code more readable and maintainable. Constants are always associated with a type, not an instance of a type. Logically, constants are always static members.

- **Fields (Chapter 7)** A field represents a read-only or read/write data value. A field can be static, in which case the field is considered part of the type's state. A field can also be instance (nonstatic), in which case it's considered part of an object's state. I strongly encourage you to make fields private so that the state of the type or object can't be corrupted by code outside of the defining type.

- **Instance constructors (Chapter 8)** An instance constructor is a special method used to initialize a new object's instance fields to a good initial state.

- **Type constructors (Chapter 8)** A type constructor is a special method used to initialize a type's static fields to a good initial state.

- **Methods (Chapter 8)**   A method is a function that performs operations that change or query the state of a type (static method) or an object (instance method). Methods typically read and write to the fields of the type or object.

- **Operator overloads (Chapter 8)**   An operator overload is a method that defines how an object should be manipulated when certain operators are applied to the object. Because not all programming languages support operator overloading, operator overload methods are not part of the Common Language Specification (CLS).

- **Conversion operators (Chapter 8)**   A conversion operator is a method that defines how to implicitly or explicitly cast or convert an object from one type to another type. As with operator overload methods, not all programming languages support conversion operators, so they're not part of the CLS.

- **Properties (Chapter 9)**   A property is a mechanism that allows a simple, field-like syntax for setting or querying part of the logical state of a type (static property) or object (instance property) while ensuring that the state doesn't become corrupt. Properties can be parameterless (very common) or parameterful (fairly uncommon but used frequently with collection classes).

- **Events (Chapter 10)**   A static event is a mechanism that allows a type to send a notification to listening types or listening objects. An instance (nonstatic) event is a mechanism that allows an object to send a notification to listening types or listening objects. Events are usually raised in response to a state change occurring in the type or object offering the event. An event consists of two methods that allow types or objects ("listeners") to register and unregister interest in the event. In addition to the two methods, events typically use a delegate field to maintain the set of registered listeners.

- **Types**   A type can define other types nested within it. This approach is typically used to break a large, complex type down into smaller building blocks to simplify the implementation.

Again, the purpose of this chapter isn't to describe these various members in detail but to set the stage and explain what these various members all have in common.

Regardless of the programming language you're using, the corresponding compiler must process your source code and produce metadata and IL code for each kind of member in the preceding list. The format of the metadata is identical regardless of the source programming language you use, and this feature is what makes the CLR a *common language* runtime. The metadata is the common information that all languages produce and consume, enabling code in one programming language to seamlessly access code written in a completely different programming language.

This common metadata format is also used by the CLR, which determines how constants, fields, constructors, methods, properties, and events all behave at run time. Simply stated, metadata is the key to the whole Microsoft .NET Framework development platform; it enables the seamless integration of languages, types, and objects.

The following C# code shows a type definition that contains an example of all the possible members. The code shown here will compile (with warnings), but it isn't representative of a type that you'd normally create; most of the methods do nothing of any real value. Right now, I just want to show you how the compiler translates this type and its members into metadata. Once again, I'll discuss the individual members in the next few chapters.

```csharp
using System;

public sealed class SomeType {                              // 1

  // Nested class
  private class SomeNestedType { }                          // 2

  // Constant, read-only, and static read/write field
  private const    Int32 SomeConstant      = 1;             // 3
  private readonly Int32 SomeReadOnlyField = 2;             // 4
  private static   Int32 SomeReadWriteField = 3;            // 5

  // Type constructor
  static SomeType() { }                                     // 6

  // Instance constructors
  public SomeType() { }                                     // 7
  public SomeType(Int32 x) { }                              // 8


  // Instance and static methods
  private String InstanceMethod() { return null; }          // 9
  public static void Main() {}                              // 10

  // Instance parameterless property
  public Int32 SomeProp {                                   // 11
    get { return 0;  }                                      // 12
    set { }                                                 // 13
  }

  // Instance parameterful property
  public Int32 this[string s] {                            // 14
    get { return 0; }                                       // 15
    set { }                                                 // 16
  }

  // Instance event
  public event EventHandler SomeEvent;                     // 17
}
```

If you were to compile the type just defined and examine the metadata in ILDasm.exe, you'd see the output shown in Figure 6-1.

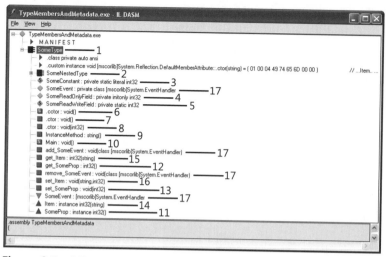

Figure 6-1   ILDasm.exe output showing metadata from preceding code

Notice that all the members defined in the source code cause the compiler to emit some metadata. In fact, some of the members cause the compiler to generate additional members as well as additional metadata. For example, the event member (17) causes the compiler to emit a field, two methods, and some additional metadata. I don't expect you to fully understand what you're seeing here now. But as you read the next few chapters, I encourage you to look back to this example to see how the member is defined and what effect that has on the metadata produced by the compiler.

Type Visibility

When defining a type at file scope (versus defining a type nested within another type), you can specify the type's visibility as being either **public** or **internal**. A **public** type is visible to all code within the defining assembly as well as all code written in other assemblies. An **internal** type is visible to all code within the defining assembly, and the type is not visible to code written in other assemblies. If you do not explicitly specify either of these when you define a type, the C# compiler sets the type's visibility to **internal** (the more restrictive of the two). Here are some examples:

```
using System;

// The type below has public visibility and can be accessed by code
// in this assembly as well as code written in other assemblies.
public class ThisIsAPublicType { ... }

// The type below has internal visibility and can be accessed by code
// in this assembly only.
internal class ThisIsAnInternalType { ... }

// The type below is internal because public/internal
// was not explicitly stated
class ThisIsAlsoAnInternalType { ... }
```

Friend Assemblies

Imagine the following scenario: A company has one team, TeamA, that is defining a bunch of utility types in one assembly, and they expect these types to be used by members in another team, TeamB. For various reasons such as time schedules or geographical location, or perhaps different cost centers or reporting structures, these two teams cannot build all of their types into a single assembly; instead, each team produces its own assembly file.

In order for TeamB's assembly to use TeamA's types, TeamA must define all of their utility types as **public**. However, this means that their types are publicly visible to any and all assemblies; developers in another company could write code that uses the public utility types, and this is not desirable. Maybe the utility types make certain assumptions that TeamB ensures when they write code that uses TeamA's types. What we'd like to have is a way for TeamA to define their types as **internal** while still allowing TeamB to access the types. The CLR and C# support this via *friend assemblies*.

When an assembly is built, it can indicate other assemblies it considers "friends" by using the **InternalsVisibleTo** attribute defined in the **System.Runtime.CompilerServices** namespace. The attribute has a string parameter that identifies the friend assembly's name and public key (the string you pass to the attribute must not include a version, culture, or processor architecture). Note that friend assemblies can access *all* of an assembly's **internal** types as well as these type's **internal** members. Here is an example of how an assembly can specify two other strongly named assemblies named "Wintellect" and "Microsoft" as its friend assemblies:

```
using System;
using System.Runtime.CompilerServices; // For InternalsVisibleTo attribute

// This assembly's internal types can be accessed by any code written
// in the following two assemblies (regardless of version or culture):
[assembly:InternalsVisibleTo("Wintellect, PublicKey=12345678...90abcdef")]
[assembly:InternalsVisibleTo("Microsoft, PublicKey=b77a5c56...1934e089")]

internal sealed class SomeInternalType { ... }
internal sealed class AnotherInternalType { ... }
```

Accessing the above assembly's **internal** types from a friend assembly is trivial. For example, here's how a friend assembly called "Wintellect" with a public key of "12345678...90abcdef" can access the internal type **SomeInternalType** in the assembly above:

```
using System;

internal sealed class Foo {
    private static Object SomeMethod() {
        // This "Wintellect" assembly accesses the other assembly's
        // internal type as if it were a public type
        SomeInternalType sit = new SomeInternalType();
        return sit;
    }
}
```

Since the `internal` members of the types in an assembly become accessible to friend assemblies, you should think carefully about what accessibility you specify for your type's members and which assemblies you declare as your friends. Note that the C# compiler requires you to use the `/out:<file>` compiler switch when compiling the friend assembly (the assembly that does not contain the `InternalsVisibleTo` attribute). The switch is required because the compiler needs to know the name of the assembly being compiled in order to determine if the resulting assembly should be considered a friend assembly. You would think that the C# compiler could determine this on its own since it normally determines the output file name on its own; however, the compiler doesn't decide on an output file name until it is finished compiling the code. So requiring the `/out:<file>` compiler switch improves the performance of compiling significantly.

Also, if you are compiling a module (as opposed to an assembly) using C#'s `/t:module` switch, and this module is going to become part of a friend assembly, you need to compile the module by using the C# compiler's `/moduleassemblyname:<string>` switch as well. This tells the compiler what assembly the module will be a part of so the compiler can allow code in the module to access the other assembly's internal types.

 Important   The friend assembly feature should be used only by assemblies that ship on the same schedule and probably even ship together. The reason is because the interdependency between friend assemblies is so high that shipping the friend assemblies on different schedules will most likely cause compatibility problems. If you expect the assemblies to ship on different schedules, you should try to design `public` classes that can be consumed by any assembly and limit accessibility via a LinkDemand requesting the `StrongNameIdentityPermission`.

Member Accessibility

When defining a type's member (which includes nested types), you can specify the member's accessibility. A member's accessibility indicates which members can be legally accessed from referent code. The CLR defines the set of possible accessibility modifiers, but each programming language chooses the syntax and term it wants developers to use when applying the accessibility to a member. For example, the CLR uses the term *Assembly* to indicate that a member is accessible to any code within the same assembly, whereas the C# term for this is `internal`.

Table 6-1 shows the six accessibility modifiers that can be applied to a member. The rows of the table are in order from most restrictive (*Private*) to least restrictive (*Public*).

Table 6-1   Member Accessibility

CLR Term	C# Term	Description
Private	`private`	The member is accessible only by methods in the defining type or any nested type.
Family	`protected`	The member is accessible only by methods in the defining type, any nested type, or one of its derived types without regard to assembly.

Table 6-1 Member Accessibility

CLR Term	C# Term	Description
Family and Assembly	(not supported)	The member is accessible only by methods in the defining type, any nested type, or by any derived types defined in the same assembly.
Assembly	`internal`	The member is accessible only by methods in the defining assembly.
Family or Assembly	`protected internal`	The member is accessible by any nested type, any derived type (regardless of assembly), or any methods in the defining assembly.
Public	`public`	The member is accessible to all methods in any assembly.

Of course, for any member to be accessible, it must be defined in a type that is visible. For example, if AssemblyA defines an **internal** type with a **public** method, code in AssemblyB cannot call the **public** method because the **internal** type is not visible to AssemblyB.

When compiling code, the language compiler is responsible for checking that the code is referencing types and members correctly. If the code references some type or member incorrectly, the compiler has the responsibility of emitting the appropriate error message. In addition, the JIT compiler also ensures that references to fields and methods are legal when compiling IL code into native CPU instructions at run time. For example, if the JIT compiler detects code that is improperly attempting to access a private field or method, the JIT compiler throws a **FieldAccessException** or a **MethodAccessException**, respectively.

Verifying the IL code ensures that a referenced member's accessibility is properly honored at run time, even if a language compiler ignored checking the accessibility. Another, more likely, possibility is that the language compiler compiled code that accessed a **public** member in another type (in another assembly); but at run time, a different version of the assembly is loaded, and in this new version, the **public** member has changed and is now **protected** or **private**.

In C#, if you do not explicitly declare a member's accessibility, the compiler usually (but not always) defaults to selecting **private** (the most restrictive of them all). The CLR requires that all members of an interface type be public. The C# compiler knows this and forbids the programmer from explicitly specifying accessibility on interface members; the compiler just makes all the members **public** for you.

 More Info See the "Declared Accessibility" section in the C# Language Specification for the complete set of C# rules about what accessibilities can be applied to types and members and what default accessibilities C# selects based on the context in which the declaration takes place.

Furthermore, you'll notice the CLR offers an accessibility called *Family and Assembly*. However, C# doesn't expose this in the language. The C# team felt that this accessibility was for the most part useless and decided not to incorporate it into the C# language.

When a derived type is overriding a member defined in its base type, the C# compiler requires that the original member and the overriding member have the same accessibility. That is, if the member in the base class is **protected**, the overriding member in the derived class must also be **protected**. However, this is a C# restriction, not a CLR restriction. When deriving from a base class, the CLR allows a member's accessibility to become less restrictive but not more restrictive. For example, a class can override a **protected** method defined in its base class and make the overridden method **public** (more accessible). However, a class cannot override a **protected** method defined in its base class and make the overridden method **private** (less accessible). The reason a class cannot make a base class method more restricted is because a user of the derived class could always cast to the base type and gain access to the base class's method. If the CLR allowed the derived type's method to be less accessible, it would be making a claim that was not enforceable.

Static Classes

There are certain classes that are never intended to be instantiated, such as **Console**, **Math**, **Environment**, and **ThreadPool**. These classes have only **static** members and, in fact, the classes exist simply as a way to group a set of related members together. For example, the **Math** class defines a bunch of methods that do math-related operations. C# allows you to define non-instantiable classes by using the C# **static** keyword. This keyword can be applied only to classes, not structures (value types) because the CLR always allows value types to be instantiated and there is no way to stop or prevent this.

The compiler enforces many restrictions on a **static** class:

- The class must be derived directly from **System.Object** because deriving from any other base class makes no sense since inheritance applies only to objects, and you cannot create an instance of a **static** class.

- The class must not implement any interfaces since interface methods are callable only when using an instance of a class.

- The class must define only **static** members (fields, methods, properties, and events). Any instance members cause the compiler to generate an error.

- The class cannot be used as a field, method parameter, or local variable because all of these would indicate a variable that refers to an instance, and this is not allowed. If the compiler detects any of these uses, the compiler issues an error.

Here is an example of a **static** class that defines some **static** members; this code compiles (with a warning) but the class doesn't do anything interesting:

```
using System;

public static class AStaticClass {
   public static void AStaticMethod() {  }

   public static String AStaticProperty {
      get { return s_AStaticField; }
      set { s_AStaticField = value; }
   }

   private static String s_AStaticField;

   public static event EventHandler AStaticEvent;
}
```

If you compile the code above into a library (DLL) assembly and look at the result by using ILDasm.exe, you'll see what is shown in Figure 6-2. As you can see in Figure 6-2, defining a class by using the **static** keyword causes the C# compiler to make the class both **abstract** and **sealed**. Furthermore, the compiler will not emit an instance constructor method into the type. Notice that there is no instance constructor (**.ctor**) method shown in Figure 6-2.

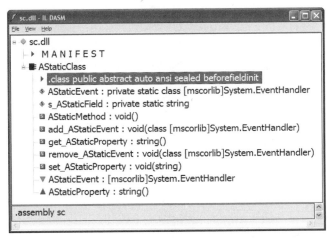

Figure 6-2   ILDasm.exe showing the class as abstract sealed in metadata

Partial Classes, Structures, and Interfaces

In this section, I discuss partial classes, structures, and interfaces. It should be noted that this feature is offered entirely by the C# compiler (other compilers also offer this feature); the CLR knows nothing about partial classes, structures, and interfaces. In fact, I offer this section more for completeness because this book really focuses on CLR features as exposed through C#.

The **partial** keyword tells the C# compiler that the source code for a single class, structure, or interface definition may span one or more source code files. There are two main reasons why you might want to split the source code for a type across multiple files:

■ **Source control** Suppose a type's definition consists of a lot of source code, and a programmer checks it out of source control to make changes. No other programmer will be able to modify the type at the same time without doing a merge later. Using the `partial` keyword allows you to split the code for the type across multiple source code files, each of which can be checked out individually so that multiple programmers can edit the type at the same time.

- **Code spitters** In Microsoft Visual Studio, when you create a new Windows Forms or Web Forms project, some source code files are created automatically as part of the project. These source code files contain templates that give you a head start at building these kinds of projects. When you use the Visual Studio designers and drag and drop controls onto the Windows form or Web form, Visual Studio writes source code for you automatically and spits this code into the source code files. This really improves your productivity. Historically, the generated code was emitted into the same source code file that you were working on. The problem with this is that you might edit the generated code accidentally and cause the designers to stop functioning correctly. Starting with Visual Studio 2005, when you create a new project, Visual Studio creates two source code files: one for your code and the other for the code generated by the designer. Since the designer code is in a separate file, you'll be far less likely to accidentally edit it.

The `partial` keyword is applied to the types in both files. When the files are compiled together, the compiler combines the code to produce one type that is in the resulting .exe or .dll assembly file (or .netmodule module file). As I stated in the beginning of this section, the partial types feature is completely implemented by the C# compiler; the CLR knows nothing about partial types at all. This is why all of the source code files for the type must use the same programming language, and they must all be compiled together as a single compilation unit.

Components, Polymorphism, and Versioning

Object-oriented programming (OOP) has been around for many, many years. When it was first used in the late 1970s/early 1980s, applications were much smaller in size and all the code to make the application run was written by one company. Sure, there were operating systems back then and applications did make use of what they could out of those operating systems, but the operating systems offered very few features compared with the operating systems of today.

Today, software is much more complex and users demand that applications offer rich features such as GUIs, menu items, mouse input, tablet input, printer output, networking, and so on. For this reason, our operating systems and development platforms have grown substantially over recent years. Furthermore, it is no longer feasible or even cost effective for application developers to write all of the code necessary for their application to work the way users expect. Today, applications consist of code produced by many different companies. This code is stitched together using an object-oriented paradigm.

Component Software Programming (CSP) is OOP brought to this level. Here are some attributes of a component:

- A component (an assembly in .NET) has the feeling of being "published."

- A component has an identity (a name, version, culture, and public key).

- A component forever maintains its identity (the code in an assembly is never statically linked into another assembly; .NET always uses dynamic linking).

- A component clearly indicates the components it depends upon (reference metadata tables).

- A component should document its classes and members. C# offers this by allowing in-source XML documentation along with the compiler's **/doc** command-line switch.

- A component must specify the security permissions it requires. The CLR's Code Access Security (CAS) facilities enable this.

- A component publishes an interface (object model) that won't change for any servicings. A servicing is a new version of a component whose intention is to be backward compatible with the original version of the component. Typically, a servicing version includes bug fixes, security patches, and possibly some small feature enhancements. But a servicing cannot require any new dependencies or any additional security permissions.

As indicated by the last bullet, a big part of CSP has to do with versioning. Components will change over time and components will ship on different time schedules. Versioning introduces a whole new level of complexity for CSP that didn't exist with OOP, with which all code was written, tested, and shipped as a single unit by a single company. In this section, I'm going to focus on component versioning.

In .NET, a version number consists of four parts: a *major* part, a *minor* part, a *build* part, and a *revision* part. For example, an assembly whose version number is 1.2.3.4 has a major part of 1, a minor part of 2, a build part of 3, and a revision part of 4. The major/minor parts are typically used to represent an assembly's identity and the build/revision parts are typically used to represent a servicing of that assembly.

Let's say that a company ships an assembly with version 2.7.0.0. If the company later wants to fix a bug in this component, they would produce a new assembly in which only the build/revision parts of the version are changed, something like version 2.7.1.34. This indicates that the assembly is a servicing whose intention is to be backward compatible with the original component (version 2.7.0.0).

On the other hand, if the company wants to make a new version of the assembly that has significant changes to it and is therefore not intended to be backward compatible with the original assembly, the company is really creating a new component and the new assembly should be given a version number in which the major/minor parts are different from the existing component (version 3.0.0.0, for example).

> **Note**   I have just described how you should think of version numbers. Unfortunately, the CLR doesn't treat version numbers this way. Today, the CLR treats a version number as an opaque value, and if an assembly depends on version 1.2.3.4 of another assembly, the CLR tries to load version 1.2.3.4 only (unless a binding redirection is in place). However, Microsoft has plans to change the CLR's loader in a future version so that it loads the latest build/revision for a given major/minor version of an assembly. For example, on a future version of the CLR, if the loader is trying to find version 1.2.3.4 of an assembly and version 1.2.5.0 exists, the loader will automatically pick up the latest available serving version. This will be a very welcome change to the CLR's loader—I for one can't wait.

Now that we've looked at how we use version numbers to update a component's identity to reflect a new version, let's take a look at some of the features offered by the CLR and programming languages (such as C#) that allow developers to write code that is resilient to changes that may be occurring in components that they are using.

Versioning issues come into play when a type defined in a component (assembly) is used as the base class for a type in another component (assembly). Obviously, if the base class versions (changes) underneath the derived class, the behavior of the derived class changes as well, probably in a way that causes the class to behave improperly. This is particularly true in polymorphism scenarios in which a derived type overrides virtual methods defined by a base type.

C# offers five keywords that you can apply to types and/or type members that impact component versioning. These keywords map directly to features supported in the CLR to support component versioning. Table 6-2 contains the C# keywords related to component versioning and indicates how each keyword affects a type or type member definition.

Table 6-2   C# Keywords and How they Affect Component Versioning

C# Keyword	Type	Method/Property/Event	Constant/Field
`abstract`	Indicates that no instances of the type can be constructed	Indicates that the derived type must override and implement this member before instances of the derived type can be constructed	(not allowed)
`virtual`	(not allowed)	Indicates that this member can be overridden by a derived type	(not allowed)
`override`	(not allowed)	Indicates that the derived type is overriding the base type's member	(not allowed)
`sealed`	Indicates that the type cannot be used as a base type	Indicates that the member cannot be overridden by a derived type. This keyword can be applied only to a method that is overriding a virtual method.	(not allowed)
`new`	When applied to a nested type, method, property, event, constant, or field, indicates that the member has no relationship to a similar member that may exist in the base class		

I will demonstrate the value and use of all these keywords in the upcoming section titled "Dealing with Virtual Methods when Versioning Types." But before we get to a versioning scenario, let's focus on how the CLR actually calls virtual methods.

How the CLR Calls Virtual Methods, Properties, and Events

In this section, I will be focusing on methods, but this discussion is relevant to virtual properties and virtual events as well. Properties and events are actually implemented as methods; this will be shown in their corresponding chapters.

Methods represent code that performs some operation on the type (static methods) or an instance of the type (nonstatic methods). All methods have a name, a signature, and a return value (that may be **void**). The CLR allows a type to define multiple methods with the same name as long as each method has a different set of parameters or a different return value. So it's possible to define two methods with the same name and same parameters as long as the methods have a different return type. However, except for IL assembly language, I'm not aware of any language that takes advantage of this "feature"; most languages (including C#) require that methods differ by parameters and ignore a method's return type when determining uniqueness. (C# actually relaxes this restriction when defining conversion operator methods; see Chapter 8 for details.)

The **Employee** class shown below defines three different kinds of methods:

```
internal class Employee {
// A non-virtual instance method
    public          Int32     GetYearsEmployed()   { ... }

    // A virtual method (virtual implies instance)
    public virtual String     GenProgressReport() { ... }

    // A static method
    public static  Employee   Lookup(String name) { ... }
}
```

When the compiler compiles this code, the compiler emits three entries in the resulting assembly's method definition table. Each entry has flags set indicating if the method is instance, virtual, or static.

When code is written to call any of these methods, the compiler emitting the calling code examines the method definition's flags to determine how to emit the proper IL code so that the call is made correctly. The CLR offers two IL instructions for calling a method:

- The **call** IL instruction can be used to call static, instance, and virtual methods. When the **call** instruction is used to call a static method, you must specify the type that defines the method that the CLR should call. When the **call** instruction is used to call an instance or virtual method, you must specify a variable that refers to an object. The **call** instruction assumes that this variable is not **null**. In other words, the type of the variable itself indicates which type defines the method that the CLR should call. If the variable's type doesn't define the method, base types are checked for a matching method. The **call** instruction is frequently used to call a virtual method non-virtually.

■   The **callvirt** IL instruction can be used to call instance and virtual methods, not static methods. When the **callvirt** instruction is used to call an instance or virtual method, you must specify a variable that refers to an object. When the **callvirt** IL instruction is used to call a non-virtual instance method, the type of the variable indicates which type defines the method that the CLR should call. When the **callvirt** IL instruction is used to call a virtual instance method, the CLR discovers the actual type of the object being used to make the call and then calls the method polymorphically. It order to determine the type, the variable being used to make the call must not be **null**. In other words, when compiling this call, the JIT compiler generates code that verifies that the variable's value is not **null**. If it is **null**, the **callvirt** instruction causes the CLR to throw a **NullReferenceException**. This additional check means that the **callvirt** IL instruction executes slightly more slowly than the **call** instruction. Note that this **null** check is performed even when the **callvirt** instruction is used to call a non-virtual instance method.

So now, let's put this together to see how C# uses these different IL instructions:

```
using System;

public sealed class Program {
    public static void Main() {
        Console.WriteLine(); // Call a static method

        Object o = new Object();
        o.GetHashCode(); // Call a virtual instance method
        o.GetType(); // Call a non-virtual instance method
    }
}
```

If you were to compile the code above and look at the resulting IL, you'd see the following:

```
.method public hidebysig static void  Main() cil managed {
  .entrypoint
  // Code size       26 (0x1a)
  .maxstack  1
  .locals init (object V_0)
  IL_0000:  call       void System.Console::WriteLine()
  IL_0005:  newobj     instance void System.Object::.ctor()
  IL_000a:  stloc.0
  IL_000b:  ldloc.0
  IL_000c:  callvirt   instance int32 System.Object::GetHashCode()
  IL_0011:  pop
  IL_0012:  ldloc.0
  IL_0013:  callvirt   instance class System.Type System.Object::GetType()
  IL_0018:  pop
  IL_0019:  ret
} // end of method Program::Main
```

Notice that the C# compiler uses the `call` IL instruction to call `Console`'s `WriteLine` method. This is expected because `WriteLine` is a static method. Next, notice that the `callvirt` IL instruction is used to call `GetHashCode`. This is also expected, since `GetHashCode` is a virtual method. Finally, notice that the C# compiler also uses the `callvirt` IL instruction to call the `GetType` method. This is surprising since `GetType` is not a virtual method. However, this works because while JIT-compiling this code, the CLR will know that `GetType` is not a virtual method, and so the JIT-compiled code will simply call `GetType` non-virtually.

Of course, the question is, why didn't the C# compiler simply emit the `call` instruction instead? The answer is because the C# team decided that the JIT compiler should generate code to verify that the object being used to make the call is not `null`. This means that calls to non-virtual instance methods are a little slower than they could be. It also means that the C# code shown below will cause a `NullReferenceException` to be thrown. In some other programming languages, the intention of the code shown below would run just fine:

```
using System;

public sealed class Program {
    public Int32 GetFive() { return 5; }
    public static void Main() {
        Program p = null;
        Int32 x = p.GetFive(); // In C#, NullReferenceException is thrown
    }
}
```

Theoretically, the code above is fine. Sure, the variable **p** is `null` but when calling a non-virtual method (`GetFive`), the CLR needs to know just the data type of **p**, which is `Program`. If `GetFive` did get called, the value of the `this` argument would be `null`. Since the argument is not used inside the `GetFive` method, no `NullReferenceException` would be thrown. However, because the C# compiler emits a `callvirt` instruction instead of a `call` instruction, the code above will end up throwing the `NullReferenceException`.

> **Important**   If you define a method as non-virtual, you should never change the method to virtual in the future. The reason is because some compilers will call the non-virtual method by using the `call` instruction instead of the `callvirt` instruction. If the method changes from non-virtual to virtual and the referencing code is not re-compiled, the virtual method will be called non-virtually, causing the application to produce unpredictable behavior. If the referencing code is written in C#, this is not a problem, since C# calls all instance methods by using `callvirt`. But this could be a problem if the referencing code was written using a different programming language.

Sometimes, the compiler will use a `call` instruction to call a virtual method instead of using a `callvirt` instruction. At first, this may seem surprising, but the code below demonstrates why this is sometimes required:

```
internal class SomeClass {
    // ToString is a virtual method defined in the base class: Object.
    public override String ToString() {
```

```
        // Compiler uses the 'call' IL instruction to call
        // Object's ToString method nonvirtually.

        // If the compiler were to use 'callvirt' instead of 'call', this
        // method would call itself recursively until the stack overflowed.
        return base.ToString();
    }
}
```

When calling **base.ToString** (a virtual method), the C# compiler emits a **call** instruction to ensure that the **ToString** method in the base type is called non-virtually. This is required because if **ToString** were called virtually, the call would execute recursively until the threads' stack overflowed, which obviously is not desired.

Compilers tend to use the **call** instruction when calling methods defined by a value type since value types are sealed. This implies that there can be no polymorphism even for their virtual methods, which causes the performance of the call to be faster. In addition, the nature of a value type instance guarantees it can never be **null**, so a **NullReferenceException** will never be thrown. Finally, if you were to call a value type's virtual method virtually, the CLR would need to have a reference to the value type's type object in order to refer to the method table within it, this requires boxing the value type. Boxing puts more pressure on the heap, forcing more frequent garbage collections and hurting performance.

Regardless of whether **call** or **callvirt** is used to call an instance or virtual method, these methods always receive a hidden **this** argument as the method's first parameter. The **this** argument refers to the object being operated on.

When designing a type, you should try to minimize the number of virtual methods you define. First, calling a virtual method is slower than calling a non-virtual method. Second, virtual methods cannot be inlined by the JIT compiler, which further hurts performance. Third, virtual methods make versioning of components more brittle, as described in the next section. Fourth, when defining a base type, it is common to offer a set of convenience overloaded methods. If you want these methods to be polymorphic, the best thing to do is to make the most complex method virtual and leave all of the convenience overloaded methods non-virtual. By the way, following this guideline will also improve the ability to version a component without adversely affecting the derived types. Here is an example:

```
public class Set {
    private Int32 m_length = 0;

    // This convenience overload is not virtual
    public Int32 Find(Object value) {
        return Find(value, 0, m_length);
    }

    // This convenience overload is not virtual
    public Int32 Find(Object value, Int32 startIndex) {
        return Find(value, 0, m_length);
    }
```

```
    // The most feature-rich method is virtual and can be overridden
    public virtual Int32 Find(Object value, Int32 startIndex, Int32 endIndex) {
        // Actual implementation that can be overridden goes here...
    }

    // Other methods go here
}
```

Using Type Visibility and Member Accessibility Intelligently

With the .NET Framework, applications are composed of types defined in multiple assemblies produced by various companies. This means that the developer has little control over the components he or she is using and the types defined within those components. The developer typically doesn't have access to the source code (and probably doesn't even know what programming language was used to create the component), and components tend to version with different schedules. Furthermore, due to polymorphism and protected members, a base class developer must trust the code written by the derived class developer. And, of course, the developer of a derived class must trust the code that he is inheriting from a base class. These are just some of the issues that you need to really think about when designing components and types.

In this section, I'd like to say just a few words about how to design a type with these issues in mind. Specifically, I'm going to focus on the proper way to set type visibility and member accessibility so that you'll be most successful.

First, when defining a new type, compilers should make the class sealed by default so that the class cannot be used as a base class. Instead, many compilers, including C#, default to unsealed classes and allow the programmer to explicitly mark a class as sealed by using the **sealed** keyword. Obviously, it is too late now, but I think that today's compilers have chosen the wrong default and it would be nice if this could change with future compilers. There are three reasons why a sealed class is better than an unsealed class:

- **Versioning** When a class is originally sealed, it can change to unsealed in the future without breaking compatibility. However, once a class is unsealed, you can never change it to sealed in the future as this would break all derived classes. In addition, if the unsealed class defines any unsealed virtual methods, ordering of the virtual method calls must be maintained with new versions or there is the potential of breaking derived types in the future.

- **Performance** As discussed in the previous section, calling a virtual method doesn't perform as well as calling a non-virtual method because the CLR must look up the type of the object at run time in order to determine which type defines the method to call. However, if the JIT compiler sees a call to a virtual method using a sealed type, the JIT compiler can produce more efficient code by calling the method non-virtually. It can do this because it knows there can't possibly be a derived class if the class is sealed.

For example, in the code below, the JIT compiler can call the virtual `ToString` method non-virtually:

```
using System;
public sealed class Point {
   private Int32 m_x, m_y;

   public Point(Int32 x, Int32 y) { m_x = x; m_y = y; }

   public override String ToString() {
      return String.Format("({0}, {1})", m_x, m_y);
   }

   public static void Main() {
      Point p = new Point(3, 4);

      // The C# compiler emits the callvirt instruction here but the
      // JIT compiler will optimize this call and produce code that
      // calls ToString non-virtually because p's type is Point,
      // which is a sealed class
      Console.WriteLine(p.ToString());
   }
}
```

- **Security and Predictability**   A class must protect its own state and not allow itself to ever become corrupted. When a class is unsealed, a derived class can access and manipulate the base class's state if any data fields or methods that internally manipulate fields are accessible and not private. In addition, a virtual method can be overridden by a derived class, and the derived class can decide whether to call the base class's implementation. By making a method, property, or event virtual, the base class is giving up some control over its behavior and its state. Unless carefully thought out, this can cause the object to behave unpredictably, and it opens up potential security holes.

The problem with a sealed class is that it can be a big inconvenience to users of the type. Occasionally, developers want to create a class derived from an existing type in order to attach some additional fields or state information for their application's own use. In fact, they may even want to define some helper or convenience methods on the derived type to manipulate these additional fields. Since sealed classes restrict this ability, I recently made a proposal to the CLR team that they introduce a new class modifier called **closed**.

A closed class can be used as a base class, but its behavior is closed and not subject to interference by a derived class. Basically, a closed base class would prohibit a derived class from accessing any of the base class's non-public members. This would allow the base class to change with the knowledge that it will not impact a derived class. Ideally, compilers would change the default access modifier for types to **closed** because this would be the safest choice without being too restrictive. It is too early to know if this idea will make its way into a future version of the CLR and programming languages. However, I am very hopeful it will.

By the way, you could almost accomplish today what **closed** is designed to do; it's just that it is very inconvenient. Basically, when you implement your class, make sure you seal all the virtual methods you inherit (including the methods defined by **System.Object**). Also, don't define any methods that may become a versioning burden in the future such as protected or virtual methods. Here is an example:

```
public class SimulatedClosedClass : Object {
    public sealed override Boolean Equals(Object obj) {
        return base.Equals(obj);
    }
    public sealed override Int32 GetHashCode() {
        return base.GetHashCode();
    }
    public sealed override String ToString() {
        return base.ToString();
    }
    // Unfortunately, C# won't let you seal the Finalize method

    // Define additional public or private members here...
    // Do not define any protected or virtual members
}
```

Unfortunately, the compilers and the CLR do not support closed types today. Here are the guidelines I follow when I define my own classes:

■ When defining a class, I always explicitly make it **sealed** unless I truly intend for the class to be a base class that allows specialization by derived classes. As stated earlier, this is the opposite of what C# and many other compilers default to today. I also default to making the class **internal** unless I want the class to be publicly exposed outside of my assembly. Fortunately, if you do not explicitly indicate a type's visibility, the C# compiler defaults to internal. If I really feel that it is important to define a class that others can derive but I do not want to allow specialization, I will simulate creating a closed class by using the above technique of sealing the virtual methods that my class inherits.

■ Inside the class, I always define my data fields as **private** and I never waver on this. Fortunately, C# does default to making fields **private**. I'd actually prefer it if C# mandated that all fields be private and that you could not make fields **protected**, **internal**, **public**, and so on. Exposing state is the easiest way to get into problems, have your object behave unpredictably, and open potential security holes. This is true even if you just declare some fields as **internal**. Even within a single assembly, it is too hard to track all code that references a field, especially if several developers are writing code that gets compiled into the same assembly.

■ Inside the class, I always define my methods, properties, and events as **private** and non-virtual. Fortunately, C# defaults to this as well. Certainly, I'll make a method, property, or event **public** to expose some functionality from the type. I try to avoid making any of these members **protected** or **internal**, as this would be exposing my type to some potential vulnerability. However, I would sooner make a member **protected** or **internal** than I would make a member **virtual** because a virtual member gives up a lot of control and really relies on the proper behavior of the derived class.

■ There is an old object-oriented programming adage that goes like this: when things get too complicated, make more types. When an implementation of some algorithm starts to get complicated, I define helper types that encapsulate discrete pieces of functionality. If I'm defining these helper types for use by a single über-type, I'll define the helper types nested within the über-type. This allows for scoping and also allows the code in the nested, helper type to reference the private members defined in the über-type. However, there is a design guideline rule (enforced by FxCop), which indicates that publicly exposed nested types should be defined at file or assembly scope and not be defined within another type. This rule exists because some developers find the syntax for referencing nest types cumbersome. I appreciate this rule and I never define public nested types.

Dealing with Virtual Methods when Versioning Types

As was stated earlier, in a Component Software Programming environment, versioning is a very important issue. I talked about some of these versioning issues in Chapter 3, "Shared Assemblies and Strongly Named Assesmbles," when I explained strongly named assemblies and discussed how an administrator can ensure that an application binds to the assemblies that it was built and tested with. However, other versioning issues cause source code compatibility problems. For example, you must be very careful when adding or modifying members of a type if that type is used as a base type. Let's look at some examples.

CompanyA has designed the following type, **Phone**:

```
namespace CompanyA {
   public class Phone {
      public void Dial() {
         Console.WriteLine("Phone.Dial");
         // Do work to dial the phone here.
      }
   }
}
```

Now imagine that CompanyB defines another type, **BetterPhone**, which uses CompanyA's **Phone** type as its base:

```
namespace CompanyB {
   public class BetterPhone : CompanyA.Phone {
      public void Dial() {
         Console.WriteLine("BetterPhone.Dial");
         EstablishConnection();
         base.Dial();
      }

      protected virtual void EstablishConnection() {
         Console.WriteLine("BetterPhone.EstablishConnection");
```

```
        // Do work to establish the connection.
      }
   }
}
```

When CompanyB attempts to compile its code, the C# compiler issues the following message: "warning CS0108: 'CompanyB.BetterPhone.Dial()' hides inherited member 'CompanyA .Phone.Dial()'. Use the new keyword if hiding was intended." This warning is notifying the developer that **BetterPhone** is defining a **Dial** method, which will hide the **Dial** method defined in **Phone**. This new method could change the semantic meaning of **Dial** (as defined by CompanyA when it originally created the **Dial** method).

It's a very nice feature of the compiler to warn you of this potential semantic mismatch. The compiler also tells you how to remove the warning by adding the **new** keyword before the definition of **Dial** in the **BetterPhone** class. Here's the fixed **BetterPhone** class:

```
namespace CompanyB {
   public class BetterPhone : CompanyA.Phone {

      // This Dial method has nothing to do with Phone's Dial method.
      public new void Dial() {
         Console.WriteLine("BetterPhone.Dial");
         EstablishConnection();
         base.Dial();
      }

      protected virtual void EstablishConnection() {
         Console.WriteLine("BetterPhone.EstablishConnection");
         // Do work to establish the connection.
      }
   }
}
```

At this point, CompanyB can use **BetterPhone.Dial** in its application. Here's some sample code that CompanyB might write:

```
public sealed class Program {
   public static void Main() {
      CompanyB.BetterPhone phone = new CompanyB.BetterPhone();
      phone.Dial();
   }
}
```

When this code runs, the following output is displayed:

```
BetterPhone.Dial
BetterPhone.EstablishConnection
Phone.Dial
```

This output shows that CompanyB is getting the behavior it desires. The call to **Dial** is calling the new **Dial** method defined by **BetterPhone**, which calls the virtual **EstablishConnection** method and then calls the **Phone** base type's **Dial** method.

Now let's imagine that several companies have decided to use CompanyA's **Phone** type. Let's further imagine that these other companies have decided that the ability to establish a connection in the **Dial** method is a really useful feature. This feedback is given to CompanyA, which now revises its **Phone** class:

```
namespace CompanyA {
   public class Phone {
      public void Dial() {
         Console.WriteLine("Phone.Dial");
         EstablishConnection();
         // Do work to dial the phone here.
      }

      protected virtual void EstablishConnection() {
         Console.WriteLine("Phone.EstablishConnection");
         // Do work to establish the connection.
      }
   }
}
```

Now when CompanyB compiles its **BetterPhone** type (derived from this new version of CompanyA's **Phone**), the compiler issues this message: "warning CS0114: 'CompanyB.BetterPhone .EstablishConnection()' hides inherited member 'CompanyA.Phone.EstablishConnection()'. To make the current member override that implementation, add the override keyword. Otherwise, add the new keyword."

The compiler is alerting you to the fact that both **Phone** and **BetterPhone** offer an **Establish-Connection** method and that the semantics of both might not be identical; simply recompiling **BetterPhone** can no longer give the same behavior as it did when using the first version of the **Phone** type.

If CompanyB decides that the **EstablishConnection** methods are not semantically identical in both types, CompanyB can tell the compiler that the **Dial** and **EstablishConnection** method defined in **BetterPhone** is the correct method to use and that it has no relationship with the **EstablishConnection** method defined in the **Phone** base type. CompanyB informs the compiler of this by adding the **new** keyword to the **EstablishConnection** method:

```
namespace CompanyB {
   public class BetterPhone : CompanyA.Phone {

      // Keep 'new' to mark this method as having no
      // relationship to the base type's Dial method.
      public new void Dial() {
         Console.WriteLine("BetterPhone.Dial");
         EstablishConnection();
         base.Dial();
      }

      // Add 'new' to mark this method as having no
```

```
    // relationship to the base type's EstablishConnection method.
    protected new virtual void EstablishConnection() {
        Console.WriteLine("BetterPhone.EstablishConnection");
        // Do work to establish the connection.
    }
  }
}
```

In this code, the **new** keyword tells the compiler to emit metadata, making it clear to the CLR that **BetterPhone**'s **EstablishConnection** method is intended to be treated as a new function that is introduced by the **BetterPhone** type. The CLR will know that there is no relationship between **Phone**'s and **BetterPhone**'s methods.

When the same application code (in the **Main** method) executes, the output is as follows:

```
BetterPhone.Dial
BetterPhone.EstablishConnection
Phone.Dial
Phone.EstablishConnection
```

This output shows that **Main**'s call to **Dial** calls the new **Dial** method defined by **BetterPhone**. **Dial**, which in turn calls the virtual **EstablishConnection** method that is also defined by **BetterPhone**. When **BetterPhone**'s **EstablishConnection** method returns, **Phone**'s **Dial** method is called. **Phone**'s **Dial** method calls **EstablishConnection**, but because **BetterPhone**'s **EstablishConnection** is marked with **new**, **BetterPhone**'s **EstablishConnection** method isn't considered an override of **Phone**'s virtual **EstablishConnection** method. As a result, **Phone**'s **Dial** method calls **Phone**'s **EstablishConnection** method—this is the expected behavior.

> **Note** Without the **new** keyword, the developer of **BetterPhone** couldn't use the method names **Dial** and **EstablishConnection**. This would most likely cause a ripple effect of changes throughout the entire source code base, breaking source and binary compatibility. This type of pervasive change is usually undesirable, especially in any moderate-to-large project. However, if changing the method name causes only moderate updates in the source code, you should change the name of the methods so the two different meanings of **Dial** and **EstablishConnection** don't confuse other developers.

Alternatively, CompanyB could have gotten the new version of CompanyA's **Phone** type and decided that **Phone**'s semantics of **Dial** and **EstablishConnection** are exactly what it's been looking for. In this case, CompanyB would modify its **BetterPhone** type by removing its **Dial** method entirely. In addition, because CompanyB now wants to tell the compiler that **Better-Phone**'s **EstablishConnection** method is related to **Phone**'s **EstablishConnection** method, the **new** keyword must be removed. Simply removing the **new** keyword isn't enough, though, because now the compiler can't tell exactly what the intention is of **BetterPhone**'s **Establish-Connection** method. To express his intent exactly, the CompanyB developer must also change

BetterPhone's **EstablishConnection** method from **virtual** to **override**. The following code shows the new version of **BetterPhone**:

```
namespace CompanyB {
   public class BetterPhone : CompanyA.Phone {

      // Delete the Dial method (inherit Dial from base).

      // Remove 'new' and change 'virtual' to 'override' to
      // mark this method as having a relationship to the base
      // type's EstablishConnection method.
      protected override void EstablishConnection() {
         Console.WriteLine("BetterPhone.EstablishConnection");
         // Do work to establish the connection.
      }
   }
}
```

Now when the same application code (in the **Main** method) executes, the output is as follows:

```
Phone.Dial
BetterPhone.EstablishConnection
```

This output shows that **Main**'s call to **Dial** calls the **Dial** method defined by **Phone** and inherited by **BetterPhone**. Then when **Phone**'s **Dial** method calls the virtual **EstablishConnection** method, **BetterPhone**'s **EstablishConnection** method is called because it overrides the virtual **EstablishConnection** method defined by **Phone**.

Chapter 7
Constants and Fields

In this chapter, I'll show you how to add data members to a type. Specifically, we'll look at constants and fields.

Constants

A constant is a symbol that has a never-changing value. When defining a constant symbol, its value must be determinable at compile time. The compiler then saves the constant's value in the assembly's metadata. This means that you can define a constant only for types that your compiler considers primitive types. In C#, the following types are primitives and can be used to define constants: `Boolean`, `Char`, `Byte`, `SByte`, `Int16`, `UInt16`, `Int32`, `UInt32`, `Int64`, `UInt64`, `Single`, `Double`, `Decimal`, and `String`.

Because a constant value never changes, constants are always considered to be part of the defining type. In other words, constants are always considered to be static members, not instance members. Defining a constant causes the creation of metadata.

When code refers to a constant symbol, compilers look up the symbol in the metadata of the assembly that defines the constant, extract the constant's value, and embed the value in the emitted IL code. Because a constant's value is embedded directly in code, constants don't require any memory to be allocated for them at run time. In addition, you can't get the address of a constant and you can't pass a constant by reference. These constraints also mean that constants don't have a good cross-assembly versioning story, so you should use them only when you know that the value of a symbol will never change. (Defining `MaxInt16` as `32767` is a good example.) Let me demonstrate exactly what I mean. First take the following code and compile it into a DLL assembly:

```
using System;

public sealed class SomeLibraryType {
    // NOTE: C# doesn't allow you to specify static for constants
    // because constants are always implicitly static.
    public const Int32 MaxEntriesInList = 50;
}
```

Then use the following code to build an application assembly:

```
using System;

public sealed class Program {
   public static void Main() {
      Console.WriteLine("Max entries supported in list: "
         + SomeLibraryType.MaxEntriesInList);
   }
}
```

You'll notice that this application code references the **MaxEntriesInList** constant defined in the **SomeLibraryType** class. When the compiler builds the application code, it sees that **MaxEntriesInList** is a constant literal with a value of **50** and embeds the **Int32** value of **50** right inside the application's IL code, as you can see in the IL code shown in Figure 7-1. In fact, after building the application assembly, the DLL assembly isn't even loaded at run time and can be deleted from the disk.

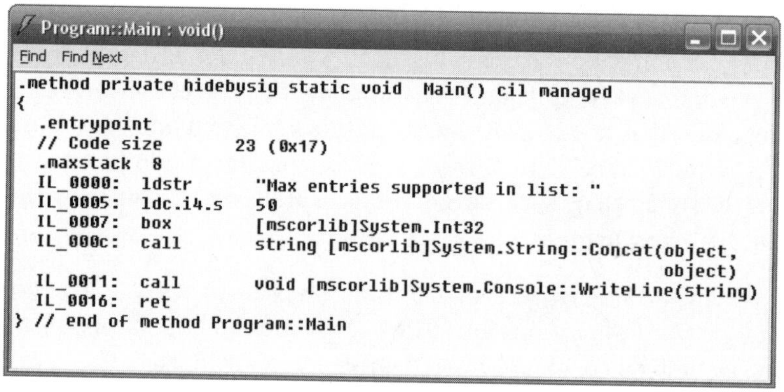

Figure 7-1   ILDasm.exe shows method's IL with constant literal embedded directly in the method

This example should make the versioning problem obvious to you. If the developer changes the **MaxEntriesInList** constant to **1000** and rebuilds the DLL assembly, the application assembly is not affected. For the application to pick up the new value, it will have to be recompiled as well. You can't use constants if you need to have a value in one assembly picked up by another assembly at run time (instead of compile time). Instead, you can use readonly fields, which I'll discuss next.

Fields

A *field* is a data member that holds an instance of a value type or a reference to a reference type. Table 7-1 shows the modifiers that can be applied to a field.

Table 7-1   Field Modifiers

CLR Term	C# Term	Description
Static	`static`	The field is part of the type's state as opposed to being part of an object's state.
Instance	(default)	The field is associated with an instance of the type, not the type itself.
InitOnly	`readonly`	The field can be written to only by code contained in a constructor method.
Volatile	`volatile`	Code that accessed the field is not subject to some thread-unsafe optimizations that may be performed by the compiler, the CLR, or by hardware. Only the following types can be marked `volatile`: all reference types, `Single`, `Boolean`, `Byte`, `SByte`, `Int16`, `UInt16`, `Int32`, `UInt32`, `Char`, and all enumerated types with an underlying type of `Byte`, `SByte`, `Int16`, `UInt16`, `Int32`, or `UInt32`. Volatile fields are discussed in Chapter 24, "Thread Synchronization."

As Table 7-1 shows, the common language runtime (CLR) supports both type (static) and instance (nonstatic) fields. For type fields, the dynamic memory required to hold the field's data is allocated inside the type object, which is created when the type is loaded into an AppDomain (see Chapter 21, "CLR Hosting and AppDomains"), which typically happens the first time any method that references the type is JIT compiled. For instance fields, the dynamic memory to hold the field is allocated when an instance of the type is constructed.

Because fields are stored in dynamic memory, their value can be obtained at run time only. Fields also solve the versioning problem that exists with constants. In addition, a field can be of any data type, so you don't have to restrict yourself to your compiler's built-in primitive types (as you do for constants).

The CLR supports readonly fields and read/write fields. Most fields are read/write fields, meaning the field's value might change multiple times as the code executes. However, readonly fields can be written to only within a constructor method (which is called only once, when an object is first created). Compilers and verification ensure that readonly fields are not written to by any method other than a constructor. Note that reflection can be used to modify a `readonly` field.

Let's take the example from the "Constants" section and fix the versioning problem by using a static readonly field. Here's the new version of the DLL assembly's code:

```
using System;

public sealed class SomeLibraryType {
    // The static is required to associate the field with the type.
    public static readonly Int32 MaxEntriesInList = 50;
}
```

This is the only change you have to make; the application code doesn't have to change at all, although you must rebuild it to see the new behavior. Now when the application's `Main` method runs, the CLR will load the DLL assembly (so this assembly is now required at run time) and grab the value of the `MaxEntriesInList` field out of the dynamic memory allocated for it. Of course, the value will be 50.

Let's say that the developer of the DLL assembly changes the 50 to 1000 and rebuilds the assembly. When the application code is reexecuted, it will automatically pick up the new value: 1000. In this case, the application code doesn't have to be rebuilt—it just works (although its performance is adversely affected). A caveat: this scenario assumes that the new version of the DLL assembly is not strongly named and the versioning policy of the application is such that the CLR loads this new version.

The following example shows how to define a readonly static field that is associated with the type itself, as well as read/write static fields and readonly and read/write instance fields, as shown here:

```
public sealed class SomeType {
   // This is a static read-only field; its value is calculated and
   // stored in memory when this class is initialized at run time.
   public static readonly Random s_random = new Random();

   // This is a static read/write field.
   private static Int32 s_numberOfWrites = 0;

   // This is an instance read-only field.
   public readonly String Pathname = "Untitled";

   // This is an instance read/write field.
   private System.IO.FileStream m_fs;

   public SomeType(String pathname) {
      // This line changes a read-only field.
      // This is OK because the code is in a constructor.
      this.Pathname = pathname;
   }

   public String DoSomething() {
      // This line reads and writes to the static read/write field.
      s_numberOfWrites = s_numberOfWrites + 1;

      // This line reads the read-only instance field.
      return Pathname;
   }
}
```

In this code, many of the fields are initialized inline. C# allows you to use this convenient inline initialization syntax to initialize a class's constants, read/write, and readonly fields. As you'll see in Chapter 8, "Methods: Constructors, Operators, Conversions, and Parameters," C# treats initializing a field inline as shorthand syntax for initializing the field in a constructor.

Also, in C#, there are some performance issues to consider when initializing fields by using inline syntax versus assignment syntax in a constructor. These performance issues are discussed in Chapter 8 as well.

Important   When a field is of a reference type and the field is marked as **readonly**, it is the reference that is immutable, not the object that the field refers to. The following code demonstrates:

```
public sealed class AType {
    // InvalidChars must always refer to the same array object
    public static readonly Char[] InvalidChars = new Char[] { 'A', 'B', 'C' };
}

public sealed class AnotherType {
    public static void M() {
        // The lines below are legal, compile, and successfully
        // change the characters in the InvalidChars array
        AType.InvalidChars[0] = 'X';
        AType.InvalidChars[1] = 'Y';
        AType.InvalidChars[2] = 'Z';

        // The line below is illegal and will not compile because
        // what InvalidChars refers to cannot be changed
        AType.InvalidChars = new Char[] { 'X', 'Y', 'Z' };
    }
}
```

Chapter 8
Methods: Constructors, Operators, Conversions, and Parameters

In this chapter, I'll talk about the different kinds of methods a type can define and the various issues related to methods. Specifically, I'll show you how to define constructor methods (both instance and type), operator overload methods, and conversion operator methods (for implicit and explicit casting). In addition, I'll cover various ways of passing parameters to a method including how to pass parameters by reference versus by value as well as how to define methods that accept a variable number of arguments.

Instance Constructors and Classes (Reference Types)

Constructors are special methods that allow an instance of a type to be initialized to a good state. Constructor methods are always called `.ctor` (for *constructor*) in a method definition metadata table. When creating an instance of a reference type, memory is allocated for the instance's data fields, the object's overhead fields (type object pointer and sync block index) are initialized, and then the type's instance constructor is called to set the initial state of the object.

When constructing a reference type object, the memory allocated for the object is always zeroed out before the type's instance constructor is called. Any fields that the constructor doesn't explicitly overwrite are guaranteed to have a value of **0** or **null**.

Unlike other methods, instance constructors are never inherited. That is, a class has only the instance constructors that the class itself defines. Since instance constructors are never inherited, you cannot apply the following modifiers to an instance constructor: **virtual**, **new**, **override**, **sealed**, or **abstract**. If you define a class that does not explicitly define any constructors, many compilers (including C#) define a default (parameterless) constructor for you whose implementation simply calls the base class's parameterless constructor.

For example, if you define the following class:

```
public class SomeType {
}
```

It is as though you wrote the code like this:

```
public class SomeType {
    public SomeType() : base() { }
}
```

If the class is **abstract**, the compiler-produced default constructor has **protected** accessibility; otherwise, the constructor is given **public** accessibility. If the base class doesn't offer a parameterless constructor, the derived class must explicitly call a base class constructor or the compiler will issue an error. If the class is **static** (**sealed** and **abstract**), the compiler will not emit a default constructor at all into the class definition.

A type can define several instance constructors. Each constructor must have a different signature, and each can have different accessibility. For verifiable code, a class's instance constructor must call its base class's constructor before accessing any of the inherited fields of the base class. Many compilers, including C#, generate the call to the base class's constructor automatically, so you typically don't have to worry or think about this at all. Ultimately, **System.Object**'s public, parameterless constructor gets called. This constructor does nothing—it simply returns. This is because **System.Object** defines no instance data fields, and therefore its constructor has nothing to do.

In a few situations, an instance of a type can be created without an instance constructor being called. In particular, calling **Object**'s **MemberwiseClone** method allocates memory, initializes the object's overhead fields, and then copies the source object's bytes to the new object. Also, a constructor is usually not called when deserializing an object.

> **Important**   You should not call any virtual methods within a constructor that can affect the object being constructed. The reason is if the virtual method is overridden in the type being instantiated, the derived type's implementation of the overridden method will execute, but all of the fields in the hierarchy have not been fully initialized. Calling a virtual method would therefore result in unpredictable behavior.

C# offers a simple syntax that allows the initialization of fields defined within a reference type when an instance of the type is constructed:

```
internal sealed class SomeType {
   private Int32 m_x = 5;
}
```

When a **SomeType** object is constructed, its **m_x** field will be initialized to **5**. How does this happen? Well, if you examine the intermediate language (IL) for **SomeType**'s constructor method (also called **.ctor**), you'll see the code shown in Figure 8-1.

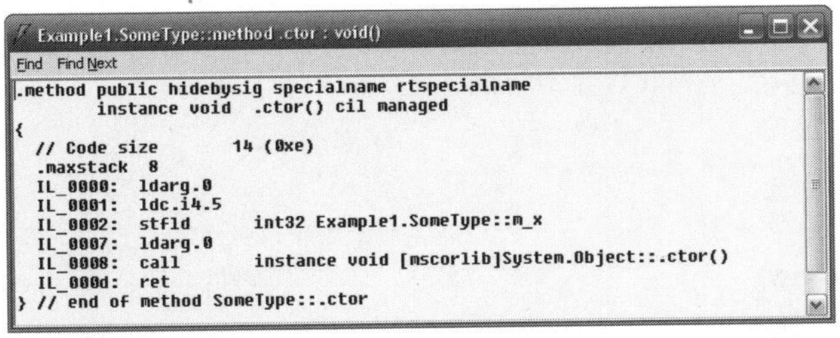

Figure 8-1   The IL code for **SomeType**'s constructor method

In Figure 8-1, you see that **SomeType**'s constructor contains code to store a **5** into **m_x** and then calls the base class's constructor. In other words, the C# compiler allows the convenient syntax that lets you initialize the instance fields inline and translates this to code in the constructor method to perform the initialization. This means that you should be aware of code explosion as illustrated by the following class definition:

```
internal sealed class SomeType {
   private Int32  m_x = 5;
   private String m_s = "Hi there";
   private Double m_d = 3.14159;
   private Byte   m_b;

   // Here are some constructors.
   public SomeType()          { ... }
   public SomeType(Int32 x)  { ... }
   public SomeType(String s) { ...; m_d = 10; }
}
```

When the compiler generates code for the three constructor methods, the beginning of each method includes the code to initialize **m_x**, **m_s**, and **m_d**. After this initialization code, the compiler appends to the method the code that appears in the constructor methods. For example, the code generated for the constructor that takes a **String** parameter includes the code to initialize **m_x**, **m_s**, and **m_d** and then overwrites **m_d** with the value **10**. Note that **m_b** is guaranteed to be initialized to **0** even though no code exists to explicitly initialize it.

Because there are three constructors in the preceding class, the compiler generates the code to initialize **m_x**, **m_s**, and **m_d** three times—once per constructor. If you have several initialized instance fields and a lot of overloaded constructor methods, you should consider defining the fields without the initialization, creating a single constructor that performs the common initialization, and having each constructor explicitly call the common initialization constructor. This approach will reduce the size of the generated code. Here is an example using C#'s ability to explicitly have a constructor call another constructor by using the **this** keyword:

```
internal sealed class SomeType {
   // Do not explicitly initialize the fields here
   private Int32  m_x;
   private String m_s;
   private Double m_d;
   private Byte   m_b;

   // This constructor sets all fields to their default.
   // All of the other constructors explicitly invoke this constructor.
   public SomeType() {
      m_x = 5;
      m_s = "Hi there";
      m_d = 3.14159;
      m_b = 0xff;
   }

   // This constructor sets all fields to their default, then changes m_x.
   public SomeType(Int32 x) : this() {
      m_x = x;
   }

   // This constructor sets all fields to their default, then changes m_s.
   public SomeType(String s) : this() {
      m_s = s;
   }

   // This constructor sets all fields to their default, then changes m_x & m_s.
   public SomeType(Int32 x, String s) : this() {
      m_x = x;
      m_s = s;
   }
}
```

Instance Constructors and Structures (Value Types)

Value type (**struct**) constructors work quite differently from reference type (**class**) constructors. The common language runtime (CLR) always allows the creation of value type instances, and there is no way to prevent a value type from being instantiated. For this reason, value types don't actually even need to have a constructor defined within them. For this reason, many compilers (including C#) don't emit default parameterless constructors for value types. Examine the following code:

```
internal struct Point {
   public Int32 m_x, m_y;
}
internal sealed class Rectangle {
   public Point m_topLeft, m_bottomRight;
}
```

To construct a `Rectangle`, the **new** operator must be used, and a constructor must be specified. In this case, the default constructor automatically generated by the C# compiler is called. When memory is allocated for the `Rectangle`, the memory includes the two instances of the `Point` value type. For performance reasons, the CLR doesn't attempt to call a constructor for each value type field contained within the reference type. But as I mentioned earlier, the fields of the value types are initialized to **0/null**.

The CLR does allow you to define constructors on value types. The only way that these constructors will execute is if you write code to explicitly call one of them, as in `Rectangle`'s constructor, shown here:

```
internal struct Point {
   public Int32 m_x, m_y;

   public Point(Int32 x, Int32 y) {
      m_x = x;
      m_y = y;
   }
}

internal sealed class Rectangle {
   public Point m_topLeft, m_bottomRight;

   public Rectangle() {
      // In C#, new on a value type calls the constructor to
      // initialize the value type's fields.
      m_topLeft     = new Point(1, 2);
      m_bottomRight = new Point(100, 200);
   }
}
```

A value type's instance constructor is executed only when explicitly called. So if `Rectangle`'s constructor didn't initialize its **m_topLeft** and **m_bottomRight** fields by using the **new** operator to call **Point**'s constructor, the **m_x** and **m_y** fields in both **Point** fields would be **0**.

In the **Point** value type defined earlier, no default parameterless constructor is defined. However, let's rewrite that code as follows:

```
internal struct Point {
   public Int32 m_x, m_y;

   public Point() {
      m_x = m_y = 5;
   }
}

internal sealed class Rectangle {
   public Point m_topLeft, m_bottomRight;

   public Rectangle() {
   }
}
```

Now when a new **Rectangle** is constructed, what do you think the **m_x** and **m_y** fields in the two **Point** fields, **m_topLeft** and **m_bottomRight**, would be initialized to: **0** or **5**? (Hint: This is a trick question.)

Many developers (especially those with a C++ background) would expect the C# compiler to emit code in **Rectangle**'s constructor that automatically calls **Point**'s default parameterless constructor for the **Rectangle**'s two fields. However, to improve the run-time performance of the application, the C# compiler doesn't automatically emit this code. In fact, many compilers will never emit code to call a value type's default constructor automatically, even if the value type offers a parameterless constructor. To have a value type's parameterless constructor execute, the developer must add explicit code to call a value type's constructor.

Based on the information in the preceding paragraph, you should expect the **m_x** and **m_y** fields in **Rectangle**'s two **Point** fields to be initialized to **0** in the code shown earlier because there are no explicit calls to **Point**'s constructor anywhere in the code.

However, I did say that my original question was a trick question. The trick part is that C# doesn't allow a value type to define a parameterless constructor. So the previous code won't actually compile. The C# compiler produces the following message when attempting to compile that code: "error CS0568: Structs cannot contain explicit parameterless constructors".

C# purposely disallows value types from defining parameterless constructors to remove any confusion a developer might have about when that constructor gets called. If the constructor can't be defined, the compiler can never generate code to call it automatically. Without a parameterless constructor, a value type's fields are always initialized to **0/null**.

> **Note**   Strictly speaking, value type fields are guaranteed to be 0/null when the value type is a field nested within a reference type. However, stack-based value type fields are not guaranteed to be 0/null. For verifiability, any stack-based value type field must be written to prior to being read. If code could read a value type's field prior to writing to the field, a security breach is possible. C# and other compilers that produce verifiable code ensure that all stack-based value types have their fields zeroed out or at least written to before being read so that a verification exception won't be thrown at run time. For the most part, this means that you can assume that your value types have their fields initialized to 0, and you can completely ignore everything in this note.

Keep in mind that although C# doesn't allow value types with parameterless constructors, the CLR does. So if the unobvious behavior described earlier doesn't bother you, you can use another programming language (such as IL assembly language) to define your value type with a parameterless constructor.

Because C# doesn't allow value types with parameterless constructors, compiling the following type produces the message: "error CS0573: 'SomeValType.m_x': cannot have instance field initializers in structs".

```
internal struct SomeValType {
   // You cannot do inline instance field initialization in a value type
   private Int32 m_x = 5;
}
```

In addition, because verifiable code requires that every field of a value type be written to prior to any field being read, any constructors that you do have for a value type must initialize all of the type's fields. The following type defines a constructor for the value type but fails to initialize all of the fields:

```
internal struct SomeValType {
   private Int32 m_x, m_y;

   // C# allows value types to have constructors that take parameters.
   public SomeValType(Int32 x) {
      m_x = x;
      // Notice that m_y is not initialized here.
   }
}
```

When compiling this type, the C# compiler produces the following: "error CS0171: Field 'SomeValType.m_y' must be fully assigned before control leaves the constructor". To fix the problem, assign a value (usually **0**) to **y** in the constructor.

Type Constructors

In addition to instance constructors, the CLR also supports type constructors (also known as *static constructors*, *class constructors*, or *type initializers*). A type constructor can be applied to interfaces (although C# doesn't allow this), reference types, and value types. Just as instance constructors are used to set the initial state of an instance of a type, type constructors are used to set the initial state of a type. By default, types don't have a type constructor defined within them. If a type has a type constructor, it can have no more than one. In addition, type constructors never have parameters. In C#, here's how to define a reference type and a value type that have type constructors:

```
internal sealed class SomeRefType {
   static SomeRefType() {
      // This executes the first time a SomeRefType is accessed.
   }
}
```

```
internal struct SomeValType {
   // C# does allow value types to define parameterless type constructors.
   static SomeValType() {
      // This executes the first time a SomeValType is accessed.
   }
}
```

You'll notice that you define type constructors just as you would parameterless instance constructors, except that you must mark them as **static**. Also, type constructors should always be private; C# makes them **private** for you automatically. In fact, if you explicitly mark a type constructor as **private** (or anything else) in your source code, the C# compiler issues the following error: "error CS0515: 'SomeValType.SomeValType()': access modifiers are not allowed on static constructors". Type constructors should be private to prevent any developer-written code from calling them; the CLR is always capable of calling a type constructor.

> **Important**   While you can define a type constructor within a value type, you should never actually do this because there are times when the CLR will not call a value type's static type constructor. Here is an example:
>
> ```
> internal struct SomeValType {
>    static SomeValType() {
>       Console.WriteLine("This never gets displayed");
>    }
>    public Int32 m_x;
> }
>
> public sealed class Program {
>    public static void Main() {
>       SomeValType[] a = new SomeValType[10];
>       a[0].m_x = 123;
>       Console.WriteLine(a[0].m_x);    // Displays 123
>    }
> }
> ```

The calling of a type constructor is a tricky thing. When the JIT compiler is compiling a method, it sees what types are referenced in the code. If any of the types define a type constructor, the JIT compiler checks if the type's type constructor has already been executed for this AppDomain. If the constructor has never executed, the JIT compiler emits a call to the type constructor into the native code that the JIT compiler is emitting. If the type constructor for the type has already executed, the JIT compiler does not emit the call since it knows that the type is already initialized. (For an example of this, see the "Type Constructor Performance" section later in this chapter.)

Now, after the method has been JIT compiled, the thread starts to execute it and will eventually get to the code that calls the type constructor. In fact, it is possible that multiple threads will be executing the same method concurrently. The CLR wants to ensure that a type's constructor executes only once per AppDomain. To guarantee this, when a type constructor is called, the calling thread acquires a mutually exclusive thread synchronization lock. So if multiple threads attempt to simultaneously call a type's static constructor, only one thread will acquire the lock and the other threads will block. The first thread will execute the code in the static constructor. After the first thread leaves the constructor, the waiting threads will wake up and will see that the constructor's code has already been executed. These threads will not execute the code again; they will simply return from the constructor method. In addition, if any of these methods ever get called again, the CLR knows that the type constructor has already executed and will ensure that the constructor is not called again.

> **Note**   Since the CLR guarantees that a type constructor executes only once per AppDomain and is thread-safe, a type constructor is a great place to initialize any singleton objects required by the type.

Within a single thread, there is a potential problem that can occur if two type constructors contain code that reference each other. For example, ClassA has a type constructor containing code that references ClassB, and ClassB has a type constructor containing code that references ClassA. In this situation, the CLR still guarantees that each type constructor's code executes only once; however, it cannot guarantee that ClassA's type constructor code has run to completion before executing ClassB's type constructor. You should certainly try to avoid writing code that sets up this scenario. In fact, since the CLR is responsible for calling type constructors, you should always avoid writing any code that requires type constructors to be called in a specific order.

Finally, if a type constructor throws an unhandled exception, the CLR considers the type to be unusable. Attempting to access any fields or methods of the type will cause a **System .TypeInitializationException** to be thrown.

The code in a type constructor has access only to a type's static fields, and its usual purpose is to initialize those fields. As it does with instance fields, C# offers a simple syntax that allows you to initialize a type's static fields:

```
internal sealed class SomeType {
    private static Int32 s_x = 5;
}
```

> **Note**   While C# doesn't allow a value type to use inline field initialization syntax for instance fields, it does allow you to use it for static fields. In other words, if you change the **SomeType** type above from a **class** to a **struct**, the code will compile and work as expected.

When this code is built, the compiler automatically generates a type constructor for **SomeType**. It's as if the source code had originally been written as follows:

```
internal sealed class SomeType {
    private static Int32 s_x;
    static SomeType() { s_x = 5; }
}
```

Using ILDasm.exe, it's easy to verify what the compiler actually produced by examining the IL for the type constructor, shown in Figure 8-2. Type constructor methods are always called **.cctor** (for *class constructor*) in a method definition metadata table.

In Figure 8-2, you see that the **.cctor** method is **private** and **static**. In addition, notice that the code in the method does in fact load a **5** into the static field **s_x**.

```
SomeType::.cctor : void()                                    _ □ ×
.method private hidebysig specialname rtspecialname static
        void   .cctor() cil managed
{
  // Code size        7 (0x7)
  .maxstack  1
  IL_0000:  ldc.i4.5
  IL_0001:  stsfld      int32 SomeType::x
  IL_0006:  ret
} // end of method SomeType::.cctor
```

Figure 8-2   The IL code for SomeType's type constructor method

Type constructors shouldn't call a base type's type constructor. Such a call isn't necessary because none of a type's static fields is shared or inherited from its base type.

> **Note**   Some languages, such as Java, expect that accessing a type causes its type constructor and all of its base type's type constructors to be called. In addition, interfaces implemented by the types must also have their type constructors called. The CLR doesn't offer this behavior. However, the CLR does offer compilers and developers the ability to provide this behavior via the RunClassConstructor method offered by the System.Runtime.CompilerServices .RuntimeHelpers type. Any language that requires this behavior would have its compiler emit code into a type's type constructor that calls this method for all base types. When using the RunClassConstructor method to call a type constructor, the CLR knows if the type constructor has executed previously and, if it has, the CLR won't call it again.

Finally, assume that you have this code:

```
internal sealed class SomeType {
   private static Int32 s_x = 5;

   static SomeType() {
      s_x = 10;
   }
}
```

In this case, the C# compiler generates a single type constructor method. This constructor first initializes s_x to 5 and then initializes s_x to 10. In other words, when the C# compiler generates IL code for the type constructor, it first emits the code required to initialize the static fields followed by the explicit code contained in your type constructor method.

> **Important**   Developers occasionally ask me if there's a way to get some code to execute when a type is unloaded. You should first know that types are unloaded only when the AppDomain shuts down. When the AppDomain shuts down, the object that identifies the type becomes unreachable, and the garbage collector reclaims the type object's memory. This behavior leads many developers to believe that they could add a static Finalize method to the type, which will automatically get called when the type is unloaded. Unfortunately, the CLR doesn't support static Finalize methods. All is not lost, however. If you want some code to execute when an AppDomain shuts down, you can register a callback method with the System.AppDomain type's DomainUnload event.

Type Constructor Performance

In the previous section, I mentioned that calling a type constructor is a tricky thing. And I explained some of the trickiness about it: the JIT compiler has to decide whether to emit the code to call it, and the CLR ensures that calls to it are thread-safe. As it turns out, this is the just the beginning of the tricky stuff. There is more about this that is performance related.

As discussed already, when compiling a method, the JIT compiler determines whether it must emit a call to execute a type constructor into the method. If the JIT compiler decides to emit the call, it must decide where it should emit the call. There are two possibilities here:

- The JIT compiler can emit the call immediately before code that would create the first instance of the type or immediately before code that accesses a noninherited field or member of the class. This is called *precise* semantics because the CLR will call the type constructor at precisely the right time.

- The JIT compiler can emit the call sometime before code that accesses a noninherited static field. This is called *before-field-init* semantics because the CLR guarantees only that the static constructor will run some time before the static field is accessed; it could run much earlier.

The before-field-init semantics is preferred since it gives the CLR a lot of freedom as to when it can call the type constructor, and the CLR takes advantage of this whenever possible to produce code that executes faster. For example, the CLR might pick different times to call the type constructor based on whether the type is loaded in an AppDomain or loaded domain-neutral or whether the code is being JIT compiled or NGen'd.

By default, language compilers choose which of these semantics makes the most sense for the type you're defining and informs the CLR of this choice by setting the **beforefieldinit** flag in the row of the type definition metadata table. In this section, I'll focus on what the C# compiler does and how this impacts performance. Let's start by examining the following code:

```
using System;
using System.Diagnostics;


///////////////////////////////////////////////////////////////////////


// Since this class doesn't explicitly define a type constructor,
// C# marks the type definition with BeforeFieldInit in the metadata.
internal sealed class BeforeFieldInit {
   public static Int32 s_x = 123;
}

// Since this class does explicitly define a type constructor,
// C# doesn't mark the type definition with BeforeFieldInit in the metadata.
internal sealed class Precise {
   public static Int32 s_x;
   static Precise() { s_x = 123; }
}
```

//

```csharp
public sealed class Program {
    public static void Main() {
        const Int32 iterations = 1000 * 1000 * 1000;
        PerfTest1(iterations);
        PerfTest2(iterations);
    }


    // When this method is JIT compiled, the type constructors for
    // the BeforeFieldInit and Precise classes HAVE NOT executed yet
    // and therefore, calls to these constructors are embedded in
    // this method's code, making it run slower
    private static void PerfTest1(Int32 iterations) {
        Stopwatch sw = Stopwatch.StartNew();
        for (Int32 x = 0; x < iterations; x++) {
            // The JIT compiler hoists the code to call BeforeFieldInit's
            // type constructor so that it executes before the loop starts
            BeforeFieldInit.s_x = 1;
        }
        Console.WriteLine("PerfTest1: {0} BeforeFieldInit", sw.Elapsed);

        sw = Stopwatch.StartNew();
        for (Int32 x = 0; x < iterations; x++) {
            // The JIT compiler emits the code to call Precise's
            // type constructor here so that it checks whether it
            // has to call the constructor with each loop iteration
            Precise.s_x = 1;
        }
        Console.WriteLine("PerfTest1: {0} Precise", sw.Elapsed);
    }

    // When this method is JIT compiled, the type constructors for
    // the BeforeFieldInit and Precise classes HAVE executed
    // and therefore, calls to these constructors are NOT embedded
    // in this method's code, making it run faster
    private static void PerfTest2(Int32 iterations) {
        Stopwatch sw = Stopwatch.StartNew();
        for (Int32 x = 0; x < iterations; x++) {
            BeforeFieldInit.s_x = 1;
        }
        Console.WriteLine("PerfTest2: {0} BeforeFieldInit", sw.Elapsed);

        sw = Stopwatch.StartNew();
        for (Int32 x = 0; x < iterations; x++) {
            Precise.s_x = 1;
        }
        Console.WriteLine("PerfTest2: {0} Precise", sw.Elapsed);
    }
}
```

///////////////////////////// End of File ////////////////////////////////////

When I build and run the code above, I get the following output:

```
PerfTest1: 00:00:02.1997770 BeforeFieldInit
PerfTest1: 00:00:07.6188948 Precise
PerfTest2: 00:00:02.0843565 BeforeFieldInit
PerfTest2: 00:00:02.0843732 Precise
```

When the C# compiler sees a class with static fields that use inline initialization (the **BeforeFieldInit** class), the compiler emits the class's type definition table entry with the **BeforeFieldInit** metadata flag. When the C# compiler sees a class with an explicit type constructor (the **Precise** class), the compiler emits the class's type definition table entry without the **BeforeFieldInit** metadata flag. The rationale behind this is as follows: initialization of static fields needs to be done before the fields are accessed, whereas an explicit type constructor can contain arbitrary code that can have observable side effects; this code may need to run at a precise time.

As you can see from the output, this decision comes with a huge performance impact. When **PerfTest1** runs, the top loop executes in about 2.20 seconds versus the bottom loop, which took about 7.62 seconds to run—the bottom loop took about 3 times longer to execute. When **PerfTest2** runs, the times are much closer in value because the JIT compiler knew that the types' constructors were already called, and therefore the native code doesn't contain any calls to the type constructor methods.

It would be nice if C# gave programmers the ability to set the **BeforeFieldInit** flag explicitly in their source code instead of the compiler making this decision based on whether a type constructor is created implicitly or explicitly. This way, developers would have more direct control over the performance and semantics of their code.

Operator Overload Methods

Some programming languages allow a type to define how operators should manipulate instances of the type. For example, a lot of types (such as **System.String**) overload the equality (==) and inequality (!=) operators. The CLR doesn't know anything about operator overloading because it doesn't even know what an operator is. Your programming language defines what each operator symbol means and what code should be generated when these special symbols appear.

For example, in C#, applying the + symbol to primitive numbers causes the compiler to generate code that adds the two numbers together. When the + symbol is applied to **String** objects, the C# compiler generates code that concatenates the two strings together. For inequality, C# uses the != symbol, while Microsoft Visual Basic uses the <> symbol. Finally, the ∧ symbol means exclusive OR (XOR) in C#, but it means exponent in Visual Basic.

Although the CLR doesn't know anything about operators, it does specify how languages should expose operator overloads so that they can be readily consumed by code written in a different programming language. Each programming language gets to decide for itself whether it will support operator overloads, and if it does, the syntax for expressing and using them. As far as the CLR is concerned, operator overloads are simply methods.

Your choice of programming language determines whether or not you get the support of operator overloading and what the syntax looks like. When you compile your source code, the compiler produces a method that identifies the behavior of the operator. The CLR specification mandates that operator overload methods be **public** and **static** methods. In addition, C# (and many other languages) requires that at least one of the operator method's parameters or return type must be the same as the type that the operator method is defined within. The reason for this restriction is that it enables the C# compiler to search for a possible operator method to bind to in a reasonable amount of time.

Here is an example of an operator overload method defined in a C# class definition:

```
public sealed class Complex {
    public static Complex operator+(Complex c1, Complex c2) { ... }
}
```

The compiler emits a method definition for a method called **op_Addition**; the method definition entry also has the **specialname** flag set, indicating that this is a "special" method. When language compilers (including the C# compiler) see a + operator specified in source code, they look to see if one of the operand's types defines a **specialname** method called **op_Addition** whose parameters are compatible with the operand's types. If this method exists, the compiler emits code to call this method. If no such method exists, a compilation error occurs.

Tables 8-1 and 8-2 show the set of unary and binary operators that C# supports being overloaded, their symbols, and the corresponding method name that the compiler emits. I'll explain the tables' third columns in the next section.

Table 8-1   C# Unary Operators and Their CLS-Compliant Method Names

C# Operator Symbol	Special Method Name	Suggested CLS-Compliant Method Name
+	op_UnaryPlus	Plus
−	op_UnaryNegation	Negate
!	op_LogicalNot	Not
~	op_OnesComplement	OnesComplement
++	op_Increment	Increment
−−	op_Decrement	Decrement
(none)	op_True	IsTrue { get; }
(none)	op_False	IsFalse { get; }

Table 8-2 C# Binary Operators and Their CLS-Compliant Method Names

C# Operator Symbol	Special Method Name	Suggested CLS-Compliant Method Name
+	op_Addition	Add
–	op_Subtraction	Subtract
*	op_Multiply	Multiply
/	op_Division	Divide
%	op_Modulus	Mod
&	op_BitwiseAnd	BitwiseAnd
|	op_BitwiseOr	BitwiseOr
^	op_ExclusiveOr	Xor
<<	op_LeftShift	LeftShift
>>	op_RightShift	RightShift
==	op_Equality	Equals
!=	op_Inequality	Compare
<	op_LessThan	Compare
>	op_GreaterThan	Compare
<=	op_LessThanOrEqual	Compare
>=	op_GreaterThanOrEqual	Compare

The CLR specification defines many additional operators that can be overloaded, but C# does not support these additional operators. Therefore, they are not in mainstream use, so I will not list them here. If you are interested in the complete list, please see the ECMA specifications (www.ecma-international.org/publications/standards/Ecma-335.htm) for the Common Language Infrastructure (CLI), Partition I, Concepts and Architecture, Sections 10.3.1 (unary operators) and 10.3.2 (binary operators).

> **Note** If you examine the FCL's core numeric types (**Int32**, **Int64**, **UInt32**, and so on), you'll see that they don't define any operator overload methods. The reason they don't is that compilers look for operations on these primitive types and emit IL instructions that directly manipulate instances of these types. If the types were to offer methods and if compilers were to emit code to call these methods, a run-time performance cost would be associated with the method call. Plus, the method would ultimately have to execute some IL instructions to perform the expected operation anyway. This is the reason why the core FCL types don't define any operator overload methods. Here's what this means to you: if the programming language you're using doesn't support one of the core FCL types, you won't be able to perform any operations on instances of that type.

Operators and Programming Language Interoperability

Operator overloading can be a very useful tool, allowing developers to express their thoughts with succinct code. However, not all programming languages support operator overloading. When using a language that doesn't support operator overloading, the language will not know how to interpret the + operator (unless the type is a primitive in that language), and the compiler will emit an error. When using languages that do not support operator overloading, the language should allow you to call the desired **op_*** method directly (such as **op_Addition**).

If you are using a language that doesn't support + operator overloading to be defined in a type, obviously, this type could still offer an **op_Addition** method. From C#, you might expect that you could call this **op_Addition** method by using the + operator, but you cannot. When the C# compiler detects the + operator, it looks for an **op_Addition** method that has the **specialname** metadata flag associated with it so that the compiler knows for sure that the **op_Addition** method is intended to be an operator overload method. Because the **op_Addition** method is produced by a language that doesn't support operator overloads, the method won't have the **specialname** flag associated with it, and the C# compiler will produce a compilation error. Of course, code in any language can explicitly call a method that just happens to be named **op_Addition**, but the compilers won't translate a usage of the + symbol to call this method.

Jeff's Opinion About Microsoft's Operator Method Name Rules

I'm sure that all of these rules about when you can and can't call an operator overload method seem very confusing and overly complicated. If compilers that supported operator overloading just didn't emit the **specialname** metadata flag, the rules would be a lot simpler, and programmers would have an easier time working with types that offer operator overload methods. Languages that support operator overloading would support the operator symbol syntax, and all languages would support calling the various **op_** methods explicitly. I can't come up with any reason why Microsoft made this so difficult, and I hope that they'll loosen these rules in future versions of their compilers.

For a type that defines operator overload methods, Microsoft recommends that the type also define friendlier public static methods that call the operator overload methods internally. For example, a public-friendly named method called **Add** should be defined by a type that overloads the **op_Addition** method. The third column in Tables 8-1 and 8-2 lists the recommended friendly name for each operator. So the **Complex** type shown earlier should be defined this way:

```
public sealed class Complex {
    public static Complex operator+(Complex c1, Complex c2) { ... }
    public static Complex Add(Complex c1, Complex c2) { return(c1 + c2); }
}
```

Certainly, code written in any programming language can call any of the friendly operator methods, such as **Add**. Microsoft's guideline that types offer these friendly method names complicates the story even more. I feel that this additional complication is unnecessary, and that calling these friendly named methods would cause an additional performance hit unless the JIT compiler is able to inline the code in the friendly named method. Inlining the code would cause the JIT compiler to optimize the code, removing the additional method call and boosting run-time performance.

> **Note** For an example of a type that overloads operators and uses the friendly method names as per Microsoft's design guidelines, see the `System.Decimal` class in the Framework Class Library.

Conversion Operator Methods

Occasionally, you need to convert an object from one type to an object of a different type. For example, I'm sure you've had to convert a `Byte` to an `Int32` at some point in your life. When the source type and the target type are a compiler's primitive types, the compiler knows how to emit the necessary code to convert the object.

If the source type or target type is not a primitive, the compiler emits code that has the CLR perform the conversion (cast). In this case, the CLR just checks if the source object's type is the same type as the target type (or derived from the target type). However, it is sometimes natural to want to convert an object of one type to a completely different type. For example, imagine that the FCL included a `Rational` data type. It might be convenient to convert an `Int32` object or a `Single` object to a `Rational` object. Moreover, it also might be nice to convert a `Rational` object to an `Int32` or a `Single` object.

To make these conversions, the `Rational` type should define public constructors that take a single parameter: an instance of the type that you're converting from. You should also define public instance `ToXxx` methods that take no parameters (just like the very popular `ToString` method). Each method will convert an instance of the defining type to the `Xxx` type. Here's how to correctly define conversion constructors and methods for a `Rational` type:

```
public sealed class Rational {
    // Constructs a Rational from an Int32
    public Rational(Int32 num) { ... }

    // Constructs a Rational from a Single
    public Rational(Single num) { ... }

    // Convert a Rational to an Int32
    public Int32 ToInt32() { ... }

    // Convert a Rational to a Single
    public Single ToSingle() { ... }
}
```

By invoking these constructors and methods, a developer using any programming language can convert an `Int32` or a `Single` object to a `Rational` object and convert a `Rational` object to an `Int32` or a `Single` object. The ability to do these conversions can be quite handy, and when designing a type, you should seriously consider what conversion constructors and methods make sense for your type.

In the previous section, I discussed how some programming languages offer operator overloading. Well, some programming languages (such as C#) also offer conversion operator overloading. *Conversion operators* are methods that convert an object from one type to another type. You define a conversion operator method by using special syntax. The CLR specification mandates that conversion overload methods be **public** and **static** methods. In addition, C# (and many other languages) requires that either the parameter or the return type must be the same as the type that the conversion method is defined within. The reason for this restriction is that it enables the C# compiler to search for a possible operator method to bind to in a reasonable amount of time. The following code adds four conversion operator methods to the **Rational** type:

```
public sealed class Rational {
    // Constructs a Rational from an Int32
    public Rational(Int32 num) { ... }

    // Constructs a Rational from a Single
    public Rational(Single num) { ... }

    // Convert a Rational to an Int32
    public Int32 ToInt32() { ... }

    // Convert a Rational to a Single
    public Single ToSingle() { ... }

    // Implicitly constructs and returns a Rational from an Int32
    public static implicit operator Rational(Int32 num) {
        return new Rational(num);
    }

    // Implicitly constructs and returns a Rational from a Single
    public static implicit operator Rational(Single num) {
        return new Rational(num);
    }

    // Explicitly returns an Int32 from a Rational
    public static explicit operator Int32(Rational r) {
        return r.ToInt32();
    }

    // Explicitly returns a Single from a Rational
    public static explicit operator Single(Rational r) {
        return r.ToSingle();
    }
}
```

For conversion operator methods, you must indicate whether a compiler can emit code to call a conversion operator method implicitly or whether the source code must explicitly indicate when the compiler is to emit code to call a conversion operator method. In C#, you use the **implicit** keyword to indicate to the compiler that an explicit cast doesn't have to appear in the source code in order to emit code that calls the method. The **explicit** keyword allows the compiler to call the method only when an explicit cast exists in the source code.

After the **implicit** or **explicit** keyword, you tell the compiler that the method is a conversion operator by specifying the **operator** keyword. After the **operator** keyword, you specify the type that an object is being cast to; in the parentheses, you specify the type that an object is being cast from.

Defining the conversion operators in the preceding `Rational` type allows you to write code like this (in C#):

```
public sealed class Program {
   public static void Main() {
      Rational r1 = 5;          // Implicit cast from Int32  to Rational
      Rational r2 = 2.5F;       // Implicit cast from Single to Rational

      Int32  x = (Int32)  r1;  // Explicit cast from Rational to Int32
      Single s = (Single) r2;  // Explicit cast from Rational to Single
   }
}
```

Under the covers, the C# compiler detects the casts (type conversions) in the code and internally generates IL code that calls the conversion operator methods defined by the `Rational` type. But what are the names of these methods? Well, compiling the `Rational` type and examining its metadata shows that the compiler produces one method for each conversion operator defined. For the `Rational` type, the metadata for the four conversion operator methods looks like this:

```
public static Rational op_Implicit(Int32 num)
public static Rational op_Implicit(Single num)
public static Int32    op_Explicit(Rational r)
public static Single   op_Explicit(Rational r)
```

As you can see, methods that convert an object from one type to another are always named `op_Implicit` or `op_Explicit`. You should define an implicit conversion operator only when precision or magnitude isn't lost during a conversion, such as when converting an `Int32` to a `Rational`. However, you should define an explicit conversion operator if precision or magnitude is lost during the conversion, as when converting a `Rational` object to an `Int32`. If an explicit conversion fails, you should indicate this by having your explicit conversion operator method throw an `OverflowException` or an `InvalidOperationException`.

> **Note**   The two `op_Explicit` methods take the same parameter, a `Rational`. However, the methods differ by their return value, an `Int32` and a `Single`. This is an example of two methods that differ only by their return type. The CLR fully supports the ability for a type to define multiple methods that differ only by return type. However, very few languages expose this ability. As you're probably aware, C++, C#, Visual Basic, and Java are all examples of languages that don't support the definition of multiple methods that differ only by their return type. A few languages (such as IL assembly language) allow the developer to explicitly select which of these methods to call. Of course, IL assembly language programmers shouldn't take advantage of this ability because the methods they define can't be callable from other programming languages. Even though C# doesn't expose this ability to the C# programmer, the compiler does take advantage of this ability internally when a type defines conversion operator methods.

C# has full support for conversion operators. When it detects code where you're using an object of one type and an object of a different type is expected, the compiler searches for an implicit conversion operator method capable of performing the conversion and generates code to call that method. If an implicit conversion operator method exists, the compiler emits a call to it in the resulting IL code. If the compiler sees source code that is explicitly casting an object from one type to another type, the compiler searches for an implicit or explicit conversion operator method. If one exists, the compiler emits the call to the method. If the compiler can't find an appropriate conversion operator method, it issues an error and doesn't compile the code.

To really understand operator overload methods and conversion operator methods, I strongly encourage you to examine the **System.Decimal** type as a role model. **Decimal** defines several constructors that allow you to convert objects from various types to a **Decimal**. It also offers several **To***Xxx* methods that let you convert a **Decimal** object to another type. Finally, the type defines several conversion operators and operator overload methods as well.

Passing Parameters by Reference to a Method

By default, the CLR assumes that all method parameters are passed by value. When reference type objects are passed, the reference (or pointer) to the object is passed (by value) to the method. This means that the method can modify the object and the caller will see the change. For value type instances, a copy of the instance is passed to the method. This means that the method gets its own private copy of the value type and the instance in the caller isn't affected.

> **Important**   In a method, you must know whether each parameter passed is a reference type or a value type because the code you write to manipulate the parameter could be markedly different.

The CLR allows you to pass parameters by reference instead of by value. In C#, you do this by using the **out** and **ref** keywords. Both keywords tell the C# compiler to emit metadata indicating that this designated parameter is passed by reference, and the compiler uses this to generate code to pass the address of the parameter rather than the parameter itself.

From the CLR's perspective, **out** and **ref** are identical—that is, the same metadata and IL are produced regardless of which keyword you use. However, the C# compiler treats the two keywords differently, and the difference has to do with which method is responsible for initializing the object being referred to. If a method's parameter is marked with **out**, the caller isn't expected to have initialized the object prior to calling the method. The called method can't read from the value, and the called method must write to the value before returning. If a method's parameter is marked with **ref**, the caller must initialize the parameter's value prior to calling the method. The called method can read from the value and/or write to the value.

Reference and value types behave very differently with **out** and **ref**. Let's look at using **out** and **ref** with value types first:

```
public sealed class Program {
   public static void Main() {
      Int32 x;                // x is uninitialized
      GetVal(out x);          // x doesn't have to be initialized.
      Console.WriteLine(x);   // Displays "10"
   }

   private static void GetVal(out Int32 v) {
      v = 10;  // This method must initialize v.
   }
}
```

In this code, x is declared in **Main**'s stack frame. The address of x is then passed to **GetVal**. **GetVal**'s v is a pointer to the **Int32** value in **Main**'s stack frame. Inside **GetVal**, the **Int32** that v points to is changed to **10**. When **GetVal** returns, **Main**'s x has a value of **10**, and *10* is displayed on the console. Using **out** with large value types is efficient because it prevents instances of the value type's fields from being copied when making method calls.

Now let's look at an example that uses **ref** instead of **out**:

```
public sealed class Program {
   public static void Main() {
      Int32 x = 5;            // x is initialized
      AddVal(ref x);          // x must be initialized.
      Console.WriteLine(x);   // Displays "15"
   }

   private static void AddVal(ref Int32 v) {
      v += 10;  // This method can use the initialized value in v.
   }
}
```

In this code, x is also declared in **Main**'s stack frame and is initialized to **5**. The address of x is then passed to **AddVal**. **AddVal**'s v is a pointer to the **Int32** value in **Main**'s stack frame. Inside **AddVal**, the **Int32** that v points to is required to have a value already. So, **AddVal** can use the initial value in any expression it desires. **AddVal** can also change the value, and the new value will be "returned" back to the caller. In this example, **AddVal** adds **10** to the initial value. When **AddVal** returns, **Main**'s x will contain *15*, which is what gets displayed in the console.

To summarize, from an IL or a CLR perspective, **out** and **ref** do exactly the same thing: they both cause a pointer to the instance to be passed. The difference is that the compiler helps ensure that your code is correct. The following code that attempts to pass an uninitialized value to a method expecting a **ref** parameter produces the following message: "error CS0165: Use of unassigned local variable 'x'".

```
public sealed class Program {
   public static void Main() {
      Int32 x;                // x is not initialized.
```

```
        // The following line fails to compile, producing
        // error CS0165: Use of unassigned local variable 'x'.
        AddVal(ref x);

        Console.WriteLine(x);
    }

    private static void AddVal(ref Int32 v) {
        v += 10;  // This method can use the initialized value in v.
    }
}
```

Important   I'm frequently asked why C# requires that a call to a method must specify **out** or **ref**. After all, the compiler knows whether the method being called requires **out** or **ref** and should be able to compile the code correctly. It turns out that the compiler can indeed do the right thing automatically. However, the designers of the C# language felt that the caller should explicitly state its intention. This way at the call site, it's obvious that the method being called is expected to change the value of the variable being passed.

In addition, the CLR allows you to overload methods based on their use of **out** and **ref** parameters. For example, in C#, the following code is legal and compiles just fine:

```
public sealed class Point {
    static void Add(Point p) { ... }
    static void Add(ref Point p) { ... }
}
```

It's not legal to overload methods that differ only by **out** and **ref** because the metadata representation of the method's signature for the methods would be identical. So I couldn't also define the following method in the preceding **Point** type:

```
    static void Add(out Point p) { ... }
```

If you attempt to include the last **Add** method in the **Point** type, the C# compiler issues error CS0663: 'Add' cannot define overloaded methods that differ only on ref and out.

Using **out** and **ref** with value types gives you the same behavior that you already get when passing reference types by value. With value types, **out** and **ref** allow a method to manipulate a single value type instance. The caller must allocate the memory for the instance, and the callee manipulates that memory. With reference types, the caller allocates memory for a pointer to a reference object, and the callee manipulates this pointer. Because of this behavior, using **out** and **ref** with reference types is useful only when the method is going to "return" a reference to an object that it knows about. The following code demonstrates:

```
using System;
using System.IO;

public sealed class Program {
    public static void Main() {
        FileStream fs;   // fs is uninitialized
```

```
      // Open the first file to be processed.
      StartProcessingFiles(out fs);

      // Continue while there are more files to process.
      for (; fs != null; ContinueProcessingFiles(ref fs)) {

         // Process a file.
         fs.Read(...);
      }
   }

   private static void StartProcessingFiles(out FileStream fs) {
      fs = new FileStream(...);    // fs must be initialized in this method
   }

   private static void ContinueProcessingFiles(ref FileStream fs) {
      fs.Close();  // Close the last file worked on.

      // Open the next file, or if no more files, "return" null.
      if (noMoreFilesToProcess) fs = null;
      else fs = new FileStream (...);
   }
}
```

As you can see, the big difference with this code is that the methods that have **out** or **ref** reference type parameters are constructing an object, and the pointer to the new object is returned to the caller. You'll also notice that the **ContinueProcessingFiles** method can manipulate the object being passed into it before returning a new object. This is possible because the parameter is marked with the **ref** keyword. You can simplify the preceding code a bit, as shown here:

```
using System;
using System.IO;

public sealed class Program {
   public static void Main() {
      FileStream fs = null;    // Initialized to null (required)

      // Open the first file to be processed.
      ProcessFiles(ref fs);

      // Continue while there are more files to process.
      for (; fs != null; ProcessFiles(ref fs)) {

         // Process a file.
         fs.Read(...);
      }
   }

   private static void ProcessFiles(ref FileStream fs) {
      // Close the previous file if one was open.
      if (fs != null) fs.Close();  // Close the last file worked on.
```

```
        // Open the next file, or if no more files, "return" null.
        if (noMoreFilesToProcess) fs = null;
        else fs = new FileStream (...);
    }
}
```

Here's another example that demonstrates how to use the **ref** keyword to implement a method that swaps two reference types:

```
public static void Swap(ref Object a, ref Object b) {
    Object t = b;
    b = a;
    a = t;
}
```

To swap references to two **string** objects, you'd probably think that you could write code like this:

```
public static void SomeMethod() {
    String s1 = "Jeffrey";
    String s2 = "Richter";

    Swap(ref s1, ref s2);
    Console.WriteLine(s1);   // Displays "Richter"
    Console.WriteLine(s2);   // Displays "Jeffrey"
}
```

However, this code won't compile. The problem is that variables passed by reference to a method must be of the same type as declared in the method signature. In other words, **Swap** expects two **Object** references, not two **String** references. To swap the two **String** references, you must do this:

```
public static void SomeMethod() {
    String s1 = "Jeffrey";
    String s2 = "Richter";

    // Variables that are passed by reference
    // must match what the method expects.
    Object o1 = s1, o2 = s2;
    Swap(ref o1, ref o2);

    // Now cast the objects back to strings.
    s1 = (String) o1;
    s2 = (String) o2;

    Console.WriteLine(s1);   // Displays "Richter"
    Console.WriteLine(s2);   // Displays "Jeffrey"
}
```

This version of **SomeMethod** does compile and execute as expected. The reason why the parameters passed must match the parameters expected by the method is to ensure that type safety is preserved. The following code, which thankfully won't compile, shows how type safety could be compromised.

```
internal sealed class SomeType {
    public Int32 m_val;
}

public sealed class Program {
    public static void Main() {
        SomeType st;

        // The following line generates error CS1503: Argument '1':
        // cannot convert from 'ref SomeType' to 'ref object'.
        GetAnObject(out st);

        Console.WriteLine(st.m_val);
    }

    private static void GetAnObject(out Object o) {
        o = new String('X', 100);
    }
}
```

In this code, **Main** clearly expects **GetAnObject** to return a **SomeType** object. However, because **GetAnObject**'s signature indicates a reference to an **Object**, **GetAnObject** is free to initialize **o** to an object of any type. In this example, when **GetAnObject** returned to **Main**, **st** would refer to a **String**, which is clearly not a **SomeType** object, and the call to **Console.WriteLine** would certainly fail. Fortunately, the C# compiler won't compile the preceding code because **st** is a reference to **SomeType**, but **GetAnObject** requires a reference to an **Object**.

You can use generics to fix these methods so that they work as you'd expect. Here is how to fix the **Swap** method shown earlier:

```
public static void Swap<T>(ref T a, ref T b) {
    T t = b;
    b = a;
    a = t;
}
```

And now, with **Swap** rewritten as above, the following code (identical to that shown before), will compile and run perfectly:

```
public static void SomeMethod() {
    String s1 = "Jeffrey";
    String s2 = "Richter";

    Swap(ref s1, ref s2);
    Console.WriteLine(s1);  // Displays "Richter"
    Console.WriteLine(s2);  // Displays "Jeffrey"
}
```

For some other examples that use generics to solve this problem, see **System.Threading**'s **Interlocked** class with its **CompareExchange** and **Exchange** generics methods.

Passing a Variable Number of Arguments to a Method

It's sometimes convenient for the developer to define a method that can accept a variable number of arguments. For example, the **System.String** type offers methods allowing an arbitrary number of strings to be concatenated together and methods allowing the caller to specify a set of strings that are to be formatted together.

To declare a method that accepts a variable number of arguments, you declare the method as follows:

```
static Int32 Add(params Int32[] values) {
   // NOTE: it is possible to pass the 'values'
   // array to other methods if you want to.

   Int32 sum = 0;
   for (Int32 x = 0; x < values.Length; x++)
      sum += values[x];
   return sum;
}
```

Everything in this method should look very familiar to you except for the **params** keyword that is applied to the last parameter of the method signature. Ignoring the **params** keyword for the moment, it's obvious that this method accepts an array of **Int32** values and iterates over the array, adding up all of the values. The resulting **sum** is returned to the caller.

Obviously, code can call this method as follows:

```
public static void Main() {
   // Displays "15"
   Console.WriteLine(Add(new Int32[] { 1, 2, 3, 4, 5 } ));
}
```

It's clear that the array can easily be initialized with an arbitrary number of elements and then passed off to **Add** for processing. Although the preceding code would compile and work correctly, it is a little ugly. As developers, we would certainly prefer to have written the call to **Add** as follows:

```
public static void Main() {
   // Displays "15"
   Console.WriteLine(Add(1, 2, 3, 4, 5));
}
```

You'll be happy to know that we can do this because of the **params** keyword. The **params** keyword tells the compiler to apply an instance of the **System.ParamArrayAttribute** custom attribute to the parameter.

When the C# compiler detects a call to a method, the compiler checks all of the methods with the specified name, where no parameter has the **ParamArray** attribute applied. If a method exists that can accept the call, the compiler generates the code necessary to call the method. However, if the compiler can't find a match, it looks for methods that have a `ParamArray` attribute to see whether the call can be satisfied. If the compiler finds a match, it emits code that constructs an array and populates its elements before emitting the code that calls the selected method.

In the previous example, no **Add** method is defined that takes five **Int32**-compatible arguments; however, the compiler sees that the source code has a call to **Add** that is being passed a list of **Int32** values and that there is an **Add** method whose array-of-**Int32** parameter is marked with the `ParamArray` attribute. So the compiler considers this a match and generates code that coerces the parameters into an **Int32** array and then calls the **Add** method. The end result is that you can write the code, easily passing a bunch of parameters to **Add**, but the compiler generates code as though you'd written the first version that explicitly constructs and initializes the array.

Only the last parameter to a method can be marked with the **params** keyword (`ParamArray-Attribute`). This parameter must also identify a single-dimension array of any type. It's legal to pass **null** or a reference to an array of **0** entries as the last parameter to the method. The following call to **Add** compiles fine, runs fine, and produces a resulting sum of **0** (as expected):

```
public static void Main() {
   // Displays "0"
   Console.WriteLine(Add());
}
```

So far, all of the examples have shown how to write a method that takes an arbitrary number of **Int32** parameters. How would you write a method that takes an arbitrary number of parameters where the parameters could be any type? The answer is very simple: just modify the method's prototype so that it takes an **Object[]** instead of an **Int32[]**. Here's a method that displays the **Type** of every object passed to it:

```
public sealed class Program {
   public static void Main() {
      DisplayTypes(new Object(), new Random(), "Jeff", 5);
   }

   private static void DisplayTypes(params Object[] objects) {
      foreach (Object o in objects)
         Console.WriteLine(o.GetType());
   }
}
```

Running this code yields the following output:

```
System.Object
System.Random
System.String
System.Int32
```

> **Important** Be aware that calling a method that takes a variable number of arguments incurs an additional performance hit. After all, an array object must be allocated on the heap, the array's elements must be initialized, and the array's memory must ultimately be garbage collected. To help reduce the performance hit associated with this, you may want to consider defining a few overloaded methods that do not use the **params** keyword. For some examples, look at the **System.String** class's **Concat** method, which have the following overloads:
>
> ```
> public sealed class String : Object, ... {
>    public static string Concat(object arg0);
>    public static string Concat(object arg0, object arg1);
>    public static string Concat(object arg0, object arg1, object arg2);
>    public static string Concat(params object[] args);
>
>    public static string Concat(string str0, string str1);
>    public static string Concat(string str0, string str1, string str2);
>    public static string Concat(string str0, string str1, string str2, string str3);
>    public static string Concat(params string[] values);
> }
> ```
>
> As you can see, the **Concat** method defines several overloads that do not use the **params** keyword. These versions of the **Concat** method are the most-frequently called overloads, and these overloads exist in order to improve performance for the most-common scenarios. The overloads that use the **params** keyword are there for the less-common scenarios; these scenarios will suffer the performance hit but fortunately, they are rare.

Declaring a Method's Parameter Types

When declaring a method's parameter types, you should specify the weakest type possible, preferring interfaces over base classes. For example, if you are writing a method that manipulates a collection of items, it would be best to declare the method's parameter by using an interface such as **IEnumerable<T>** rather than using a strong data type such as **List<T>** or even a stronger interface type such as **ICollection<T>** or **IList<T>**:

```
// Desired: This method uses a weak parameter type
public void ManipulateItems<T>(IEnumerable<T> collection) { ... }

// Undesired: This method uses a strong parameter type
public void ManipulateItems<T>(List<T> collection) { ... }
```

The reason, of course, is that someone can call the first method passing in an array object, a **List<T>** object, a **String** object, and so on—any object whose type implements **IEnumerable<T>**. The second method allows only **List<T>** objects to be passed in; it will not accept an array or a **String** object. Obviously, the first method is better because it is much more flexible and can be used in a much wider range of scenarios.

Naturally, if you are writing a method that requires a list (not just any enumerable object), then you should declare the parameter type as an **IList<T>**. You should still avoid declaring the parameter type as `List<T>`. Using `IList<T>` allows the caller to pass arrays and any other objects whose type implements `IList<T>`.

Note that my examples talked about collections, which are designed using an interface architecture. If we were talking about classes designed using a base class architecture, the concept still applies. So, for example, if I were implementing a method that processed bytes from a stream, we'd have this:

```
// Desired: This method uses a weak parameter type
public void ProcessBytes(Stream someStream) { ... }

// Undesired: This method uses a strong parameter type
public void ProcessBytes(FileStream fileStream) { ... }
```

The first method can process bytes from any kind of stream: a `FileStream`, a `NetworkStream`, a `MemoryStream`, and so on. The second method can operate only on a `FileStream`, making it far more limited.

On the flip side, it is usually best to declare a method's return type by using the strongest type possible (trying not to commit yourself to a specific type). For example, it is better to declare a method that returns a `FileStream` object as opposed to returning a `Stream` object:

```
// Desired: This method uses a strong return type
public FileStream OpenFile() { ... }

// Undesired: This method uses a weak return type
public Stream OpenFile() { ... }
```

Here, the first method is preferred because it allows the method's caller the option of treating the returned object as either a `FileStream` object or as a `Stream` object. Meanwhile, the second method requires that the caller treat the returned object as a `Stream` object. Basically, it is best to let the caller have as much flexibility as possible when calling a method, allowing the method to be used in the widest range of scenarios.

Sometimes you want to retain the ability to change the internal implementation of a method without affecting the callers. In the example just shown, the `OpenFile` method is unlikely to ever change its internal implementation to return anything other than a `FileStream` object (or an object whose type is derived from `FileStream`). However, if you have a method that returns a `List<String>` object, you might very well want to change the internal implementation of this method in the future so that it would instead return a `string[]`. In the cases in which you want to leave yourself some flexibility to change what your method returns, choose a weaker return type. For example,

```
// Flexible: This method uses a weaker return type
public IList<String> GetStringCollection() { ... }

// Inflexible: This method uses a stronger return type
public List<String> GetStringCollection() { ... }
```

In this example, even though the **GetStringCollection** method uses a **List<String>** object internally and returns it, it is better to prototype the method as returning an **IList<String>** instead. In the future, the **GetStringCollection** method could change its internal collection to use a **String[]**, and callers of the method won't be required to change any of their source code. In fact, they won't even have to recompile their code. Notice in this example that I'm using the strongest of the weakest types. For instance, I'm not using an **IEnumerable<String>** or even **ICollection<String>**.

Constant Methods and Parameters

In some languages, such as unmanaged C++, it is possible to declare methods or parameters as a constant that forbids the code in an instance method from changing any of the object's fields or prevents the code from modifying any of the objects passed into the method. The CLR does not provide for this, and many programmers have been lamenting this missing feature. Since the CLR doesn't offer this feature, no language (including C#) can offer this feature.

First, you should note that in unmanaged C++, marking an instance method or parameter as **const** ensured only that the programmer could not write normal code that would modify the object or parameter. Inside the method, it was always possible to write code that could mutate the object/parameter by either casting away the **const**-ness or by getting the address of the object/argument and then writing to the address. In a sense, unmanaged C++ lied to programmers, making them believe that their constant objects/arguments couldn't be written to even though they could.

When designing a type's implementation, the developer can just avoid writing code that manipulates the object/arguments. For example, strings are immutable because the **String** class doesn't offer any methods that can change a string object.

Also, it would be very difficult for Microsoft to endow the CLR with the ability to verify that a constant object/argument isn't being mutated. The CLR would have to verify at each write that the write was not occurring to a constant object, and this would hurt performance significantly. Of course, a detected violation would result in the CLR throwing some exception. Furthermore, constant support adds a lot of complexity for developers. For example, if a type is immutable, all derived types would have to respect this. In addition, an immutable type would probably have to consist of fields that are also of immutable types.

These are just some of the reasons why the CLR does not support constant objects/arguments.

Chapter 9
Properties

In this chapter, I'll talk about properties. Properties allow source code to call a method by using a simplified syntax. The common language runtime (CLR) offers two kinds of properties: parameterless properties, which are simply called *properties*, and parameterful properties, which are called different names by different programming languages. For example, C# calls parameterful properties *indexers*, and Microsoft Visual Basic calls them *default properties*.

Parameterless Properties

Many types define state information that can be retrieved or altered. Frequently, this state information is implemented as field members of the type. For example, here's a type definition that contains two fields:

```
public sealed class Employee {
    public String Name;  // The employee's name
    public Int32  Age;   // The employee's age
}
```

If you were to create an instance of this type, you could easily get or set any of this state information with code similar to the following:

```
Employee e = new Employee();
e.Name = "Jeffrey Richter"; // Set the employee's Name.
e.Age  = 41;                // Set the employee's Age.

Console.WriteLine(e.Name); // Displays "Jeffrey Richter"
```

Querying and setting an object's state information in the way I just demonstrated is very common. However, I would argue that the preceding code should never be implemented as shown. One of the hallmarks of object-oriented design and programming is *data encapsulation*. Data encapsulation means that your type's fields should never be publicly exposed because it's too easy to write code that improperly uses the fields, corrupting the object's state. For example, a developer could easily corrupt an **Employee** object with code like this:

```
e.Age = -5; // How could someone be -5 years old?
```

There are additional reasons for encapsulating access to a type's data field. For example, you might want access to a field to execute some side effect, cache some value, or lazily create some internal object. You might also want access to the field to be thread safe. Or perhaps the field is a logical field whose value isn't represented by bytes in memory but whose value is instead calculated using some algorithm.

For any of these reasons, when designing a type, I strongly suggest that all of your fields be **private**. Then, to allow a user of your type to get or set state information, you expose methods for that specific purpose. Methods that wrap access to a field are typically called *accessor methods*. These accessor methods can optionally perform sanity checking and ensure that the object's state is never corrupted. For example, I'd rewrite the previous class as follows:

```
public sealed class Employee {
   private String m_Name;    // Field is now private
   private Int32  m_Age;     // Field is now private

   public String GetName() {
      return(m_Name);
   }

   public void SetName(String value) {
      m_Name = value;
   }

   public Int32 GetAge() {
      return(m_Age);
   }

   public void SetAge(Int32 value) {
      if (value < 0)
         throw new ArgumentOutOfRangeException("value",
            value.ToString(),
            "The value must be greater than or equal to 0");
      m_Age = value;
   }
}
```

Although this is a simple example, you should still be able to see the enormous benefit you get from encapsulating the data fields. You should also be able to see how easy it is to make read-only or write-only properties: just don't implement one of the accessor methods.

Encapsulating the data as shown earlier has two disadvantages. First, you have to write more code because you now have to implement additional methods. Second, users of the type must now call methods rather than simply refer to a single field name.

```
e.SetName("Jeffrey Richter");      // updates the employee's name
String EmployeeName = e.GetName();// retrieves the employee's name
```

```
e.SetAge(41);                           // Updates the employee's age
e.SetAge(-5);                           // Throws ArgumentOutOfRangeException
Int32 EmployeeAge = e.GetAge();         // retrieves the employee's age
```

Personally, I think these disadvantages are quite minor. Nevertheless, programming languages and the CLR offer a mechanism called *properties* that alleviates the first disadvantage a little and removes the second disadvantage entirely.

The class shown here uses properties and is functionally identical to the class shown earlier:

```
public sealed class Employee {
   private String m_Name;
   private Int32  m_Age;

   public String Name {
      get { return(m_Name); }
      set { m_Name = value; } // The 'value' keyword always identifies the new value.
   }

   public Int32 Age {
      get { return(m_Age); }
      set {
         if (value < 0)     // The 'value' keyword always identifies the new value.
            throw new ArgumentOutOfRangeException("value",
               value.ToString(),
               "The value must be greater than or equal to 0");
         m_Age = value;
      }
   }
}
```

As you can see, properties complicate the definition of the type slightly, but the fact that they allow you to write your code as follows more than compensates for the extra work:

```
e.Name = "Jeffrey Richter";   // "sets" the employee name
String EmployeeName = e.Name; // "gets" the employee's name
e.Age = 41;                   // "sets" the employee's age
e.Age = -5;                   // Throws ArgumentOutOfRangeException
Int32 EmployeeAge = e.Age;    // "gets" the employee's age
```

You can think of properties as *smart fields*: fields with additional logic behind them. The CLR supports static, instance, abstract and virtual properties. In addition, properties can be marked with any accessibility modifier (discussed in Chapter 6, "Type and Member Basics") and defined within an interface (discussed in Chapter 14, "Interfaces").

Each property has a name and a type (which can't be **void**). It isn't possible to overload properties (that is, have two properties with the same name if their types are different). When you define a property, you typically specify both a **get** and a **set** method. However, you can leave out the **set** method to define a read-only property or leave out the **get** method to define a write-only property.

It's also quite common for the property's **get**/**set** methods to manipulate a private field defined within the type. This field is commonly referred to as the *backing field*. The **get** and **set** methods don't have to access a backing field, however. For example, the **System.Threading .Thread** type offers a **Priority** property that communicates directly with the operating system; the **Thread** object doesn't maintain a field for a thread's priority. Another example of properties without backing fields are those read-only properties calculated at run time—for example, the length of a zero-terminated array or the area of a rectangle when you have its height and width.

When you define a property, depending on its definition, the compiler will emit either two or three of the following items into the resulting managed assembly:

■ A method representing the property's **get** accessor method. This is emitted only if you define a **get** accessor method for the property.

■ A method representing the property's **set** accessor method. This is emitted only if you define a **set** accessor method for the property.

■ A property definition in the managed assembly's metadata. This is always emitted.

Refer back to the **Employee** type shown earlier. As the compiler compiles this type, it comes across the **Name** and **Age** properties. Because both properties have **get** and **set** accessor methods, the compiler emits four method definitions into the **Employee** type. It's as though the original source were written as follows:

```
public sealed class Employee {
    private String m_Name;
    private Int32  m_Age;

    public String get_Name(){
       return m_Name;
    }
    public void   set_Name(String value) {
       m_Name = value; // The argument 'value' always identifies the new value.
    }

    public Int32 get_Age() {
       return m_Age;
    }

    public void  set_Age(Int32 value) {
       if (value < 0) {     // The 'value' always identifies the new value.
          throw new ArgumentOutOfRangeException("value",
            value.ToString(),
            "The value must be greater than or equal to 0");
       }
       m_Age = value;
    }
}
```

The compiler automatically generates names for these methods by prepending **get_** or **set_** to the property name specified by the developer.

C# has built-in support for properties. When the C# compiler sees code that's trying to get or set a property, the compiler actually emits a call to one of these methods. If you're using a programming language that doesn't directly support properties, you can still access properties by calling the desired accessor method. The effect is exactly the same; it's just that the source code doesn't look as pretty.

In addition to emitting the accessor methods, compilers also emit a property definition entry into the managed assembly's metadata for each property defined in the source code. This entry contains some flags and the type of the property, and it refers to the **get** and **set** accessor methods. This information exists simply to draw an association between the abstract concept of a "property" and its accessor methods. Compilers and other tools can use this metadata, which can be obtained by using the **System.Reflection.PropertyInfo** class. The CLR doesn't use this metadata information and requires only the accessor methods at run time.

Defining Properties Intelligently

Personally, I don't like properties and I wish that they were not supported in the Microsoft .NET Framework and its programming languages. The reason is because properties look like fields but they are methods. This has been known to cause a phenomenal amount of confusion. When a programmer sees code that appears to be accessing a field, there are many assumptions that the programmer makes that may not be true for a property. For example,

- A property may be read-only or write-only; field access is always readable and writable. If you define a property, it is best to offer both **get** and **set** accessor methods.

- A property method may throw an exception; field access never throws an exception.

- A property cannot be passed as an **out** or **ref** parameter to a method; a field can. For example, the following code will not compile:

```
using System;

public sealed class SomeType {
   private static String Name {
      get { return null; }
      set {}
   }

   static void MethodWithOutParam(out String n) { n = null; }

   public static void Main() {
      // For the line of code below, the C# compiler emits the following:
      // error CS0206: A property or indexer may not
      // be passed as an out or ref parameter
      MethodWithOutParam(out Name);
   }
}
```

- A property method can take a long time to execute; field access always completes immediately. A common reason to use properties is to perform thread synchronization, which can stop the thread forever, and therefore, a property should not be used if thread synchronization is required. In that situation, a method is preferred. Also, if your class can be accessed remotely (for example, your class is derived from `System.MashalByRefObject`), calling the property method will be very slow, and therefore, a method is preferred to a property. In my opinion, classes derived from `MarshalByRefObject` should never use properties.

- If called multiple times in a row, a property method may return a different value each time; a field returns the same value each time. The `System.DateTime` class has a read-only `Now` property that returns the current date and time. Each time you query this property, it will return a different value. This is a mistake, and Microsoft wishes that they could fix the class by making `Now` a method instead of a property.

- A property method may cause observable side effects; field access never does. In other words, a user of a type should be able to set various properties defined by a type in any order he or she chooses without noticing any different behavior in the type.

- A property method may require additional memory or return a reference to something that is not actually part of the object's state, so modifying the returned object has no effect on the original object; querying a field always returns a reference to an object that is guaranteed to be part of the original object's state. Working with a property that returns a copy can be very confusing to developers, and this characteristic is frequently not documented.

It has come to my attention that people use properties far more often than they should. If you examine this list of differences between properties and fields, you'll see that there are very few circumstances in which defining a property is actually useful and will not cause confusion for developers. The only thing that properties buy you is some simplified syntax; there is no performance benefit, and understandability of the code is reduced. If I had been involved in the design of the .NET Framework and compilers, I would have not offered properties at all; instead, I would have programmers actually implement **Get***Xxx* and **Set***Xxx* methods as desired. Then, if compilers wanted to offer some special, simplified syntax for calling these methods, so be it. But I'd want the compiler to use syntax that is different from field access syntax so that programmers really understand what they are doing—a method call.

Parameterful Properties

In the previous section, the **get** accessor methods for the properties accepted no parameters. For this reason, I called these properties *parameterless properties*. These properties are easy to understand because they have the feel of accessing a field. In addition to these field-like properties, programming languages also support what I call *parameterful properties*, whose **get** accessor methods accept one or more parameters and whose **set** accessor methods accept two or more parameters. Different programming languages expose parameterful properties in different ways. Also, languages use different terms to refer to parameterful properties: C# calls them *indexers* and Visual Basic calls them *default properties*. In this section, I'll focus on how C# exposes its indexers by using parameterful properties.

In C#, parameterful properties (indexers) are exposed using an array-like syntax. In other words, you can think of an indexer as a way for the C# developer to overload the `[]` operator. Here's an example of a `BitArray` class that allows array-like syntax to index into the set of bits maintained by an instance of the class:

```
using System;

public sealed class BitArray {
   // Private array of bytes that hold the bits
   private Byte[] m_byteArray;
   private Int32  m_numBits;

   // Constructor that allocates the byte array and sets all bits to 0
   public BitArray(Int32 numBits) {
      // Validate arguments first.
      if (numBits <= 0)
         throw new ArgumentOutOfRangeException("numBits",
            numBits.ToString(),
            "numBits must be > 0");

      // Save the number of bits.
      m_numBits = numBits;

      // Allocate the bytes for the bit array.
      m_byteArray = new Byte[(numBits + 7) / 8];
   }

   // This is the indexer (parameterful property).
   public Boolean this[Int32 bitPos] {

      // This is the indexer's get accessor method.
      get {
         // Validate arguments first
         if ((bitPos < 0) || (bitPos >= m_numBits))
            throw new ArgumentOutOfRangeException("bitPos");

         // Return the state of the indexed bit.
         return (m_byteArray[bitPos / 8] & (1 << (bitPos % 8))) != 0;
      }

      // This is the indexer's set accessor method.
      set {
         if ((bitPos < 0) || (bitPos >= m_numBits))
            throw new ArgumentOutOfRangeException("bitPos",
               bitPos.ToString());

         if (value) {
            // Turn the indexed bit on.
            m_byteArray[bitPos / 8] = (Byte)
               (m_byteArray[bitPos / 8] | (1 << (bitPos % 8)));
```

```
            } else {
               // Turn the indexed bit off.
               m_byteArray[bitPos / 8] = (Byte)
                  (m_byteArray[bitPos / 8] & ~(1 << (bitPos % 8)));
            }
         }
      }
   }
}
```

Using the **BitArray** class's indexer is incredibly simple:

```
// Allocate a BitArray that can hold 14 bits.
BitArray ba = new BitArray(14);

// Turn all the even-numbered bits on by calling the set accessor.
for (Int32 x = 0; x < 14; x++) {
   ba[x] = (x % 2 == 0);
}

// Show the state of all the bits by calling the get accessor.
for (Int32 x = 0; x < 14; x++) {
   Console.WriteLine("Bit " + x + " is " + (ba[x] ? "On" : "Off"));
}
```

In the **BitArray** example, the indexer takes one **Int32** parameter, **bitPos**. All indexers must have at least one parameter, but they can have more. These parameters (as well as the return type) can be of any data type (except **void**).

It's quite common to create an indexer to look up values in an associative array. In fact, the **System.Collections.Generic.Dictionary** type offers an indexer that takes a key and returns the value associated with the key. Unlike parameterless properties, a type can offer multiple, overloaded indexers as long as their signatures differ.

Like a parameterless property's **set** accessor method, an indexer's **set** accessor method also contains a hidden parameter, called **value** in C#. This parameter indicates the new value desired for the "indexed element."

The CLR doesn't differentiate parameterless properties and parameterful properties; to the CLR, each is simply a pair of methods and a piece of metadata defined within a type. As mentioned earlier, different programming languages require different syntax to create and use parameterful properties. The fact that C# requires **this[...]** as the syntax for expressing an indexer was purely a choice made by the C# team. What this choice means is that C# allows indexers to be defined only on instances of objects. C# doesn't offer syntax allowing a developer to define a static indexer property, although the CLR does support static parameterful properties.

Because the CLR treats parameterful properties just as it does parameterless properties, the compiler will emit either two or three of the following items into the resulting managed assembly:

■ A method representing the parameterful property's **get** accessor method. This is emitted only if you define a **get** accessor method for the property.

- A method representing the parameterful property's **set** accessor method. This is emitted only if you define a **set** accessor method for the property.

- A property definition in the managed assembly's metadata, which is always emitted. There's no special parameterful property metadata definition table because, to the CLR, parameterful properties are just properties.

For the **BitArray** class shown earlier, the compiler compiles the indexer as though the original source code were written as follows:

```
public sealed class BitArray {

    // This is the indexer's get accessor method.
    public Boolean get_Item(Int32 bitPos) { /* ... */ }

    // This is the indexer's set accessor method.
    public void    set_Item(Int32 bitPos, Boolean value)  { /* ... */ }
}
```

The compiler automatically generates names for these methods by prepending **get_** and **set_** to the *indexer name*. Because the C# syntax for an indexer doesn't allow the developer to specify an *indexer name*, the C# compiler team had to choose a default name to use for the accessor methods; they chose **Item**. Therefore, the method names emitted by the compiler are **get_Item** and **set_Item**.

When examining the .NET Framework Reference documentation, you can tell if a type offers an indexer by looking for a property named **Item**. For example, the **System.Collections .Generic.List** type offers a public instance property named **Item**; this property is **List**'s indexer.

When you program in C#, you never see the name of **Item**, so you don't normally care that the compiler has chosen this name for you. However, if you're designing an indexer for a type that code written in other programming languages will be accessing, you might want to change the default name, **Item**, given to your indexer's **get** and **set** accessor methods. C# allows you to rename these methods by applying the **System.Runtime.CompilerServices.IndexerName-Attribute** custom attribute to the indexer. The following code demonstrates how:

```
using System;
using System.Runtime.CompilerServices;

public sealed class BitArray {

    [IndexerName("Bit")]
    public Boolean this[Int32 bitPos] {
        // At least one accessor method is defined here
    }
}
```

Now the compiler will emit methods called **get_Bit** and **set_Bit** instead of **get_Item** and **set_Item**. When compiling, the C# compiler sees the **IndexerName** attribute, and this tells the compiler how to name the methods and the property metadata; the attribute itself is not emitted into the assembly's metadata.[1]

Here's some Visual Basic code that demonstrates how to access this C# indexer:

```
' Construct an instance of the BitArray type.
Dim ba as New BitArray(10)

' Visual Basic uses () instead of [] to specify array elements.
Console.WriteLine(ba(2))        ' Displays True or False

' Visual Basic also allows you to access the indexer by its name.
Console.WriteLine(ba.Bit(2))    ' Displays same as previous line
```

In C#, a single type can define multiple indexers as long as the indexers all take different parameter sets. In other programming languages, the **IndexerName** attribute allows you to define multiple indexers with the same signature because each can have a different name. The reason C# won't allow you to do this is because its syntax doesn't refer to the indexer by name; the compiler wouldn't know which indexer you were referring to. Attempting to compile the following C# source code causes the compiler to generate the following: "error C0111: Type 'SomeType' already defines a member called 'this' with the same parameter types".

```
using System;
using System.Runtime.CompilerServices;

public sealed class SomeType {

    // Define a get_Item accessor method.
    public Int32 this[Boolean b] {
        get { return 0; }
    }

    // Define a get_Jeff accessor method.
    [IndexerName("Jeff")]
    public String this[Boolean b] {
        get { return null; }
    }
}
```

You can clearly see that C# thinks of indexers as a way to overload the **[]** operator, and this operator can't be used to disambiguate parameterful properties with different method names and identical parameter sets.

By the way, the **System.String** type is an example of a type that changed the name of its indexer. The name of **String**'s indexer is **Chars** instead of **Item**. This read-only property allows you to get an individual character within a string. For programming languages that don't use **[]** operator syntax to access this property, **Chars** was decided to be a more meaningful name.

---

[1]. For this reason, the **IndexerNameAttribute** class is not part of the ECMA standardization of the CLI and the C# language.

> ### Selecting the Primary Parameterful Property
>
> C#'s limitations with respect to indexers brings up the following two questions:
>
> - What if a type is defined in a programming language that does allow the developer to define several parameterful properties?
>
> - How can this type be consumed from C#?
>
> The answer to both questions is that a type must select one of the parameterful property names to be the default property by applying an instance of `System.Reflection.DefaultMemberAttribute` to the class itself. For the record, `DefaultMemberAttribute` can be applied to a class, a structure, or an interface. In C#, when you compile a type that defines a parameterful property, the compiler automatically applies an instance of `DefaultMemberAttribute` to the defining type and takes it into account when you use the `IndexerNameAttribute`. This attribute's constructor specifies the name that is to be used for the type's default parameterful property.
>
> So, in C#, if you define a type that has a parameterful property and you don't specify the `IndexerName` attribute, the defining type will have a `DefaultMember` attribute indicating `Item`. If you apply the `IndexerName` attribute to a parameterful property, the defining type will have a `DefaultMember` attribute indicating the string name specified in the `IndexerName` attribute. Remember, C# won't compile the code if it contains parameterful properties with different names.
>
> For a language that supports several parameterful properties, one of the property method names must be selected and identified by the type's `DefaultMember` attribute. This is the only parameterful property that C# will be able to access.

When the C# compiler sees code that is trying to get or set an indexer, the compiler actually emits a call to one of these methods. Some programming languages might not support parameterful properties. To access a parameterful property from one of these languages, you must call the desired accessor method explicitly. To the CLR, there's no difference between parameterless properties and parameterful properties, so you use the same `System.Reflection.PropertyInfo` class to find the association between a parameterful property and its accessor methods.

The Performance of Calling Property Accessor Methods

For simple **get** and **set** accessor methods, the JIT compiler *inlines* the code so that there's no run-time performance hit as a result of using properties rather than fields. Inlining is when the code for a method (or accessor method, in this case) is compiled directly in the method that is making the call. This removes the overhead associated with making a call at run time at the expense of making the compiled method's code bigger. Because property accessor methods typically contain very little code, inlining them can make the native code smaller and can make it execute faster.

Note that the JIT compiler does not inline property methods when debugging code because inlined code is harder to debug. This means that the performance of accessing a property can be fast in a release build and slow in a debug build. Field access is fast in both debug and release builds.

Property Accessor Accessibility

Occasionally, when designing a type, it is desired to have one accessibility for a **get** accessor method and a different accessibility for a **set** accessor method. The most common scenario is to have a public **get** accessor and a protected **set** accessor:

```
public class SomeType {
   public String Name {
      get { return null; }
      protected set {}
   }
}
```

As you can see from the code above, the **Name** property is itself declared as a **public** property, and this means that the **get** accessor method will be public and therefore callable by all code. However, notice that the **set** accessor is declared as **protected** and will be callable only from code defined within **SomeType** or from code in a class that is derived from **SomeType**.

When defining a property with accessor methods that have different accessibilities, C# syntax requires that the property itself must be declared with the least-restrictive accessibility and that more restrictive accessibility be applied to just one of the accessor methods. In the example above, the property is **public**, and the **set** accessor is **protected** (more restrictive than **public**).

Generic Property Accessor Methods

Since properties are really just methods, and because C# and the CLR allow methods to be generic, sometimes people try to define generic property accessor methods. However, C# does not allow this. The main reason why generic properties are not allowed is because they don't make sense conceptually. A property is supposed to represent a characteristic of an object that can be queried or set. Adding a generic type parameter would mean that the behavior of the querying/setting could be changed, but conceptually, a property is not supposed to have behavior. If you want your object to expose some behavior—generic or not—define a method, not a property.

Chapter 10

Events

In this chapter, I'll talk about the last kind of member a type can define: events. A type that defines an event member allows the type (or instances of the type) to notify other objects that something special has happened. For example, the `Button` class offers an event called `Click`. When a `Button` object is clicked, one or more objects in an application may want to receive notification about this event in order to perform some action. Events are type members that allow this interaction. Specifically, defining an event member means that a type is offering the following capabilities:

■ A type's static method or an object's instance method can register its interest in the type's event.

■ A type's static method or an object's instance method can unregister its interest in the type's event.

■ Registered methods will be notified when the event occurs.

Types can offer this functionality when defining an event because they maintain a list of the registered methods. When the event occurs, the type notifies all of the registered methods in the list.

The common language runtime's (CLR's) event model is based on *delegates*. A delegate is a type-safe way to invoke a callback method. Callback methods are the means by which objects receive the notifications they subscribed to. In this chapter, I'll be using delegates, but I won't fully explain all their details until Chapter 15, "Delegates."

To help you fully understand the way events work within the CLR, I'll start with a scenario in which events are useful. Suppose you want to design an e-mail application. When an e-mail message arrives, the user might like the message to be forwarded to a fax machine or a pager. In architecting this application, let's say that you'll first design a type, called `MailManager`, that receives the incoming e-mail messages. **MailManager** will expose an event called **NewMail**. Other types (such as **Fax** and **Pager**) may register interest in this event. When **MailManager** receives a new e-mail message, it will raise the event, causing the message to be distributed to each of the registered objects. Each object can process the message in any way it desires.

When the application initializes, let's instantiate just one **MailManager** instance—the application can then instantiate any number of **Fax** and **Pager** types. Figure 10-1 shows how the application initializes and what happens when a new e-mail message arrives.

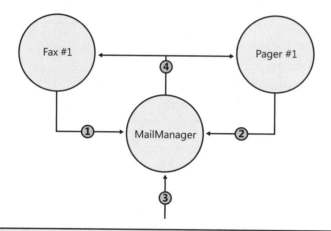

1. A Fax object registers interest with the MailManager's event.
2. A Pager object registers interest with the MailManager's event.
3. A new mail message arrives at MailManager.
4. The MailManager object fires the notification off to all the registered objects, which process the mail message as desired.

Figure 10-1   Architecting an application to use events

Here's how the application illustrated in Figure 10-1 works: The application initializes by constructing an instance of **MailManager**. **MailManager** offers a **NewMail** event. When the **Fax** and **Pager** objects are constructed, they register themselves with **MailManager**'s **NewMail** event so that **MailManager** knows to notify the **Fax** and **Pager** objects when new e-mail messages arrive. Now, when **MailManager** receives a new e-mail message (sometime in the future), it will raise the **NewMail** event, giving all of the registered objects an opportunity to process the new message in any way they want.

Designing a Type That Exposes an Event

There are many steps a developer must take in order to define a type that exposes one or more event members. In this section, I'll walk through each of the necessary steps. The **MailManager** sample application (which can be downloaded from *http://wintellect.com*) shows all of the source code for the **MailManager** type, the **Fax** type, and the **Pager** type. You'll notice that the **Pager** type is practically identical to the **Fax** type.

Step #1: Define a type that will hold any additional information that should be sent to receivers of the event notification

When an event is raised, the object raising the event may want to pass some additional information to the objects receiving the event notification. This additional information needs to be encapsulated into its own class, which typically contains a bunch of private fields along with some read-only public properties to expose these fields. By convention, classes that hold event information to be passed to the event handler should be derived from **System.EventArgs**, and the name of the class should be suffixed with **EventArgs**. In this example, the **NewMail-EventArgs** class has fields identifying who sent the message (**m_from**), who is receiving the message (**m_to**), and the subject of the message (**m_subject**).

```
// Step #1: Define a type that will hold any additional information that
// should be sent to receivers of the event notification
internal class NewMailEventArgs : EventArgs {

    private readonly String m_from, m_to, m_subject;

    public NewMailEventArgs(String from, String to, String subject) {
        m_from = from; m_to = to; m_subject = subject;
    }

    public String From    { get { return m_from;    } }
    public String To      { get { return m_to;      } }
    public String Subject { get { return m_subject; } }
}
```

> **Note**   The **EventArgs** class is defined in the Microsoft .NET Framework Class Library (FCL) and is implemented like this:
>
> ```
> [ComVisible(true)]
> [Serializable]
> public class EventArgs {
>     public static readonly EventArgs Empty = new EventArgs();
>     public EventArgs() {  }
> }
> ```
>
> As you can see, this type is nothing to write home about. It simply serves as a base type from which other types can derive. Many events don't have any additional information to pass on. For example, when a **Button** notifies its registered receivers that it has been clicked, just invoking the callback method is enough information. When you're defining an event that doesn't have any additional data to pass on, just use **EventArgs.Empty** rather than constructing a new **EventArgs** object.

Step #2: Define the event member

An event member is defined using the C# keyword **event**. Each event member is given accessibility (which is almost always **public** so that other code can access the event member), a type of delegate indicating the prototype of the method(s) that will be called, and a name (which can be any valid identifier). Here is what the event member in our **NewMail** class looks like:

```
internal class MailManager {

    // Step #2: Define the event member
    public event EventHandler<NewMailEventArgs> NewMail;
    ...
}
```

NewMail is the name of this event. The type of the event member is **EventHandler<NewMail-EventArgs>**, which means that all receivers of the event notification must supply a callback method whose prototype matches that of the **EventHandler<NewMailEventArgs>** delegate type. Since the generic **System.EventHandler** delegate is defined as follows:

```
public delegate void EventHandler<TEventArgs>
    (Object sender, TEventArgs e) where TEventArgs: EventArgs;
```

the method prototypes must look like this:

```
void MethodName(Object sender, NewMailEventArgs e);
```

> **Note**   A lot of people wonder why the event pattern requires the sender parameter to always be of type **Object**. After all, since the **MailManager** will be the only type raising an event with a **NewMailEventArgs** object, it makes more sense for the callback method to be prototyped like this:
>
> ```
> void MethodName(MailManager sender, NewMailEventArgs e);
> ```
>
> The pattern requires the **sender** parameter to be of type **Object** mostly because of inheritance. What if **MailManager** were used as a base class for **SmtpMailManager**? In this case, the callback method should have the **sender** parameter prototyped as an **SmtpMailManager** instead of **MailManager**, but this can't happen because **SmtpMailManager** just inherited the **NewMail** event. So the code that was expecting an **SmtpMailManager** to raise the event must still have to cast the **sender** argument to an **SmtpMailManager**. In other words, the cast is still required, so the **sender** parameter might as well be typed as **Object**.
>
> The next reason for typing the **sender** parameter as **Object** is just flexibility. It allows the delegate to be used by multiple types that offer an event that passes a **NewMailEventArgs** object. For example, a **PopMailManager** class could use the delegate even if this class were not derived from **MailManager**.
>
> One more thing: the event pattern also requires that the delegate definition and the callback method name the **EventArgs**-derived parameter **e**. The only reason for this is to add additional consistency to the pattern, making it easier for developers to learn and implement the pattern. Tools that spit out source code (such as Microsoft Visual Studio) also know to call the parameter **e**.
>
> Finally, the event pattern requires all event handlers to have a return type of **void**. This is nec-essary because raising an event might call several callback methods, and there is no way to get the return values from all of them. Having a return type of **void** doesn't allow the callbacks to return a value. Unfortunately, there are some event handlers in the Framework Class Library, such as **ResolveEventHandler**, that did not follow Microsoft's own prescribed pattern because it returns an object of type **Assembly**.

Step #3: Define a method responsible for raising the event to notify registered objects that the event has occurred

By convention, the class should define a protected, virtual method that is called by code internally within the class and its derived classes when the event is to be raised. This method takes one parameter, a **NewMailEventArgs** object, which includes the information passed to the objects receiving the notification. The default implementation of this method simply checks if any objects have registered interest in the event and, if so, the event will be raised, thereby notifying the registered methods that the event has occurred. Here is what the method in our **MailManager** class looks like:

```
internal class MailManager {
    ...
    // Step #3: Define a method responsible for raising the event
    // to notify registered objects that the event has occurred
    // If this class is sealed, make this method private and non-virtual
    protected virtual void OnNewMail(NewMailEventArgs e) {

        // Save the delegate field in a temporary field for thread safety
        EventHandler<NewMailEventArgs> temp = NewMail;

        // If any objects registered interest with our event, notify them
        if (temp != null) temp(this, e);
    }
    ...
}
```

You'll notice the **OnNewMail** method defines a temporary local variable, called **temp**, which is initialized to the event member itself. Next, the **temp** variable is compared to **null**. If **temp** is found to not be equal to **null**, it will be used to raise the event. This temporary variable is necessary in order to prevent a possible thread synchronization issue. You see, if instead of using **temp**, the method simply referred to **NewMail**, it's possible that the thread would see that **NewMail** is not **null**, but then, just before raising the event, another thread could cause it to become **null**. If this were to happen, attempting to raise the event would cause the CLR to throw a **NullReferenceException**. Using the temporary variable **temp** solves this problem and ensures that a **NullReferenceException** is not thrown.

A class that uses **MailManager** as a base type is free to override the **OnNewMail** method. This capability gives the derived class control over the raising of the event. The derived class can handle the new e-mail message in any way it sees fit. Usually, a derived type calls the base type's **OnNewMail** method so that the registered method(s) receive the notification. However, the derived class might decide to disallow the event from being forwarded.

Step #4: Define a method that translates the input into the desired event

Your class must have some method that takes some input and translates it into the raising of the event. In my `MailManager` example, the `SimulateNewMail` method is called to indicate that a new e-mail message has arrived into `MailManager`:

```
internal class MailManager {

    // Step #4: Define a method that translates the
    // input into the desired event
    public void SimulateNewMail(String from, String to, String subject) {

        // Construct an object to hold the information we wish
        // to pass to the receivers of our notification
        NewMailEventArgs e = new NewMailEventArgs(from, to, subject);

        // Call our virtual method notifying our object that the event
        // occurred. If no type overrides this method, our object will
        // notify all the objects that registered interest in the event
        OnNewMail(e);
    }
}
```

`SimulateNewMail` accepts information about the message and constructs a `NewMailEventArgs` object, passing the message information to its constructor. `MailManager`'s own virtual `OnNew-Mail` method is then called to formally notify the `MailManager` object of the new e-mail message. Usually, this causes the event to be raised, notifying all of the registered methods. (As mentioned before, a class using `MailManager` as a base class can override this behavior.)

How Events Are Implemented

Now that you know how to define a class that offers an event member, let's now take a closer look at what an event really is and how it works. In the `MailManager` class, we have a line of code that defines the event member itself:

```
public event EventHandler<NewMailEventArgs> NewMail;
```

When the C# compiler compiles the line above, it translates this single line of source code into the following three constructs:

```
// 1. A PRIVATE delegate field that is initialized to null
private EventHandler<NewMailEventArgs> NewMail = null;

// 2. A PUBLIC add_Xxx method (where Xxx is the Event name)
//    Allows objects to register interest in the event.
[MethodImpl(MethodImplOptions.Synchronized)]
public void add_NewMail(EventHandler<NewMailEventArgs> value) {
    NewMail = (EventHandler<NewMailEventArgs>)
        Delegate.Combine(NewMail, value);
}
```

```
// 3. A PUBLIC remove_Xxx method (where Xxx is the Event name)
//    Allows objects to unregister interest in the event.
[MethodImpl(MethodImplOptions.Synchronized)]
public void remove_NewMail(EventHandler<NewMailEventArgs> value) {
   NewMail = (EventHandler<NewMailEventArgs>)
      Delegate.Remove(NewMail, value);
}
```

The first construct is simply a field of the appropriate delegate type. This field is a reference to the head of a list of delegates that will be notified when this event occurs. This field is initialized to **null**, meaning that no listeners have registered interest in the event. When a method registers interest in the event, this field refers to an instance of the **EventHandler<NewMailEventArgs>** delegate, which may refer to additional **EventHandler<NewMailEventArgs>** delegates. When a listener registers interest in an event, the listener is simply adding an instance of the delegate type to the list. Obviously, unregistering means removing the delegate from the list.

You'll notice that the delegate field, **NewMail** in this example, is always **private** even though the original line of source code defines the event as **public**. The reason for making the delegate field private is to prevent code outside the defining class from manipulating it improperly. If the field were public, any code could alter the value in the field and potentially wipe out all of the delegates that have registered interest in the event.

The second construct the C# compiler generates is a method that allows other objects to register their interest in the event. The C# compiler automatically names this function by prepending **add_** to the event's name (**NewMail**). The C# compiler automatically generates the code that is inside this method. The code always calls **System.Delegate**'s static **Combine** method, which adds the instance of a delegate to the list of delegates and returns the new head of the list, which gets saved back in the field.

The third and final construct the C# compiler generates is a method that allows an object to unregister its interest in the event. Again, the C# compiler automatically names this function by prepending **remove_** to the event's name (**NewMail**). The code inside this method always calls **Delegate**'s static **Remove** method, which removes the instance of a delegate from the list of delegates and returns the new head of the list, which gets saved back in the field.

You should also notice that both the **add** and **remove** methods have a **MethodImplAttribute** attribute (defined in the **System.Runtime.CompilerServices** namespace) applied to them. More specifically, these methods are marked as synchronized, making them thread safe: multiple listeners can register or unregister themselves with the event at the same time without corrupting the list. For more about thread safety and events, see the "Events and Thread Safety" section later in this chapter.

In this example, the **add** and **remove** methods are **public**. The reason they are **public** is that the original line of source code declared the event to be **public**. If the event had been declared **protected**, the **add** and **remove** methods generated by the compiler would also have been declared **protected**. So, when you define an event in a type, the accessibility of the event determines what code can register and unregister interest in the event, but only the type itself can ever access the delegate field directly. Event members can also be declared as **static** or **virtual**, in which case the **add** and **remove** methods generated by the compiler would be either **static** or **virtual**, respectively.

In addition to emitting the aforementioned three constructs, compilers also emit an event definition entry into the managed assembly's metadata. This entry contains some flags and the underlying delegate type, and refers to the **add** and **remove** accessor methods. This information exists simply to draw an association between the abstract concept of an "event" and its accessor methods. Compilers and other tools can use this metadata, and this information can also be obtained by using the **System.Reflection.EventInfo** class. However, the CLR itself doesn't use this metadata information and requires only the accessor methods at run time.

Designing a Type That Listens for an Event

The hard work is definitely behind you at this point. In this section, I'll show you how to define a type that uses an event provided by another type. Let's start off by examining the code for the **Fax** type:

```
internal sealed class Fax {
    // Pass the MailManager object to the constructor
    public Fax(MailManager mm) {

        // Construct an instance of the EventHandler<NewMailEventArgs>
        // delegate that refers to our FaxMsg callback method.
        // Register our callback with MailManager's NewMail event
        mm.NewMail += FaxMsg;
    }

    // This is the method the MailManager will call
    // when a new e-mail message arrives
    private void FaxMsg(Object sender, NewMailEventArgs e) {

        // 'sender' identifies the MailManager object in case
        // we want to communicate back to it.

        // 'e' identifies the additional event information
        // the MailManager wants to give us.

        // Normally, the code here would fax the e-mail message.
        // This test implementation displays the info in the console
        Console.WriteLine("Faxing mail message:");
        Console.WriteLine("   From={0}, To={1}, Subject={2}",
            e.From, e.To, e.Subject);
    }

    // This method could be executed to have the Fax object unregister
    // itself with the NewMail event so that it no longer receives
    // notifications
    public void Unregister(MailManager mm) {
```

```
        // Unregister with MailManager's NewMail event
        mm.NewMail -= FaxMsg;
    }
}
```

When the e-mail application initializes, it would first construct a `MailManager` object and save the reference to this object in a variable. Then the application would construct a `Fax` object, passing the reference to the `MailManager` object as a parameter. In the `Fax` constructor, the `Fax` object registers its interest in `MailManager`'s `NewMail` event using C#'s `+=` operator:

```
mm.NewMail += FaxMsg;
```

Because the C# compiler has built-in support for events, the compiler translates the use of the `+=` operator into the following line of code to add the object's interest in the event:

```
mm.add_NewMail(new EventHandler<NewMailEventArgs>(this.FaxMsg));
```

As you can see, the C# compiler is generating code that will construct an `EventHandler<NewMailEventArgs>` delegate object that wraps the `Fax` class's `FaxMsg` method. Then, the C# compiler calls the `MailManager`'s `add_NewMail` method, passing it the new delegate. Of course, you can verify all of this by compiling the code and looking at the IL with a tool such as ILDasm.exe.

Even if you're using a programming language that doesn't directly support events, you can still register a delegate with the event by calling the **add** accessor method explicitly. The effect is identical; the source code will just not look as pretty. It's the **add** method that registers the delegate with the event by adding it to the event's list of delegates.

When the `MailManager` object raises the event, the `Fax` object's `FaxMsg` method gets called. The method is passed a reference to the `MailManager` object as the first parameter, **sender**. Most of the time, this parameter is ignored, but it can be used if the `Fax` object wants to access members of the `MailManager` object in response to the event notification. The second parameter is a reference to a `NewMailEventArgs` object. This object contains any additional information the designer of `MailManager` and `NewMailEventArgs` thought would be useful to the event receivers.

From the `NewMailEventArgs` object, the `FaxMsg` method has easy access to the message's sender, the message's recipient, and the message's subject. In a real `Fax` object, this information would be faxed somewhere. In this example, the information is simply displayed in the console window.

When an object is no longer interested in receiving event notifications, it should unregister its interest. For example, the `Fax` object would unregister its interest in the `NewMail` event if the user no longer wanted his or her e-mail forwarded to a fax. As long as an object has registered one of its methods with an event, the object can't be garbage collected. If your type implements `IDisposable`'s `Dispose` method, the implementation should cause it to unregister interest in all events. (See Chapter 20, "Automatic Memory Management (Garbage Collection)," for more information about `IDisposable`.)

Code that demonstrates how to unregister for an event is shown in **Fax**'s **Unregister** method. This method is practically identical to the code shown in the **Fax** constructor. The only difference is that this code uses -= instead of +=. When the C# compiler sees code using the -= operator to unregister a delegate with an event, the compiler emits a call to the event's **remove** method:

```
mm.remove_NewMail(new EventHandler<NewMailEventArgs>(FaxMsg));
```

As with the += operator, even if you're using a programming language that doesn't directly support events, you can still unregister a delegate with the event by calling the **remove** accessor method explicitly. The **remove** method unregisters the delegate from the event by scanning the list for a delegate that wraps the same method as the one passed in. If a match is found, the existing delegate is removed from the event's list of delegates. If a match isn't found, no error occurs, and the list is unaltered.

By the way, C# requires your code to use the += and -= operators to add and remove delegates from the list. If you try to call the **add** or **remove** method explicitly, the C# compiler produces a CS0571: "cannot explicitly call operator or accessor" error.

Events and Thread Safety

In the previous section, I showed how the C# compiler adds the [MethodImpl(Method-ImplOptions.Synchronized)] attribute to the event's **add** and **remove** methods. The purpose of this attribute is to ensure that only one **add** or **remove** method can be executing at any one time for any single object when manipulating an instance event member. This attribute also ensures that only one **add** or **remove** method can be executing at any one time for a type when manipulating an static event member. This thread synchronization is required so that the list of delegate objects doesn't become corrupted. However, you should be aware that there are many issues with the way the CLR accomplishes this thread synchronization.

When the **MethodImpl** attribute is applied to an instance (non-static) method, the CLR uses the object itself as the thread-synchronization lock. This means that if a class defines many events, all **add** and **remove** methods use the same lock, and this hurts scalability if you have multiple threads registering and unregistering interest on different events simultaneously. This is very rare however, and for almost all applications, this is not a problem. However, the thread-synchronization guidelines state that methods should not take a lock on the object itself because the lock is exposed publicly to any and all code. This means that anyone could write code that locks the object, potentially causing other threads to deadlock. If you want to code your type defensively to make it more robust, a different object should be used to accomplish the locking. In the next section, I'll demonstrate how to accomplish this.

When the [MethodImpl(MethodImplOptions.Synchronized)] attribute is applied to a static method, the CLR uses the type object as the thread-synchronization lock. Again, this means that if a class defines many static events, all **add** and **remove** methods use the same lock, and this hurts the performance of your code if you have multiple threads registering and unregistering interest on different events simultaneously. Again, this is rare.

However, there is a much more severe problem: The thread-synchronization guidelines state that methods should never take a lock on a type object because the lock is exposed publicly to any and all code. In addition, there is a bug in the CLR that occurs when the type is loaded domain neutral. This situation causes the lock to be shared across all AppDomains using the type, thus giving code in one AppDomain the ability to adversely affect code running in another AppDomain. In reality, the C# compiler should be doing something completely different in order to achieve thread safety for static **add** and **remove** methods. In the next section, I'll discuss a mechanism that you can use to correct this deficiency in the C# compiler.

C# and the CLR allow you to define a value type (structure) with one or more instance (non-static) event members in it. However, you must be aware that in this case, the C# compiler will give you no thread safety at all. The reason is because unboxed value types do not have a lock object associated with them. In fact, the C# compiler knows not to emit the `[Method-Impl(MethodImplOptions.Synchronized)]` attribute to the **add** and **remove** methods because this attribute would have no effect on instance methods of a value type. Unfortunately, there is no good way to add thread safety for instance events when they are defined as members of a value type. Therefore, it is recommended that you avoid doing this. Note it is OK (with the limitations presented just above) to define static events in a value type because they lock on the type object (which is a reference type). However, if you care about coding this robustly, you should use the mechanism I show in the next section.

Explicitly Controlling Event Registration and Unregistration

Sometimes the **add** and **remove** methods the compiler generates are not ideal. For example, in the previous section, I mentioned all of the thread-safety issues that exist when using Microsoft's C# compiler. In fact, Microsoft's C# compiler never does the safest thing here in terms of defensive coding and robustness. To create rock-solid components, I'd recommend that you always use the technique explained in this section—this technique can be used to solve all of the thread-safety issues. However, the technique can also be applied for other purposes as well. For example, a common reason for explicitly implementing **add** and **remove** methods is if your type defines many events, and you'd like to use storage more efficiently. I'll cover this scenario specifically in the next section, "Designing a Type That Defines Lots of Events."

Fortunately, C# and many other compilers allow the developer to create explicit implementations of the **add** and **remove** accessor methods. To make the registering and unregistering events on a **MailManager** object thread safe, we'd modify the code in the class to look like this:

```
internal class MailManager {

   // Private instance field created to serve as thread synchronization lock
   private readonly Object m_eventLock = new Object();

   // Add private field that refers to the head of the delegate list
   private EventHandler<NewMailEventArgs> m_NewMail;

   // Add an event member to the class
   public event EventHandler<NewMailEventArgs> NewMail {
      // Explicitly implement the 'add' method
      add {
         // Take the private lock and add a handler
         // (passed as 'value') to the delegate list
         lock (m_eventLock) { m_NewMail += value; }
      }

      // Explicitly implement the 'remove' method
      remove {
         // Take the private lock and remove a handler
         // (passed as 'value') from the delegate list
         lock (m_eventLock) { m_NewMail -= value; }
      }
   }


   // Step #3: Define a method responsible for raising the event
   // to notify registered objects that the event has occurred
   // If this class is sealed, make this method private and non-virtual
   protected virtual void OnNewMail(NewMailEventArgs e) {

      // Save the delegate field in a temporary field for thread safety
      EventHandler<NewMailEventArgs> temp = m_NewMail;

      // If any objects registered interest with our event, notify them
      if (temp != null) temp(this, e);
   }

   // Step #4: Define a method that translates the
   // input into the desired event
   public void SimulateNewMail(String from, String to, String subject) {

      // Construct an object to hold the information we wish
      // to pass to the receivers of our notification
      NewMailEventArgs e = new NewMailEventArgs(from, to, subject);

      // Call our virtual method notifying our object that the event
      // occurred. If no type overrides this method, our object will
      // notify all the objects that registered interest in the event
      OnNewMail(e);
   }
}
```

In this new version of **MailManager**, the private field, **m_NewMail**, that refers to the delegate list must be explicitly defined. In the original event syntax, the C# compiler automatically defined a **private** field for you. Using this new event syntax, when the developer explicitly supplies implementations for the **add** and **remove** accessor methods, the field must also be explicitly declared.

The field is just a reference to an **EventHandler<NewMailEventArgs>** delegate. There's nothing that makes this field an event. The new extended syntax after the **event** keyword is actually what defines an event within the type. The code in the **add** and **remove** blocks provides the implementation for the accessor methods. Notice that each method accepts a hidden parameter, called **value**, which is of the **EventHandler<NewMailEventArgs>** type. Inside, these methods implement the code necessary to add a delegate to or remove a delegate from the list. Unlike properties, which can have a **get** accessor method, a **set** accessor method, or both, events must always have both **add** and **remove** accessor methods.

The explicit implementations shown in the preceding example have exactly the same behavior as the methods the C# compiler would have provided except that the **[MethodImpl(Method-ImplOptions.Synchronized)]** attribute is omitted, and instead, the C# **lock** statement is used with a reference to a privately defined **Object** (**m_eventLock**). This is how I fix the thread-safety problem mentioned in the previous section. Since the **m_eventLock** field is declared as **private**, no code outside the **MailManager** class can access it; this is what makes the **MailManager** class more robust.

The event can be declared as a **static** member, which would make the **add** and **remove** accessor methods **static** as well. Of course, the private field, **m_NewMail**, would also have to become **static**. Then, to get proper thread safety, the **m_eventLock** field should also be declared as **static**. This will work for reference types or value types that want to expose a static event in a thread-safe way. Unfortunately, as stated in the previous section, there is no good way to make instance events on a value type thread safe because there is no good way to initialize an instance field within a value type. See Chapter 5, "Primitive, Reference, and Value Types," for an explanation as to why this is.

Code that is registering or unregistering with an event cannot tell whether the event's **add** and **remove** methods were created automatically by the compiler or were explicitly implemented by a programmer. In fact, registering and unregistering code can still use the += and -= operators, and the compiler will know to emit calls to the explicitly defined methods.

The last thing to point out is the **OnNewMail** method. Semantically, this method is identical to the previous version. The only difference is that the name of the event (**NewMail**) has been replaced with the name of the delegate field, **m_NewMail**.

Designing a Type That Defines Lots of Events

In the previous section, I described a scenario in which you might want to explicitly provide **add** and **remove** accessor methods for an event. However, when you're implementing the explicit accessor methods yourself, you can get a bit more creative with their implementation. Let's see how implementing these explicit methods can reduce the memory usage of an application.

The `System.Windows.Forms.Control` type defines about 70 events. If the `Control` type implemented the events by allowing the compiler to implicitly generate the **add** and **remove** accessor methods and delegate fields, every `Control` object would have 70 delegate fields in it just for the events! Because one never registers interest in most of these events, an enormous amount of memory would be wasted for each object created from a `Control`-derived type. By the way, the `System.Web.UI.Control` type also uses the following technique to reduce the memory wasted by unused events.

By explicitly implementing the event's **add** and **remove** methods creatively, you can greatly reduce the amount of space wasted by each event. In this section, I'll show you how to define a type that exposes many events efficiently.

The basic idea is that each object will maintain a collection (usually a dictionary) with some sort of event identifier as the key and a delegate list as the value. When a new object is constructed, this collection is empty. When interest in an event is registered, the event's identifier is looked up in the collection. If the event identifier is there, the new delegate is combined with the list of delegates for this event. If the event identifier isn't in the collection, the event identifier is added with the delegate.

When the object needs to raise an event, the event identifier is looked up in the collection. If the collection doesn't have an entry for the event identifier, nothing has registered interest in the event, and no delegates need to be called back. If the event identifier is in the collection, the delegate list associated with the event identifier is invoked. Implementing this design pattern is the responsibility of the developer who is designing the type that defines the events; the developer using the type has no idea how the events are implemented internally.

The `TypeWithLotsOfEvents` sample application, which can be downloaded from *http://wintellect.com*, demonstrates how to do all of this. The code is heavily commented, and if you understand everything that was said in this chapter, you should have no trouble understanding the code and adapting it to your own needs.

> **Note**   My code uses a reusable helper class called `EventSet`, which maintains the dictionary of event identifier keys and delegate values. The FCL defines a type, `System.ComponentModel.EventHandlerList`, that does essentially the same thing as my `EventSet` class. The `System.Windows.Forms.Control` and `System.Web.UI.Control` types use the `EventHandlerList` type internally to maintain their sparse set of events. You're certainly welcome to use the FCL's `EventHandlerList` type if you'd like. The difference between the `EventHandlerList` type and my `EventSet` type is that `EventHandlerList` uses a linked list instead of a hash table. This means that accessing elements managed by the `EventHandlerList` is slower than using my `EventSet`. In addition, the `EventHandlerList` doesn't offer any thread-safe way to access the events; you would have to implement your own thread-safe wrapper around the `EventHandlerList` collection if you need this. My `EventSet` class is fully thread safe.

Part IV
Essential Types

Chapter 11

Chars, Strings, and Working with Text

In this chapter, I'll explain the mechanics of working with individual characters and strings in the Microsoft .NET Framework. I'll start by talking about the `System.Char` structure and the various ways that you can manipulate a character. Then I'll go over the more useful `System.String` class, which allows you to work with immutable strings. (Once created, strings can't be modified in any way.) After examining strings, I'll show you how to perform various operations efficiently to build a string dynamically via the `System.Text.StringBuilder` class. With the string basics out of the way, I'll then describe how to format objects into strings and how to efficiently persist or transmit strings by using various encodings. Finally, I'll discuss the `System.Security.SecureString` class, which can be used to protect sensitive string data such as passwords and credit card information.

Characters

In the .NET Framework, characters are always represented in 16-bit Unicode code values, easing the development of global applications. A character is represented with an instance of the `System.Char` structure (a value type). The `System.Char` type is pretty simple. It offers two public read-only constant fields: `MinValue`, defined as `'\0'`, and `MaxValue`, defined as `'\uffff'`.

Given an instance of a `Char`, you can call the static `GetUnicodeCategory` method, which returns a value of the `System.Globalization.UnicodeCategory` enumerated type. This value indicates whether the character is a control character, a currency symbol, a lowercase letter, an uppercase letter, a punctuation character, a math symbol, or another character (as defined by the Unicode standard).

To ease developing, the **Char** type also offers several static methods, such as **IsDigit**, **IsLetter**, **IsWhiteSpace**, **IsUpper**, **IsLower**, **IsPunctuation**, **IsLetterOrDigit**, **IsControl**, **IsNumber**, **IsSeparator**, **IsSurrogate**, **IsLowSurrogate**, **IsHighSurrogate**, and **IsSymbol**. Most of these methods call **GetUnicodeCategory** internally and simply return **true** or **false** accordingly. Note that all of these methods take either a single character for a parameter or a **String** and the index of a character within the **String** as parameters.

In addition, you can convert a single character to its lowercase or uppercase equivalent in a culture-agnostic way by calling the static **ToLowerInvariant** or **ToUpperInvariant** method. Alternatively, the **ToLower** and **ToUpper** methods convert the character by using the culture information associated with the calling thread (which the methods obtain internally by querying the static **CurrentCulture** property of the **System.Threading.Thread** class). You can also specify a particular culture by passing an instance of the **CultureInfo** class to these methods. **ToLower** and **ToUpper** require culture information because letter casing is a culture-dependent operation. For example, Turkish considers the uppercase of U+0069 (LATIN LOWERCASE LETTER I) to be U+0130 (LATIN UPPERCASE LETTER I WITH DOT ABOVE), whereas other cultures consider the result to be U+0049 (LATIN CAPITAL LETTER I).

Besides these static methods, the **Char** type also offers a few instance methods of its own. The **Equals** method returns **true** if two **Char** instances represent the same 16-bit Unicode code point. The **CompareTo** methods (defined by the **IComparable/IComparable<Char>** interfaces) return a comparison of two **Char** instances; this comparison is not culture-sensitive. The **ToString** method returns a **String** consisting of a single character. The opposite of **ToString** is **Parse/TryParse**, which takes a single-character **String** and returns its UTF-16 code point.

The last method, **GetNumericValue**, returns the numeric equivalent of a character. I demonstrate this method in the following code:

```
using System;

public static class Program {
   public static void Main() {
      Double d;                           // '\u0033' is the "digit 3"
      d = Char.GetNumericValue('\u0033'); // '3' would work too
      Console.WriteLine(d.ToString());    // Displays "3"

      // '\u00bc' is the "vulgar fraction one quarter ('¼')"
      d = Char.GetNumericValue('\u00bc');
      Console.WriteLine(d.ToString());    // Displays "0.25"

      // 'A' is the "Latin capital letter A"
      d = Char.GetNumericValue('A');
      Console.WriteLine(d.ToString());    // Displays "-1"
   }
}
```

Finally, three techniques allow you to convert between various numeric types to **Char** instances and vice versa. The techniques are listed here in order of preference:

- **Casting**   The easiest way to convert a **Char** to a numeric value such as an **Int32** is simply by casting. Of the three techniques, this is the most efficient because the compiler emits intermediate language (IL) instructions to perform the conversion, and no methods have to be called. In addition, some languages (such as C#) allow you to indicate whether the conversion should be performed using checked or unchecked code (discussed in Chapter 5, "Primitive, Reference, and Value Types").

■ **Use the `Convert` type**   The `System.Convert` type offers several static methods that are capable of converting a `Char` to a numeric type and vice versa. All of these methods perform the conversion as a checked operation, causing an `OverflowException` to be thrown if the conversion results in the loss of data.

■ **Use the `IConvertible` interface**   The `Char` type and all of the numeric types in the .NET Framework Class Library (FCL) implement the `IConvertible` interface. This interface defines methods such as `ToUInt16` and `ToChar`. This technique is the least efficient of the three because calling an interface method on a value type requires that the instance be boxed—`Char` and all of the numeric types are value types. The methods of `IConvertible` throw a `System.InvalidCastException` if the type can't be converted (such as converting a `Char` to a `Boolean`) or if the conversion results in a loss of data. Note that many types (including the FCL's `Char` and numeric types) implement `IConvertible`'s methods as explicit interface member implementations (described in Chapter 14, "Interfaces"). This means that you must explicitly cast the instance to an `IConvertible` before you can call any of the interface's methods. All of the methods of `IConvertible` except `GetTypeCode` accept a reference to an object that implements the `IFormatProvider` interface. This parameter is useful if for some reason the conversion needs to take culture information into account. For most conversions, you can pass `null` for this parameter because it would be ignored anyway.

The following code demonstrates how to use these three techniques:

```
using System;

public static class Program {
   public static void Main() {
      Char   c;
      Int32 n;

      // Convert number <-> character using C# casting
      c = (Char) 65;
      Console.WriteLine(c);                // Displays "A"

      n = (Int32) c;
      Console.WriteLine(n);                // Displays "65"

      c = unchecked((Char) (65536 + 65));
      Console.WriteLine(c);                // Displays "A"


      // Convert number <-> character using Convert
      c = Convert.ToChar(65);
      Console.WriteLine(c);                // Displays "A"
```

```
    n = Convert.ToInt32(c);
    Console.WriteLine(n);                    // Displays "65"


    // This demonstrates Convert's range checking
    try {
        c = Convert.ToChar(70000);           // Too big for 16 bits
        Console.WriteLine(c);                // Doesn't execute
    }
    catch (OverflowException) {
        Console.WriteLine("Can't convert 70000 to a Char.");
    }


    // Convert number <-> character using IConvertible
    c = ((IConvertible) 65).ToChar(null);
    Console.WriteLine(c);                    // Displays "A"

    n = ((IConvertible) c).ToInt32(null);
    Console.WriteLine(n);                    // Displays "65"
    }
}
```

The System.String Type

One of the most used types in any application is **System.String**. A **string** represents an immutable ordered set of characters. The **string** type is derived immediately from **Object**, making it a reference type, and therefore, **string** objects (its array of characters) always live in the heap, never on a thread's stack. The **string** type also implements several interfaces (**IComparable/IComparable<String>**, **ICloneable**, **IConvertible**, **IEnumerable/ IEnumerable<Char>**, and **IEquatable<String>**).

Constructing Strings

Many programming languages (including C#) consider **string** to be a primitive type—that is, the compiler lets you express literal strings directly in your source code. The compiler places these literal strings in the module's metadata, and they are then loaded and referenced at run time.

In C#, you can't use the **new** operator to construct a **string** object from a literal string:

```
using System;

public static class Program {
    public static void Main() {
        String s = new String("Hi there.");  // <-- Error
        Console.WriteLine(s);
    }
}
```

Instead, you must use the following simplified syntax:

```
using System;

public static class Program {
   public static void Main() {
      String s = "Hi there.";
      Console.WriteLine(s);
   }
}
```

If you compile this code and examine its IL (using ILDasm.exe), you'd see the following:

```
.method public hidebysig static void  Main() cil managed
{
  .entrypoint
  // Code size       13 (0xd)
  .maxstack  1
  .locals init (string V_0)
  IL_0000:  ldstr      "Hi there."
  IL_0005:  stloc.0
  IL_0006:  ldloc.0
  IL_0007:  call       void [mscorlib]System.Console::WriteLine(string)
  IL_000c:  ret
} // end of method Program::Main
```

The **newobj** IL instruction constructs a new instance of an object. However, no **newobj** instruction appears in the IL code example. Instead, you see the special **ldstr** (load string) IL instruction, which constructs a **String** object by using a literal string obtained from metadata. This shows you that the common language runtime (CLR) does, in fact, have a special way of constructing literal **String** objects.

If you are using unsafe code, you can construct a **String** object from a **Char*** or **SByte***. To accomplish this, you would use C#'s **new** operator and call one of the constructors provided by the **String** type that takes **Char*** or **SByte*** parameters. These constructors create a **String** object, initializing the string from an array of **Char** instances or signed bytes. The other constructors don't have any pointer parameters and can be called using safe (verifiable) code written in any managed programming language.

C# offers some special syntax to help you enter literal strings into the source code. For special characters such as new lines, carriage returns, and backspaces, C# uses the escape mechanism familiar to C/C++ developers:

```
// String containing carriage-return and newline characters
String s = "Hi\r\nthere.";
```

> **Important**   Although the preceding example hard-codes carriage-return and newline
> characters into the string, I don't recommend this practice. Instead, the `System.Environment`
> type defines a read-only `NewLine` property that returns a string consisting of these characters
> when your application is running on Microsoft Windows. However, the `NewLine` property is plat-
> form sensitive, and it returns the appropriate string required to obtain a newline by the underlying
> platform. So, for example, when the Common Language Infrastructure (CLI) is ported to a UNIX
> system, the `NewLine` property would return a string consisting of just a single character `\n`. Here's
> the proper way to define the previous string so that it works correctly on any platform:
>
> ```
> String s = "Hi" + Environment.NewLine + "there.";
> ```

You can concatenate several strings to form a single string by using C#'s **+** operator as follows:

```
// Three literal strings concatenated to form a single literal string
String s = "Hi" + " " + "there.";
```

In this code, because all of the strings are literal strings, the C# compiler concatenates them at compile time and ends up placing just one string—**"Hi there."**—in the module's metadata. Using the **+** operator on nonliteral strings causes the concatenation to be performed at run time. To concatenate several strings together at run time, avoid using the **+** operator because it creates multiple string objects on the garbage-collected heap. Instead, use the **System.Text.StringBuilder** type (which I'll explain later in this chapter).

Finally, C# also offers a special way to declare a string in which all characters between quotes are considered part of the string. These special declarations are called *verbatim strings* and are typically used when specifying the path of a file or directory or when working with regular expressions. Here is some code showing how to declare the same string with and without using the verbatim string character (**@**).

```
// Specifying the pathname of an application
String file = "C:\\Windows\\System32\\Notepad.exe";
```

```
// Specifying the pathname of an application by using a verbatim string
String file = @"C:\Windows\System32\Notepad.exe";
```

You could use either one of the preceding code lines in a program because they produce identical strings in the assembly's metadata. However, the **@** symbol before the string on the second line tells the compiler that the string is a verbatim string. In effect, this tells the compiler to treat backslash characters as backslash characters instead of escape characters, making the path much more readable in your source code.

Now that you've seen how to construct a string, let's talk about some of the operations you can perform on **String** objects.

Strings Are Immutable

The most important thing to know about a **String** object is that it is immutable. That is, once created, a string can never get longer, get shorter, or have any of its characters changed. Having immutable strings offers several benefits. First, it allows you to perform operations on a string without actually changing the string:

```
if (s.ToUpperInvariant().Substring(10, 21).EndsWith("EXE")) {
   ...
}
```

Here, **ToUpperInvariant** returns a new string; it doesn't modify the characters of the string **s**. **Substring** operates on the string returned by **ToUpperInvariant** and also returns a new string, which is then examined by **EndsWith**. The two temporary strings created by **ToUpper-Invariant** and **Substring** are not referenced for long by the application code, and the garbage collector will reclaim their memory at the next collection. If you perform a lot of string manipulations, you end up creating a lot of **String** objects on the heap, which causes more frequent garbage collections, thus hurting your application's performance. To perform a lot of string manipulations efficiently, use the **StringBuilder** class.

Having immutable strings also means that there are no thread synchronization issues when manipulating or accessing a string. In addition, it's possible for the CLR to share multiple identical **String** contents through a single **String** object. This can reduce the number of strings in the system—thereby conserving memory usage—and it is what string interning (discussed later in the chapter) is all about.

For performance reasons, the **String** type is tightly integrated with the CLR. Specifically, the CLR knows the exact layout of the fields defined within the **String** type, and the CLR accesses these fields directly. This performance and direct access come at a small development cost: the **String** class is sealed. If you were able to define your own type, using **String** as a base type, you could add your own fields, which would break the CLR's assumptions. In addition, you could break some assumptions that the CLR team has made about **string** objects being immutable.

Comparing Strings

Comparing is probably the most common operation performed on strings. There are two reasons to compare two strings with each other. We compare two strings to determine equality or to sort them (usually for presentation to a user).

In determining string equality or when comparing strings for sorting, I highly recommend that you call one of these methods (defined by the **String** class):

```
Boolean Equals(String value, StringComparison comparisonType)
static Boolean Equals(String a, String b,
   StringComparison comparisonType)

static Int32 Compare(String strA, String strB,
   StringComparison comparisonType)
static Int32 Compare(string strA, string strB,
   Boolean ignoreCase, CultureInfo culture)
```

```
static Int32 Compare(String strA, Int32 indexA,
    String strB, Int32 indexB, Int32 length, StringComparison comparisonType)
static Int32 Compare(String strA, Int32 indexA, String strB,
    Int32 indexB, Int32 length, Boolean ignoreCase, CultureInfo culture)

Boolean StartsWith(String value, StringComparison comparisonType)
Boolean StartsWith(String value,
    Boolean ignoreCase, CultureInfo culture)

Boolean EndsWith(String value, StringComparison comparisonType)
Boolean EndsWith(String value, Boolean ignoreCase, CultureInfo culture)
```

When sorting, you should always perform case-sensitive comparisons. The reason is that if two strings differing only by case are considered to be equal, they could be ordered differently each time you sort them; this would confuse the user.

The **comparisonType** argument (in most of the methods shown above) is one of the values defined by the **StringComparison** enumerated type, which is defined as follows:

```
public enum StringComparison {
    CurrentCulture = 0,
    CurrentCultureIgnoreCase = 1,
    InvariantCulture = 2,
    InvariantCultureIgnoreCase = 3,
    Ordinal = 4,
    OrdinalIgnoreCase = 5
}
```

Many programs use strings for internal programmatic purposes such as path names, file names, URLs, registry keys and values, environment variables, reflection, XML tags, XML attributes, and so on. Often, these strings are not shown to a user and are used only within the program. When comparing programmatic strings, you should always use **StringComparison.Ordinal** or **StringComparison.OrdinalIgnoreCase**. This is the fastest way to perform a comparison that is not to be affected in any linguistic way because culture information is not taken into account when performing the comparison.

On the other hand, when you want to compare strings in a linguistically correct manner (usually for display to an end user), you should use **StringComparison.CurrentCulture** or **StringComparison.CurrentCultureIgnoreCase**.

Important   For the most part, **StringComparison.InvariantCulture** and **StringComparison.InvariantCultureIgnoreCase** should not be used. Although these values cause the comparison to be linguistically correct, using them to compare programmatic strings takes longer than performing an ordinal comparison. Furthermore, the invariant culture is culture agnostic, which makes it an incorrect choice when working with strings that you want to show to an end user.

> **Important**   If you want to change the case of a string's characters before performing an ordinal comparison, you should use `String`'s `ToUpperInvariant` or `ToLowerInvariant` method. When normalizing strings, it is highly recommended that you use `ToUpperInvariant` instead of `ToLowerInvariant` because Microsoft has optimized the code for performing uppercase comparisons. In fact, the FCL normalizes strings to uppercase prior to performing case-insensitive comparisons.

Sometimes, when you compare strings in a linguistically correct manner, you want to specify a specific culture rather than use a culture that is associated with the calling thread. In this case, you can use the overloads of the `StartsWith`, `EndsWith`, and `Compare` methods shown earlier, all of which take `Boolean` and `CultureInfo` arguments.

> **Important**   The `String` type defines several overloads of the `Equals`, `StartsWith`, `EndsWith`, and `Compare` methods in addition to the versions shown earlier. Microsoft recommends that these other versions (not shown in this book) be avoided. Furthermore, `String`'s other comparison methods—`CompareTo` (required by the `IComparable` interface), `CompareOrdinal`, and the `==` and `!=` operators—should also be avoided. The reason for avoiding these methods and operators is because the caller does not explicitly indicate how the string comparison should be performed, and you cannot determine from the name of the method what the default comparison will be. For example, by default, `CompareTo` performs a culture-sensitive comparison, whereas `Equals` performs an ordinal comparison. Your code will be easier to read and maintain if you always indicate explicitly how you want to perform your string comparisons.

Now, let's talk about how to perform linguistically correct comparisons. The .NET Framework uses the `System.Globalization.CultureInfo` type to represent a language/country pair (as described by the RFC 1766 standard). For example, "en-US" identifies English as written in the United States, "en-AU" identifies English as written in Australia, and "de-DE" identifies German as written in Germany. In the CLR, every thread has two properties associated with it. Each of these properties refers to a `CultureInfo` object. The two properties are:

- `CurrentUICulture`   This property is used to obtain resources that are shown to an end user. It is most useful for Windows Forms or Web Forms applications because it indicates the language that should be used when displaying UI elements such as labels and buttons. When retrieving resources, only the language part inside the `CultureInfo` object is used; the country part is ignored. By default, when you create a thread, this thread property is set to a `CultureInfo` object that identifies the language of the Windows version the application is running on using the Win32 `GetUserDefaultUI-Language` function. If you're running an MUI (Multilingual User Interface) version of Windows, you can set this via the "Regional and Language Options" Control Panel Settings dialog box.

■ **CurrentCulture**   This property is used for everything that **CurrentUICulture** isn't used for, including number and date formatting, string casing, and string comparing. When formatting, both the language and country parts of the **CultureInfo** object are used. By default, when you create a thread, this thread property is set to a **CultureInfo** object, whose value is determined by calling the Win32 **GetUserDefaultLCID** method, whose value is also set in the Regional Options tab of the Regional and Language Options application in Windows Control Panel.

In many applications, the thread's **CurrentUICulture** and **CurrentCulture** properties will be set to the same **CultureInfo** object, which means that they both use the same language/country information. However, they can be set differently. For example: an application running in the United States could use Spanish for all of its menu items and other GUI elements while properly displaying all of the currency and date formatting for the United States. To do this, the thread's **CurrentUICulture** property should be set to a **CultureInfo** object initialized with a language of "es" (for Spanish) while the thread's **CurrentCulture** property should be set to a **CultureInfo** object initialized with a language/country pair of "en-US".

Internally, a **CultureInfo** object refers to a **System.Globalization.CompareInfo** object, which encapsulates the culture's character sorting table information as defined by the Unicode standard. These tables are part of the .NET Framework itself, and therefore, all versions of the .NET Framework (regardless of underlying operating system platform) will compare and sort the strings in the same way.

The following code demonstrates the difference between performing an ordinal comparison and a culturally aware string comparison:

```
using System;
using System.Globalization;

public static class Program {
    public static void Main() {
        String s1 = "Strasse";
        String s2 = "Straße";
        Boolean eq;

        // CompareOrdinal returns nonzero.
        eq = String.Compare(s1, s2, StringComparison.Ordinal) == 0;
        Console.WriteLine("Ordinal   comparison: '{0}' {2} '{1}'", s1, s2,
            eq ? "==" : "!=");

        // Compare Strings appropriately for people
        // who speak German (de) in Germany (DE)
        CultureInfo ci = new CultureInfo("de-DE");

        // Compare returns zero.
        eq = String.Compare(s1, s2, true, ci) == 0;
        Console.WriteLine("Cultural comparison: '{0}' {2} '{1}'", s1, s2,
            eq ? "==" : "!=");
    }
}
```

Building and running this code produces the following output:

```
Ordinal  comparison: 'Strasse' != 'Straße'
Cultural comparison: 'Strasse' == 'Straße'
```

> **Note** When the **Compare** method is not performing an ordinal comparison, it performs *character expansions*. A character expansion is when a character is expanded to multiple characters regardless of culture. In the above case, the German *Eszet* character 'ß' is always expanded to 'ss.' Similarly, the 'Æ' ligature character is always expanded to 'AE.' So in the code example, the second call to **Compare** will always return 0 regardless of which culture I actually pass in to it.

In some rare circumstances, you may need to have even more control when comparing strings for equality or for sorting. This could be necessary when comparing strings consisting of Japanese characters. This additional control can be accessed via the **CultureInfo** object's **CompareInfo** property. As mentioned earlier, a **CompareInfo** object encapsulates a culture's character comparison tables, and there is just one **CompareInfo** object per culture.

When you call **String**'s **Compare** method, if the caller specifies a culture, the specified culture is used, or if no culture is specified, the value in the calling thread's **CurrentCulture** property is used. Internally, the **Compare** method obtains the reference to the **CompareInfo** object for the appropriate culture and calls the **Compare** method of the **CompareInfo** object, passing along the appropriate options (such as case insensitivity). Naturally, you could call the **Compare** method of a specific **CompareInfo** object yourself if you need the additional control.

The **Compare** method of the **CompareInfo** type takes as a parameter a value from the **Compare-Options** enumerated type, which defines the following symbols: **IgnoreCase**, **IgnoreKanaType**, **IgnoreNonSpace**, **IgnoreSymbols**, **IgnoreWidth**, **None**, **Ordinal**, and **StringSort**. These symbols represent bit flags that you can OR together to gain significantly greater control when performing string comparisons. For a complete description of these symbols, consult the .NET Framework documentation.

The following code demonstrates how important culture is to sorting strings and shows various ways of performing string comparisons:

```
using System;
using System.Text;
using System.Windows.Forms;
using System.Globalization;
using System.Threading;

public sealed class Program {
    public static void Main() {
        String output = String.Empty;
        String[] symbol = new String[] { "<", "=", ">" };
        Int32 x;
        CultureInfo ci;
```

```
// The code below demonstrates how strings compare
// differently for different cultures.
String s1 = "coté";
String s2 = "côte";

// Sorting strings for French in France.
ci = new CultureInfo("fr-FR");
x = Math.Sign(ci.CompareInfo.Compare(s1, s2));
output += String.Format("{0} Compare: {1} {3} {2}",
    ci.Name, s1, s2, symbol[x + 1]);
output += Environment.NewLine;

// Sorting strings for Japanese in Japan.
ci = new CultureInfo("ja-JP");
x = Math.Sign(ci.CompareInfo.Compare(s1, s2));
output += String.Format("{0} Compare: {1} {3} {2}",
    ci.Name, s1, s2, symbol[x + 1]);
output += Environment.NewLine;

// Sorting strings for the thread's culture
ci = Thread.CurrentThread.CurrentCulture;
x = Math.Sign(ci.CompareInfo.Compare(s1, s2));
output += String.Format("{0} Compare: {1} {3} {2}",
    ci.Name, s1, s2, symbol[x + 1]);
output += Environment.NewLine + Environment.NewLine;

// The code below demonstrates how to use CompareInfo.Compare's
// advanced options with 2 Japanese strings. One string represents
// the word "shinkansen" (the name for the Japanese high-speed
// train) in hiragana (one subtype of Japanese writing), and the
// other represents the same word in katakana (another subtype of
// Japanese writing).
s1 = "しんかんせん";  // ("\u3057\u3093\u304b\u3093\u305b\u3093")
s2 = "シンカンセン";  // ("\u30b7\u30f3\u30ab\u30f3\u30bb\u30f3")

// Here is the result of a default comparison
ci = new CultureInfo("ja-JP");
x = Math.Sign(String.Compare(s1, s2, true, ci));
output += String.Format("Simple {0} Compare: {1} {3} {2}",
    ci.Name, s1, s2, symbol[x + 1]);
output += Environment.NewLine;

// Here is the result of a comparison that ignores
// kana type (a type of Japanese writing)
CompareInfo compareInfo = CompareInfo.GetCompareInfo("ja-JP");
x = Math.Sign(compareInfo.Compare(s1, s2, CompareOptions.IgnoreKanaType));
output += String.Format("Advanced {0} Compare: {1} {3} {2}",
    ci.Name, s1, s2, symbol[x + 1]);

MessageBox.Show(output, "Comparing Strings For Sorting");
    }
}
```

Building and running this code produces the output shown in Figure 11-1.

Figure 11-1   String sorting results

Japanese Characters

To see Japanese characters in the source code and in the message box, Windows must have the East Asian Language files installed (which use approximately 230 MB of disk space). To install these files, open the Regional And Language Options dialog box (shown in Figure 11-2) in Control Panel, and on the Languages tab, select the Install Files For East Asian Languages check box, and then click OK. This causes Windows to install the East Asian language fonts and Input Method Editor (IME) files.

Figure 11-2   Installing East Asian Language files by using the Regional and Language Options Control Panel dialog box

Also, the source code file can't be saved in ANSI; I used UTF-8, which the Microsoft Visual Studio editor and Microsoft's C# compiler handle just fine.

In addition to **Compare**, the **CompareInfo** class offers the **IndexOf**, **LastIndexOf**, **IsPrefix**, and **IsSuffix** methods. Because all of these methods offer overloads that take a **CompareOptions** enumeration value as a parameter, they give you more control than the **Compare**, **IndexOf**, **LastIndexOf**, **StartsWith**, and **EndsWith** methods defined by the **String** class. Also, you should be aware that the FCL includes a **System.StringComparer** class that you can also use for performing string comparisons. This class is useful when you want to perform the same kind of comparison repeatedly for many different strings.

String Interning

As I said in the preceding section, checking strings for equality is a common operation for many applications—this task can hurt performance significantly. When performing an ordinal equality check, the CLR quickly tests to see if both strings have the same number of characters. If they don't, the strings are definitely not equal; if they do, the strings might be equal, and the CLR must then compare each individual character to determine for sure. When performing a culturally aware comparison, the CLR must always compare all of the individual characters because strings of different lengths might be considered equal.

In addition, if you have several instances of the same string duplicated in memory, you're wasting memory because strings are immutable. You'll use memory much more efficiently if there is just one instance of the string in memory and all variables needing to refer to the string can just point to the single string object.

If your application frequently compares strings for equality using case-sensitive, ordinal comparisons, or if you expect to have many string objects with the same value, you can enhance performance substantially if you take advantage of the *string interning* mechanism in the CLR. When the CLR initializes, it creates an internal hash table in which the keys are strings and the values are references to **string** objects in the managed heap. Initially, the table is empty (of course). The **string** class offers two methods that allow you to access this internal hash table:

```
public static String Intern(String str);
public static String IsInterned(String str);
```

The first method, **Intern**, takes a **String**, obtains a hash code for it, and checks the internal hash table for a match. If an identical string already exists, a reference to the already existing **String** object is returned. If an identical string doesn't exist, a copy of the string is made, the copy is added to the internal hash table, and a reference to this copy is returned. If the application no longer holds a reference to the original **String** object, the garbage collector is able to free the memory of that string. Note that the garbage collector can't free the strings that the internal hash table refers to because the hash table holds the reference to those **String** objects. **string** objects referred to by the internal hash table can't be freed until the AppDomain is unloaded or the process terminates.

As does the **Intern** method, the **IsInterned** method takes a **String** and looks it up in the internal hash table. If a matching string is in the hash table, **IsInterned** returns a reference to the interned string object. If a matching string isn't in the hash table, however, **IsInterned** returns **null**; it doesn't add the string to the hash table.

By default, when an assembly is loaded, the CLR interns all of the literal strings described in the assembly's metadata. Microsoft learned that this hurts performance significantly due to the additional hash table lookups, so it is now possible to turn this "feature" off. If an assembly is marked with a **System.Runtime.CompilerServices.CompilationRelaxationsAttribute** specifying the **System.Runtime.CompilerServices.CompilationRelaxations.NoString-Interning** flag value, the CLR *may*, according to the ECMA specification, choose not to intern all of the strings defined in that assembly's metadata. Note that, in an attempt to improve your application's performance, the C# compiler always specifies this attribute/flag whenever you compile an assembly.

Even if an assembly has this attribute/flag specified, the CLR may chose to intern the strings, but you should not count on this. In fact, you really should never write code that relies on strings being interned unless you have written code that explicitly calls the **String**'s **Intern** method yourself. The following code demonstrates string interning:

```
String s1 = "Hello";
String s2 = "Hello";
Console.WriteLine(Object.ReferenceEquals(s1, s2));    // Should be 'False'

s1 = String.Intern(s1);
s2 = String.Intern(s2);
Console.WriteLine(Object.ReferenceEquals(s1, s2));    // 'True'
```

In the first call to the **ReferenceEquals** method, **s1** refers to a **"Hello"** string object in the heap, and **s2** refers to a different **"Hello"** string object in the heap. Since the references are different, **False** should be displayed. However, if you run this on version 2.0 of the CLR, you'll see that **True** is displayed. The reason is because this version of the CLR chooses to ignore the attribute/flag emitted by the C# compiler, and the CLR interns the literal **"Hello"** string when the assembly is loaded into the AppDomain. This means that **s1** and **s2** refer to the single **"Hello"** string in the heap. However, as mentioned previously, you should never write code that relies on this behavior because a future version of the CLR might honor the attribute/flag and not intern the **"Hello"** string. In fact, version 2.0 of the CLR does honor the attribute/flag when this assembly's code has been compiled using the NGen.exe utility.

Before the second call to the **ReferenceEquals** method, the **"Hello"** string has been explicitly interned, and **s1** now refers to an interned **"Hello"**. Then by calling **Intern** again, **s2** is set to refer to the same **"Hello"** string as **s1**. Now, when **ReferenceEquals** is called the second time, we are guaranteed to get a result of **True** regardless of whether the assembly was compiled with the attribute/flag.

So now, let's look at an example to see how you can use string interning to improve performance and reduce memory usage. The **NumTimesWordAppearsEquals** method below takes two arguments: a word and an array of strings in which each array element refers to a single word. This method then determines how many times the specified word appears in the word list and returns this count:

```
private static Int32 NumTimesWordAppearsEquals(String word, String[] wordlist) {
    Int32 count = 0;
    for (Int32 wordnum = 0; wordnum < wordlist.Length; wordnum++) {
        if (word.Equals(wordlist[wordnum], StringComparison.Ordinal))
            count++;
    }
    return count;
}
```

As you can see, this method calls **String**'s **Equals** method, which internally compares the strings' individual characters and checks to ensure that all characters match. This comparison can be slow. In addition, the wordlist array might have multiple entries that refer to multiple **String** objects containing the same set of characters. This means that multiple identical strings might exist in the heap and are surviving ongoing garbage collections.

Now, let's look at a version of this method that was written to take advantage of string interning:

```
private static Int32 NumTimesWordAppearsIntern(String word, String[] wordlist) {
    // This method assumes that all entries in wordlist refer to interned strings.
    word = String.Intern(word);
    Int32 count = 0;
    for (Int32 wordnum = 0; wordnum < wordlist.Length; wordnum++) {
        if (Object.ReferenceEquals(word, wordlist[wordnum]))
            count++;
    }
    return count;
}
```

This method interns the word and assumes that the wordlist contains references to interned strings. First, this version might be saving memory if a word appears in the word list multiple times because, in this version, **wordlist** would now contain multiple references to the same single **String** object in the heap. Second, this version will be faster because determining if the specified word is in the array is simply a matter of comparing pointers.

Although the **NumTimesWordAppearsIntern** method is faster than the **NumTimesWordAppears-Equals** method, the overall performance of the application might be slower when using the **NumTimesWordAppearsIntern** method because of the time it takes to intern all of the strings when they were added to the **wordlist** array (code not shown). The **NumTimesWordAppears-Intern** method will really show its performance and memory improvement if the application needs to call the method multiple times using the same wordlist. The point of this discussion is to make it clear that string interning is useful, but it should be used with care and caution. In fact, this is why the C# compiler indicates that it doesn't want string interning to be enabled.

String Pooling

When compiling source code, your compiler must process each literal string and emit the string into the managed module's metadata. If the same literal string appears several times in your source code, emitting all of these strings into the metadata will bloat the size of the resulting file.

To remove this bloat, many compilers (include the C# compiler) write the literal string into the module's metadata only once. All code that references the string will be modified to refer to the one string in the metadata. This ability of a compiler to merge multiple occurrences of a single string into a single instance can reduce the size of a module substantially. This process is nothing new—C/C++ compilers have been doing it for years. (Microsoft's C/C++ compiler calls this *string pooling*.) Even so, string pooling is another way to improve the performance of strings and just one more piece of knowledge that you should have in your repertoire.

Examining a String's Characters and Text Elements

Although comparing strings is useful for sorting them or for detecting equality, sometimes you need just to examine the characters within a string. The **string** type offers several properties and methods to help you do this, including **Length**, **Chars** (an indexer in C#), **GetEnumerator**, **ToCharArray**, **Contains**, **IndexOf**, **LastIndexOf**, **IndexOfAny**, and **LastIndexOfAny**.

In reality, a **System.Char** represents a single 16-bit Unicode code value that doesn't necessarily equate to an abstract Unicode character. For example, some abstract Unicode characters are a combination of two code values. When combined, the U+0625 (Arabic letter *Alef* with *Hamza* below) and U+0650 (Arabic *Kasra*) characters form a single abstract character or *text element*.

In addition, some Unicode text elements require more than a 16-bit value to represent them. These text elements are represented using two 16-bit code values. The first code value is called the *high surrogate,* and the second code value is called the *low surrogate*. High surrogates have a value between U+D800 and U+DBFF, and low surrogates have a value between U+DC00 and U+DFFF. The use of surrogates allows Unicode to express more than a million different characters.

Surrogates are rarely used in the United States and Europe but are more commonly used in East Asia. To properly work with text elements, you should use the **System.Globalization .StringInfo** type. The easiest way to use this type is to construct an instance of it, passing its constructor a string. Then you can see how many text elements are in the string by querying the **StringInfo**'s **LengthInTextElements** property. You can then call **StringInfo**'s **Substring-ByTextElements** method to extract the text element or the number of consecutive text elements that you desire.

In addition, the **StringInfo** class offers a static **GetTextElementEnumerator** method, which acquires a **System.Globalization.TextElementEnumerator** object that allows you to enumerate through all of the abstract Unicode characters contained in the string. Finally, you could call **StringInfo**'s static **ParseCombiningCharacters** method to obtain an array of **Int32** values. The length of the array indicates how many text elements are contained in the string. Each element of the array identifies an index into the string where the first code value for a new text element can be found.

The following code demonstrates the various ways of using the **StringInfo** class to manipulate a string's text elements:

```
using System;
using System.Text;
using System.Globalization;
using System.Windows.Forms;


public sealed class Program {
    public static void Main() {
        // The string below contains combining characters
        String s = "a\u0304\u0308bc\u0327";
```

```
    SubstringByTextElements(s);
    EnumTextElements(s);
    EnumTextElementIndexes(s);
}

private static void SubstringByTextElements(String s) {
    String output = String.Empty;

    StringInfo si = new StringInfo(s);
    for (Int32 element = 0; element < si.LengthInTextElements; element++) {
        output += String.Format(
            "Text element {0} is '{1}'{2}",
            element, si.SubstringByTextElements(element, 1),
            Environment.NewLine);
    }
    MessageBox.Show(output, "Result of SubstringByTextElements");
}

private static void EnumTextElements(String s) {
    String output = String.Empty;

    TextElementEnumerator charEnum =
        StringInfo.GetTextElementEnumerator(s);
    while (charEnum.MoveNext()) {
        output += String.Format(
            "Character at index {0} is '{1}'{2}",
            charEnum.ElementIndex, charEnum.GetTextElement(),
            Environment.NewLine);
    }
    MessageBox.Show(output, "Result of GetTextElementEnumerator");
}

private static void EnumTextElementIndexes(String s) {
    String output = String.Empty;

    Int32[] textElemIndex = StringInfo.ParseCombiningCharacters(s);
    for (Int32 i = 0; i < textElemIndex.Length; i++) {
        output += String.Format(
            "Character {0} starts at index {1}{2}",
            i, textElemIndex[i], Environment.NewLine);
    }
    MessageBox.Show(output, "Result of ParseCombiningCharacters");
}
}
```

Building and running this code produces the message boxes shown in Figures 11-3, 11-4, and 11-5.

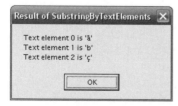

Figure 11-3 Result of `SubstringByTextElements`

Figure 11-4   Result of `GetTextElementEnumerator`

Figure 11-5   Result of `ParseCombiningCharacters`

> **Note**   To see the message box text in Figures 11-3 and 11-4 correctly, I had to open the
> Display Properties dialog box in Control Panel, and on the Appearance tab, click the Advanced
> button to change the font used by message box text to Lucida Sans Unicode because this font
> contains glyphs for these combining characters. This is also why I don't have the code display
> the results to the console.

Other String Operations

The `string` type also offers methods that allow you to copy a string or parts of it. Table 11-1
summarizes these methods.

Table 11-1   Methods for Copying Strings

Member	Method Type	Description
`Clone`	Instance	Returns a reference to the same object (`this`). This is OK because `String` objects are immutable. This method implements `String`'s `ICloneable` interface.
`Copy`	Static	Returns a new duplicate string of the specified string. This method is rarely used and exists to help applications that treat strings as tokens. Normally, strings with the same set of characters are interned to a single string. This method creates a new string object so that the references (pointers) are different even though the strings contain the same characters.
`CopyTo`	Instance	Copies a portion of the string's characters to an array of characters.
`Substring`	Instance	Returns a new string that represents a portion of the original string.
`ToString`	Instance	Returns a reference to the same object (`this`).

In addition to these methods, `string` offers many static and instance methods that manipulate a string, such as `Insert`, `Remove`, `PadLeft`, `Replace`, `Split`, `Join`, `ToLower`, `ToUpper`, `Trim`,
`Concat`, `Format`, and so on. Again, the important thing to remember about all of these methods

is that they return new string objects; because strings are immutable, once they're created, they can't be modified (using safe code).

Dynamically Constructing a String Efficiently

Because the **String** type represents an immutable string, the FCL provides another type, **System.Text.StringBuilder**, which allows you to perform dynamic operations efficiently with strings and characters to create a **String**. Think of **StringBuilder** as a fancy constructor to create a **String** that can be used with the rest of the framework. In general, you should design methods that take **String** parameters, not **StringBuilder** parameters, unless you define a method that "returns" a string dynamically constructed by the method itself.

Logically, a **StringBuilder** object contains a field that refers to an array of **Char** structures. **StringBuilder**'s members allow you to manipulate this character array, effectively shrinking the string or changing the characters in the string. If you grow the string past the allocated array of characters, the **StringBuilder** automatically allocates a new, larger array, copies the characters, and starts using the new array. The previous array is garbage collected.

When finished using the **StringBuilder** object to construct your string, "convert" the **String-Builder**'s character array into a **String** simply by calling the **StringBuilder**'s **ToString** method. Internally, this method just returns a reference to the string field maintained inside the **StringBuilder**. This makes the **StringBuilder**'s **ToString** method very fast because the array of characters isn't copied.

The **String** returned from **StringBuilder**'s **ToString** method must not be changed. So if you ever call a method that attempts to modify the string field maintained by the **StringBuilder**, the **StringBuilder**'s methods will have the information that **ToString** was called on the string field and they will internally create and use a new character array, allowing you to perform manipulations without affecting the string returned by the previous call to **ToString**.

Constructing a StringBuilder Object

Unlike with the **String** class, the CLR has no special information about the **StringBuilder** class. In addition, most languages (including C#) don't consider the **StringBuilder** class to be a primitive type. You construct a **StringBuilder** object as you would any other nonprimitive type:

```
StringBuilder sb = new StringBuilder();
```

The **StringBuilder** type offers many constructors. The job of each constructor is to allocate and initialize the state maintained by each **StringBuilder** object:

- **Maximum capacity** An **Int32** value that specifies the maximum number of characters that can be placed in the string. The default is **Int32.MaxValue** (approximately 2 billion). It's unusual to change this value. However, you might specify a smaller maximum capacity to ensure that you never create a string over a certain length. Once constructed, a **StringBuilder**'s maximum capacity value can't be changed.

- **Capacity**   An **Int32** value indicating the size of the character array being maintained by the **StringBuilder**. The default is 16. If you have some idea of how many characters you'll place in the **StringBuilder**, you should use this number to set the capacity when constructing the **StringBuilder** object.

  When appending characters to the character array, the **StringBuilder** detects if the array is trying to grow beyond the array's capacity. If it is, the **StringBuilder** automatically doubles the capacity field, allocates a new array (the size of the new capacity), and copies the characters from the original array into the new array. The original array will be garbage collected in the future. Dynamically growing the array hurts performance; avoid this by setting a good initial capacity.

- **Character array**   An array of **Char** structures that maintains the set of characters in the "string." The number of characters is always less than or equal to the capacity and maximum capacity values. You can use the **StringBuilder**'s **Length** property to obtain the number of characters used in the array. The **Length** is always less than or equal to the **StringBuilder**'s capacity value. When constructing a **StringBuilder**, you can pass a **String** to initialize the character array. If you don't specify a string, the array initially contains no characters—that is, the **Length** property returns **0**.

StringBuilder Members

Unlike a **String**, a **StringBuilder** represents a mutable string. This means that most of **StringBuilder**'s members change the contents in the array of characters and don't cause new objects to be allocated on the managed heap. A **StringBuilder** allocates a new object on only two occasions:

- You dynamically build a string whose length is longer than the capacity you've set.

- You attempt to modify the array after **StringBuilder**'s **ToString** method has been called.

Table 11-2 summarizes **StringBuilder**'s members.

Table 11-2   **StringBuilder** **Members**

Member	Member Type	Description
MaxCapacity	Read-only property	Returns the largest number of characters that can be placed in the string.
Capacity	Read/write property	Gets or sets the size of the character array. Trying to set the capacity smaller than the string's length or bigger than **MaxCapacity** throws an **ArgumentOutOfRange-Exception**.
EnsureCapacity	Method	Guarantees that the character array is at least the size specified. If the value passed is larger than the **StringBuilder**'s current capacity, the current capacity increases. If the current capacity is already larger than the value passed to this property, no change occurs.

Table 11-2 `StringBuilder` **Members**

Member	Member Type	Description
`Length`	Read/write property	Gets or sets the number of characters in the "string." This will likely be smaller than the character array's current capacity. Setting this property to 0 resets the `StringBuilder`'s contents to an empty string.
`ToString`	Method	The parameterless version of this method returns a `String` representing the `StringBuilder`'s character array. This method is efficient because it doesn't create a new `String` object. Any attempt to modify the `StringBuilder`'s array causes the `StringBuilder` to allocate and use a new array (initializing it from the old array). The version of `ToString` that takes `startIndex` and `length` parameters creates a new `String` object representing the desired portion of the `StringBuilder`'s string.
`Chars`	Read/write indexer property	Gets or sets the character at the specified index into the character array. In C#, this is an indexer (parameterful property) that you access using array syntax (`[]`).
`Append`	Method	Appends a single object to the end of the character array, growing the array if necessary. The object is converted to a string by using the general format and the culture associated with the calling thread.
`Insert`	Method	Inserts a single object into the character array, growing the array if necessary. The object is converted to a string by using the general format and the culture associated with the calling thread.
`AppendFormat`	Method	Appends the specified objects to the end of the character array, growing the array if necessary. The objects are converted to strings by using the formatting and culture information provided by the caller. `Append-Format` is one of the most common methods used with `StringBuilder` objects.
`AppendLine`	Method	Appends a blank line or a string with a blank line to the end of the character array, increasing the capacity of the array if necessary.
`Replace`	Method	Replaces one character with another or one string with another from within the character array.
`Remove`	Method	Removes a range of characters from the character array.
`Equals`	Method	Returns `true` only if both `StringBuilder` objects have the same maximum capacity, capacity, and characters in the array.
`CopyTo`	Method	Copies a subset of the `StringBuilder`'s characters to a `Char` array.

One important thing to note about **StringBuilder**'s methods is that most of them return a reference to the same **StringBuilder** object. This allows a convenient syntax to chain several operations together:

```
StringBuilder sb = new StringBuilder();
String s = sb.AppendFormat("{0} {1}", "Jeffrey", "Richter").
   Replace(' ', '-').Remove(4, 3).ToString();
Console.WriteLine(s);  // "Jeff-Richter"
```

You'll notice that the **String** and **StringBuilder** classes don't have full method parity; that is, **String** has **ToLower**, **ToUpper**, **EndsWith**, **PadLeft**, **PadRight**, **Trim**, and so on. The **String-Builder** class doesn't offer any of these methods. On the other hand, the **StringBuilder** class offers a richer **Replace** method that allows you to replace characters or strings in a portion of the string (not the whole string). It's unfortunate that there isn't complete parity between these two classes because now you must convert between **String** and **StringBuilder** to accomplish certain tasks. For example, to build up a string, convert all characters to uppercase, and then insert a string requires code like this:

```
// Construct a StringBuilder to perform string manipulations.
StringBuilder sb = new StringBuilder();

// Perform some string manipulations by using the StringBuilder.
sb.AppendFormat("{0} {1}", "Jeffrey", "Richter").Replace(" ", "-");

// Convert the StringBuilder to a String in
// order to uppercase all the characters.
String s = sb.ToString().ToUpper();

// Clear the StringBuilder (allocates a new Char array).
sb.Length = 0;

// Load the uppercase String into the StringBuilder,
// and perform more manipulations.
sb.Append(s).Insert(8, "Marc-");

// Convert the StringBuilder back to a String.
s = sb.ToString();

// Display the String to the user.
Console.WriteLine(s);  // "JEFFREY-Marc-RICHTER"
```

It's inconvenient and inefficient to have to write this code just because **StringBuilder** doesn't offer all of the operations that **String** does. In the future, I hope that Microsoft will add more string operation methods to **StringBuilder** to make it a more complete class.

Obtaining a String Representation of an Object

You frequently need to obtain a string representation of an object. Usually, this is necessary when you want to display a numeric type (such as **Byte**, **Int32**, and **Single**) or a **DateTime** object to the user. Because the .NET Framework is an object-oriented platform, every type is responsible for providing code that converts an instance's value to a string equivalent. When designing how types should accomplish this, the designers of the FCL devised a pattern that would be used consistently throughout. In this section, I'll describe this pattern.

You can obtain a string representation for any object by calling the **ToString** method. A public, virtual, parameterless **ToString** method is defined by **System.Object** and is therefore callable using an instance of any type. Semantically, **ToString** returns a string representing the object's current value, and this string should be formatted for the calling thread's current culture; that is, the string representation of a number should use the proper decimal separator, digit-grouping symbol, and other elements associated with the culture assigned to the calling thread.

System.Object's implementation of **ToString** simply returns the full name of the object's type. This value isn't particularly useful, but it is a reasonable default for the many types that can't offer a sensible string. For example, what should a string representation of a **FileStream** or a **Hashtable** object look like?

All types that want to offer a reasonable way to obtain a string representing the current value of the object should override the **ToString** method. All base types built into the FCL (**Byte**, **Int32**, **UInt64**, **Double**, and so on) override their **ToString** method and return a culturally aware string.

Specific Formats and Cultures

The parameterless **ToString** method has two problems. First, the caller has no control over the formatting of the string. For example, an application might want to format a number into a currency string, decimal string, percent string, or hexadecimal string. Second, the caller can't easily choose to format a string by using a specific culture. This second problem is more troublesome for server-side application code than for client-side code. On rare occasions, an application needs to format a string by using a culture other than the culture associated with the calling thread. To have more control over string formatting, you need a version of the **ToString** method that allows you to specify precise formatting and culture information.

Types that offer the caller a choice in formatting and culture implement the **System.IFormattable** interface:

```
public interface IFormattable {
    String ToString(String format, IFormatProvider formatProvider);
}
```

In the FCL, all of the base types (**Byte**, **SByte**, **Int16/UInt16**, **Int32/UInt32**, **Int64/UInt64**, **Single**, **Double**, **Decimal**, and **DateTime**) implement this interface. In addition, some other types, such as **GUID**, implement it. Finally, every enumerated type definition will automatically implement the **IFormattable** interface so that a meaningful string symbol from an instance of the enumerated type can be obtained.

IFormattable's **ToString** method takes two parameters. The first, **format**, is a string that tells the method how the object should be formatted. **ToString**'s second parameter, **formatProvider**, is an instance of a type that implements the **System.IFormatProvider** interface. This type supplies specific culture information to the **ToString** method. I'll discuss how shortly.

The type implementing the **IFormattable** interface's **ToString** method determines which format strings it's going to recognize. If you pass a format string that the type doesn't recognize, the type is supposed to throw a **System.FormatException**.

Many of the types Microsoft has defined in the FCL recognize several formats. For example, the **DateTime** type supports "d" for short date, "D" for long date, "g" for general, "M" for month/day, "s" for sortable, "T" for time, "u" for universal time in ISO 8601 format, "U" for universal time in long date format, "Y" for year/month, and others. All enumerated types support "G" for general, "F" for flags, "D" decimal, and "X" for hexadecimal. I'll cover formatting enumerated types in more detail in Chapter 12, "Enumerated Types and Bit Flags."

Also, all of the built-in numeric types support "C" for currency, "D" for decimal, "E" for exponential (scientific) notation, "F" for fixed-point, "G" for general, "N" for number, "P" for percent, "R" for round-trip, and "X" for hexadecimal. In fact, the numeric types also support picture format strings just in case the simple format strings don't offer you exactly what you're looking for. Picture format strings contain special characters that tell the type's **ToString** method exactly how many digits to show, exactly where to place a decimal separator, exactly how many digits to place after the decimal separator, and so on. For complete information about format strings, see "Formatting Types" in the .NET Framework SDK.

For most types, calling **ToString** and passing **null** for the format string is identical to calling **ToString** and passing "G" for the format string. In other words, objects format themselves using the "General format" by default. When implementing a type, choose a format that you think will be the most commonly used format; this format is the "General format." By the way, the **ToString** method that takes no parameters assumes that the caller wants the "General format."

So now that format strings are out of the way, let's turn to culture information. By default, strings are formatted using the culture information associated with the calling thread. The parameterless **ToString** method certainly does this, and so does **IFormattable**'s **ToString** if you pass **null** for the **formatProvider** parameter.

Culture-sensitive information applies when you're formatting numbers (including currency, integers, floating point, percentages, dates, and times). A type that represents a **GUID** has a **ToString** method that returns only a string representing the **GUID**'s value. There's no need to consider a culture when generating the **GUID**'s string because **GUID**s are used for programmatic purposes only.

When formatting a number, the **ToString** method sees what you've passed for the **format-Provider** parameter. If **null** is passed, **ToString** determines the culture associated with the calling thread by reading the `System.Threading.Thread.CurrentThread.CurrentCulture` property. This property returns an instance of the `System.Globalization.CultureInfo` type.

Using this object, `ToString` reads its `NumberFormat` or `DateTimeFormat` property, depending on whether a number or date/time is being formatted. These properties return an instance of `System.Globalization.NumberFormatInfo` or `System.Globalization.DateTimeFormatInfo`, respectively. The `NumberFormatInfo` type defines a bunch of properties, such as `Currency-DecimalSeparator`, `CurrencySymbol`, `NegativeSign`, `NumberGroupSeparator`, and `PercentSymbol`. Likewise, the `DateTimeFormatInfo` type defines an assortment of properties, such as `Calendar`, `DateSeparator`, `DayNames`, `LongDatePattern`, `ShortTimePattern`, and `TimeSeparator`. `ToString` reads these properties when constructing and formatting a string.

When calling `IFormattable`'s `ToString` method, instead of passing `null`, you can pass a reference to an object whose type implements the `IFormatProvider` interface:

```
public interface IFormatProvider {
    Object GetFormat(Type formatType);
}
```

Here's the basic idea behind the `IFormatProvider` interface: when a type implements this interface, it is saying that an instance of the type is able to provide culture-specific formatting information and that the culture information associated with the calling thread should be ignored.

The `System.Globalization.CultureInfo` type is one of the very few types defined in the FCL that implements the `IFormatProvider` interface. If you want to format a string for, say, Vietnam, you'd construct a `CultureInfo` object and pass that object in as `ToString`'s `format-Provider` parameter. The following code obtains a string representation of a `Decimal` numeric value formatted as currency appropriate for Vietnam:

```
Decimal price = 123.54M;
String s = price.ToString("C", new CultureInfo("vi-VN"));
MessageBox.Show(s);
```

If you build and run this code, the message box shown in Figure 11-6 appears.

Figure 11-6   Numeric value formatted correctly to represent Vietnamese currency

Internally, `Decimal`'s `ToString` method sees that the `formatProvider` argument is not `null` and calls the object's `GetFormat` method as follows:

```
NumberFormatInfo nfi = (NumberFormatInfo)
    formatProvider.GetFormat(typeof(NumberFormatInfo));
```

This is how **ToString** requests the appropriate number-formatting information from the (**CultureInfo**) object. Number types (such as **Decimal**) request only number-formatting information. But other types (such as **DateTime**) could call **GetFormat** like this:

```
DateTimeFormatInfo dtfi = (DateTimeFormatInfo)
    formatProvider.GetFormat(typeof(DateTimeFormatInfo));
```

Actually, because **GetFormat**'s parameter can identify any type, the method is flexible enough to allow any type of format information to be requested. The types in version 2 of the .NET Framework call **GetFormat**, requesting only number or date/time information; in the future, other kinds of formatting information could be requested.

By the way, if you want to obtain a string for an object that isn't formatted for any particular culture, you should call **System.Globalization.CultureInfo**'s static **InvariantCulture** property and pass the object returned as **ToString**'s **formatProvider** parameter:

```
Decimal price = 123.54M;
String s = price.ToString("C", CultureInfo.InvariantCulture);
MessageBox.Show(s);
```

If you build and run this code, the message box shown in Figure 11-7 appears. Notice the first character in the resulting string: ¤. This is the international sign for currency (U+00A4).

Figure 11-7   Numeric value formatted to represent a culture-neutral currency

Normally, you wouldn't display a string formatted by using the invariant culture to a user. Typically, you'd just save this string in a data file so that it could be parsed later.

In the FCL, just three types implement the **IFormatProvider** interface. The first is **CultureInfo**, which I've already explained. The other two are **NumberFormatInfo** and **DateTimeFormatInfo**. When **GetFormat** is called on a **NumberFormatInfo** object, the method checks if the type being requested is a **NumberFormatInfo**. If it is, **this** is returned; if it's not, **null** is returned. Similarly, calling **GetFormat** on a **DateTimeFormatInfo** object returns **this** if a **DateTimeFormatInfo** is requested and **null** if it's not. These two types implement this interface simply as a programming convenience. When trying to obtain a string representation of an object, the caller commonly specifies a format and uses the culture associated with the calling thread. For this reason, you often call **ToString**, passing a string for the format parameter and **null** for the **formatProvider** parameter. To make calling **ToString** easier for you, many types offer several overloads of the **ToString** method. For example, the **Decimal** type offers four different **ToString** methods:

```
// This version calls ToString(null, null).
// Meaning: General numeric format, thread's culture information
public override String ToString();
```

```
// This version is where the actual implementation of ToString goes.
// This version implements IFormattable's ToString method.
// Meaning: Caller-specified format and culture information
public String ToString(String format, IFormatProvider formatProvider);

// This version simply calls ToString(format, null).
// Meaning: Caller-specified format, thread's culture information
public String ToString(String format);

// This version simply calls ToString(null, formatProvider).
// This version implements IConvertible's ToString method.
// Meaning: General format, caller-specified culture information
public String ToString(IFormatProvider formatProvider);
```

Formatting Multiple Objects into a Single String

So far, I've explained how an individual type formats its own objects. At times, however, you want to construct strings consisting of many formatted objects. For example, the following string has a date, a person's name, and an age:

```
String s = String.Format("On {0}, {1} is {2} years old.",
    new DateTime(2006, 4, 22, 14, 35, 5), "Aidan", 3);
Console.WriteLine(s);
```

If you build and run this code where "en-US" is the thread's current culture, you'll see the following line of output:

```
On 4/22/2006 2:35:05 PM, Aidan is 3 years old.
```

String's static **Format** method takes a format string that identifies replaceable parameters using numbers in braces. The format string used in this example tells the **Format** method to replace **{0}** with the first parameter after the format string (the date/time), replace **{1}** with the second parameter after the format string ("Aidan"), and replace **{2}** with the third parameter after the format string (3).

Internally, the **Format** method calls each object's **ToString** method to obtain a string representation for the object. Then the returned strings are all appended and the complete, final string is returned. This is all fine and good, but it means that all of the objects are formatted by using their general format and the calling thread's culture information.

You can have more control when formatting an object if you specify format information within braces. For example, the following code is identical to the previous example except that I've added formatting information to replaceable parameters 0 and 2:

```
String s = String.Format("On {0:D}, {1} is {2:E} years old.",
    new DateTime(2006, 4, 22, 14, 35, 5), "Aidan", 3);
Console.WriteLine(s);
```

If you build and run this code where "en-US" is the thread's current culture, you'll see the following line of output:

```
On Saturday, April 22, 2006, Aidan is 3.000000E+000 years old.
```

When the **Format** method parses the format string, it sees that replaceable parameter 0 should have its **IFormattable** interface's **ToString** method called passing **"D"** and **null** for its two parameters. Likewise, **Format** calls replaceable parameter 2's **IFormattable ToString** method, passing **"E"** and **null**. If the type doesn't implement the **IFormattable** interface, **Format** calls its parameterless **ToString** method inherited from **Object** (and possibly overridden), and the default format is appended into the resulting string.

The **String** class offers several overloads of the static **Format** method. One version takes an object that implements the **IFormatProvider** interface so that you can format all of the replaceable parameters by using caller-specified culture information. Obviously, **Format** calls each object's **IFormattable ToString** method, passing it whatever **IFormatProvider** object was passed to **Format**.

If you're using **StringBuilder** instead of **String** to construct a string, you can call **String-Builder**'s **AppendFormat** method. This method works exactly as **String**'s **Format** method except that it formats a string and appends to the **StringBuilder**'s character array. As does **String**'s **Format**, **AppendString** takes a format string, and there's a version that takes an **IFormatProvider**.

System.Console offers **Write** and **WriteLine** methods that also take format strings and replaceable parameters. However, there are no overloads of **Console**'s **Write** and **WriteLine** methods that allow you to pass an **IFormatProvider**. If you want to format a string for a specific culture, you have to call **String**'s **Format** method, first passing the desired **IFormat-Provider** object and then passing the resulting string to **Console**'s **Write** or **WriteLine** method. This shouldn't be a big deal because, as I said earlier, it's rare for client-side code to format a string by using a culture other than the one associated with the calling thread.

Providing Your Own Custom Formatter

By now it should be clear that the formatting capabilities in the .NET Framework were designed to offer you a great deal of flexibility and control. However, we're not quite finished. It's possible for you to define a method that **StringBuilder**'s **AppendFormat** method will call whenever any object is being formatted into a string. In other words, instead of calling **ToString** for each object, **AppendFormat** can call a function you define, allowing you to format any or all of the objects in any way you want. What I'm about to describe also works with **String**'s **Format** method.

Let me explain this mechanism by way of an example. Let's say that you're formatting HTML text that a user will view in an Internet browser. You want all **Int32** values to appear in bold. To accomplish this, every time an **Int32** value is formatted into a **String**, you want to surround the string with HTML bold tags: **<B>** and **</B>**. The following code demonstrates how easy it is to do this:

```
using System;
using System.Text;
using System.Threading;

public static class Program {
    public static void Main() {
        StringBuilder sb = new StringBuilder();
        sb.AppendFormat(new BoldInt32s(), "{0} {1} {2:M}", "Jeff", 123, DateTime.Now);
        Console.WriteLine(sb);
    }
}

internal sealed class BoldInt32s : IFormatProvider, ICustomFormatter {
    public Object GetFormat(Type formatType) {
        if (formatType == typeof(ICustomFormatter)) return this;
        return Thread.CurrentThread.CurrentCulture.GetFormat(formatType);
    }

    public String Format(String format, Object arg, IFormatProvider formatProvider) {
        String s;

        IFormattable formattable = arg as IFormattable;

        if (formattable == null) s = arg.ToString();
        else s = formattable.ToString(format, formatProvider);

        if (arg.GetType() == typeof(Int32))
            return "<B>" + s + "</B>";
        return s;
    }
}
```

When you compile and run this code where "en-US" is the thread's current culture, it displays the following output (your date may be different, of course):

```
Jeff <B>123</B> January 23
```

In **Main**, I'm constructing an empty **StringBuilder** and then appending a formatted string into it. When I call **AppendFormat**, the first parameter is an instance of the **BoldInt32s** class. This class implements the **IFormatProvider** interface that I discussed earlier. In addition, this class implements the **ICustomFormatter** interface:

```
public interface ICustomFormatter {
    String Format(String format, Object arg,
        IFormatProvider formatProvider);
}
```

This interface's **Format** method is called whenever **StringBuilder**'s **AppendFormat** needs to obtain a string for an object. You can do some pretty clever things inside this method that give you a great deal of control over string formatting. Let's look inside the `AppendFormat` method to see exactly how it works. The following pseudocode shows how `AppendFormat` works:

```
public StringBuilder AppendFormat(IFormatProvider formatProvider,
   String format, params Object[] args) {

   // If an IFormatProvider was passed, find out
   // whether it offers an ICustomFormatter object.
   ICustomFormatter cf = null;

   if (formatProvider != null)
      cf = (ICustomFormatter)
         formatProvider.GetFormat(typeof(ICustomFormatter));

   // Keep appending literal characters (not shown in this pseudocode)
   // and replaceable parameters to the StringBuilder's character array.
   Boolean MoreReplaceableArgumentsToAppend = true;
   while (MoreReplaceableArgumentsToAppend) {
      // argFormat refers to the replaceable format string obtained
      // from the format parameter
      String argFormat = /* ... */;

      // argObj refers to the corresponding element
      // from the args array parameter
      Object argObj = /* ... */;

      // argStr will refer to the formatted string to be appended
      // to the final, resulting string
      String argStr = null;

      // If a custom formatter is available, let it format the argument.
      if (cf != null)
         argStr = cf.Format(argFormat, argObj, formatProvider);

      // If there is no custom formatter or if it didn't format
      // the argument, try something else.
      if (argStr == null) {
         // Does the argument's type support rich formatting?
         IFormattable formattable = argObj as IFormattable;
         if (formattable != null) {
            // Yes; pass the format string and provider to
            // the type's IFormattable ToString method.
            argStr = formattable.ToString(argFormat, formatProvider);
         } else {
            // No; get the default format by using
            // the thread's culture information.
            if (argObj != null) argStr = argObj.ToString();
            else argStr = String.Empty;
         }
      }
      // Append argStr's characters to the character array field member.
      /* ... */

      // Check if any remaining parameters to format
```

```
        MoreReplaceableArgumentsToAppend = /* ... */;
    }
    return this;
}
```

When **Main** calls **AppendFormat**, **AppendFormat** calls my format provider's **GetFormat** method, passing it the **ICustomFormatter** type. The **GetFormat** method defined in my **BoldInt32s** type sees that the **ICustomFormatter** is being requested and returns a reference to itself because it implements this interface. If my **GetFormat** method is called and is passed any other type, I call the **GetFormat** method of the **CultureInfo** object associated with the calling thread.

Whenever **AppendFormat** needs to format a replaceable parameter, it calls **ICustomFormatter**'s **Format** method. In my example, **AppendFormat** calls the **Format** method defined by my **BoldInt32s** type. In my **Format** method, I check whether the object being formatted supports rich formatting via the **IFormattable** interface. If the object doesn't, I then call the simple, parameterless **ToString** method (inherited from **Object**) to format the object. If the object does support **IFormattable**, I then call the rich **ToString** method, passing it the format string and the format provider.

Now that I have the formatted string, I check whether the corresponding object is an **Int32** type, and if it is, I wrap the formatted string in **<B>** and **</B>** HTML tags and return the new string. If the object is not an **Int32**, I simply return the formatted string without any further processing.

Parsing a String to Obtain an Object

In the preceding section, I explained how to take an object and obtain a string representation of that object. In this section, I'll talk about the opposite: how to take a string and obtain an object representation of it. Obtaining an object from a string isn't a very common operation, but it does occasionally come in handy. Microsoft felt it necessary to formalize a mechanism by which strings can be parsed into objects.

Any type that can parse a string offers a public, static method called **Parse**. This method takes a **String** and returns an instance of the type; in a way, **Parse** acts as a factory. In the FCL, a **Parse** method exists on all of the numeric types as well as for **DateTime**, **TimeSpan**, and a few other types (such as the SQL data types).

Let's look at how to parse a string into a number type. All of the numeric types (**Byte**, **SByte**, **Int16/UInt16**, **Int32/UInt32**, **Int64/UInt64**, **Single**, **Double**, and **Decimal**) offer at least one **Parse** method. Here I'll show you just the **Parse** method defined by the **Int32** type. (The **Parse** methods for the other numeric types work similarly to **Int32**'s **Parse** method.)

```
public static Int32 Parse(String s, NumberStyles style,
    IFormatProvider provider);
```

Just from looking at the prototype, you should be able to guess exactly how this method works. The **String** parameter, **s**, identifies a string representation of a number you want parsed into an **Int32** object. The **System.Globalization.NumberStyles** parameter, **style**, is a set of bit flags that identify characters that **Parse** should expect to find in the string. And the **IFormatProvider** parameter, **provider**, identifies an object that the **Parse** method can use to obtain culture-specific information as discussed earlier in this chapter.

For example, the following code causes **Parse** to throw a **System.FormatException** because the string being parsed contains a leading space:

```
Int32 x = Int32.Parse(" 123", NumberStyles.None, null);
```

To allow **Parse** to skip over the leading space, change the **style** parameter as follows:

```
Int32 x = Int32.Parse(" 123", NumberStyles.AllowLeadingWhite, null);
```

See the .NET Framework SDK documentation for a complete description of the bit symbols and common combinations that the **NumberStyles** enumerated type defines.

Here's a code fragment showing how to parse a hexadecimal number:

```
Int32 x = Int32.Parse("1A", NumberStyles.HexNumber, null);
Console.WriteLine(x);  // Displays "26"
```

This **Parse** method accepts three parameters. For convenience, many types offer additional overloads of **Parse** so you don't have to pass as many arguments. For example, **Int32** offers four overloads of the **Parse** method:

```
// Passes NumberStyles.Integer for style
// and thread's culture's provider information.
public static Int32 Parse(String s);

// Passes thread's culture's provider information.
public static Int32 Parse(String s, NumberStyles style);

// Passes NumberStyles.Integer for the style parameter.
public static Int32 Parse(String s, IFormatProvider provider);

// This is the method I've been talking about in this section.
public static Int32 Parse(String s, NumberStyles style,
   IFormatProvider provider);
```

The **DateTime** type also offers a **Parse** method:

```
public static DateTime Parse(String s,
   IFormatProvider provider, DateTimeStyles styles);
```

This method works just as the **Parse** method defined on the number types except that **DateTime**'s **Parse** method takes a set of bit flags defined by the **System.Globalization .DateTimeStyles** enumerated type instead of the **NumberStyles** enumerated type. See the .NET Framework SDK documentation for a complete description of the bit symbols and common combinations the **DateTimeStyles** type defines.

For convenience, the **DateTime** type offers three overloads of the **Parse** method:

```
// Passes thread's culture's provider information
// and DateTimeStyles.None for the style
public static DateTime Parse(String s);

// Passes DateTimeStyles.None for the style
public static DateTime Parse(String s, IFormatProvider provider);

// This is the method I've been talking about in this section.
public static DateTime Parse(String s,
    IFormatProvider provider, DateTimeStyles styles);
```

Parsing dates and times is complex. Many developers have found the **Parse** method of the **DateTime** type too forgiving in that it sometimes parses strings that don't contain dates or times. For this reason, the **DateTime** type also offers a **ParseExact** method that accepts a picture format string that indicates exactly how the date/time string should be formatted and how it should be parsed. For more information about picture format strings, see the **DateTimeFormatInfo** class in the .NET Framework SDK.

> **Note**   Some developers have reported the following back to Microsoft: when their application calls **Parse** frequently, and **Parse** throws exceptions repeatedly (due to invalid user input), performance of the application suffers. For these performance-sensitive uses of **Parse**, Microsoft added **TryParse** methods to all of the numeric data types, **DateTime**, **TimeSpan**, and even **IPAddress**. This is what one of the two **Int32**'s two **TryParse** method overloads looks like:
>
> ```
> public static Boolean TryParse(String s, NumberStyles style,
>     IFormatProvider provider, out Int32 result);
> ```
>
> As you can see, this method returns **true** or **false** indicating whether the specified string can be parsed into an **Int32**. If the method returns **true**, the variable passed by reference to the result parameter will contain the parsed numeric value. The **Try*Xxx*** pattern is discussed in Chapter 19, "Exception Handling."

Encodings: Converting Between Characters and Bytes

In Win32, programmers all too frequently have to write code to convert Unicode characters and strings to Multi-Byte Character Set (MBCS) characters and strings. I've certainly written my share of this code, and it's very tedious to write and error prone to use. In the CLR, all characters are represented as 16-bit Unicode code values and all strings are composed of 16-bit Unicode code values. This makes working with characters and strings easy at run time.

At times, however, you want to save strings to a file or transmit them over a network. If the strings consist mostly of characters readable by English-speaking people, saving or transmitting a set of 16-bit values isn't very efficient because half of the bytes written would contain zeros. Instead, it would be more efficient to *encode* the 16-bit values into a compressed array of bytes and then *decode* the array of bytes back into an array of 16-bit values.

Encodings also allow a managed application to interact with strings created by non-Unicode systems. For example, if you want to produce a file readable by an application running on a Japanese version of Windows 95, you have to save the Unicode text by using the Shift-JIS (code page 932) encoding. Likewise, you'd use Shift-JIS encoding to read a text file produced on a Japanese Windows 95 system into the CLR.

Encoding is typically done when you want to send a string to a file or network stream by using the `System.IO.BinaryWriter` or `System.IO.StreamWriter` type. Decoding is typically done when you want to read a string from a file or network stream by using the `System.IO.BinaryReader` or `System.IO.StreamReader` type. If you don't explicitly select an encoding, all of these types default to using UTF-8. (UTF stands for Unicode Transformation Format.) However, at times, you might want to explicitly encode or decode a string. Even if you don't want to explicitly do this, this section will give you more insight into the reading and writing of strings from and to streams.

Fortunately, the FCL offers some types to make character encoding and decoding easy. The two most frequently used encodings are UTF-16 and UTF-8.

- UTF-16 encodes each 16-bit character as 2 bytes. It doesn't affect the characters at all, and no compression occurs—its performance is excellent. UTF-16 encoding is also referred to as Unicode encoding. Also note that UTF-16 can be used to convert from little-endian to big-endian and vice versa.

- UTF-8 encodes some characters as 1 byte, some characters as 2 bytes, some characters as 3 bytes, and some characters as 4 bytes. Characters with a value below 0x0080 are compressed to 1 byte, which works very well for characters used in the United States. Characters between 0x0080 and 0x07FF are converted to 2 bytes, which works well for European and Middle Eastern languages. Characters of 0x0800 and above are converted to 3 bytes, which works well for East Asian languages. Finally, surrogate pairs are written out as 4 bytes. UTF-8 is an extremely popular encoding, but it's less efficient than UTF-16 if you encode many characters with values of 0x0800 or above.

Although the UTF-16 and UTF-8 encodings are by far the most common, the FCL also supports some encodings that are used less frequently:

- UTF-32 encodes all characters as 4 bytes. This encoding is useful when you want to write a simple algorithm to traverse characters and you don't want to have to deal with characters taking a variable number of bytes. For example, with UTF-32, you do not need to think about surrogates because every character is 4 bytes. Obviously, UTF-32 is not an efficient encoding in terms of memory usage and is therefore rarely used for saving or transmitting strings to a file or network. This encoding is typically used inside the program itself. Also note that UTF-32 can be used to convert from little-endian to big-endian and vice versa.

- UTF-7 encoding is typically used with older systems that work with characters that can be expressed using 7-bit values. You should avoid this encoding because it usually ends up expanding the data rather than compressing it. The Unicode Consortium has deprecated this encoding.

- ASCII encodes the 16-bit characters into ASCII characters; that is, any 16-bit character with a value of less than 0x0080 is converted to a single byte. Any character with a value greater than 0x007F can't be converted, so that character's value is lost. For strings consisting of characters in the ASCII range (0x00 to 0x7F), this encoding compresses the data in half and is very fast (because the high byte is just cut off). This encoding isn't appropriate if you have characters outside of the ASCII range because the character's values will be lost.

Finally, the FCL also allows you to encode 16-bit characters to an arbitrary code page. As is the ASCII encoding, encoding to a code page is dangerous because any character whose value can't be expressed in the specified code page is lost. You should always use UTF-16 or UTF-8 encoding unless you must work with some legacy files or applications that already use one of the other encodings.

When you need to encode or decode a set of characters, you should obtain an instance of a class derived from **System.Text.Encoding**. **Encoding** is an abstract base class that offers several static readonly properties, each of which returns an instance of an **Encoding**-derived class.

Here's an example that encodes and decodes characters by using UTF-8:

```
using System;
using System.Text;

public static class Program {
    public static void Main() {
        // This is the string we're going to encode.
        String s = "Hi there.";

        // Obtain an Encoding-derived object that knows how
        // to encode/decode using UTF8
        Encoding encodingUTF8 = Encoding.UTF8;

        // Encode a string into an array of bytes.
        Byte[] encodedBytes = encodingUTF8.GetBytes(s);

        // Show the encoded byte values.
        Console.WriteLine("Encoded bytes: " +
            BitConverter.ToString(encodedBytes));

        // Decode the byte array back to a string.
        String decodedString = encodingUTF8.GetString(encodedBytes);

        // Show the decoded string.
        Console.WriteLine("Decoded string: " + decodedString);
    }
}
```

This code yields the following output:

```
Encoded bytes: 48-69-20-74-68-65-72-65-2E
Decoded string: Hi there.
```

In addition to the **UTF8** static property, the **Encoding** class also offers the following static properties: **Unicode**, **BigEndianUnicode**, **UTF32**, **UTF7**, **ASCII**, and **Default**. The **Default** property returns an object that is able to encode/decode using the user's code page as specified by the Advanced tab of the Regional And Language Options dialog box in Control Panel. (See the **GetACP** Win32 function for more information.) However, using the **Default** property is discouraged because your application's behavior would be machine-setting dependent, so if you change the system's default code page or if your application runs on another machine, your application will behave differently.

In addition to these properties, **Encoding** also offers a static **GetEncoding** method that allows you to specify a code page (by integer or by string) and returns an object that can encode/decode using the specified code page. You can call **GetEncoding**, passing **"Shift-JIS"** or 932, for example.

When you first request an encoding object, the **Encoding** class's property or **GetEncoding** method constructs a single object for the requested encoding and returns this object. If an already-requested encoding object is requested in the future, the encoding class simply returns the object it previously constructed; it doesn't construct a new object for each request. This efficiency reduces the number of objects in the system and reduces pressure in the garbage-collected heap.

Instead of calling one of **Encoding**'s static properties or its **GetEncoding** method, you could also construct an instance of one of the following classes: **System.Text.UnicodeEncoding**, **System.Text.UTF8Encoding**, **System.Text.UTF32Encoding**, **System.Text.UTF7Encoding**, or **System.Text.ASCIIEncoding**. However, keep in mind that constructing any of these classes creates new objects in the managed heap, which hurts performance.

Four of these classes, **UnicodeEncoding**, **UTF8Encoding**, **UTF32Encoding**, and **UTF7Encoding**, offer multiple constructors, providing you with more control over the encoding and preamble. (Preamble is sometimes referred to as a *byte order mark* or BOM.) The first three aforementioned classes also offer constructors that let you tell the class to throw exceptions when decoding an invalid byte sequence; you should use these constructors when you want your application to be secure and resistant to invalid incoming data.

You might want to explicitly construct instances of these encoding types when working with a **BinaryWriter** or a **StreamWriter**. The **ASCIIEncoding** class has only a single constructor and therefore doesn't offer any more control over the encoding. If you need an **ASCIIEncoding** object, always obtain it by querying **Encoding**'s **ASCII** property; this returns a reference to a single **ASCIIEncoding** object. If you construct **ASCIIEncoding** objects yourself, you are creating more objects on the heap, which hurts your application's performance.

Once you have an **Encoding**-derived object, you can convert a string or an array of characters to an array of bytes by calling the **GetBytes** method. (Several overloads of this method exist.) To convert an array of bytes to an array of characters, call the **GetChars** method or the more useful **GetString** method. (Several overloads exist for both of these methods.) The preceding code demonstrated calls to the **GetBytes** and **GetString** methods.

All **Encoding**-derived types offer a **GetByteCount** method that obtains the number of bytes necessary to encode a set of characters without actually encoding. Although **GetByteCount** isn't especially useful, you can use this method to allocate an array of bytes. There's also a **GetCharCount** method that returns the number of characters that would be decoded without actually decoding them. These methods are useful if you're trying to save memory and reuse an array.

The **GetByteCount/GetCharCount** methods aren't that fast because they must analyze the array of characters/bytes in order to return an accurate result. If you prefer speed to an exact result, you can call the **GetMaxByteCount** or **GetMaxCharCount** method instead. Both methods take an integer specifying the number of characters or number of bytes and return a worst-case value.

Each **Encoding**-derived object offers a set of public read-only properties that you can query to obtain detailed information about the encoding. See the .NET Framework SDK documentation for a description of these properties.

To illustrate most of the properties and their meanings, I wrote the following program that displays the property values for several different encodings:

```
using System;
using System.Text;

public static class Program {
    public static void Main() {
        foreach (EncodingInfo ei in Encoding.GetEncodings()) {
            Encoding e = ei.GetEncoding();
            Console.WriteLine("{1}{0}" +
                "\tCodePage={2}, WindowsCodePage={3}{0}" +
                "\tWebName={4}, HeaderName={5}, BodyName={6}{0}" +
                "\tIsBrowserDisplay={7}, IsBrowserSave={8}{0}" +
                "\tIsMailNewsDisplay={9}, IsMailNewsSave={10}{0}",

                Environment.NewLine,
                e.EncodingName, e.CodePage, e.WindowsCodePage,
                e.WebName, e.HeaderName, e.BodyName,
                e.IsBrowserDisplay, e.IsBrowserSave,
                e.IsMailNewsDisplay, e.IsMailNewsSave);
        }
    }
}
```

Running this program yields the following output (abridged to conserve paper):

```
IBM EBCDIC (US-Canada)
        CodePage=37, WindowsCodePage=1252
        WebName=IBM037, HeaderName=IBM037, BodyName=IBM037
        IsBrowserDisplay=False, IsBrowserSave=False
        IsMailNewsDisplay=False, IsMailNewsSave=False

OEM United States
        CodePage=437, WindowsCodePage=1252
        WebName=IBM437, HeaderName=IBM437, BodyName=IBM437
```

```
                IsBrowserDisplay=False, IsBrowserSave=False
                IsMailNewsDisplay=False, IsMailNewsSave=False

IBM EBCDIC (International)
                CodePage=500, WindowsCodePage=1252
                WebName=IBM500, HeaderName=IBM500, BodyName=IBM500
                IsBrowserDisplay=False, IsBrowserSave=False
                IsMailNewsDisplay=False, IsMailNewsSave=False

Arabic (ASMO 708)
                CodePage=708, WindowsCodePage=1256
                WebName=ASMO-708, HeaderName=ASMO-708, BodyName=ASMO-708
                IsBrowserDisplay=True, IsBrowserSave=True
                IsMailNewsDisplay=False, IsMailNewsSave=False

Unicode
                CodePage=1200, WindowsCodePage=1200
                WebName=utf-16, HeaderName=utf-16, BodyName=utf-16
                IsBrowserDisplay=False, IsBrowserSave=True
                IsMailNewsDisplay=False, IsMailNewsSave=False

Unicode (Big-Endian)
                CodePage=1201, WindowsCodePage=1200
                WebName=unicodeFFFE, HeaderName=unicodeFFFE, BodyName=unicodeFFFE
                IsBrowserDisplay=False, IsBrowserSave=False
                IsMailNewsDisplay=False, IsMailNewsSave=False

Western European (DOS)
                CodePage=850, WindowsCodePage=1252
                WebName=ibm850, HeaderName=ibm850, BodyName=ibm850
                IsBrowserDisplay=False, IsBrowserSave=False
                IsMailNewsDisplay=False, IsMailNewsSave=False

Unicode (UTF-8)
                CodePage=65001, WindowsCodePage=1200
                WebName=utf-8, HeaderName=utf-8, BodyName=utf-8
                IsBrowserDisplay=True, IsBrowserSave=True
                IsMailNewsDisplay=True, IsMailNewsSave=True
```

Table 11-3 covers the most commonly used methods offered by all **Encoding**-derived classes.

Table 11-3   Methods of the Encoding-Derived Classes

Method	Description
GetPreamble	Returns an array of bytes indicating what should be written to a stream before writing any encoded bytes. Frequently, these bytes are referred to as the *byte order mark* (BOM) bytes. When you start reading from a stream, the BOM bytes automatically help detect the encoding that was used when the stream was written so that the correct decoder can be used. For some **Encoding**-derived classes, this method returns an array of 0 bytes— that is, no preamble bytes. A **UTF8Encoding** object can be explicitly constructed so that this method returns a 3-byte array of 0xEF, 0xBB, 0xBF. A **UnicodeEncoding** object can be explicitly constructed so that this method returns a 2-byte array of 0xFE, 0xFF for big-endian encoding or a 2-byte array of 0xFF, 0xFE for little-endian encoding. The default is little-endian.

Table 11-3   Methods of the Encoding-Derived Classes

Method	Description
Convert	Converts an array of bytes specified in a source encoding to an array of bytes specified by a destination encoding. Internally, this static method calls the source encoding object's GetChars method and passes the result to the destination encoding object's GetBytes method. The resulting byte array is returned to the caller.
Equals	Returns **true** if two Encoding-derived objects represent the same code page and preamble setting.
GetHashCode	Returns the encoding object's code page.

Encoding/Decoding Streams of Characters and Bytes

Imagine that you're reading a UTF-16 encoded string via a System.Net.Sockets.Network-Stream object. The bytes will very likely stream in as chunks of data. In other words, you might first read 5 bytes from the stream, followed by 7 bytes. In UTF-16, each character consists of 2 bytes. So calling Encoding's GetString method passing the first array of 5 bytes will return a string consisting of just two characters. If you later call GetString, passing in the next 7 bytes that come in from the stream, GetString will return a string consisting of three characters, and all of the code points will have the wrong values!

This data corruption problem occurs because none of the Encoding-derived classes maintains any state in between calls to their methods. If you'll be encoding or decoding characters/bytes in chunks, you must do some additional work to maintain state between calls, preventing any loss of data.

To decode chunks of bytes, you should obtain a reference to an Encoding-derived object (as described in the previous section) and call its GetDecoder method. This method returns a reference to a newly constructed object whose type is derived from the System.Text.Decoder class. Like the Encoding class, the Decoder class is an abstract base class. If you look in the .NET Framework SDK documentation, you won't find any classes that represent concrete implementations of the Decoder class. However, the FCL does define a bunch of Decoder-derived classes. These classes are all internal to the FCL, but the GetDecoder method can construct instances of these classes and return them to your application code.

All Decoder-derived classes offer two important methods: GetChars and GetCharCount. Obviously, these methods are used for decoding an array of bytes and work similarly to Encoding's GetChars and GetCharCount methods, discussed earlier. When you call one of these methods, it decodes the byte array as much as possible. If the byte array doesn't contain enough bytes to complete a character, the leftover bytes are saved inside the decoder object. The next time you call one of these methods, the decoder object uses the leftover bytes plus the new byte array passed to it—this ensures that the chunks of data are decoded properly. Decoder objects are very useful when reading bytes from a stream.

An Encoding-derived type can be used for stateless encoding and decoding. However, a Decoder-derived type can be used only for decoding. If you want to encode strings in chunks, call **GetEncoder** instead of calling the **Encoding** object's **GetDecoder** method. **GetEncoder** returns a newly constructed object whose type is derived from the abstract base class **System .Text.Encoder**. Again, the .NET Framework SDK documentation doesn't contain any classes representing concrete implementations of the **Encoder** class. However, the FCL does define some **Encoder**-derived classes. As with the **Decoder**-derived classes, these classes are all internal to the FCL, but the **GetEncoder** method can construct instances of these classes and return them to your application code.

All **Encoder**-derived classes offer two important methods: **GetBytes** and **GetByteCount**. On each call, the **Encoder**-derived object maintains any leftover state information so that you can encode data in chunks.

Base-64 String Encoding and Decoding

As of this writing, the UTF-16 and UTF-8 encodings are becoming quite popular. It is also quite popular to encode a sequence of bytes to a base-64 string. The FCL does offer methods to do base-64 encoding and decoding, and you might expect that this would be accomplished via an **Encoding**-derived type. However, for some reason, base-64 encoding and decoding is done using some static methods offered by the **System.Convert** type.

To encode a base-64 string as an array of bytes, you call **Convert**'s static **FromBase64String** or **FromBase64CharArray** method. Likewise, to decode an array of bytes as a base-64 string, you call **Convert**'s static **ToBase64String** or **ToBase64CharArray** method. The following code demonstrates how to use some of these methods:

```
using System;

public static class Program {
    public static void Main() {
        // Get a set of 10 randomly generated bytes
        Byte[] bytes = new Byte[10];
        new Random().NextBytes(bytes);

        // Display the bytes
        Console.WriteLine(BitConverter.ToString(bytes));

        // Decode the bytes into a base-64 string and show the string
        String s = Convert.ToBase64String(bytes);
        Console.WriteLine(s);

        // Encode the base-64 string back to bytes and show the bytes
        bytes = Convert.FromBase64String(s);
        Console.WriteLine(BitConverter.ToString(bytes));
    }
}
```

Compiling this code and running the executable file produces the following output (your output might vary from mine because of the randomly generated bytes):

```
3B-B9-27-40-59-35-86-54-5F-F1
O7knQFk1hlRf8Q==
3B-B9-27-40-59-35-86-54-5F-F1
```

Secure Strings

Often, **string** objects are used to contain sensitive data such as a user's password or credit-card information. Unfortunately, **string** objects contain an array of characters in memory, and if some unsafe or unmanaged code is allowed to execute, the unsafe/unmanaged code could snoop around the process's address space, locate the string containing the sensitive information, and use this data in an unauthorized way. Even if the **string** object is used for just a short time and then garbage collected, the CLR might not immediately reuse the **string** object's memory (especially if the **string** object was in an older generation), leaving the **string**'s characters in the process' memory, where the information could be compromised. In addition, since strings are immutable, as you manipulate them, the old copies linger in memory and you end up with different versions of the string scattered all over memory.

Some governmental departments have stringent security requirements that require very specific security guarantees. To meet these requirements, Microsoft added a more secure string class to the FCL: **System.Security.SecureString**. When you construct a **SecureString** object, it internally allocates a block of unmanaged memory that contains an array of characters. Unmanaged memory is used so that the garbage collector isn't aware of it.

These string's characters are encrypted, protecting the sensitive information from any malicious unsafe/unmanaged code. You can append, insert, remove, or set a character in the secure string by using any of these methods: **AppendChar**, **InsertAt**, **RemoveAt**, and **SetAt**. Whenever you call any of these methods, internally, the method decrypts the characters, performs the operation, and then re-encrypts the characters. This means that the characters are in an unencrypted state for a very short period of time. This also means that these operations mutate the string's characters in place and that their performance is less than stellar, so you should perform as few of these operations as possible.

The **SecureString** class implements the **IDisposable** interface to provide an easy way to deterministically destroy the string's secured contents. When your application no longer needs the sensitive string information, you simply call **SecureString**'s **Dispose** method. Internally, **Dispose** zeroes out the contents of the memory buffer to make sure that the sensitive information is not accessible to malicious code, and then the buffer is freed. You'll also notice that the **SecureString** class is derived from **CriticalFinalizerObject**, discussed in Chapter 20, "Automatic Memory Management (Garbage Collection)," which ensures that a garbage-collected **SecureString** object has its **Finalize** method called, guaranteeing that the string's characters are zeroed out and that its buffer is freed. Unlike a **string** object, when a **SecureString** object is collected, the encrypted string's characters will no longer be in memory.

Now that you know how to create and modify a **SecureString** object, let's talk about how you use one. Unfortunately, the most recent FCL has limited support for the **SecureString** class. In other words, there are only a few methods that accept a **SecureString** argument. In version 2 of the .NET Framework, you can pass a **SecureString** as a password when

■ Working with a cryptographic service provider (CSP). See the **System.Security .Cryptography.CspParameters** class.

- Creating, importing, or exporting an X.509 certificate. See the `System.Security` `.Cryptography.X509Certificates.X509Certificate` and `System.Security` `.Cryptography.X509Certificates.X509Certificate2` classes.

- Starting a new process under a specific user account. See the `System.Diagnostics` `.Process` and `System.Diagnostics.ProcessStartInfo` classes.

In the future, the .NET Framework will add more support for `SecureString`. For example, one would expect to be able to use a `SecureString` for text boxes in a Windows Forms, Windows Presentation Foundation, or Web Form application, allowing end users to enter the secure string information in your application UI. You should also expect to be able to pass a `SecureString` as the connection string to open a database connection or to establish a network connection. There are many other scenarios in the FCL in which `SecureString` would be useful.

Finally, you can create your own methods that can accept a `SecureString` object parameter. Inside your method, you must have the `SecureString` object create an unmanaged memory buffer that contains the decrypted characters before your method uses the buffer. To keep the window of opportunity for malicious code to access the sensitive data as small as possible, your code should require access to the decrypted string for as short a period of time as possible. When finished using the string, your code should zero the buffer and free it as soon as possible. Also, never put the contents of a `SecureString` into a `String`: if you do, the `String` lives unencrypted in the heap and will not have its characters zeroed out until the memory is reused after a garbage collection. The `SecureString` class does not override the `ToString` method specifically to avoid exposing the sensitive data (which converting it to a `String` would do).

Here is some sample code demonstrating how to initialize and use a `SecureString` (when compiling this, you'll need to specify the `/unsafe` switch to the C# compiler):

```
using System;
using System.Security;
using System.Runtime.InteropServices;

public static class Program {
   public static void Main() {
      using (SecureString ss = new SecureString()) {
         Console.Write("Please enter password: ");
         while (true) {
            ConsoleKeyInfo cki = Console.ReadKey(true);
            if (cki.Key == ConsoleKey.Enter) break;

            // Append password characters into the SecureString
            ss.AppendChar(cki.KeyChar);
            Console.Write("*");
         }
         Console.WriteLine();

         // Password entered, display it for demonstration purposes
         DisplaySecureString(ss);
      }
```

```
      // After 'using', the SecureString is Disposed; no sensitive data in memory
   }

   // This method is unsafe because it accesses unmanaged memory
   private unsafe static void DisplaySecureString(SecureString ss) {
      Char* pc = null;
      try {
         // Decrypt the SecureString into an unmanaged memory buffer
         pc = (Char*) Marshal.SecureStringToCoTaskMemUnicode(ss);

         // Access the unmanaged memory buffer that
         // contains the decrypted SecureString
         for (Int32 index = 0; pc[index] != 0; index++)
            Console.Write(pc[index]);
      }
      finally {
         // Make sure we zero and free the unmanaged memory buffer that contains
         // the decrypted SecureString characters
         if (pc != null)
            Marshal.ZeroFreeCoTaskMemUnicode((IntPtr) pc);
      }
   }
}
```

The `System.Runtime.InteropServices.Marshal` class offers five methods that you can call to decrypt a `SecureString`'s characters into an unmanaged memory buffer. All of these methods are static, all accept a `SecureString` argument, and all return an `IntPtr`. Each of these methods has a corresponding method that you must call in order to zero the internal buffer and free it. Table 11-4 shows the `System.Runtime.InteropServices.Marshal` class's methods to decrypt a `SecureString` into a memory buffer and the corresponding method to zero and free the buffer.

Table 11-4   Methods of the `Marshal` Class for Working with Secure Strings

Method to Decrypt `SecureString` to Buffer	Method to Zero and Free Buffer
SecureStringToBSTR	ZeroFreeBSTR
SecureStringToCoTaskMemAnsi	ZeroFreeCoTaskMemAnsi
SecureStringToCoTaskMemUnicode	ZeroFreeCoTaskMemUnicode
SecureStringToGlobalAllocAnsi	ZeroFreeGlobalAllocAnsi
SecureStringToGlobalAllocUnicode	ZeroFreeGlobalAllocUnicode

Chapter 12
Enumerated Types and Bit Flags

In this chapter, I'll discuss enumerated types and bit flags. Since Windows has used these constructs for so many years, I'm sure that many of you are already familiar with how to use enumerated types and bit flags. However, the common language runtime (CLR) and the Framework Class Library (FCL) work together to make enumerated types and bit flags real object-oriented types that offer cool new features that I suspect most developers aren't familiar with. It's amazing to me how these new features, which are the focus of this chapter, make developing application code so much easier.

Enumerated Types

An *enumerated type* is a type that defines a set of symbolic name and value pairs. For example, the **Color** type shown here defines a set of symbols, with each symbol identifying a single color:

```
internal enum Color {
    White,      // Assigned a value of 0
    Red,        // Assigned a value of 1
    Green,      // Assigned a value of 2
    Blue,       // Assigned a value of 3
    Orange      // Assigned a value of 4
}
```

Of course, programmers can always write a program using 0 to represent white, 1 to represent red, and so on. However, programmers shouldn't hard-code numbers into their code and should use an enumerated type instead, for at least two reasons:

- Enumerated types make the program much easier to write, read, and maintain. With enumerated types, the symbolic name is used throughout the code, and the programmer doesn't have to mentally map the meaning of each hard-coded value (for example, white is 0 or vice versa). Also, should a symbol's numeric value change, the code can simply be recompiled without requiring any changes to the source code. In addition, documentation tools and other utilities, such as a debugger, can show meaningful symbolic names to the programmer.

■ Enumerated types are strongly typed. For example, the compiler will report an error if I attempt to pass **Color.Orange** as a value to a method requiring a **Fruit** enumerated type as a parameter.

In the Microsoft .NET Framework, enumerated types are more than just symbols that the compiler cares about. Enumerated types are treated as first-class citizens in the type system, which allows for very powerful operations that simply can't be done with enumerated types in other environments (such as in unmanaged C++, for example).

Every enumerated type is derived directly from **System.Enum**, which is derived from **System .ValueType**, which in turn is derived from **System.Object**. So enumerated types are value types (described in Chapter 5, "Primitive, Reference, and Value Types") and can be represented in unboxed and boxed forms. However, unlike other value types, an enumerated type can't define any methods, properties, or events.

When an enumerated type is compiled, the C# compiler turns each symbol into a constant field of the type. For example, the compiler treats the **Color** enumeration shown earlier as if you had written code similar to the following:

```
internal struct Color : System.Enum {
    // Below are public constants defining Color's symbols and values
    public const Color White  = (Color) 0;
    public const Color Red    = (Color) 1;
    public const Color Green  = (Color) 2;
    public const Color Blue   = (Color) 3;
    public const Color Orange = (Color) 4;

    // Below is a public instance field containing a Color variable's value
    // You cannot write code that references this instance field directly
    public Int32 value__;
}
```

The C# compiler won't actually compile this code because it forbids you from defining a type derived from the special **System.Enum** type. However, this pseudo-type definition shows you what's happening internally. Basically, an enumerated type is just a structure with a bunch of constant fields defined in it and one instance field. The constant fields are emitted to the assembly's metadata and can be accessed via reflection. This means that you can get all of the symbols and their values associated with an enumerated type at run time. It also means that you can convert a string symbol into its equivalent numeric value. These operations are made available to you by the **System.Enum** base type, which offers several static and instance methods that can be performed on an instance of an enumerated type, saving you the trouble of having to use reflection. I'll discuss some of these operations next.

> **Important**   Symbols defined by an enumerated type are constant values. So when a compiler sees code that references an enumerated type's symbol, the compiler substitutes the symbol's numeric value at compile time, and this code no longer references the enumerated type that defined the symbol. This means that the assembly that defines the enumerated type may not be required at run time; it was required only when compiling. If you have code that references the enumerated type—rather than just having references to symbols defined by the type—the assembly containing the enumerated type's definition will be required at run time. Some versioning issues arise because enumerated type symbols are constants instead of read-only values. I explained these issues in the "Constants" section of Chapter 7, "Constants and Fields."

For example, the **Enum** type has a static method called **GetUnderlyingType**:

```
public static Type GetUnderlyingType(Type enumType);
```

This method returns the core type used to hold an enumerated type's value. Every enumerated type has an underlying type, which can be a **byte**, **sbyte**, **short**, **ushort**, **int** (the most common and what C# chooses by default), **uint**, **long**, or **ulong**. Of course, these C# primitive types correspond to FCL types. However, the C# compiler requires you to specify a primitive type name here; using an FCL type name (such as **Int32**) generates the following: "error CS1008: Type byte, sbyte, short, ushort, int, uint, long, or ulong expected." The following code shows how to declare an enumerated type with an underlying type of **byte** (**System.Byte**):

```
internal enum Color : byte {
    White,
    Red,
    Green,
    Blue,
    Orange
}
```

With the **Color** enumerated type defined in this way, the following code shows what **GetUnderlyingType** will return:

```
// The following line displays "System.Byte".
Console.WriteLine(Enum.GetUnderlyingType(typeof(Color)));
```

The C# compiler treats enumerated types as primitive types. As such, you can use many of the familiar operators (==, !=, <, >, <=, >=, +, -, ^, &, |, ~, ++, and --) to manipulate enumerated type instances. All of these operators actually work on the **value__** instance field inside each enumerated type instance. Furthermore, the C# compiler allows you to explicitly cast instances of an enumerated type to a different enumerated type. You can also implicitly or explicitly cast an enumerated type instance to a numeric type.

Given an instance of an enumerated type, it's possible to map that value to one of several string representations by calling the **ToString** method inherited from **System.Enum**:

```
Color c = Color.Blue;
Console.WriteLine(c);                  // "Blue" (General format)
Console.WriteLine(c.ToString());       // "Blue" (General format)
Console.WriteLine(c.ToString("G"));    // "Blue" (General format)
Console.WriteLine(c.ToString("D"));    // "3"    (Decimal format)
Console.WriteLine(c.ToString("X"));    // "03"   (Hex format)
```

> **Note**   When using hex formatting, **ToString** always outputs uppercase letters. In addition, the number of digits outputted depends on the enum's underlying type: 2 digits for **byte/sbyte**, 4 digits for **short/ushort**, 8 digits for **int/uint**, and 16 digits for **long/ulong**. Leading zeros are outputted if necessary.

In addition to the **ToString** method, the **System.Enum** type offers a static **Format** method that you can call to format an enumerated type's value:

```
public static String Format(Type enumType, Object value, String format);
```

Generally, I prefer to call the **ToString** method because it requires less code and it's easier to call. But using **Format** has one advantage over **ToString**: **Format** lets you pass a numeric value for the value parameter; you don't have to have an instance of the enumerated type. For example, the following code will display "Blue":

```
// The following line displays "Blue".
Console.WriteLine(Enum.Format(typeof(Color), 3, "G"));
```

> **Note**   It's possible to declare an enumerated type that has multiple symbols, all with the same numeric value. When converting a numeric value to a symbol by using general formatting, **Enum**'s methods return one of the symbols. However, there's no guarantee of which symbol name is returned. Also, if no symbol is defined for the numeric value you're looking up, a string containing the numeric value is returned.

It's also possible to call **System.Enum**'s static **GetValues** method to obtain an array that contains one element for each symbolic name in an enumerated type; each element contains the symbolic name's numeric value:

```
public static Array GetValues(Type enumType);
```

Using this method along with the **ToString** method, you can display all of an enumerated type's symbolic and numeric values, like so:

```
Color[] colors = (Color[]) Enum.GetValues(typeof(Color));
Console.WriteLine("Number of symbols defined: " + colors.Length);
Console.WriteLine("Value\tSymbol\n-----\t------");
```

```
foreach (Color c in colors) {
   // Display each symbol in Decimal and General format.
   Console.WriteLine("{0,5:D}\t{0:G}", c);
}
```

The previous code produces the following output:

```
Number of symbols defined: 5
Value    Symbol
-----    ------
    0    White
    1    Red
    2    Green
    3    Blue
    4    Orange
```

This discussion shows some of the cool operations that can be performed on enumerated types. I suspect that the **ToString** method with the general format will be used quite frequently to show symbolic names in a program's user interface elements (list boxes, combo boxes, and the like), as long as the strings don't need to be localized (since enumerated types offer no support for localization). In addition to the **GetValues** method, the **Enum** type also offers the following two static methods that return an enumerated type's symbols:

```
// Returns a String representation for the numeric value
public static String   GetName(Type enumType, Object value);

// Returns an array of Strings: one per symbol defined in the enum
public static String[] GetNames(Type enumType);
```

I've discussed a lot of methods that you can use to look up an enumerated type's symbol. But you also need a method that can look up a symbol's equivalent value, an operation that could be used to convert a symbol that a user enters into a text box, for example. Converting a symbol to an instance of an enumerated type is easily accomplished by using one of **Enum**'s static **Parse** methods:

```
public static Object Parse(Type enumType, String value);
public static Object Parse(Type enumType,
   String value, Boolean ignoreCase);
```

Here's some code demonstrating how to use this method:

```
// Because Orange is defined as 4, 'c' is initialized to 4.
Color c = (Color) Enum.Parse(typeof(Color), "orange", true);

// Because Brown isn't defined, an ArgumentException is thrown.
Color c = (Color) Enum.Parse(typeof(Color), "Brown", false);

// Creates an instance of the Color enum with a value of 1
Color c = (Color) Enum.Parse(typeof(Color), "1", false);

// Creates an instance of the Color enum with a value of 23
Color c = (Color) Enum.Parse(typeof(Color), "23", false);
```

Finally, using **Enum**'s static **IsDefined** method,

```
public static Boolean IsDefined(Type enumType, Object value);
```

you can determine whether a numeric value is legal for an enumerated type:

```
// Displays "True" because Color defines Red as 1
Console.WriteLine(Enum.IsDefined(typeof(Color),  1));

// Displays "True" because Color defines White as 0
Console.WriteLine(Enum.IsDefined(typeof(Color), "White"));

// Displays "False" because a case-sensitive check is performed
Console.WriteLine(Enum.IsDefined(typeof(Color), "white"));

// Displays "False" because Color doesn't have a symbol of value 10
Console.WriteLine(Enum.IsDefined(typeof(Color),  10));
```

The **IsDefined** method is frequently used for parameter validation. Here's an example:

```
public void SetColor(Color c) {
    if (!Enum.IsDefined(typeof(Color), c)) {
        throw(new ArgumentOutOfRangeException("c", c, "Invalid Color value."));
    }
    // Set color to White, Red, Green, Blue, or Orange
    ...
}
```

The parameter validation is useful because someone could call **SetColor** like this:

```
SetColor((Color) 547);
```

Because no symbol has a corresponding value of 547, the **SetColor** method will throw an **ArgumentOutOfRangeException** exception, indicating which parameter is invalid and why.

> **Important**   The **IsDefined** method is very convenient, but you must use it with caution. First, **IsDefined** always does a case-sensitive search, and there is no way to get it to perform a case-insensitive search. Second, **IsDefined** is pretty slow because it uses reflection internally; if you wrote code to manually check each possible value, your application's performance would most certainly be better. Third, you should really use **IsDefined** only if the enum type itself is defined in the same assembly that is calling **IsDefined**. Here's why: Let's say the **Color** enum is defined in one assembly and the **SetColor** method is defined in another assembly. The **SetColor** method calls **IsDefined**, and if the color is **White**, **Red**, **Green**, **Blue**, or **Orange**, **SetColor** performs its work. However, if the **Color** enum changes in the future to include **Purple**, **SetColor** will now allow **Purple**, which it never expected before, and the method might execute with unpredictable results.

Finally, the **System.Enum** type offers a set of static **ToObject** methods that convert an instance of a **Byte**, **SByte**, **Int16**, **UInt16**, **Int32**, **UInt32**, **Int64**, or **UInt64** to an instance of an enumerated type.

Enumerated types are always used in conjunction with some other type. Typically, they're used for the type's method parameters or return type, properties, and fields. A common question that arises is whether to define the enumerated type nested within the type that requires it or to define the enumerated type at the same level as the type that requires it. If you examine the FCL, you'll see that an enumerated type is usually defined at the same level as the class that requires it. The reason is simply to make the developer's life a little easier by reducing the amount of typing required. So you should define your enumerated type at the same level unless you're concerned about name conflicts.

Bit Flags

Programmers frequently work with sets of bit flags. When you call the **System.IO.File** type's **GetAttributes** method, it returns an instance of a **FileAttributes** type. A **FileAttributes** type is an instance of an **Int32**-based enumerated type, in which each bit reflects a single attribute of the file. The **FileAttributes** type is defined in the FCL as follows:

```
[Flags, Serializable]
public enum FileAttributes {
    ReadOnly          = 0x0001,
    Hidden            = 0x0002,
    System            = 0x0004,
    Directory         = 0x0010,
    Archive           = 0x0020,
    Device            - 0x0040,
    Normal            = 0x0080,
    Temporary         = 0x0100,
    SparseFile        = 0x0200,
    ReparsePoint      = 0x0400,
    Compressed        = 0x0800,
    Offline           = 0x1000,
    NotContentIndexed = 0x2000,
    Encrypted         = 0x4000
}
```

To determine whether a file is hidden, you would execute code like this:

```
String file = @"C:\Boot.ini";
FileAttributes attributes = File.GetAttributes(file);
Console.WriteLine("Is {0} hidden? {1}", file,
    (attributes & FileAttributes.Hidden) == FileAttributes.Hidden);
```

And here's code demonstrating how to change a file's attributes to read-only and hidden:

```
File.SetAttributes(@"C:\Boot.ini",
    FileAttributes.ReadOnly | FileAttributes.Hidden);
```

As the **FileAttributes** type shows, it's common to use enumerated types to express the set of bit flags that can be combined. However, although enumerated types and bit flags are similar, they don't have exactly the same semantics. For example, enumerated types represent single numeric values, and bit flags represent a set of bits, some of which are on, and some of which are off.

When defining an enumerated type that is to be used to identify bit flags, you should, of course, explicitly assign a numeric value to each symbol. Usually, each symbol will have an individual bit turned on. It is also common to see a symbol called **None** defined with a value of **0**, and you can also define symbols that represent commonly used combinations (see the **ReadWrite** symbol below). It's also highly recommended that you apply the **System.Flags-Attribute** custom attribute type to the enumerated type, as shown here:

```
[Flags]    // The C# compiler allows either "Flags" or "FlagsAttribute".
internal enum Actions {
    None      = 0
    Read      = 0x0001,
    Write     = 0x0002,
    ReadWrite = Actions.Read | Actions.Write,
    Delete    = 0x0004,
    Query     = 0x0008,
    Sync      = 0x0010
}
```

Because **Actions** is an enumerated type, you can use all of the methods described in the previous section when working with bit-flag enumerated types. However, it would be nice if some of those functions behaved a little differently. For example, let's say you had the following code:

```
Actions actions = Actions.Read | Actions.Delete; // 0x0005
Console.WriteLine(actions.ToString());           // "Read, Delete"
```

When **ToString** is called, it attempts to translate the numeric value into its symbolic equivalent. The numeric value is 0x0005, which has no symbolic equivalent. However, the **ToString** method detects the existence of the **[Flags]** attribute on the **Actions** type, and **ToString** now treats the numeric value not as a single value but as a set of bit flags. Because the 0x0001 and 0x0004 bits are set, **ToString** generates the following string: "Read, Delete". If you remove the **[Flags]** attribute from the **Actions** type, **ToString** would return "5".

I discussed the **ToString** method in the previous section, and I showed that it offered three ways to format the output: "G" (general), "D" (decimal), and "X" (hex). When you're formatting an instance of an enumerated type by using the general format, the type is first checked to see if the **[Flags]** attribute is applied to it. If this attribute is not applied, a symbol matching the numeric value is looked up and returned. If the **[Flags]** attribute is applied, **ToString** works like this:

1. The set of numeric values defined by the enumerated type is obtained, and the numbers are sorted in descending order.

2. Each numeric value is bitwise-ANDed with the value in the enum instance, and if the result equals the numeric value, the string associated with the numeric value is appended to the output string, and the bits are considered accounted for and are turned off. This step is repeated until all numeric values have been checked or until the enum instance has all of its bits turned off.

3. If, after all the numeric values have been checked, the enum instance is still not 0, the enum instance has some bits turned on that do not correspond to any defined symbols. In this case, **ToString** returns the original number in the enum instance as a string.

4. If the enum instance's original value wasn't 0, the string with the comma-separated set of symbols is returned.

5. If the enum instance's original value was 0 and if the enumerated type has a symbol defined with a corresponding value of 0, the symbol is returned.

6. If we reach this step, "0" is returned.

If you prefer, you could define the **Actions** type without the **[Flags]** attribute and still get the correct string by using the "F" format:

```
// [Flags]     // Commented out now
internal enum Actions {
    None      = 0
    Read      = 0x0001,
    Write     = 0x0002,
    ReadWrite = Actions.Read | Actions.Write,
    Delete    = 0x0004,
    Query     = 0x0008,
    Sync      = 0x0010
}

Actions actions = Actions.Read | Actions.Delete; // 0x0005
Console.WriteLine(actions.ToString("F"));        // "Read, Delete"
```

If the numeric value has a bit that cannot be mapped to a symbol, the returned string will contain just a decimal number indicating the original numeric value; no symbols will appear in the string.

Note that the symbols you define in your enumerated type don't have to be pure powers of 2. For example, the **Actions** type could define a symbol called **All** with a value of 0x001F. If an instance of the **Actions** type has a value of 0x001F, formatting the instance will produce a string that contains "All". The other symbol strings won't appear.

So far, I've discussed how to convert numeric values into a string of flags. It's also possible to convert a string of comma-delimited symbols into a numeric value by calling **Enum**'s static **Parse** method. Here's some code demonstrating how to use this method:

```
// Because Query is defined as 8, 'a' is initialized to 8.
Actions a = (Actions) Enum.Parse(typeof(Actions), "Query", true);
Console.WriteLine(a.ToString());  // "Query"

// Because Query and Read are defined, 'a' is initialized to 9.
a = (Actions) Enum.Parse(typeof(Actions), "Query, Read", false);
Console.WriteLine(a.ToString());  // "Read, Query"

// Creates an instance of the Actions enum with a value of 28
a = (Actions) Enum.Parse(typeof(Actions), "28", false);
Console.WriteLine(a.ToString());  // "Delete, Query, Sync"
```

When **Parse** is called, it performs the following actions internally:

1. Removes all whitespace characters from the start and end of the string

2. If the first character of the string is a digit, plus sign ('+'), or minus sign ('-'), the string is assumed to be a number, and **Parse** returns an enum instance whose numeric value is equal to the string converted to its numeric equivalent.

3. The passed string is split into a set of tokens (separated by commas), and all white space is trimmed away from each token.

4. Each token string is looked up in the enum type's defined symbols. If the symbol is not found, a **System.ArgumentException** is thrown. If the symbol is found, bitwise-OR its numeric value into a running result, and then look up the next token.

5. If all tokens have been sought and found, return the running result.

You should never use the **IsDefined** method with bit flag enumerated types. It won't work for two reasons:

- If you pass a string to **IsDefined**, it doesn't split the string into separate tokens to look up; it will attempt to look up the string as through it were one big symbol with commas in it. Since you can't define an enum with a symbol that has commas in it, the symbol will never be found.

- If you pass a numeric value to **IsDefined**, it checks if the enumerated type defines a single symbol whose numeric value matches the passed-in number. Since this is unlikely for bit flags, **IsDefined** will usually return **false**.

Chapter 13

Arrays

Arrays are mechanisms that allow you to treat several items as a single collection. The Microsoft .NET common language runtime (CLR) supports single-dimensional arrays, multi-dimensional arrays, and jagged arrays (that is, arrays of arrays). All array types are implicitly derived from the **System.Array** abstract class, which itself is derived from **System.Object**. This means that arrays are always reference types that are allocated on the managed heap and that your application's variable or field contains a reference to the array and not the elements of the array itself. The following code makes this clearer:

```
Int32[] myIntegers;        // Declares a reference to an array
myIntegers = new Int32[100]; // Creates an array of 100 Int32s
```

On the first line, **myIntegers** is a variable that's capable of pointing to a single-dimensional array of **Int32**s. Initially, **myIntegers** will be set to **null** because I haven't allocated an array. The second line of code allocates an array of 100 **Int32** values; all of the **Int32**s are initialized to 0. Since arrays are reference types, the memory block required to hold the 100 unboxed **Int32**s is allocated on the managed heap. Actually, in addition to the array's elements, the memory block occupied by an array object also contains a type object pointer, a sync block index, and some additional overhead members as well. The address of this array's memory block is returned and saved in the variable **myIntegers**.

You can also create arrays of reference types:

```
Control[] myControls;        // Declares a reference to an array
myControls = new Control[50]; // Creates an array of 50 Control references
```

On the first line, **myControls** is a variable capable of pointing to a single-dimensional array of **Control** references. Initially, **myControls** will be set to **null** because I haven't allocated an array. The second line allocates an array of 50 **Control** references; all of these references are initialized to **null**. Because **Control** is a reference type, creating the array creates only a bunch of references; the actual objects aren't created at this time. The address of this memory block is returned and saved in the variable **myControls**.

Figure 13-1 shows how arrays of value types and arrays of reference types look in the managed heap.

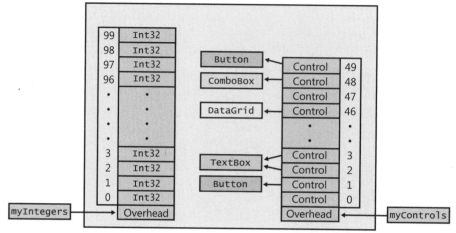

Figure 13-1   Arrays of value and reference types in the managed heap

In the figure, the **Controls** array shows the result after the following lines have executed:

```
myControls[1]  = new Button();
myControls[2]  = new TextBox();
myControls[3]  = myControls[2];   // Two elements refer to the same object.
myControls[46] = new DataGrid();
myControls[48] = new ComboBox();
myControls[49] = new Button();
```

Common Language Specification (CLS) compliance requires all arrays to be zero-based. This allows a method written in C# to create an array and pass the array's reference to code written in another language, such as Microsoft Visual Basic .NET. In addition, because zero-based arrays are, by far, the most common arrays, Microsoft has spent a lot of time optimizing their performance. However, the CLR does support non-zero-based arrays even though their use is discouraged. For those of you who don't care about performance or cross-language portability, I'll demonstrate how to create and use non-zero-based arrays later in this chapter.

Notice in Figure 13-1 that each array has some additional overhead information associated with it. This information contains the rank of the array (number of dimensions), the lower bounds for each dimension of the array (almost always 0), and the length of each dimension. The overhead also contains the array's element type. I'll mention the methods that allow you to query this overhead information later in this chapter.

So far, I've shown examples demonstrating how to create single-dimensional arrays. When possible, you should stick with single-dimensional, zero-based arrays, sometimes referred to as *SZ arrays*, or *vectors*. Vectors give the best performance because you can use specific IL instructions—such as **newarr**, **ldelem**, **ldelema**, **ldlen**, and **stelem**—to manipulate them. However, if you prefer to work with multi-dimensional arrays, you can. Here are some examples of multi-dimensional arrays:

```
// Create a 2-dimensional array of Doubles.
Double[,] myDoubles = new Double[10, 20];

// Create a 3-dimensional array of String references.
String[,,] myStrings = new String[5, 3, 10];
```

The CLR also supports jagged arrays, which are arrays of arrays. Zero-based, single-dimensional jagged arrays have the same performance as normal vectors. However, accessing the elements of a jagged array means that two or more array accesses must occur. Here are some examples of how to create an array of polygons with each polygon consisting of an array of **Point** instances:

```
// Create a single-dimensional array of Point arrays.
Point[][] myPolygons = new Point[3][];

// myPolygons[0] refers to an array of 10 Point instances.
myPolygons[0] = new Point[10];

// myPolygons[1] refers to an array of 20 Point instances.
myPolygons[1] = new Point[20];

// myPolygons[2] refers to an array of 30 Point instances.
myPolygons[2] = new Point[30];

// Display the Points in the first polygon.
for (Int32 x = 0; x < myPolygons[0].Length; x++)
   Console.WriteLine(myPolygons[0][x]);
```

> **Note**   The CLR verifies that an index into an array is valid. In other words, you can't create an array with 100 elements in it (numbered 0 through 99) and then try to access the element at index –5 or 100. Doing so will cause a **System.IndexOutOfRangeException** to be thrown. Allowing access to memory outside the range of an array would be a breach of type safety and a potential security hole, and the CLR doesn't allow verifiable code to do this. Usually, the performance degradation associated with index checking is insubstantial because the JIT (just-in-time) compiler normally checks array bounds once before a loop executes instead of at each loop iteration. However, if you're still concerned about the performance hit of the CLR's index checks, you can use unsafe code in C# to access the array. The "Array Access Performance" section later in this chapter demonstrates how to do this.

Casting Arrays

For arrays with reference type elements, the CLR allows you to implicitly cast the source array's element type to a target type. For the cast to succeed, both array types must have the same number of dimensions, and an implicit or explicit conversion from the source element type to the target element type must exist. The CLR doesn't allow the casting of arrays with value type elements to any other type. (However, by using the **Array.Copy** method, you can create a new array and populate its elements in order to obtain the desired effect.) The following code demonstrates how array casting works:

```
// Create a 2-dimensional FileStream array.
FileStream[,] fs2dim = new FileStream[5, 10];

// Implicit cast to a 2-dimensional Object array
Object[,] o2dim = fs2dim;

// Can't cast from 2-dimensional array to 1-dimensional array
// Compiler error CS0030: Cannot convert type 'object[*,*]' to
// 'System.IO.Stream[]'
Stream[] s1dim = (Stream[]) o2dim;

// Explicit cast to 2-dimensional Stream array
Stream[,] s2dim = (Stream[,]) o2dim;

// Explicit cast to 2-dimensional String array
// Compiles but throws InvalidCastException at run time
String[,] st2dim = (String[,]) o2dim;

// Create a 1-dimensional Int32 array (value types).
Int32[] i1dim = new Int32[5];

// Can't cast from array of value types to anything else
// Compiler error CS0030: Cannot convert type 'int[]' to 'object[]'
Object[] o1dim = (Object[]) i1dim;

// Create a new array, then use Array.Copy to coerce each element in the
// source array to the desired type in the destination array.
// The following code creates an array of references to boxed Int32s.
Object[] ob1dim = new Object[i1dim.Length];
Array.Copy(i1dim, ob1dim, i1dim.Length);
```

The **Array.Copy** method is not just a method that copies elements from one array to another. The **Copy** method handles overlapping regions of memory correctly, as does C's **memmove** function. C's **memcpy** function, on the other hand, doesn't handle overlapping regions correctly. The **Copy** method can also convert each array element as it is copied if conversion is required. The **Copy** method is capable of performing the following conversions:

- Boxing value type elements to reference type elements, such as copying an **Int32[]** to an **Object[]**.

- Unboxing reference type elements to value type elements, such as copying an **Object[]** to an **Int32[]**.

- Widening CLR primitive value types, such as copying elements from an **Int32[]** to a **Double[]**.

- Downcasting elements when copying between array types that can't be proven to be compatible based on the array's type, such as when casting from an **Object[]** to an **IFormattable[]**. If every object in the **Object[]** implements **IFormattable[]**, **Copy** will succeed.

Here's another example showing the usefulness of **Copy**:

```
// Define a value type that implements an interface.
internal struct MyValueType : IComparable {
    public Int32 CompareTo(Object obj) {
        ...
    }
}
```

```
public static class Program {
    public static void Main() {
        // Create an array of 100 value types.
        MyValueType[] src = new MyValueType[100];

        // Create an array of IComparable references.
        IComparable[] dest = new IComparable[src.Length];

        // Initialize an array of IComparable elements to refer to boxed
        // versions of elements in the source array.
        Array.Copy(src, dest, src.Length);
    }
}
```

As you might imagine, the Framework Class Library (FCL) takes advantage of **Array**'s **Copy** method quite frequently.

In some situations, it is useful to cast an array from one type to another. This kind of functionality is called *array covariance*. When you take advantage of array covariance, you should be aware of an associated performance penalty. Let's say you have the following code:

```
String[] sa = new String[100];
Object[] oa = sa;    // oa refers to an array of String elements
oa[5] = "Jeff";      // Perf hit: CLR checks oa's element type for String; OK
oa[3] = 5;           // Perf hit: CLR checks oa's element type for Int32; throws
                     // ArrayTypeMismatchException
```

In the code above, the **oa** variable is typed as an **Object[]**; however, it really refers to a **String[]**. The compiler will allow you to write code that attempts to put a 5 into an array element because 5 is an **Int32**, which is derived from **Object**. Of course, the CLR must ensure type safety, and when assigning to an array element, the CLR must ensure that the assignment is legal. So the CLR must check at run time whether the array contains **Int32** elements. In this case, it doesn't, and the assignment cannot be allowed; the CLR will throw an **ArrayTypeMismatchException**.

> **Note** If you just need to make a copy of some array elements to another array, `System.Buffer`'s `BlockCopy` method executes faster than `Array`'s `Copy` method. However, `Buffer`'s `BlockCopy` supports only primitive types; it does not offer the same casting abilities as `Array`'s `Copy` method. The `Int32` parameters are expressed as byte offsets within the array, not as element indexes. `BlockCopy` is really designed for copying data that is bitwise compatible from one array type to another blittable array type, such as copying a `Byte[]` containing Unicode characters (in the proper byte order) to a `Char[]`. This method allows programmers to partially make up for the lack of the ability to treat an array as a block of memory of any type.
>
> If you need to reliably copy a set of array elements from one array to another array, you should use `System.Array`'s `ConstrainedCopy` method. This method guarantees that the copy operation will either complete or throw an exception without destroying any data within the destination array. This allows `ConstrainedCopy` to be used in a constrained execution region (CER). In order to offer this guarantee, `ConstrainedCopy` requires that the source array's element type be the same as or derived from the destination array's element type. In addition, it will not perform any boxing, unboxing, or downcasting.

All Arrays Are Implicitly Derived from `System.Array`

When you declare an array variable like this:

```
FileStream[] fsArray;
```

then the CLR automatically creates a `FileStream[]` type for the AppDomain. This type will be implicitly derived from the `System.Array` type, and therefore, all of the instance methods and properties defined on the `System.Array` type will be inherited by the `FileStream[]` type, allowing these methods and properties to be called using the `fsArray` variable. This makes working with arrays extremely convenient because there are many helpful instance methods and properties defined by `System.Array`, such as `Clone`, `CopyTo`, `GetLength`, `GetLongLength`, `GetLowerBound`, `GetUpperBound`, `Length`, `Rank`, and others.

The `System.Array` type also exposes a large number of extremely useful static methods that operate on arrays. These methods all take a reference to an array as a parameter. Some of the useful static methods are: `AsReadOnly`, `BinarySearch`, `Clear`, `ConstrainedCopy`, `ConvertAll`, `Copy`, `Exists`, `Find`, `FindAll`, `FindIndex`, `FindLast`, `FindLastIndex`, `ForEach`, `IndexOf`, `LastIndexOf`, `Resize`, `Reverse`, `Sort`, and `TrueForAll`. There are many overloads for each of these methods. In fact, many of the methods provide generic overloads for compile-time type safety as well as good performance. I encourage you to examine the SDK documentation to get an understanding of how useful and powerful these methods are.

All Arrays Implicitly Implement `IEnumerable`, `ICollection`, and `IList`

There are many methods that operate on various collection objects because the methods are declared with parameters such as `IEnumerable`, `ICollection`, and `IList`. It is possible to pass arrays to these methods because `System.Array` also implements these three interfaces.

`System.Array` implements these non-generic interfaces because they treat all elements as `System.Object`. However, it would be nice to have `System.Array` implement the generic equivalent of these interfaces, providing better compile-time type safety as well as better performance.

The CLR team didn't want `System.Array` to implement `IEnumerable<T>`, `ICollection<T>`, and `IList<T>`, though, because of issues related to multi-dimensional arrays and non-zero-based arrays. Defining these interfaces on `System.Array` would have enabled these interfaces for all array types. Instead, the CLR performs a little trick: when a single-dimensional, zero-lower bound array type is created, the CLR automatically makes the array type implement `IEnumerable<T>`, `ICollection<T>`, and `IList<T>` (where `T` is the array's element type) and also implements the three interfaces for all of the array type's base types as long as they are reference types. The following hierarchy diagram helps make this clear:

```
Object
    Array (non-generic IEnumerable, ICollection, IList)
        Object[]            (IEnumerable, ICollection, IList of Object)
            String[]        (IEnumerable, ICollection, IList of String)
            Stream[]        (IEnumerable, ICollection, IList of Stream)
                FileStream[] (IEnumerable, ICollection, IList of FileStream)
            .
            .               (other arrays of reference types)
            .
```

So, for example, if you have the following line of code

```
FileStream[] fsArray;
```

then when the CLR creates the `FileStream[]` type, it will cause this type to automatically implement the `IEnumerable<FileStream>`, `ICollection<FileStream>`, and `IList<FileStream>` interfaces. Furthermore, the `FileStream[]` type will also implement the interfaces for the base types: `IEnumerable<Stream>`, `IEnumerable<Object>`, `ICollection<Stream>`, `ICollection<Object>`, `IList<Stream>`, and `IList<Object>`. Since all of these interfaces are automatically implemented by the CLR, the **fsArray** variable could be used wherever any of these interfaces exist. For example, the **fsArray** variable could be passed to methods that have any of the following prototypes:

```
void M1(IList<FileStream> fsList) { … }
void M2(ICollection<Stream> sCollection) { … }
void M3(IEnumerable<Object> oEnumerable) { … }
```

Note that if the array contains value type elements, the array type will not implement the interfaces for the element's base types. For example, if you have the following line of code:

```
DateTime[] dtArray; // An array of value types
```

then the `DateTime[]` type will implement `IEnumerable<DateTime>`, `ICollection<DateTime>`, and `IList<DateTime>` only; it will not implement versions of these interfaces that are generic over `System.ValueType` or `System.Object`. This means that the **dtArray** variable cannot be passed as an argument to the **M3** method shown earlier. The reason for this is because arrays of value types are laid out in memory differently than arrays of reference types. Array memory layout was discussed earlier in this chapter.

Passing and Returning Arrays

Arrays are always passed by reference to a method, and the called method is able to modify the elements in the array. If you don't want to allow this, you must make a copy of the array and pass the copy into the method. Note that the **Array.Copy** method performs a shallow copy, and therefore, if the array's elements are reference types, the new array refers to the already-existing objects.

Similarly, some methods return a reference to an array. If the method constructs and initializes the array, returning a reference to the array is fine. But if the method wants to return a reference to an internal array maintained by a field, you must decide if you want the method's caller to have direct access to this array and its elements. If you do, just return the array's reference. But most often, you won't want the method's caller to have such access, so the method should construct a new array and call **Array.Copy**, returning a reference to the new array. Again, be aware that **Array.Copy** makes a shallow copy of the original array.

If you define a method that returns a reference to an array, and if that array has no elements in it, your method can return either **null** or a reference to an array with zero elements in it. When you're implementing this kind of method, Microsoft strongly recommends that you implement the method by having it return a zero-length array because doing so simplifies the code that a developer calling the method must write. For example, this easy-to-understand code runs correctly even if there are no appointments to iterate over:

```
// This code is easier to write and understand.
Appointment[] appointments = GetAppointmentsForToday();
for (Int32 a = 0; a < appointments.Length; a++) {
   ...
}
```

The following code also runs correctly if there are no appointments to iterate over. However, this code is slightly more difficult to write and understand:

```
// This code is harder to write and understand.
Appointment[] appointments = GetAppointmentsForToday();
if (appointments != null) {
   for (Int32 a = 0, a < appointments.Length; a++) {
      // Do something with appointments[a]
   }
}
```

If you design your methods to return arrays with zero elements instead of **null**, callers of your methods will have an easier time working with them. By the way, you should do the same for fields. If your type has a field that's a reference to an array, you should consider having the field refer to an array even if the array has no elements in it.

Creating Non-Zero–Lower Bound Arrays

Earlier I mentioned that it's possible to create and work with arrays that have non-zero lower bounds. You can dynamically create your own arrays by calling **Array**'s static **CreateInstance** method. Several overloads of this method exist, allowing you to specify the type of the elements in the array, the number of dimensions in the array, the lower bounds of each dimension, and the number of elements in each dimension. **CreateInstance** allocates memory for the array, saves the parameter information in the overhead portion of the array's memory block, and returns a reference to the array. If the array has two or more dimensions, you can cast the reference returned from **CreateInstance** to an *ElementType*[] variable (where *ElementType* is some type name), making it easier for you to access the elements in the array. If the array has just one dimension, in C#, you have to use **Array**'s **GetValue** and **SetValue** methods to access the elements of the array.

Here's some code that demonstrates how to dynamically create a 2-dimensional array of **System.Decimal** values. The first dimension represents calendar years from 2005 to 2009 inclusive, and the second dimension represents quarters from 1 to 4 inclusive. The code iterates over all the elements in the dynamic array. I could have hard-coded the array's bounds into the code, which would have given better performance, but I decided to use **System.Array**'s **GetLowerBound** and **GetUpperBound** methods to demonstrate their use.

```
using System;

public sealed class DynamicArrays {
    public static void Main() {
        // I want a 2-dimensional array [2005..2009][1..4].
        Int32[] lowerBounds = { 2005, 1 };
        Int32[] lengths     = {    5, 4 };
        Decimal[,] quarterlyRevenue = (Decimal[,])
            Array.CreateInstance(typeof(Decimal), lengths, lowerBounds);

        Console.WriteLine("{0,4}  {1,9}  {2,9}  {3,9}  {4,9}",
            "Year", "Q1", "Q2", "Q3", "Q4");
        Int32 firstYear    = quarterlyRevenue.GetLowerBound(0);
        Int32 lastYear     = quarterlyRevenue.GetUpperBound(0);
        Int32 firstQuarter = quarterlyRevenue.GetLowerBound(1);
        Int32 lastQuarter  = quarterlyRevenue.GetUpperBound(1);

        for (Int32 year = firstYear; year <= lastYear; year++) {
            Console.Write(year + "  ");
            for (Int32 quarter = firstQuarter; quarter <= lastQuarter; quarter++) {
                Console.Write("{0,9:C}  ", quarterlyRevenue[year, quarter]);
            }
            Console.WriteLine();
        }
    }
}
```

If you compile and run this code, you get the following output:

Year	Q1	Q2	Q3	Q4
2005	$0.00	$0.00	$0.00	$0.00
2006	$0.00	$0.00	$0.00	$0.00
2007	$0.00	$0.00	$0.00	$0.00
2008	$0.00	$0.00	$0.00	$0.00
2009	$0.00	$0.00	$0.00	$0.00

Array Access Performance

Internally, the CLR actually supports two different kinds of arrays:

- Single-dimensional arrays with a lower-bound of 0. These arrays are sometimes called SZ (for single-dimensional, zero-based) arrays or vectors.

- Single-dimensional and multi-dimensional arrays with an unknown lower-bound.

You can actually see the different kinds of arrays by executing the following code (the output is shown in the code's comments):

```
using System;

public sealed class Program {
    public static void Main() {
    Array a;

    // Create a 1-dim, 0-based array, with no elements in it
    a = new String[0];
    Console.WriteLine(a.GetType());   // "System.String[]"

    // Create a 1-dim, 0-based array, with no elements in it
    a = Array.CreateInstance(typeof(String),
       new Int32[] { 0 }, new Int32[] { 0 });
    Console.WriteLine(a.GetType());   // "System.String[]"

    // Create a 1-dim, 1-based array, with no elements in it
    a = Array.CreateInstance(typeof(String),
       new Int32[] { 0 }, new Int32[] { 1 });
    Console.WriteLine(a.GetType());   // "System.String[*]"  <-- INTERESTING!

    Console.WriteLine();

    // Create a 2-dim, 0-based array, with no elements in it
    a = new String[0, 0];
    Console.WriteLine(a.GetType());   // "System.String[,]"

    // Create a 2-dim, 0-based array, with no elements in it
    a = Array.CreateInstance(typeof(String),
       new Int32[] { 0, 0 }, new Int32[] { 0, 0 });
    Console.WriteLine(a.GetType());   // "System.String[,]"
```

```
    // Create a 2-dim, 1-based array, with no elements in it
    a = Array.CreateInstance(typeof(String),
        new Int32[] { 0, 0 }, new Int32[] { 1, 1 });
    Console.WriteLine(a.GetType());    // "System.String[,]"
  }
}
```

Next to each **Console.WriteLine** is a comment that indicates the output. For the single-dimensional arrays, the zero-based arrays display a type name of **System.String[]**, whereas the 1-based array displays a type name of **System.String[*]**. The * indicates that the CLR knows that this array is not zero-based. Note that C# does not allow you to declare a variable of type **String[*]**, and therefore it is not possible to use C# syntax to access a single-dimensional, non-zero-based array. Although you can call **Array**'s **GetValue** and **SetValue** methods to access the elements of the array, this access will be slow due to the overhead of the method call.

For multi-dimensional arrays, the zero-based and 1-based arrays all display the same type name: **System.String[,]**. The CLR treats all multi-dimensional arrays as though they are *not* zero-based at run time. This would make you think that the type name should display as **System.String[*,*]**; however, the CLR doesn't use the *s for multi-dimensional arrays because they would always be present, and the asterisks would just confuse most developers.

Accessing the elements of a single-dimensional, zero-based array is much faster than accessing the elements of a non-zero-based, single-dimensional array or a multi-dimensional array. There are several reasons for this. First, there are specific IL instructions—such as **newarr**, **ldelem**, **ldelema**, **ldlen**, and **stelem**—to manipulate single-dimensional, zero-based arrays, and these special IL instructions cause the JIT compiler to emit optimized code. For example, the JIT compiler will emit code that assumes that the array is zero-based, and this means that an offset doesn't have to be subtracted from the specified index when accessing an element. Second, in common situations, the JIT compiler is able to hoist the index range–checking code out of the loop, causing it to execute just once. For example, look at the following commonly written code:

```
using System;

public static class Program {
  public static void Main() {
    Int32[] a = new Int32[5];
    for(Int32 index = 0; index < a.Length; index++) {
      // Do something with a[index]
    }
  }
}
```

The first thing to notice about this code is the call to the array's **Length** property in the **for** loop's test expression. Since **Length** is a property, querying the length actually represents a method call. However, the JIT compiler knows that **Length** is a property on the **Array** class, and the JIT compiler will actually generate code that calls the property just once and stores the result in a temporary variable that will be checked with each iteration of the loop. The result is that the JITted code is fast. In fact, some developers have underestimated the abilities of the JIT compiler and have tried to write "clever code" in an attempt to help the JIT compiler. However, any clever attempts that you come up with will almost certainly impact performance negatively and make your code harder to read, reducing its maintainability. You are better off leaving the call to the array's **Length** property in the code above instead of attempting to cache it in a local variable yourself.

The second thing to notice about the code above is that the JIT compiler knows that the **for** loop is accessing array elements 0 through **Length - 1**. So the JIT compiler produces code that, at run time, tests that all array accesses will be within the array's valid range. Specifically, the JIT compiler produces code to check if **((Length - 1) <= a.GetUpperBound(0))**. This check occurs just before the loop. If the check is good, the JIT compiler will not generate code inside the loop to verify that each array access is within the valid range. This allows array access within the loop to be very fast.

Unfortunately, as I alluded to earlier in this chapter, accessing elements of a non-zero-based single-dimensional array or of a multi-dimensional array is much slower than single-dimensional, zero-based array. For these array types, the JIT compiler doesn't hoist index checking outside of loops, so each array access validates the specified indices. In addition, the JIT compiler adds code to subtract the array's lower bounds from the specified index, which also slows the code down, even if you're using a multi-dimensional array that happens to be zero-based.

So if performance is a concern to you, you might want to consider using an array of arrays (a jagged array) instead of a rectangular array. C# and the CLR also allow you to access an array by using unsafe (non-verifiable) code, which is, in effect, a technique that allows you to turn off the index bounds checking when accessing an array. Note that this unsafe array manipulation technique is usable with arrays whose elements are **SByte**, **Byte**, **Int16**, **UInt16**, **Int32**, **UInt32**, **Int64**, **UInt64**, **Char**, **Single**, **Double**, **Decimal**, **Boolean**, an enumerated type, or a value type structure whose fields are any of the aforementioned types.

This is a very powerful feature that should be used with extreme caution because it allows you to perform direct memory accesses. If these memory accesses are outside the bounds of the array, an exception will not be thrown; instead, you will be corrupting memory, violating type safety, and possibly opening a security hole! For this reason, the assembly containing the unsafe code must either be granted full trust or at least have the SecurityPermission with Skip Verification turned on.

The following C# code demonstrates three techniques (safe, jagged, and unsafe), for accessing a 2-dimensional array:

```
using System;
using System.Diagnostics;

public static class Program {
    public static void Main() {
        const Int32 numElements = 100;
        const Int32 testCount = 10000;
        Stopwatch sw;
```

```csharp
   // Declare a 2-dimensional array
   Int32[,] a2Dim = new Int32[numElements, numElements];

   // Declare a 2-dimensional array as a jagged array (a vector of vectors)
   Int32[][] aJagged = new Int32[numElements][];
   for (Int32 x = 0; x < numElements; x++)
      aJagged[x] = new Int32[numElements];


   // 1: Access all elements of the array by using the usual, safe technique
   sw = Stopwatch.StartNew();
   for (Int32 test = 0; test < testCount; test++)
      Safe2DimArrayAccess(a2Dim);
   Console.WriteLine("{0}: Safe2DimArrayAccess", sw.Elapsed);

   // 2: Access all elements of the array by using the jagged array technique
   sw = Stopwatch.StartNew();
   for (Int32 test = 0; test < testCount; test++)
      SafeJaggedArrayAccess(aJagged);
   Console.WriteLine("{0}: SafeJaggedArrayAccess", sw.Elapsed);

   // 3: Access all elements of the array by using the unsafe technique
   sw = Stopwatch.StartNew();
   for (Int32 test = 0; test < testCount; test++)
      Unsafe2DimArrayAccess(a2Dim);
   Console.WriteLine("{0}: Unsafe2DimArrayAccess", sw.Elapsed);
}

private static void Safe2DimArrayAccess(Int32[,] a) {
   for (Int32 x = 0; x < a.GetLength(0); x++) {
      for (Int32 y = 0; y < a.GetLength(1); y++) {
         Int32 element = a[x, y];
      }
   }
}

private static void SafeJaggedArrayAccess(Int32[][] a) {
   for (Int32 x = 0; x < a.GetLength(0); x++) {
      for (Int32 y = 0; y < a[x].GetLength(0); y++) {
         Int32 element = a[x][y];
      }
   }
}

private static unsafe void Unsafe2DimArrayAccess(Int32[,] a) {
   Int32 dim0LowIndex  = 0;    // a.GetLowerBound(0);
   Int32 dim0HighIndex = a.GetUpperBound(0);

   Int32 dim1LowIndex  = 0;    // a.GetLowerBound(1);
   Int32 dim1HighIndex = a.GetUpperBound(1);

   Int32 dim0Elements = dim0HighIndex - dim0LowIndex;

   fixed (Int32* pi = &a[0, 0]) {
      for (Int32 x = dim0LowIndex; x <= dim0HighIndex; x++) {
         Int32 baseOfDim = x * dim0Elements;
```

```
        for (Int32 y = dim1LowIndex; y <= dim1HighIndex; y++) {
            Int32 element = pi[baseOfDim + y];
        }
    }
  }
}
```

The `Unsafe2DimArrayAccess` method is marked with the **unsafe** modifier, which is required to use C#'s **fixed** statement. To compile this code, you'll have to specify the **/unsafe** switch when invoking the C# compiler or check the "Allow Unsafe Code" check box on the Build tab of the Project Properties pane in Microsoft Visual Studio.

When I run this program on my machine, I get the following output:

```
00:00:02.7977902: Safe2DimArrayAccess
00:00:02.2690798: SafeJaggedArrayAccess
00:00:00.2265131: Unsafe2DimArrayAccess
```

As you can see, the safe array technique is the slowest. The jagged array access takes a little less time to complete than the safe access. However, you should note that creating the jagged array is more time consuming than creating the multi-dimensional array because creating the jagged array requires an object to be allocated on the heap for each dimension, causing the garbage collector to kick in periodically. So there is a trade-off: If you need to create a lot of "multi-dimensional arrays" and you intend to access the elements infrequently, it is quicker to create a multi-dimensional array. If you need to create the "multi-dimensional array" just once, and you access its elements frequently, a jagged array will give you better performance. Certainly, in most applications, the latter scenario is the more common of the two.

Finally, notice that the unsafe array access technique is extremely fast. In fact, it accesses the elements in less than 1/10 of the time of the jagged array access and it also uses a real 2-dimensional array, making creation of an unsafe array much cheaper than creation of a jagged array. Obviously, the unsafe technique wins hands-down, but there are three serious downsides to using this technique:

- The code that accesses the array elements is more complicated to read and write than with the other techniques because you are using C#'s **fixed** statement and performing memory-address calculations.

- If you make a mistake in the calculation, you are accessing memory that is not part of the array. This can result in an incorrect calculation, corruption of memory, a type-safety violation, and a potential security hole.

- Due to the potential problems, the CLR will allow unsafe code to run only if the administrator or end-user grants permission. By default, an assembly that is locally installed on the machine is granted this permission. However, by default, an assembly that loads via the intranet or Internet will not be granted this permission, and the CLR will throw an exception when it attempts to load an assembly with unsafe code. These defaults can be changed by using the CASPol.exe tool that ships with the .NET Framework.

Unsafe Array Access and Fixed-Size Array

Unsafe array access is very powerful because it allows you to access:

- Elements within a managed array object that resides on the heap (as the previous section demonstrated).

- Elements within an array that resides on an unmanaged heap. The `SecureString` example in Chapter 11, "Chars, Strings, and Working with Text," demonstrated using unsafe array access on an array returned from calling `System.Runtime.InteropServices.Marshal` class's `SecureStringToCoTaskMemUnicode` method.

- Elements within an array that resides on the thread's stack.

In cases in which performance is extremely critical, you could avoid allocating a managed array object on the heap and instead allocate the array on the thread's stack by using C#'s `stackalloc` statement (which works a lot like C's `alloca` function). The `stackalloc` statement can be used to create a single-dimensional, zero-based array of value type elements only, and the value type must not contain any reference type fields. Really, you should think of this as allocating a block of memory that you can manipulate by using unsafe pointers, and therefore, you cannot pass the address of this memory buffer to the vast majority of FCL methods. Of course, the stack-allocated memory (array) will automatically be freed when the method returns; this is where we get the performance improvement. Using this feature also requires you specify the `/unsafe` switch to the C# compiler.

The `StackallocDemo` method in the code below shows an example of how to use C#'s `stackalloc` statement:

```
using System;

public static class Program {
   public static void Main() {
      StackallocDemo();
      InlineArrayDemo();
   }

   private static void StackallocDemo() {
      unsafe {
         const Int32 width = 20;
         Char* pc = stackalloc Char[width]; // Allocates array on stack

         String s = "Jeffrey Richter";      // 15 characters

         for (Int32 index = 0; index < width; index++) {
            pc[width - index - 1] =
               (index < s.Length) ? s[index] : '.';
         }

         // The line below displays ".....rethciR yerffeJ"
         Console.WriteLine(new String(pc, 0, width));
```

```
        }
    }

    private static void InlineArrayDemo() {
        unsafe {
            CharArray ca;                    // Allocates array on stack
            Int32 widthInBytes = sizeof(CharArray);
            Int32 width = widthInBytes / 2;

            String s = "Jeffrey Richter"; // 15 characters

            for (Int32 index = 0; index < width; index++) {
                ca.Characters[width - index - 1] =
                    (index < s.Length) ? s[index] : '.';
            }

            // The line below displays ".....rethciR yerffeJ"
            Console.WriteLine(new String(ca.Characters, 0, width));
        }
    }
}

internal unsafe struct CharArray {
    // This array is embedded inline inside the structure
    public fixed Char Characters[20];
}
```

Normally, because arrays are reference types, an array field defined in a structure is really just a pointer or reference to an array; the array itself lives outside of the structure's memory. However, it is possible to embed an array directly inside a structure as shown by the **CharArray** structure in the preceding code. To embed an array directly inside a structure, there are several requirements:

- The type must be a structure (value type); you cannot embed an array inside a class (reference type).

- The field or its defining structure must be marked with the **unsafe** keyword.

- The array field must be marked with the **fixed** keyword.

- The array must be single-dimensional and zero-based.

- The array's element type must be one of the following types: **Boolean**, **Char**, **SByte**, **Byte**, **Int32**, **UInt32**, **Int64**, **UInt64**, **Single**, or **Double**.

Inline arrays are typically used for scenarios that involve interoperating with unmanaged code where the unmanaged data structure also has an inline array. However, inline arrays can be used in other scenarios as well. The **InlineArrayDemo** method in the code shown earlier offers an example of how to use an inline array. The **InlineArrayDemo** method performs the same function as the **StackallocDemo** method; it just does it in a different way.

Chapter 14

Interfaces

Many programmers are familiar with the concept of multiple inheritance: the ability to define a class that is derived from two or more base classes. For example, imagine a class named `TransmitData`, whose function is to transmit data, and another class named `ReceiveData`, whose function is to receive data. Now imagine that you want to create a class named `Socket-Port`, whose function is to transmit and receive data. In order to accomplish this, you would want to derive `SocketPort` from both `TransmitData` and `ReceiveData`.

Some programming languages allow multiple inheritance, making it possible for the `Socket-Port` class to be derived from the two base classes, `TransmitData` and `ReceiveData`. However, the common language runtime (CLR)—and therefore all managed programming languages—does not support multiple inheritance. Rather than not offer any kind of multiple inheritance at all, the CLR does offer scaled-down multiple inheritance via *interfaces*. This chapter will discuss how to define and use interfaces as well as provide some guidelines to help you determine when to use an interface rather than a base class.

Class and Interface Inheritance

In the Microsoft .NET Framework, there is a class called `System.Object` that defines four public instance methods: `ToString`, `Equals`, `GetHashCode`, and `GetType`. This class is the root or ultimate base class of all other classes—all classes will inherit `object`'s four instance methods. This also means that code written to operate on an instance of the `object` class can actually perform operations on an instance of any class.

Since someone at Microsoft has implemented `object`'s methods, any class derived from `object` is actually inheriting the following:

- **The method signatures**   This allows code to think that it is operating on an instance of the `object` class, when in fact, it could be operating on an instance of some other class.

- **The implementation of these methods**   This allows the developer defining a class derived from `object` not to be required to implement `object`'s methods manually.

In the CLR, a class is always derived from one and only one class (that must ultimately be derived from `object`). This base class provides a set of method signatures and implementations for these methods. And a cool thing about defining a new class is that it can become the base class for another class defined in the future by some other developer—all of the method signatures and their implementations will be inherited by the new derived class.

The CLR also allows developers to define an *interface*, which is really just a way to give a name to a set of method signatures. These methods do not come with any implementation at all. A class inherits an interface by specifying the interface's name, and the class must explicitly provide implementations of the interface's methods before the CLR will consider the type definition to be valid. Of course, implementing interface methods can be tedious, which is why I referred to interface inheritance as a scaled-down mechanism to achieve multiple inheritance. The C# compiler and the CLR actually allow a class to inherit several interfaces, and of course, the class must provide implementations for all of the inherited interface methods.

One of the great features of class inheritance is that it allows instances of a derived type to be substituted in all contexts that expect instances of a base type. Similarly, interface inheritance allows instances of a type that implements the interface to be substituted in all contexts that expect instances of the named interface type. We will now look at how to define interfaces to make our discussion more concrete.

Defining an Interface

As mentioned in the previous section, an interface is a named set of method signatures. Note that interfaces can also define events, parameterless properties, and parameterful properties (indexers in C#) because all of these are just syntax shorthands that map to methods anyway as shown in previous chapters. However, an interface cannot define any constructor methods. In addition, an interface is not allowed to define any instance fields.

Although the CLR does allow an interface to define static methods, static fields, constants, and static constructors, a CLS-compliant interface must not have any of these static members because some programming languages aren't able to define or access them. In fact, C# prevents an interface from defining any of these static members.

In C#, you use the **interface** keyword to define an interface, giving it a name and its set of instance method signatures. Here are the definitions of a few interfaces defined in the Framework Class Library:

```
public interface IDisposable {
   void Dispose();
}

public interface IEnumerable {
   IEnumerator GetEnumerator();
}

public interface IEnumerable<T> : IEnumerable {
   IEnumerator<T> GetEnumerator();
}

public interface ICollection<T> : IEnumerable<T>, IEnumerable {
   void    Add(T item);
   void    Clear();
   Boolean Contains(T item);
   void    CopyTo(T[] array, Int32 arrayIndex);
   Boolean Remove(T item);
   Int32   Count      { get; } // Read-only property
   Boolean IsReadOnly { get; } // Read-only property
}
```

To the CLR, an interface definition is just like a type definition. That is, the CLR will define an internal data structure for the interface type object, and reflection can be used to query features of the interface type. Like types, an interface can be defined at file scope or defined nested within another type. When defining the interface type, you can specify whatever visibility/accessibility (**public**, **protected**, **internal**, etc.) you desire.

By convention, interface type names are prefixed with an uppercase **I**, making it easy to spot an interface type in source code. The CLR does support generic interfaces (as you can see from some of the previous examples) as well as generic methods in an interface. I will discuss some of the many features offered by generic interfaces later in this chapter and in Chapter 16, "Generics," in which I cover generics more broadly.

An interface definition can "inherit" other interfaces. However, I use the word *inherit* here rather loosely because interface inheritance doesn't work exactly as does class inheritance. I prefer to think of interface inheritance as including the contract of other interfaces. For example, the **ICollection<T>** interface definition includes the contracts of the **IEnumerable<T>** and **IEnumerable** interfaces. This means that:

- Any class that inherits the **ICollection<T>** interface must implement all of the methods defined by the **ICollection<T>**, **IEnumerable<T>**, and **IEnumerable** interfaces.

■ Any code that expects an object whose type implements the **ICollection<T>** interface can assume that the object's type also implements the methods of the **IEnumerable<T>** and **IEnumerable** interfaces.

Inheriting an Interface

In this section, I'll show how to define a type that implements an interface, and then I'll show how to create an instance of this type and use the object to call the interface's methods. C# actually makes this pretty simple, but what happens behind the scenes is a bit more complicated. I'll explain what is happening behind the scenes later in this chapter.

The **System.IComparable<T>** interface is defined (in MSCorLib.dll) as follows:

```
public interface IComparable<T> {
    Int32 CompareTo(T other);
}
```

The following code shows how to define a type that implements this interface and also shows code that compares two **Point** objects:

```
using System;


// Point is derived from System.Object and implements IComparable<T> for Point.
public sealed class Point : IComparable<Point> {
    private Int32 m_x, m_y;

    public Point(Int32 x, Int32 y) {
        m_x = x;
        m_y = y;
    }

    // This method implements IComparable<T> for Point
    public Int32 CompareTo(Point other) {
        return Math.Sign(Math.Sqrt(m_x * m_x + m_y * m_y)
            - Math.Sqrt(other.m_x * other.m_x + other.m_y * other.m_y));
    }

    public override String ToString() {
        return String.Format("({0}, {1})", m_x, m_y);
    }
}


public static class Program {
    public static void Main() {
        Point[] points = new Point[] {
            new Point(3, 3),
            new Point(1, 2),
        };
```

```
   // Here is a call to Point's IComparable<T> CompareTo method
   if (points[0].CompareTo(points[1]) > 0) {
      Point tempPoint = points[0];
      points[0] = points[1];
      points[1] = tempPoint;
   }
   Console.WriteLine("Points from closest to (0, 0) to farthest:");
   foreach (Point p in points)
      Console.WriteLine(p);
   }
}
```

The C# compiler requires that a method that implements an interface be marked as **public**. The CLR requires that interface methods be marked as virtual. If you do not explicitly mark the method as **virtual** in your source code, the compiler marks the method as virtual and sealed; this prevents a derived class from overriding the interface method. If you explicitly mark the method as **virtual**, the compiler marks the method as virtual (and leaves it unsealed); this allows a derived class to override the interface method.

If an interface method is sealed, a derived class cannot override the method. However, a derived class can re-inherit the same interface and can provide its own implementation for the interface's methods. When calling an interface's method on an object, the implementation associated with the object's type is called. Here is an example that demonstrates this:

```
using System;

public static class Program {
   public static void Main() {
      /************************** First Example **************************/
      Base b = new Base();

      // Calls Dispose by using b's type: "Base's Dispose"
      b.Dispose();

      // Calls Dispose by using b's object's type: "Base's Dispose"
      ((IDisposable)b).Dispose();


      /************************** Second Example **************************/
      Derived d = new Derived();

      // Calls Dispose by using d's type: "Derived's Dispose"
      d.Dispose();

      // Calls Dispose by using d's object's type: "Derived's Dispose"
      ((IDisposable)d).Dispose();


      /************************** Third Example **************************/
      b = new Derived();

      // Calls Dispose by using b's type: "Base's Dispose"
      b.Dispose();
```

```
        // Calls Dispose by using b's object's type: "Derived's Dispose"
        ((IDisposable)b).Dispose();
    }
}

// This class is derived from Object and it implements IDisposable
internal class Base : IDisposable {
    // This method is implicitly sealed and cannot be overridden
    public void Dispose() {
        Console.WriteLine("Base's Dispose");
    }
}

// This class is derived from Base and it re-implements IDisposable
internal class Derived : Base, IDisposable {
    // This method cannot override Base's Dispose. 'new' is used to indicate
    // that this method re-implements IDisposable's Dispose method
    new public void Dispose() {
        Console.WriteLine("Derived's Dispose");

        // NOTE: The next line shows how to call a base class's implementation (if desired)
        // base.Dispose();
    }
}
```

More About Calling Interface Methods

The FCL's **System.String** type inherits **System.Object**'s method signatures and their implementations. In addition, the **String** type also implements several interfaces: **IComparable**, **ICloneable**, **IConvertible**, **IEnumerable**, **IComparable<String>**, **IEnumerable<Char>**, and **IEquatable<String>**. This means that the **String** type isn't required to implement (or override) the methods its **Object** base type offers. However, the **String** type must implement the methods declared in all of the interfaces.

The CLR allows you to define field, parameter, or local variables that are of an interface type. Using a variable of an interface type allows you to call methods defined by that interface. In addition, the CLR will allow you to call methods defined by **Object** because all classes inherit **Object**'s methods. The following code demonstrates:

```
// The s variable refers to a String object.
String s = "Jeffrey";
// Using s, I can call any method defined in
// String, Object, IComparable, ICloneable, IConvertible, IEnumerable, etc.

// The cloneable variable refers to the same String object
ICloneable cloneable = s;
// Using cloneable, I can call any method declared by the
// ICloneable interface (or any method defined by Object) only.
```

```
// The comparable variable refers to the same String object
IComparable comparable = s;
// Using comparable, I can call any method declared by the
// IComparable interface (or any method defined by Object) only.

// The enumerable variable refers to the same String object
// At run time, you can cast a variable from one interface to another as
// long as the object's type implements both interfaces.
IEnumerable enumerable = (IEnumerable) comparable;
// Using enumerable, I can call any method declared by the
// IEnumerable interface (or any method defined by Object) only.
```

In this code, all of the variables refer to the same "Jeffrey" **String** object that is in the managed heap, and therefore, any method that I call while using any of these variables affects the one "Jeffrey" **String** object. However, the type of the variable indicates the action that I can perform on the object. The **s** variable is of type **String**, and therefore, I can use **s** to call any members defined by the **String** type (such as the **Length** property). I can also use the variable **s** to call any methods inherited from **Object** (such as **GetType**).

The **cloneable** variable is of the **ICloneable** interface type, and therefore, using the **cloneable** variable, I can call the **Clone** method defined by this interface. In addition, I can call any method defined by **Object** (such as **GetType**) because the CLR knows that all types derive from **Object**. However, using the **cloneable** variable, I cannot call public methods defined by **String** itself or any methods defined by any other interface that **String** implements. Similarly, using the **comparable** variable, I can call **CompareTo** or any method defined by **Object**, but no other methods are callable using this variable.

> **Important** Like a reference type, a value type can implement zero or more interfaces. However, when you cast an instance of a value type to an interface type, the value type instance must be boxed. This is because an interface variable is a reference that must point to an object on the heap so that the CLR can examine the object's type object pointer to determine the exact type of the object. Then, when calling an interface method with a boxed value type, the CLR will follow the object's type object pointer to find the type object's method table in order to call the proper method.

Implicit and Explicit Interface Method Implementations (What's Happening Behind the Scenes)

When a type is loaded into the CLR, a method table is created and initialized for the type (as discussed in Chapter 1, "The CLR's Execution Model"). This method table contains one entry for every new method introduced by the type as well as entries for any methods inherited by the type. Inherited methods include methods defined by the base types in the inheritance hierarchy as well as any methods defined by the interface types. So if you have a simple type defined like this:

```
internal sealed class SimpleType : IDisposable {
    public void Dispose() { Console.WriteLine("Dispose"); }
}
```

the type's method table contains entries for the following:

- All the instance methods defined by **object**, the implicitly inherited base class.

- All the interface methods defined by **IDisposable**, the inherited interface. In this example, there is only one method, **Dispose**, since the **IDisposable** interface defines just one method.

- The new method, **Dispose**, introduced by **SimpleType**.

To make things simple for the programmer, the C# compiler assumes that the **Dispose** method introduced by **SimpleType** is the implementation for **IDisposable**'s **Dispose** method. The C# compiler makes this assumption because the method is **public**, and the signatures of the interface method and the newly introduced method are identical. That is, the methods have the same parameter and return types. By the way, if the new **Dispose** method were marked as **virtual**, the C# compiler would still consider this method to be a match for the interface method.

When the C# compiler matches a new method to an interface method, it emits metadata indicating that both entries in **SimpleType**'s method table should refer to the same implementation. To help make this clearer, here is some code that demonstrates how to call the class's public **Dispose** method as well as how to call the class's implementation of **IDisposable**'s **Dispose** method:

```
public sealed class Program {
    public static void Main() {
        SimpleType st = new SimpleType();

        // This calls the public Dispose method implementation
        st.Dispose();

        // This calls IDisposable's Dispose method implementation
        IDisposable d = st;
        d.Dispose();
    }
}
```

In the first call to **Dispose**, the **Dispose** method defined by **SimpleType** is called. Then I define a variable, **d**, which is of the **IDisposable** interface type. I initialize the **d** variable to refer to the **SimpleType** object. Now when I call **d.Dispose()**, I am calling the **IDisposable** interface's **Dispose** method. Since C# requires the public **Dispose** method to also be the implementation for **IDisposable**'s **Dispose** method, the same code will execute, and, in this example, you can't see any observable difference. The output is as follows:

```
Dispose
Dispose
```

Now, let me rewrite the **SimpleType** from above so that you can see an observable difference:

```
internal sealed class SimpleType : IDisposable {
    public void Dispose() { Console.WriteLine("public Dispose"); }
    void IDisposable.Dispose() { Console.WriteLine("IDisposable Dispose"); }
}
```

Without changing the **Main** method shown earlier, if we just recompile and rerun the program, the output will be this:

```
public Dispose
IDisposable Dispose
```

In C#, when you prefix the name of a method with the name of the interface that defines the method (**IDisposable.Dispose** as in this example), you are creating an *explicit interface method implementation* (EIMI). Note that when you define an explicit interface method in C#, you are not allowed to specify any accessibility (such as **public** or **private**). However, when the compiler generates the metadata for the method, its accessibility is set to private, preventing any code using an instance of the class from simply calling the interface method. The only way to call the interface method is through a variable of the interface's type.

Also note that an EIMI method cannot be marked as **virtual** and therefore cannot be overridden. This is because the EIMI method is not really part of the type's object model; it's a way of attaching an interface (set of behaviors or methods) onto a type without making the behaviors/ methods obvious. If all of this seems a bit kludgy to you, you *are* understanding it correctly— this is all a bit kludgy. Later in this chapter, I'll show some valid reasons for using EIMIs.

Generic Interfaces

C#'s and the CLR's support of generic interfaces offers many great features for developers. In this section, I'd like to discuss the benefits offered when using generic interfaces.

First, generic interfaces offer great compile-time type safety. Some interfaces (such as the non-generic **IComparable** interface) define methods that have **Object** parameters or return types. When code calls these interface methods, a reference to an instance of any type can be passed. But this is usually not desired. The following code demonstrates:

```
private void SomeMethod1() {
   Int32 x = 1, y = 2;
   IComparable c = x;

   // CompareTo expects an Object; passing y (an Int32) is OK
   c.CompareTo(y);      // Boxing occurs here

   // CompareTo expects an Object; passing "2" (a String) compiles
   // but an ArgumentException is thrown at runtime
   c.CompareTo("2");
}
```

Obviously, it is preferable to have the interface method strongly typed, and this is why the FCL includes a generic **IComparable<T>** interface. Here is the new version of the code revised by using the generic interface:

```
private void SomeMethod2() {
   Int32 x = 1, y = 2;
   IComparable<Int32> c = x;
```

```
    // CompareTo expects an Int32; passing y (an Int32) is OK
    c.CompareTo(y);      // Boxing occurs here

    // CompareTo expects an Int32; passing "2" (a String) results
    // in a compiler error indicating that String cannot be cast to an Int32
    c.CompareTo("2");
}
```

The second benefit of generic interfaces is that much less boxing will occur when working with value types. Notice in **SomeMethod1** that the non-generic **IComparable** interface's **CompareTo** method expects an **Object**; passing **y** (an **Int32** value type) causes the value in **y** to be boxed. However, in **SomeMethod2**, the generic **IComparable<T>** interface's **CompareTo** method expects an **Int32**; passing **y** causes it to be passed by value, and no boxing is necessary.

> **Note**   The FCL defines non-generic and generic versions of the **IComparable**, **ICollection**, **IList**, and **IDictionary** interfaces as well as some others. If you are defining a type, and you want to implement any of these interfaces, you should typically implement the generic versions of these interfaces. The non-generic versions are in the FCL for backward compatibility to work with code written before the .NET Framework supported generics. The non-generic versions also provide users a way of manipulating the data in a more general, less type-safe fashion.
>
> Some of the generic interfaces inherit the non-generic versions, so your class will have to implement both the generic and non-generic versions of the interfaces. For example, the generic **IEnumerable<T>** interface inherits the non-generic **IEnumerable** interface. So if your class implements **IEnumerable<T>**, your class must also implement **IEnumerable**.
>
> Sometimes when integrating with other code, you may have to implement a non-generic interface because a generic version of the interface simply doesn't exist. In this case, if any of the interface's methods take or return **Object**, you will lose compile-time type safety, and you will get boxing with value types. You can alleviate this situation to some extent by using a technique I describe in the "Improving Compile-Time Type Safety with Explicit Interface Method Implementations" section near the end of this chapter.

The third benefit of generic interfaces is that a class can implement the same interface multiple times as long as different type parameters are used. The following code shows an example of how useful this could be:

```
using System;

// This class implements the generic IComparable<T> interface twice
public sealed class Number: IComparable<Int32>, IComparable<String> {
    private Int32 m_val = 5;

    // This method implements IComparable<Int32>'s CompareTo
    public Int32 CompareTo(Int32 n) {
        return m_val.CompareTo(n);
    }
```

```
    // This method implements IComparable<String>'s CompareTo
    public Int32 CompareTo(String s) {
        return m_val.CompareTo(Int32.Parse(s));
    }
}

public static class Program {
    public static void Main() {
        Number n = new Number();

        // Here, I compare the value in n with an Int32 (5)
        IComparable<Int32> cInt32 = n;
        Int32 result = cInt32.CompareTo(5);

        // Here, I compare the value in n with a String ("5")
        IComparable<String> cString = n;
        result = cString.CompareTo("5");
    }
}
```

Generics and Interface Constraints

In the previous section, I discussed the benefits of using generic interfaces. In this section, I'll discuss the benefits of constraining generic type parameters to interfaces.

The first benefit is that you can constrain a single generic type parameter to multiple interfaces. When you do this, the type of parameter you are passing in must implement *all* of the interface constraints. Here is an example:

```
public static class SomeType {
    private static void Test() {
        Int32 x = 5;
        Guid g = new Guid();

        // This call to M compiles fine because
        // Int32 implements IComparable AND IConvertible
        M(x);

        // This call to M causes a compiler error because
        // Guid implements IComparable but it does not implement IConvertible
        M(g);
    }

    // M's type parameter, T, is constrained to work only with types that
    // implement both the IComparable AND IConvertible interfaces
    private static Int32 M<T>(T t) where T : IComparable, IConvertible {
        ...
    }
}
```

This is actually quite cool! When you define a method's parameters, each parameter's type indicates that the argument passed must be of the parameter's type or be derived from it. If the parameter type is an interface, this indicates that the argument can be of any class type as long as the class implements the interface. Using multiple interface constraints actually lets the method indicate that the passed argument must implement multiple interfaces.

In fact, if we constrained T to a class and two interfaces, we are saying that the type of argument passed must be of the specified base class (or derived from it), and it must also implement the two interfaces. This flexibility allows the method to really dictate what callers can pass, and compiler errors will be generated if callers do not meet these constraints.

The second benefit of interface constraints is reduced boxing when passing instances of value types. In the previous code fragment, the M method was passed x (an instance of an Int32, which is a value type). No boxing will occur when x is passed to M. If code inside M does call t.CompareTo(...), still no boxing occurs to make the call (boxing may still happen for arguments passed to CompareTo).

On the other hand, if M had been declared like this:

```
private static Int32 M(IComparable t) {
   ...
}
```

then in order to pass x to M, x would have to be boxed.

For interface constraints, the C# compiler emits certain IL instructions that result in calling the interface method on the value type directly without boxing it. Aside from using interface constraints, there is no other way to get the C# compiler to emit these IL instructions, and therefore, calling an interface method on a value type always causes boxing.

Implementing Multiple Interfaces That Have the Same Method Name and Signature

Occasionally, you might find yourself defining a type that implements multiple interfaces that define methods with the same name and signature. For example, imagine that there are two interfaces defined as follows:

```
public interface IWindow {
   Object GetMenu();
}

public interface IRestaurant {
   Object GetMenu();
}
```

Let's say that you want to define a type that implements both of these interfaces. You'd have to implement the type's members by using explicit interface method implementations as follows:

```
// This type is derived from System.Object and
// implements the IWindow and IRestaurant interfaces.
public sealed class MarioPizzeria : IWindow, IRestaurant {
```

```
   // This is the implementation for IWindow's GetMenu method.
   Object IWindow.GetMenu() { ... }

   // This is the implementation for IRestaurant's GetMenu method.
   Object IRestaurant.GetMenu() { ... }

   // This (optional method) is a GetMenu method that has nothing
   // to do with an interface.
   public Object GetMenu() { ... }
}
```

Because this type must implement multiple and separate **GetMenu** methods, you need to tell the C# compiler which **GetMenu** method contains the implementation for a particular interface.

Code that uses a **MarioPizzeria** object must cast to the specific interface to call the desired method. The following code demonstrates:

```
MarioPizzeria mp = new MarioPizzeria();

// This line calls MarioPizzeria's public GetMenu method
mp.GetMenu();

// These lines call MarioPizzeria's IWindow.GetMenu method
IWindow window = mp;
window.GetMenu();

// These lines call MarioPizzeria's IRestaurant.GetMenu method
IRestaurant restaurant = mp;
restaurant.GetMenu();
```

Improving Compile-Time Type Safety with Explicit Interface Method Implementations

Interfaces are great because they define a standard way for types to communicate with each other. Earlier, I talked about generic interfaces and how they improve compile-time type safety and reduce boxing. Unfortunately, there may be times when you need to implement a non-generic interface because a generic version doesn't exist. If any of the interface's method(s) accept parameters of type **System.Object** or return a value whose type is **System.Object**, you will lose compile-time type safety, and you will get boxing. In this section, I'll show you how you can use EIMI to improve this situation somewhat.

Look at the very common **IComparable** interface:

```
public interface IComparable {
    Int32 CompareTo(Object other);
}
```

This interface defines one method that accepts a parameter of type `System.Object`. If I define my own type that implements this interface, the type definition might look like this:

```
internal struct SomeValueType : IComparable {
   private Int32 m_x;
   public SomeValueType(Int32 x) { m_x = x; }
   public Int32 CompareTo(Object other) {
      return(m_x - ((SomeValueType) other).m_x);
   }
}
```

Using `SomeValueType`, I can now write the following code:

```
public static void Main() {
   SomeValueType v = new SomeValueType(0);
   Object o = new Object();
   Int32 n = v.CompareTo(v); // Undesired boxing
   n = v.CompareTo(o);       // InvalidCastException
}
```

There are two characteristics of this code that are not ideal:

- **Undesired boxing** When **v** is passed as an argument to the `CompareTo` method, it must be boxed because `CompareTo` expects an `Object`.

- **The lack of type safety** This code compiles, but an `InvalidCastException` is thrown inside the `CompareTo` method when it attempts to cast **other** to `SomeValueType`.

Both of these issues can be fixed by using EIMIs. Here's a modified version of `SomeValueType` that has an EIMI added to it:

```
internal struct SomeValueType : IComparable {
   private Int32 m_x;
   public SomeValueType(Int32 x) { m_x = x; }

   public Int32 CompareTo(SomeValueType other) {
      return(m_x - other.m_x);
   }

   // NOTE: No public/private used on the next line
   Int32 IComparable.CompareTo(Object other) {
      return CompareTo((SomeValueType) other);
   }
}
```

Notice several changes in this new version. First, it now has two `CompareTo` methods. The first `CompareTo` method no longer takes an `Object` as a parameter; it now takes a `SomeValueType` instead. Because this parameter has changed, the code that casts **other** to `SomeValueType` is no longer necessary and has been removed. Second, changing the first `CompareTo` method to make it type safe means that `SomeValueType` no longer adheres to the contract placed on it by implementing the `IComparable` interface. So `SomeValueType` must implement a `CompareTo`

method that satisfies the **IComparable** contract. This is the job of the second **IComparable**
.CompareTo method, which is an EIMI.

Having made these two changes means that we now get compile-time type safety and no boxing:

```
public static void Main() {
    SomeValueType v = new SomeValueType(0);
    Object o = new Object();
    Int32  n = v.CompareTo(v); // No boxing
    n = v.CompareTo(o);        // compile-time error
}
```

If, however, we define a variable of the interface type, we will lose compile-time type safety and
experience undesired boxing again:

```
public static void Main() {
    SomeValueType v = new SomeValueType(0);
    IComparable c = v;         // Boxing!

    Object o = new Object();
    Int32  n = c.CompareTo(v); // Undesired boxing
    n = c.CompareTo(o);        // InvalidCastException
}
```

In fact, as mentioned earlier in this chapter, when casting a value type instance to an interface
type, the CLR must box the value type instance. Because of this fact, two boxings will occur in
the previous **Main** method.

EIMIs are frequently used when implementing interfaces such as **IConvertible**, **ICollection**,
IList, and **IDictionary**. They let you create type-safe versions of these interfaces' methods,
and they enable you to reduce boxing operations for value types.

Be Careful with Explicit Interface Method Implementations

It is critically important for you to understand some ramifications that exist when using
EIMIs. And because of these ramifications, you should try to avoid EIMIs as much as possible.
Fortunately, generic interfaces help you avoid EIMIs quite a bit. But there may still be times
when you will need to use them (such as implementing two interface methods with the same
name and signature). Here are the big problems with EIMIs:

- There is no documentation explaining how a type specifically implements an EIMI
  method, and there is no Microsoft Visual Studio IntelliSense support.

- Value type instances are boxed when cast to an interface.

- An EIMI cannot be called by a derived type.

Let's take a closer look at these problems.

When examining the methods for a type in the .NET Framework reference documentation, explicit interface method implementations are listed, but no type-specific help exists; you can just read the general help about the interface methods. For example, the documentation for the **Int32** type shows that it implements all of **IConvertible** interface's methods. This is good because developers know that these methods exist; however, this has been very confusing to developers because you can't call an **IConvertible** method on an **Int32** directly. For example, the following method won't compile:

```
public static void Main() {
   Int32 x = 5;
   Single s = x.ToSingle(null); // Trying to call an IConvertible method
}
```

When compiling this method, the C# compiler produces the following: "error CS0117: 'int' does not contain a definition for 'ToSingle'". This error message confuses the developer because it's clearly stating that the **Int32** type doesn't define a **ToSingle** method when, in fact, it does.

To call **ToSingle** on an **Int32**, you must first cast the **Int32** to an **IConvertible**, as shown in the following method:

```
public static void Main() {
   Int32 x = 5;
   Single s = ((IConvertible) x).ToSingle(null);
}
```

Requiring this cast isn't obvious at all, and many developers won't figure this out on their own. But an even more troublesome problem exists: casting the **Int32** value type to an **IConvertible** also boxes the value type, wasting memory and hurting performance. This is the second of the big problems I mentioned at the beginning of this section.

The third and perhaps the biggest problem with EIMIs is that they cannot be called by a derived class. Here is an example:

```
internal class Base : IComparable {

   // Explicit Interface Method Implementation
   Int32 IComparable.CompareTo(Object o) {
      Console.WriteLine("Base's CompareTo");
      return 0;
   }
}

internal sealed class Derived : Base, IComparable {

   // A public method that is also the interface implementation
   public Int32 CompareTo(Object o) {
      Console.WriteLine("Derived's CompareTo");
```

```
        // This attempt to call the base class's EIMI causes a compiler error:
        // error CS0117: 'Base' does not contain a definition for 'CompareTo'
        base.CompareTo(o);
        return 0;
    }
}
```

In **Derived**'s **CompareTo** method, I try to call **base.CompareTo**, but this causes the C# compiler to issue an error. The problem is that the **Base** class doesn't offer a public or protected **CompareTo** method that can be called; it offers a **CompareTo** method that can be called only by using a variable that is of the **IComparable** type. I could modify **Derived**'s **CompareTo** method so that it looks like this:

```
// A public method that is also the interface implementation
public Int32 CompareTo(Object o) {
    Console.WriteLine("Derived's CompareTo");

    // This attempt to call the base class's EIMI causes infinite recursion
    IComparable c = this;
    c.CompareTo(o);

    return 0;
}
```

In this version, I am casting **this** to an **IComparable** variable, **c**. And then, I use **c** to call **CompareTo**. However, the **Derived**'s public **CompareTo** method serves as the implementation for **Derived**'s **IComparable CompareTo** method, and therefore, infinite recursion occurs. This could be fixed by declaring the **Derived** class without the **IComparable** interface, like this:

```
internal sealed class Derived : Base /*, IComparable */ { ... }
```

Now the previous **CompareTo** method will call the **CompareTo** method in **Base**. But sometimes you cannot simply remove the interface from the type because you want the derived type to implement an interface method. The best way to fix this is for the base class to provide a virtual method in addition to the interface method that it has chosen to implement explicitly. Then the **Derived** class can override the virtual method. Here is the correct way to define the **Base** and **Derived** classes:

```
internal class Base : IComparable {

    // Explicit Interface Method Implementation
    Int32 IComparable.CompareTo(Object o) {
        Console.WriteLine("Base's IComparable CompareTo");
        return CompareTo(o);   // This now calls the virtual method
    }

    // Virtual method for derived classes (this method could have any name)
    public virtual Int32 CompareTo(Object o) {
        Console.WriteLine("Base's virtual CompareTo");
        return 0;
    }
}
```

```
internal sealed class Derived : Base, IComparable {

   // A public method that is also the interface implementation
   public override Int32 CompareTo(Object o) {
      Console.WriteLine("Derived's CompareTo");

      // Now, we can call Base's virtual method
      return base.CompareTo(o);
   }
}
```

Note that I have defined the virtual method above as a **public** method, but in some cases, you will prefer to make the method **protected** instead. It is fine to make this method **protected** instead of **public**, but that will necessitate other minor changes. This discussion clearly shows you that EIMIs should be used with great care. When many developers first learn about EIMIs, they think that they're cool and they start using them whenever possible. Don't do this! EIMIs are useful in some circumstances, but you should avoid them whenever possible because they make using a type much more difficult.

Design: Base Class or Interface?

I often hear the question, "Should I design a base type or an interface?" The answer isn't always clear-cut. Here are some guidelines that might help you:

- **IS-A vs. CAN-DO relationship**   A type can inherit only one implementation. If the derived type can't claim an IS-A relationship with the base type, don't use a base type; use an interface. Interfaces imply a CAN-DO relationship. If the CAN-DO functionality appears to belong with various object types, use an interface. For example, a type can convert instances of itself to another type (**IConvertible**), a type can serialize an instance of itself (**ISerializable**), etc. Note that value types must be derived from **System.ValueType**, and therefore, they cannot be derived from an arbitrary base class. In this case, you must use a CAN-DO relationship and define an interface.

- **Ease of use**   It's generally easier for you as a developer to define a new type derived from a base type than to implement all of the methods of an interface. The base type can provide a lot of functionality, so the derived type probably needs only relatively small modifications to its behavior. If you supply an interface, the new type must implement all of the members.

- **Consistent implementation**   No matter how well an interface contract is documented, it's very unlikely that everyone will implement the contract 100 percent correctly. In fact, COM suffers from this very problem, which is why some COM objects work correctly only with Microsoft Office Word or with Microsoft Internet Explorer. By providing a base type with a good default implementation, you start off using a type that works and is well tested; you can then modify parts that need modification.

- **Versioning**   If you add a method to the base type, the derived type inherits the new method's default implementation for free. In fact, the user's source code doesn't even have to be recompiled. Adding a new member to an interface forces the inheritor of the interface to change its source code and recompile.

In the FCL, the classes related to streaming data use an implementation inheritance design. The `System.IO.Stream` class is the abstract base class. It provides a bunch of methods, such as `Read` and `Write`. Other classes—`System.IO.FileStream`, `System.IO.MemoryStream`, and `System.Net.Sockets.NetworkStream`—are derived from `Stream`. Microsoft chose an IS-A relationship between each of these three classes and the `Stream` class because it made implementing the concrete classes easier. For example, the derived classes need to implement only synchronous I/O operations; they inherit the ability to perform asynchronous I/O operations from the `Stream` base class.

Admittedly, choosing to use inheritance for the stream classes isn't entirely clear-cut; the `Stream` base class actually provides very little implementation. However, if you consider the Microsoft Windows Forms control classes, in which `Button`, `CheckBox`, `ListBox`, and all of the other controls are derived from `System.Windows.Forms.Control`, it's easy to imagine all of the code that `Control` implements, which the various control classes simply inherit to function correctly.

By contrast, Microsoft designed the FCL collections to be interface based. The `System.Collections.Generic` namespace defines several collection-related interfaces: `IEnumerable<T>`, `ICollection<T>`, `IList<T>`, and `IDictionary<TKey, TValue>`. Then Microsoft provided a number of classes, such as `List<T>`, `Dictionary<TKey, TValue>`, `Queue<T>`, `Stack<T>`, and so on, that implement combinations of these interfaces. Here the designers chose a CAN-DO relationship between the classes and the interfaces because the implementations of these various collection classes are radically different from one another. In other words, there isn't a lot of sharable code between a `List<T>`, a `Dictionary<TKey, TValue>`, and a `Queue<T>`.

The operations these collection classes offer are, nevertheless, pretty consistent. For example, they all maintain a set of elements that can be enumerated, and they all allow adding and removing of elements. If you have a reference to an object whose type implements the `IList<T>` interface, you can write code to insert elements, remove elements, and search for an element without having to know exactly what type of collection you're working with. This is a very powerful mechanism.

Finally, it should be pointed out that you can actually do both: define an interface *and* provide a base class that implements the interface. For example, the FCL defines the `IComparer<T>` interface, and any type can choose to implement this interface. In addition, the FCL provides an abstract base class, `Comparer<T>`, that implements this interface (abstractly) and provides some additional methods as well. Having both an interface definition and a base class offers great flexibility because developers can now choose whichever they prefer.

Chapter 15
Delegates

In this chapter, I talk about callback functions. Callback functions are an extremely useful programming mechanism that has been around for years. The Microsoft .NET Framework exposes a callback function mechanism by using *delegates*. Unlike callback mechanisms used in other platforms, such as unmanaged C++, delegates offer much more functionality. For example, delegates ensure that the callback method is type-safe (in keeping with one of the most important goals of the common language runtime [CLR]). Delegates also integrate the ability to call multiple methods sequentially and support the calling of static methods as well as instance methods.

A First Look at Delegates

The C runtime's `qsort` function takes a pointer to a callback function to sort elements within an array. In Microsoft Windows, callback functions are required for window procedures, hook procedures, asynchronous procedure calls, and more. In the .NET Framework, callback methods are used for a whole slew of things. For example, you can register callback methods to get a variety of notifications such as unhandled exceptions, window state changes, menu item selections, file system changes, form control events, and completed asynchronous operations.

In unmanaged C/C++, the address of a non-member function is just a memory address. This address doesn't carry any additional information such as the number of parameters the function expects, the types of these parameters, the function's return value type, and the function's calling convention. In short, unmanaged C/C++ callback functions are not type-safe (although they are a very lightweight mechanism).

In the .NET Framework, callback functions are just as useful and pervasive as in unmanaged Windows programming. However, the .NET Framework provides a type-safe mechanism

called *delegates*. I'll start off the discussion of delegates by showing you how to use them. The
following code demonstrates how to declare, create, and use delegates.

```
using System;
using System.Windows.Forms;
using System.IO;


// Declare a delegate type; instances refer to a method that
// takes an Int32 parameter and returns void.
internal delegate void Feedback(Int32 value);


public sealed class Program {
    public static void Main() {
        StaticDelegateDemo();
        InstanceDelegateDemo();
        ChainDelegateDemo1(new Program());
        ChainDelegateDemo2(new Program());
    }

    private static void StaticDelegateDemo() {
        Console.WriteLine("----- Static Delegate Demo -----");
        Counter(1, 3, null);
        Counter(1, 3, new Feedback(Program.FeedbackToConsole));
        Counter(1, 3, new Feedback(FeedbackToMsgBox)); // "Program." is optional
        Console.WriteLine();
    }

    private static void InstanceDelegateDemo() {
        Console.WriteLine("----- Instance Delegate Demo -----");
        Program p = new Program();
        Counter(1, 3, new Feedback(p.FeedbackToFile));

        Console.WriteLine();
    }

    private static void ChainDelegateDemo1(Program p) {
        Console.WriteLine("----- Chain Delegate Demo 1 -----");
        Feedback fb1 = new Feedback(FeedbackToConsole);
        Feedback fb2 = new Feedback(FeedbackToMsgBox);
        Feedback fb3 = new Feedback(p.FeedbackToFile);

        Feedback fbChain = null;
        fbChain = (Feedback) Delegate.Combine(fbChain, fb1);
        fbChain = (Feedback) Delegate.Combine(fbChain, fb2);
        fbChain = (Feedback) Delegate.Combine(fbChain, fb3);
        Counter(1, 2, fbChain);

        Console.WriteLine();
        fbChain = (Feedback)
            Delegate.Remove(fbChain, new Feedback(FeedbackToMsgBox));
        Counter(1, 2, fbChain);
    }
```

```
private static void ChainDelegateDemo2(Program p) {
    Console.WriteLine("----- Chain Delegate Demo 2 -----");
    Feedback fb1 = new Feedback(FeedbackToConsole);
    Feedback fb2 = new Feedback(FeedbackToMsgBox);
    Feedback fb3 = new Feedback(p.FeedbackToFile);

    Feedback fbChain = null;
    fbChain += fb1;
    fbChain += fb2;
    fbChain += fb3;
    Counter(1, 2, fbChain);

    Console.WriteLine();
    fbChain -= new Feedback(FeedbackToMsgBox);
    Counter(1, 2, fbChain);
}

private static void Counter(Int32 from, Int32 to, Feedback fb) {
    for (Int32 val = from; val <= to; val++) {
        // If any callbacks are specified, call them
        if (fb != null)
            fb(val);
    }
}

private static void FeedbackToConsole(Int32 value) {
    Console.WriteLine("Item=" + value);
}

private static void FeedbackToMsgBox(Int32 value) {
    MessageBox.Show("Item=" + value);
}

private void FeedbackToFile(Int32 value) {
    StreamWriter sw = new StreamWriter("Status", true);
    sw.WriteLine("Item=" + value);
    sw.Close();
}
}
```

Now I'll describe what this code is doing. At the top, notice the declaration of the internal delegate, **Feedback**. A delegate indicates the signature of a callback method. In this example, a **Feedback** delegate identifies a method that takes one parameter (an **Int32**) and returns **void**. In a way, a delegate is very much like an unmanaged C/C++ **typedef** that represents the address of a function.

The **Program** class defines a private, static method named **Counter**. This method counts integers from the **from** argument to the **to** argument. The **Counter** method also takes an **fb**, which is a reference to a **Feedback** delegate object. **Counter** iterates through all of the integers, and for each integer, if the **fb** variable is not **null**, the callback method (specified by the **fb** variable) is called. This callback method is passed the value of the item being processed, the item number. The callback method can be designed and implemented to process each item in any manner deemed appropriate.

Using Delegates to Call Back Static Methods

Now that you understand how the **Counter** method is designed and how it works, let's see how to use delegates to call back static methods. The **StaticDelegateDemo** method that appears in the previous code sample is the focus of this section.

The **StaticDelegateDemo** method calls the **Counter** method, passing **null** in the third parameter, which corresponds to **Counter**'s **fb** parameter. Because **Counter**'s **fb** parameter receives **null**, each item is processed without calling any callback method.

Next, the **StaticDelegateDemo** method calls **Counter** a second time, passing a newly constructed **Feedback** delegate object in the third parameter of the method call. This delegate object is a wrapper around a method, allowing the method to be called back indirectly via the wrapper. In this example, the name of the static method, **Program.FeedbackToConsole**, is passed to the **Feedback** type's constructor, indicating that it is the method to be wrapped. The reference returned from the **new** operator is passed to **Counter** as its third parameter. Now when **Counter** executes, it will call the **Program** type's static **FeedbackToConsole** method for each item in the series. **FeedbackToConsole** simply writes a string to the console indicating the item being processed.

> **Note**   The **FeedbackToConsole** method is defined as **private** inside the **Program** type, but the **Counter** method is able to call **Program**'s private method. In this case, you might not expect a problem because both **Counter** and **FeedbackToConsole** are defined in the same type. However, this code would work just fine even if the **Counter** method was defined in another type. In short, it is not a security or accessibility violation for one type to have code that calls another type's private member via a delegate as long as the delegate object is created by code that has ample security/accessibility.

The third call to **Counter** in the **StaticDelegateDemo** method is almost identical to the second call. The only difference is that the **Feedback** delegate object wraps the static **Program.FeedbackToMsgBox** method. **FeedbackToMsgBox** builds a string indicating the item being processed. This string is then displayed in a message box.

Everything in this example is type-safe. For instance, when constructing a **Feedback** delegate object, the compiler ensures that the signatures of **Program**'s **FeedbackToConsole** and **FeedbackToMsgBox** methods are compatible with the signature defined by the **Feedback** delegate. Specifically, both methods must take one argument (an **Int32**), and both methods must have the same return type (**void**). If **FeedbackToConsole** had been defined like this:

```
private static Boolean FeedbackToConsole(String value) {
    ...
}
```

the C# compiler wouldn't compile the code and would issue the following error: "error CS0123: No overload for 'FeedbackToConsole' matches delegate 'Feedback'".

Both C# and the CLR allow for covariance and contra-variance of reference types when binding a method to a delegate. *Covariance* means that a method can return a type that is derived from the delegate's return type. *Contra-variance* means that a method can take a parameter that is a base of the delegate's parameter type. For example, given a delegate defined like this:

```
delegate Object MyCallback(FileStream s);
```

it is possible to construct an instance of this delegate type bound to a method that is prototyped like this:

```
String SomeMethod(Stream s);
```

Here, **SomeMethod**'s return type (**String**) is a type that is derived from the delegate's return type (**Object**); this covariance is allowed. **SomeMethod**'s parameter type (**Stream**) is a type that is a base class of the delegate's parameter type (**FileStream**); this contra-variance is allowed.

Note that covariance and contra-variance are supported only for reference types, not for value types or for **void**. So, for example, I cannot bind the following method to the **MyCallback** delegate:

```
Int32 SomeOtherMethod(Stream s);
```

Even though **SomeOtherMethod**'s return type (**Int32**) is derived from **MyCallback**'s return type (**Object**), this form of covariance is not allowed because **Int32** is a value type. Obviously, the reason why value types and **void** cannot be used for covariance and contra-variance is because the memory structure for these things varies, whereas the memory structure for reference types is always a pointer. Fortunately, the C# compiler will produce an error if you attempt to do something that is not supported.

Using Delegates to Call Back Instance Methods

I just explained how delegates can be used to call static methods, but they can also be used to call instance methods for a specific object. To understand how calling back an instance method works, look at the **InstanceDelegateDemo** method that appears in the code shown at the beginning of this chapter.

Notice that a **Program** object named **p** is constructed in the **InstanceDelegateDemo** method. This **Program** object doesn't have any instance fields or properties associated with it; I created it merely for demonstration purposes. When the new **Feedback** delegate object is constructed in the call to the **Counter** method, its constructor is passed **p.FeedbackToFile**. This causes the delegate to wrap a reference to the **FeedbackToFile** method, which is an instance method (not a static method). When **Counter** calls the callback method identified by its **fb** argument, the **FeedbackToFile** instance method is called, and the address of the recently constructed object **p** will be passed as the implicit **this** argument to the instance method.

The **FeedbackToFile** method works as the **FeedbackToConsole** and **FeedbackToMsgBox** methods, except that it opens a file and appends the string to the end of the file. (The Status file the method creates can be found in the application's AppBase directory).

Again, the purpose of this example is to demonstrate that delegates can wrap calls to instance methods as well as static methods. For instance methods, the delegate needs to know the instance of the object the method is going to operate on. Wrapping an instance method is useful because code inside the object can access the object's instance members. This means that the object can have some state that can be used while the callback method is doing its processing.

Demystifying Delegates

On the surface, delegates seem easy to use: you define them by using C#'s **delegate** keyword, you construct instances of them by using the familiar **new** operator, and you invoke the callback by using the familiar method-call syntax (except instead of a method name, you use the variable that refers to the delegate object).

However, what's really going on is quite a bit more complex than what the earlier examples illustrate. The compilers and the CLR do a lot of behind-the-scenes processing to hide the complexity. In this section, I'll focus on how the compiler and the CLR work together to implement delegates. Having this knowledge will improve your understanding of delegates and will teach you how to use them efficiently and effectively. I'll also touch on some additional features delegates make available.

Let's start by reexamining this line of code:

```
internal delegate void Feedback(Int32 value);
```

When it sees this line, the compiler actually defines a complete class that looks something like this:

```
internal class Feedback : System.MulticastDelegate {
   // Constructor
   public Feedback(Object object, IntPtr method);

   // Method with same prototype as specified by the source code
   public virtual void Invoke(Int32 value);

   // Methods allowing the callback to be called asynchronously
   public virtual IAsyncResult BeginInvoke(Int32 value,
      AsyncCallback callback, Object object);
   public virtual void EndInvoke(IAsyncResult result);
}
```

The class defined by the compiler has four methods: a constructor, **Invoke**, **BeginInvoke**, and **EndInvoke**. In this chapter, I'll concentrate on the constructor and **Invoke** methods. I'll address the **BeginInvoke** and **EndInvoke** methods in Chapter 23, "Performing Asynchronous Operations," when I discuss the Asynchronous Programming Model.

In fact, you can verify that the compiler did indeed generate this class automatically by examining the resulting assembly with ILDasm.exe, as shown in Figure 15-1.

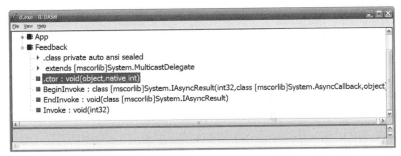

Figure 15-1   ILDasm.exe showing the metadata produced by the compiler for the delegate

In this example, the compiler has defined a class called **Feedback** that is derived from the **System.MulticastDelegate** type defined in the Framework Class Library (FCL). (All delegate types are derived from **MulticastDelegate**.)

> **Important**   The **System.MulticastDelegate** class is derived from **System.Delegate**, which is itself derived from **System.Object**. The reason why there are two delegate classes is historical and unfortunate; there should be just one delegate class in the FCL. Sadly, you need to be aware of both of these classes because even though all delegate types you create have **MulticastDelegate** as a base class, you'll occasionally manipulate your delegate types by using methods defined by the **Delegate** class instead of the **MulticastDelegate** class. For example, the **Delegate** class has static methods called **Combine** and **Remove**. (I explain what these methods do later.) The signatures for both of these methods indicate that they take **Delegate** parameters. Because your delegate type is derived from **MulticastDelegate**, which is derived from **Delegate**, instances of your delegate type can be passed to these methods.

The class has private visibility because the delegate is declared as **internal** in the source code. If the source code had indicated **public** visibility, the **Feedback** class the compiler generated would also be public. You should be aware that delegate types can be defined within a type (nested within another type) or at global scope. Basically, because delegates are classes, a delegate can be defined anywhere a class can be defined.

Because all delegate types are derived from **MulticastDelegate**, they inherit **Multicast-Delegate**'s fields, properties, and methods. Of all of these members, three non-public fields are probably most significant. Table 15-1 describes these significant fields.

Table 15-1   **MulticastDelegate**'s **Significant Non-Public Fields**

Field	Type	Description
_target	System.Object	When the delegate object wraps a static method, this field is **null**. When the delegate objects wraps an instance method, this field refers to the object that should be operated on when the callback method is called. In other words, this field indicates the value that should be passed for the instance method's implicit **this** parameter.

Table 15-1 MulticastDelegate's **Significant Non-Public Fields**

Field	Type	Description
_methodPtr	System.IntPtr	An internal integer the CLR uses to identify the method that is to be called back.
_invocationList	System.Object	This field is usually null. It can refer to an array of delegates when building a delegate chain (discussed later in this chapter).

Notice that all delegates have a constructor that takes two parameters: a reference to an object and an integer that refers to the callback method. However, if you examine the source code, you'll see that I'm passing in values such as **Program.FeedbackToConsole** or **p.FeedbackToFile**. Everything you've learned about programming tells you that this code shouldn't compile!

However, the C# compiler knows that a delegate is being constructed and parses the source code to determine which object and method are being referred to. A reference to the object is passed for the constructor's **object** parameter, and a special **IntPtr** value (obtained from a **MethodDef** or **MemberRef** metadata token) that identifies the method is passed for the **method** parameter. For static methods, **null** is passed for the **object** parameter. Inside the constructor, these two arguments are saved in the **_target** and **_methodPtr** private fields, respectively. In addition, the constructor sets the **_invocationList** field to **null**. I'll postpone discussing this **_invocationList** field until the next section, "Using Delegates to Call Back Many Methods (Chaining)."

So each delegate object is really a wrapper around a method and an object to be operated on when the method is called. So if I have two lines of code that look like this:

```
Feedback fbStatic   = new Feedback(Program.FeedbackToConsole);
Feedback fbInstance = new Feedback(new Program().FeedbackToFile);
```

the **fbStatic** and **fbInstance** variables refer to two separate **Feedback** delegate objects that are initialized, as shown in Figure 15-2:

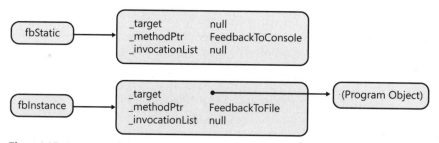

Figure 15-2 A variable that refers to a delegate to a static method and a variable that refers to a delegate to an instance method

The **Delegate** class defines two read-only public instance properties: **Target** and **Method**. Given a reference to a delegate object, you can query these properties. The **Target** property returns a reference to the object that will be operated on if the method is called back. Basically, the **Target** property returns the value stored in the private **_target** field. If the delegate object wraps a static method, **Target** returns **null**. The **Method** property returns a reference to a **System.Reflection.MethodInfo** object that identifies the callback method. Basically, the **Method** property has an internal mechanism that converts the value in the private **_methodPtr** field to a **MethodInfo** object and returns it.

You could use this information in several ways. For example, you could check to see if a delegate object refers to an instance method of a specific type:

```
Boolean DelegateRefersToInstanceMethodOfType(MulticastDelegate d, Type type) {
    return((d.Target != null) && d.Target.GetType() == type);
}
```

You could also write code to check if the callback method has a specific name (such as **FeedbackToMsgBox**):

```
Boolean DelegateRefersToMethodOfName(MulticastDelegate d, String methodName) {
    return(d.Method.Name == methodName);
}
```

There are many other potential uses of these properties.

Now that you know how delegate objects are constructed and what their internal structure looks like, let's talk about how the callback method is invoked. For convenience, I've repeated the code for the **Counter** method here:

```
private static void Counter(Int32 from, Int32 to, Feedback fb) {
    for (Int32 val = from; val <= to; val++) {
        // If any callbacks are specified, call them
        if (fb != null)
            fb(val);
    }
}
```

Look at the line of code just below the comment. The **if** statement first checks to see if **fb** is not **null**. If **fb** is not **null**, on the next line, you see the code that invokes the callback method. The **null** check is required because **fb** is really just a variable that *can* refer to a **Feedback** delegate object; it could also be **null**. It might seem as if I'm calling a function named **fb** and passing it one parameter (**val**). However, there is no function called **fb**. Again, because it knows that **fb** is a variable that refers to a delegate object, the compiler generates code to call the delegate object's **Invoke** method. In other words, the compiler sees this:

```
fb(val);
```

But the compiler generates code as though the source code said this:

```
fb.Invoke(val);
```

You can verify that the compiler produces code to call the delegate type's **Invoke** method by using ILDasm.exe to examine the IL code created for the **Counter** method. Figure 15-3 shows the intermediate language (IL) for the **Counter** method. The instruction at IL_0009 in the figure indicates the call to **Feedback**'s **Invoke** method.

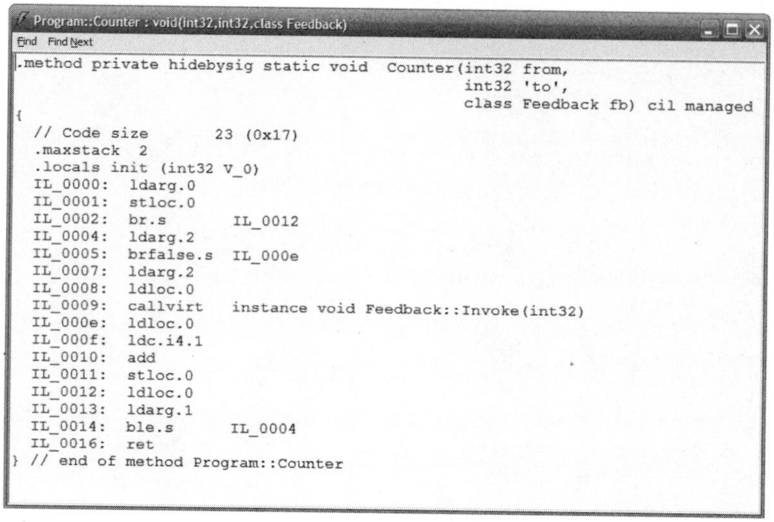

Figure 15-3   ILDasm.exe proves that the compiler emitted a call to the *Feedback* delegate type's *Invoke* method

In fact, you could modify the **Counter** method to call **Invoke** explicitly, as shown here:

```
private static void Counter(Int32 from, Int32 to, Feedback fb) {
    for (Int32 val = from; val <= to; val++) {
        // If any callbacks are specified, call them
        if (fb != null)
            fb.Invoke(val);
    }
}
```

You'll recall that the compiler defined the **Invoke** method when it defined the **Feedback** class. When **Invoke** is called, it uses the private **_target** and **_methodPtr** fields to call the desired method on the specified object. Note that the signature of the **Invoke** method matches the signature of the delegate; because the **Feedback** delegate takes one **Int32** parameter and returns **void**, the **Invoke** method (as produced by the compiler) takes one **Int32** parameter and returns **void**.

Using Delegates to Call Back Many Methods (Chaining)

By themselves, delegates are incredibly useful. But add in their support for chaining, and delegates become even more useful. *Chaining* is a set or collection of delegate objects, and it provides the ability to invoke, or call, all of the methods represented by the delegates in the set. To understand this, see the `ChainDelegateDemo1` method that appears in the code shown at the beginning of this chapter. In this method, after the `Console.WriteLine` statement, I construct three delegate objects and have variables—**fb1**, **fb2**, and **fb3**—refer to each object, as shown in Figure 15-4:

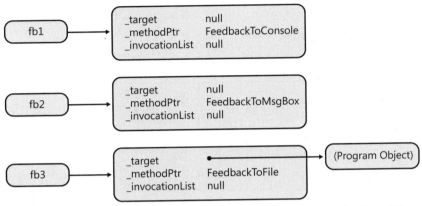

Figure 15-4   Initial state of the delegate objects referred to by the **fb1**, **fb2**, and **fb3** variables

The reference variable to a **Feedback** delegate object, **fbChain**, is intended to refer to a chain or set of delegate objects that wrap methods that can be called back. Initializing **fbChain** to **null** indicates that there currently are no methods to be called back. The **Delegate** class's public, static **Combine** method is used to add a delegate to the chain:

```
fbChain = (Feedback) Delegate.Combine(fbChain, fb1);
```

When this line of code executes, the **Combine** method sees that we are trying to combine **null** and **fb1**. Internally, **Combine** will simply return the value in **fb1**, and the **fbChain** variable will be set to refer to the same delegate object referred to by the **fb1** variable, as shown in Figure 15-5:

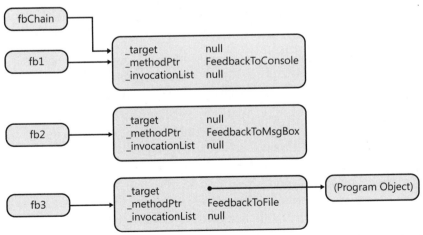

Figure 15-5   State of the delegate objects after inserting the first delegate in the chain

To add another delegate to the chain, the **Combine** method is called again:

```
fbChain = (Feedback) Delegate.Combine(fbChain, fb2);
```

Internally, the **Combine** method sees that **fbChain** already refers to a delegate object, so **Combine** will construct a new delegate object. This new delegate object initializes its private **_target** and **_methodPtr** fields to values that are not important for this discussion. However, what is important is that the **_invocationList** field is initialized to refer to an array of delegate objects. The first element of this array (index 0) will be initialized to refer to the delegate that wraps the **FeedbackToConsole** method (this is the delegate that **fbChain** currently refers to). The second element of the array (index 1) will be initialized to refer to the delegate that wraps the **FeedbackToMsgBox** method (this is the delegate that **fb2** refers to). Finally, **fbChain** will be set to refer to the newly created delegate object, shown in Figure 15-6:

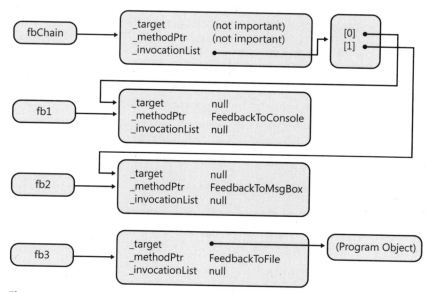

Figure 15-6   State of the delegate objects after inserting the second delegate in the chain

To add the third delegate to the chain, the **Combine** method is called once again:

```
fbChain = (Feedback) Delegate.Combine(fbChain, fb3);
```

Again, **Combine** sees that **fbChain** already refers to a delegate object, and this causes a new delegate object to be constructed, as shown in Figure 15-7. As before, this new delegate object initializes the private **_target** and **_methodPtr** fields to values unimportant to this discussion, and the **_invocationList** field is initialized to refer to an array of delegate objects. The first and second elements of this array (indexes 0 and 1) will be initialized to refer to the same delegates the previous delegate object referred to in its array. The third element of the array (index 2) will be initialized to refer to the delegate that wraps the **FeedbackToFile** method (this is the delegate that **fb3** refers to). Finally, **fbChain** will be set to refer to this newly created delegate object. Note that the previously created delegate and the array referred to by its **_invocationList** field are now candidates for garbage collection.

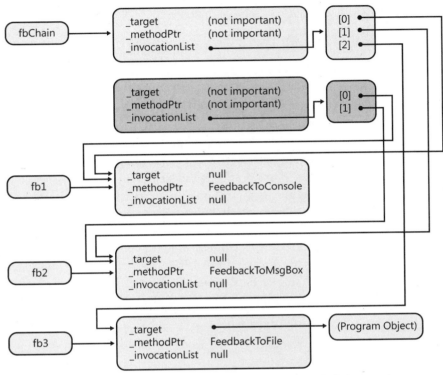

Figure 15-7   Final state of the delegate objects when the chain is complete

After all of the code has executed to set up the chain, the **fbChain** variable is then passed to the **Counter** method:

```
Counter(1, 2, fbChain);
```

Inside the **Counter** method is the code that implicitly calls the **Invoke** method on the **Feedback** delegate object as I detailed earlier in Figure 15-3. When **Invoke** is called on the delegate referred to by **fbChain**, the delegate sees that the private **_invocationList** field is not **null**, causing it to execute a loop that iterates through all of the elements in the array, calling the method wrapped by each delegate. In this example, **FeedbackToConsole** will get called first, followed by **FeedbackToMsgBox**, followed by **FeedbackToFile**.

Feedback's **Invoke** method is essentially implemented something like this (in pseudocode):

```
public void Invoke(Int32 value) {
    Delegate[] delegateSet = _invocationList as Delegate[];
    if (delegateSet != null) {
        // This delegate's array indicates the delegates that should be called
        foreach (Feedback d in delegateSet)
            d(value);   // Call each delegate
    } else {
```

```
        // This delegate identifies a single method to be called back
        // Call the callback method on the specified target object.
        _methodPtr.Invoke(_target, value);
        // The line above is an approximation of the actual code.
        // What really happens cannot be expressed in C#.
    }
}
```

Note that it is also possible to remove a delegate from a chain by calling **Delegate**'s public, static **Remove** method. This is demonstrated toward the end of the **ChainDelegateDemo1** method:

```
fbChain = (Feedback) Delegate.Remove(fbChain, new Feedback(FeedbackToMsgBox));
```

When **Remove** is called, it scans the delegate array (from the end toward index 0) maintained inside the delegate object referred to by the first parameter (**fbChain**, in my example). **Remove** is looking for a delegate entry whose **_target** and **_methodPtr** fields match those in the second argument (the new **Feedback** delegate, in my example). If a match is found and there is only one item left in the array, that array item is returned. If a match is found and there are multiple items left in the array, a new delegate object is constructed—the **_invocationList** array created and initialized will refer to all items in the original array except for the item being removed, of course—and a reference to this new delegate object is returned. If you are removing the only element in the chain, **Remove** returns **null**. Note that each call to **Remove** removes just one delegate from the chain; it does not remove all delegates that have matching **_target** and **_methodPtr** fields.

So far, I've shown examples in which my delegate type, **Feedback**, is defined as having a **void** return value. However, I could have defined my **Feedback** delegate as follows:

```
public delegate Int32 Feedback(Int32 value);
```

If I had, its **Invoke** method would have internally looked like this (again, in pseudocode):

```
public Int32 Invoke(Int32 value) {
    Int32 result;
    Delegate[] delegateSet = _invocationList as Delegate[];
    if (delegateSet != null) {
        // This delegate's array indicates the delegates that should be called
        foreach (Feedback d in delegateSet)
            result = d(value);    // Call each delegate
    } else {
        // This delegate identifies a single method to be called back
        // Call the callback method on the specified target object.
        result = _methodPtr.Invoke(_target, value);
        // The line above is an approximation of the actual code.
        // What really happens cannot be expressed in C#.
    }
    return result;
}
```

As each delegate in the array is called, its return value is saved in the result variable. When the loop is complete, the **result** variable will contain only the result of the last delegate called (previous return values are discarded); this value is returned to the code that called **Invoke**.

C#'s Support for Delegate Chains

To make things easier for C# developers, the C# compiler automatically provides overloads of the += and -= operators for instances of delegate types. These operators call `Delegate.Combine` and `Delegate.Remove`, respectively. Using these operators simplifies the building of delegate chains. The `ChainDelegateDemo1` and `ChainDelegateDemo2` methods in the source code shown at the beginning of this chapter produce absolutely identical IL code. The only difference between the methods is that the `ChainDelegateDemo2` method simplifies the source code by taking advantage of C#'s += and -= operators.

If you require proof that the resulting IL code is identical for the two methods, you can build the code and look at its IL for both methods by using ILDasm.exe. This will confirm that the C# compiler did in fact replace all += and -= operators with calls to the `Delegate` type's public static `Combine` and `Remove` methods, respectively.

Having More Control over Delegate Chain Invocation

At this point, you understand how to build a chain of delegate objects and how to invoke all of the objects in that chain. All items in the chain are invoked because the delegate type's `Invoke` method includes code to iterate through all of the items in the array, invoking each item. This is obviously a very simple algorithm. And although this simple algorithm is good enough for a lot of scenarios, it has many limitations. For example, the return values of the callback methods are all discarded except for the last one. Using this simple algorithm, there's no way to get the return values for all of the callback methods called. But this isn't the only limitation. What happens if one of the invoked delegates throws an exception or blocks for a very long time? Because the algorithm invoked each delegate in the chain serially, a "problem" with one of the delegate objects stops all of the subsequent delegates in the chain from being called. Clearly, this algorithm isn't robust.

For those scenarios in which this algorithm is insufficient, the `MulticastDelegate` class offers an instance method, `GetInvocationList`, that you can use to call each delegate in a chain explicitly, using any algorithm that meets your needs:

```
public abstract class MulticastDelegate : Delegate {
    // Creates a delegate array where each elements refers
    // to a delegate in the chain.
    public sealed override Delegate[] GetInvocationList();
}
```

The `GetInvocationList` method operates on a `MulticastDelegate`-derived object and returns an array of `Delegate` references where each reference points to one of the chain's delegate objects. Internally, `GetInvocationList` constructs an array and initializes it with each element referring to a delegate in the chain; a reference to the array is then returned. If the `_invocationList` field is `null`, the returned array contains one element that references the only delegate in the chain; the delegate instance itself.

You can easily write an algorithm that explicitly calls each object in the array. The following code demonstrates:

```csharp
using System;
using System.Text;

// Define a Light component.
internal sealed class Light {
   // This method returns the light's status.
   public String SwitchPosition() {
      return "The light is off";
   }
}

// Define a Fan component.
internal sealed class Fan {
   // This method returns the fan's status.
   public String Speed() {
      throw new InvalidOperationException("The fan broke due to overheating");
   }
}

// Define a Speaker component.
internal sealed class Speaker {
   // This method returns the speaker's status.
   public String Volume() {
      return "The volume is loud";
   }
}

public sealed class Program {

   // Definition of delegate that allows querying a component's status.
   private delegate String GetStatus();

   public static void Main() {
      // Declare an empty delegate chain.
      GetStatus getStatus = null;

      // Construct the three components, and add their status methods
      // to the delegate chain.
      getStatus += new GetStatus(new Light().SwitchPosition);
      getStatus += new GetStatus(new Fan().Speed);
      getStatus += new GetStatus(new Speaker().Volume);

      // Show consolidated status report reflecting
      // the condition of the three components.
      Console.WriteLine(GetComponentStatusReport(getStatus));
   }

   // Method that queries several components and returns a status report
   private static String GetComponentStatusReport(GetStatus status) {

      // If the chain is empty, there is nothing to do.
      if (status == null) return null;
```

```
    // Use this to build the status report.
    StringBuilder report = new StringBuilder();

    // Get an array where each element is a delegate from the chain.
    Delegate[] arrayOfDelegates = status.GetInvocationList();

    // Iterate over each delegate in the array.
    foreach (GetStatus getStatus in arrayOfDelegates) {

        try {
            // Get a component's status string, and append it to the report.
            report.AppendFormat("{0}{1}{1}", getStatus(), Environment.NewLine);
        }
        catch (InvalidOperationException e) {
            // Generate an error entry in the report for this component.
            Object component = getStatus.Target;
            report.AppendFormat(
                "Failed to get status from {1}{2}{0}    Error: {3}{0}{0}",
                Environment.NewLine,
                ((component == null) ? "" : component.GetType() + "."),
                getStatus.Method.Name,
                e.Message);
        }
    }

    // Return the consolidated report to the caller.
    return report.ToString();
  }
}
```

When you build and run this code, the following output appears:

```
The light is off

Failed to get status from Fan.Speed
    Error: The fan broke due to overheating

The volume is loud
```

C#'s Syntactical Sugar for Delegates

Most programmers find working with delegates to be cumbersome. The reason for this is that the syntax is so strange. For example, take this line of code:

```
button1.Click += new EventHandler(button1_Click);
```

where **button1.Click** is a method that looks something like this:

```
void button1_Click(Object sender, EventArgs e) {
    // Do something, the button was clicked...
}
```

The idea behind the first line of code is to register the address of the **button1_Click** method with a button control so that when the button is clicked, the method will be called. To most programmers, it feels quite unnatural to construct an **EventHandler** delegate object just to specify the address of the **button1_Click** method. However, constructing the **EventHandler** delegate object is required for the CLR because this object provides a wrapper that ensures that the method can be called only in a type-safe fashion. The wrapper also allows the calling of instance methods and chaining. Unfortunately, most programmers don't want to think about these details. Programmers would prefer to write the code above as follows:

```
button1.Click += button1_Click;
```

Fortunately, Microsoft's C# compiler offers programmers some syntax shortcuts when working with delegates. I'll explain all of these shortcuts in this section. One last point before we begin: what I'm about to describe really boils down to C# syntactical sugar; these new syntax shortcuts are really just giving programmers an easier way to produce the IL that must be generated so that the CLR and other programming languages can work with delegates. This also means that what I'm about to describe is specific to C#; other compilers might not offer the additional delegate syntax shortcuts.

Syntactical Shortcut #1: No Need to Construct a Delegate Object

As demonstrated already, C# allows you to specify the name of a callback method without having to construct a delegate object wrapper. Here is another example:

```
internal sealed class AClass {
    public static void CallbackWithoutNewingADelegateObject() {
        ThreadPool.QueueUserWorkItem(SomeAsyncTask, 5);
    }

    private static void SomeAsyncTask(Object o) {
        Console.WriteLine(o);
    }
}
```

Here, the **ThreadPool** class's static **QueueUserWorkItem** method expects a reference to a **WaitCallback** delegate object that contains a reference to the **SomeAsyncTask** method. Since the C# compiler is capable of inferring this on its own, it allows me to omit code that constructs the **WaitCallback** delegate object, making the code much more readable and understandable. Of course, when the code is compiled, the C# compiler does produce IL that does, in fact, new up the **WaitCallback** delegate object—we just got a syntactical shortcut.

Syntactical Shortcut #2: No Need to Define a Callback Method

In the code above, the name of the callback method, **SomeAsyncTask**, is passed to the **ThreadPool**'s **QueueUserWorkItem** method. C# allows you to write the code for the callback method in-line so it doesn't have to be written inside its very own method. For example, the code above could be rewritten as follows:

```
internal sealed class AClass {
    public static void CallbackWithoutNewingADelegateObject() {
```

```
      ThreadPool.QueueUserWorkItem(
         delegate(Object obj) { Console.WriteLine(obj); },
         5);
   }
}
```

Notice that the first "argument" to the **QueueUserWorkItem** method is a block of code! When the C# compiler sees the **delegate** keyword used wherever a reference to a delegate object is expected, the compiler automatically defines a new private method in the class (**AClass** in this example). This new method is called an *anonymous method* because the compiler creates the name of the method for you automatically, and normally, you wouldn't know its name. However, you could use a tool such as ILDasm.exe to examine the compiler-generated code. After I wrote the code above and compiled it, I was able to see, by using ILDasm.exe, that my C# compiler decided to name this method **<CallbackWithoutNewingADelegateObject>b__0**. But beware: you should never write code that expects this method name because a future version of the C# compiler might use a different algorithm for generating the method name.

Using ILDasm.exe, you might also notice that the C# compiler applies the **System.Runtime .CompilerServices.CompilerGeneratedAttribute** attribute to this method to indicate to tools that this method was produced by a compiler as opposed to a programmer. The code in the "argument" is then placed in this compiler-generated method.

> **Note** There is no limit to the number of statements or kinds of statements you may have in the callback code (an anonymous method). However, when writing an anonymous method, there is no way to apply a custom attribute to the method. Furthermore, you cannot apply any method modifiers (such as **unsafe**) to the method. But this is usually not a problem because anonymous methods generated by the compiler always end up being private, and the method is either static or non-static depending on whether the method accesses any instance members. So there is no need to apply modifiers such as **public**, **protected**, **internal**, **virtual**, **sealed**, **override**, or **abstract** to the method.

Finally, if you write the code shown above and compile it, it's as if the C# compiler rewrote your code to look like this (comments inserted by me):

```
internal sealed class AClass {
   // This private field is created to cache the delegate object.
   // Pro: CallbackWithoutNewingADelegateObject will not create
   //       a new object each time it is called.
   // Con: The cached object never gets garbage collected
   [CompilerGenerated]
   private static WaitCallback <>9__CachedAnonymousMethodDelegate1;

   public static void CallbackWithoutNewingADelegateObject() {
      if (<>9__CachedAnonymousMethodDelegate1 == null) {
         // First time called, create the delegate object and cache it.
         <>9__CachedAnonymousMethodDelegate1 =
            new WaitCallback(<CallbackWithoutNewingADelegateObject>b__0);
      }
```

```
      ThreadPool.QueueUserWorkItem(<>9__CachedAnonymousMethodDelegate1, 5);
   }

   [CompilerGenerated]
   private static void <CallbackWithoutNewingADelegateObject>b__0(Object obj) {
      Console.WriteLine(obj);
   }
}
```

The prototype of the anonymous method must match that of the **WaitCallback** delegate: it returns **void** and takes an **Object** parameter. However, I specified the name of the parameter by placing **(Object obj)** after the **delegate** keyword in my code as I was writing the anonymous method.

It is also worth noting that the anonymous method is marked as **private**; this forbids any code not defined within the type from accessing the method (although reflection will reveal that the method does exist). Also, note that the anonymous method is marked as **static**; this is because the code doesn't access any instance members (which it can't since **CallbackWithoutNewingADelegateObject** is itself a static method. However, the code can reference any static fields or static methods defined within the class. Here is an example:

```
internal sealed class AClass {
   private static String sm_name;  // A static field

   public static void CallbackWithoutNewingADelegateObject() {
      ThreadPool.QueueUserWorkItem(
         // The callback code can reference static members.
         delegate(Object obj) { Console.WriteLine(sm_name+ ": " + obj); },
         5);
   }
}
```

If the **CallbackWithoutNewingADelegateObject** method had not been static, the anonymous method's code could contain references to instance members. If it doesn't contain references to instance members, the compiler will still produce a static anonymous method since this is more efficient than an instance method because the additional **this** parameter is not necessary. But, if the anonymous method's code does reference an instance member, the compiler will produce a non-static anonymous method:

```
internal sealed class AClass {
   private String m_name;  // An instance field

   // An instance method
   public void CallbackWithoutNewingADelegateObject() {
      ThreadPool.QueueUserWorkItem(
         // The callback code can reference instance members.
         delegate(Object obj) { Console.WriteLine(m_name+ ": " + obj); },
         5);
   }
}
```

Syntactical Shortcut #3: No Need to Specify Callback Method Parameters

A common way to use the previous syntactical shortcut is when you want to have some code execute when a button is clicked:

```
button1.Click +=
    delegate(Object sender, EventArgs e)
        { MessageBox.Show("The Button was clicked!"); };
```

It's nice to be able to specify the callback code inline without having to manually define another method. But in this example, the callback code doesn't refer to the callback method's arguments, **sender** and **e**, at all. If your callback code doesn't care about the arguments, C# allows the code above to be shortened to this:

```
button1.Click +=
    delegate { MessageBox.Show("The Button was clicked!"); };
```

Notice that I just deleted the **(Object sender, EventArgs e)** portion of the original code. When the compiler emits the anonymous method, it still emits a method whose prototype matches the delegate exactly—the CLR absolutely requires this for type safety. In this case, the compiler still emits an anonymous method that matches an **EventHandler** delegate (the delegate type expected by **Button**'s **Click** event). However, the delegate's arguments won't be referenced by this example's anonymous method's code.

If the callback code references any of the parameters, you must include the parentheses, parameter types, and variable names after the **delegate** keyword. The return type is still inferred from the delegate's type and, if the return type is not **void**, you must have a **return** statement inside the inline callback code.

Syntactical Shortcut #4: No Need to Manually Wrap Local Variables in a Class to Pass them to a Callback Method

I've already shown how the callback code can reference other members defined in the class. However, sometimes, you might like the callback code to reference local parameters or variables that exist in the defining method. Here's an interesting example:

```
internal sealed class AClass {
    public static void UsingLocalVariablesInTheCallbackCode(Int32 numToDo) {
        // Some local variables
        Int32[] squares = new Int32[numToDo];
        AutoResetEvent done = new AutoResetEvent(false);

        // Do a bunch of tasks on other threads
        for (Int32 n = 0; n < squares.Length; n++) {
            ThreadPool.QueueUserWorkItem(
                delegate(Object obj) {
                    Int32 num = (Int32) obj;
```

```
            // This task would normally be more time consuming
            squares[num] = num * num;

            // If last task, let main thread continue running
            if (Interlocked.Decrement(ref numToDo) == 0)
                done.Set();
        },
        n);
    }

    // Wait for all the other threads to finish
    done.WaitOne();

    // Show the results
    for (Int32 n = 0; n < squares.Length; n++)
        Console.WriteLine("Index {0}, Square={1}", n, squares[n]);
    }
}
```

This example really shows off how easy C# makes implementing what used to be a pretty complex task. The method above defines one parameter, **numToDo**, and two local variables, **squares** and **done**. And the delegate callback code refers to these variables.

Now imagine that the callback code is placed in a separate method (as is required by the CLR). How would the values of the variables be passed to the callback method? The only way to do this is to define a new helper class that also defines a field for each value you want passed to the callback code. In addition, the callback code would have to be defined as an instance method in this helper class. Then, the **UsingLocalVariablesInTheCallbackCode** method would have to construct an instance of the helper class, initialize the fields from the values in its local variables, and then construct the delegate object bound to the helper object/ instance method.

This is very tedious and error-prone work, and, of course, the C# compiler does all this for you automatically. When you write the code shown above, it's as if the C# compiler rewrites your code so that it looks like this (comments inserted by me):

```
internal sealed class AClass {
    public static void UsingLocalVariablesInTheCallbackCode(Int32 numToDo) {

        // Some local variables
        WaitCallback callback1 = null;

        // Construct an instance of the helper class
        <>c__DisplayClass2 class1 = new <>c__DisplayClass2();

        // Initialize the helper class' fields
        class1.numToDo = numToDo;
        class1.squares = new Int32[class1.numToDo];
        class1.done = new AutoResetEvent(false);

        // Do a bunch of tasks on other threads
        for (Int32 n = 0; n < class1.squares.Length; n++) {
```

```
        if (callback1 == null) {
            // New up delegate object bound to the helper object and
            // its anonymous instance method
            callback1 = new WaitCallback(
                class1.<UsingLocalVariablesInTheCallbackCode>b__0);
        }

        ThreadPool.QueueUserWorkItem(callback1, n);
    }

    // Wait for all the other threads to finish
    class1.done.WaitOne();

    // Show the results
    for (Int32 n = 0; n < class1.squares.Length; n++)
        Console.WriteLine("Index {0}, Square={1}", n, class1.squares[n]);
}

// The helper class is given a strange name to avoid potential
// conflicts and is private to forbid access from outside AClass
[CompilerGenerated]
private sealed class <>c__DisplayClass2 : Object {

    // One public field per local variable used in the callback code
    public Int32[] squares;
    public Int32 numToDo;
    public AutoResetEvent done;

    // public parameterless constructor
    public <>c__DisplayClass2 { }

    // Public instance method containing the callback code
    public void <UsingLocalVariablesInTheCallbackCode>b__0(Object obj) {
        Int32 num = (Int32) obj;
        squares[num] = num * num;
        if (Interlocked.Decrement(ref numToDo) == 0)
            done.Set();
    }
}
}
```

Important   Without a doubt, it doesn't take much for programmers to start abusing C#'s anonymous method feature. When I first started using anonymous methods, it definitely took me some getting used to. After all, the code that you write in a method is not actually inside that method, and this also can make debugging and single-stepping though the code a bit more challenging. In fact, I'm amazed at how well the Visual Studio debugger actually handles stepping through anonymous methods in my source code.

I've set up a rule for myself: if I need my callback method to contain more than three lines of code in it, I will not use an anonymous method; instead, I'll write the method manually and assign it a name of my own creation. But, used judiciously, anonymous methods can greatly increase programmer productivity as well as maintainability of your code. Below is some code in which using anonymous methods just feels very natural. Without anonymous methods, this code would be tedious to write, harder to read, and harder to maintain.

```
// Create an initialize a String array
String[] names = { "Jeff", "Kristin", "Aidan" };

// Get just the names that have a lowercase 'i' in them.
Char charToFind = 'i';
names = Array.FindAll(names, delegate(String name)
    { return (name.IndexOf(charToFind) >= 0); });

// Convert each string's characters to uppercase
names = Array.ConvertAll<String, String>(names, delegate(String name)
    { return name.ToUpper(); });

// Sort the names
Array.Sort(names, String.Compare);

// Display the results
Array.ForEach(names, Console.WriteLine);
```

Delegates and Reflection

So far in this chapter, the use of delegates has required the developer to know up front the prototype of the method that is to be called back. For example, if **fb** is a variable that references a **Feedback** delegate (see this chapter's first program listing), to invoke the delegate, the code would look like this:

```
fb(item);    // item is defined as Int32
```

As you can see, the developer must know when coding how many parameters the callback method requires and the types of those parameters. Fortunately, the developer almost always has this information, so writing code like the preceding code isn't a problem.

In some rare circumstances, however, the developer doesn't have this information at compile time. I showed an example of this in Chapter 10, "Events," when I discussed the **EventSet** type. In this example, a dictionary maintained a set of different delegate types. At run time, to raise an event, one of the delegates was looked up in the dictionary and invoked. At compile time, it wasn't possible to know exactly which delegate would be called and which parameters were necessary to pass to the delegate's callback method.

Fortunately, **System.Delegate** offers a few methods that allow you to create and invoke a delegate when you just don't have all the necessary information about the delegate at compile time. Here are the corresponding methods that **Delegate** defines:

```
public abstract class Delegate {
    // Construct a 'type' delegate wrapping the specified static method.
    public static Delegate CreateDelegate(Type type, MethodInfo method);
    public static Delegate CreateDelegate(Type type, MethodInfo method,
        Boolean throwOnBindFailure);

    // Construct a 'type' delegate wrapping the specified instance method.
    public static Delegate CreateDelegate(Type type,
        Object firstArgument, MethodInfo method); // firstArgument means 'this'
```

```
    public static Delegate CreateDelegate(Type type,
        Object firstArgument, MethodInfo method, Boolean throwOnBindFailure);

    // Invoke a delegate passing it parameters
    public Object DynamicInvoke(params Object[] args);
}
```

All of the **CreateDelegate** methods here construct a new object of a **Delegate**-derived type identified by the first parameter, **type**. The **MethodInfo** parameter indicates the method that should be called back; you'd use reflection APIs (discussed in Chapter 22, "Assembly Loading and Reflection") to obtain this value. If you want the delegate to wrap an instance method, you will also pass to **CreateDelegate** a **firstArgument** parameter indicating the object that should be passed as the **this** parameter (first argument) to the instance method. Finally, **CreateDelegate** normally throws an **ArgumentException** if the delegate cannot bind to the method specified by the **method** parameter. This can happen if the signature of the method identified by **method** doesn't match the signature required by the delegate identified by the **type** parameter. However, if you pass **false** for the **throwOnBindFailure** parameter, an **ArgumentException** will not be thrown; **null** will be returned instead.

> **Important** The **System.Delegate** class has many more overloads of the **CreateDelegate** method that I do not show here. You should never call any of these other methods. As a matter of fact, Microsoft regrets even defining them in the first place. The reason is because these other methods identify the method to bind to by using a **String** instead of a **MethodInfo**. This means that an ambiguous bind is possible causing your application to behave unpredictably.

System.Delegate's **DynamicInvoke** method allows you to invoke a delegate object's callback method, passing a set of parameters that you determine at run time. When you call **DynamicInvoke**, it internally ensures that the parameters you pass are compatible with the parameters the callback method expects. If they're compatible, the callback method is called. If they're not, an **ArgumentException** is thrown. **DynamicInvoke** returns the object the callback method returned.

The following code shows how to use the **CreateDelegate** and **DynamicInvoke** methods:

```
using System;
using System.Reflection;
using System.IO;


// Here are some different delegate definitions
internal delegate Object TwoInt32s(Int32 n1, Int32 n2);
internal delegate Object OneString(String s1);


public static class Program {
    public static void Main(String[] args) {
        if (args.Length < 2) {
```

```csharp
      String fileName = Path.GetFileNameWithoutExtension(
         Assembly.GetEntryAssembly().Location);
   String usage =
      @"Usage:" +
      "{0}{1} delType methodName [Arg1] [Arg2]" +
      "{0}   where delType must be TwoInt32s or OneString"+
      "{0}   if delType is TwoInt32s, methodName must be Add or Subtract" +
      "{0}   if delType is OneString, methodName must be NumChars or Reverse" +
      "{0}" +
      "{0}Examples:" +
      "{0}   {1} TwoInt32s Add 123 321" +
      "{0}   {1} TwoInt32s Subtract 123 321" +
      "{0}   {1} OneString NumChars \"Hello there\"" +
      "{0}   {1} OneString Reverse  \"Hello there\"";
   Console.WriteLine(usage, Environment.NewLine, fileName);
   return;
}

// Convert the delType argument to a delegate type
Type delType = Type.GetType(args[0]);
if (delType == null) {
   Console.WriteLine("Invalid delType argument: " + args[0]);
   return;
}

Delegate d;
try {
   // Convert the Arg1 argument to a method
   MethodInfo mi = typeof(Program).GetMethod(args[1],
      BindingFlags.NonPublic | BindingFlags.Static);

   // Create a delegate object that wraps the static method
   d = Delegate.CreateDelegate(delType, mi);
}
catch (ArgumentException) {
   Console.WriteLine("Invalid methodName argument: " + args[1]);
   return;
}

// Create an array that will contain just the arguments
// to pass to the method via the delegate object
Object[] callbackArgs = new Object[args.Length - 2];

if (d.GetType() == typeof(TwoInt32s)) {
   try {
      // Convert the String arguments to Int32 arguments
      for (Int32 a = 2; a < args.Length; a++)
         callbackArgs[a - 2] = Int32.Parse(args[a]);
   }
   catch (FormatException) {
      Console.WriteLine("Parameters must be integers.");
      return;
   }
}

if (d.GetType() == typeof(OneString)) {
```

```
         // Just copy the String argument
         Array.Copy(args, 2, callbackArgs, 0, callbackArgs.Length);
      }

      try {
         // Invoke the delegate and show the result
         Object result = d.DynamicInvoke(callbackArgs);
         Console.WriteLine("Result = " + result);
      }
      catch (TargetParameterCountException) {
         Console.WriteLine("Incorrect number of parameters specified.");
      }
   }


   // This callback method takes 2 Int32 arguments
   private static Object Add(Int32 n1, Int32 n2) {
      return n1 + n2;
   }

   // This callback method takes 2 Int32 arguments
   private static Object Subtract(Int32 n1, Int32 n2) {
      return n1 - n2;
   }

   // This callback method takes 1 String argument
   private static Object NumChars(String s1) {
      return s1.Length;
   }

   // This callback method takes 1 String argument
   private static Object Reverse(String s1) {
      Char[] chars = s1.ToCharArray();
      Array.Reverse(chars);
      return new String(chars);
   }
}
```

Chapter 16

Generics

Developers who are familiar with object-oriented programming know the benefits it offers. One of the big benefits that make developers extremely productive is code re-use, which is the ability to derive a class that inherits all of the capabilities of a base class. The derived class can simply override virtual methods or add some new methods to customize the behavior of the base class to meet the developer's needs. *Generics* is another mechanism offered by the common language runtime (CLR) and programming languages that provides one more form of code re-use: algorithm re-use.

Basically, one developer defines an algorithm such as sorting, searching, swapping, comparing, or converting. However, the developer defining the algorithm doesn't specify what data type(s) the algorithm operates on; the algorithm can be generically applied to objects of different types. Another developer can then use this existing algorithm as long as he or she indicates the specific data type(s) the algorithm should operate on, for example, a sorting algorithm that operates on `Int32`s, `String`s, etc., or a comparing algorithm that operates on `DateTime`s, `Version`s, etc.

Most algorithms are encapsulated in a type, and the CLR allows the creation of generic reference types as well as generic value types, but it does not allow the creation of generic enumerated types. In addition, the CLR allows the creation of generic interfaces and generic delegates. Occasionally, a single method can encapsulate a useful algorithm, and therefore, the CLR allows the creation of generic methods that are defined in a reference type, value type, or interface.

Let's look at a quick example. The Framework Class Library (FCL) defines a generic list algorithm that knows how to manage a set of objects; the data type of these objects is not specified by the generic algorithm. Someone wanting to use the generic list algorithm can specify the exact data type to use with it later.

The FCL class that encapsulates the generic list algorithm is called **List<T>** (pronounced *List of Tee*), and this class is defined in the **System.Collections.Generic** namespace. Here is what the source code for this class definition looks like (severely abbreviated):

```
[Serializable]
public class List<T> : IList<T>, ICollection<T>, IEnumerable<T>,
    IList, ICollection, IEnumerable {

    public List();
    public void Add(T item);
    public Int32 BinarySearch(T item);
    public void Clear();
    public Boolean Contains(T item);
    public Int32 IndexOf(T item);
    public Boolean Remove(T item);
    public void Sort();
    public void Sort(IComparer<T> comparer);
    public void Sort(Comparison<T> comparison);
    public T[] ToArray();

    public Int32 Count { get; }
    public T this[Int32 index] { get; set; }
}
```

The programmer who defined the generic **List** class indicates that it works with an unspecified data type by placing the **<T>** immediately after the class name. When defining a generic type or method, any variables it specifies for types (such as **T**) are called *type parameters*. **T** is a variable name that can be used in source code anywhere a data type can be used. For example, in the **List** class definition, you see **T** being used for method parameters (the **Add** method accepts a parameter of type **T**) and return values (the **ToArray** method returns a single-dimension array of type **T**). Another example is the indexer method (called **this** in C#). The indexer has a **get** accessor method that returns a value of type **T** and a **set** accessor method that accepts a parameter of type **T**. Since the **T** variable can be used anywhere that a data type can be specified, it is also possible to use **T** when defining local variables inside a method or when defining fields inside a type.

Now that the generic **List<T>** type has been defined, other developers can use this generic algorithm by specifying the exact data type they would like the algorithm to operate on. When using a generic type or method, the specified data types are referred to as *type arguments*. For example, a developer might want to work with the **List** algorithm by specifying a **DateTime** type argument. Here is some code that shows this:

```
private static void SomeMethod() {
    // Construct a List that operates on DateTime objects
    List<DateTime> dtList = new List<DateTime>();

    // Add a DateTime object to the list
    dtList.Add(DateTime.Now);         // No boxing
```

```
    // Add another DateTime object to the list
    dtList.Add(DateTime.MinValue); // No boxing

    // Attempt to add a String object to the list
    dtList.Add("1/1/2004");          // Compile-time error

    // Extract a DateTime object out of the list
    DateTime dt = dtList[0];          // No cast required
}
```

Generics provide the following big benefits to developers as exhibited by the code just shown:

- **Source code protection**   The developer using a generic algorithm doesn't need to have access to the algorithm's source code. With C++ templates or Java's generics, however, the algorithm's source code must be available to the developer who is using the algorithm.

- **Type Safety**   When a generic algorithm is used with a specific type, the compiler and the CLR understand this and ensure that only objects compatible with the specified data type are used with the algorithm. Attempting to use an object of an incompatible type will result in either a compiler error or a run-time exception being thrown. In the example, attempting to pass a **String** object to the **Add** method results in the compiler issuing an error.

- **Cleaner Code**   Since the compiler enforces type safety, fewer casts are required in your source code, meaning that your code is easier to write and maintain. In the last line of **SomeMethod**, a developer doesn't need to use a **(DateTime)** cast to put the result of the indexer (querying element at index 0) into the **dt** variable.

- **Better Performance**   Before generics, the way to define a generalized algorithm was to define all of its members to work with the **object** data type. If you wanted to use the algorithm with value type instances, the CLR had to box the value type instance prior to calling the members of the algorithm. As discussed in Chapter 5, "Primitive, Reference, and Value Types," boxing causes memory allocations on the managed heap, which causes more frequent garbage collections, which, in turn, hurt an application's performance. Since a generic algorithm can now be created to work with a specific value type, the instances of the value type can be passed by value, and the CLR no longer has to do any boxing. In addition, since casts are not necessary (see the previous bullet), the CLR doesn't have to check the type safety of the attempted cast, and this results in faster code too.

To drive home the performance benefits of generics, I wrote a program that tests the performance of the generic **List** algorithm against the FCL's non-generic **ArrayList** algorithm. In fact, I tested the performance of these two algorithms by using both value type objects and reference type objects. Here is the program itself:

```
using System;
using System.Collections;
using System.Collections.Generic;
using System.Diagnostics;
```

```
public static class Program {
    public static void Main() {
        ValueTypePerfTest();
        ReferenceTypePerfTest();
    }

    private static void ValueTypePerfTest() {
        const Int32 count = 10000000;

        using (new OperationTimer("List<Int32>")) {
            List<Int32> l = new List<Int32>(count);
            for (Int32 n = 0; n < count; n++) {
                l.Add(n);
                Int32 x = l[n];
            }
            l = null;   // Make sure this gets GC'd
        }

        using (new OperationTimer("ArrayList of Int32")) {
            ArrayList a = new ArrayList();
            for (Int32 n = 0; n < count; n++) {
                a.Add(n);
                Int32 x = (Int32) a[n];
            }
            a = null;   // Make sure this gets GC'd
        }
    }

    private static void ReferenceTypePerfTest() {
        const Int32 count = 10000000;

        using (new OperationTimer("List<String>")) {
            List<String> l = new List<String>();
            for (Int32 n = 0; n < count; n++) {
                l.Add("X");
                String x = l[n];
            }
            l = null;   // Make sure this gets GC'd
        }

        using (new OperationTimer("ArrayList of String")) {
            ArrayList a = new ArrayList();
            for (Int32 n = 0; n < count; n++) {
                a.Add("X");
                String x = (String) a[n];
            }
            a = null;   // Make sure this gets GC'd
        }
    }
}

// This is useful for doing operation performance timing
internal sealed class OperationTimer : IDisposable {
    private Int64  m_startTime;
    private String m_text;
    private Int32  m_collectionCount;
```

```
public OperationTimer(String text) {
   PrepareForOperation();

   m_text = text;
   m_collectionCount = GC.CollectionCount(0);

   // This should be the last statement in this
   // method to keep timing as accurate as possible
   m_startTime = Stopwatch.GetTimestamp();
}

public void Dispose() {
   Console.WriteLine("{0,6:###.00} seconds (GCs={1,3}) {2}",
      (Stopwatch.GetTimestamp() - m_startTime) /
         (Double) Stopwatch.Frequency,
      GC.CollectionCount(0) - m_collectionCount, m_text);
}

private static void PrepareForOperation() {
   GC.Collect();
   GC.WaitForPendingFinalizers();
   GC.Collect();
}
}
```

When I compile and run a release build (with optimizations turned on) of this program on my computer, I get the following output:

```
 .10 seconds (GCs=  0) List<Int32>
2.02 seconds (GCs= 30) ArrayList of Int32
 .52 seconds (GCs=  6) List<String>
 .53 seconds (GCs=  6) ArrayList of String
```

The output here shows that using the generic **List** algorithm with the **Int32** type is much faster than using the non-generic **ArrayList** algorithm with **Int32**. In fact, the difference is phenomenal: .1 second versus 2 seconds. That's 20 times faster! In addition, using a value type (**Int32**) with **ArrayList** causes a lot of boxing operations to occur, which results in 30 garbage collections. Meanwhile, the **List** algorithm required 0 garbage collections.

The result of the test using reference types is not as momentous. Here we see that the times and number of garbage collections are about the same. So it doesn't appear that the generic **List** algorithm is of any benefit here. However, keep in mind that when using a generic algorithm, you also get cleaner code and compile-time type safety. So while the performance improvement is not huge, the other benefits you get when using a generic algorithm are usually an improvement.

 Note You do need to realize that the CLR generates native code for each method the first time the method is called for a particular data type. This will increase an application's working set size, which will hurt performance. I will talk about this more in the "Generics Infrastructure" section of this chapter.

Generics in the Framework Class Library

Certainly, the most obvious use of generics is with collection classes, and the FCL defines several generic collection classes available for your use. Microsoft recommends that programmers use the new generic collection classes and now discourages use of the non-generic collection classes for several reasons. First, the non-generic collection classes are not generic, and so you don't get the type safety, cleaner code, and better performance that you get when you use generic collection classes. Second, the generic classes have a better object model than the non-generic classes. For example, fewer methods are virtual, resulting in better performance, and new members have been added to the generic collections to provide new functionality. Table 16-1 shows the generic collection classes and the non-generic collection classes they substitute.

Table 16-1   Generic Collection Classes and Their Non-Generic Counterparts

Generic Collection Class	Non-Generic Collection Class
`List<T>`	`ArrayList`
`Dictionary<TKey, TValue>`	`Hashtable`
`SortedDictionary<TKey, TValue>`	`SortedList`
`Stack<T>`	`Stack`
`Queue<T>`	`Queue`
`LinkedList<T>`	`(none)`

Many of these collection classes use helper classes. The `Dictionary` and `SortedDictionary` classes use the `KeyValuePair<TKey,TValue>` class, which is the generic equivalent of the non-generic `DictionaryEntry` class. Also, the `LinkedListNode<T>` class is used by the `LinkedList` class.

> **Note**   Microsoft's design guidelines state that generic parameter variables should either be called `T` or at least start with an uppercase `T` (as in `TKey` and `TValue`). The uppercase `T` stands for *type* just as an uppercase `I` stands for *interface* (as in `IComparable`).

The collection classes implement many interfaces, and the objects that you place into the collections can implement interfaces that the collection classes use for operations such as sorting and searching. The FCL ships with many generic interface definitions so that the benefits of generics can be realized when working with interfaces as well. Table 16-2 shows the generic interfaces and their equivalent non-generic interfaces.

Table 16-2   Generic Collection Interfaces and Their Non-Generic Counterparts

Generic Interfaces	Non-Generic Interfaces
`IList<T>`	`IList`
`IDictionary<TKey, TValue>`	`IDictionary`
`ICollection<T>`	`ICollection`

Table 16-2   Generic Collection Interfaces and Their Non-Generic Counterparts

Generic Interfaces	Non-Generic Interfaces
IEnumerator<T>	IEnumerator
IEnumerable<T>	IEnumerable
IComparer<T>	IComparer
IComparable<T>	IComparable

The new generic interfaces are not a replacement for the old non-generic interfaces; in many scenarios, you will have to use both. The reason is backward compatibility. For example, if the List<T> class implemented only the IList<T> interface, no code could consider a List<DateTime> object an IList.

I should also point out that the System.Array class, the base class of all array types, offers many static generic methods, such as AsReadOnly, BinarySearch, ConvertAll, Exists, Find, FindAll, FindIndex, FindLast, FindLastIndex, ForEach, IndexOf, LastIndexOf, Resize, Sort, and TrueForAll. Here are examples showing what some of these methods look like:

```
public abstract class Array : ICloneable, IList, ICollection, IEnumerable {
   public static void  Sort<T>(T[] array);
   public static void  Sort<T>(T[] array, IComparer<T> comparer);

   public static Int32 BinarySearch<T>(T[] array, T value);
   public static Int32 BinarySearch<T>(T[] array, T value,
      IComparer<T> comparer);
   ...
}
```

Here is code that demonstrates how to use some of these methods:

```
public static void Main() {
   // Create & initialize a byte array
   Byte[] byteArray = new Byte[] { 5, 1, 4, 2, 3 };

   // Call Byte[] sort algorithm
   Array.Sort<Byte>(byteArray);

   // Call Byte[] binary search algorithm
   Int32 i = Array.BinarySearch<Byte>(byteArray, 1);
   Console.WriteLine(i);   // Displays "0"
}
```

Wintellect's Power Collections Library

At Microsoft's request, Wintellect has produced the Power Collections library to bring some of the C++ Standard Template Library's collection classes to the CLR programmer. This library is a set of collection classes that anyone can download and use free of charge. See *http://Wintellect.com* for details. These collection classes are generic themselves and make extensive use of generics. Table 16-3 shows a list of some of the collection classes you'll find in the Power Collections library.

Table 16-3   Generic Collection Classes from Wintellect's Power Collections Library

Collection Class	Description
BigList<T>	Collection of ordered T objects. Very efficient when working with >100 items.
Bag<T>	Collection of unordered T objects. The collection is hashed, and duplicates are allowed.
OrderedBag<T>	Collection of ordered T objects. Duplicates are allowed.
Set<T>	Collection of unordered T items. Duplicates are not allowed.
OrderedSet<T>	Collection of ordered T items. Duplicates are not allowed.
Deque<T>	Double-ended queue. Similar to a list but more efficient for adding/removing items at the beginning than a list.
OrderedDictionary<TKey,TValue>	Dictionary in which keys are ordered, and each can have one value.
MultiDictionary<TKey,TValue>	Dictionary in which a key can have multiple values. Keys are hashed, duplicates are allowed, and items are unordered.
OrderedMultiDictionary<TKey,TValue>	Dictionary in which keys are ordered, and each can have multiple values (also maintained in sorted order). Duplicate keys are allowed.

Generics Infrastructure

Adding generics to the CLR was a major task that took many people a lot of time. Specifically, to make generics work, Microsoft had to do the following:

- Create new IL instructions that are aware of type arguments.

- Modify the format of existing metadata tables so that type names and methods with generic parameters could be expressed.

- Modify the various programming languages (C#, Microsoft Visual Basic .NET, etc.) to support the new syntax, allowing developers to define and reference generic types and methods.

- Modify the compilers to emit the new IL instructions and the modified metadata format.

- Modify the JIT compiler to process the new type-argument–aware IL instructions that produce the correct native code.

- Create new reflection members so that developers can query types and members to determine if they have generic parameters. Also, new reflection emit members had to be defined so that developers could create generic type and method definitions at run time.

- Modify the debugger to show and manipulate generic types, members, fields, and local variables.

- Modify the Microsoft Visual Studio IntelliSense feature to show specific member prototypes when using a generic type or a method with a specific data type.

Now let's spend some time discussing how the CLR handles generics internally. This information could impact how you architect and design a generic algorithm. It could also impact your decision to use an existing generic algorithm or not.

Open and Closed Types

In various chapters throughout this book, I have discussed how the CLR creates an internal data structure for each and every type in use by an application. These data structures are called *type objects*. Well, a type with generic type parameters is still considered a type, and the CLR will create an internal type object for each of these. This applies to reference types (classes), value types (structs), interface types, and delegate types. However, a type with generic type parameters is called an *open type*, and the CLR does not allow any instance of an open type to be constructed (similar to how the CLR prevents an instance of an interface type from being constructed).

When code references a generic type, it can specify a set of generic type arguments. If actual data types are passed in for all of the type arguments, the type is called a *closed type*, and the CLR does allow instances of a closed type to be constructed. However, it is possible for code referencing a generic type to leave some generic type arguments unspecified. This creates a new open type object in the CLR, and instances of this type cannot be created. The following code should make this clear:

```
using System;
using System.Collections.Generic;

// A partially specified open type
internal sealed class DictionaryStringKey<TValue> :
   Dictionary<String, TValue> {
}

public static class Program {
   public static void Main() {
      Object o = null;

      // Dictionary<,> is an open type having 2 type parameters
      Type t = typeof(Dictionary<,>);

      // Try to create an instance of this type (fails)
      o = CreateInstance(t);
      Console.WriteLine();

      // DictionaryStringKey<> is an open type having 1 type parameter
      t = typeof(DictionaryStringKey<>);
```

```
      // Try to create an instance of this type (fails)
      o = CreateInstance(t);
      Console.WriteLine();

      // DictionaryStringKey<Guid> is a closed type
      t = typeof(DictionaryStringKey<Guid>);

      // Try to create an instance of this type (succeeds)
      o = CreateInstance(t);

      // Prove it actually worked
      Console.WriteLine("Object type=" + o.GetType());
   }

   private static Object CreateInstance(Type t) {
      Object o = null;
      try {
         o = Activator.CreateInstance(t);
         Console.Write("Created instance of {0}", t.ToString());
      }
      catch (ArgumentException e) {
         Console.WriteLine(e.Message);
      }
      return o;
   }
}
```

When I compile the code above and run it, I get the following output:

```
Cannot create an instance of System.Collections.Generic.
Dictionary`2[TKey,TValue] because Type.ContainsGenericParameters is true.

Cannot create an instance of DictionaryStringKey`1[TValue] because
Type.ContainsGenericParameters is true.

Created instance of DictionaryStringKey`1[System.Guid]
Object type=DictionaryStringKey`1[System.Guid]
```

As you can see, **Activator**'s **CreateInstance** method throws an **ArgumentException** when you ask it to construct an instance of an open type. In fact, the exception's string message indicates that the type still contains some generic parameters.

In the output, you'll notice that the type names end with a backtick (`) followed by a number. The number indicates the type's *arity*, which indicates the number of type parameters required by the type. For example, the **Dictionary** class has an arity of 2 since it requires that types be specified for **TKey** and **TValue**. The **DictionaryStringKey** class has an arity of 1 since it requires just one type to be specified for **TValue**.

I should also point out that the CLR allocates a type's static fields inside the type object (as discussed in Chapter 4, "Type Fundamentals"). So each closed type has its own static fields. In other words, if **List<T>** defined any static fields, these fields are not shared between a

`List<DateTime>` and a `List<String>`; each closed type object has its own static fields. Also, if a generic type defines a static constructor (discussed in Chapter 8, "Methods: Constructors, Operators, Conversions, and Parameters"), this constructor will execute once per closed type. Sometimes people define a static constructor on a generic type to ensure that the type arguments will meet certain criteria. For example, if you wanted to define a generic type that can be used only with enumerated types, you could do the following:

```
internal sealed class GenericTypeThatRequiresAnEnum<T> {
    static GenericTypeThatRequiresAnEnum() {
        if (!typeof(T).IsEnum) {
            throw new ArgumentException("T must be an enumerated type");
        }
    }
}
```

The CLR has a feature, called *constraints*, that offers a better way for you to define a generic type indicating what type arguments are valid for it. I'll discuss constraints later in this chapter. Unfortunately, constraints do not support the ability to limit a type argument to enumerated types only, which is why the previous example requires a static constructor to ensure that the type is an enumerated type.

Generic Types and Inheritance

A generic type is a type, and as such, it can be derived from any other type. When you use a generic type and specify type arguments, you are defining a new type object in the CLR, and the new type object is derived from whatever type the generic type was derived from. In other words, since `List<T>` is derived from `Object`, `List<String>` and `List<Guid>` are also derived from `Object`. Similarly, since `DictionaryStringKey<TValue>` is derived from `Dictionary<String, TValue>`, `DictionaryStringKey<Guid>` is also derived from `Dictionary<String, Guid>`. Understanding that specifying type arguments doesn't have anything to do with inheritance hierarchies will help you to recognize what kind of casting you can and can't do.

For example, if a linked-list node class is defined like this:

```
internal sealed class Node<T> {
    public T m_data;
    public Node<T> m_next;

    public Node(T data) : this(data, null) {
    }

    public Node(T data, Node<T> next) {
        m_data = data; m_next = next;
    }

    public override String ToString() {
        return m_data.ToString() +
            ((m_next != null) ? m_next.ToString() : null);
    }
}
```

then I can write some code to build up a linked list that would look something like this:

```
private static void SameDataLinkedList() {
    Node<Char> head = new Node<Char>('C');
    head = new Node<Char>('B', head);
    head = new Node<Char>('A', head);
    Console.WriteLine(head.ToString());
}
```

In the **Node** class just shown, the **m_next** field must refer to another node that has the same kind of data type in its **m_data** field. This means that the linked list must contain nodes in which all data items are of the same type (or derived type). For example, I can't use the **Node** class to create a linked list in which one element contains a **Char**, another element contains a **DateTime**, and another element contains a **String**.

However, by defining a non-generic **Node** base class and then defining a generic **TypedNode** class (using the **Node** class as a base class), I can now have a linked list in which each node can be of any data type. Here are the new class definitions:

```
internal class Node {
    protected Node m_next;

    public Node(Node next) {
        m_next = next;
    }
}

internal sealed class TypedNode<T> : Node {
    public T m_data;

    public TypedNode(T data) : this(data, null) {
    }

    public TypedNode(T data, Node next) : base(next) {
        m_data = data;
    }

    public override String ToString() {
        return m_data.ToString() +
            ((m_next != null) ? m_next.ToString() : null);
    }
}
```

I can now write code to create a linked list in which each node is a different data type. The code could look something like this:

```
private static void DifferentDataLinkedList() {
    Node head = new TypedNode<Char>('.');
    head = new TypedNode<DateTime>(DateTime.Now, head);
    head = new TypedNode<String>("Today is ", head);
    Console.WriteLine(head.ToString());
}
```

Generic Type Identity

Sometimes generic syntax confuses developers. After all, there can be a lot of less-than (<) and greater-than (>) signs sprinkled throughout your source code, and this hurts readability. To improve syntax, some developers define a new non-generic class type that is derived from a generic type and that specifies all of the type arguments. For example, to simplify code like this:

```
List<DateTime> dt = new List<DateTime>();
```

Some developers might first define a class like this:

```
internal sealed class DateTimeList : List<DateTime> {
    // No need to put any code in here!
}
```

Now, the code that creates a list can be rewritten more simply (without less-than and greater-than signs) like this:

```
DateTimeList dt = new DateTimeList();
```

While this seems like a convenience, especially if you use the new type for parameters, local variables, and fields, you should never define a new class explicitly for the purpose of making your source code easier to read. The reason is because you lose type identity and equivalence, as you can see in the following code:

```
Boolean sameType = (typeof(List<DateTime>) == typeof(DateTimeList));
```

When the code above runs, **sameType** will be initialized to **false** because you are comparing two different type objects. This also means that a method prototyped as accepting a **DateTimeList** will not be able to have a **List<DateTime>** passed to it. However, a method prototyped as accepting a **List<DateTime>** can have a **DateTimeList** passed to it since **DateTimeList** is derived from **List<DateTime>**. Programmers may become easily confused by all of this.

Fortunately, C# does offer a way to use simplified syntax to refer to a generic closed type while not affecting type equivalence at all; you can use the good old **using** directive at the top of your source code file. Here is an example:

```
using DateTimeList = System.Collections.Generic.List<System.DateTime>;
```

Here, the **using** directive is really just defining a symbol called **DateTimeList**. As the code compiles, the compiler substitutes all occurrences of **DateTimeList** with **System.Collections .Generic.List<System.DateTime>**. This just allows developers to use a simplified syntax without affecting the actual meaning of the code, and therefore, type identity and equivalence are maintained. So now, when the following line executes, **sameType** will be initialized to **true**.

```
Boolean sameType = (typeof(List<DateTime>) == typeof(DateTimeList));
```

Code Explosion

When a method that uses generic type parameters is JIT-compiled, the CLR takes the method's IL, substitutes the specified type arguments, and then creates native code that is specific to that method operating on the specified data types. This is exactly what you want and is one of the main features of generics. However, there is a downside to this: the CLR keeps generating native code for every method/type combination. This is referred to as *code explosion*. This can end up increasing the application's working set substantially, thereby hurting performance.

Fortunately, the CLR has some optimizations built into it to reduce code explosion. First, if a method is called for a particular type argument, and later, the method is called again using the same type argument, the CLR will compile the code for this method/type combination just once. So if one assembly uses `List<DateTime>`, and a completely different assembly (loaded in the same AppDomain) also uses `List<DateTime>`, the CLR will compile the methods for `List<DateTime>` just once. This reduces code explosion substantially.

The CLR has another optimization: the CLR considers all reference type arguments to be identical, and so again, the code can be shared. For example, the code compiled by the CLR for `List<String>`'s methods can be used for `List<Stream>`'s methods, since `String` and `Stream` are both reference types. In fact, for any reference type, the same code will be used. The CLR can perform this optimization because all reference type arguments or variables are really just pointers (all 32 bits on a 32-bit Windows system and 64 bits on a 64-bit Windows system) to objects on the heap, and object pointers are all manipulated in the same way.

But if any type argument is a value type, the CLR must produce native code specifically for that value type. The reason is because value types can vary in size. And even if two value types are the same size (such as `Int32` and `UInt32`, which are both 32 bits), the CLR still can't share the code because different native CPU instructions can be used to manipulate these values.

Generic Interfaces

Obviously, the ability to define generic reference and value types was the main feature of generics. However, it was critical for the CLR to also allow generic interfaces. Without generic interfaces, any time you tried to manipulate a value type by using a non-generic interface (such as `IComparable`), boxing and a loss of compile-time type safety would happen again. This would severely limit the usefulness of generic types. And so the CLR does support generic interfaces. A reference or value type can implement a generic interface by specifying type arguments, or a type can implement a generic interface by leaving the type arguments unspecified. Let's look at some examples.

Here is the definition of a generic interface that ships as part of the FCL (in the `System .Collections.Generic` namespace):

```
public interface IEnumerator<T> : IDisposable, IEnumerator {
   T Current { get; }
}
```

Here is an example of a type that implements this generic interface and that specifies type arguments. Notice that a **Triangle** object can enumerate a set of **Point** objects. Also note that the **Current** property is of the **Point** data type:

```
internal sealed class Triangle : IEnumerator<Point> {
   private Point[] m_vertices;

   // IEnumerator<Point>'s Current property is of type Point
   Point Current { get { ... } }
}
```

Now let's look at an example of a type that implements the same generic interface but with the type arguments left unspecified:

```
internal sealed class ArrayEnumerator<T> : IEnumerator<T> {
   private T[] m_array;

   // IEnumerator<T>'s Current property is of type T
   T Current { get { ... } }
}
```

Notice that an **ArrayEnumerator** object can enumerate a set of **T** objects (where **T** is unspecified allowing code using the generic **ArrayEnumerator** type to specify a type for **T** later). Also note that the **Current** property is now of the unspecified data type **T**. Much more information about generic interfaces is presented in Chapter 14, "Interfaces."

Generic Delegates

The CLR supports generic delegates to ensure that any type of object can be passed to a callback method in a type-safe way. Furthermore, generic delegates allow a value type instance to be passed to a callback method without any boxing. As discussed in Chapter 15, "Delegates," a delegate is really just a class definition with four methods: a constructor, an **Invoke** method, a **BeginInvoke** method, and an **EndInvoke** method. When you define a delegate type that specifies type parameters, the compiler defines the delegate class's methods, and the type parameters are applied to any methods having parameters/return values of the specified type parameter.

For example, if you define a generic delegate like this:

```
public delegate TReturn CallMe<TReturn, TKey, TValue>(TKey key, TValue value);
```

The compiler turns that into a class that logically looks like this:

```
public sealed class CallMe<TReturn, TKey, TValue> : MulticastDelegate {
   public CallMe(Object object, IntPtr method);
   public TReturn Invoke(TKey key, TValue value);
   public IAsyncResult BeginInvoke(TKey key, TValue value,
      AsyncCallback callback, Object object);
   public TReturn EndInvoke(IAsyncResult result);
}
```

The FCL ships with a handful of generic delegate types. Most of these are used when working with collections. Examples include:

```
// Typically used to perform an action on an collection item
public delegate void Action<T>(T obj);

// Typically used to compare 2 collection items for sorting
public delegate Int32 Comparison<T>(T x, T y);

// Typically used to convert a collection item from one type to another
public delegate TOutput Converter<TInput, TOutput>(TInput input);

// Typically used to decide whether a collection item passes some test
public delegate Boolean Predicate<T>(T obj);
```

Another generic delegate that ships with the FCL is used for events. This delegate (shown below) is discussed in Chapter 10, "Events":

```
public delegate void EventHandler<TEventArgs>(
    object sender, TEventArgs e) where TEventArgs : EventArgs;
```

The **where** clause above is called a *constraint*. Constraints are discussed later in this chapter.

Generic Methods

When you define a generic reference type, value type, or interface, any methods defined in these types can refer to a type parameter specified by the type. A type parameter can be used as a method's parameter, a method's return value, or as a local variable defined inside the method. However, the CLR also supports the ability for a method to specify its very own type parameters. And these type parameters can be used for parameters, return values, or local variables. Here is a somewhat contrived example of a type that defines a type parameter and a method that has its very own type parameter:

```
internal sealed class GenericType<T> {
   private T m_value;

   public GenericType(T value) { m_value = value; }

   public TOutput Converter<TOutput>() {
      TOutput result = (TOutput) Convert.ChangeType(m_value, typeof(TOutput));
      return result;
   }
}
```

In this example, you can see that the **GenericType** class defines its own type parameter (**T**), and the **Converter** method defines its own type parameter (**TOutput**). This allows a **GenericType** to be constructed to work with any type. The **Converter** method can convert the object referred to by the **m_value** field to various types depending on what type argument is passed to it when called. The ability to have type parameters and method parameters allows for phenomenal flexibility.

A reasonably good example of a generic method is the `Swap` method:

```
private static void Swap<T>(ref T o1, ref T o2) {
    T temp = o1;
    o1 = o2;
    o2 = temp;
}
```

Code can now call `Swap` like this:

```
private static void CallingSwap() {
    Int32 n1 = 1, n2 = 2;
    Console.WriteLine("n1={0}, n2={1}", n1, n2);
    Swap<Int32>(ref n1, ref n2);
    Console.WriteLine("n1={0}, n2={1}", n1, n2);

    String s1 = "Aidan", s2 = "Kristin";
    Console.WriteLine("s1={0}, s2={1}", s1, s2);
    Swap<String>(ref s1, ref s2);
    Console.WriteLine("s1={0}, s2={1}", s1, s2);
}
```

Using generic types with methods that take **out** and **ref** parameters can be particularly interesting because the variable you pass as an **out**/**ref** argument must be the same type as the method's parameter to avoid a potential type safety exploit. This issue related to **out**/**ref** parameters is discussed toward the end of Chapter 8's "Passing Parameters by Reference to a Method" section. In fact, the `Interlocked` class's `Exchange` and `CompareExchange` methods offer generic overloads for precisely this reason:

```
public static class Interlocked {
    public static T Exchange<T>(ref T location1, T value) where T: class;
    public static T CompareExchange<T>(
        ref T location1, T value, T comparand) where T: class;
}
```

Generic Methods and Type Inference

For many developers, the C# generic syntax can be confusing with all of its less-than and greater-than signs. To help improve code creation, readability, and maintainability, the C# compiler offers *type inference* when calling a generic method. Type inference means that the compiler attempts to determine (or infer) the type to use automatically when calling a generic method. Here is some code that demonstrates type inference:

```
private static void CallingSwapUsingInference() {
    Int32 n1 = 1, n2 = 2;
    Swap(ref n1, ref n2);// Calls Swap<Int32>

    String s1 = "Aidan";
    Object s2 = "Kristin";
    Swap(ref s1, ref s2);// Error, type can't be inferred
}
```

In this code, notice that the calls to **Swap** do not specify type arguments in less-than/greater-than signs. In the first call to **Swap**, the C# compiler was able to infer that **n1** and **n2** are **Int32**s, and therefore, it should call **Swap** by using an **Int32** type argument.

When performing type inference, C# uses the variable's data type, not the actual type of the object referred to by the variable. So in the second call to **Swap**, C# sees that **s1** is a **String** and **s2** is an **Object** (even though it happens to refer to a **String**). Since **s1** and **s2** are variables of different data types, the compiler can't accurately infer the type to use for **Swap**'s type argument, and it issues the following: "error CS0411: The type arguments for method 'Program.Swap<T>(ref T, ref T)' cannot be inferred from the usage. Try specifying the type arguments explicitly."

A type can define multiple methods with one of its methods taking a specific data type and another taking a generic type parameter, as in the following example:

```
private static void Display(String s) {
   Console.WriteLine(s);
}

private static void Display<T>(T o) {
   Display(o.ToString());  // Calls Display(String)
}
```

Here are some ways to call the **Display** method:

```
Display("Jeff");          // Calls Display(String)
Display(123);             // Calls Display<T>(T)
Display<String>("Aidan"); // Calls Display<T>(T)
```

In the first call, the compiler could actually call either the **Display** method that takes a **String** or the generic **Display** method (replacing **T** with **String**). However, the C# compiler always prefers a more explicit match over a generic match, and therefore, it generates a call to the non-generic **Display** method that takes a **String**. For the second call, the compiler can't call the non-generic **Display** method that takes a **String**, so it must call the generic **Display** method. By the way, it is fortunate that the compiler always prefers the more explicit match; if the compiler had preferred the generic method, because the generic **Display** method calls **ToString**, which returns a **String**, there would have been infinite recursion.

The third call to **Display** specifies a generic type argument, **String**. This tells the compiler not to try to infer type arguments but instead to use the type arguments I specified. In this case, the compiler also assumes that I must really want to call the generic **Display** method, so the generic **Display** will be called. Internally, the generic **Display** method will call **ToString** on the passed-in string, which results in a string that is then passed to the non-generic **Display** method.

Generics and Other Members

In C#, properties, indexers, events, operator methods, constructors, and finalizers cannot themselves have type parameters. However, they can be defined within a generic type, and the code in these members can use the type's type parameters.

C# doesn't allow these members to specify their own generic type parameters because Microsoft's C# team believes that developers would rarely have a need to use these members as generic. Furthermore, the cost of adding generic support to these members would be quite high in terms of designing adequate syntax into the language. For example, when you use a **+** operator in code, the compiler could call an operator overload method. There is no way to indicate any type arguments in your code along with the **+** operator.

Verifiability and Constraints

When compiling generic code, the C# compiler analyzes it and ensures that the code will work for any type that exists today or that may be defined in the future. Let's look at the following method:

```
private static Boolean MethodTakingAnyType<T>(T o) {
    T temp = o;
    Console.WriteLine(o.ToString());
    Boolean b = temp.Equals(o);
    return b;
}
```

This method declares a temporary variable (**temp**) of type **T**, and then the method performs a couple of variable assignments and a few method calls. This method works for any type. If **T** is a reference type, it works. If **T** is a value or enumeration type, it works. If **T** is an interface or delegate type, it works. This method works for all types that exist today or that will be defined tomorrow because every type supports assignment and calls to methods defined by **Object** (such as **ToString** and **Equals**).

Now look at the following method:

```
private static T Min<T>(T o1, T o2) {
    if (o1.CompareTo(o2) < 0) return o1;
    return o2;
}
```

The **Min** method attempts to call use the **o1** variable to call the **CompareTo** method. But there are lots of types that do not offer a **CompareTo** method, and therefore, the C# compiler can't compile this code and guarantee that this method would work for all types. If you attempt to compile the above code, the compiler issues the following: "error CS0117: 'T' does not contain a definition for 'CompareTo'".

So it would seem that when using generics, you can declare variables of a generic type, perform some variable assignments, call methods defined by **Object**, and that's about it! This makes generics practically useless. Fortunately, compilers and the CLR support a mechanism called *constraints* that you can take advantage of to make generics useful again.

A constraint is a way to limit the number of types that can be specified for a generic argument. Limiting the number of types allows you to do more with those types. Here is a new version of the **Min** method that specifies a constraint (in bold):

```
public static T Min<T>(T o1, T o2) where T : IComparable<T> {
   if (o1.CompareTo(o2) < 0) return o1;
   return o2;
}
```

The C# **where** token tells the compiler that any type specified for **T** must implement the generic **IComparable** interface of the same type (**T**). Because of this constraint, the compiler now allows the method to call the **CompareTo** method since this method is defined by the **IComparable<T>** interface.

Now, when code references a generic type or method, the compiler is responsible for ensuring that a type argument that meets the constraints is specified. For example, the following code causes the compiler to issue the following: "error CS0309: The type 'object' must be convertible to 'System.IComparable<object>' in order to use it as parameter 'T' in the generic type or method 'Program.Min<T>(T, T)'".

```
private static void CallMin() {
   Object o1 = "Jeff", o2 = "Richter";
   Object oMin = Min<Object>(o1, o2);   // Error CS0309
}
```

The compiler issues the error because **System.Object** doesn't implement the **IComparable<Object>** interface. In fact, **System.Object** doesn't implement any interfaces at all.

Now that you have a sense of what constraints are and how they work, we'll start to look a little deeper into them. Constraints can be applied to a generic type's type parameters as well as to a generic method's type parameters (as shown in the **Min** method). The CLR doesn't allow overloading based on type parameter names or constraints; you can overload types or methods based only on arity. The following examples show what I mean:

```
// It is OK to define the following types:
internal sealed class AType {}
internal sealed class AType<T> {}
internal sealed class AType<T1, T2> {}

// Error: conflicts with AType<T> that has no constraints
internal sealed class AType<T> where T : IComparable<T> {}
```

```
// Error: conflicts with AType<T1, T2>
internal sealed class AType<T3, T4> {}

internal sealed class AnotherType {
    // It is OK to define the following methods:
    private static void M() {}
    private static void M<T>() {}
    private static void M<T1, T2>() {}

    // Error: conflicts with M<T> that has no constraints
    private static void M<T>() where T : IComparable<T> {}

    // Error: conflicts with M<T1, T2>
    private static void M<T3, T4>() {}
}
```

When overriding a virtual generic method, the overriding method must specify the same number of type parameters, and these type parameters will inherit the constraints specified on them by the base class's method. In fact, the overriding method is not allowed to specify any constraints on its type parameters at all. However, it can change the names of the type parameter. Similarly, when implementing an interface method, the method must specify the same number of type parameters as the interface method, and these type parameters will inherit the constraints specified on them by the interface's method. Here is an example that demonstrates this rule by using virtual methods:

```
internal class Base {
    public virtual void M<T1, T2>()
        where T1 : struct
        where T2 : class {
    }
}

internal sealed class Derived : Base {
    public override void M<T3, T4>()
        where T3 : EventArgs  // Error
        where T4 : class      // Error
        { }
}
```

Attempting to compile the code above causes the compiler to issue the following: "error CS0460: Constraints for override and explicit interface implementation methods are inherited from the base method so cannot be specified directly". If we remove the two **where** lines from the **Derived** class' **M<T3, T4>** method, the code will compile just fine. Notice that you can change the names of the type parameters (as in the example: from **T1** to **T3** and **T2** to **T4**); however, you cannot change (or even specify) constraints.

Now let's talk about the different kinds of constraints the compiler/CLR allows you to apply to a type parameter. A type parameter can be constrained using a *primary constraint*, a *secondary constraint*, and/or a *constructor constraint*. I'll talk about these three kinds of constraints in the next three sections.

Primary Constraints

A type parameter can specify zero or one primary constraints. A primary constraint can be a reference type that identifies a class that is not sealed. You cannot specify one of the following special reference types: `System.Object`, `System.Array`, `System.Delegate`, `System.Multicast-Delegate`, `System.ValueType`, `System.Enum`, or `System.Void`.

When specifying a reference type constraint, you are promising the compiler that a specified type argument will either be of the same type or of a type derived from the constraint type. For example, see the following generic class:

```
internal sealed class PrimaryConstraintOfStream<T> where T : Stream {
   public void M(T stream) {
      stream.Close();// OK
   }
}
```

In this class definition, the type parameter `T` has a primary constraint of `Stream` (defined in the `System.IO` namespace). This tells the compiler that code using `PrimaryConstraintOfStream` must specify a type argument of `Stream` or a type derived from `Stream` (such as `FileStream`). If a type parameter doesn't specify a primary constraint, `System.Object` is assumed. However, the C# compiler issues an error ("error CS0702: Constraint cannot be special class 'object'") if you explicitly specify `System.Object` in your source code.

There are two special primary constraints: `class` and `struct`. The `class` constraint promises the compiler that a specified type argument will be a reference type. Any class type, interface type, delegate type, or array type satisfies this constraint. For example, see the following generic class:

```
internal sealed class PrimaryConstraintOfClass<T> where T : class {
   public void M() {
      T temp = null;// Allowed because T must be a reference type
   }
}
```

In this example, setting `temp` to `null` is legal because `T` is known to be a reference type, and all reference type variables can be set to `null`. If `T` were unconstrained, the code above would not compile because `T` could be a value type, and value type variables cannot be set to `null`.

The `struct` constraint promises the compiler that a specified type argument will be a value type. Any value type, including enumerations, satisfies this constraint. However, the compiler and the CLR treat any `System.Nullable<T>` value type as a special type, and nullable types do not satisfy this constraint. The reason is because the `Nullable<T>` type constrains its type parameter to `struct`, and the CLR wants to prohibit a recursive type such as `Nullable<Nullable<T>>`. Nullable types are discussed in Chapter 18, "Nullable Value Types."

Here is an example class that constrains its type parameter by using the **struct** constraint:

```
internal sealed class PrimaryConstraintOfStruct<T> where T : struct {
    public static T Factory() {
        // Allowed because all value types implicitly
        // have a public, parameterless constructor
        return new T();
    }
}
```

In this example, **new**ing up a **T** is legal because **T** is known to be a value type, and all value types implicitly have a public, parameterless constructor. If **T** were unconstrained, constrained to a reference type, or constrained to **class**, the above code would not compile because some reference types do not have public, parameterless constructors.

Secondary Constraints

A type parameter can specify zero or more secondary constraints where a secondary constraint represents an interface type. When specifying an interface type constraint, you are promising the compiler that a specified type argument will be a type that implements the interface. And since you can specify multiple interface constraints, the type argument must specify a type that implements all of the interface constraints (and all of the primary constraints too, if specified). Chapter 15 discusses interface constraints in detail.

There is another kind of secondary constraint called a *type parameter constraint* (sometimes referred to as a *naked type constraint*). This kind of constraint is used much less often than an interface constraint. It allows a generic type or method to indicate that there must be a relationship between specified type arguments. A type parameter can have zero or more type constraints applied to it. Here is a generic method that demonstrates the use of a type parameter constraint:

```
private static List<TBase> ConvertIList<T, TBase>(IList<T> list)
    where T : TBase {
    List<TBase> baseList = new List<TBase>(list.Count);
    for (Int32 index = 0; index < list.Count; index++) {
        baseList.Add(list[index]);
    }
    return baseList;
}
```

The **ConvertIList** method specifies two type parameters in which the **T** parameter is constrained by the **TBase** type parameter. This means that whatever type argument is specified for **T**, the type argument must be compatible with whatever type argument is specified for **TBase**. Here is a method showing some legal and illegal calls to **ConvertIList**:

```
private static void CallingConvertIList() {
    // Construct and initialize a List<String> (which implements IList<String>)
    IList<String> ls = new List<String>();
    ls.Add("A String");
```

```
// Convert the IList<String> to an IList<Object>
IList<Object> lo = ConvertIList<String, Object>(ls);

// Convert the IList<String> to an IList<IComparable>
IList<IComparable> lc = ConvertIList<String, IComparable>(ls);

// Convert the IList<String> to an IList<IComparable<String>>
IList<IComparable<String>> lcs =
    ConvertIList<String, IComparable<String>>(ls);

// Convert the IList<String> to an IList<String>
IList<String> ls2 = ConvertIList<String, String>(ls);

// Convert the IList<String> to an IList<Exception>
IList<Exception> le = ConvertIList<String, Exception>(ls);// Error
}
```

In the first call to `ConvertIList`, the compiler ensures that `String` is compatible with `Object`. Since `String` is derived from `Object`, the first call adheres to the type parameter constraint. In the second call to `ConvertIList`, the compiler ensures that `String` is compatible with `IComparable`. Since `String` implements the `IComparable` interface, the second call adheres to the type parameter constraint. In the third call to `ConvertIList`, the compiler ensures that `String` is compatible with `IComparable<String>`. Since `String` implements the `IComparable<String>` interface, the third call adheres to the type parameter constraint. In the fourth call to `ConvertIList`, the compiler knows that `String` is compatible with itself. In the fifth call to `ConvertIList`, the compiler ensures that `String` is compatible with `Exception`. Since `String` is not compatible with `Exception`, the fifth call doesn't adhere to the type parameter constraint, and the compiler issues the following: "error CS0309: The type 'string' must be convertible to 'System.Exception' in order to use it as parameter 'T' in the generic type or method SomeType.ConvertIList<T,TBase>(System.Collections.Generic.IList<T>)'".

Constructor Constraints

A type parameter can specify zero or one constructor constraints. When specifying a constructor constraint, you are promising the compiler that a specified type argument will be a non-abstract type that implements a public, parameterless constructor. Note that the C# compiler considers it an error to specify a constructor constraint with the `struct` constraint because it is redundant; all value types implicitly offer a public, parameterless constructor. Here is an example class that constrains its type parameter by using the constructor constraint:

```
internal sealed class ConstructorConstraint<T> where T : new() {
    public static T Factory() {
        // Allowed because all value types implicitly
        // have a public, parameterless constructor and because
        // the constraint requires that any specified reference
```

```
        // type also have a public, parameterless constructor
        return new T();
    }
}
```

In this example, **new**ing up a **T** is legal because **T** is known to be a type that has a public, parameterless constructor. This is certainly true of all value types, and the constructor constraint
requires that it be true of any reference type specified as a type argument.

Sometimes, developers would like to declare a type parameter by using a constructor constraint
whereby the constructor takes various parameters itself. As of today, the CLR (and therefore
the C# compiler) supports only parameterless constructors. Microsoft feels that this will
be good enough for almost all scenarios, and I agree.

Other Verifiability Issues

In the remainder of this section, I'd like to point out a few other code constructs that have
unexpected behavior when used with generics due to verifiability issues and how constraints
can be used to make the code verifiable again.

Casting a Generic Type Variable

Casting a generic type variable to another type is illegal unless you are casting to a type compatible with a constraint:

```
private static void CastingAGenericTypeVariable1<T>(T obj) {
    Int32  x = (Int32) obj ;  // Error
    String s = (String) obj;  // Error
}
```

The compiler issues an error on both lines above because **T** could be any type, and there is no
guarantee that the casts will succeed. You can modify this code to get it to compile by casting
to **Object** first:

```
private static void CastingAGenericTypeVariable2<T>(T obj) {
    Int32  x = (Int32) (Object) obj ;  // No error
    String s = (String) (Object) obj;  // No error
}
```

While this code will now compile, it is still possible for the CLR to throw an **InvalidCast-**
Exception at run time.

If you are trying to cast to a reference type, you can also use the C# **as** operator. Here is code
modified to use the **as** operator with **String** (since **Int32** is a value type):

```
private static void CastingAGenericTypeVariable3<T>(T obj) {
    String s = obj as String;  // No error
}
```

Setting a Generic Type Variable to a Default Value

Setting a generic type variable to **null** is illegal unless the generic type is constrained to a reference type.

```
private static void SettingAGenericTypeVariableToNull<T>() {
   T temp = null;    // CS0403 - Cannot convert null to type parameter 'T'
                     // because it could be a value type...
}
```

Since **T** is unconstrained, it could be a value type, and setting a variable of a value type to **null** is not possible. If **T** were constrained to a reference type, setting **temp** to **null** would compile and run just fine.

Microsoft's C# team felt that it would be useful to give developers the ability to set a variable to a default value. So the C# compiler allows you to use the **default** keyword to accomplish this:

```
private static void SettingAGenericTypeVariableToDefaultValue<T>() {
   T temp = default(T);  // OK
}
```

The use of a the **default** keyword above tells the C# compiler and the CLR's JIT compiler to produce code to set **temp** to **null** if **T** is a reference type and to set **temp** to all-bits-zero if **T** is a value type.

Comparing a Generic Type Variable with null

Comparing a generic type variable to **null** by using the **==** or **!=** operators is legal regardless of whether the generic type is constrained:

```
private static void ComparingAGenericTypeVariableWithNull<T>(T obj) {
   if (obj == null) { /* Never executes for a value type */ }
}
```

Since **T** is unconstrained, it could be a reference type or a value type. If **T** is a value type, **obj** can never be **null**. Normally, you'd expect the C# compiler to issue an error because of this. However, the C# compiler does not issue an error; instead, it compiles the code just fine. When this method is called using a type argument that is a value type, the JIT compiler sees that the **if** statement can never be true, and the JIT compiler will not emit the native code for the **if** test or the code in the braces. If I had used the **!=** operator, the JIT compiler would not emit the code for the **if** test (since it is always true), and it will emit the code inside the **if**'s braces.

By the way, if **T** had been constrained to a **struct**, the C# compiler would issue an error because you shouldn't be writing code that compares a value type variable with **null** since the result is always the same.

Comparing Two Generic Type Variables with Each Other

Comparing two variables of the same generic type is illegal if the generic type parameter is not known to be a reference type:

```
private static void ComparingTwoGenericTypeVariables<T>(T o1, T o2) {
   if (o1 == o2) { }  // Error
}
```

In this example, **T** is unconstrained, and whereas it is legal to compare two reference type variables with one another, it is not legal to compare two value type variables with one another unless the value type overloads the **==** operator. If **T** were constrained to **class**, this code would compile, and the **==** operator would return **true** if the variables referred to the same object, checking for exact identity. Note that if **T** were constrained to a reference type that overloaded the **operator==** method, the compiler would emit calls to this method when it sees the **==** operator. Obviously, this whole discussion applies to uses of the **!=** operator too.

When you write code to compare the primitive value types—**Byte**, **Int32**, **Single**, **Decimal**, etc.—the C# compiler knows how to emit the right code. However, for non-primitive value types, the C# compiler doesn't know how to emit the code to do comparisons. So if **ComparingTwoGenericTypeVariables** method's **T** were constrained to **struct**, the compiler would issue an error. And you're not allowed to constrain a type parameter to a value type because they are implicitly sealed. Theoretically you could get the method to compile if you specified a specific value type as the constraint, but if you did this, the method would no longer be generic; it would be tied to a specific data type, and of course, the compiler won't compile a generic method that is constrained to a single type.

Using Generic Type Variables as Operands

Finally, it should be noted that there are a lot of issues about using operators with generic type operands. In Chapter 5, I talked about C# and how it handles its primitive types: **Byte**, **Int16**, **Int32**, **Int64**, **Decimal**, and so on. In particular, I mentioned that C# knows how to interpret operators (such as +, -, *, and /) when applied to the primitive types. Well, these operators can't be applied to variables of a generic type because the compiler doesn't know the type at compile time. This means that you can't use any of these operators with variables of a generic type. So it is impossible to write a mathematical algorithm that works on an arbitrary numeric data type. Here is an example of a generic method that I'd like to write:

```
private static T Sum<T>(T num) where T : struct {
   T sum = default(T) ;
   for (T n = default(T) ; n < num ; n++)
      sum += n;
   return sum;
}
```

I've done everything possible to try to get this method to compile. I've constrained T to **struct**, and I'm using **default(T)** to initialize **sum** and **n** to **0**. But when I compile this code, I get the following three errors:

- error CS0019: Operator '<' cannot be applied to operands of type 'T' and 'T'
- error CS0023: Operator '++' cannot be applied to operand of type 'T'
- error CS0019: Operator '+=' cannot be applied to operands of type 'T' and 'T'

This is a severe limitation on the CLR's generic support, and many developers (especially in the scientific and mathematical world) are very disappointed by this limitation. Many people have tried to come up with techniques to work around this limitation by using reflection (Chapter 22, "Assembly Loading and Reflection"), operator overloading, and so on. But all of these cause a severe performance penalty or hurt readability of the code substantially. Hopefully, this is an area that Microsoft will address in a future version of the CLR and the compilers.

Chapter 17
Custom Attributes

In this chapter, I'll discuss one of the most innovative features the Microsoft .NET Framework has to offer: *custom attributes*. Custom attributes allow for a relatively new kind of programming known as *declarative programming*. Declarative programming is when you use data rather than write source code to instruct your application or component to do something. (The act of writing source code is sometimes called *imperative programming*.)

An example of declarative programming is when a person creates a text file and explicitly enters HTML tags into the file by using an editor such as Notepad.exe. In this scenario, the HTML tags act as instructions that are eventually processed by the Internet browser so that it can lay out the page in a window. The HTML tags are declaring how the program (Web page) should be displayed and operate, and it's the programmer who decides what tags to use and where. Many hard-core programmers don't consider HTML programming to be real programming, but I do.

Custom attributes is a technology that allows declarative programming to be used in conjunction with imperative programming (C# source code). Combining these two kinds of programming offers incredible flexibility to the programmer and provides for a very succinct way of expressing your coding intentions. I think that declarative programming is going to become much more mainstream as time goes on. We can already see examples of this in technologies such as Microsoft ASP.NET and Microsoft Windows Communication Foundation. Even the Windows Presentation Foundation technology allows programmers to develop a user interface by declaring its layout and behavior using the XAML markup language.

Custom attributes allow information to be defined and applied to almost any metadata table entry. This extensible metadata information can be queried at run time to dynamically alter the way code executes. As you use the various .NET Framework technologies (Windows Forms, Web Forms, XML Web services, and so on), you'll see that they all take advantage of custom attributes, allowing developers to express their intentions within code (but without coding) very easily. A solid understanding of custom attributes is necessary for any .NET Framework developer.

Using Custom Attributes

Attributes, such as **public**, **private**, **static**, and so on, can be applied to types and members. I think we'd all agree on the usefulness of applying attributes, but wouldn't it be even more useful if we could define our own attributes? For example, what if I could define a type and somehow indicate that the type can be remoted via serialization? Or maybe I could apply an attribute to a method to indicate that certain security permissions must be granted before the method can execute.

Of course, creating and applying user-defined attributes to types and methods would be great and convenient, but it would require the compiler to be aware of these attributes so it would emit the attribute information into the resulting metadata. Because compiler vendors usually prefer not to release the source code for their compiler, Microsoft came up with another way to allow user-defined attributes. This mechanism, called *custom attributes*, is an incredibly powerful mechanism that's useful at both application design time and run time. Anyone can define and use custom attributes, and all compilers that target the common language runtime (CLR) must be designed to recognize custom attributes and emit them into the resulting metadata.

The first thing you should realize about custom attributes is that they're just a way to associate additional information with a target. The compiler emits this additional information into the managed module's metadata. Most attributes have no meaning for the compiler; the compiler simply detects the attributes in the source code and emits the corresponding metadata.

The .NET Framework Class Library (FCL) defines literally hundreds of custom attributes that can be applied to items in your own source code. Here are some examples:

- Applying the **DllImport** attribute to a method informs the CLR that the implementation of the method is actually in unmanaged code contained in the specified DLL.

- Applying the **Serializable** attribute to a type informs the serialization formatters that an instance's fields may be serialized and deserialized.

- Applying the **AssemblyVersion** attribute to an assembly sets the version number of the assembly.

- Applying the **Flags** attribute to an enumerated type causes the enumerated type to act as a set of bit flags.

Following is some C# code with many attributes applied to it. In C#, you apply a custom attribute to a target by placing the attribute in square brackets immediately before the target. It's not important to understand what this code does. I just want you to see what attributes look like.

```
using System;
using System.Runtime.InteropServices;

[StructLayout(LayoutKind.Sequential, CharSet = CharSet.Auto)]
internal sealed class OSVERSIONINFO {
    public OSVERSIONINFO() {
        OSVersionInfoSize = (UInt32) Marshal.SizeOf(this);
    }

    public UInt32 OSVersionInfoSize = 0;
    public UInt32 MajorVersion     = 0;
    public UInt32 MinorVersion     = 0;
    public UInt32 BuildNumber      = 0;
    public UInt32 PlatformId       = 0;

    [MarshalAs(UnmanagedType.ByValTStr, SizeConst = 128)]
    public String CSDVersion        = null;
}

internal sealed class MyClass {
    [DllImport("Kernel32", CharSet = CharSet.Auto, SetLastError = true)]
    public static extern Boolean GetVersionEx(
        [In, Out] OSVERSIONINFO ver);
}
```

In this case, the **StructLayout** attribute is applied to the **OSVERSIONINFO** class, the **MarshalAs** attribute is applied to the **CSDVersion** field, the **DllImport** attribute is applied to the **GetVersionEx** method, and the **In** and **Out** attributes are applied to **GetVersionEx**'s **ver** parameter. Every programming language defines the syntax a developer must use in order to apply a custom attribute to a target. Microsoft Visual Basic .NET, for example, requires angle brackets (<, >) instead of square brackets.

The CLR allows attributes to be applied to just about anything that can be represented in a file's metadata. Most commonly, attributes are applied to entries in the following definition tables: TypeDef (classes, structures, enumerations, interfaces, and delegates), MethodDef (including constructors), ParamDef, FieldDef, PropertyDef, EventDef, AssemblyDef, and ModuleDef. Specifically, C# allows you to apply an attribute only to source code that defines any of the following targets: assembly, module, type (class, struct, enum, interface, delegate), field, method (including constructors), method parameter, method return value, property, event, and generic type parameter.

When you're applying an attribute, C# allows you to specify a prefix specifically indicating the target the attribute applies to. The following code shows all of the possible prefixes. In many cases, if you leave out the prefix, the compiler can still determine the target an attribute applies to, as shown in the previous example. In some cases, the prefix must be specified to make your intentions clear to the compiler. The prefixes shown in italics below are mandatory.

```
using System;

[assembly: SomeAttr]            // Applied to assembly
[module:   SomeAttr]            // Applied to module

[type:     SomeAttr]            // Applied to type
internal sealed class SomeType
   <[typevar: SomeAttr] T> {    // Applied to generic type variable

   [field: SomeAttr]            // Applied to field
   public Int32 SomeField = 0;

   [return: SomeAttr]           // Applied to return value
   [method: SomeAttr]           // Applied to method
   public Int32 SomeMethod(
      [param: SomeAttr]         // Applied to parameter
      Int32 SomeParam) { return SomeParam; }

   [property: SomeAttr]         // Applied to property
   public String SomeProp {
      [method: SomeAttr]        // Applied to get accessor method
      get { return null; }
   }

   [event:  SomeAttr]           // Applied to event
   [field:  SomeAttr]           // Applied to compiler-generated field
   [method: SomeAttr]           // Applied to compiler-generated add & remove methods
   public event EventHandler SomeEvent;
}
```

Now that you know how to apply a custom attribute, let's find out what an attribute really is. A custom attribute is simply an instance of a type. For Common Language Specification (CLS) compliance, custom attribute classes must be derived, directly or indirectly, from the public abstract **System.Attribute** class. C# allows only CLS-compliant attributes. By examining the .NET Framework SDK documentation, you'll see that the following classes (from the earlier example) are defined: **StructLayoutAttribute**, **MarshalAsAttribute**, **DllImportAttribute**, **InAttribute**, and **OutAttribute**. All of these classes happen to be defined in the **System .Runtime.InteropServices** namespace, but attribute classes can be defined in any namespace. Upon further examination, you'll notice that all of these classes are derived from **System .Attribute**, as all CLS-compliant attribute classes must be.

> **Note** When applying an attribute to a target in source code, the C# compiler allows you to omit the **Attribute** suffix to reduce programming typing and to improve the readability of the source code. My code examples in this chapter take advantage of this C# convenience. For example, my source code contains [**DllImport(...)**] instead of [**DllImportAttribute(...)**].

As I mentioned earlier, an attribute is an instance of a class. The class must have a public constructor so that instances of it can be created. So when you apply an attribute to a target, the syntax is similar to that for calling one of the class's instance constructors. In addition, a language might permit some special syntax to allow you to set any public fields or properties associated with the attribute class. Let's look at an example. Recall the application of the **DllImport** attribute as it was applied to the **GetVersionEx** method earlier:

```
[DllImport("Kernel32", CharSet = CharSet.Auto, SetLastError = true)]
```

The syntax of this line should look pretty strange to you because you could never use syntax like this when calling a constructor. If you examine the **DllImportAttribute** class in the documentation, you'll see that its constructor requires a single **String** parameter. In this example, **"Kernel32"** is being passed for this parameter. A constructor's parameters are called *positional parameters* and are mandatory; the parameter must be specified when the attribute is applied.

What are the other two "parameters"? This special syntax allows you to set any public fields or properties of the **DllImportAttribute** object after the object is constructed. In this example, when the **DllImportAttribute** object is constructed and **"Kernel32"** is passed to the constructor, the object's public instance fields, **CharSet** and **SetLastError**, are set to **CharSet .Auto** and **true**, respectively. The "parameters" that set fields or properties are called *named parameters* and are optional because the parameters don't have to be specified when you're applying an instance of the attribute. A little later on, I'll explain what causes an instance of the **DllImportAttribute** class to actually be constructed.

Also note that it's possible to apply multiple attributes to a single target. For example, in this chapter's first program listing, the **GetVersionEx** method's **ver** parameter has both the **In** and **Out** attributes applied to it. When applying multiple attributes to a single target, be aware that the order of attributes has no significance. Also, in C#, each attribute can be enclosed in square brackets, or multiple attributes can be comma-separated within a single set of square brackets. If the attribute class's constructor takes no parameters, the parentheses are optional. Finally, as mentioned earlier, the **Attribute** suffix is also optional. The following lines behave identically and demonstrate all of the possible ways of applying multiple attributes:

```
[Serializable][Flags]
[Serializable, Flags]
[FlagsAttribute, SerializableAttribute]
[FlagsAttribute()][Serializable()]
```

Defining Your Own Attribute Class

You know that an attribute is an instance of a class derived from **System.Attribute**, and you also know how to apply an attribute. Let's now look at how to define your own custom attribute classes. Say you're the Microsoft employee responsible for adding the bit flag support

to enumerated types. To accomplish this, the first thing you have to do is define a
FlagsAttribute class:

```
namespace System {
    public class FlagsAttribute : System.Attribute {
        public FlagsAttribute() {
        }
    }
}
```

Notice that the **FlagsAttribute** class inherits from **Attribute**; this is what makes the
FlagsAttribute class a CLS-compliant custom attribute. In addition, the class's name
has a suffix of **Attribute**; this follows the standard convention but is not mandatory.
Finally, all nonabstract attributes must contain at least one public constructor. The simple
FlagsAttribute constructor takes no parameters and does absolutely nothing.

> **Important**   You should think of an attribute as a logical state container. That is, while an
> attribute type is a class, the class should be simple. The class should offer just one public
> constructor that accepts the attribute's mandatory (or positional) state information, and the
> class can offer public fields/properties that accept the attribute's optional (or named) state
> information. The class should not offer any public methods, events, or other members.
>
> In general, I always discourage the use of public fields, and I still discourage them for attributes.
> It is much better to use properties because this allows more flexibility if you ever decide to
> change how the attribute class is implemented.

So far, instances of the **FlagsAttribute** class can be applied to any target, but this attribute
should really be applied to enumerated types only. It doesn't make sense to apply the attribute
to a property or a method. To tell the compiler where this attribute can legally be applied, you
apply an instance of the **System.AttributeUsageAttribute** class to the attribute class. Here's
the new code:

```
namespace System {
    [AttributeUsage(AttributeTargets.Enum, Inherited = false)]
    public class FlagsAttribute : System.Attribute {
        public FlagsAttribute() {
        }
    }
}
```

In this new version, I've applied an instance of **AttributeUsageAttribute** to the attribute.
After all, the attribute type is just a class, and a class can have attributes applied to it. The
AttributeUsage attribute is a simple class that allows you to specify to a compiler where your
custom attribute can legally be applied. All compilers have built-in support for this attribute
and generate errors when a user-defined custom attribute is applied to an invalid target. In
this example, the **AttributeUsage** attribute specifies that instances of the **Flags** attribute can
be applied only to enumerated type targets.

Because all attributes are just types, you can easily understand the **AttributeUsageAttribute** class. Here's what the FCL source code for the class looks like:

```
[Serializable]
[AttributeUsage(AttributeTargets.Class, Inherited=true)]
public sealed class AttributeUsageAttribute : Attribute {
    internal static AttributeUsageAttribute Default =
        new AttributeUsageAttribute(AttributeTargets.All);

    internal Boolean m_allowMultiple = false;
    internal AttributeTargets m_attributeTarget = AttributeTargets.All;
    internal Boolean m_inherited = true;

    // This is the one public constructor
    public AttributeUsageAttribute(AttributeTargets validOn) {
        m_attributeTarget = validOn;
    }

    internal AttributeUsageAttribute(AttributeTargets validOn,
        Boolean allowMultiple, Boolean inherited) {
        m_attributeTarget = validOn;
        m_allowMultiple = allowMultiple;
        m_inherited = inherited;
    }

    public Boolean AllowMultiple {
        get { return m_allowMultiple; }
        set { m_allowMultiple = value; }
    }

    public Boolean Inherited {
        get { return m_inherited; }
        set { m_inherited = value; }
    }

    public AttributeTargets ValidOn {
        get { return m_attributeTarget; }
    }
}
```

As you can see, the **AttributeUsageAttribute** class has a public constructor that allows you to pass bit flags that indicate where your attribute can legally be applied. The **System .AttributeTargets** enumerated type is defined in the FCL as follows:

```
[Flags, Serializable]
public enum AttributeTargets {
    Assembly        = 0x0001,
    Module          = 0x0002,
    Class           = 0x0004,
    Struct          = 0x0008,
    Enum            = 0x0010,
    Constructor     = 0x0020,
    Method          = 0x0040,
    Property        = 0x0080,
```

```
    Field         = 0x0100,
    Event         = 0x0200,
    Interface     = 0x0400,
    Parameter     = 0x0800,
    Delegate      = 0x1000,
    ReturnValue   = 0x2000,
    GenericParameter = 0x4000,
    All           = Assembly   | Module   | Class    | Struct | Enum  |
                    Constructor | Method   | Property | Field  | Event |
                    Interface  | Parameter | Delegate | ReturnValue |
                    GenericParameter
}
```

The **AttributeUsageAttribute** class offers two additional public properties that can option-ally be set when the attribute is applied to an attribute class: **AllowMultiple** and **Inherited**.

For most attributes, it makes no sense to apply them to a single target more than once. For example, nothing is gained by applying the **Flags** or **Serializable** attributes more than once to a single target. In fact, if you tried to compile the code below, the compiler would report the following: "error CS0579: Duplicate 'Flags' attribute".

```
[Flags][Flags]
internal enum Color {
    Red
}
```

For a few attributes, however, it does make sense to apply the attribute multiple times to a single target. In the FCL, the **ConditionalAttribute** attribute class and lots of permission attribute classes (such as **EnvironmentPermissionAttribute**, **FileIOPermissionAttribute**, **ReflectionPermissionAttribute**, **RegistryPermissionAttribute**, and so on) allow multiple instances of themselves to be applied to a single target. If you don't explicitly set **AllowMultiple** to **true**, your attribute can be applied no more than once to a selected target.

AttributeUsageAttribute's other property, **Inherited**, indicates if the attribute should be applied to derived classes and overriding methods when applied on the base class. The fol-lowing code demonstrates what it means for an attribute to be inherited:

```
[AttributeUsage(AttributeTargets.Class | AttributeTargets.Method,
    Inherited=true)]
internal class TastyAttribute : Attribute {
}

[Tasty][Serializable]
internal class BaseType {

    [Tasty] protected virtual void DoSomething() { }
}

internal class DerivedType : BaseType {
    protected override void DoSomething() { }
}
```

In this code, **DerivedType** and its **DoSomething** method are both considered **Tasty** because the **TastyAttribute** class is marked as inherited. However, **DerivedType** is not serializable because the FCL's **SerializableAttribute** class is marked as a noninherited attribute.

Be aware that the .NET Framework considers targets only of classes, methods, properties, events, fields, method return values, and parameters to be inheritable. So when you're defining an attribute type, you should set **Inherited** to **true** only if your targets include any of these targets. Note that inherited attributes do not cause additional metadata to be emitted for the derived types into the managed module. I'll say more about this a little later in the "Detecting the Use of a Custom Attribute" section.

> **Note**   If you define your own attribute class and forget to apply an **AttributeUsage** attribute to your class, the compiler and the CLR will assume that your attribute can be applied to all targets, can be applied only once to a single target, and is inherited. These assumptions mimic the default field values in the **AttributeUsageAttribute** class.

Attribute Constructor and Field/Property Data Types

When defining your own custom attribute class, you can define its constructor to take parameters that must be specified by developers when they apply an instance of your attribute type. In addition, you can define nonstatic public fields and properties in your type that identify settings that a developer can optionally choose for an instance of your attribute class.

When defining an attribute class's instance constructor, fields, and properties, you must restrict yourself to a small subset of data types. Specifically, the legal set of data types is limited to the following: **Boolean**, **Char**, **Byte**, **SByte**, **Int16**, **UInt16**, **Int32**, **UInt32**, **Int64**, **UInt64**, **Single**, **Double**, **String**, **Type**, **Object**, or an enumerated type. In addition, you can use a single-dimensional, zero-based array of any of these types. However, you should avoid using arrays because a custom attribute class whose constructor takes an array is not CLS-compliant.

When applying an attribute, you must pass a compile-time constant expression that matches the type defined by the attribute class. Wherever the attribute class defines a **Type** parameter, **Type** field, or **Type** property, you must use C#'s **typeof** operator, as shown in the following code. Wherever the attribute class defines an **Object** parameter, **Object** field, or **Object** property, you can pass an **Int32**, **String**, or any other constant expression (including **null**). If the constant expression represents a value type, the value type will be boxed at run time when an instance of the attribute is constructed.

Here's an example of an attribute and its usage:

```
using System;

internal enum Color { Red }

[AttributeUsage(AttributeTargets.All)]
internal sealed class SomeAttribute : Attribute {
```

```
    public SomeAttribute(String name, Object o, Type[] types) {
        // 'name'  refers to a String
        // 'o'     refers to one of the legal types (boxing if necessary)
        // 'types' refers to a 1-dimension, 0-based array of Types
    }
}

[Some("Jeff", Color.Red, new Type[] { typeof(Math), typeof(Console) })]
internal sealed class SomeType {
}
```

Logically, when a compiler detects a custom attribute applied to a target, the compiler constructs an instance of the attribute class by calling its constructor, passing it any specified parameters. Then the compiler initializes any public fields and properties using the values specified via the enhanced constructor syntax. Now that the custom attribute object is initialized, the compiler serializes the attribute object's state out to the target's metadata table entry.

> **Important**   I've found this to be the best way for developers to think of custom attributes: instances of classes that have been serialized to a byte stream that resides in metadata. Later, at run time, an instance of the class can be constructed by deserializing the bytes contained in the metadata. In reality, what actually happens is that the compiler emits the information necessary to create an instance of the attribute class into metadata. Each constructor parameter is written out with a 1-byte type ID followed by the value. After "serializing" the constructor's parameters, the compiler emits each of the specified field and property values by writing out the field/property name followed by a 1-byte type ID and then the value. For arrays, the count of elements is saved first, followed by each individual element.

Detecting the Use of a Custom Attribute

Defining an attribute class is useless by itself. Sure, you could define attribute classes all you want and apply instances of them all you want, but this would just cause additional metadata to be written out to the assembly—the behavior of your application code wouldn't change.

In Chapter 12, "Enumerated Types and Bit Flags," you saw that applying the **Flags** attribute to an enumerated type altered the behavior of **System.Enum**'s **ToString** and **Format** methods. The reason that these methods behave differently is that they check at run time if the enumerated type that they're operating on has the **Flags** attribute metadata associated with it. Code can look for the presence of attributes by using a technology called *reflection*. I'll give some brief demonstrations of reflection here, but I'll discuss it fully in Chapter 22, "Assembly Loading and Reflection."

If you were the Microsoft employee responsible for implementing **Enum**'s **Format** method, you would implement it like this:

```
public static String Format(Type enumType, Object value, String format) {

    // Does the enumerated type have an instance of
    // the FlagsAttribute type applied to it?
```

```
    if (enumType.IsDefined(typeof(FlagsAttribute), false)) {
        // Yes; execute code treating value as a bit flag enumerated type.
        ...
    } else {
        // No; execute code treating value as a normal enumerated type.
        ...
    }
    ...
}
```

This code calls **Type**'s **IsDefined** method, effectively asking the system to look up the meta-data for the enumerated type and see whether an instance of the **FlagsAttribute** class is associated with it. If **IsDefined** returns **true**, an instance of **FlagsAttribute** is associated with the enumerated type, and the **Format** method knows to treat the value as though it contained a set of bit flags. If **IsDefined** returns **false**, **Format** treats the value as a normal enumerated type.

So if you define your own attribute classes, you must also implement some code that checks for the existence of an instance of your attribute class (on some target) and then execute some alternate code path. This is what makes custom attributes so useful!

The FCL offers many ways to check for the existence of an attribute. If you're checking for the existence of an attribute via a **System.Type** object, you can use the **IsDefined** method as shown earlier. However, sometimes you want to check for an attribute on a target other than a type, such as an assembly, a module, or a method. For this discussion, let's concentrate on the methods defined by the **System.Attribute** class. You'll recall that all CLS-compliant attributes are derived from **System.Attribute**. This class defines three static methods for retrieving the attributes associated with a target: **IsDefined**, **GetCustomAttributes**, and **GetCustomAttribute**. Each of these functions has several overloaded versions. For example, each method has a version that works on type members (classes, structs, enums, interfaces, delegates, constructors, methods, properties, fields, events, and return types), parameters, modules, and assemblies. There are also versions that allow you to tell the system to walk up the derivation hierarchy to include inherited attributes in the results. Table 17-1 briefly describes what each method does.

Table 17-1 **System.Attribute**'s Methods That Reflect over Metadata Looking for Instances of CLS-Compliant Custom Attributes

Method	Description
IsDefined	Returns **true** if there is at least one instance of the specified **Attribute**-derived class associated with the target. This method is efficient because it doesn't construct (deserialize) any instances of the attribute class.
GetCustomAttributes	Returns an array in which each element is an instance of the specified attribute class that was applied to the target. If no attribute class is given to the method, the array contains the instances of all applied attributes, whatever class they have. Each instance is constructed (deserialized) by using the parameters, fields, and properties specified during compilation. If the target has no instances of the specified attribute class, an empty array is returned. This method is typically used with attributes that have **AllowMultiple** set to **true** or to list all applied attributes.

Table 17-1   `System.Attribute`'s Methods That Reflect over Metadata Looking for Instances of CLS-Compliant Custom Attributes

Method	Description
`GetCustomAttribute`	Returns an instance of the specified attribute class that was applied to the target. The instance is constructed (deserialized) by using the parameters, fields, and properties specified during compilation. If the target has no instances of the specified attribute class, `null` is returned. If the target has multiple instances of the specified attribute applied to it, a `System.Reflection.AmbiguousMatch-Exception` exception is thrown. This method is typically used with attributes that have `AllowMultiple` set to `false`.

If you just want to see if an attribute has been applied to a target, you should call `IsDefined` because it's more efficient than the other two methods. However, you know that when an attribute is applied to a target, you can specify parameters to the attribute's constructor and optionally set fields and properties. Using `IsDefined` won't construct an attribute object, call its constructor, or set its fields and properties.

If you want to construct an attribute object, you must call either `GetCustomAttributes` or `GetCustomAttribute`. Every time one of these methods is called, it constructs new instances of the specified attribute type and sets each of the instance's fields and properties based on the values specified in the source code. These methods return references to fully constructed instances of the applied attribute classes.

When you call any of these methods, internally, they must scan the managed module's metadata, performing string comparisons to locate the specified custom attribute class. Obviously, these operations take time. If you're performance conscious, you should consider caching the result of calling these methods rather than calling them repeatedly asking for the same information.

The `System.Reflection` namespace defines several classes that allow you to examine the contents of a module's metadata: `Assembly`, `Module`, `ParameterInfo`, `MemberInfo`, `Type`, `Method-Info`, `ConstructorInfo`, `FieldInfo`, `EventInfo`, `PropertyInfo`, and their respective `*Builder` classes. All of these classes also offer `IsDefined` and `GetCustomAttributes` methods. Only `System.Attribute` offers the very convenient `GetCustomAttribute` method.

The version of `GetCustomAttributes` defined by the reflection classes returns an array of `Object` instances (`Object[]`) instead of an array of `Attribute` instances (`Attribute[]`). This is because the reflection classes are able to return objects of non-CLS-compliant attribute classes. You shouldn't be concerned about this inconsistency because non-CLS-compliant attributes are incredibly rare. In fact, in all of the time I've been working with the .NET Framework, I've never even seen one.

> **Note**   Be aware that only `Attribute`, `Type`, and `MethodInfo` classes implement reflection methods that honor the `Boolean inherit` parameter. All other reflection methods that look up attributes ignore the `inherit` parameter and do not check the inheritance hierarchy. If you need to check the presence of an inherited attribute for events, properties, fields, constructors, or parameters, you must call one of `Attribute`'s methods.

There's one more thing you should be aware of: When you pass a class to `IsDefined`, `GetCustomAttribute`, or `GetCustomAttributes`, these methods search for the application of the attribute class you specify or any attribute class derived from the specified class. If your code is looking for a specific attribute class, you should perform an additional check on the returned value to ensure that what these methods returned is the exact class you're looking for. You might also want to consider defining your attribute class to be **sealed** to reduce potential confusion and eliminate this extra check.

Here's some sample code that lists all of the methods defined within a type and displays the attributes applied to each method. The code is for demonstration purposes; normally, you wouldn't apply these particular custom attributes to these targets as I've done here.

```
using System;
using System.Diagnostics;
using System.Reflection;


[assembly: CLSCompliant(true)]


[Serializable]
[DefaultMemberAttribute("Main")]
[DebuggerDisplayAttribute("Richter", Name = "Jeff", Target = typeof(Program))]
public sealed class Program {
    [Conditional("Debug")]
    [Conditional("Release")]
    public void DoSomething() { }

    public Program() {
    }

    [CLSCompliant(true)]
    [STAThread]
    public static void Main() {
        // Show the set of attributes applied to this type
        ShowAttributes(typeof(Program));

        // Get the set of methods associated with the type
        MemberInfo[] members = typeof(Program).FindMembers(
            MemberTypes.Constructor | MemberTypes.Method,
            BindingFlags.DeclaredOnly | BindingFlags.Instance |
            BindingFlags.Public | BindingFlags.Static,
            Type.FilterName, "*");

        foreach (MemberInfo member in members) {
            // Show the set of attributes applied to this member
            ShowAttributes(member);
        }
    }

    private static void ShowAttributes(MemberInfo attributeTarget) {
        Attribute[] attributes = Attribute.GetCustomAttributes(attributeTarget);
```

```csharp
            Console.WriteLine("Attributes applied to {0}: {1}",
                attributeTarget.Name, (attributes.Length == 0 ? "None" : String.Empty));

            foreach (Attribute attribute in attributes) {
                // Display the type of each applied attribute
                Console.WriteLine("  {0}", attribute.GetType().ToString());

                if (attribute is DefaultMemberAttribute)
                    Console.WriteLine("    MemberName={0}",
                        ((DefaultMemberAttribute) attribute).MemberName);

                if (attribute is ConditionalAttribute)
                    Console.WriteLine("    ConditionString={0}",
                        ((ConditionalAttribute) attribute).ConditionString);

                if (attribute is CLSCompliantAttribute)
                    Console.WriteLine("    IsCompliant={0}",
                        ((CLSCompliantAttribute) attribute).IsCompliant);

                DebuggerDisplayAttribute dda = attribute as DebuggerDisplayAttribute;
                if (dda != null) {
                    Console.WriteLine("    Value={0}, Name={1}, Target={2}",
                        dda.Value, dda.Name, dda.Target);
                }
            }
            Console.WriteLine();
        }
    }
```

Building and running this application yields the following output:

```
Attributes applied to Program:
  System.SerializableAttribute
  System.Diagnostics.DebuggerDisplayAttribute
    Value=Richter, Name=Jeff, Target=Program
  System.Reflection.DefaultMemberAttribute
    MemberName=Main

Attributes applied to DoSomething:
  System.Diagnostics.ConditionalAttribute
    ConditionString=Release
  System.Diagnostics.ConditionalAttribute
    ConditionString=Debug

Attributes applied to Main:
  System.STAThreadAttribute
  System.CLSCompliantAttribute
    IsCompliant=True

Attributes applied to .ctor: None
```

Matching Two Attribute Instances Against Each Other

Now that your code knows how to check if an instance of an attribute is applied to a target, it might want to check the fields of the attribute to see what values they have. One way to do this is to write code that checks the values of the attribute class's fields. However, your attribute class could also override **System.Attribute**'s **Match** method to take into account the fact that each time an attribute is returned by reflection, a new instance is created. Since the default **Attribute.Match** implementation simply calls **Equal**, you need to be cautious. Once this is done, your code could construct an instance of the attribute class and call **Match** to compare it to the instance that reflects what was applied to the target. The following code demonstrates this:

```
using System;


[Flags]
internal enum Accounts {
    Savings   = 0x0001,
    Checking  = 0x0002,
    Brokerage = 0x0004
}


[AttributeUsage(AttributeTargets.Class)]
internal sealed class AccountsAttribute : Attribute {
    private Accounts m_accounts;

    public AccountsAttribute(Accounts accounts) {
      m_accounts = accounts;
    }


    public override Boolean Match(Object obj) {
        // If the base class implements Match and the base class
        // is not Attribute, then uncomment the line below.
        // if (!base.Match(obj)) return false;

        // Since 'this' isn't null, if obj is null,
        // then the objects can't match
        // NOTE: This line may be deleted if you trust
        // that the base type implemented Match correctly.
        if (obj == null) return false;

        // If the objects are of different types, they can't match
        // NOTE: This line may be deleted if you trust
        // that the base type implemented Match correctly.
        if (this.GetType() != obj.GetType()) return false;

        // Cast obj to our type to access fields. NOTE: This cast
        // can't fail since we know objects are of the same type
        AccountsAttribute other = (AccountsAttribute) obj;
```

```
            // Compare the fields as you see fit
            // This example checks if 'this' accounts is a subset
            // of others' accounts
            if ((other.m_accounts & m_accounts) != m_accounts)
                return false;

            return true;   // Objects match
        }


    public override Boolean Equals(Object obj) {
        // If the base class implements Equals, and the base class
        // is not Object, then uncomment the line below.
        // if (!base.Equals(obj)) return false;

        // Since 'this' isn't null, if obj is null,
        // then the objects can't be equal
        // NOTE: This line may be deleted if you trust
        // that the base type implemented Equals correctly.
        if (obj == null) return false;

        // If the objects are of different types, they can't be equal
        // NOTE: This line may be deleted if you trust
        // that the base type implemented Equals correctly.
        if (this.GetType() != obj.GetType()) return false;

        // Cast obj to our type to access fields. NOTE: This cast
        // can't fail since we know objects are of the same type
        AccountsAttribute other = (AccountsAttribute) obj;

        // Compare the fields to see if they have the same value
        // This example checks if 'this' accounts is the same
        // as other's accounts
        if (other.m_accounts != m_accounts)
            return false;

        return true;   // Objects are equal
    }


    // Override GetHashCode since we override Equals
    public override Int32 GetHashCode() {
        return (Int32) m_accounts;
    }
}


[Accounts(Accounts.Savings)]
internal sealed class ChildAccount { }


[Accounts(Accounts.Savings | Accounts.Checking | Accounts.Brokerage)]
internal sealed class AdultAccount { }
```

```
public sealed class Program {
    public static void Main() {
        CanWriteCheck(new ChildAccount());
        CanWriteCheck(new AdultAccount());

        // This just demonstrates that the method works correctly on a
        // type that doesn't have the AccountsAttribute applied to it.
        CanWriteCheck(new Program());
    }

    private static void CanWriteCheck(Object obj) {
        // Construct an instance of the attribute type and initialize it
        // to what we are explicitly looking for.
        Attribute checking = new AccountsAttribute(Accounts.Checking);

        // Construct the attribute instance that was applied to the type
        Attribute validAccounts = Attribute.GetCustomAttribute(
            obj.GetType(), typeof(AccountsAttribute), false);

        // If the attribute was applied to the type AND the
        // attribute specifies the "Checking" account, then the
        // type can write a check
        if ((validAccounts != null) && checking.Match(validAccounts)) {
            Console.WriteLine("{0} types can write checks.", obj.GetType());
        } else {
            Console.WriteLine("{0} types can NOT write checks.", obj.GetType());
        }
    }
}
```

Building and running this application yields the following output:

```
ChildAccount types can NOT write checks.
AdultAccount types can write checks.
Program types can NOT write checks.
```

If you define a custom attribute and you don't override the **Match** method, you'll inherit the implementation of **Attribute**'s **Match** method. This implementation simply calls **Equals** and is not appropriate to compare new instances of attributes, even with the same contents.

Detecting the Use of a Custom Attribute Without Creating Attribute-Derived Objects

In this section, I discuss an alternate technique for detecting custom attributes applied to a metadata entry. In some security-conscious scenarios, this alternate technique ensures that no code in an **Attribute**-derived class will execute. After all, when you call **Attribute**'s **GetCustomAttribute(s)** methods, internally, these methods call the attribute class's constructor and can also call property set accessor methods. In addition, the first access to a type causes the CLR to invoke the type's type constructor (if it exists). The constructor, set accessor, and type constructor methods could contain code that will execute whenever code is just looking for an attribute. This allows unknown code to run in the AppDomain, and this is a potential security vulnerability.

To discover attributes without allowing attribute class code to execute, you use the `System .Reflection.CustomAttributeData` class. This class defines one static method for retrieving the attributes associated with a target: `GetCustomAttributes`. This method has four overloads: one that takes an `Assembly`, one that takes a `Module`, one that takes a `ParameterInfo`, and one that takes a `MemberInfo`. This class is defined in the `System.Reflection` namespace, which is discussed in Chapter 22. Typically, you'll use the `CustomAttributeData` class to analyze attributes in metadata for an assembly that is loaded via `Assembly`'s static `ReflectionOnlyLoad` method (also discussed in Chapter 22). Briefly, `ReflectionOnlyLoad` loads an assembly in such a way that prevents the CLR from executing any code in it; this includes type constructors.

`CustomAttributeData`'s `GetCustomAttributes` method acts as a factory. That is, when you call it, it returns a collection of `CustomAttributeData` objects in an object of type `IList<Custom-AttributeData>`. The collection contains one element per custom attribute applied to the specified target. For each `CustomAttributeData` object, you can query some read-only properties to determine how the attribute object *would be* constructed and initialized. Specifically, the `Constructor` property indicates which constructor method *would be* called, the `Constructor-Arguments` property returns the arguments that *would be* passed to this constructor as an instance of `IList<CustomAttributeTypedArgument>`, and the `NamedArguments` property returns the fields/properties that *would be* set as an instance of `IList<CustomAttribute-NamedArgument>`. Notice that I say "would be" in the previous sentences because the constructor and set accessor methods will not actually be called—we get the added security by preventing any attribute class methods from executing.

Here's a modified version of a previous code sample that uses the `CustomAttributeData` class to securely obtain the attributes applied to various targets:

```
using System;
using System.Diagnostics;
using System.Reflection;
using System.Collections.Generic;


[assembly: CLSCompliant(true)]


[Serializable]
[DefaultMemberAttribute("Main")]
[DebuggerDisplayAttribute("Richter", Name="Jeff", Target=typeof(Program))]
public sealed class Program {
   [Conditional("Debug")]
   [Conditional("Release")]
   public void DoSomething() { }

   public Program() {
   }
```

```
[CLSCompliant(true)]
[STAThread]
public static void Main() {
    // Show the set of attributes applied to this type
    ShowAttributes(typeof(Program));

    // Get the set of methods associated with the type
    MemberInfo[] members = typeof(Program).FindMembers(
        MemberTypes.Constructor | MemberTypes.Method,
        BindingFlags.DeclaredOnly | BindingFlags.Instance |
        BindingFlags.Public | BindingFlags.Static,
        Type.FilterName, "*");

    foreach (MemberInfo member in members) {
        // Show the set of attributes applied to this member
        ShowAttributes(member);
    }
}

private static void ShowAttributes(MemberInfo attributeTarget) {
    IList<CustomAttributeData> attributes =
        CustomAttributeData.GetCustomAttributes(attributeTarget);

    Console.WriteLine("Attributes applied to {0}: {1}",
        attributeTarget.Name, (attributes.Count == 0 ? "None" : String.Empty));

    foreach (CustomAttributeData attribute in attributes) {
        // Display the type of each applied attribute
        Type t = attribute.Constructor.DeclaringType;
        Console.WriteLine("  {0}", t.ToString());
        Console.WriteLine("    Constructor called={0}", attribute.Constructor);

        IList<CustomAttributeTypedArgument> posArgs = attribute.ConstructorArguments;
        Console.WriteLine("    Positional arguments passed to constructor:" +
            ((posArgs.Count == 0) ? " None" : String.Empty));
        foreach (CustomAttributeTypedArgument pa in posArgs) {
            Console.WriteLine("      Type={0}, Value={1}", pa.ArgumentType, pa.Value);
        }


        IList<CustomAttributeNamedArgument> namedArgs = attribute.NamedArguments;
        Console.WriteLine("    Named arguments set after construction:" +
            ((namedArgs.Count == 0) ? " None" : String.Empty));
        foreach(CustomAttributeNamedArgument na in namedArgs) {
            Console.WriteLine("      Name={0}, Type={1}, Value={2}",
                na.MemberInfo.Name, na.TypedValue.ArgumentType, na.TypedValue.Value);
        }

        Console.WriteLine();
    }
    Console.WriteLine();
}
}
```

Building and running this application yields the following output:

```
Attributes applied to Program:
  System.SerializableAttribute
    Constructor called=Void .ctor()
    Positional arguments passed to constructor: None
    Named arguments set after construction: None

  System.Diagnostics.DebuggerDisplayAttribute
    Constructor called=Void .ctor(System.String)
    Positional arguments passed to constructor:
      Type=System.String, Value=Richter
    Named arguments set after construction:
     Name=Name, Type=System.String, Value=Jeff
     Name=Target, Type=System.Type, Value=Program

  System.Reflection.DefaultMemberAttribute
    Constructor called=Void .ctor(System.String)
    Positional arguments passed to constructor:
      Type=System.String, Value=Main
    Named arguments set after construction: None


Attributes applied to DoSomething:
  System.Diagnostics.ConditionalAttribute
    Constructor called=Void .ctor(System.String)
    Positional arguments passed to constructor:
      Type=System.String, Value=Release
    Named arguments set after construction: None

  System.Diagnostics.ConditionalAttribute
    Constructor called=Void .ctor(System.String)
    Positional arguments passed to constructor:
      Type=System.String, Value=Debug
    Named arguments set after construction: None


Attributes applied to Main:
  System.CLSCompliantAttribute
    Constructor called=Void .ctor(Boolean)
    Positional arguments passed to constructor:
      Type=System.Boolean, Value=True
    Named arguments set after construction: None

  System.STAThreadAttribute
    Constructor called=Void .ctor()
    Positional arguments passed to constructor: None
    Named arguments set after construction: None


Attributes applied to .ctor: None
```

Conditional Attribute Classes

Over time, the ease of defining, applying, and reflecting over attributes has caused developers to use them more and more. Using attributes is also a very easy way to annotate your code while simultaneously implementing rich features. Lately, developers have been using attributes to assist them with design time and debugging. For example, users of NUnit apply attributes—such as `TestFixtureSetUp`, `Setup`, `TearDown`, `TestFixtureTearDown`, and `Test`—to types and methods that should be accessed by the NUnit utility in order to perform unit testing.

These attributes are looked for only by the NUnit utility; the attributes are never looked for when the program is running normally. When not using NUnit, having the NUnit attributes sitting in the metadata just bloats the metadata, which makes your file bigger, increases your process's working set, and hurts your application's performance. It would be great if there were an easy way to have the compiler emit the NUnit attributes only when you intend to perform unit testing with NUnit. Fortunately, there is a way to do this by using conditional attribute classes.

An attribute class that has the `System.Diagnostics.ConditionalAttribute` applied to it is called a *conditional attribute class*. Here is an example:

```
//#define TEST
#define VERIFY

using System;
using System.Diagnostics;


[Conditional("TEST")][Conditional("VERIFY")]
public sealed class CondAttribute : Attribute {
}

[Cond]
public sealed class Program {
   public static void Main() {
      Console.WriteLine("CondAttribute is {0}applied to Program type.",
         Attribute.IsDefined(typeof(Program),
            typeof(CondAttribute)) ? "" : "not ");
   }
}
```

When a compiler sees an instance of the `CondAttribute` being applied to a target, the compiler will emit the attribute information into the metadata only if the `TEST` or `VERIFY` symbol is defined when the code containing the target is compiled. However, the attribute class definition metadata and implementation is still present in the assembly.

Chapter 18
Nullable Value Types

As you know, a variable of a value type can never be `null`; it always contains the value type's value itself. In fact, this is why they call value types value types. Unfortunately, there are some scenarios in which this is a problem. For example, when designing a database, it's possible to define a column's data type to be a 32-bit integer that would map to the FCL's `Int32` data type. But a column in a database can indicate that the value is nullable. That is, it is OK to have no value in the row's column. Working with database data by using the Microsoft .NET Framework can be quite difficult because in the common language runtime (CLR), there is no way to represent an `Int32` value as `null`.

Note Microsoft ADO.NET's table adapters do support nullable types. But unfortunately, the types in the `System.Data.SqlTypes` namespace are not replaced by nullable types, partially because there isn't a one-to-one correspondence between types. For example, the `SqlDecimal` type has a maximum of 38 digits, whereas the regular `Decimal` type can reach only 29. In addition, the `SqlString` type supports its own locale and compare options, which are not supported by the normal `String` type.

Note Microsoft's Language Integrated Query (LINQ) technologies take advantage of nullable types to integrate data queries very naturally into the programming language.

Here is another example: in Java, the `java.util.Date` class is a reference type, and therefore, a variable of this type can be set to `null`. However, in the CLR, a `System.DateTime` is a value type, and a `DateTime` variable can never be `null`. If an application written in Java wants to communicate a date/time to a Web service running the CLR, there is a problem if the Java application sends `null` because the CLR has no way to represent this and operate on it.

To improve this situation, Microsoft added the concept of nullable value types to the CLR. To understand how they work, we first need to look at the `System.Nullable<T>` class, which is

409

defined in the FCL. Here is the logical representation of how the `System.Nullable<T>` type is defined:

```
[Serializable, StructLayout(LayoutKind.Sequential)]
public struct Nullable<T> where T : struct {

    // These 2 fields represent the state
    private Boolean hasValue = false; // Assume null
    internal T value = default(T);    // Assume all bits zero

    public Nullable(T value) {
        this.value = value;
        this.hasValue = true;
    }

    public Boolean HasValue { get { return hasValue; } }

    public T Value {
        get {
            if (!hasValue) {
                throw new InvalidOperationException(
                    "Nullable object must have a value.");
            }
            return value;
        }
    }

    public T GetValueOrDefault() { return value; }

    public T GetValueOrDefault(T defaultValue) {
        if (!HasValue) return defaultValue;
        return value;
    }

    public override Boolean Equals(Object other) {
        if (!HasValue) return (other == null);
        if (other == null) return false;
        return value.Equals(other);
    }

    public override int GetHashCode() {
        if (!HasValue) return 0;
        return value.GetHashCode();
    }

    public override string ToString() {
        if (!HasValue) return "";
        return value.ToString();
    }

    public static implicit operator Nullable<T>(T value) {
        return new Nullable<T>(value);
    }
```

```
    public static explicit operator T(Nullable<T> value) {
        return value.Value;
    }
}
```

As you can see, this class encapsulates the notion of a value type than can also be **null**. Since **Nullable<T>** is itself a value type, instances of it are still fairly lightweight. That is, instances can still be on the stack, and an instance is the same size as the original value type plus the size of a **Boolean** field. Notice that **Nullable**'s type parameter, **T**, is constrained to **struct**. This was done because reference type variables can already be **null**.

So now, if you want to use a nullable **Int32** in your code, you can write something like this:

```
Nullable<Int32> x = 5;
Nullable<Int32> y = null;
Console.WriteLine("x: HasValue={0}, Value={1}",
    x.HasValue, x.Value);
Console.WriteLine("y: HasValue={0}, Value={1}",
    y.HasValue, y.GetValueOrDefault());
```

When I compile and run this code, I get the following output:

```
x: HasValue=True, Value=5
y: HasValue=False, Value=0
```

C#'s Support for Nullable Value Types

Notice in the code that C# allows you to use fairly simple syntax to initialize the two **Nullable<Int32>** variables, **x** and **y**. In fact, the C# team wants to integrate nullable value types into the C# language, making them first-class citizens. To that end, C# offers an (arguably) cleaner syntax for working with nullable value types. C# allows the code to declare and initialize the **x** and **y** variables to be written using question-mark notation:

```
Int32? x = 5;
Int32? y = null;
```

In C#, **Int32?** is a synonym notation for **Nullable<Int32>**. But C# takes this further. C# allows you to perform conversions and casts on nullable instances. And C# also supports applying operators to nullable instances. The following code shows examples of these:

```
private static void ConversionsAndCasting() {
    // Implicit conversion from non-nullable Int32 to Nullable<Int32>
    Int32? a = 5;

    // Implicit conversion from 'null' to Nullable<Int32>
    Int32? b = null;
```

```
// Explicit conversion from Nullable<Int32> to non-nullable Int32
Int32 c = (Int32) a;

// Casting between nullable primitive types
Double? d = 5; // Int32->Double?  (d is 5.0 as a double)
Double? e = b; // Int32?->Double? (e is null)
}
```

C# also allows you to apply operators to nullable instances. The following code shows examples of this:

```
private static void Operators() {
    Int32? a = 5;
    Int32? b = null;

    // Unary operators (+  ++  -  --  !  ~)
    a++;      // a = 6
    b = -b;   // b = null

    // Binary operators (+  -  *  /  %  &  |  ^  <<  >>)
    a = a + 3;  // a = 9
    b = b * 3;  // b = null;

    // Equality operators (==  !=)
    if (a == null) { /* no  */ } else { /* yes */ }
    if (b == null) { /* yes */ } else { /* no  */ }
    if (a != b)    { /* yes */ } else { /* no  */ }

    // Comparison operators (<  >  <=  >=)
    if (a < b)     { /* no  */ } else { /* yes */ }
}
```

Here is how C# interprets the operators:

- Unary operators (+ ++ - -- ! ~). If the operand is **null**, the result is **null**.

- Binary operators (+ - * / % & | ^ << >>). If either operand is **null**, the result is **null**.

- Equality operators (== !=). If both operands are **null**, they are equal. If one operand is **null**, they are not equal. If neither operand is **null**, compare the values to determine if they are equal.

- Comparison operators (< > <= >=). If either operand is **null**, the result is **false**. If neither operand is **null**, compare the values.

You should be aware that manipulating nullable instances does cause the generation of a lot of code. For example, see the following method:

```
private static Int32? NullableCodeSize(Int32? a, Int32? b) {
    return a + b;
}
```

When I compile this method, there is quite a bit of resulting IL code. Here is the C# equivalent of the compiler-produced IL code:

```
private static Nullable<Int32> NullableCodeSize(
    Nullable<Int32> a, Nullable<Int32> b) {

    Nullable<Int32> nullable1 = a;
    Nullable<Int32> nullable2 = b;
    if (!(nullable1.HasValue & nullable2.HasValue)) {
        return new Nullable<Int32>();
    }
    return new Nullable<Int32>(
        nullable1.GetValueOrDefault() + nullable2.GetValueOrDefault());
}
```

C#'s Null-Coalescing Operator

C# has an operator called the *null-coalescing operator* (**??**), which takes two operands. If the operand on the left is not **null**, the operand's value is returned. If the operand on the left is **null**, the value of the right operand is returned. The null-coalescing operator offers a very convenient way to set a variable's default value.

A cool feature of the null-coalescing operator is that it can be used with reference types as well as nullable value types. Here is some code that demonstrates the use of the null-coalescing operator:

```
private static void NullCoalescingOperator() {
    Int32? b = null;

    // The line below is equivalent to:
    // x = (b.HasValue) ? b.Value : 123
    Int32 x = b ?? 123;
    Console.WriteLine(x);  // "123"

    // The line below is equivalent to:
    // String temp = GetFilename();
    // filename = (temp != null) ? temp : "Untitled";
    String filename = GetFilename() ?? "Untitled";
}
```

The CLR Has Special Support for Nullable Value Types

The CLR has built-in support for nullable value types. This special support is provided for boxing, unboxing, calling **GetType**, and calling interface methods, and it is given to nullable types to make them fit more seamlessly into the CLR. This also makes them behave more naturally and as most developers would expect. Let's take a closer look at the CLR's special support for nullable types.

Boxing Nullable Value Types

Imagine a **Nullable\<Int32>** variable that is logically set to **null**. If this variable is passed to a method prototyped as expecting an **Object**, the variable must be boxed, and a reference to the boxed **Nullable\<Int32>** is passed to the method. This is not ideal because the method is now being passed a non-**null** value even though the **Nullable\<Int32>** variable logically contained the value of **null**. To fix this, the CLR executes some special code when boxing a nullable variable to keep up the illusion that nullable types are first-class citizens in the environment.

Specifically, when the CLR is boxing a **Nullable\<T>** instance, it checks to see if it is **null**, and if so, the CLR doesn't actually box anything, and **null** is returned. If the nullable instance is not **null**, the CLR takes the value out of the nullable instance and boxes it. In other words, a **Nullable\<Int32>** with a value of **5** is boxed into a boxed-**Int32** with a value of **5**. Here is some code that demonstrates this behavior:

```
// Boxing Nullable<T> is null or boxed T
Int32? n = null;
Object o = n;  // o is null
Console.WriteLine("o is null={0}", o == null);  // "True"

n = 5;
o = n;   // o refers to a boxed Int32
Console.WriteLine("o's type={0}", o.GetType()); // "System.Int32"
```

Unboxing Nullable Value Types

The CLR allows a boxed value type **T** to be unboxed into a **T** or a **Nullable\<T>**. If the reference to the boxed value type is **null**, and you are unboxing it to a **Nullable\<T>**, the CLR sets **Nullable\<T>**'s value to **null**. Here is some code to demonstrate this behavior:

```
// Create a boxed Int32
Object o = 5;

// Unbox it into a Nullable<Int32> and into an Int32
Int32? a = (Int32?) o;  // a = 5
Int32  b = (Int32) o;  // b = 5

// Create a reference initialized to null
o = null;

// "Unbox" it into a Nullable<Int32> and into an Int32
a = (Int32?) o;       // a = null
b = (Int32) o;        // NullReferenceException
```

When unboxing a value type into a nullable version of the value type, the CLR might have to allocate memory. This is very unusual because in all other situations, unboxing never causes memory to be allocated. Here is some code that demonstrates this behavior:

```
private static void UnboxingAllocations() {
   const Int32 count = 1000000;

   // Create a boxed Int32
   Object o = 5;

   Int32 numGCs = GC.CollectionCount(0);
   for (Int32 x = 0; x < count; x++) {
      Int32 unboxed = (Int32) o;
   }
   Console.WriteLine("Number of GCs={0}", GC.CollectionCount(0) - numGCs);

   numGCs = GC.CollectionCount(0);
   for (Int32 x = 0; x < count; x++) {
      Int32? unboxed = (Int32?) o;
   }
   Console.WriteLine("Number of GCs={0}", GC.CollectionCount(0) - numGCs);
}
```

When I compile and run this method, I get the following output:

```
Number of GCs=0
Number of GCs=30
```

The only difference between the two loops in the code above is that one unboxes **o** to an **Int32**, whereas the other unboxes **o** to a **Nullable<Int32>**. But in the second loop, 30 garbage collections occurred, clearly indicating that objects are being created on the heap during the unboxing. As discussed in Chapter 5, "Primitive, Reference, and Value Types," unboxing is simply the act of obtaining a reference to the unboxed portion of a boxed object. The problem is that a boxed value type cannot simply be unboxed into a nullable version of that value type because the boxed value type doesn't have the **Boolean hasValue** field in it. So when unboxing a value type to a nullable version, the CLR must allocate a **Nullable<T>** object, initialize the **hasValue** field to **true**, and set the **value** field to the same value that is in the boxed value type. This impacts your application's performance.

Calling GetType via a Nullable Value Type

When calling **GetType** on a **Nullable<T>** object, the CLR actually lies and returns the type **T** instead of the type **Nullable<T>**. Here is some code that demonstrates this behavior:

```
Int32? x = 5;

// The line below displays "System.Int32"; not "System.Nullable<Int32>"
Console.WriteLine(x.GetType());
```

Calling Interface Methods via a Nullable Value Type

In the code below, I'm casting **n**, a **Nullable<Int32>**, to **IComparable<Int32>**, an interface type. However, the **Nullable<T>** type does not implement the **IComparable<Int32>** interface as **Int32** does. The C# compiler allows this code to compile anyway, and the CLR's verifier considers this code verifiable to allow you a more convenient syntax.

```
Int32? n = 5;
Int32 result = ((IComparable) n).CompareTo(5);   // Compiles & runs OK
Console.WriteLine(result);                        // 0
```

If the CLR didn't provide this special support, it would be more cumbersome for you to write code to call an interface method on a nullable value type. You'd have to cast the unboxed value type first before casting to the interface to make the call:

```
Int32 result = ((IComparable) (Int32) n).CompareTo(5);   // Cumbersome
```

Part V
CLR Facilities

Chapter 19
Exceptions

In this chapter, I'll talk about a powerful mechanism that allows you to write more maintainable and robust code: *exception handling*. Here are just a few of the benefits provided by exception handling:

- **The ability to keep cleanup code in a dedicated location and the assurance that this cleanup code will execute**   By moving cleanup code out of an application's main logic to a dedicated location, the application is easier to write, understand, and maintain. The assurance that cleanup code will run means that the application is more likely to remain in a consistent state. For example, when the code writing to the files can no longer continue because an exception is thrown in the program, the files will be closed.

- **The ability to keep code that deals with exceptional situations in a central place**   A line of code can fail for many reasons. Some examples of situations that cause code to fail are: arithmetic overflow, stack overflow, insufficient memory, an out-of-range argument, an out-of-range index into an array, and an attempt to access a resource after it has been released (such as accessing a file after it has been closed). Without using exception handling, it's very difficult, if not impossible, to write code that gracefully detects and recovers from such failures. Sprinkling your application's logic with code to detect these potential failures makes the code difficult to write, understand, and maintain. In most circumstances, adding code to check for these potential failures seriously impacts an application's performance.

By using exception handling, you don't need to write code to detect these potential failures. Instead, you can simply write your code assuming that failures won't occur. This certainly makes code easier to write, understand, and maintain. In addition, the code runs faster than code that is sprinkled with tests for exceptional conditions. After you've written your block of code, you next put all of your recovery code in a central location. Only if a failure occurs will the exception-handling mechanism step in to execute your recovery code.

■ **The ability to locate and fix bugs in the code**   When a failure occurs, the common language runtime (CLR) walks up the thread's call stack looking for code capable of handling the exception. If the CLR does not find code that handles the exception, you will receive a notification of this unhandled exception. You can then easily locate the source code that issued the failure, determine why the failure happened, and modify the source code to fix the bug. This means that bugs are more likely to be detected during development and testing of an application and fixed prior to the application's deployment. Once deployed, the application will be more stable, thus improving the end user's experience.

When used properly, exception handling is a great tool that eases the burden on software developers. However, if used improperly, exception handling can bring much sorrow and pain by hiding serious problems in the code or by misinforming you instead of telling you about the actual problem. The bulk of this chapter is dedicated to explaining how to properly use exception handling.

The Evolution of Exception Handling

When designing the Win32 API and COM, Microsoft decided not to use exceptions to notify the callers of Win32 functions when a problem occurred. Instead, most Win32 functions return a **BOOL** set to **FALSE** to indicate that something went wrong, and then it's up to the caller to call **GetLastError** to find the reason for the failure. On the other hand, COM methods return an **HRESULT** with the high bit set to 1 to indicate failure. The remaining bits represent a value that helps you determine the cause of the failure.

Microsoft avoided using exceptions with Win32 and COM APIs for many reasons:

■ Most developers were not familiar with exception handling.

■ Many programming languages, including C and early versions of C++, did not support exceptions.

■ Some developers felt that exceptions were difficult to use and understand, and Microsoft didn't want to alienate developers. (Personally, I feel the benefit of exceptions far outweighs the exception-handling learning curve.)

■ Exception handling can hurt the performance of an application. In some situations, exception handling doesn't perform as well as simply returning an error code. However, if exceptions are rarely thrown, this overhead isn't noticeable. Again, I feel that the benefit of exceptions outweighs the slight performance hit that sometimes occurs. I also believe that when exception handling is used correctly throughout an application, performance can improve. I'll address performance later in this chapter. In addition, exceptions in managed code are far less expensive than in some unmanaged languages, such as C++.

The old ways of reporting violations are too limiting because the caller gets back only a 32-bit number. If the number is the code for an invalid argument, the caller doesn't know which argument is invalid. And if the number is the code for a division by zero, the caller doesn't know exactly which line of code caused the division by zero and thus can't fix the code easily. Developing software is hard enough without losing important details about problems! If the application code detects a problem, you want to receive as much information as possible about the problem so that you can correct the situation quickly and easily.

The exception-handling mechanism offers several advantages over a 32-bit number. An exception includes a string description of the problem; for example if an invalid argument exception occurs, you will know exactly which argument is causing the problem. The string might also include additional information giving you guidance as to how to improve the code. Exceptions also include a stack trace that tells you which path the application took when the exception occurred.

Another advantage of exceptions is that they don't have to be caught or detected at the place they occur; any code in the thread's call stack can handle a thrown exception. This simplifies coding substantially because you don't have to associate error detection and correction code with every statement or method call that might fail.

Closely related to the previous advantage is perhaps the biggest benefit of all: an exception can't be easily ignored. If a Win32 function is called and returns a failure code, it's all too easy for the caller to ignore the return code, assume that the function worked as expected, and allow the application to continue running as if all is fine. However, when a managed-code method throws an exception, it indicates that the method couldn't work as expected. If the application doesn't catch the exception, the CLR terminates the application. To some, this behavior might seem radical and severe. However, I think it's the right thing to do because if a method is called and an exception is thrown, it's not OK for the application to continue running. The rest of the application assumes that the previous operations all completed as expected. If this isn't the case, the application will continue running, but with unpredictable results. For example, if the user's data in the application is corrupt, this data shouldn't continue to be manipulated. With the Win32 and COM return values, the possibility of an application running with unpredictable results is too strong. With exceptions, it's not possible.

All of the methods defined by types in the Microsoft .NET Framework throw exceptions to indicate that the method couldn't complete; no 32-bit status values are returned. All programmers must therefore have a full understanding of exceptions and how to handle them in their code. Microsoft made a great decision here! Using exception handling in your code is straightforward and allows you to write code that's easy to implement, easy to read, and easy to maintain. In addition, exception handling allows you to write robust code that's capable of recovering from any application situation. Used correctly, exception handling can prevent application crashes and keep your users happy.

The Mechanics of Exception Handling

In this section, I'll introduce the mechanics and C# constructs needed in order to use exception handling, but it's not my intention to explain them in great detail. The purpose of this chapter is to offer useful guidelines for when and how to use exception handling in your code. If you want more information about the mechanics and language constructs for using exception handling, see the .NET Framework documentation and the C# language specification. Also, the .NET Framework exception-handling mechanism is built using the Structured Exception Handling (SEH) mechanism offered by Microsoft Windows. SEH has been discussed in many resources, including my own book, *Programming Applications for Microsoft Windows* (4th ed., Microsoft Press, 1999), which contains three chapters devoted to SEH.

The following C# code shows a standard usage of the exception-handling mechanism. This code gives you an idea of what exception-handling blocks look like and what their purpose is. In the subsections after the code, I'll formally describe the **try**, **catch**, and **finally** blocks and their purpose and provide some notes about their use.

```csharp
private void SomeMethod() {

    try {
        // Inside the try block is where you put code requiring
        // graceful recovery or common cleanup operations.
    }
    catch (InvalidOperationException) {
        // Inside this catch block is where you put code that recovers
        // from an InvalidOperationException (or any exception type derived
        // from InvalidOperationException).
    }
    catch (IOException) {
        // Inside this catch block is where you put code that recovers
        // from an IOException (or any exception type derived
        // from IOException).
    }
    catch {
        // Inside this catch block is where you put code that recovers
        // from any kind of exception.

        // When catching any exception, you usually re-throw
        // the exception. I explain re-throwing later in this chapter.
        throw;
    }
    finally {
        // Inside the finally block is where you put code that
        // cleans up any operations started within the try block.
        // The code in this block ALWAYS executes, regardless of
        // whether an exception is thrown.
    }
```

```
    // Code below the finally block executes if no exception is thrown
    // within the try block or if a catch block catches the exception
    // and doesn't throw or re-throw an exception.
}
```

This code demonstrates one possible way to use exception-handling blocks. Don't let the code scare you—most methods have simply a **try** block matched with a single **finally** block or a **try** block matched with a single **catch** block. It's unusual to have as many **catch** blocks as in this example. I put them there for illustration purposes.

The try Block

A *try* block contains code that requires common cleanup or exception-recovery operations or both. The cleanup code should be placed in a single **finally** block. A **try** block can also contain code that might potentially throw an exception. The exception recovery code should be placed in one or more **catch** blocks. You create one **catch** block for each kind of exception that your application can safely recover from. A **try** block must be associated with at least one **catch** or **finally** block; it makes no sense to have a **try** block that stands by itself, and C# will prevent you from doing this.

The catch Block

A *catch* block contains code to execute in response to an exception. A **try** block can have zero or more **catch** blocks associated with it. If the code in a **try** block doesn't cause an exception to be thrown, the CLR will never execute the code contained within any of its **catch** blocks. The thread will simply skip over all of the **catch** blocks and execute the code in the **finally** block (if one exists). After the code in the **finally** block executes, execution continues with the statement following the **finally** block.

The parenthetical expression appearing after the **catch** keyword is called the *catch type*. In C#, you must specify a catch type of **System.Exception** or a type derived from **System.Exception**. For example, the previous code contains **catch** blocks for handling an **InvalidOperationException** (or any exception derived from it) and an **IOException** (or any exception derived from it). The last **catch** block (which doesn't specify a catch type) handles any exception at all; this is equivalent to having a **catch** block that specifies a catch type of **System.Exception** except that you cannot access the exception information via code inside the **catch** block's braces.

> **Note** When debugging through a **catch** block by using Microsoft Visual Studio, you can see the currently thrown exception object by adding the special "$exception" variable name to a watch window.

The CLR searches from top to bottom for a matching **catch** type, and therefore, you should place the more specific exception types at the top. The most-derived exception types should appear first, followed by their base types (if any), down to **System.Exception** (or an exception block that doesn't specify a catch type). In fact, the C# compiler generates an error if more specific **catch** blocks appear closer to the bottom because the **catch** block would be unreachable.

If an exception is thrown by code executing within the **try** block (or any method called from within the **try** block), the CLR starts searching for **catch** blocks whose catch type matches the thrown exception. If none of the catch types matches the exception, the CLR continues searching up the call stack looking for a catch type that matches the exception. If after reaching the top of the call stack, no **catch** block is found with a matching catch type, an unhandled exception will occur. I'll talk more about unhandled exceptions later in this chapter.

Once the CLR locates a **catch** block with a matching catch type, it executes the code in all inner **finally** blocks, starting from within the **try** block whose code threw the exception and stopping with the **catch** block that matched the exception. Note that any **finally** block associated with the **catch** block that matched the exception is not executed yet. The code in this **finally** block won't execute until after the code in the handling **catch** block has executed.

After all the code in the inner **finally** blocks has executed, the code in the handling **catch** block executes. This code typically performs some operations to recover from the exception. At the end of the **catch** block, you have three choices:

- Re-throw the same exception, notifying code higher up in the call stack of the exception.

- Throw a different exception, giving richer exception information to code higher up in the call stack.

- Let the thread fall out of the bottom of the **catch** block.

Later in this chapter, I'll offer some guidelines for when you should use each of these techniques.

If you choose either of the first two techniques, you're throwing an exception, and the CLR behaves just as it did before: it walks up the call stack looking for a **catch** block whose type matches the type of the exception thrown.

If you pick the last technique, when the thread falls out of the bottom of the **catch** block, it immediately starts executing code contained in the **finally** block (if one exists). After all of the code in the **finally** block executes, the thread drops out of the **finally** block and starts executing the statements immediately following the **finally** block. If no **finally** block exists, the thread continues execution at the statement following the last **catch** block.

In C#, you can specify a variable name after a catch type. When an exception is caught, this variable refers to the **System.Exception**-derived object that was thrown. The **catch** block's code can reference this variable to access information specific to the exception (such as the stack trace leading up to the exception). Although it's possible to modify this object, you shouldn't; consider the object to be read-only. I'll explain the **Exception** type and what you can do with it later in this chapter.

The `finally` Block

A `finally` block contains code that's guaranteed to execute. Typically, the code in a `finally` block performs the cleanup operations required by actions taken in the **try** block. For example, if you open a file in a **try** block, you'd put the code to close the file in a `finally` block:

```
private void ReadData(String pathname) {

    FileStream fs = null;
    try {
        fs = new FileStream(pathname, FileMode.Open);
        // Process the data in the file.
        ...
    }
    catch (IOException) {
        // Inside this catch block is where you put code that recovers
        // from an IOException (or any exception type derived
        // from IOException).
        ...
    }
    finally {
        // Make sure that the file gets closed.
        if (fs != null) fs.Close();
    }
}
```

If the code in the **try** block executes without throwing an exception, the file is guaranteed to be closed. If the code in the **try** block does throw an exception, the code in the `finally` block still executes, and the file is guaranteed to be closed, regardless of whether the exception is caught. It's improper to put the statement to close the file after the `finally` block; the statement wouldn't execute if an exception were thrown and not caught, which would result in the file being left open.

A **try** block doesn't require a `finally` block associated with it; sometimes the code in a **try** block just doesn't require any cleanup code. However, if you do have a `finally` block, it must appear after any and all **catch** blocks. A **try** block can have no more than one `finally` block associated with it.

When a thread reaches the end of the code contained in a `finally` block, the thread simply starts executing the statements immediately following the `finally` block. Remember that the code in the `finally` block is cleanup code. This code should execute only what is necessary to clean up operations initiated in the **try** block. Avoid putting in code that might throw an exception in a `finally` block. If an exception is inadvertently thrown within a `finally` block, the world will not come to an end—the CLR's exception mechanism will execute as though the exception were thrown after the `finally` block. However, the CLR does not keep track of the first exception that was thrown in the corresponding **try** block if any, and you will lose any and all information (such as the stack trace) available about the first exception.

Common Language Specification (CLS) and Non-CLS Exceptions

All programming languages for the CLR must support the throwing of **Exception**-derived objects because the Common Language Specification mandates this. However, the CLR actually allows an instance of any type to be thrown, and some programming languages will allow code to throw non-CLS-compliant exception objects such as a **String**, **Int32**, **DateTime**, or whatever. The C# compiler allows code to throw only **Exception**-derived objects, whereas code written in IL assembly language and C++/CLI allow code to throw **Exception**-derived objects as well as objects that are not derived from **Exception**.

Many programmers are not aware that the CLR allows any object to be thrown to report an exception. Most developers believe that only **Exception**-derived objects can be thrown. Prior to version 2.0 of the CLR, when programmers wrote **catch** blocks to catch exceptions, they were catching CLS-compliant exceptions only. If a C# method called a method written in another language, and that method threw a non-CLS-compliant exception, the C# code would not catch this exception at all, leading to some security vulnerabilities.

In version 2.0 of the CLR, Microsoft has introduced a new **RuntimeWrappedException** class (defined in the **System.Runtime.CompilerServices** namespace). This class is derived from **Exception**, so it is a CLS-compliant exception type. The **RuntimeWrappedException** class contains a private field of type **Object** (which can be accessed by using **RuntimeWrappedException**'s **WrappedException** read-only property). In version 2.0 of the CLR, when a non-CLS-compliant exception is thrown, the CLR automatically constructs an instance of the **RuntimeWrapped-Exception** class and initializes its private field to refer to the object that was actually thrown. In effect, the CLR now turns all non-CLS-compliant exceptions into CLS-compliant exceptions. Any code that now catches an **Exception** type will catch non-CLS-compliant exceptions, which fixes the potential security vulnerability problem.

Although the C# compiler allows developers to throw **Exception**-derived objects only, prior to C# version 2.0, the C# compiler did allow developers to catch non-CLS-compliant exceptions by using code like this:

```
private void SomeMethod() {
   try {
      // Inside the try block is where you put code requiring
      // graceful recovery or common cleanup operations.
   }
   catch (Exception e) {
      // Before C# 2.0, this block catches CLS-compliant exceptions only
      // In C# 2.0, this block catches CLS- & non-CLS- compliant exceptions
      throw; // Re-throws whatever got caught
   }
   catch {
      // In all versions of C#, this block catches
      // CLS- & non-CLS- compliant exceptions
      throw; // Re-throws whatever got caught
   }
}
```

Now, some developers were aware that the CLR supports both CLS- and non-CLS-compliant exceptions, and these developers might have written the two **catch** blocks (shown above) in order to catch both kinds of exceptions. If the above code is recompiled for CLR 2.0, the second **catch** block will never execute, and the C# compiler will indicate this by issuing a warning: "CS1058: A previous catch clause already catches all exceptions. All non-exceptions thrown will be wrapped in a System.Runtime.CompilerServices.RuntimeWrappedException."

There are two ways for developers to migrate code from an earlier version of the .NET Framework to version 2.0:

■ You can merge the code from the two **catch** blocks into a single **catch** block and delete one of the **catch** blocks.

■ You can tell the CLR that the code in your assembly wants to play by the old rules. That is, tell the CLR that your **catch (Exception)** blocks should not catch an instance of the new **RuntimeWrappedException** class. And instead, the CLR should unwrap the non-CLS-compliant object and call your code only if you have a **catch** block that doesn't specify any type at all. You tell the CLR that you want the old behavior by applying an instance of the **RuntimeCompatibilityAttribute** to your assembly like this:

```
using System.Runtime.CompilerServices;
[assembly:RuntimeCompatibility(WrapNonExceptionThrows = false)]
```

> **Note** This attribute has an assembly-wide impact. There is no way to mix wrapped and unwrapped exception styles in the same assembly. Be careful when adding new code (that expects the CLR to wrap exceptions) to an assembly containing old code (in which the CLR didn't wrap exceptions).

What Exactly Is an Exception?

Over the years, I've run into many developers who think an exception identifies something that rarely happens: *an exceptional event*. I always ask them to define *exceptional event*. They respond, "You know, something you don't expect to happen." Then they add, "If you're reading bytes from a file, eventually you'll reach the end of the file. So because you expect this, an exception shouldn't be thrown when you reach the end of the file. Instead, the **Read** method should return some special value when the end of the file is reached."

Here's my response: "I have an application that needs to read a 20-byte data structure from a file. However, for some reason, the file contains only 10 bytes. In this case, I'm not expecting to reach the end of the file while reading. But because I'll reach the end of the file prematurely, I'd expect an exception to be thrown. Wouldn't you?" In fact, most files contain structured data. It's rare for applications to read bytes from a file and process them one at a time until the end of the file is reached. For this reason, I think it makes more sense to have the **Read** method always throw an exception when attempting to read past the end of a file.

Important   Many developers are misguided by the term *exception handling*. These developers believe that the word *exception* is related to how *frequently* something happens. For example, a developer designing a file **Read** method is likely to say the following: "When reading from a file, you will eventually reach the end of its data. Since reaching the end will *always* happen, I'll design my **Read** method so that it reports the end by returning a special value; I won't have it throw an exception." The problem with this statement is that it is being made by the developer designing the **Read** method, not by the developer calling the **Read** method.

When designing the **Read** method, it is impossible for the developer to know all of the possible situations in which the method gets called. Therefore, the developer can't possibly know how *often* the caller of the **Read** method will attempt to read past the end of the file. In fact, since most files contain structured data, attempting to read past the end of a file is something that *rarely* happens.

Another common misconception is that an exception identifies an error. The term *error* implies that the programmer did something wrong. However, again, it isn't possible for the developer designing the **Read** method to know when the caller has called the method incorrectly for the application. Only the developer calling the method can determine this. Therefore, only the caller can decide if the results of the call indicate an error. So you should avoid thinking "I'll throw an exception here in my code to report an error." In fact, because exceptions don't necessarily indicate errors, I've avoided using the term *error handling* throughout this entire chapter (except for this sentence, of course).

The preceding note explained what "exception" does *not* mean. Now I'll describe what it *does* mean. When designing a type, you first imagine the various situations for how the type will be used. The type name is usually a noun such as **FileStream** or **StringBuilder**. Then you define the properties, methods, events, and so on for the type. The way you define these members (property data types, method parameters, return values, and so forth) becomes the programmatic interface for your type. These members indicate actions that can be performed by the type itself or on an instance of the type. These action members are usually verbs such as **Read**, **Write**, **Flush**, **Append**, **Insert**, **Remove**, etc.

When an action member cannot complete its task, the member should throw an exception. An exception means that an action member failed to complete the task it was supposed to perform as indicated by its name. Look at the following class definition:

```
internal class Account {
    public static void Transfer(Account from, Account to, Decimal amount) {
        ...
    }
}
```

The **Transfer** method accepts two **Account** objects and a **Decimal** value that identifies an amount of money to transfer between accounts. Obviously, the goal of the **Transfer** method is to subtract money from one account and add money to another. The **Transfer** method could fail for many reasons: the **from** or **to** argument might be **null**; the **from** or **to** argument might not refer to an open account; the **from** account might have insufficient funds; the **to** account might have so much money in it that adding more would cause it to overflow; or the amount argument might be **0**, negative, or have more than two digits after the decimal place.

When the **Transfer** method is called, its code must check for all of these possibilities, and if any of them are detected, it cannot transfer the money and should notify the caller that it failed by throwing an exception. In fact, notice that the **Transfer** method's return type is **void**. This is because the **Transfer** method has no meaningful value to return; if it returns at all, it was successful. If it fails, it throws a meaningful exception.

Calling a Method Could Always Result in Failure

When calling a method, there are many reasons why an exception might be thrown:

- If there is insufficient stack space, a StackOverflowException is thrown.
- If the assembly defining the type can't be found, a FileNotFoundException is thrown.
- If the method's IL code is not verifiable, a VerificationException is thrown.
- If there is insufficient memory to JIT compile the IL, an OutOfMemoryException is thrown.

The list goes on and on. The important point to take away from this section is that an exception can be thrown at any time. For example, imagine the following method:

```
private void InfiniteLoop() {
   while (true) ;
}
```

The loop in the preceding method could execute successfully 1000 times, but on the 1001st time, an exception could be thrown. How could this happen? Well, another thread could attempt to abort this thread by calling **Thread**'s **Abort** method. This causes the thread executing the infinite loop to be suspended and forced to throw a **Thread-AbortException**. In fact, in CLR-hosting scenarios such as Microsoft ASP.NET and Microsoft SQL Server, aborting threads is a fairly common occurrence.

The System.Exception Class

The common language runtime (CLR) allows an instance of any type to be thrown for an exception—from an **Int32** to a **string** and beyond. However, Microsoft decided against forcing all programming languages to throw and catch exceptions of any type. So Microsoft defined the **System.Exception** type and decreed that all CLS-compliant programming languages must be able to throw and catch exceptions whose type is derived from this type. Exception types that are derived from **System.Exception** are said to be CLS-compliant. C# and many other language compilers allow your code to throw only CLS-compliant exceptions.

The System.Exception type is a very simple type that contains the properties described in Table 19-1.

Table 19-1   Public Properties of the System.Exception Type

Property	Access	Type	Description
Message	Read-only	String	Contains helpful text indicating why the exception was thrown. The message is typically written to a log when a thrown exception is unhandled. Since end users do not see this message, the message should be as technical as possible so that developers viewing the log can use the information in the message to fix the code when producing a new version.
Data	Read-only	IDictionary	A reference to a collection of key-value pairs. Usually, the code throwing the exception adds entries to this collection prior to throwing it; code that catches the exception can query the entries and use the information in its exception-recovery processing.
Source	Read/write	String	Contains the name of the assembly that generated the exception.
StackTrace	Read-only	String	Contains the names and signatures of methods called that led up to the exception being thrown. This property is invaluable for debugging.
TargetSite	Read-only	MethodBase	Contains the method that threw the exception.
HelpLink	Read-only	String	Contains a URL (such as file://C:\MyApp\ Help.htm#MyExceptionHelp) to documentation that can help a user understand the exception. Keep in mind that sound programming and security practices prevent users from ever being able to see raw unhandled exceptions, so unless you are trying to convey information to other programmers, this property is seldom used.
InnerException	Read-only	Exception	Indicates the previous exception if the current exception were raised while handling an exception. This read-only property is usually **null**. The **Exception** type also offers a public **GetBaseException** method that traverses the linked list of inner exceptions and returns the originally thrown exception.

FCL-Defined Exception Classes

The Framework Class Library (FCL) defines many exception types (all ultimately derived from **System.Exception**). The following hierarchy shows the exception types defined in the MSCorLib.dll assembly; other assemblies define even more exception types. (The application used to obtain this hierarchy is shown in Chapter 22, "Assembly Loading and Reflection.")

```
System.Exception
   System.ApplicationException
      System.Reflection.InvalidFilterCriteriaException
      System.Reflection.TargetException
```

```
        System.Reflection.TargetInvocationException
        System.Reflection.TargetParameterCountException
        System.Threading.WaitHandleCannotBeOpenedException
   System.IO.IsolatedStorage.IsolatedStorageException
   System.Runtime.CompilerServices.RuntimeWrappedException
   System.SystemException
       System.AccessViolationException
       System.AppDomainUnloadedException
       System.ArgumentException
           System.ArgumentNullException
           System.ArgumentOutOfRangeException
           System.DuplicateWaitObjectException
           System.Text.DecoderFallbackException
           System.Text.EncoderFallbackException
       System.ArithmeticException
           System.DivideByZeroException
           System.NotFiniteNumberException
           System.OverflowException
       System.ArrayTypeMismatchException
       System.BadImageFormatException
       System.CannotUnloadAppDomainException
       System.Collections.Generic.KeyNotFoundException
       System.ContextMarshalException
       System.DataMisalignedException
       System.ExecutionEngineException
       System.FormatException
           System.Reflection.CustomAttributeFormatException
       System.IndexOutOfRangeException
       System.InvalidCastException
       System.InvalidOperationException
           System.ObjectDisposedException
       System.InvalidProgramException
       System.IO.IOException
           System.IO.DirectoryNotFoundException
           System.IO.DriveNotFoundException
           System.IO.EndOfStreamException
           System.IO.FileLoadException
           System.IO.FileNotFoundException
           System.IO.PathTooLongException
       System.MemberAccessException
           System.FieldAccessException
           System.MethodAccessException
           System.MissingMemberException
               System.MissingFieldException
               System.MissingMethodException
       System.MulticastNotSupportedException
       System.NotImplementedException
       System.NotSupportedException
           System.PlatformNotSupportedException
       System.NullReferenceException
       System.OperationCanceledException
       System.OutOfMemoryException
           System.InsufficientMemoryException
       System.RankException
       System.Reflection.AmbiguousMatchException
       System.Reflection.ReflectionTypeLoadException
```

```
System.Resources.MissingManifestResourceException
System.Resources.MissingSatelliteAssemblyException
System.Runtime.InteropServices.ExternalException
    System.Runtime.InteropServices.COMException
    System.Runtime.InteropServices.SEHException
System.Runtime.InteropServices.InvalidComObjectException
System.Runtime.InteropServices.InvalidOleVariantTypeException
System.Runtime.InteropServices.MarshalDirectiveException
System.Runtime.InteropServices.SafeArrayRankMismatchException
System.Runtime.InteropServices.SafeArrayTypeMismatchException
System.Runtime.Remoting.RemotingException
    System.Runtime.Remoting.RemotingTimeoutException
System.Runtime.Remoting.ServerException
System.Runtime.Serialization.SerializationException
System.Security.Cryptography.CryptographicException
System.Security.Cryptography.CryptographicUnexpectedOperationException
System.Security.HostProtectionException
System.Security.Policy.PolicyException
System.Security.Principal.IdentityNotMappedException
System.Security.SecurityException
System.Security.VerificationException
System.Security.XmlSyntaxException
System.StackOverflowException
System.Threading.AbandonedMutexException
System.Threading.SynchronizationLockException
System.Threading.ThreadAbortException
System.Threading.ThreadInterruptedException
System.Threading.ThreadStartException
System.Threading.ThreadStateException
System.TimeoutException
System.TypeInitializationException
System.TypeLoadException
    System.DllNotFoundException
    System.EntryPointNotFoundException
System.TypeUnloadedException
System.UnauthorizedAccessException
    System.Security.AccessControl.PrivilegeNotHeldException
```

Microsoft's original idea was that `System.Exception` would be the base type for all exceptions and that two other types, `System.SystemException` and `System.ApplicationException`, would be the only two types immediately derived from `Exception`. Furthermore, exceptions thrown by the CLR would be derived from `SystemException`, and all application-thrown exceptions would be derived from `ApplicationException`. This way, developers could write a **catch** block that catches all CLR-thrown exceptions or all application-thrown exceptions.

However, as you can see, this rule was not followed very well; some exception types are immediately derived from `Exception` (`IsolatedStorageException`), some CLR-thrown exceptions are derived from `ApplicationException` (`TargetInvocationException`), and some application-thrown exceptions are derived from `SystemException` (`FormatException`). So it is all a big mess, and the result is that the `SystemException` and `ApplicationException` types have no special meaning at all. At this point, Microsoft would like to remove them from the exception class hierarchy, but they can't because it would break any code that already references these two types.

Throwing an Exception

When implementing your own methods, you should throw an exception when the method cannot complete its task as indicated by its name. When you want to throw an exception, there are two issues that you really need to think about and consider:

- **What `Exception`-derived type are you going to throw?**   You really want to select a type that is meaningful here. Consider the code that is higher up the call stack and how that code might want to determine that a method failed in order to execute some graceful recovery code. You can use a type that is already defined in the FCL, but there may not be one in the FCL that matches your exact semantics. So you'll probably need to define your own type, derived directly from `System.Exception`. If you want to define an exception type hierarchy, it is highly recommended that the hierarchy be shallow and wide in order to create as few base classes as possible. The reason is that base classes act as a way of treating lots of errors as one error, and this is usually dangerous. Along these lines, you should never throw a `System.Exception` type, and you should use extreme caution if you do throw any other base class exception type.

- **What string message are you going to pass to the exception type's constructor?**   When you throw an exception, you should include a string message with detailed information indicating why the method couldn't complete its task. If the exception is caught and handled, this string message is not seen. However, if the exception becomes an unhandled exception, this message is usually logged. An unhandled exception indicates a true bug in the application, and a developer must get involved to fix the bug. An end user will not have the source code or the ability to fix the code and re-compile it. In fact, this string message should not be shown to an end user. So these string messages can be very technically detailed and as geeky as is necessary to help developers fix their code. Furthermore, since all developers have to speak English (at least to some degree, since programming languages and the FCL classes and methods are in English), there is usually no need to localize exception string messages. However, you may want to localize the strings if you are building a class library that will be used by developers who speak different languages. Microsoft localizes the exception messages thrown by the FCL, since developers all over the world will be using this class library.

Defining Your Own Exception Class

Let's say that you're defining a method that receives a reference to an object whose type must implement the `IFormattable` and `IComparable` interfaces. You might implement the method like this:

```
internal sealed class SomeType {
    public void SomeMethod(Object o) {
        if (!((o is IFormattable) && (o is IComparable))) {
            throw new MissingInterfaceException(...);
        }
        // Code that operates on o goes here.
        ...
    }
}
```

Because the FCL doesn't define an appropriate exception type, you must define the `Missing-InterfaceException` type yourself. Note that by convention, the name of an exception type should end with `Exception`. When defining this type, you must decide what its base type will be. Should you choose `Exception`, `ArgumentException`, or a different type entirely? I've spent years thinking about this question, but unfortunately, I can't come up with a good rule of thumb to offer you because of the normal limitations intrinsic in any inheritance-based object model.

If you derive `MissingInterfaceException` from `ArgumentException`, any existing code that's already catching `ArgumentException` will catch your new exception, too. In some ways, this is a feature, and in some ways, this is a bug. It's a feature because any code that wants to catch any kind of argument exception (via `ArgumentException`) now catches this new kind of argument exception (`MissingInterfaceException`) automatically. It's a bug because a `Missing-InterfaceException` identifies a new event that wasn't anticipated when code was written to catch an `ArgumentException`. When you define the `MissingInterfaceException` type, you might think it's so similar to an `ArgumentException` that it should be handled the same way. However, this unanticipated relationship might cause unpredictable behavior.

On the other hand, if you derive `MissingInterfaceException` directly from `Exception`, the code throws a new type that the application couldn't have known about. Most likely, this will become an unhandled exception that causes the application to terminate. I could easily consider this as desired behavior because a method can't complete its task, and the application never considered a remedy for it. Catching this new exception, swallowing it, and continuing execution might cause the application to run with unpredictable results and security holes.

Answering questions such as these is one of the reasons that application design is more of an art form than a science. When defining a new exception type, carefully consider how application code will catch your type (or base types of your type), and then choose a base type that has the least negative effect on your callers.

When defining your own exception types, feel free to define your own sub-hierarchies, if they're applicable to what you're doing. You can define them directly from `Exception` or from some other base type. Again, just make sure that where you're putting the sub-hierarchy types makes sense to your callers. If you define an exception type that's not going to be the base of other exception types, mark the type as `sealed`.

The `Exception` base type defines four standard constructors:

- A public parameterless (default) constructor that creates an instance of the type and sets all fields and properties to default values.

- A public constructor that takes a `String` that creates an instance of the type and sets a specific message.

- A public constructor that takes a `String` and an instance of an `Exception`-derived type that creates an instance of the type and sets a specific message and an inner exception.

■ A protected constructor that takes a **SerializationInfo** and a **StreamingContext** that deserializes instances of the **Exception**-derived object. Note that this method should be **private**
if the **Exception**-derived type is sealed, and make sure that this constructor calls the same
constructor in the base class so that the base class's fields are deserialized correctly.

When defining your own exception type, your type should implement a set of four matching
constructors with each one calling the base type's corresponding constructor. Of course, your
exception type will inherit all of the fields and properties defined by **Exception**. In addition,
you can add fields and properties of your own to your type. For example, when the **System
.ArgumentException** type was defined, it added a virtual **String** property called **ParamName**
(in addition to everything it inherited from the **Exception** type). The **ArgumentException** type
also defines two new constructors (in addition to the four standard constructors) that take an
extra **String** parameter so that the **ParamName** property can be initialized to identify the name
of the parameter that violated the expectation of the method.

When an **ArgumentException** is caught, the **ParamName** property can be read to determine
exactly which parameter caused the problem. Let me tell you, this is incredibly handy when
you're trying to debug an application! If you do add fields to your exception type, make sure
that you define some additional constructors that will initialize your new fields. Also, be sure
that you define properties or other members that can return the fields' value to application
code that catches your exception type.

Exception-derived types should always be serializable so that the exception object can be marshaled across an AppDomain boundary. Making an exception type serializable also allows it
to persist in a log or a database. To make your exception type serializable, you must take two
steps: first, apply the **[Serializable]** custom attribute to the type, and second, implement
the **ISerializable** interface along with its **GetObjectData** method (that has a **Security-
Permission** attribute on it) and a constructor, both of which take a **SerializationInfo** and
a **StreamingContext** parameter. Note that if the class is **sealed**, the constructor should be
private; otherwise, the constructor should be **protected**. The following code shows how to
properly define your own exception type:

```
using System;
using System.Text;
using System.Runtime.Serialization;
using System.Security.Permissions;


// Allow instances of DiskFullException to be serialized
[Serializable]
public sealed class DiskFullException : Exception, ISerializable {
    // Define a private field
    private String m_diskpath;

    // Define a read-only property that returns the field
    public String DiskPath { get { return m_diskpath; } }
```

```csharp
   // Override the Message property to include our field (if set)
   public override String Message {
      get {
         if (m_diskpath == null) return base.Message;
         StringBuilder msg = new StringBuilder(base.Message);
         msg.AppendFormat(
            " (DiskPath={0}){1}",
            m_diskpath, Environment.NewLine);
         return msg.ToString();
      }
   }


   // The three public constructors
   public DiskFullException() : base() {  }
   public DiskFullException(String message) : base(message) { }
   public DiskFullException(String message, Exception innerException)
      : base(message, innerException) { }

   // Define additional constructors that set the field
   public DiskFullException(String message, String diskpath)
      : this(message) { m_diskpath = diskpath; }

   public DiskFullException(String message, String diskpath, Exception innerException)
      : this(message, innerException) { m_diskpath = diskpath; }

   // The one constructor for deserialization
   // Since this class is sealed, this constructor is private
   // If this class were not sealed, this constructor should be protected
   private DiskFullException(SerializationInfo info, StreamingContext context)
      : base(info, context) {
      // Deserialize each field
      m_diskpath = info.GetString("DiskPath");
   }

   // The method for serialization; the SecurityPermission ensures that
   // callers are allowed to obtain the internal state of this object
   [SecurityPermission(SecurityAction.Demand, SerializationFormatter = true)]
   public override void GetObjectData(
      SerializationInfo info, StreamingContext context) {
      // Let the base type serialize its fields
      base.GetObjectData(info, context);

      // Serialize this type's fields
      info.AddValue("DiskPath", m_diskpath);
   }
}
```

How to Use Exceptions Properly

Understanding the exception mechanism is certainly important. It is equally important to understand how to use exceptions wisely. All too often I see library developers catching all kinds of exceptions, preventing the application developer from knowing that a problem occurred. In this section, I offer some guidelines for developers to be aware of when using exceptions.

> **Important**   If you're a *class library developer* developing types that will be used by other developers, take these guidelines very seriously. You have a huge responsibility: you're trying to design the type's interface so that it makes sense for a wide variety of applications. Remember that you don't have intimate knowledge of the code that you're calling back (via delegates, virtual methods, or interface methods). And you don't know which code is calling you. It's not feasible to anticipate every situation in which your type will be used, so don't make any policy decisions. Your code must not decide what conditions constitute an error; let the caller make that decision. If you follow the guidelines in this chapter, application developers will not have a difficult time using the types in your class library.
>
> If you're an *application developer*, define whatever policy you think is appropriate. Following the design guidelines in this chapter will help you discover problems in your code before it is released, allowing you to fix them and make your application more robust. However, feel free to diverge from these guidelines after careful consideration. You get to set the policy. For example, application code can get more aggressive about catching exceptions.

Validate Your Method's Arguments

For types that are part of a reusable class library, it is highly recommended that public types have their public and protected methods validate their arguments before the method attempts to perform any operation. There are two reasons for this. First, it allows developers calling the method to know if they are calling the method correctly. Second, if all the arguments are correct, it is much more likely for the method to run to completion and return instead of throwing an exception. This also means that it is more likely that objects will remain in a consistent state.

For example, recall the **Account** type's public, static **Transfer** method shown on page 428. This method transfers money from one account to another. If this method doesn't validate its arguments right away, the method could subtract money from the **from** account successfully, and then discover that the **to** account argument is **null**. At this point, the method would throw an exception because it cannot transfer the money. However, the method must also add the money back to the **from** account. If it fails to do this, the state of the **from** account is incorrect. Having a method validate its arguments early allows for easier programming because the developer does not have to think about and write code to compensate for an aborted transaction or other complex conditions.

When you implement a method in a reusable class, the method should validate its arguments and for any invalid argument, an exception derived from **System.ArgumentException** should be thrown. The most useful exception classes derived from **System.ArgumentException** are **System.ArgumentNullException**, **System.ArgumentOutOfRangeException**, and **System.DuplicateWaitObjectException**. If none of these exceptions works for you, you can either define your own exception type derived from **ArgumentException**, or you can simply throw **ArgumentException** itself. Note that **System.ComponentModel.InvalidEnumArgumentException** is also derived from **ArgumentException**; however, Microsoft considers this exception type to be a mistake and is discouraging its use because it is in an unusual namespace, and it is defined in System.dll instead of in MSCorLib.dll.

> **Note**   If your methods validate their arguments upon entry, you could choose to use fewer `Debug.Assert` calls in your code. You should consider an assert to be a development tool that you use to validate some assumption in your own assembly that you always expect to be true. Using an assert can help you detect some programmer errors at development time, allowing you to correct the source code, rebuild, and test the new version. There never is code in place to catch or recover from a failed assertion. Remember that `Debug.Assert` calls vanish out of the code for a release build, whereas exceptions will still get thrown. For this and other reasons, an assembly should not use `Debug.Assert` calls to ensure that code in another assembly is calling a method correctly; use exceptions for this. However, you may want to include calls to `Debug.Assert` in addition to throwing an exception because a failed assert allows you to connect the debugger immediately to the failed code, allowing you to examine argument and local variables easily.

While we're on the subject of argument validation, I'd like to point out something very important. As you know, a method can be declared using both value type and reference type parameters. When value type arguments are passed, the value of the argument cannot be changed by code outside of the method itself. On the other hand, when reference type arguments are passed to a method, the actual object referred to by the argument can be changed outside the method (this does not apply to **String** objects since strings are immutable). This can, for example, happen in a multithreaded application.

To build a secure and robust class library, methods that accept mutable reference types should actually make a copy of these arguments, validate the copy, and then use the copy inside the method itself. This ensures that the method operates on immutable input. The following code demonstrates the potential problem:

```
#define BADCODE

using System;
using System.Threading;

public static class Program {
    public static void Main() {
        Int32[] denominators = { 1, 2, 3 };

        // Have another thread do the work
        ThreadPool.QueueUserWorkItem(Divide100By, denominators);

        // DEMO: Give Divide100By a chance to validate the array elements
        Thread.Sleep(50);

        // Make an array element no longer valid for the Divide100By method
        denominators[2] = 0;

        Console.WriteLine("Press <Enter> when you see the results.");
        Console.ReadLine();
    }
```

```
        private static void Divide100By(Object o) {

#if BADCODE
        // This code demonstrates the problem
        Int32[] denominators = (Int32[]) o;
#else
        // This code fixes the problem by making a copy of the array
        // The copy is validated and used throughout the rest of the method
        Int32[] denominatorsInput = (Int32[]) o;
        Int32[] denominators = new Int32[denominatorsInput.Length];
        Array.Copy(denominatorsInput, denominators, denominators.Length);
#endif

        // Validate all the elements in the array argument
        for (Int32 index = 0; index < denominators.Length; index++) {
            if (denominators[index] == 0)
                throw new ArgumentOutOfRangeException("denominators",
                    String.Format("Index {0} contains 0", index));
        }
        Console.WriteLine(
            "All denominators are valid; DivideByZeroException can't occur.");

        // DEMO: Give Main a chance to invalidate an array element
        Thread.Sleep(100);

        // All elements are valid, now do the work
        for (Int32 index = 0; index < denominators.Length; index++) {
            Console.WriteLine("100 / {0} = {1}",
                denominators[index], 100 / denominators[index]);
        }
    }
}
```

When you build and run the code above, you get the following output:

```
All denominators are valid; DivideByZeroException can't occur.
Press <Enter> when you see the results.
100 / 1 = 100
100 / 2 = 50

Unhandled Exception: System.DivideByZeroException: Attempted to divide by zero.
    at Program.Divide100By(Object o) in C:\...\ArgumentValidation.cs:line 50
    at System.Threading._ThreadPoolWaitCallback.WaitCallback_Context(Object state)
    at System.Threading.ExecutionContext.Run(ExecutionContext executionContext, ContextCall
back callback, Object state)
    at System.Threading._ThreadPoolWaitCallback.PerformWaitCallback(Object state)
```

As you can see, the elements in the array were validated correctly, so the method began operating on its input. But the **Main** method modified the last element of the array after the array was validated, so **Divide100By** ends up throwing a **DivideByZeroException** even though that was supposedly impossible!

The code above includes the code necessary to fix this problem—just delete the line that defines the **BADCODE** symbol. Deleting this line causes **Divide100By** to make a copy of the array;

the copy is then validated and used throughout the rest of the method. Now, a **DivideBy-ZeroException** will really not occur. When you build and run the version of the code without **BADCODE** defined, you get the following output:

```
All denominators are valid; DivideByZeroException can't occur.
Press <Enter> when you see the results.
100 / 1 = 100
100 / 2 = 50
100 / 3 = 33
```

Use **finally** Blocks Liberally

I think **finally** blocks are awesome! They allow you to specify a block of code that's guaranteed to execute no matter what kind of exception the thread throws. You should use **finally** blocks to clean up from any operation that successfully started before returning to your caller or allowing code following the **finally** block to execute. You also frequently use **finally** blocks to explicitly dispose of any objects to avoid resource leaking. Here's an example that has all cleanup code (closing the file) in a **finally** block:

```csharp
using System;
using System.IO;

public sealed class SomeType {
   private void SomeMethod() {

      // Open a file.
      FileStream fs = new FileStream(@"C:\Data.bin ", FileMode.Open);
      try {
         // Display 100 divided by the first byte in the file.
         Console.WriteLine(100 / fs.ReadByte());
      }
      finally {
         // Put cleanup code in a finally block to ensure that
         // the file gets closed regardless of whether or not an
         // exception occurs (for example, the first byte was 0).
         fs.Close();
      }
   }
}
```

Ensuring that cleanup code always executes is so important that many programming languages offer constructs that make writing cleanup code easier. For example, the C# language provides the **lock** and **using** statements. These statements provide the developer with a simple syntax that causes the compiler to automatically generate **try** and **finally** blocks, with the cleanup code placed inside the **finally** block. For example, the following C# code takes advantage of the **using** statement. This code is shorter than the code shown in the previous example, but the code that the compiler generates is identical to the code generated in the previous example.

```
using System;
using System.IO;

internal sealed class SomeType {
   private void SomeMethod() {

      // Open a file.
      using (FileStream fs =
         new FileStream(@"C:\Data.bin", FileMode.Open)) {

         // Display 100 divided by the first byte in the file.
         Console.WriteLine(100 / fs.ReadByte());
      }
   }
}
```

For more about the **using** statement, see Chapter 20, "Automatic Memory Management (Garbage Collection)"; and for more about the **lock** statement, see Chapter 24, "Thread Synchronization."

Don't Catch Everything

A ubiquitous mistake made by developers who have not been properly trained on the proper use of exceptions is to use **catch** blocks too often and improperly. When you catch an exception, you're stating that you expected this exception, you understand why it occurred, and you know how to deal with it. In other words, you're defining a policy for the application.

All too often, I see code like this:

```
try {
   // try to execute code that the programmer knows might fail...
}
catch (Exception) {
   ...
}
```

This code indicates that it was expecting *any* and *all* exceptions and knows how to recover from *any* and *all* situations. How can this possibly be? A type that's part of a class library should *never, ever, under any circumstance* catch and swallow all exceptions because there is no way for the type to know exactly how the application intends to respond to an exception. In addition, the type will frequently call out to application code via a delegate or a virtual method. If the application code throws an exception, another part of the application is probably expecting to catch this exception. The exception should be allowed to filter its way up the call stack and let the application code handle the exception as it sees fit.

In addition, it is possible that an exception was thrown because some object was in a bad state. If library code catches and swallows the exception, the program continues running with unpredictable results and with potential security vulnerabilities! It is better for the exception to be unhandled and for the application to terminate. (I'll discuss unhandled exceptions later in this chapter.) In fact, most unhandled exceptions will be discovered during testing of your code. To fix these unhandled exceptions, you will either modify the code to look for a specific exception, or you will rewrite the code to eliminate the conditions that cause the exception to be thrown. The final version of the code that will be running in a production environment should see very few (if any) unhandled exceptions and will be extremely robust.

> **Note** In some cases, a method that can't complete its task will detect that some object's state has been corrupted and cannot be restored. Allowing the application to continue running might result in unpredictable behavior or security vulnerabilities. When this situation is detected, that method should not throw an exception; instead, it should force the process to terminate immediately by calling `System.Environment`'s `FailFast` method.

By the way, it *is* OK to catch `System.Exception` and execute some code inside the **catch** block's braces as long as you re-throw the exception at the bottom of that code. Catching `System.Exception` and swallowing the exception (not re-throwing it) should never be done because it results in hiding failures that allow the application to run with unpredictable results and potential security vulnerabilities. Microsoft's FxCop tool will flag any code that contains a **catch** **(Exception)** block unless there is a **throw** statement included in the block's code. The "Backing Out of a Partially Completed Operation When an Unrecoverable Exception Occurs" section coming shortly in this chapter will discuss this pattern.

Finally, it is OK to catch an exception occurring in one thread and re-throw the exception in another thread. The Asynchronous Programming Model (discussed in Chapter 23, "Performing Asynchronous Operations") supports this. For example, if a thread pool thread executes code that throws an exception, the CLR catches and swallows the exception and allows the thread to return to the thread pool. Later, some thread should call an **End***Xxx* method to determine the result of the asynchronous operation. The **End***Xxx* method will throw the same exception object that was thrown by the thread pool thread that did the actual work. In this scenario, the exception is being swallowed by the first thread; however, the exception is being re-thrown by the thread that called the **End***Xxx* method, so it is not being hidden from the application.

Gracefully Recovering from an Exception

Sometimes you call a method knowing in advance some of the exceptions that the method might throw. Because you expect these exceptions, you might want to have some code that allows your application to recover gracefully from the situation and continue running. Here's an example in pseudocode:

```
public String CalculateSpreadsheetCell(Int32 row, Int32 column) {
   String result;
   try {
      result = /* Code to calculate value of a spreadsheet's cell */
   }
```

```
    catch (DivideByZeroException) {
        result = "Can't show value: Divide by zero";
    }
    catch (OverflowException) {
        result = "Can't show value: Too big";
    }
    return result;
}
```

This pseudocode calculates the contents of a cell in a spreadsheet and returns a string representing the value back to the caller so that the caller can display the string in the application's window. However, a cell's contents might be the result of dividing one cell by another cell. If the cell containing the denominator contains 0, the CLR will throw a **DivideByZeroException** object. In this case, the method catches this specific exception and returns a special string that will be displayed to the user. Similarly, a cell's contents might be the result of multiplying one cell by another. If the multiplied value doesn't fit in the number of bits allowed, the CLR will throw an **OverflowException** object, and again, a special string will be displayed to the user.

When you catch specific exceptions, fully understand the circumstances that cause the exception to be thrown, and know what exception types are derived from the exception type you're catching. Don't catch and handle **System.Exception** (without re-throwing) because it's not feasible for you to know all of the possible exceptions that could be thrown within your **try** block (especially if you consider the **OutOfMemoryException** or the **StackOverflowException**, to name two).

Backing Out of a Partially Completed Operation When an Unrecoverable Exception Occurs

Usually, methods call several other methods to perform a single abstract operation. Some of the individual methods might complete successfully, and some might not. For example, let's say that you're serializing a set of objects to a disk file. After serializing 10 objects, an exception is thrown. (Perhaps the disk is full or the next object to be serialized isn't marked with the **Serializable** custom attribute.) At this point, the exception should filter up to the caller, but what about the state of the disk file? The file is now corrupt because it contains a partially serialized object graph. It would be great if the application could back out of the partially completed operation so that the file would be in the state it was in before any objects were serialized into it. The following code demonstrates the correct way to implement this:

```
public void SerializeObjectGraph(FileStream fs,
    IFormatter formatter, Object rootObj) {

    // Save the current position of the file.
    Int64 beforeSerialization = fs.Position;
```

```
try {
   // Attempt to serialize the object graph to the file.
   formatter.Serialize(fs, rootObj);
}
catch {  // Catch any and all exceptions.
   // If ANYTHING goes wrong, reset the file back to a good state.
   fs.Position = beforeSerialization;

   // Truncate the file.
   fs.SetLength(fs.Position);

   // NOTE: The preceding code isn't in a finally block because
   // the stream should be reset only when serialization fails.

   // Let the caller(s) know what happened by
   // re-throwing the SAME exception.
   throw;
}
}
```

To properly back out of the partially completed operation, write code that catches all exceptions. Yes, catch *all* exceptions here because you don't care what kind of error occurred; you need to put your data structures back into a consistent state. After you've caught and handled the exception, don't swallow it—let the caller know that the exception occurred. You do this by re-throwing the same exception. In fact, C# and many other languages make this easy. Just use C#'s **throw** keyword without specifying anything after **throw**, as shown in the previous code.

Notice that the **catch** block in the previous example doesn't specify any exception type because I want to catch any and all exceptions. In addition, the code in the **catch** block doesn't need to know exactly what kind of exception was thrown, just that something went wrong. Fortunately, C# lets me do this easily just by not specifying any exception type and by making the **throw** statement re-throw whatever object is caught.

Hiding an Implementation Detail to Maintain a "Contract"

In some situations, you might find it useful to catch one exception and re-throw a different exception. Here's an example:

```
public Int32 SomeMethod(Int32 x){
   try {
      return 100 / x;
   }
   catch (DivideByZeroException e) {
      throw new ArgumentOutOfRangeException("x can't be 0", e);
   }
}
```

When **SomeMethod** is called, the caller passes in an **Int32** value, and the method returns 100 divided by this value. Upon entry into this public method, code could check to see whether **x** is **0**, and if it is, throw an **ArgumentOutOfRangeException** exception. This check would be performed every time, and because there is an implicit assumption that **x** is rarely **0**, the check would cause an unnecessary performance hit. The better performing strategy in the **SomeMethod** example assumes that **x** is not **0** and attempts to perform the division. In the less likely circumstance in which **x** does happen to be **0**, the specific **DivideByZeroException** exception is caught and is re-thrown as an **ArgumentOutOfRangeException** exception. By catching one exception and throwing another exception, **SomeMethod** is maintaining its contract with its callers. Note that the **DivideByZeroException** exception is set as the **ArgumentOutOfRangeException**'s **InnerException** property via the constructor's second argument. This additional information can be handy in debugging scenarios because it allows the programmer to know which exception actually occurred.

This technique results in catches similar to those discussed in the earlier section "Gracefully Recovering from an Exception" You catch specific exceptions, you fully understand the circumstances that cause the exception to be thrown, and you know what exception types are derived from the exception type you're catching.

Again, class library developers shouldn't catch **System.Exception** and other base class exceptions. Doing so means that you're converting all specific exception types into a single exception type. It discards all meaningful information (the type of the exception) and throws a single exception type that doesn't contain any useful information about what really happened. Without this information, it's much harder for code higher up the call stack to catch and handle a specific exception. Give the code higher up the call stack a chance to catch **System .Exception** or some other exception that's a base type for more specific exceptions.

Basically, the only reason to catch an exception and re-throw a different exception is to maintain the meaning of a method's contract. Also, the new exception type you throw should be a specific exception (an exception that's not used as the base type of any other exception type). Imagine a **PhoneBook** type that defines a method that looks up a phone number from a name, as shown in the following pseudocode:

```
internal sealed class PhoneBook {
    private String m_pathname;  // pathname of file containing the address book

    // Other methods go here.

    public String GetPhoneNumber(String name) {
        String phone;
        FileStream fs = null;
        try {
            fs = new FileStream(m_pathname, FileMode.Open);
            (Code to read from fs until name is found)
            phone = /* the phone # found */
        }
        catch (FileNotFoundException e) {
            // Throw a different exception containing the name, and
            // set the originating exception as the inner exception.
            throw new NameNotFoundException(name, e);
        }
```

```
        catch (IOException e) {
           // Throw a different exception containing the name, and
           // set the originating exception as the inner exception.
           throw new NameNotFoundException(name, e);
        }
        finally {
           if (fs != null) fs.Close();
        }
        return phone;
     }
}
```

The phone book data is obtained from a file (versus a network connection or database). However, the user of the **PhoneBook** type doesn't know this because this is an implementation detail that could change in the future. So if the file isn't found or can't be read for any reason, the caller would see a **FileNotFoundException** or **IOException**, which wouldn't be anticipated. In other words, the file's existence and ability to be read is not part of the method's implied contract: there is no way the caller could have guessed this. So the **GetPhoneNumber** method catches these two exception types and throws a new **NameNotFoundException**.

Throwing an exception still lets the caller know that the method cannot complete its task, and the **NameNotFoundException** type gives the caller an abstracted view as to why. Setting the inner exception to **FileNotFoundException** or **IOException** is important so that the real cause of the exception isn't lost. Besides, knowing what caused the exception could be useful to the developer of the **PhoneBook** type and possibly to a developer using the **PhoneBook** type.

> **Important**   When you use this technique, you are lying to callers about two things. First, you are lying about what actually went wrong. In my example, a file was not found but I'm reporting that a name was not found. Second, you are lying about where the failure occurred. If the **FileNotFoundException** were allowed to propagate up the call stack, its **StackTrace** property would reflect that the error occurred inside **FileStream**'s constructor. But when I swallow this exception and throw a new **NameNotFoundException**, the stack trace will indicate that the error occurred inside the **catch** block, several lines away from where the real exception was thrown. This can make debugging very difficult, so therefore, this technique should be used with great care.

Now let's say that the **PhoneBook** type was implemented a little differently. Assume that the type offers a public **PhoneBookPathname** property that allows the user to set or get the pathname of the file in which to look up a phone number. Because the user is aware of the fact that the phone book data comes from a file, I would modify the **GetPhoneNumber** method so that it doesn't catch any exceptions; instead, I let whatever exception is thrown propagate out of the method. Note that I'm not changing any parameters of the **GetPhoneNumber** method, but I am changing how it's abstracted to users of the **PhoneBook** type. Users now expect a path to be part of the **PhoneBook**'s contract.

Performance Considerations

The developer community actively debates the performance of exception handling. My experience is that the benefit of exception handling far outweighs any performance penalties. In this section, I'll address some of the performance issues related to exception handling.

It's difficult to compare performance between exception handling and the more conventional means of reporting exceptions (such as **HRESULT**s, special return codes, and so forth). If you write code to check the return value of every method call and filter the return value up to your own callers, your application's performance will be seriously affected. But performance aside, the amount of additional coding you must do and the potential for mistakes is incredibly high when you write code to check the return value of every method. Exception handling is a much better alternative.

Unmanaged C++ compilers must generate code to track which objects have been constructed successfully. The compiler must also generate code that, when an exception is caught, calls the destructor of each successfully constructed object. It's great that the compiler takes on this burden, but it generates a lot of bookkeeping code in your application, adversely affecting code size and execution time.

On the other hand, managed compilers have it much easier because managed objects are allocated in the managed heap, which is monitored by the garbage collector (GC). If an object is successfully constructed and an exception is thrown, the GC will eventually free the object's memory. Compilers don't need to emit any bookkeeping code to track which objects are constructed successfully and don't need to ensure that a destructor has been called. Compared to unmanaged C++, this means that less code is generated by the compiler, and less code has to execute at run time, resulting in better performance for your application.

Over the years, I've used exception handling in different languages, different operating systems, and different CPU architectures. In each case, exception handling is implemented differently with each implementation having its pros and cons with respect to performance. Some implementations compile exception handling constructs directly into a method, whereas other implementations store information related to exception handling in a data table associated with the method—this table is accessed only if an exception is thrown. Some compilers can't inline methods that contain exception handlers, and some compilers won't enregister variables if the method contains exception handlers.

The point is that you can't determine how much additional overhead is added to an application when using exception handling. In the managed world, it's even more difficult to tell because your assembly's code can run on any platform that supports the .NET Framework. So the code produced by the JIT compiler to manage exception handling when your assembly is running on an x86 machine will be very different from the code produced by the JIT compiler when your code is running on an IA64 processor or the code produced by the .NET Compact Framework's JIT compiler.

Actually, I've been able to test some of my own code with a few different JIT compilers that Microsoft has internally, and the difference in performance that I've observed has been quite dramatic and surprising. The point is that you must test your code on the various platforms that you expect your users to run on, and make changes accordingly. Again, I wouldn't worry about the performance of using exception handling; as I've said, the benefits far outweigh any negative performance impact.

If you're interested in seeing how exception handling impacts the performance of your code, you can use PerfMon.exe or the System Monitor ActiveX control that comes with Windows. The screen in Figure 19-1 shows the exception-related counters that are installed along with the .NET Framework.

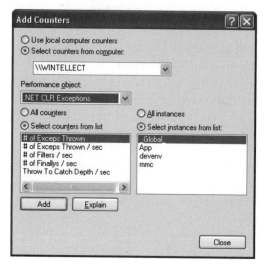

Figure 19-1   PerfMon.exe showing the .NET CLR exception counters

Occasionally, you come across a method that you call frequently that has a high failure rate. In this situation, the performance hit of having exceptions thrown can be intolerable. For example, Microsoft heard back from several customers who were calling **Int32**'s **Parse** method, frequently passing in data entered from an end user that could not be parsed. Since **Parse** was called frequently, the performance hit of throwing and catching the exceptions was taking a large toll on the application's overall performance.

To address customers' concerns and to keep with all the guidelines described in this chapter, Microsoft added new methods to the **Int32** class. These new methods are called **TryParse**, and their signatures look like this:

```
public static Boolean TryParse(String s, out Int32 result) { … }
public static Boolean TryParse(String s, NumberStyles styles,
    IFormatProvider, provider, out Int32 result) { … }
```

You'll notice that these methods return a **Boolean** that indicates whether the **string** passed in contains characters that can be parsed into an **Int32**. These methods also return an output parameter named **result**. If the methods return **true**, **result** will contain the result of parsing the string into a 32-bit integer. If the methods return **false**, **result** will contain **0**, but you really shouldn't execute any code that looks at it anyway.

One thing I want to make absolutely clear: A **Try***Xxx* method's **Boolean** return value returns **false** to indicate one and only one type of failure. The method should still throw exceptions for any other type of failure. For example, **Int32**'s **TryParse** throws an **ArgumentException** if the styles argument is not valid, and it is certainly still possible to have an **OutOfMemory-Exception** thrown when calling **TryParse**.

I also want to make it clear that object-oriented programming allows programmers to be productive. One way that it does this is by not exposing error codes in a type's members. In other words, constructors, methods, properties, etc. are all defined with the idea that calling them won't fail. And, if defined correctly, for most uses of a member, it will not fail, and there will be no performance hit because an exception will not be thrown.

When defining types and their members, you should define the members so that it is unlikely that they will fail for the common scenarios in which you expect your types to be used. If you later hear back from users that the performance is not meeting with their approval due to exceptions being thrown, then and only then should you consider adding **Try***Xxx* methods. In other words, you should produce the best object model first and then, if users push back, add some **Try***Xxx* methods to your type so that the users who experience performance trouble can benefit. Users who are not experiencing performance trouble should continue to use the non-**Try***Xxx* versions of the methods because this is the better object model.

Unhandled Exceptions

When an exception is thrown, the CLR climbs up the call stack looking for **catch** blocks that match the type of the exception object being thrown. If no **catch** block matches the thrown exception type, an *unhandled exception* occurs. When the CLR detects that any thread in the process has had an unhandled exception, the CLR terminates the process. An unhandled exception identifies a situation that the application didn't anticipate and is considered to be a true bug in the application. At this point, the bug should be reported back to the company that publishes the application. Hopefully, the publisher will fix the bug and distribute a new version of the application.

Class library developers should not even think about unhandled exceptions. Only application developers need to concern themselves with unhandled exceptions, and the application should have a policy in place for dealing with unhandled exceptions. Microsoft actually recommends that application developers just accept the CLR's default policy. That is, when an application gets an unhandled exception, the message box shown in Figure 19-2 appears, and the end user has the option of sending this information to Microsoft servers. This is called *Windows Error Reporting*, and more information about it can be found at the Windows Quality Web site (*http://WinQual.Microsoft.com*).

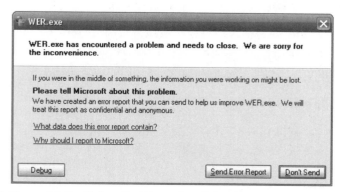

Figure 19-2   Unhandled Exception dialog box, which can send an application log to Windows Error Reporting

Companies can optionally sign up with Microsoft to view this information about their own applications and components. Signing up is free, but it does require that your assemblies be signed with a VeriSign ID (also called a Software Publisher's Digital ID for Authenticode). The VeriSign ID is required to ensure that only your company can see the results of your applications and components.

If you prefer not to have your application's failure information sent to Microsoft's server, you could use Microsoft's Shareware Starter Kit (*http://msdn.microsoft.com/vstudio/downloads/starterkits/*). This kit includes the ability to set up your own Web server and then to have your application's unhandled exceptions be reported to your own Web server. In effect, you are setting up, running, and administering your own stripped-down version of Microsoft's Windows Error Reporting system.

Naturally, you could also develop your own system for getting unhandled exception information back to you so that you can fix bugs in your code. When your application initializes, you can inform the CLR that you have a method that you want to be called whenever any thread in your application experiences an unhandled exception.

The members that you want to look up in the FCL documentation are:

- For any application, look at `System.AppDomain`'s `UnhandledException` event.

- For a Windows Forms application, look at `System.Windows.Forms.NativeWindow`'s `OnThreadException` virtual method, `System.Windows.Forms.Application`'s `OnThread-Exception` virtual method, and `System.Windows.Forms.Application`'s `ThreadException` event.

■ For an ASP.NET Web Form application, look at `System.Web.UI.TemplateControl`'s `Error` event. `TemplateControl` is the base class of the `System.Web.UI.Page` and `System.Web.UI.UserControl` classes. Furthermore, you should also look at `System.Web.HTTPApplication`'s `Error` event.

Unfortunately, every application model Microsoft produces (ASP.NET Web Services, WSE Web Services, Windows Communication Foundation Web Services, Windows Presentation Foundation, etc.) has its own way of tapping into unhandled exceptions.

Before I leave this section, I'd like to say a few words about unhandled exceptions that could occur in a distributed application such as a Web site or Web service. In an ideal world, a server application that experiences an unhandled exception should log it, send some kind of notification back to the client indicating that the requested operation could not complete, and then the server should terminate. Unfortunately, we don't live in an ideal world, and therefore, it may not be possible to send a failure notification back to the client. For some stateful servers (such as Microsoft SQL Server), it may not be practical to terminate the server and start up a brand new instance.

For a server application, information about the unhandled exception should not be returned to the client because there is little a client could do about it, especially if the client is implemented by a different company. Furthermore, the server should divulge as little information about itself as possible to its clients to reduce that potential of the server being hacked.

Exception Stack Traces

As I mentioned earlier, the `System.Exception` type offers a public, read-only `StackTrace` property. A `catch` block can read this property to obtain the stack trace indicating what events led up to the exception. This information can be extremely valuable when you're trying to detect the cause of an exception so that you can correct your code. In this section, I'll discuss some issues related to the stack trace that aren't immediately obvious.

The `Exception` type's `StackTrace` property is magical. When you access this property, you're actually calling into code in the CLR; the property doesn't simply return a string. When you construct a new object of an `Exception`-derived type, the `StackTrace` property is initialized to `null`. If you were to read the property, you wouldn't get back a stack trace; you would get back `null`.

When an exception is thrown, the CLR internally records where the **throw** instruction occurred. When a **catch** block accepts the exception, the CLR records where the exception was caught. If, inside a **catch** block, you now access the thrown exception object's `StackTrace` property, the code that implements the property calls into the CLR, which builds a string identifying all of the methods between the place where the exception was thrown and the filter that caught the exception.

Important   When you throw an exception, the CLR resets the starting point for the exception; that is, the CLR remembers only the location where the most recent exception object was thrown. The following code throws the same exception object that it caught and causes the CLR to reset its starting point for the exception:

```
private void SomeMethod() {
   try { ... }
   catch (Exception e) {
      ...
      throw e;  // CLR thinks this is where exception originated.
               // FxCop reports this as an error
   }
}
```

In contrast, if you re-throw an exception object by using the **throw** keyword by itself, the CLR doesn't reset the stack's starting point. The following code re-throws the same exception object that it caught, causing the CLR to not reset its starting point for the exception:

```
private void SomeMethod() {
   try { ... }
   catch (Exception e) {
      ...
      throw;  // This has no effect on where the CLR thinks the exception
             // originated. FxCop does NOT report this as an error
   }
}
```

In fact, the only difference between these two code fragments is what the CLR thinks is the original location where the exception was thrown. Unfortunately, when you throw or re-throw an exception, Windows does reset the stack's starting point. So if the exception becomes unhandled, the stack location that gets reported to Windows Error Reporting is the location of the last throw or re-throw, even though the CLR knows the stack location where the original exception was thrown. This is unfortunate because it makes debugging applications that have failed in the field much more difficult. Some developers have found this so intolerable that they have chosen a different way to implement their code to ensure that the stack trace truly reflects the location where an exception was originally thrown:

```
private void SomeMethod() {
   Boolean trySucceeds = false;
   try {
      ...
      trySucceeds = true;
   }
   finally {
      if (!trySucceeds) { /* catch code goes in here */ }
   }
}
```

The string returned from the **StackTrace** property doesn't include any of the methods in the call stack that are above the point where the **catch** block accepted the exception object. If you want the complete stack trace from the start of the thread up to the exception handler, you can use the `System.Diagnostics.StackTrace` type. This type defines some properties and methods that allow a developer to programmatically manipulate a stack trace and the frames that make up the stack trace.

You can construct a `StackTrace` object by using several different constructors. Some constructors build a `StackTrace` object representing the frames from the start of the thread to the point where the object is constructed. Other constructors initialize the frames of the `StackTrace` object by using an `Exception`-derived object.

If the CLR can find debug symbols (located in the .pdb files) for your assemblies, the string returned by `System.Exception`'s `StackTrace` property or `System.Diagnostics.StackTrace`'s `ToString` method will include source code file paths and line numbers. This information is incredibly useful for debugging.

Whenever you obtain a stack trace, you might find that some methods in the actual call stack don't appear in the stack trace string. The reason for their absence is that the JIT compiler can inline methods to avoid the overhead of calling and returning from a separate method. Many compilers (including the C# compiler) offer a **/debug** command-line switch. When this switch is used, these compilers embed information into the resulting assembly to tell the JIT compiler not to inline any of the assembly's methods, making stack traces more complete and meaningful to the developer debugging the code.

Note   The JIT compiler examines the `System.Diagnostics.DebuggableAttribute` custom attribute applied to the assembly. The C# compiler applies this attribute automatically. If this attribute has `true` specified for the `DebuggableAttribute` constructor's `isJITOptimizer-Disabled` parameter, the JIT compiler won't inline the assembly's methods. Using the C# compiler's **/debug** switch sets this parameter to `true`. By applying the `System.Runtime.CompilerServices.MethodImplAttribute` custom attribute to a method, you can forbid the JIT compiler from inlining the method for both debug and release builds. The following method definition shows how to forbid the method from being inlined:

```
using System;
using System.Runtime.CompilerServices;

internal sealed class SomeType {

    [MethodImpl(MethodImplOptions.NoInlining)]
    public void SomeMethod() {
        ...
    }
}
```

Debugging Exceptions

The Microsoft Visual Studio debugger offers special support for exceptions. With a solution open, choose the Debug.Exceptions menu item, and you'll see the dialog box shown in Figure 19-3.

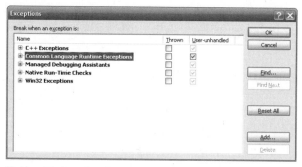

Figure 19-3   Visual Studio Exceptions dialog box showing the different kinds of exceptions

This dialog box shows the different kinds of exceptions that Visual Studio is aware of. For Common Language Runtime Exceptions, expanding the corresponding branch in the dialog box, as in Figure 19-4, shows the set of namespaces that the Visual Studio debugger is aware of.

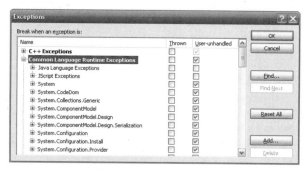

Figure 19-4   Visual Studio's Exceptions dialog box showing CLR exceptions by namespace

If you expand a namespace, you'll see all of the **System.Exception**-derived types defined within that namespace. For example, Figure 19-5 shows what you'll see if you open the **System** namespace.

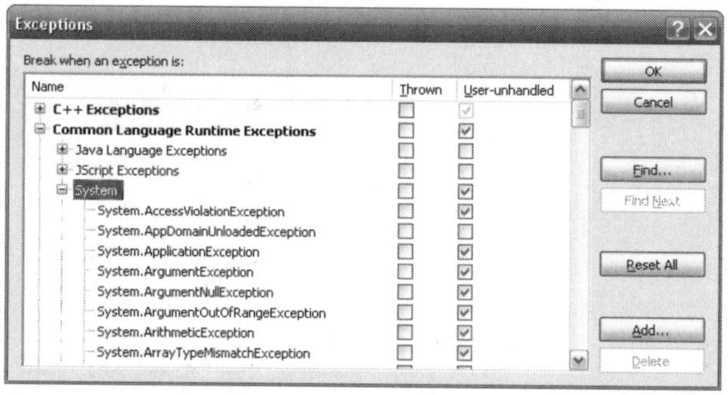

Figure 19-5   Visual Studio's Exceptions dialog box showing CLR exceptions defined in the **System** namespace

For any exception type, if its Thrown check box is selected, the debugger will break as soon as that exception is thrown. At this point, the CLR has not tried to find any matching `catch` blocks. This is useful if you want to debug your code that catches and handles an exception. It is also useful when you suspect that a component or library may be swallowing or re-throwing exceptions, and you are uncertain where exactly to set a break point to catch it in the act.

If an exception type's Thrown check box is not selected, the debugger will break only if the exception type is thrown and becomes unhandled. This option is the most common one to select because a handled exception indicates that the application anticipated the situation and dealt with it; the application continues running normally.

If you define your own exception types, you can add them to this dialog box by clicking the **Add** button. This causes the dialog box in Figure 19-6 to appear.

Figure 19-6   Making Visual Studio aware of your own exception type: New Exception dialog box

In this dialog box, you first select the type of exception to be Common Language Runtime Exceptions, and then, you can enter the fully qualified name of your own exception type. Note that the type you enter doesn't have to be a type derived from `System.Exception`; non-CLS-compliant types are fully supported. If you have two or more types with the same name but in different assemblies, there is no way to distinguish the types from one another. Fortunately, this situation rarely happens.

If your assembly defines several exception types, you must add them one at a time. In the future, I'd like to see this dialog box allow me to browse for an assembly and automatically import all `Exception`-derived types into Visual Studio's debugger. Each type could then be identified by assembly as well, which would fix the problem of having two types with the same name in different assemblies.

In addition, it might be nice if this dialog box also allowed me to individually select types not derived from `Exception` so that I could add any non-CLS-compliant exceptions that I might define. However, non-CLS-compliant exception types are strongly discouraged, so this isn't a must-have feature.

Chapter 20

Automatic Memory Management (Garbage Collection)

In this chapter, I'll discuss how managed applications construct new objects, how the managed heap controls the lifetime of these objects, and how the memory for these objects gets reclaimed. In short, I'll explain how the garbage collector in the common language runtime (CLR) works, and I'll explain various performance issues related to it. I'll also discuss how to design applications so that they use memory most efficiently.

Understanding the Basics of Working in a Garbage-Collected Platform

Every program uses resources of one sort or another, be they files, memory buffers, screen space, network connections, database resources, and so on. In fact, in an object-oriented environment, every type identifies some resource available for a program's use. To use any of these resources requires memory to be allocated to represent the type. The following steps are required to access a resource:

1. Allocate memory for the type that represents the resource by calling the intermediate language's **newobj** instruction, which is emitted when you use the **new** operator in C#.

2. Initialize the memory to set the initial state of the resource and to make the resource usable. The type's instance constructor is responsible for setting this initial state.

3. Use the resource by accessing the type's members (repeating as necessary).

4. Tear down the state of a resource to clean up. I'll address this topic in the section "The Dispose Pattern: Forcing an Object to Clean Up" later in this chapter.

5. Free the memory. The garbage collector is solely responsible for this step.

This seemingly simple paradigm has been one of the major sources of programming errors. How many times have programmers forgotten to free memory when it is no longer needed? How many times have programmers attempted to use memory after it had already been freed?

With unmanaged programming, these two application bugs are worse than most others because you usually can't predict the consequences or the timing of them. For other bugs, when you see your application misbehaving, you just fix the problem. But these two bugs cause resource leaks (memory consumption) and object corruption (destabilization), making the application perform unpredictably. In fact, there are many tools (such as the Microsoft Windows Task Manager, the System Monitor ActiveX Control, NuMega BoundsChecker from Compuware, and Rational's Purify) that are specifically designed to help developers locate these types of bugs.

Proper resource management is very difficult and quite tedious. It distracts developers from concentrating on the real problems that they're trying to solve. It would be wonderful if some mechanism existed that simplified the mind-numbing memory-management task for developers. Fortunately, there is: garbage collection.

Garbage collection completely absolves the developer from having to track memory usage and know when to free memory. However, the garbage collector doesn't know anything about the resource represented by the type in memory, which means that a garbage collector can't know how to perform Step 4 in the preceding list: tear down the state of a resource to clean up. To get a resource to clean up properly, the developer must write code that knows how to properly clean up a resource. The developer writes this code in the **Finalize**, **Dispose**, and **Close** methods, as described later in this chapter. However, as you'll see, the garbage collector can offer some assistance here too, allowing developers to skip Step 4 in many circumstances.

Also, most types, including **String**, **Attribute**, **Delegate**, and **Exception**, represent resources that don't require any special cleanup. For example, a **String** resource can be completely cleaned up simply by destroying the character array maintained in the object's memory.

On the other hand, a type that represents (or wraps) an unmanaged or native resource, such as a file, a database connection, a socket, a mutex, a bitmap, an icon, and so on, always requires the execution of some cleanup code when the object is about to have its memory reclaimed. In this chapter, I'll explain how to properly define types that require explicit clean up, and I'll show you how to properly use types that offer this explicit clean-up. For now, let's examine how memory is allocated and how resources are initialized.

Allocating Resources from the Managed Heap

The CLR requires that all resources to be allocated from a heap called the *managed heap*. This heap is similar to a C-runtime heap, except that you never delete objects from the managed heap—objects are automatically deleted when the application no longer needs them. This, of course, raises the question, "How does the managed heap know when the application is no longer using an object?" I'll address this question shortly.

Several garbage-collection algorithms are in use today. Each algorithm is fine-tuned for a particular environment to provide the best performance. In this chapter, I'll concentrate on the garbage-collection algorithm used by the Microsoft .NET Framework's CLR. Let's start off with the basic concepts.

When a process is initialized, the CLR reserves a contiguous region of address space that initially contains no backing storage. This address space region is the managed heap. The heap also maintains a pointer, which I'll call **NextObjPtr**. This pointer indicates where the next object is to be allocated within the heap. Initially, **NextObjPtr** is set to the base address of the reserved address space region.

The **newobj** intermediate language (IL) instruction creates an object. Many languages (including C#, C++/CLI, and Microsoft Visual Basic) offer a **new** operator that causes the compiler to emit a **newobj** instruction into the method's IL code. The **newobj** instruction causes the CLR to perform the following steps:

1. Calculate the number of bytes required for the type's (and all of its base type's) fields.

2. Add the bytes required for an object's overhead. Each object has two overhead fields: a type object pointer and a sync block index. For a 32-bit application, each of these fields requires 32 bits, adding 8 bytes to each object. For a 64-bit application, each field is 64 bits, adding 16 bytes to each object.

3. The CLR then checks that the bytes required to allocate the object are available in the reserved region (committing storage if necessary). If there is enough free space in the managed heap, the object will fit, starting at the address pointed to by **NextObjPtr**, and these bytes are zeroed out. The type's constructor is called (passing **NextObjPtr** for the **this** parameter), and the **newobj** IL instruction (or C#'s **new** operator) returns the address of the object. Just before the address is returned, **NextObjPtr** is advanced past the object and now points to the address where the next object will be placed in the heap.

Figure 20-1 shows a managed heap consisting of three objects: A, B, and C. If a new object were to be allocated, it would be placed where **NextObjPtr** points to (immediately after object C).

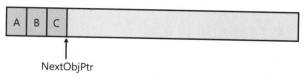

Figure 20-1   Newly initialized managed heap with three objects constructed in it

By contrast, let's look at how the C-runtime heap allocates memory. In a C-runtime heap, allocating memory for an object requires walking through a linked list of data structures. Once a large enough block is found, that block is split, and pointers in the linked-list nodes are modified to keep everything intact. For the managed heap, allocating an object simply means adding a value to a pointer—this is blazingly fast by comparison. In fact, allocating an object from the managed heap is nearly as fast as allocating memory from a thread's stack! In addition, most heaps (such as the C-runtime heap) allocate objects wherever they find free space. Therefore, if I create several objects consecutively, it's quite possible for these objects to be separated by megabytes of address space. In the managed heap, however, allocating several objects consecutively ensures that the objects are contiguous in memory.

In many applications, objects allocated around the same time tend to have strong relationships to each other and are frequently accessed around the same time. For example, it's very common to allocate a **FileStream** object immediately before a **BinaryWriter** object is created. Then the application would use the **BinaryWriter** object, which internally uses the **FileStream** object. In a garbage-collected environment, new objects are allocated contiguously in memory, providing performance gains resulting from locality of reference. Specifically, this means that your process' working set will be smaller than a similar application running in a non-managed environment. It's also likely that the objects that your code is using can all reside in the CPU's cache. Your application will access these objects with phenomenal speed because the CPU will be able to perform most of its manipulations without having cache misses that would force slower access to RAM.

So far, it sounds as if the managed heap is far superior to the C-runtime heap because of its simplicity of implementation and speed. But there's one little detail you should know about before getting too excited. The managed heap gains these advantages because it makes one really big assumption: that address space and storage are infinite. Obviously, this assumption is ridiculous, and the managed heap must employ a mechanism to allow it to make this assumption. This mechanism is the garbage collector. Here's how it works:

When an application calls the **new** operator to create an object, there might not be enough address space left in the region to allocate to the object. The heap detects this lack of space by adding the bytes that the object requires to the address in **NextObjPtr**. If the resulting value is beyond the end of the address space region, the heap is full, and a garbage collection must be performed.

> **Important**   What I've just said is an oversimplification. In reality, a garbage collection occurs when generation 0 is full. Some garbage collectors use generations, a mechanism whose sole purpose is to improve performance. The idea is that newly created objects are part of a young generation and objects created early in the application's lifecycle are in an old generation. Objects in Generation 0 are objects that have recently been allocated and have never been examined by the garbage collector algorithm. Objects that survive a collection are promoted to another generation (such as Generation 1). Separating objects into generations allows the garbage collector to collect specific generations instead of collecting all of the objects in the managed heap. I'll explain generations in more detail later in this chapter. Until then, it's easiest for you to think that a garbage collection occurs when the heap is full.

The Garbage Collection Algorithm

The garbage collector checks to see if any objects in the heap are no longer being used by the application. If such objects exist, the memory used by these objects can be reclaimed. (If no more memory is available in the heap after a garbage collection, **new** throws an **OutOfMemory-Exception**.) How does the garbage collector know whether the application is using an object? As you might imagine, this isn't a simple question to answer.

Every application has a set of *roots*. A single root is a storage location containing a memory pointer to a reference type object. This pointer either refers to an object in the managed heap or is set to **null**. For example, a static field (defined within a type) is considered a root. In addition, any method parameter or local variable is also considered a root. Only variables that are of a reference type are considered roots; value type variables are never considered roots. Now, let's look at a concrete example starting with the following class definition:

```
internal sealed class SomeType {
   private TextWriter m_textWriter;

   public SomeType(TextWriter tw) {
      m_textWriter = tw;
   }

   public void WriteBytes(Byte[] bytes) {
      for (Int32 x = 0; x < bytes.Length; x++) {
         m_textWriter.Write(bytes[x]);
      }
   }
}
```

The first time the **WriteBytes** method is called, the JIT compiler converts the method's IL code into native CPU instructions. Let's say the CLR is running on an *x86* CPU, and the JIT compiler compiles the **WriteBytes** method into the CPU instructions shown in Figure 20-2. (I added comments on the right to help you understand how the native code maps back to the original source code.)

```
              00000000 push  edi                           // Prolog
              00000001 push  esi
              00000002 push  ebx
      EBX
              00000003 mov   ebx,ecx                       // ebx = this (argument)
              00000005 mov   esi,edx                       // esi = bytes array (argument)
      ESI     00000007 xor   edi,edi                       // edi = x (a value type)
              00000009 cmp   dword ptr [esi+4],0           // compare bytes.Length with 0
              0000000d jle   0000002A                      // if bytes.Length <=0, go to 2a
      ECX
              0000000f mov   ecx,dword ptr [ebx+4]         // ecx = m_textWriter (field)
              00000012 cmp   edi,dword ptr [esi+4]         // compare x with bytes.Length
              00000015 jae   0000002E                      // if x >= bytes.Length, go to 2e

      EAX     00000017 movzx edx,byte prt [esi+edi+8]      // edx = bytes[x]
              0000001c mov   eax,dword ptr [ecx]           // eax = m_textWriter's type object
              0000001e call  dword ptr [eax+000000BCh]     // Call m_textWriter's Write method

              00000024 inc   edi                           // x++
              00000025 cmp   dword ptr [esi+4],edi         // compare bytes.Length with x
              00000028 jg    0000000F                      // if bytes.Length > x, go to f

              0000002a pop   ebx                           // Epilog
              0000002b pop   esi
              0000002c pop   edi
              0000002d ret                                 // return to caller

              0000002e call  76B6E337                      // Throw IndexOutOfRangeException
              00000033 int   3                             // Break in debugger
```

Figure 20-2   Native code produced by the JIT compiler with ranges of roots shown

As the JIT compiler produces the native code, it also creates an internal table. Logically, each entry in the table indicates a range of byte offsets in the method's native CPU instructions, and for each range, a set of memory addresses and CPU registers that contain roots.

For the **WriteBytes** method, this table reflects that the EBX register starts being a root at offset 0x00000003, the ESI register starts being a root at offset 0x00000005, and the ECX register starts being a root at offset 0x0000000f. All three of these registers stop being roots at the end of the loop (offset 0x00000028). Also note that the EAX register is a root from 0x0000001c to 0x0000001e. The EDI register is used to hold the **Int32** value represented by the variable **x** in the original source code. Since **Int32** is a value type, the JIT compiler doesn't consider the EDI register to be a root.

The **WriteBytes** method is a fairly simple method, and all of the variables that it uses can be enregistered. A more complex method could use all of the available CPU registers, and some roots would be in memory locations relative to the method's stack frame. Also note that on an *x86* architecture, the CLR passes the first two arguments to a method via the ECX and EDX registers. For instance methods, the first argument is the **this** pointer, which is always passed in the ECX register. For the **WriteBytes** method, this is how I know that the **this** pointer is passed in the ECX register and stored in the EBX register right after the method prolog. This is also how I know that the **bytes** argument is passed in the EDX register and stored in the ESI register after the prolog.

If a garbage collection were to start while code was executing at offset 0x00000017 in the **writeBytes** method, the garbage collector would know that the objects referred to by the EBX (**this** argument), ESI (**bytes** argument), and ECX (the **m_textWriter** field) registers were all roots and refer to objects in the heap that shouldn't be considered garbage. In addition, the garbage collector can walk up the thread's call stack and determine the roots for all of the calling methods by examining each method's internal table. The garbage collector iterates through all the type objects to obtain the set of roots stored in static fields.

When a garbage collection starts, it assumes that all objects in the heap are garbage. In other words, it is assumed that the thread's stack contains no variables that refer to objects in the heap, that no CPU registers refer to objects in the heap, and that no static fields refer to objects in the heap. The garbage collector starts what is called the *marking* phase of the collection. This is when the collector walks up the thread's stack checking all of the roots. If a root is found to refer to an object, a bit will be turned on in the object's sync block index field—this is how the object is *marked*. For example, the garbage collector might locate a local variable that points to an object in the heap. Figure 20-3 shows a heap containing several allocated objects, and the application's roots refer directly to objects A, C, D, and F. All of these objects are marked. When marking object D, the garbage collector notices that this object contains a field that refers to object H, causing object H to be marked as well. The garbage collector continues to walk through all reachable objects recursively.

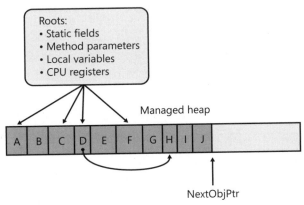

Figure 20-3   Managed heap before a collection

After a root and the objects referenced by its fields are marked, the garbage collector checks the next root and continues marking objects. If the garbage collector is going to mark an object that it previously marked, it can stop walking down that path. This behavior serves two purposes. First, performance is enhanced significantly because the garbage collector doesn't walk through a set of objects more than once. Second, infinite loops are prevented if you have any circular linked lists of objects.

Once all of the roots have been checked, the heap contains a set of marked and unmarked objects. The marked objects are reachable via the application's code, and the unmarked objects are unreachable. The unreachable objects are considered garbage, and the memory that they occupy can be reclaimed. The garbage collector now starts what is called the *compact phase* of the collection. This is when the collector traverses the heap linearly looking for contiguous blocks of unmarked (garbage) objects.

If small blocks are found, the garbage collector leaves the blocks alone. If large free contiguous blocks are found, however, the garbage collector shifts the nongarbage objects down in memory to compact the heap.

Naturally, moving the objects in memory invalidates all variables and CPU registers that contain pointers to the objects. So the garbage collector must revisit all of the application's roots and modify them so that each root's value points to the objects' new memory location. In addition, if any object contains a field that refers to another moved object, the garbage collector is responsible for correcting these fields as well. After the heap memory is compacted, the managed heap's `NextObjPtr` pointer is set to point to a location just after the last nongarbage object. Figure 20-4 shows the managed heap after a collection.

As you can see, a garbage collection generates a considerable performance hit, which is the major downside of using a managed heap. But keep in mind that garbage collections occur only when generation 0 is full, and until then, the managed heap is significantly faster than a C-runtime heap. Finally, the CLR's garbage collector offers some optimizations that greatly improve the performance of garbage collection. I'll discuss these optimizations later in this chapter, in the "Generations" and "Other Garbage Collector Performance Topics" sections.

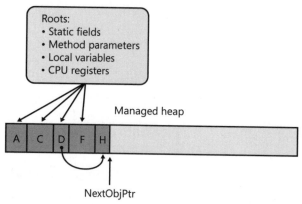

Figure 20-4   Managed heap after a collection

As a programmer, you should take away a couple of important points from this discussion. To start, you no longer have to implement any code to manage the lifetime of objects your application uses. And notice how the two bugs described at the beginning of this chapter no longer exist. First, it's not possible to leak objects because any object not accessible from your application's roots can be collected at some point. Second, it's not possible to access an object that is freed because the object won't be freed if it is reachable, and if it's not reachable, your application has no way to access it. Also, since a collection causes memory compaction, it is not possible for managed objects to fragment your process' virtual address space. This would sometimes be a severe problem with unmanaged heaps but is no longer an issue when using the managed heap. Using large objects (discussed later in this chapter) is an exception to this, and fragmentation of the large object heap is possible.

> **Note**   If garbage collection is so great, you might be wondering why it isn't in ANSI C++. The reason is that a garbage collector must be able to identify an application's roots and must also be able to find all object pointers. The problem with unmanaged C++ is that it allows casting a pointer from one type to another, and there's no way to know what a pointer refers to. In the CLR, the managed heap always knows the actual type of an object and uses the metadata information to determine which members of an object refer to other objects.

Garbage Collections and Debugging

In Figure 20-2, notice that the method's **bytes** argument (stored in the ESI register) isn't referred to after the CPU instruction at offset 0x00000028. This means that the **Byte** array object that the **bytes** argument refers to can be collected any time after the instruction at offset 0x00000028 executes (assuming that there are no other roots in the application that also refer to this array object). In other words, as soon as an object becomes unreachable, it is a candidate for collection—objects aren't guaranteed to live throughout a method's lifetime. This can have an interesting impact on your application. For example, examine the following code:

```
using System;
using System.Threading;

public static class Program {
   public static void Main() {
      // Create a Timer object that knows to call our TimerCallback
      // method once every 2000 milliseconds.
      Timer t = new Timer(TimerCallback, null, 0, 2000);

      // Wait for the user to hit <Enter>
      Console.ReadLine();
   }

   private static void TimerCallback(Object o) {
      // Display the date/time when this method got called.
      Console.WriteLine("In TimerCallback: " + DateTime.Now);

      // Force a garbage collection to occur for this demo.
      GC.Collect();
   }
}
```

Compile this code from the command prompt without using any special compiler switches. When you run the resulting executable file, you'll see that the **TimerCallback** method is called just once!

From examining the code above, you'd think that the **TimerCallback** method would get called once every 2000 milliseconds. After all, a **Timer** object is created, and the variable **t** refers to this object. As long as the timer object exists, the timer should keep firing. But you'll notice in the **TimerCallback** method that I force a garbage collection to occur by calling **GC.Collect()**.

When the collection starts, it first assumes that all objects in the heap are unreachable (garbage); this includes the **Timer** object. Then, the collector examines the application's roots and sees that **Main** doesn't use the **t** variable after the initial assignment to it. Therefore, the application has no variable referring to the **Timer** object, and the garbage collection reclaims the memory for it; this stops the timer and explains why the **TimerCallback** method is called just once.

Let's say that you're using a debugger to step through **Main**, and a garbage collection just happens to occur just after **t** is assigned the address of the new **Timer** object. Then, let's say that you try to view the object that **t** refers to by using the debugger's Quick Watch window. What do you think will happen? The debugger can't show you the object because it was just garbage collected. This behavior would be considered very unexpected and undesirable by most developers, so Microsoft has come up with a solution.

When the JIT compiler compiles the IL for a method into native code, it checks to see if the assembly defining the method was compiled without optimizations and if the process is currently being executed under a debugger. If both are true, the JIT compiler generates the method's internal root table in such a way as to artificially extend the lifetime of all of the variables to the end of the method. In other words, the JIT compiler will trick itself into believing that the **t** variable in **Main** must live until the end of the method. So, if a garbage collection were to occur, the garbage collector now thinks that **t** is still a root and that the **Timer** object that **t** refers to will continue to be reachable. The **Timer** object will survive the collection, and the **TimerCallback** method will get called repeatedly until **Console.ReadLine** returns and **Main** exits. This is easy to see. Just run the same executable file under a debugger, and you'll see that the **TimerCallback** method is called repeatedly!

Now, recompile the program from a command prompt, but this time, specify the C# compiler's **/debug+** compiler-line switch. When you run the resulting executable file, you'll now see that the **TimerCallback** method is called repeatedly—even if you don't run this program under a debugger! What is happening here?

Well, when the JIT compiler compiles a method, the JIT compiler looks to see if the assembly that defines the method contains the **System.Diagnostics.DebuggableAttribute** attribute with its constructor's **isJITOptimizerDisabled** argument set to **true**. If the JIT compiler sees this attribute set, it also compiles the method, artificially extending the lifetime of all variables until the end of the method. When you specify the **/debug+** compiler switch, the C# compiler emits this attribute for you into the resulting assembly. Note, the C# compiler's **/optimize+** compiler switch can turn optimizations back on so this compiler switch should not be specified when performing this experiment.

The JIT compiler does this to help you with just-in-time debugging. You may now start your application normally (without a debugger), and if the method is called, the JIT compiler will artificially extend the lifetime of the variables to the end of the method. Later, if you decide to attach a debugger to the process, you can put a breakpoint in a previously compiled method and examine the variables.

So now you know how to build a program that works in a debug build but doesn't work correctly when you make a release build! Since no developer wants a program that works only when debugging it, there should be something we can do to the program so that it works all of the time regardless of the type of build.

You could try modifying the **Main** method to this:

```
public static void Main() {
    // Create a Timer object that knows to call our TimerCallback
    // method once every 2000 milliseconds.
    Timer t = new Timer(TimerCallback, null, 0, 2000);

    // Wait for the user to hit <Enter>
    Console.ReadLine();

    // Refer to t after ReadLine (this gets optimized away)
    t = null;
}
```

However, if you compile this (without the **/debug+** switch) and run the resulting executable file (not under the debugger), you'll see that the **TimerCallback** method is still called just once. The problem here is that the JIT compiler is an optimizing compiler, and setting a local variable or parameter variable to **null** is the same as not referencing the variable at all. In other words, the JIT compiler optimizes the **t = null;** line out of the code completely, and therefore, the program still does not work as we desire. The correct way to modify the **Main** method is as follows:

```
public static void Main() {
    // Create a Timer object that knows to call our TimerCallback
    // method once every 2000 milliseconds.
    Timer t = new Timer(TimerCallback, null, 0, 2000);

    // Wait for the user to hit <Enter>
    Console.ReadLine();

    // Refer to t after ReadLine (t will survive GCs until Dispose returns)
    t.Dispose();
}
```

Now, if you compile this code (without the **/debug+** switch) and run the resulting executable file (not under the debugger), you'll see that the **TimerCallback** method is called multiple times, and the program is fixed. What's happening here is that the object **t** refers to is required to stay alive so that the **Dispose** instance method can be called on it (the value in **t** needs to be passed as the **this** argument to **Dispose**).

Using Finalization to Release Native Resources

At this point, you should have a basic understanding of garbage collection and the managed heap, including how the garbage collector reclaims an object's memory. Fortunately for us, most types need only memory to operate. For example, the **String**, **Attribute**, **Delegate**, and **Exception** types are really just types that manipulate bytes in memory. However, some types require more than just memory to be useful; some types require the use of a native resource in addition to memory.

The **System.IO.FileStream** type, for example, needs to open a file (a native resource) and store the file's handle. Then the type's **Read** and **Write** methods use this handle to manipulate the file. Similarly, the **System.Threading.Mutex** type opens a Windows mutex kernel object (a native resource) and stores its handle, using it when the **Mutex**'s methods are called.

Finalization is a mechanism offered by the CLR that allows an object to perform some graceful cleanup prior to the garbage collector reclaiming the object's memory. Any type that wraps a native resource, such as a file, network connection, socket, mutex, or other type, must support finalization. Basically, the type implements a method named **Finalize**. When the garbage collector determines that an object is garbage, it calls the object's **Finalize** method (if it exists). I think of it this way: any type that implements the **Finalize** method is in effect stating that all of its objects want a last meal before they are killed.

Microsoft's C# team felt that **Finalize** methods were a special kind of method requiring special syntax in the programming language (similar to how C# uses requires special syntax to define a constructor). So, in C#, you must define a **Finalize** method by placing a tilde symbol "~" in front of the class name, as shown in the following code sample:

```
internal sealed class SomeType {
   // This is the Finalize method
   ~SomeType() {
      // The code here is inside the Finalize method
   }
}
```

If you were to compile this code and examine the resulting assembly with ILDasm.exe, you'd see that the C# compiler did, in fact, emit a method named **Finalize** into the module's metadata. If you examined the **Finalize** method's IL code, you'd also see that the code inside the method's body is emitted into a **try** block, and that a call to **base.Finalize** is emitted into a **finally** block.

> **Important**   If you're familiar with C++, you'll notice that the special syntax C# requires for defining a `Finalize` method looks just like the syntax you'd use to define a C++ destructor. In fact, the earlier versions of the C# Programming Language Specification called this method a *destructor*. However, a `Finalize` method doesn't work like an unmanaged C++ destructor at all, and this has caused a great deal of confusion for developers migrating from one language to another.
>
> The problem is that developers mistakenly believe that using the C# destructor syntax means that the type's objects will be deterministically destructed, just as they would be in C++. However, the CLR doesn't support deterministic destruction, which makes it difficult for C# to provide this mechanism.
>
> In version 2 of the C# Programming Language Specification, a method using this syntax is now officially called a *finalizer*. The C# team would have liked to have changed the syntax of the method to avoid using the tilde (~), but doing so would break existing code. Therefore, only the term has changed; the syntax stays the same.

A `Finalize` method is usually implemented to call the Win32 `CloseHandle` function, passing in the handle of the native resource. The `FileStream` type defines a file handle field, which identifies the native resource. The `FileStream` type also defines a `Finalize` method, which internally calls `CloseHandle`, passing it the file handle field; this ensures that the native file handle is closed when the managed `FileStream` object is determined to be garbage. If a type that wraps a native resource fails to define a `Finalize` method, the native resource won't be closed and will cause a resource leak that will exist until the process terminates, at which time the operating system will reclaim the native resources.

Guaranteed Finalization Using `CriticalFinalizerObject` Types

To make things simpler for developers, the `System.Runtime.ConstrainedExecution` namespace defines a `CriticalFinalizerObject` class that looks like this:

```
public abstract class CriticalFinalizerObject {
   protected CriticalFinalizerObject() { /* there is no code in here */ }

   // This is the Finalize method
   ~CriticalFinalizerObject() { /* there is no code in here */ }
}
```

I know that you're thinking that this class doesn't look too exciting, but the CLR treats this class and classes derived from it in a very special manner. In particular, the CLR endows this class with three cool features:

■   The first time an object of any `CriticalFinalizerObject`-derived type is constructed, the CLR immediately JIT compiles all of the `Finalize` methods in the inheritance hierarchy. Compiling these methods upon object construction guarantees that the native resource will be released when the object is determined to be garbage. Without this eager compiling of the `Finalize` method, it would be possible to allocate the native resource and use it, but not to get rid of it. Under low memory conditions, the CLR might not be able to find enough memory in order to compile the `Finalize` method, which would prevent it from executing causing the native resource to leak. Or the resource might not be freed if the `Finalize` method contained code that referred to a type in another assembly, and the CLR failed to locate this other assembly.

■ The CLR calls the `Finalize` method of `CriticalFinalizerObject`-derived types after calling the `Finalize` methods of non-`CriticalFinalizerObject`-derived types. This ensures that managed resource classes that have a `Finalize` method can access `CriticalFinalizerObject`-derived objects within their `Finalize` methods successfully. For example, the `FileStream` class' `Finalize` method can flush data from a memory buffer to an underlying disk with confidence that the disk file has not been closed yet.

■ The CLR calls the `Finalize` method of `CriticalFinalizerObject`-derived types if an AppDomain is rudely aborted by a host application (such as Microsoft SQL Server or Microsoft ASP.NET). This also is part of ensuring that the native resource is released even in a case in which a host application no longer trusts the managed code running inside of it.

SafeHandle and Its Derived Types

Now, Microsoft realizes that the most-used native resources are those resources provided by Windows. And Microsoft also realizes that most Windows resources are manipulated by way of handles (32-bit values on a 32-bit system and 64-bit values on a 64-bit system). Again, to make life easier and safer for developers, the `System.Runtime.InteropServices` namespace includes a class called `SafeHandle`, which looks like this (I've added comments in the methods to indicate what they do):

```
public abstract class SafeHandle : CriticalFinalizerObject, IDisposable {
   // This is the handle to the native resource
   protected IntPtr handle;

   protected SafeHandle(IntPtr invalidHandleValue, Boolean ownsHandle) {
      this.handle = invalidHandleValue;
      // If ownsHandle is true, then the native resource is closed when
      // this SafeHandle-derived object is collected
   }

   protected void SetHandle(IntPtr handle) {
      this.handle = handle;
   }


   // You can explicitly release the resource by calling Dispose or Close
   public void Dispose() { Dispose(true); }
   public void Close()   { Dispose(true); }
```

```
    // The default Dispose implementation (shown here) is exactly
    // what you want. Overriding this method is very strongly discouraged.
    protected virtual void Dispose(Boolean disposing) {
        // The default implementation ignores the disposing argument
        // If resource was already released, just return
        // If ownsHandle is false, return
        // Set flag indicating that this resource has been released
        // Call the virtual ReleaseHandle method
        // Call GC.SuppressFinalize(this) to prevent Finalize from being called
        // If ReleaseHandle returned true, return
        // Fire the ReleaseHandleFailed Managed Debugging Assistant (MDA)
    }

    // The default Finalize implementation (shown here) is exactly
    // what you want. Overriding this method is very strongly discouraged.
    ~SafeHandle() { Dispose(false); }

    // A derived class overrides this method to
    // implement the code that releases the resource
    protected abstract Boolean ReleaseHandle();

    public void SetHandleAsInvalid() {
        // Set flag indicating that this resource has been released
        // Call GC.SuppressFinalize(this) to prevent Finalize from being called
    }

    public Boolean IsClosed {
        get {
            // Returns flag indicating whether resource was released
        }
    }

    public abstract Boolean IsInvalid {
        get {
            // A derived class overrides this property.
            // The implementation should return true if the handle's value doesn't
            // represent a resource (this usually means that the handle is 0 or -1)
        }
    }

    // These three methods have to do with security and reference counting;
    // I'll talk about them at the end of this section in this chapter
    public void    DangerousAddRef(ref Boolean success) {...}
    public IntPtr DangerousGetHandle() {...}
    public void    DangerousRelease() {...}
}
```

The first thing to notice about the **SafeHandle** class is that it is derived from **Critical-FinalizerObject**; this ensures it gets the CLR's special treatment. The second thing to notice is that the class is abstract; it is expected that another class will be derived from **SafeHandle**, and this class will override the protected constructor, the abstract method **ReleaseHandle**, and the abstract **IsInvalid** property **get** accessor method.

In Windows, most handles are invalid if they have a value of **0** or **-1**. The **Microsoft .Win32.SafeHandles** namespace contains another helper class called **SafeHandleZeroOr-MinusOneIsInvalid**, which looks like this:

```
public abstract class SafeHandleZeroOrMinusOneIsInvalid : SafeHandle {
    protected SafeHandleZeroOrMinusOneIsInvalid(Boolean ownsHandle)
        : base(IntPtr.Zero, ownsHandle) {
    }

    public override Boolean IsInvalid {
        get {
            if (base.handle == IntPtr.Zero) return true;
            if (base.handle == (IntPtr) (-1)) return true;
            return false;
        }
    }
}
```

Again, you'll notice that the **SafeHandleZeroOrMinusOneIsInvalid** class is abstract, and therefore, another class must be derived from this one to override the protected constructor and the abstract method **ReleaseHandle**. The Microsoft .NET Framework provides two public classes derived from **SafeHandleZeroOrMinusOneIsInvalid**: **SafeFileHandle** and **SafeWait-Handle**. Both of these classes are also in the **Microsoft.Win32.SafeHandles** namespace. Here is what the **SafeFileHandle** class looks like:

```
public sealed class SafeFileHandle : SafeHandleZeroOrMinusOneIsInvalid {
    public SafeFileHandle(IntPtr preexistingHandle, Boolean ownsHandle)
        : base(ownsHandle) {
        base.SetHandle(preexistingHandle);
    }

    protected override Boolean ReleaseHandle() {
        // Tell Windows that we want the native resource closed.
        return Win32Native.CloseHandle(base.handle);
    }
}
```

The **SafeWaitHandle** class is implemented similarly to the **SafeFileHandle** class shown above. The only reason why there are different classes with similar implementations is to achieve type safety; the compiler won't let you use a file handle as an argument to a method that expects a wait handle, and vice versa.

It would be nice if the .NET Framework included additional classes that wrap various native resources. For example, one could imagine classes such as **SafeProcessHandle**, **SafeThread-Handle**, **SafeTokenHandle**, **SafeFileMappingHandle**, **SafeFileMapViewHandle** (its **ReleaseHandle** method would call the Win32 **UnmapViewOfFile** function), **SafeRegistryHandle** (its **Release-Handle** method would call the Win32 **RegCloseKey** function), **SafeLibraryHandle** (its **ReleaseHandle** method would call the Win32 **FreeLibrary** function), **SafeLocalAllocHandle** (its **ReleaseHandle** method would call the Win32 **LocalFree** function), and so on.

All of the classes just listed (and more) actually do ship with the Framework Class Library. However, only the **SafeFileHandle** and **SafeWaitHandle** classes are publicly exposed; all of the other classes are internal to MSCorLib.dll or System.dll. Microsoft didn't expose these classes publicly because they didn't want to do full testing of them, and they didn't want to have to take the time to document them. However, if you need any of these classes for your own work, I'd recommend that you use a tool such as ILDasm.exe or some IL decompiler tool to extract the code for these classes and integrate that code into your own project's source code. All of these classes are trivial to implement, and writing them yourself from scratch would also be quite easy.

Interoperating with Unmanaged Code by Using SafeHandle Types

As already shown, the **SafeHandle**-derived classes are extremely useful because they ensure that the native resource is freed when a garbage collection occurs. In addition to what we've already discussed, **SafeHandle** offers two more capabilities. First, the CLR gives **SafeHandle**-derived types special treatment when used in scenarios in which you are interoperating with unmanaged code. For example, let's examine the following code:

```
using System;
using System.Runtime.InteropServices;
using Microsoft.Win32.SafeHandles;

internal static class SomeType {
    [DllImport("Kernel32", CharSet=CharSet.Unicode, EntryPoint="CreateEvent")]
    // This prototype is not robust
    private static extern IntPtr CreateEventBad(
        IntPtr pSecurityAttributes, Boolean manualReset,
        Boolean initialState, String name);

    // This prototype is robust
    [DllImport("Kernel32", CharSet=CharSet.Unicode, EntryPoint="CreateEvent")]
    private static extern SafeWaitHandle CreateEventGood(
        IntPtr pSecurityAttributes, Boolean manualReset,
        Boolean initialState, String name);

    public static void SomeMethod() {
        IntPtr handle = CreateEventBad(IntPtr.Zero, false, false, null);
        SafeWaitHandle swh = CreateEventGood(IntPtr.Zero, false, false, null);
    }
}
```

You'll notice that the **CreateEventBad** method is prototyped as returning an **IntPtr**. Prior to version 2.0 of the .NET Framework, the **SafeHandle** class didn't exist, and you'd have to use the **IntPtr** type to represent handles. What Microsoft's CLR team discovered was that this code was not robust. You see, after **CreateEventBad** was called (which creates the native event resource), it was possible that a **ThreadAbortException** could be thrown prior to the handle being assigned to the **handle** variable. In the rare cases when this would happen, the managed code would be leaking the native resource. The only way to get the event closed would be to terminate the process.

Now, with version 2.0 of the .NET Framework, we can use the **SafeHandle** class to fix this potential resource leak. Notice that the **CreateEventGood** method is prototyped as returning a **SafeWaitHandle** (instead of an **IntPtr**). When **CreateEventGood** is called, the CLR calls the Win32 **CreateEvent** function. As the **CreateEvent** function returns back to managed code, the CLR knows that **SafeWaitHandle** is derived from **SafeHandle**, causing the CLR to automatically construct an instance of the **SafeWaitHandle** class, passing in the handle value returned from **CreateEvent**. The newing up of the **SafeWaitHandle** object and the assignment of the handle happens in unmanaged code, which cannot be interrupted by a **ThreadAbortException**. Now, it is impossible for managed code to leak this native resource. Eventually, the **SafeWaitHandle** object will be garbage collected and its **Finalize** method will be called, ensuring that the resource is released.

One last feature of **SafeHandle**-derived classes is that they prevent someone from trying to exploit a potential security hole. The problem is that one thread could be trying to use a native resource while another thread tries to free the resource. This could manifest itself as a handle-recycling exploit. The **SafeHandle** class prevents this security vulnerability by using reference counting. Internally, the **SafeHandle** class defines a private field that maintains a count. When a **SafeHandle**-derived object is set to a valid handle, the count is set to 1. Whenever a **SafeHandle**-derived object is passed as an argument to an unmanaged method, the CLR knows to automatically increment the counter. When the unmanaged method returns back to managed code, the CLR knows to decrement the counter. For example, you would prototype the Win32 **SetEvent** function as follows:

```
[DllImport("Kernel32", ExactSpelling=true)]
private static extern Boolean SetEvent(SafeWaitHandle swh);
```

Now when you call this method passing in a reference to a **SafeWaitHandle** object, the CLR will increment the counter just before the call and decrement the counter just after the call. Of course, the manipulation of the counter is performed in a thread-safe fashion. How does this improve security? Well, if another thread tries to release the native resource wrapped by the **SafeHandle** object, the CLR knows that it cannot actually release it because the resource is being used by an unmanaged function. When the unmanaged function returns, the counter is decremented to 0, and the resource will be released.

If you are writing or calling code to manipulate a handle as an **IntPtr**, you can access it out of a **SafeHandle** object, but you should manipulate the reference counting explicitly. You accomplish this via **SafeHandle**'s **DangerousAddRef** and **DangerousRelease** methods. You gain access to the raw handle via the **DangerousGetHandle** method.

I would be remiss if I didn't mention that the **System.Runtime.InteropServices** namespace also defines a **CriticalHandle** class. This class works exactly as the **SafeHandle** class in all ways except that it does not offer the reference-counting feature. The **CriticalHandle** class and the classes derived from it sacrifice security for better performance when you use it (since counters don't get manipulated). As does **SafeHandle**, the **CriticalHandle** class has two types derived from it: `CriticalHandleMinusOneIsInvalid` and `CriticalHandleZeroOrMinus-OneIsInvalid`. Since Microsoft favors a more secure system over a faster system, the class library includes no types derived from either of these two classes. For your own work, I would recommend that you use `CriticalHandle`-derived types only if performance is an issue. If you can justify reducing security, you can switch to a `CriticalHandle`-derived type.

Using Finalization with Managed Resources

> **Important** There are some people who are of the mindset that you should never use finalization with managed resources. For the most part, I agree with these people. Therefore, you may want to skip this section entirely. Using finalization with managed resources is a super-advanced way of coding and should be used only in very rare circumstances. You must have complete and intimate knowledge of the code you are calling from within a `Finalize` method. Furthermore, you must know that the behavior of code you are calling will not change with future versions. Specifically, you must know that any code you call from within a `Finalize` method does not use any other object that could have already been finalized.

While finalization is almost exclusively used to release a native resource, it can occasionally be useful with managed resources too. Here's a class that causes the computer to beep every time the garbage collector performs a collection:

```
internal sealed class GCBeep {
   // This is the Finalize method
   ~GCBeep() {
      // We're being finalized, beep.
      Console.Beep();

      // If the AppDomain isn't unloading and if the process isn't
      // shutting down, create a new object that will get finalized
      // at the next collection.
      if (!AppDomain.CurrentDomain.IsFinalizingForUnload() &&
         !Environment.HasShutdownStarted)
         new GCBeep();
   }
}
```

To use this class, you need just to construct one instance of the class. Then whenever a garbage collection occurs, the object's `Finalize` method is called, which calls `Beep` and constructs a new `GCBeep` object. This new `GCBeep` object will have its `Finalize` method called when the next garbage collection occurs. Here's a sample program that demonstrates the `GCBeep` class:

```
public static class Program {
   public static void Main() {
      // Constructing a single GCBeep object causes a beep to
      // occur every time a garbage collection starts.
      new GCBeep();
```

```
    // Construct a lot of 100-byte objects.
    for (Int32 x = 0; x < 10000; x++) {
        Console.WriteLine(x);
        Byte[] b = new Byte[100];
    }
  }
}
```

Also be aware that a type's **Finalize** method is called even if the type's instance constructor throws an exception. So your **Finalize** method shouldn't assume that the object is in a good, consistent state. The following code demonstrates:

```
internal sealed class TempFile {
    private String m_filename = null;
    private FileStream m_fs;

    public TempFile(String filename) {
        // The following line might throw an exception.
        m_fs = new FileStream(filename, FileMode.Create);

        // Save the name of this file.
        m_filename = filename;
    }

    // This is the Finalize method
    ~TempFile() {
        // The right thing to do here is to test filename
        // against null because you can't be sure that
        // filename was initialized in the constructor.
        if (m_filename != null)
            File.Delete(m_filename);
    }
}
```

You could write the following code instead:

```
internal sealed class TempFile {
    private String m_filename;
    private FileStream m_fs;

    public TempFile(String filename) {
        try {
            // The following line might throw an exception.
            m_fs = new FileStream(filename, FileMode.Create);

            // Save the name of this file.
            m_filename = filename;
        }
        catch {
            // If anything goes wrong, tell the garbage collector
            // not to call the Finalize method. I'll discuss
            // SuppressFinalize later in this chapter.
            GC.SuppressFinalize(this);
```

```
        // Let the caller know something failed.
        throw;
    }
}

// This is the Finalize method
~TempFile() {
    // No if statement is necessary now because this code
    // executes only if the constructor ran successfully.
    File.Delete(m_filename);
}
}
```

When designing a type, it's best if you avoid using a **Finalize** method for several reasons all related to performance:

- Finalizable objects take longer to allocate because pointers to them must be placed on the finalization list (which I'll discuss in the "Finalization Internals" section a little later).

- Finalizable objects get promoted to older generations, which increases memory pressure and prevents the object's memory from being collected at the time the garbage collector determines that the object is garbage. In addition, all objects referred to directly or indirectly by this object get promoted as well. (I'll talk about generations and promotions later in this chapter.)

- Finalizable objects cause your application to run slower since extra processing must occur for each object when collected.

Furthermore, be aware of the fact that you have no control over when the **Finalize** method will execute. **Finalize** methods run when a garbage collection occurs, which may happen when your application requests more memory. Also, the CLR doesn't make any guarantees as to the order in which **Finalize** methods are called, so you should avoid writing a **Finalize** method that accesses other objects whose type defines a **Finalize** method; those other objects could have been finalized already. However, it is perfectly OK to access value type instances or reference type objects that do not define a **Finalize** method. You also need to be careful when calling static methods because these methods can internally access objects that have been finalized, causing the behavior of the static method to become unpredictable.

What Causes Finalize Methods to Be Called

Finalize methods are called at the completion of a garbage collection, which is started by one of the following five events:

- **Generation 0 is full**   When generation 0 is full, a garbage collection starts. This event is by far the most common way for **Finalize** methods to be called because it occurs naturally as the application code runs, allocating new objects. I'll discuss generations later in this chapter.

- **Code explicitly calls** `System.GC`'s static `Collect` method   Code can explicitly request that the CLR perform a collection. Although Microsoft strongly discourages such requests, at times it might make sense for an application to force a collection. I'll talk about this later in the chapter.

- **Windows is reporting low memory conditions**   The CLR internally uses the Win32 `CreateMemoryResourceNotification` and `QueryMemoryResourceNotification` functions to monitor system memory overall. If Windows reports low memory, the CLR will force a garbage collection in an effort to free up dead objects to reduce the size of a process' working set.

- **The CLR is unloading an AppDomain**   When an AppDomain unloads, the CLR considers nothing in the AppDomain to be a root, and a garbage collection consisting of all generations is performed. I'll discuss AppDomains in Chapter 21, "CLR Hosting and AppDomains."

- **The CLR is shutting down**   The CLR shuts down when a process terminates normally (as opposed to an external shutdown via Task Manager, for example). During this shutdown, the CLR considers nothing in the process to be a root and calls the `Finalize` method for all objects in the managed heap. Note that the CLR does not attempt to compact or free memory here because the whole process is terminating, and Windows will reclaim all of the processes' memory.

The CLR uses a special, dedicated thread to call `Finalize` methods. For the first four events, if a `Finalize` method enters an infinite loop, this special thread is blocked, and no more `Finalize` methods can be called. This is a very bad situation because the application will never be able to reclaim the memory occupied by the finalizable objects—the application will leak memory as long as it runs.

For the fifth event, each `Finalize` method is given approximately two seconds to return. If a `Finalize` method doesn't return within two seconds, the CLR just kills the process—no more `Finalize` methods are called. Also, if it takes more than 40 seconds to call all objects' `Finalize` methods, again, the CLR just kills the process.

> **Note**   These timeout values were correct at the time I wrote this text, but Microsoft might change them in the future. Code in a `Finalize` method can construct new objects. If this happens during CLR shutdown, the CLR continues collecting objects and calling their `Finalize` methods until no more objects exist or until the 40 seconds have elapsed.

Recall the **GCBeep** type presented earlier in this chapter. If a **GCBeep** object is being finalized because of the first, second, or third garbage collection reason, a new **GCBeep** object is constructed. This is OK because the application continues to run, assuming that more collections will occur in the future. However, if a **GCBeep** object is being finalized because of the fourth or fifth garbage collection reason, a new **GCBeep** object shouldn't be constructed because this object would be created while the AppDomain is unloading or the CLR is shutting down. If these new objects are created, the CLR will have a bunch of useless work to do because it will continue to call **Finalize** methods.

To prevent the construction of new **GCBeep** objects, **GCBeep**'s **Finalize** method calls **AppDomain**'s **IsFinalizingForUnload** method and also queries **System.Environment**'s **HasShutdownStarted** property. The **IsFinalizingForUnload** method returns **true** if the object's **Finalize** method is being called because the AppDomain is unloading. The **HasShutdownStarted** property returns **true** if the object's **Finalize** method is being called because the process is terminating.

Finalization Internals

On the surface, finalization seems pretty straightforward: you create an object and its **Finalize** method is called when it is collected. But once you dig in, finalization is more complicated than this.

When an application creates a new object, the **new** operator allocates the memory from the heap. If the object's type defines a **Finalize** method, a pointer to the object is placed on the *finalization list* just before the type's instance constructor is called. The finalization list is an internal data structure controlled by the garbage collector. Each entry in the list points to an object that should have its **Finalize** method called before the object's memory can be reclaimed.

Figure 20-5 shows a heap containing several objects. Some of these objects are reachable from the application's roots, and some are not. When objects C, E, F, I, and J were created, the system detected that these objects' types defined a **Finalize** method and so added pointers to these objects in the finalization list.

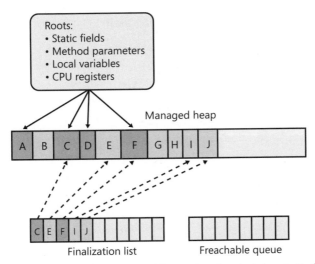

Figure 20-5   The managed heap showing pointers in its finalization list

Note   Even though `System.Object` defines a `Finalize` method, the CLR knows to ignore it; that is, when constructing an instance of a type, if the type's `Finalize` method is the one inherited from `System.Object`, the object isn't considered finalizable. One of the derived types must override `Object`'s `Finalize` method.

When a garbage collection occurs, objects B, E, G, H, I, and J are determined to be garbage. The garbage collector scans the finalization list looking for pointers to these objects. When a pointer is found, the pointer is removed from the finalization list and appended to the *freachable queue*. The freachable queue (pronounced "F-reachable") is another of the garbage collector's internal data structures. Each pointer in the freachable queue identifies an object that is ready to have its `Finalize` method called. After the collection, the managed heap looks like Figure 20-6.

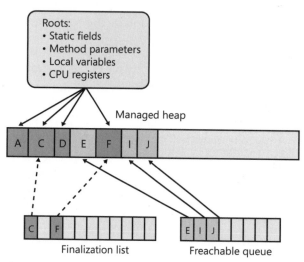

Figure 20-6   The managed heap showing pointers that moved from the finalization list to the freachable queue

In this figure, you see that the memory occupied by objects B, G, and H has been reclaimed because these objects didn't have a `Finalize` method. However, the memory occupied by objects E, I, and J couldn't be reclaimed because their `Finalize` methods haven't been called yet.

A special high-priority CLR thread is dedicated to calling `Finalize` methods. A dedicated thread is used to avoid potential thread synchronization situations that could arise if one of the application's normal-priority threads were used instead. When the freachable queue is empty (the usual case), this thread sleeps. But when entries appear, this thread wakes, removes each entry from the queue, and then calls each object's `Finalize` method. Because of the way this thread works, you shouldn't execute any code in a `Finalize` method that makes any assumptions about the thread that's executing the code. For example, avoid accessing thread-local storage in the `Finalize` method.

In the future, the CLR may use multiple finalizer threads. So you should avoid writing any code that assumes that `Finalize` methods will be called serially. In other words, you will need to use thread synchronization locks if code in a `Finalize` method touches shared state. With just one finalizer thread, there could be performance and scalability issues in the scenario in which you have multiple CPUs allocating finalizable objects but only one thread executing `Finalize` methods—the one thread might not be able to keep up with the allocations.

The interaction between the finalization list and the freachable queue is fascinating. First I'll tell you how the freachable queue got its name. Well, the "f" is obvious and stands for *finalization*; every entry in the freachable queue is a reference to an object in the managed heap that should have its `Finalize` method called. But the *reachable* part of the name means that the objects are reachable. To put it another way, the freachable queue is considered a root just as static fields are roots. So if an object is in the freachable queue, the object is reachable and is *not* garbage.

In short, when an object isn't reachable, the garbage collector considers the object to be garbage. Then when the garbage collector moves an object's reference from the finalization list to the freachable queue, the object is no longer considered garbage and its memory can't be reclaimed. As freachable objects are marked, objects referred to by their reference type fields are also marked recursively; all these objects must survive the collection. At this point, the garbage collector has finished identifying garbage. Some of the objects identified as garbage have been reclassified as not garbage—in a sense, the object has become *resurrected*. The garbage collector compacts the reclaimable memory, and the special CLR thread empties the freachable queue, executing each object's `Finalize` method.

The next time the garbage collector is invoked, it will see that the finalized objects are truly garbage because the application's roots don't point to it and the freachable queue no longer points to it either. The memory for the object is simply reclaimed. The important point to get from all of this is that two garbage collections are required to reclaim memory used by objects that require finalization. In reality, more than two collections will be necessary because the objects get promoted to another generation (which I'll explain later). Figure 20-7 shows what the managed heap looks like after the second garbage collection.

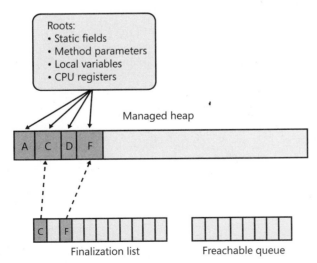

Figure 20-7   Status of managed heap after second garbage collection

The Dispose Pattern: Forcing an Object to Clean Up

The `Finalize` method is incredibly useful because it ensures that native resources aren't leaked when managed objects have their memory reclaimed. However, the problem with the `Finalize` method is there is no guarantee of when it will be called, and because it isn't a public method, a user of the class can't call it explicitly.

The capability to deterministically dispose of or close an object is frequently useful when you're working with managed types that wrap native resources such as files, database connections, and bitmaps. For example, you might want to open a database connection, query some records, and close the database connection—you wouldn't want the database connection to stay open until the next garbage collection occurs, especially because the next garbage collection could occur hours or even days after you retrieve the database records.

Types that offer the capability to be deterministically disposed of or closed implement what is known as the *dispose pattern*. The dispose pattern defines conventions a developer should adhere to when defining a type that wants to offer explicit cleanup to a user of the type. In addition, if a type implements the dispose pattern, a developer using the type knows exactly how to explicitly dispose of the object when it's no longer needed.

> **Note**   Any type that defines a `Finalize` method should also implement the dispose pattern as described in this section so that users of the type have a lot of control over the lifetime of the resource. However, a type can implement the dispose pattern and not define a `Finalize` method. For example, the `System.IO.BinaryWriter` class falls into this category. I'll explain the reason for this exception in the section "An Interesting Dependency Issue" later in this chapter.

Earlier I showed you the `SafeHandle` class. This class implements a `Finalize` method that ensures that a native resource wrapped by the object is closed (or released) when the object is collected. However, a developer using a `SafeHandle` object has a way to explicitly close the native resource because the `SafeHandle` class implements the `IDisposable` interface.

Let's take another look at the `SafeHandle` class. But for brevity, let's just focus on the parts that have to do with the dispose pattern:

```
// Implementing the IDisposable interface signals users of
// this class that it offers the dispose pattern.
public abstract class SafeHandle : CriticalFinalizerObject, IDisposable {

    // This public method can be called to deterministically close
    // the resource. This method implements IDisposable's Dispose.
    public void Dispose() {
        // Call the method that actually does the cleanup.
        Dispose(true);
    }
```

```
// This public method can be called instead of Dispose.
public void Close() {
    Dispose(true);
}

// When garbage collected, this Finalize method runs to close the resource
~SafeHandle() {
    // Call the method that actually does the cleanup.
    Dispose(false);
}

// This is the common method that does the actual cleanup.
// Finalize, Dispose, and Close call this method.
// Because this class isn't sealed, this method is protected & virtual.
// If this class were sealed, this method should be private.
protected virtual void Dispose(Boolean disposing) {
    if (disposing) {
        // The object is being explicitly disposed/closed, not
        // finalized. It is therefore safe for code in this if
        // statement to access fields that reference other
        // objects because the Finalize method of these other objects
        // hasn't yet been called.

        // For the SafeHandle class, there is nothing to do in here.
    }

    // The object is being disposed/closed or finalized, do the following:
    // If resource was already released, just return
    // If ownsHandle is false, return
    // Set flag indicating that this resource has been released
    // Call the virtual ReleaseHandle method
    // Call GC.SuppressFinalize(this) to prevent Finalize from being called
    }
}
```

Implementing the dispose pattern is hardly trivial. Now let me explain what all this code does. First, the **SafeHandle** class implements the **System.IDisposable** interface. This interface is defined in the FCL as follows:

```
public interface IDisposable {
    void Dispose();
}
```

Any type that implements this interface is stating that it adheres to the dispose pattern. Simply put, this means that the type offers a public, parameterless **Dispose** method that can be explicitly called to release the resource wrapped by the object. Note that the memory for the object itself is *not* freed from the managed heap's memory; the garbage collector is still responsible for freeing the object's memory, and there's no telling exactly when this will happen. The parameterless **Dispose** and **Close** methods should be both public and nonvirtual.

Note You might notice that this `SafeHandle` class also offers a public `Close` method. This method simply calls `Dispose`. Some classes that offer the dispose pattern also offer a `Close` method for convenience; but the dispose pattern doesn't require this method. For example, the `System.IO.FileStream` class offers the dispose pattern, and this class also offers a `Close` method. Programmers find it more natural to close a file rather than dispose of a file. However, the `System.Threading.Timer` class doesn't offer a `Close` method even though it adheres to the dispose pattern.

Important If a class defines a field in which the field's type implements the dispose pattern, the class itself should also implement the dispose pattern. The `Dispose` method should dispose of the object referred to by the field. This allows someone using the class to call `Dispose` on it, which in turn, releases the resources used by the object itself. In fact, this is one of the main reasons why types might implement the dispose pattern but not implement the `Finalize` method.

For example, the `BinaryWriter` class implements the dispose pattern. When `Dispose` is called on a `BinaryWriter` object, `BinaryWriter`'s `Dispose` method calls `Dispose` on the stream object maintained as a field inside the `BinaryWriter` object. So when the `BinaryWriter` object is disposed, the underlying stream is disposed, which, in turn, releases the native stream resource.

So now you know three ways to clean up a `SafeHandle` object: a programmer can write code to call `Dispose`, a programmer can write code to call `Close`, or the garbage collector can call the object's `Finalize` method. The cleanup code is placed in a separate, protected, virtual method, which is also called `Dispose`, but this `Dispose` method takes a `Boolean` parameter named `disposing`.

This `Dispose` method is where you put all of the cleanup code. In the `SafeHandle` example, the method sets a flag indicating that the resource has been released and then calls the virtual `ReleaseHandle` method to actually perform the releasing of the resource. Note that the dispose pattern states that a single object can have `Dispose` or `Close` called on it multiple times; the first time, the resource should be released, for future calls, the method should just return (no exception should be thrown).

Note It is possible to have multiple threads call `Dispose/Close` on a single object simultaneously. However, the dispose pattern states that thread synchronization is not required. The reason is because code should be calling `Dispose/Close` only if the code knows for a fact that no other thread is using the object. If you don't know if an object is still in use at a certain point in your code, you should not be calling `Dispose/Close`. Instead, wait for a garbage collection to kick in so that it can determine if the object is no longer being used, and then release the resource.

When an object's `Finalize` method is called by the CLR, the `Dispose` method's `disposing` parameter is set to `false`. This tells the `Dispose` method that it shouldn't execute any code that references other managed objects whose classes implement a **Finalize** method. Imagine that the CLR is shutting down, and inside a **Finalize** method, you attempt to write to a **FileStream**. This might not work because the **FileStream** might have already had its **Finalize** method called, closing the underlying disk file.

On the other hand, when you call **Dispose** or **Close** in your code, the **Dispose** method's **disposing** parameter must be set to **true**. This indicates that the object is being explicitly disposed of, not finalized. In this case, the **Dispose** method is allowed to execute code that references another object (such as a **FileStream**); because you have control over the program's logic, you know that the **FileStream** object is still open.

By the way, if the **SafeHandle** class were sealed, the **Dispose** method that takes a **Boolean** should be implemented as a private method instead of a protected virtual method. But since the **Safe-Handle** class is not sealed, any class that derives from **SafeHandle** can override the **Dispose** method that takes a **Boolean** in order to override the cleanup code. The derived class wouldn't implement the parameterless **Dispose** or **Close** methods, and it wouldn't override the **Finalize** method. The derived class would simply inherit the implementation of all of these methods. Note that the derived class' override of the **Dispose** method that takes a **Boolean** should call the base class' version of the **Dispose** method that takes a **Boolean**, allowing the base class to perform whatever cleanup it needs to do. This is exactly the case of the **FileStream** type that I used as an example: it derives from **Stream** that implements the **Close** and the parameterless **IDisposable** .**Dispose** method. **FileStream** simply overrides the **Dispose** method, which takes a **Boolean** parameter to dispose of the **SafeHandle** field wrapping the unmanaged file resource.

> **Important**   You need to be aware of some versioning issues here. If in version 1, a base type doesn't implement the **IDisposable** interface, it can never implement this interface in a later version. If the base type were to add the **IDisposable** interface in the future, all of the derived types wouldn't know to call the base type's methods, and the base type wouldn't get a chance to clean itself up properly. On the other hand, if in version 1, a base type implements the **IDisposable** interface, it can never remove this interface in a later version because the derived type would try to call methods that no longer exist in the base type.

Another noteworthy part of this code is the call to **GC**'s static **SuppressFinalize** method inside the **Dispose** method that takes a **Boolean**. You see, if code using a **SafeHandle** object explicitly calls **Dispose** or **Close**, there is no need for the object's **Finalize** method to execute, because if **Finalize** did execute, there would be an unnecessary attempt to release the resource a second time. The call to **GC**'s **SuppressFinalize** turns on a bit flag associated with the object referred to by its single **this** parameter. When this flag is on, the CLR knows not to move this object's pointer from the finalization list to the freachable queue, preventing the object's **Finalize** method from being called and ensuring that the object doesn't live until the next garbage collection. Note that the **SafeHandle** class calls **SuppressFinalize** even when the object is being finalized. This has no ill effect because the object is already in the process of being finalized.

Using a Type That Implements the Dispose Pattern

Now that you know how a type implements the dispose pattern, let's take a look at how a developer uses a type that offers the dispose pattern. Instead of talking about the **SafeHandle** class, let's talk about the more common **System.IO.FileStream** class. The **FileStream** class offers the ability to open a file, read bytes from the file, write bytes to the file, and close the file. When a **FileStream** object is constructed, the Win32 **CreateFile** function is called, the returned handle is saved in a **SafeFileHandle** object, and a reference to this object is maintained via a private field in the **FileStream** object. The **FileStream** class also offers several additional properties (such as **Length**, **Position**, **CanRead**) and methods (such as **Read**, **Write**, **Flush**).

Let's say that you want to write some code that creates a temporary file, writes some bytes to the file, and then deletes the file. You might start writing the code like this:

```
using System;
using System.IO;

public static class Program {
    public static void Main() {
        // Create the bytes to write to the temporary file.
        Byte[] bytesToWrite = new Byte[] { 1, 2, 3, 4, 5 };

        // Create the temporary file.
        FileStream fs = new FileStream("Temp.dat", FileMode.Create);

        // Write the bytes to the temporary file.
        fs.Write(bytesToWrite, 0, bytesToWrite.Length);

        // Delete the temporary file.
        File.Delete("Temp.dat");  // Throws an IOException
    }
}
```

Unfortunately, if you build and run this code, it might work, but most likely it won't. The problem is that the call to **File**'s static **Delete** method requests that Windows delete a file while it is still open. And so **Delete** throws a **System.IO.IOException** exception with the following string message: "The process cannot access the file "Temp.dat" because it is being used by another process."

Be aware that in some cases, the file might actually be deleted! If another thread somehow caused a garbage collection to start after the call to **Write** and before the call to **Delete**, the **FileStream**'s **SafeFileHandle** field would have its **Finalize** method called, which would close the file and allow **Delete** to work. The likelihood of this situation is extremely rare, however, and therefore the previous code will fail more than 99 percent of the time.

Fortunately, the `FileStream` class implements the dispose pattern, allowing you to modify the source code to explicitly close the file. Here's the corrected source code:

```
using System;
using System.IO;

public static class Program {
    public static void Main() {
        // Create the bytes to write to the temporary file.
        Byte[] bytesToWrite = new Byte[] { 1, 2, 3, 4, 5 };

        // Create the temporary file.
        FileStream fs = new FileStream("Temp.dat", FileMode.Create);

        // Write the bytes to the temporary file.
        fs.Write(bytesToWrite, 0, bytesToWrite.Length);

        // Explicitly close the file when finished writing to it.
        fs.Dispose();

        // Delete the temporary file.
        File.Delete("Temp.dat");  // This always works now.
    }
}
```

The only difference here is that I've added a call to `FileStream`'s `Dispose` method. The `Dispose` method calls the `Dispose` method that takes a `Boolean` as parameter, which calls `Dispose` on the `SafeFileHandle` object, which ends up calling the Win32 `CloseHandle` function, which causes Windows to close the file. Now, when `File`'s `Delete` method is called, Windows sees that the file isn't open and successfully deletes it.

Because the `FileStream` class also offers a public `Close` method, the earlier code could be written as follows with identical results:

```
using System;
using System.IO;

public static class Program {
    public static void Main() {
        // Create the bytes to write to the temporary file.
        Byte[] bytesToWrite = new Byte[] { 1, 2, 3, 4, 5 };

        // Create the temporary file.
        FileStream fs = new FileStream("Temp.dat", FileMode.Create);

        // Write the bytes to the temporary file.
        fs.Write(bytesToWrite, 0, bytesToWrite.Length);

        // Explicitly close the file when finished writing to it.
        fs.Close();

        // Delete the temporary file.
        File.Delete("Temp.dat");  // This always works now.
    }
}
```

> **Note**   Again, remember that the **Close** method isn't officially part of the dispose pattern; some types will offer it and some won't.

Keep in mind that calling **Dispose** or **Close** simply gives the programmer a way to force the object to do its cleanup at a deterministic time; these methods have no control over the lifetime of the memory used by the object in the managed heap. This means you can still call methods on the object even though it has been cleaned up. The following code calls the **Write** method after the file is closed, attempting to write more bytes to the file. Obviously, the bytes can't be written, and when the code executes, the second call to the **Write** method throws a **System.ObjectDisposedException** exception with the following string message: "Cannot access a closed file."

```
using System;

using System.IO;

public static class Program {
    public static void Main() {
        // Create the bytes to write to the temporary file.
        Byte[] bytesToWrite = new Byte[] { 1, 2, 3, 4, 5 };

        // Create the temporary file.
        FileStream fs = new FileStream("Temp.dat", FileMode.Create);

        // Write the bytes to the temporary file.
        fs.Write(bytesToWrite, 0, bytesToWrite.Length);

        // Explicitly close the file when finished writing to it.
        fs.Close();

        // Try to write to the file after closing it.
        // The following line throws an ObjectDisposedException.
        fs.Write(bytesToWrite, 0, bytesToWrite.Length);

        // Delete the temporary file.
        File.Delete("Temp.dat");
    }
}
```

No memory corruption has occurred here because the memory for the **FileStream** object still exists; it's just that the object can't successfully execute its methods after it is explicitly disposed.

> **Important**   When defining your own type that implements the dispose pattern, be sure to write code in all of your methods and properties to throw a **System.ObjectDisposed-Exception** if the object has been explicitly cleaned up. The **Dispose** and **Close** methods should never throw an **ObjectDisposedException** if called multiple times, though; these methods should just return.

> **Important** In general, I strongly discourage the use of calling a `Dispose` or `Close` method. The reason is that the CLR's garbage collector is well written, and you should let it do its job. The garbage collector knows when an object is no longer accessible from application code, and only then will it collect the object. When application code calls `Dispose` or `Close`, it is effectively saying that it knows when the application no longer has a need for the object. For many applications, it is impossible to know for sure when an object is no longer required.
>
> For example, if you have code that constructs a new object, and you then pass a reference to this object to another method, the other method could save a reference to the object in some internal field variable (a root). There is no way for the calling method to know that this has happened. Sure, the calling method can call `Dispose` or `Close`, but later, some other code might try to access the object, causing an `ObjectDisposedException` to be thrown.
>
> I recommend that you call `Dispose` or `Close` either at a place in your code where you know you must clean up the resource (as in the case of attempting to delete an open file) or at a place where you know it is safe to call one of the methods and you want to improve performance by removing the object from the finalization list, thus preventing object promotion.

C#'s using **Statement**

The previous code examples show how to explicitly call a type's `Dispose` or `Close` method. If you decide to call either of these methods explicitly, I highly recommend that you place the call in an exception-handling **finally** block. This way, the cleanup code is guaranteed to execute. So it would be better to write the previous code example as follows:

```
using System;
using System.IO;

public static class Program {
    public static void Main() {
        // Create the bytes to write to the temporary file.
        Byte[] bytesToWrite = new Byte[] { 1, 2, 3, 4, 5 };

        // Create the temporary file.
        FileStream fs = new FileStream("Temp.dat", FileMode.Create);
        try {
            // Write the bytes to the temporary file.
            fs.Write(bytesToWrite, 0, bytesToWrite.Length);
        }
        finally {
            // Explicitly close the file when finished writing to it.
            if (fs != null)
                fs.Dispose();
        }

        // Delete the temporary file.
        File.Delete("Temp.dat");
    }
}
```

Adding the exception-handling code is the right thing to do, and you must have the diligence to do it. Fortunately, the C# language provides a **using** statement, which offers a simplified syntax that produces code identical to the code just shown. Here's how the preceding code would be rewritten using C#'s **using** statement:

```
using System;
using System.IO;

public static class Program {
   public static void Main() {
      // Create the bytes to write to the temporary file.
      Byte[] bytesToWrite = new Byte[] { 1, 2, 3, 4, 5 };

      // Create the temporary file.
      using (FileStream fs = new FileStream("Temp.dat", FileMode.Create)) {
         // Write the bytes to the temporary file.
         fs.Write(bytesToWrite, 0, bytesToWrite.Length);
      }

      // Delete the temporary file.
      File.Delete("Temp.dat");
   }
}
```

In the **using** statement, you initialize an object and save its reference in a variable. Then you access the variable via code contained inside **using**'s braces. When you compile this code, the compiler automatically emits the **try** and **finally** blocks. Inside the **finally** block, the compiler emits code to cast the object to an **IDisposable** and calls the **Dispose** method. Obviously, the compiler allows the **using** statement to be used only with types that implement the **IDisposable** interface.

> **Note**   C#'s **using** statement supports the capability to initialize multiple variables as long as the variables are all of the same type. It also supports the capability to use just an already initialized variable. For more information about this topic, refer to the **using** statement topic in the C# Programmer's Reference.

The **using** statement also works with value types that implement the **IDisposable** interface. This allows you to create an extremely efficient and useful mechanism to encapsulate the code necessary to begin and end an operation. For example, let's say that you want to lock a block of code by using a **Mutex** object. The **Mutex** class does implement the **IDisposable** interface, but calling **Dispose** on it releases the native resource; it has nothing to do with the lock itself. To get efficient mutex locking and unlocking, you can define a value type that encapsulates the locking and unlocking of a **Mutex** object. The **MutexLock** structure below is an example of this, and the **Main** method following it demonstrates how to use the **MutexLock** effectively:

```
using System;
using System.Threading;

// This value type encapsulates mutex locking and unlocking
// Note that this is a non-public structure to help my
// own code; this type is not part of a library
internal struct MutexLock : IDisposable {
    private Mutex m_mutex;

    // This constructor acquires a lock on the mutex
    public MutexLock(Mutex m) {
        m_mutex = m;
        m_mutex.WaitOne();
    }

    // This Dispose method releases the lock on the mutex
    public void Dispose() {
        m_mutex.ReleaseMutex();
    }
}

public static class Program {
    // This method demonstrates how to use the MutexLock effectively
    public static void Main() {
        // Construct a mutex object
        Mutex m = new Mutex();

        // Lock the mutex, do something, and unlock the mutex
        using (new MutexLock(m)) {
            // Perform some thread-safe operation in here...
        }
    }
}
```

Important   Having a value type implement **IDisposable** as in the **MutexLock** example is very efficient. However, value types that implement **IDisposable** should be defined and used only in your own private code; do not define public values types that implement **IDisposable** in reusable class library code. The reason is because value types are copied when boxed or when passed as arguments to methods. This means that there are multiple instances, all referring to a single resource. A user of an instance might end the operation but there might be other code using another instance. This other instance could be used to end the operation twice, affecting the stability of the application. If in library code you want to offer a helper class such as the **MutexLock** type, you should define the type as a reference type (class), and you should also implement additional logic to ensure that the end operation executes only once even if **Dispose** is called multiple times.

An Interesting Dependency Issue

The `System.IO.FileStream` type allows the user to open a file for reading and writing. To improve performance, the type's implementation makes use of a memory buffer. Only when the buffer fills does the type flush the contents of the buffer to the file. A `FileStream` supports the writing of bytes only. If you want to write characters and strings, you can use a `System.IO.StreamWriter`, as is demonstrated in the following code:

```
FileStream fs = new FileStream("DataFile.dat", FileMode.Create);
StreamWriter sw = new StreamWriter(fs);
sw.Write("Hi there");

// The following call to Close is what you should do.
sw.Close();
// NOTE: StreamWriter.Close closes the FileStream.
// The FileStream doesn't have to be explicitly closed.
```

Notice that the `StreamWriter`'s constructor takes a reference to a `Stream` object as a parameter, allowing a reference to a `FileStream` object to be passed as an argument. Internally, the `StreamWriter` object saves the `Stream`'s reference. When you write to a `StreamWriter` object, it internally buffers the data in its own memory buffer. When the buffer is full, the `StreamWriter` object writes the data to the `Stream`.

When you're finished writing data via the `StreamWriter` object, you should call `Dispose` or `Close`. (Because the `StreamWriter` type implements the dispose pattern, you can also use it with C#'s `using` statement.) Both of these methods do exactly the same thing: cause the `StreamWriter` object to flush its data to the `Stream` object and close the `Stream` object. In my example, when the `FileStream` object is closed, it flushes its buffer to disk just prior to calling the Win32 `CloseHandle` function.

> **Note**   You don't have to explicitly call `Dispose` or `Close` on the `FileStream` object because the `StreamWriter` calls it for you. However, if you do call `Dispose`/`Close` explicitly, the `FileStream` will see that the object has already been cleaned up—the methods do nothing and just return.

What do you think would happen if there were no code to explicitly call `Dispose` or `Close`? Well, at some point, the garbage collector would correctly detect that the objects were garbage and finalize them. But the garbage collector doesn't guarantee the order in which the `Finalize` methods are called. So if the `FileStream` object were finalized first, it would close the file. Then when the `StreamWriter` object was finalized, it would attempt to write data to the closed file, throwing an exception. If, on the other hand, the `StreamWriter` object were finalized first, the data would be safely written to the file.

How was Microsoft to solve this problem? Making the garbage collector finalize objects in a specific order would have been impossible because objects could contain references to each other, and there would be no way for the garbage collector to correctly guess the order in which to finalize these objects. Here is Microsoft's solution: the **StreamWriter** type does not implement a **Finalize** method, missing the opportunity to flush the data in its buffer to the underlying **FileStream** object. This means that if you forget to explicitly close the **Stream-Writer** object, data is guaranteed to be lost. Microsoft expects developers to see this consistent loss of data and fix the code by inserting an explicit call to **Close**/**Dispose**.

> **Note**   Version 2.0 of the .NET Framework offers a feature called Managed Debugging Assistants (MDA). When an MDA is enabled, the .NET Framework looks for certain common programmer errors and fires a corresponding MDA. In the debugger, it looks like an exception has been thrown. There is an MDA available to detect when a **StreamWriter** object is garbage collected without having prior been explicitly closed. To enable this MDA in Visual Studio, open your project and select the Debug.Exceptions menu item. In the Exceptions dialog box, expand the Managed Debugging Assistants node and scroll to the bottom. There you will see the StreamWriterBufferedDataLost MDA. Select the Thrown checkbox to have the Visual Studio debugger stop whenever a **StreamWriter** object's data is lost.

Manually Monitoring and Controlling the Lifetime of Objects

The CLR provides each AppDomain with a *GC handle table*. This table allows an application to monitor the lifetime of an object or manually control the lifetime of an object. When an AppDomain is created, the table is empty. Each entry on the table consists of a pointer to an object on the managed heap and a flag indicating how you want to monitor or control the object. An application adds and removes entries from the table via the **System.Runtime .InteropServices.GCHandle** type shown below. Since the GC handle table is used mostly in scenarios when you are interoperating with unmanaged code, most of **GCHandle**'s members have a link demand for **SecurityPermission** with the **UnmanagedCode** flag.

```
// This type is defined in the System.Runtime.InteropServices namespace
public struct GCHandle {
    // Static methods that create an entry in the table
    public static GCHandle Alloc(object value);
    public static GCHandle Alloc(object value, GCHandleType type);

    // Static methods that convert a GCHandle to an IntPtr
    public static explicit operator IntPtr(GCHandle value);
    public static IntPtr ToIntPtr(GCHandle value);

    // Static methods that convert an IntPtr to a GCHandle
    public static explicit operator GCHandle(IntPtr value);
    public static GCHandle FromIntPtr(IntPtr value);

    // Static methods that compare two GCHandles
    public static Boolean operator ==(GCHandle a, GCHandle b);
    public static Boolean operator !=(GCHandle a, GCHandle b);

    // Instance method to free the entry in the table (index is set to 0)
    public void Free();
```

```
// Instance property to get/set the entry's object reference
public object Target { get; set; }

// Instance property that returns true if index is not 0
public Boolean IsAllocated { get; }

// For a pinned entry, this returns the address of the object
public IntPtr AddrOfPinnedObject();

public override Int32 GetHashCode();
public override Boolean Equals(object o);
}
```

Basically, to control or monitor an object's lifetime, you call **GCHandle**'s static **Alloc** method, passing a reference to the object that you want to monitor/control, and a **GCHandleType**, which is a flag indicating how you want to monitor/control the object. The **GCHandleType** type is an enumerated type defined as follows:

```
public enum GCHandleType {
    Weak = 0,    // Used for monitoring an object
    WeakTrackResurrection = 1// Used for monitoring an object
    Normal = 2, // Used for controlling object lifetime
    Pinned = 3  // Used for controlling object lifetime
}
```

Now, here's what each flag means:

- **Weak** This flag allows you to *monitor* the lifetime of an object. Specifically, you can detect when the garbage collector has determined this object to be unreachable from application code. Note that the object's **Finalize** method may or may not have executed yet and therefore, the object may still be in memory.

- **WeakTrackResurrection** This flag allows you to *monitor* the lifetime of an object. Specifically, you can detect when the garbage collector has determined that this object is unreachable from application code. Note that the object's **Finalize** method (if it exists) has definitely executed, and the object's memory has been reclaimed.

- **Normal** This flag allows you to *control* the lifetime of an object. Specifically, you are telling the garbage collector that this object must remain in memory even though there may be no variables (roots) in the application that refer to this object. When a garbage collection runs, the memory for this object can be compacted (moved). The **Alloc** method that doesn't take a **GCHandleType** flag assumes that **GCHandleType.Normal** is specified.

- **Pinned** This flag allows you to *control* the lifetime of an object. Specifically, you are telling the garbage collector that this object must remain in memory even though there might be no variables (roots) in the application that refer to this object. When a garbage collection runs, the memory for this object cannot be compacted (moved). This is typically useful when you want to hand the address of the memory out to unmanaged code. The unmanaged code can write to this memory in the managed heap knowing that the location of the managed object will not be moved due to a garbage collection.

When you call **GCHandle**'s static **Alloc** method, it scans the AppDomain's GC handle table, looking for an available entry where the address of the object you passed to **Alloc** is stored, and a flag is set to whatever you passed for the **GCHandleType** argument. Then, **Alloc** returns a **GCHandle** instance back to you. A **GCHandle** is a lightweight value type that contains a single instance field in it, an **IntPtr**, that refers to the index of the entry in the table. When you want to free this entry in the GC handle table, you take the **GCHandle** instance and call the **Free** method (which also invalidates the instance by setting the **IntPtr** field to zero).

Here's how the garbage collector makes use of the GC handle table. When a garbage collection occurs:

1. The garbage collector marks all of the reachable objects (as described at the beginning of this chapter). Then, the garbage collector scans the GC handle table; all **Normal** or **Pinned** objects are considered roots, and these objects are marked as well (including any objects that these objects refer to via their fields).

2. The garbage collector scans the GC handle table looking for all of the **Weak** entries. If a **Weak** entry refers to an object that isn't marked, the pointer identifies an unreachable object (garbage), and the entry has its pointer value changed to **null**.

3. The garbage collector scans the finalization list. If a pointer in the list refers to an unmarked object, the pointer identifies an unreachable object, and the pointer is moved from the finalization list to the freachable queue. At this point, the object is marked because the object is now considered reachable.

4. The garbage collector scans the GC handle table looking for all of the **WeakTrack-Resurrection** entries. If a **WeakTrackResurrection** entry refers to an object that isn't marked (which now is an object pointed to by an entry in the freachable queue), the pointer identifies an unreachable object (garbage), and the entry has its pointer value changed to **null**.

5. The garbage collector compacts the memory, squeezing out the holes left by the unreachable objects. Note that the garbage collector sometimes decides not to compact memory if it determines that the amount of fragmentation isn't worth the time to compact. **Pinned** objects are not compacted (moved); the garbage collector will move other objects around them.

Now that you have an understanding of the mechanism, let's take a look at when you'd use them. The easiest flags to understand are the **Normal** and **Pinned** flags, so let's start with these two. Both of these flags are typically used when interoperating with unmanaged code.

The **Normal** flag is used when you need to hand a reference to a managed object to unmanaged code because, at some point in the future, the unmanaged code is going to call back into managed code, passing it the reference. You can't actually pass a pointer to a managed object out to unmanaged code because, if a garbage collection occurs, the object could move in memory, invalidating the pointer. So to work around this, you would call **GCHandle**'s **Alloc** method, passing in a reference to the object and the **Normal** flag. Then you'd cast the returned **GCHandle** instance to an **IntPtr** and pass the **IntPtr** into the unmanaged code. When the unmanaged code calls back into managed code, the managed code would cast the passed **IntPtr** back to a **GCHandle** and then query the **Target** property to get the reference (or current address) of the managed object. When the unmanaged code no longer needs the reference, you'd call **GCHandle**'s **Free** method, which will allow a future garbage collection to free the object (assuming no other root exists to this object).

Notice that in this scenario, the unmanaged code is not actually using the managed object itself; the unmanaged code wants a way just to reference the object. In some scenarios, the unmanaged code needs to actually use the managed object. In these scenarios, the managed object must be pinned. Pinning prevents the garbage collector from moving/compacting the object. A common example is when you want to pass a managed **String** object to a Win32 function. In this case, the **String** object must be pinned because you can't pass the reference of a managed object to unmanaged code and then have the garbage collector move the object in memory. If the **String** object were moved, the unmanaged code would either be reading or writing to memory that no longer contained the **String** object's characters—this will surely cause the application to run unpredictably.

When you use the CLR's P/Invoke mechanism to call a method, the CLR pins the arguments for you automatically and unpins them when the unmanaged method returns. So, in most cases, you never have to use the **GCHandle** type to explicitly pin any managed objects yourself. You do have to use the **GCHandle** type explicitly when you need to pass the address of a managed object to unmanaged code and then, the unmanaged function returns, but unmanaged code might still need to use the object later. The most common example of this is when performing asynchronous I/O operations.

Let's say that you allocate a byte array that should be filled as data comes in from a socket. Then, you would call **GCHandle**'s **Alloc** method, passing in a reference to the array object and the **Pinned** flag. Then, using the returned **GCHandle** instance, you call the **AddrOfPinnedObject** method. This returns an **IntPtr** that is the actual address of the pinned object in the managed heap; you'd then pass this address into the unmanaged function, which will return back to managed code immediately. While the data is coming from the socket, this byte array buffer should not move in memory; preventing this buffer from moving is accomplished by using the **Pinned** flag. When the asynchronous I/O operation has completed, you'd call **GCHandle**'s **Free** method, which will allow a future garbage collection to move the buffer. Your managed code should still have a reference to the buffer so that you can access the data, and this reference will prevent a garbage collection from freeing the buffer from memory completely.

Now, let's talk about the next two flags, **Weak** and **WeakTrackResurrection**. These two flags can be used in scenarios when interoperating with unmanaged code, but they can also be used in scenarios that use only managed code. The **Weak** flag is used in scenarios when you don't want one object to keep another object from being garbage collected. For example, let's say that you construct a **Fax** object, and you want this object to receive notifications whenever a **MailManager** object receives a new e-mail message. However, you want to allow the `Fax` object to get garbage collected at some point if no other code wants to keep it alive. Naturally, if the `Fax` object did get garbage collected, then the `MailManager` object would just not notify it whenever a new e-mail message arrives.

The way the garbage collector works, implementing this scenario is actually quite tricky. The problem is that the object that sends the notifications needs to have a reference to the object that receives the notifications. This reference forces the object that receives notifications to stay alive, preventing it from being garbage collected. However, this problem can be fixed using the `Weak` and `WeakTrackResurrection` flags.

Here's how to make this work. When the `Fax` object is constructed, it will register itself with the `MailManager` object by passing it a delegate that identifies the callback method defined inside the `Fax` class. The `MailManager` object will call `GCHandle`'s `Alloc` method, passing in the reference to the delegate object and the `Weak` flag. The `MailManager` object will save the returned `GCHandle` instance in a collection instead of saving the reference to the delegate object. Since the `MailManager` object has no reference to the delegate object, a garbage collection can collect the delegate object and the `Fax` object that the delegate object refers to if there are no other references to keep the `Fax` object alive.

When the `MailManager` object wants to notify the `Fax` object that new mail has arrived, it would take the saved `GCHandle` instance and use it to query the `Target` property. If the `Target` property returns `null`, the `Fax` object has been garbage collected and the `MailManager` object should now use the saved `GCHandle` instance to call `Free` and remove it from its internal list of listeners. If the `Target` property returns a non-`null` value, the `Fax` object is still alive, and the variable that has the value returned from the `Target` property is actually a reference to the delegate wrapping an instance method of the `Fax` object that will now keep the `Fax` object from being garbage collected. The `MailManager` object can now use this variable to notify the `Fax` object that new e-mail has arrived. When the variable goes out of scope, the `Fax` object becomes subject to garbage collection again.

As mentioned earlier, the only difference between the `Weak` and `WeakTrackResurrection` flags is when the CLR indicates that the object has been garbage collected. In the real world, I've never actually seen anyone use the `WeakTrackResurrection` flag.

Note It would actually be pretty cool if the .NET Framework included a weak reference delegate mechanism, but there is no such thing in existence today. However, it has been bantered about in the CLR team at Microsoft, and it is likely that such a thing will be part of a future version.

Since working with the `GCHandle` type can be a bit cumbersome, the `System` namespace includes a `WeakReference` class to help you. This class is really just an object-oriented wrapper around a `GCHandle` instance: logically, its constructor calls `GCHandle`'s `Alloc`, its `Target` property calls **GCHandle**'s **Target** property, and its **Finalize** method calls **GCHandle**'s **Free** method. In addition, no special permissions are required for code to use the **WeakReference** class because the class supports only weak references; it doesn't support the behavior provided by **GCHandle** instances allocated with a **GCHandleType** of **Normal** or **Pinned**.

The downside of the **WeakReference** class is that it is a class. So the **WeakReference** class is a heavier-weight object than a **GCHandle** instance. Also, the **WeakReference** class doesn't implement the dispose pattern (which is a bug), so there is no way for you to free the **GCHandle** table entry explicitly; you have to wait for a garbage collection to kick in so that its **Finalize** method is called.

The following code demonstrates how to use the **WeakReference** class to implement the scenario just described:

```
using System;
using System.Collections.Generic;

public static class Program {
    public static void Main() {
        // Construct a MailManager object
        MailManager mm = new MailManager();

        // Construct a Fax object
        Fax f = new Fax(mm);

        // Since no GCs have occurred, the Fax object
        // will receive the event notification
        mm.SimulateNewMail();

        // Force a GC
        GC.Collect();

        // Since a GC has occurred, the Fax object
        // will not receive the event notification
        mm.SimulateNewMail();
    }
}

internal sealed class MailManager {
    // The collection maintains the set of WeakReferences to delegates
    private List<WeakReference> m_NewMailCallbacks = new List<WeakReference>();

    // This event is raised when new e-mail arrives
    public event EventHandler NewMail {
        add {
            lock (m_NewMailCallbacks) {
                // Construct a WeakReference around the passed-in delegate
                // and add the WeakReference to our collection
                m_NewMailCallbacks.Add(new WeakReference(value));
            }
        }
```

```
remove {
   lock (m_NewMailCallbacks) {

      // Scan collection looking for a matching delegate and remove it
      for (Int32 n = 0; n < m_NewMailCallbacks.Count; n++) {

         // Pull the WeakReference out of the collection
         WeakReference wr = m_NewMailCallbacks[n];

         // Try to turn the weak reference into a strong reference
         EventHandler eh = (EventHandler) wr.Target;

         if (eh == null) {
            // The object was garbage collected
            // Remove this entry from the collection
            m_NewMailCallbacks.RemoveAt(n);
            n--;          // Go back an entry
            continue;     // Try the next entry
         }

         // The object was not garbage collected
         // Does collection delegate match passed-in delegate
         if ((eh.Target == value.Target) && (eh.Method == value.Method)) {
            // Yes, they match. Remove it and return
            m_NewMailCallbacks.RemoveAt(n);
            break;
         }
      }
   }
}

// Call this method to simulate new mail arriving
public void SimulateNewMail() {
   Console.WriteLine("About to raise the NewMail event");
   OnNewMail(EventArgs.Empty);
}

// This method raises the NewMail event
private void OnNewMail(EventArgs e) {
   lock (m_NewMailCallbacks) {

      // Scan our collection, calling back each delegate
      for (Int32 n = 0; n < m_NewMailCallbacks.Count; n++) {

         // Pull the WeakReference out of the collection
         WeakReference wr = m_NewMailCallbacks[n];

         // Try to turn the weak reference into a strong reference
         EventHandler eh = (EventHandler)wr.Target;

         if (eh == null) {
            // The object was garbage collected
            // Remove this entry from the collection
            m_NewMailCallbacks.RemoveAt(n);
            n--;           // Go back an entry
         } else {
```

```
                  // The object was not garbage collected
                  // Invoke the delegate
                  eh(this, e);
               }
            }
         }
      }
   }


internal sealed class Fax {
   // When constructed, register interest in the MailManager's NewMail event
   public Fax(MailManager mm) {
      mm.NewMail += GotMail;
   }

   // The method is called when NewMail arrives
   public void GotMail(Object sender, EventArgs e) {
      // Just prove that we got here
      Console.WriteLine("In Fax.GotMail");
   }
}
```

When you compile and run the code above, you get the following output:

```
About to raise the NewMail event
In Fax.GotMail
About to raise the NewMail event
```

Important   When developers start learning about weak references, they immediately start thinking that they are useful in caching scenarios. For example, they think it would be cool to construct a bunch of objects that contain a lot of data and then to create weak references to these objects. When the program needs the data, the program checks the weak reference to see if the object that contains the data is still around, and if it is, the program just uses it; the program experiences high performance. However, if a garbage collection occurred, the objects that contain the data will be destroyed, and when the program has to re-create the data, the program experiences lower performance.

The problem with this technique is the following: Garbage collections do not occur when memory is full or close to full. Instead, garbage collections occur whenever generation 0 is full, which occurs approximately after every 256 KB of memory is allocated. So objects are being tossed out of memory much more frequently than desired, and your application's performance suffers greatly.

Weak references can be used quite effectively in caching scenarios, but building a good cache algorithm that finds the right balance between memory consumption and speed is very complex. Basically, you want your cache to keep strong references to all of your objects and then, when you see that memory is getting tight, you start turning strong references into weak references. Currently, the CLR offers no mechanism to notify an application that memory is getting tight. But some people have had much success by periodically calling the Win32 `GlobalMemory-StatusEx` function and checking the returned `MEMORYSTATUSEX` structure's `dwMemoryLoad` member. If this member reports a value above 80, memory is getting tight, and you can start converting strong references to weak references based on whether you want a least-recently used algorithm, a most-frequently used algorithm, a time-base algorithm, or whatever.

Resurrection

When we talked about finalization, you'll recall that when an object requiring finalization is considered dead, the garbage collector forces the object back to life so that its `Finalize` method can be called. Then, after its `Finalize` method is called, the object is permanently dead. To summarize: An object requiring finalization dies, lives, and then dies again. Bringing a dead object back to life is called *resurrection*.

The act of preparing to call an object's `Finalize` method is a form of resurrection. When the garbage collector places a reference to the object on the freachable queue, the object is now reachable from a root and has come back to life. This is required so that the code in the `Finalize` method can access the object's fields. Eventually, the object's `Finalize` method returns, no roots point to the object because it is removed from the freachable queue, and the object is dead forever after.

But what if an object's `Finalize` method executed code that placed a pointer to the object in a static field, as demonstrated in the following code?

```
internal sealed class SomeType {
   ~SomeType() {
      Program.s_ObjHolder = this;
   }
}

public static class Program {
   public static Object s_ObjHolder;      // Defaults to null
   ...
}
```

In this case, when a `SomeType` object has its `Finalize` method called, a reference to the object is placed in a root, and the object is reachable from the application's code. This object is now resurrected, and the garbage collector won't consider the object to be garbage. The application is free to use the object—but you must remember that the object *has* been finalized, so using it can cause unpredictable results. Also keep in mind that if `SomeType` contained fields that referenced other objects (either directly or indirectly), all objects would be resurrected because they are all reachable from the application's roots. However, be aware that some of these other objects might also have had their `Finalize` method called.

As in real life (or death), resurrection is not considered a good thing, and you should avoid writing code that takes advantage of this "feature" of the CLR. The few scenarios in which resurrection can be useful are when an application's architecture requires use of the same object over and over again. When the object is finished being used, a garbage collection will occur. In the object's `Finalize` method, it assigns its `this` pointer to another root, preventing the object from dying. But you'll want to tell the garbage collector to call the object's `Finalize` method again after the next usage. To make this possible, the `GC` type offers a static method named `ReRegisterForFinalize`. This method takes a single parameter: a reference to an object.

The following code demonstrates how to fix `SomeType`'s `Finalize` method so that the `Finalize` method is called after each use of the object:

```
internal sealed class SomeType {
   ~SomeType() {
      Program.s_ObjHolder = this;
      GC.ReRegisterForFinalize(this);
   }
}
```

When the `Finalize` method is called, it resurrects the object by making a root refer to the object. The `Finalize` method then calls `ReRegisterForFinalize`, which appends the address of the specified object (`this`) to the end of the finalization list. When the garbage collector determines that this object is unreachable (some time in the future when the static field is set to `null`), it will move the object's pointer from the finalization list to the freachable queue, and the `Finalize` method will be called again. Again, remember that resurrecting an object resurrects all of the objects it refers to; you may need to call `ReRegisterForFinalize` for all of these objects, and in many situations, this is impossible because you won't have access to the private fields of the other objects!

This example shows how to create an object that constantly resurrects itself and never dies—but you don't usually want objects to do this. It's far more common to conditionally set a root to reference the object inside the `Finalize` method.

> **Note** Make sure that you call `ReRegisterForFinalize` no more than once per resurrection, or the object will have its `Finalize` method called multiple times. The reason is that each call to `ReRegisterForFinalize` appends a new entry to the end of the finalization list. When an object is determined to be garbage, all of these entries move from the finalization list to the freachable queue, making the object's `Finalize` method called multiple times.

Generations

As I mentioned near the beginning of the chapter, generations are a mechanism within the CLR garbage collector whose sole reason for being is to improve an application's performance. A *generational garbage collector* (also known as an *ephemeral garbage collector*, although I don't use the latter term in this book) makes the following assumptions:

- The newer an object is, the shorter its lifetime will be.

- The older an object is, the longer its lifetime will be.

- Collecting a portion of the heap is faster than collecting the whole heap.

Numerous studies have demonstrated the validity of these assumptions for a very large set of existing applications, and these assumptions have influenced how the garbage collector is implemented. In this section, I'll describe how generations work.

When initialized, the managed heap contains no objects. Objects added to the heap are said to be in generation 0. Stated simply, objects in generation 0 are newly constructed objects that the garbage collector has never examined. Figure 20-8 shows a newly started application with five objects allocated (A through E). After a while, objects C and E become unreachable.

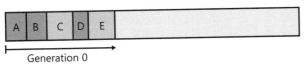

Figure 20-8   A newly initialized heap containing some objects, all in generation 0. No collections have occurred yet.

When the CLR initializes, it selects a budget size for generation 0 of, say, 256 KB. (The exact size is subject to change.) So if allocating a new object causes generation 0 to surpass its budget, a garbage collection must start. Let's say that objects A through E occupy 256 KB. When object F is allocated, a garbage collection must start. The garbage collector will determine that objects C and E are garbage and will compact object D, causing it to be adjacent to object B. Incidentally, generation 0's budget of 256 KB was chosen because it is likely that all of these objects will fit entirely into a CPU's L2 cache so that compacting memory happens incredibly fast. The objects that survive the garbage collection (objects A, B, and D) are said to be in generation 1. Objects in generation 1 have been examined by the garbage collector once. The heap now looks like Figure 20-9.

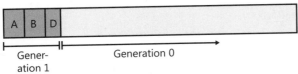

Figure 20-9   After one collection: generation 0 survivors are promoted to generation 1; generation 0 is empty.

After a garbage collection, generation 0 contains no objects. As always, new objects will be allocated in generation 0. Figure 20-10 shows the application running and allocating objects F through K. In addition, while the application was running, objects B, H, and J became unreachable and should have their memory reclaimed at some point.

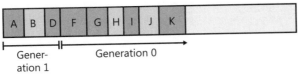

Figure 20-10   New objects are allocated in generation 0; generation 1 has some garbage.

Now let's say that attempting to allocate object L would put generation 0 over its 256-KB budget. Because generation 0 has reached its budget, a garbage collection must start. When starting a garbage collection, the garbage collector must decide which generations to examine. Earlier, I said that when the CLR initializes, it selects a budget for generation 0. Well, it also selects a budget for generation 1. Let's say that the budget selected for generation 1 is 2 MB.

When starting a garbage collection, the garbage collector also sees how much memory is occupied by generation 1. In this case, generation 1 occupies much less than 2 MB, so the garbage collector examines only the objects in generation 0. Look again at the assumptions that the generational garbage collector makes. The first assumption is that newly created objects have a short lifetime. So generation 0 is likely to have a lot of garbage in it, and collecting generation 0 will therefore reclaim a lot of memory. The garbage collector will just ignore the objects in generation 1, which will speed up the garbage collection process.

Obviously, ignoring the objects in generation 1 improves the performance of the garbage collector. However, the garbage collector improves performance more because it doesn't traverse every object in the managed heap. If a root or an object refers to an object in an old generation, the garbage collector can ignore any of the older objects' inner references, decreasing the amount of time required to build the graph of reachable objects. Of course, it's possible that an old object refers to a new object. To ensure that the updated fields of these old objects are examined, the garbage collector uses a mechanism internal to the JIT compiler that sets a bit when an object's reference field changes. This support lets the garbage collector know which old objects (if any) have been written to since the last collection. Only old objects that have had fields change need to be examined to see whether they refer to any new object in generation 0.

> **Note** Microsoft's performance tests show that it takes less than 1 millisecond to perform a garbage collection of generation 0. Microsoft's goal is to have garbage collections take no more time than an ordinary page fault.

A generational garbage collector also assumes that objects that have lived a long time will continue to live. So it's likely that the objects in generation 1 will continue to be reachable from the application. Therefore, if the garbage collector were to examine the objects in generation 1, it probably wouldn't find a lot of garbage. As a result, it wouldn't be able to reclaim much memory. So it is likely that collecting generation 1 is a waste of time. If any garbage happens to be in generation 1, it just stays there. The heap now looks like Figure 20-11.

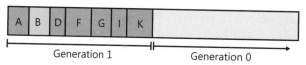

Figure 20-11　After two collections: generation 0 survivors are promoted to generation 1 (growing the size of generation 1); generation 0 is empty.

As you can see, all of the generation 0 objects that survived the collection are now part of generation 1. Because the garbage collector didn't examine generation 1, object B didn't have its memory reclaimed even though it was unreachable at the time of the last garbage collection. Again, after a collection, generation 0 contains no objects and is where new objects will be placed. In fact, let's say that the application continues running and allocates objects L through

O. And while running, the application stops using objects G, L, and M, making them all unreachable. The heap now looks like Figure 20-12.

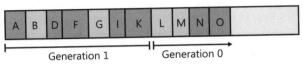

Figure 20-12   New objects are allocated in generation 0; generation 1 has more garbage.

Let's say that allocating object P causes generation 0 to exceed its budget, causing a garbage collection to occur. Because the memory occupied by all of the objects in generation 1 is less than 2 MB, the garbage collector again decides to collect only generation 0, ignoring the unreachable objects in generation 1 (objects B and G). After the collection, the heap looks like Figure 20-13.

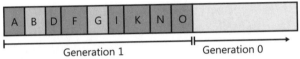

Figure 20-13   After three collections: generation 0 survivors are promoted to generation 1 (growing the size of generation 1 again); generation 0 is empty.

In Figure 20-13, you see that generation 1 keeps growing slowly. In fact, let's say that generation 1 has now grown to the point in which all of the objects in it occupy 2 MB of memory. At this point, the application continues running (because a garbage collection just finished) and starts allocating objects P through S, which fill generation 0 up to its budget. The heap now looks like Figure 20-14.

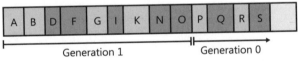

Figure 20-14   New objects are allocated in generation 0; generation 1 has more garbage.

When the application attempts to allocate object T, generation 0 is full, and a garbage collection must start. This time, however, the garbage collector sees that the objects in generation 1 are occupying so much memory that generation 1's 2-MB budget has been reached. Over the several generation 0 collections, it's likely that a number of objects in generation 1 have become unreachable (as in our example). So this time, the garbage collector decides to examine all of the objects in generation 1 and generation 0. After both generations have been garbage collected, the heap now looks like Figure 20-15.

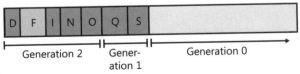

Figure 20-15   After four collections: generation 1 survivors are promoted to generation 2, generation 0 survivors are promoted to generation 1, and generation 0 is empty

As before, any objects that were in generation 0 that survived the garbage collection are now in generation 1; any objects that were in generation 1 that survived the collection are now in generation 2. As always, generation 0 is empty immediately after a garbage collection and is where new objects will be allocated. Objects in generation 2 are objects that the garbage collector has examined two or more times. There might have been several collections, but the objects in generation 1 are examined only when generation 1 reaches its budget, which usually requires several garbage collections of generation 0.

The managed heap supports only three generations: generation 0, generation 1, and generation 2; there is no generation 3. When the CLR initializes, it selects budgets for all three generations. As I mentioned earlier, the budget for generation 0 is about 256 KB, and the budget for generation 1 is about 2 MB. The budget for generation 2 is around 10 MB. Again, the budget sizes are selected to improve performance. The larger the budget, the less frequently a garbage collection will occur. And again, the performance improvement comes because of the initial assumptions: new objects have short lifetimes, and older objects are likely to live longer.

The CLR's garbage collector is a self-tuning collector. This means that the garbage collector learns about your application's behavior whenever it performs a garbage collection. For example, if your application constructs a lot of objects and uses them for a very short period of time, it's possible that garbage collecting generation 0 will reclaim a lot of memory. In fact, it's possible that the memory for all objects in generation 0 can be reclaimed.

If the garbage collector sees that there are very few surviving objects after collecting generation 0, it might decide to reduce the budget of generation 0 from 256 KB to 128 KB. This reduction in the allotted space will mean that garbage collections occur more frequently but will require less work for the garbage collector, so your process' working set will be small. In fact, if all objects in generation 0 are garbage, a garbage collection doesn't have to compact any memory; it can simply set `NextObjPtr` back to the beginning of generation 0, and then the garbage collection is performed. Wow, this is a fast way to reclaim memory!

> **Note** The garbage collector works extremely well for applications with threads that sit idle at the top of their stack most of the time. Then, when the thread has something to do, it wakes up, creates a bunch of short-lived objects, returns, and then goes back to sleep. Many applications follow this architecture including Windows Forms, ASP.NET Web Forms, and XML Web service applications.
>
> For ASP.NET applications, a client request comes in, a bunch of new objects are constructed, the objects perform work on the client's behalf, and the result is sent back to the client. At this point, all of the objects used to satisfy the client's request are garbage. In other words, each ASP.NET application request causes a lot of garbage to be created. Because these objects are unreachable almost immediately after they're created, each garbage collection reclaims a lot of memory. This keeps the process's working set very low, and the garbage collector's performance is phenomenal.
>
> In fact, most of an application's roots live on the thread's stack in arguments or local variables. If a thread's stack is short, it takes very little time for the garbage collector to examine the roots and mark the reachable objects. In other words, garbage collections go much faster if you avoid deeps stacks. One way to avoid a deep stack is to avoid using recursive methods.

On the other hand, if the garbage collector collects generation 0 and sees that there are a lot of surviving objects, not a lot of memory was reclaimed in the garbage collection. In this case, the garbage collector will grow generation 0's budget to maybe 512 KB. Now, fewer collections will occur, but when they do, a lot more memory should be reclaimed. By the way, if insufficient memory has been reclaimed after a collection, the garbage collector will perform a full collection before throwing an `OutOfMemoryException`.

Throughout this discussion, I've been talking about how the garbage collector dynamically modifies generation 0's budget after every collection. But the garbage collector also modifies the budgets of generation 1 and generation 2 by using similar heuristics. When these generations are garbage collected, the garbage collector again sees how much memory is reclaimed and how many objects survived. Based on the garbage collector's findings, it might grow or shrink the thresholds of these generations as well to improve the overall performance of the application. The end result is that the garbage collector fine-tunes itself automatically based on the memory load required by your application—this is very cool!

Other Garbage Collection Features for Use with Native Resources

Sometimes, a native resource consumes a lot of memory, but the managed object wrapping that resource occupies very little memory. The quintessential example of this is the bitmap. A bitmap can occupy several megabytes of native memory, but the managed object is tiny because it contains only an `HBITMAP` (a 4- or 8-byte value). From the CLR's perspective, a process could allocate hundreds of bitmaps (using little managed memory) before performing a collection. But if the process is manipulating many bitmaps, the process' memory consumption will grow at a phenomenal rate. To fix this situation, the `GC` class offers the following two static methods:

```
public static void AddMemoryPressure(Int64 bytesAllocated);
public static void RemoveMemoryPressure(Int64 bytesAllocated);
```

A class that wraps a potentially large native resource should use these methods to give the garbage collector a hint as to how much memory is really being consumed. Internally, the garbage collector monitors this pressure, and when it gets high, a garbage collection is forced.

There are some native resources that are fixed in number. For example, Windows formerly had a restriction that it could create only five device contexts. There had also been a restriction on the number of files that an application could open. Again, from the CLR's perspective, a process could allocate hundreds of objects (that use little memory) before performing a collection. But if the number of these native resources is limited, attempting to use more than are available will typically result in exceptions being thrown. To fix this situation, the `System.Runtime` `.InteropServices` namespace offers the `HandleCollector` class:

```
public sealed class HandleCollector {
   public HandleCollector(String name, Int32 initialThreshold);
   public HandleCollector(String name, Int32 initialThreshold,
      Int32 maximumThreshold);
```

```
    public void Add();
    public void Remove();

    public Int32 Count { get; }
    public Int32 InitialThreshold { get; }
    public Int32 MaximumThreshold { get; }
    public String Name { get; }
}
```

A class that wraps a native resource that has a limited quantity available should use an instance of this class to give the garbage collector a hint as to how many instances of the resource are really being consumed. Internally, this class object monitors the count, and when it gets high, a garbage collection is forced.

Note Internally, the `GC.AddMemoryPressure` and `HandleCollector.Add` methods call `GC.Collect`, forcing a garbage collection to start prior to generation 0 reaching its budget. Normally, forcing a garbage collection to start is strongly discouraged because it usually has an adverse affect on your application's performance. However, classes that call these methods are doing so in an effort to keep limited native resources available for the application. If the native resources run out, the application will fail. For most applications, it is better to work with reduced performance than not working at all.

Here is some code that demonstrates the use and effect of the memory pressure methods and the `HandleCollector` class:

```
using System;
using System.Runtime.InteropServices;

public static class Program {
    public static void Main() {
        // Passing 0 causes infrequent GCs
        MemoryPressureDemo(0);

        // Passing 10MB causes frequent GCs
        MemoryPressureDemo(10 * 1024 * 1024);

        // Handle Collector
        HandleCollectorDemo();
    }

    private static void MemoryPressureDemo(Int32 size) {
        Console.WriteLine();
        Console.WriteLine("MemoryPressureDemo, size={0}", size);
        // Create a bunch of objects specifying their logical size
        for (Int32 count = 0; count < 15; count++) {
            new BigNativeResource(size);
        }

        // For demo purposes, force everything to be cleaned-up
        GC.Collect();
        GC.WaitForPendingFinalizers();
    }
```

```
private sealed class BigNativeResource {
    private Int32 m_size;

    public BigNativeResource(Int32 size) {
        m_size = size;
        if (m_size > 0) {
            // Make the GC think the object is physically bigger
            GC.AddMemoryPressure(m_size);
        }
        Console.WriteLine("BigNativeResource create.");
    }

    ~BigNativeResource() {
        if (m_size > 0) {
            // Make the GC think the object released more memory
            GC.RemoveMemoryPressure(m_size);
        }
        Console.WriteLine("BigNativeResource destroy.");
    }
}


private static void HandleCollectorDemo() {
    Console.WriteLine();
    Console.WriteLine("HandleCollectorDemo");
    for (Int32 count = 0; count < 10; count++) {
        new LimitedResource();
    }

    // For demo purposes, force everything to be cleaned-up
    GC.Collect();
    GC.WaitForPendingFinalizers();
}

private sealed class LimitedResource {
    // Create a HandleCollector telling it that collections should
    // occur when two or more of these objects exist in the heap
    private static HandleCollector s_hc = new HandleCollector("LimitedResource", 2);

    public LimitedResource() {
        // Tell the HandleCollector that 1 more LimitedResource
        // object has been added to the heap
        s_hc.Add();
        Console.WriteLine("LimitedResource create.  Count={0}", s_hc.Count);
    }
    ~LimitedResource() {
        // Tell the HandleCollector that 1 less LimitedResource
        // object has been removed from the heap
        s_hc.Remove();
        Console.WriteLine("LimitedResource destroy. Count={0}", s_hc.Count);
    }
}
}
```

If you compile and run the code above, your output will be similar to the following output:

```
MemoryPressureDemo, size=0
BigNativeResource create.
BigNativeResource create.
BigNativeResource create.
BigNativeResource create.
BigNativeResource create.
BigNativeResource create.
BigNativeResource create.
BigNativeResource create.
BigNativeResource create.
BigNativeResource create.
BigNativeResource create.
BigNativeResource create.
BigNativeResource create.
BigNativeResource create.
BigNativeResource destroy.
BigNativeResource destroy.
BigNativeResource destroy.
BigNativeResource destroy.
BigNativeResource destroy.
BigNativeResource destroy.
BigNativeResource destroy.
BigNativeResource destroy.
BigNativeResource destroy.
BigNativeResource destroy.
BigNativeResource destroy.
BigNativeResource destroy.
BigNativeResource destroy.
BigNativeResource destroy.
BigNativeResource destroy.

MemoryPressureDemo, size=10485760
BigNativeResource create.
BigNativeResource create.
BigNativeResource create.
BigNativeResource create.
BigNativeResource create.
BigNativeResource create.
BigNativeResource create.
BigNativeResource create.
BigNativeResource destroy.
BigNativeResource destroy.
BigNativeResource destroy.
BigNativeResource destroy.
BigNativeResource destroy.
BigNativeResource create.
BigNativeResource create.
BigNativeResource destroy.
BigNativeResource destroy.
BigNativeResource destroy.
BigNativeResource destroy.
BigNativeResource create.
```

```
BigNativeResource create.
BigNativeResource create.
BigNativeResource destroy.
BigNativeResource destroy.
BigNativeResource create.
BigNativeResource create.
BigNativeResource destroy.
BigNativeResource destroy.
BigNativeResource destroy.
BigNativeResource destroy.

HandleCollectorDemo
LimitedResource create.  Count=1
LimitedResource create.  Count=2
LimitedResource create.  Count=3
LimitedResource destroy. Count=3
LimitedResource destroy. Count=2
LimitedResource destroy. Count=1
LimitedResource create.  Count=1
LimitedResource create.  Count=2
LimitedResource destroy. Count=2
LimitedResource create.  Count=2
LimitedResource create.  Count=3
LimitedResource destroy. Count=3
LimitedResource destroy. Count=2
LimitedResource destroy. Count=1
LimitedResource create.  Count=1
LimitedResource create.  Count=2
LimitedResource destroy. Count=2
LimitedResource create.  Count=2
LimitedResource destroy. Count=1
LimitedResource destroy. Count=0
```

Predicting the Success of an Operation that Requires a Lot of Memory

Occasionally you find yourself implementing an algorithm that you know will require a number of objects that together will occupy a good bit of memory. You could start executing the algorithm, and, if you run out of memory, the CLR will throw an OutOfMemoryException. In that case, you have done a lot of work that now must be thrown away. Plus, you need to catch this exception and allow your program to recover gracefully.

In the System.Runtime namespace, there is a MemoryFailPoint class that offers you the ability to check for sufficient memory prior to starting a memory-hungry algorithm. Here is what the class looks like:

```
public sealed class MemoryFailPoint : CriticalFinalizerObject, IDisposable {
   public MemoryFailPoint(Int32 sizeInMegabytes);
   ~MemoryFailPoint();
   public void Dispose();
}
```

The way you use this class is pretty simple. First, you construct an instance of it by passing in the number of megabytes you think your algorithm is going to require (round up if you're not completely sure). Internally, the constructor performs the following checks that trigger actions in consequence:

1. Is there enough available space in the system's paging file, and is there enough contiguous virtual address space in the process to satisfy the request? Note that the constructor subtracts any amount of memory that has been logically reserved by another call to **MemoryFailPoint**'s constructor.

2. If there isn't enough space, a garbage collection is forced in an attempt to free up some space.

3. If there is still not enough paging file space, an attempt is made to expand the paging file. If the paging file cannot grow enough, an **InsufficientMemoryException** is thrown.

4. If there still isn't enough contiguous virtual address space, an **InsufficientMemory-Exception** is thrown.

5. If enough paging file space and virtual address space has been found, the requested number of megabytes are reserved by adding the number of megabytes to a private static field defined within the **MemoryFailPoint** class. The addition is done in a thread-safe way so that multiple threads can construct an instance of this class simultaneously and be guaranteed that they have logically reserved the memory they requested as long as no exception is thrown in the constructor.

If **MemoryFailPoint**'s constructor throws an **InsufficientMemoryException**, your application can release some resources it is currently using, or it can reduce its performance (perform less caching of data) in order to reduce the chance of the CLR throwing an **OutOf-MemoryException** in the future. By the way, **InsufficientMemoryException** is derived from **OutOfMemoryException**.

> **Important**   If **MemoryFailPoint**'s constructor doesn't throw an exception, you have logically reserved the memory you have requested and you can execute your memory-hungry algorithm. However, be aware that you have not physically allocated this memory. This means that it is just *more likely* for your algorithm to run successfully, getting the memory it needs. The **MemoryFailPoint** class cannot guarantee that your algorithm will get the memory it needs even if the constructor doesn't throw an exception. This class exists to *help* you make a more robust application.

When you have completed executing the algorithm, you should call **Dispose** on the **Memory-FailPoint** object you constructed. Internally, **Dispose** just subtracts (in a thread-safe way) the number of megabytes you reserved from the **MemoryFailPoint**'s static field. The code below demonstrates the use of the `MemoryFailPoint` class:

```
using System;
using System.Runtime;

public static class Program {
   public static void Main() {
      try {
         // Logically reserve 1.5 GB of memory
         using (MemoryFailPoint mfp = new MemoryFailPoint(1500)) {
            // Perform memory-hungry algorithm in here

         } // Dispose will logically free the 1.5 GB of memory
      }
      catch (InsufficientMemoryException e) {
         // The memory could not be reserved
         Console.WriteLine(e);
      }
   }
}
```

Programmatic Control of the Garbage Collector

The `System.GC` type allows your application some direct control over the garbage collector. For starters, you can query the maximum generation supported by the managed heap by reading the `GC.MaxGeneration` property; this property always returns 2.

You can also force the garbage collector to perform a collection by calling one of the following two static methods:

```
void GC.Collect(Int32 Generation)
void GC.Collect()
```

The first method allows you to specify which generation(s) to collect. You can pass any integer from 0 to `GC.MaxGeneration` inclusive. Passing 0 causes generation 0 to be collected, passing 1 causes generations 1 and 0 to be collected, and passing 2 causes generations 2, 1, and 0 to be collected. The version of the `Collect` method that takes no parameters forces a full collection of all generations and is equivalent to calling:

```
GC.Collect(GC.MaxGeneration);
```

Under most circumstances, you should avoid calling any of the `Collect` methods; it's best just to let the garbage collector run on its own accord and fine-tune its generation budgets based on actual application behavior. However, if you're writing a CUI or GUI application, your application code owns the process and the CLR in that process. For these application types, you *might* want to force a garbage collection to occur at certain times.

For example, you might consider calling the `Collect` method if some non-recurring event has just occurred that has likely caused a lot of old objects to die. The reason that calling `Collect` in such a circumstance may not be so bad is that the garbage collector's predictions of the future based on the past are not likely to be accurate for non-recurring events.

For example, it might make sense for your application to force a full garbage collection of all generations after your application initializes or after the user saves a data file. When a Windows Form control is hosted on a Web page, a full collection is performed each time a page is unloaded. Don't explicitly call **Collect** to try to improve your application's response time; call it to reduce your process' working set.

The **GC** type also offers a **WaitForPendingFinalizers** method. This method simply suspends the calling thread until the thread processing the freachable queue has emptied the queue, calling each object's **Finalize** method. In most applications, it's unlikely that you'll ever have to call this method. Occasionally, though, I've seen code like this:

```
GC.Collect();
GC.WaitForPendingFinalizers();
GC.Collect();
```

This code forces a garbage collection. When the collection is complete, the memory for objects that don't require finalization is reclaimed. But the objects that do require finalization can't have their memory reclaimed yet. After the first call to **Collect** returns, the special, dedicated finalization thread is calling **Finalize** methods asynchronously. The call to **WaitForPending-Finalizers** puts the application's thread to sleep until all **Finalize** methods are called. When **WaitForPendingFinalizers** returns, all of the finalized objects are now truly garbage. At this point, the second call to **Collect** forces another garbage collection, which reclaims all of the memory occupied by the now-finalized objects.

Finally, the **GC** class offers two static methods to allow you to determine which generation an object is currently in:

```
Int32 GetGeneration(Object obj)
Int32 GetGeneration(WeakReference wr)
```

The first version of **GetGeneration** takes an object reference as a parameter, and the second version takes a **WeakReference** reference as a parameter. The value returned will be between **0** and **GC.MaxGeneration** inclusively.

The following code will help you understand how generations work. The code also demonstrates the use of the **GC** methods just discussed.

```
using System;

internal sealed class GenObj {
   ~GenObj() {
      Console.WriteLine("In Finalize method");
   }
}
```

```csharp
public static class Program {
    public static void Main() {
        Console.WriteLine("Maximum generations: " + GC.MaxGeneration);

        // Create a new GenObj in the heap.
        Object o = new GenObj();

        // Because this object is newly created, it is in generation 0.
        Console.WriteLine("Gen " + GC.GetGeneration(o)); // 0

        // Performing a garbage collection promotes the object's generation.
        GC.Collect();
        Console.WriteLine("Gen " + GC.GetGeneration(o)); // 1

        GC.Collect();
        Console.WriteLine("Gen " + GC.GetGeneration(o)); // 2

        GC.Collect();
        Console.WriteLine("Gen " + GC.GetGeneration(o)); // 2 (max)


        o = null; // Destroy the strong reference to this object.

        Console.WriteLine("Collecting Gen 0");
        GC.Collect(0);                      // Collect generation 0.
        GC.WaitForPendingFinalizers();      // Finalize is NOT called.

        Console.WriteLine("Collecting Gens 0, and 1");
        GC.Collect(1);                      // Collect generations 0 & 1.
        GC.WaitForPendingFinalizers();      // Finalize is NOT called.

        Console.WriteLine("Collecting Gens 0, 1, and 2");
        GC.Collect(2);                      // Same as Collect()
        GC.WaitForPendingFinalizers();      // Finalize IS called.
    }
}
```

Building and running this code yields the following output:

```
Maximum generations: 2
Gen 0
Gen 1
Gen 2
Gen 2
Collecting Gen 0
Collecting Gens 0, and 1
Collecting Gens 0, 1, and 2
In Finalize method
```

Other Garbage Collector Performance Topics

Earlier in this chapter, I explained the garbage collection algorithm. However, I made a big assumption during that discussion: that only one thread is running. In the real world, it's likely for multiple threads to be accessing the managed heap or at least manipulating objects allocated within the managed heap. When one thread sparks a garbage collection, other threads must not access any objects (including object references on its own stack) because the garbage collector is likely to move these objects, changing their memory locations.

So when the garbage collector wants to start a garbage collection, all threads executing managed code must be suspended. The CLR has a few different mechanisms that it uses to safely suspend threads so that a garbage collection can be performed. The reason that there are multiple mechanisms is to keep threads running as long as possible and to reduce overhead as much as possible. I don't want to get into all of the details here, but suffice it to say that Microsoft has done a lot of work to reduce the overhead involved with a garbage collection. Microsoft will continue to modify these mechanisms over time to ensure efficient garbage collections in the future.

When the CLR wants to start a garbage collection, it immediately suspends all threads that are executing managed code. The CLR then examines each thread's instruction pointer to determine where the thread is executing. The instruction pointer address is then compared with the JIT compiler–produced tables in an effort to determine what code the thread is executing.

If the thread's instruction pointer is at an offset identified by a table, the thread is said to have reached a *safe point*. A safe point is a place where it's OK to leave a thread suspended until a garbage collection completes. If the thread's instruction pointer isn't at an offset identified by an internal method table, the thread isn't at a safe point, and the CLR can't perform a garbage collection. In this case, the CLR *hijacks* the thread: the CLR modifies the thread's stack so that the return address points to a special function implemented inside the CLR. The thread is then resumed. When the currently executing method returns, the special function will execute, suspending the thread.

However, the thread might not return from its method for quite some time. So after the thread resumes execution, the CLR waits about 250 milliseconds for the thread to be hijacked. After this time, the CLR suspends the thread again and checks its instruction pointer. If the thread has reached a safe point, the garbage collection can start. If the thread still hasn't reached a safe point, the CLR checks to see whether another method has been called; if one has, the CLR modifies the stack again so that the thread is hijacked when it returns from the most recently executing method. Then the CLR resumes the thread and waits another few milliseconds before trying again.

When all of the threads have reached a safe point or have been hijacked, the garbage collection can begin. When the garbage collection is completed, all threads are resumed, and the application continues running. The hijacked threads return to the method that originally called them.

This algorithm has one small twist. When the CLR wants to start a GC, it suspends all threads that are executing managed code, but it does not suspend threads that are executing unmanaged code. Once all of the threads that are executing managed code are at a safe point or are hijacked, the garbage collection is allowed to start. The threads executing unmanaged code are allowed to continue running because any object that they are using should have been pinned. If a thread currently executing unmanaged code returns to managed code, the thread is immediately suspended until the garbage collection has completed.

As it turns out, the CLR uses hijacking most of the time rather than using the JIT compiler–produced tables to determine if the thread is at a safe point. The reason is the JIT compiler–produced tables require a lot of memory and increase the working set, which in turn hurts performance significantly. So, the JIT compiler–produced tables contain information for sections of code having loops that do not call other methods. If the method has a loop that calls other methods or if there are no loops, the JIT compiler–produced tables do not have much information in them, and hijacking is used to suspend the threads.

In addition to the mechanisms mentioned earlier (generations, safe points, and hijacking), the garbage collector offers some additional mechanisms that improve the performance of object allocations and collections.

Synchronization-Free Allocations

On a multiprocessor system, generation 0 of the managed heap is partitioned into multiple memory arenas, one arena per thread. This allows multiple threads to make allocations simultaneously so that exclusive access to the heap isn't required.

Scalable Parallel Collections

A host application (such as ASP.NET or Microsoft SQL Server) can load the CLR and request it to tweak the way it performs garbage collections so that the collections perform better for a typical server application. This tweak causes the managed heap to be split into several sections, one per CPU. When a garbage collection is initiated, the garbage collector has one thread per CPU; each thread collects its own section in parallel with the other threads. Parallel collections work well for server applications in which the worker threads tend to exhibit uniform behavior. This feature requires the application to be running on a computer with multiple CPUs in it so that the threads can truly be working simultaneously—this is how the performance improvement is attained.

You can tell the CLR to use the server collector by creating a configuration file (as discussed in Chapters 2 and 3) that contains a **gcServer** element for the application. Here's an example of a configuration file:

```
<configuration>
    <runtime>
        <gcServer enabled="true"/>
    </runtime>
</configuration>
```

When an application is running, it can ask the CLR if it is running with the scalable, parallel collector by querying the **GCSettings** class's **IsServerGC** property:

```
using System;
using System.Runtime; // GCSettings is in this namespace

public static class Program {
   public static void Main() {
      Console.WriteLine("Application is running with server GC=" +
         GCSettings.IsServerGC);
   }
}
```

Concurrent Collections

On a multiprocessor system running the workstation version of the execution engine, the garbage collector has an additional background thread to collect objects concurrently while the application runs. When a thread allocates an object that pushes generation 0 over its budget, the garbage collector first suspends all threads and then determines which generations to collect. If the garbage collector needs to collect generation 0 or 1, it proceeds as normal. However, if generation 2 needs collecting, the size of generation 0 will be increased beyond its budget to allocate the new object, and then the application's threads are resumed.

While the application threads are running, the garbage collector has a normal priority background thread that marks unreachable objects. This thread competes for CPU time with the application's threads, causing the application's tasks to execute more slowly; however, the concurrent collector runs only on multiprocessor systems, so you shouldn't see much of a degradation. Once the objects are marked, the garbage collector suspends all threads again and decides whether to compact memory. If the garbage collector decides to compact memory, memory is compacted, root references are fixed up, and the application's threads are resumed—this garbage collection takes less time than usual because the set of unreachable objects has already been built. However, the garbage collector might decide not to compact memory; in fact, the garbage collector favors this approach. If you have a lot of free memory, the garbage collector won't compact the heap; this improves performance but grows your application's working set. When using the concurrent garbage collector, you'll typically find that your application is consuming more memory than it would with the nonconcurrent garbage collection.

To summarize: concurrent collection makes for a better interactive experience for users and is therefore best for interactive CUI or GUI applications. For some applications, however, concurrent collection will actually hurt performance and will cause more memory to be used. When testing your application, you should experiment with and without concurrent collection and see which approach gives the best performance and memory usage for your application.

You can tell the CLR not to use the concurrent collector by creating a configuration file for the application (as discussed in Chapters 2 and 3) that contains a **gcConcurrent** element. Here's an example of a configuration file:

```
<configuration>
   <runtime>
      <gcConcurrent enabled="false"/>
   </runtime>
</configuration>
```

Large Objects

There is one more performance improvement you might want to be aware of. Any objects that are 85,000 bytes or more in size are considered to be *large objects*. Large objects are allocated from a special large object heap. Objects in this heap are finalized and freed just as the small objects I've been talking about. However, large objects are never compacted because it would waste too much CPU time shifting 85,000 byte blocks of memory down in the heap. However, you should never write code that assumes that large objects do not move in memory, because the size of large objects could change from 85,000 bytes to something else in the future. To guarantee that an object doesn't move in memory, pin it as discussed in the "Manually Monitoring and Controlling the Lifetime of Objects" section of this chapter.

Large objects are always considered part of generation 2, so you should create large objects only for resources that you need to keep alive for a long time. Allocating short-lived large objects will cause generation 2 to be collected more frequently, which will hurt performance. The following program proves that large objects are always allocated in generation 2:

```
using System;

public static class Program {
   public static void Main() {
      Object o = new Byte[85000];
      Console.WriteLine(GC.GetGeneration(o));   // Displays 2; not 0
   }
}
```

All of these mechanisms are transparent to your application code. To you, the developer, it appears as if there is just one managed heap; these mechanisms exist simply to improve application performance.

Monitoring Garbage Collections

Within a process, there are a few methods that you can call to monitor the garbage collector. Specifically, the **GC** class offers the following static methods, which you can call to see how many collections have occurred of a specific generation or how much memory is currently being used by objects in the managed heap:

```
Int64 GetTotalMemory(Boolean forceFullCollection);
Int32 CollectionCount(Int32 generation);
```

To profile a particular code block, I have frequently written code to call these methods before and after the code block and then calculate the difference. This gives me a very good indication of how my code block has affected my process' working set and indicates how many garbage collections occurred while executing the code block. If the numbers are high, I know to spend more time tuning the algorithms in my code block.

When you install the .NET Framework, it installs a set of performance counters that offer a lot of real-time statistics about the CLR's operations. These statistics are visible via the PerfMon.exe tool or the System Monitor ActiveX control that ships with Windows. The easiest way to access the System Monitor control is to run PerfMon.exe and click the + toolbar button, which causes the Add Counters dialog box shown in Figure 20-16 to appear.

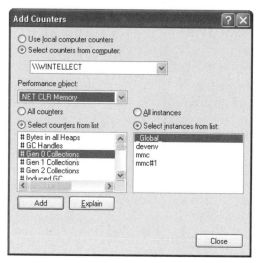

Figure 20-16   PerfMon.exe showing the .NET CLR memory counters

To monitor the CLR's garbage collector, select the .NET CLR Memory performance object. Then select a specific application from the instance list box. Finally, select the set of counters that you're interested in monitoring, click Add, and then click Close. At this point, the System Monitor will graph the selected real-time statistics. For an explanation of a particular counter, select the desired counter, and then click Explain.

Another great tool for monitoring your application's object allocations is the CLR Profiler. This tool offers call profiling, heap snapshots, and memory-use timelines. There is even an API that can be used from test code to start and stop profiling and inject comments into the logs. Also, the source code for this tool is available so that you can modify the tool for your own needs. The best way to acquire this tool is for you to search the Web for *CLR profiler*. This tool is invaluable, and I highly recommend it.

Chapter 21

CLR Hosting and AppDomains

In this chapter, I'll discuss two main topics that really show off the incredible value provided by the Microsoft .NET Framework: *hosting* and *AppDomains*. Hosting allows any application to utilize the features of the common language runtime (CLR). In particular, this allows existing applications to at least be partially written using managed code. Furthermore, hosting allows applications the ability to offer customization and extensibility via programming.

Allowing extensibility means that third-party code will be running inside your process. In Microsoft Windows, loading another third-party's DLLs into a process has been fraught with peril. The DLL could easily have code in it that could compromise the application's data structures and code. The DLL could also try to use the security context of the application to gain access to resources it should not have access to. The CLR's AppDomain feature solves all of these problems. AppDomains allow third-party untrusted code to run in an existing process, and the CLR guarantees that the data structures, code, and security context will not be exploited or compromised.

Programmers typically use hosting and AppDomains along with assembly loading and reflection. Using these four technologies together makes the CLR an incredibly rich and powerful platform. In this chapter, I'll focus on hosting and AppDomains. In the next chapter, I'll focus on assembly loading and reflection. When you learn and understand all of these technologies, you'll see how your investment in the .NET Framework today will certainly pay off down the line.

CLR Hosting

The .NET Framework runs on top of Microsoft Windows. This means that the .NET Framework must be built using technologies that Windows can interface with. For starters, all managed module and assembly files must use the Windows portable executable (PE) file format and be either a Windows EXE file or a dynamic-link library (DLL).

When developing the CLR, Microsoft implemented it as a COM server contained inside a DLL; that is, Microsoft defined a standard COM interface for the CLR and assigned GUIDs to this interface and the COM server. When you install the .NET Framework, the COM server representing the CLR is registered in the Windows registry just as any other COM server. If you want more information about this topic, refer to the MSCorEE.h C++ header file that ships with the .NET Framework SDK. This header file defines the GUIDs and the unmanaged **ICLRRuntimeHost** interface definition.

Any Windows application can host the CLR. However, you shouldn't create an instance of the CLR COM server by calling **CoCreateInstance**; instead, your unmanaged host should call the **CorBindToRuntimeEx** function or another similar function, all of which are declared in MSCorEE.h. The **CorBindToRuntimeEx** function is implemented in the MSCorEE.dll file, which is usually found in the C:\Windows\System32 directory. This DLL is called the *shim*, and its job is to determine which version of the CLR to create; the shim DLL doesn't contain the CLR COM server itself.

A single machine may have multiple versions of the CLR installed, but there will be only one version of the MSCorEE.dll file (the shim) (see the following note for exceptions). The version of MSCorEE.dll installed on the machine is the version that shipped with the latest version of the CLR installed on the machine. Therefore, this version of MSCorEE.dll knows how to find any previous versions of the CLR that may be installed.

> **Note**   If you are using a 64-bit version of Windows that has version 2.0 of the .NET Framework installed, there are actually two versions of the MSCorEE.dll file installed. One version is the 32-bit x86 version, and the other version is the 64-bit x64 or IA64 version, depending on your computer's CPU architecture.

The CLR itself isn't implemented in MSCorEE.dll; it is implemented in a file called MSCorWks.dll. If you have version 1.0, 1.1, and 2.0 of the CLR installed on a machine, there is a version of MSCorWks.dll in the following directories:

- Version 1.0 is in C:\Windows\Microsoft.NET\Framework\v1.0.3705
- Version 1.1 is in C:\Windows\Microsoft.NET\Framework\v1.0.4322
- Version 2.0 is in C:\Windows\Microsoft.NET\Framework\v2.0.50727

When **CorBindToRuntimeEx** is called, its arguments allow the host to specify the version of the CLR it would like to create, as well as some other settings. **CorBindToRuntimeEx** uses the specified version information and gathers some additional information of its own (such as how many CPUs are installed in the machine) to decide which version of the CLR to load—the shim might not load the version that the host requested.

By default, when a managed executable starts, the shim examines the executable file and extracts the information indicating the version of the CLR that the application was built and tested with. However, an application can override this default behavior by placing `required-Runtime` and `supportedRuntime` entries in its XML configuration file (described in Chapter 2, "Building, Packaging, Deploying, and Administering Applications and Types," and Chapter 3, "Shared Assemblies and Strongly Named Assemblies").

The `CorBindToRuntimeEx` function returns a pointer to the unmanaged `ICLRRuntimeHost` interface. The hosting application can call methods defined by this interface to:

- **Set Host managers**   Tell the CLR that the host wants to be involved in making decisions related to memory allocations, thread scheduling/synchronization, assembly loading, and more. The host can also state that it wants notifications of garbage collection starts and stops and when certain operations time out.

- **Get CLR managers**   Tell the CLR to prevent the use of some classes/members. In addition, the host can tell which code can and can't be debugged and which methods in the host should be called when a special event—such as an AppDomain unload, CLR stop, or stack overflow exception—occurs.

- Initialize and start the CLR.

- Load an assembly and execute code in it.

- Stop the CLR, thus preventing any more managed code from running in the Windows process.

There are many reasons why hosting the CLR is useful. Hosting allows any application to offer CLR features and a programmability story, and be at least partially written in managed code. Any application that hosts the runtime offers many benefits to developers who are trying to extend the application. Here are some of the benefits:

- Programming can be done in any programming language.

- Code is JIT-compiled for speed (versus being interpreted).

- Code uses garbage collection to avoid memory leaks and corruption.

- Code runs in a secure sandbox.

- The host doesn't need to worry about providing a rich development environment. The host makes use of existing technologies: languages, compilers, editors, debuggers, profilers, and more.

If you are interesting in using the CLR for hosting scenarios, I highly recommend that you get Steven Pratschner's excellent book: *Customizing the Microsoft .NET Framework Common Language Runtime* (Microsoft Press, 2005).

> **Note** Of course, a Windows process does not need to load the CLR at all: it needs to be
> loaded only if you want to execute managed code in a process. A single Windows process can
> load only one version of the CLR; it is not possible to have two or more versions of the CLR
> loaded in a single process. If a single host process calls **CorBindToRuntimeEx** multiple times,
> the same **ICLRRuntimeHost** pointer is returned every time.
>
> Once a CLR is loaded into the Windows process, it can never be unloaded; calling the **AddRef**
> and **Release** methods on the **ICLRRuntimeHost** interface has no effect. The only way for the
> CLR to be unloaded from a process is for the process to terminate, causing Windows to clean
> up all resources used by the process.

The following unmanaged C++ code demonstrates how easy it is to write an unmanaged host
that loads the CLR and executes some code in it.

```
#include <Windows.h>
#include <MSCorEE.h>
#include <stdio.h>

void main(int argc, WCHAR **argv) {
    // Load the CLR
    ICLRRuntimeHost *pClrHost;
    HRESULT hr = CorBindToRuntimeEx(
        NULL,                    // desired CLR version (NULL=latest)
        NULL,                    // desired GC flavor (NULL=workstation)
        0,                       // desired startup flags
        CLSID_CLRRuntimeHost,    // CLSID of CLR
        IID_ICLRRuntimeHost,     // IID of ICLRRuntimeHost
        (PVOID*) &pClrHost);     // returned COM interface

    // (This is where you would set Host managers)
    // (This is where you could get CLR managers)

    // Initialize and start the CLR
    pClrHost->Start();

    // Load an assembly and call a static method that
    // takes a String and returns an Int32
    DWORD retVal;
    hr = pClrHost->ExecuteInDefaultAppDomain(
            L"SomeMgdAssem.dll",
            L"Wintellect.SomeType", L"SomeMethod", L"Jeff", &retVal);

    // Show the result returned from managed code
    wprintf(L"Managed code returned %d", retVal);

    // Terminate this process (destroying the CLR loaded in it)
}
```

In this code, the unmanaged host has hard-coded some information about the managed assembly to load. Specifically, the managed assembly must be compiled into a SomeMgdAssem.dll file
that is in the process's working directory. This assembly must define a type called **Wintellect**
.SomeType. This type must define a static method called **SomeMethod**. Furthermore, the

ExecuteInDefaultAppDomain method requires that the SomeMethod method take one String argument and return an Int32. Here is the code for a simple C# library that can be called by this unmanaged host:

```
// Compile this C# code into a library assembly named SomeMgdAssem.dll
using System;

namespace Wintellect {
   public sealed class SomeType {
      public static Int32 SomeMethod(String s) {
         Console.WriteLine("Managed assembly: {0}", s);
         return s.Length;
      }
   }
}
```

AppDomains

When the CLR COM server initializes, it creates an *AppDomain*. An AppDomain is a logical container for a set of assemblies. The first AppDomain created when the CLR is initialized is called the *default AppDomain*; this AppDomain is destroyed only when the Windows process terminates.

In addition to the default AppDomain, a host using either unmanaged COM interface methods or managed type methods can instruct the CLR to create additional AppDomains. The whole purpose of an AppDomain is to provide isolation. Here are the specific features offered by an AppDomain:

- **Objects created by code in one AppDomain cannot be accessed directly by code in another AppDomain** When code in an AppDomain creates an object, that object is "owned" by that AppDomain. In other words, the object is not allowed to live beyond the lifetime of the AppDomain whose code constructed it. Code in other AppDomains can access another AppDomain's object only by using marshal-by-reference or marshal-by-value semantics. This enforces a clean separation and boundary because code in one AppDomain can't have a direct reference to an object created by code in a different AppDomain. This isolation allows AppDomains to be easily unloaded from a process without affecting code running in other AppDomains.

- **AppDomains can be unloaded** The CLR doesn't support the ability to unload a single assembly from an AppDomain. However, you can tell the CLR to unload an AppDomain, which will cause all of the assemblies currently contained in it to be unloaded as well.

- **AppDomains can be individually secured** When created, an AppDomain can have a permission set applied to it that determines the maximum rights granted to assemblies running in the AppDomain. This allows a host to load some code and be ensured that the code cannot corrupt or read important data structures used by the host itself.

- **AppDomains can be individually configured** When created, an AppDomain can have a bunch of configuration settings associated with it. These settings mostly affect how the CLR loads assemblies into the AppDomain. There are configuration settings related to search paths, version binding redirects, shadow copying, and loader optimizations.

> **Important**   A great feature of Windows is that it runs each application in its own process address space. This ensures that code in one application cannot access code or data in use by another application. Process isolation prevents security holes, data corruption, and other unpredictable behaviors from occurring, making Windows and the applications running on it robust. Unfortunately, creating processes in Windows is very expensive. The Win32 **CreateProcess** function is very slow, and Windows requires a lot of memory to virtualize a process's address space.
>
> However, if an application consists entirely of managed code that is verifiably safe and doesn't call out into unmanaged code, there are no problems related to running multiple managed applications in a single Windows process. And AppDomains provide the isolation required to secure, configure, and terminate each of these applications.

Figure 21-1 shows a single Windows process that has one CLR COM server running in it. This CLR is currently managing two AppDomains (although there is no hard-coded limit to the number of AppDomains that could be running in a single Windows process). Each AppDomain has its own loader heap, each of which maintains a record of which types have been accessed since the AppDomain was created. These type objects were discussed in Chapter 4, "Type Fundamentals"; each type object in the loader heap has a method table, and each entry in the method table points to JIT-compiled native code if the method has been executed at least once.

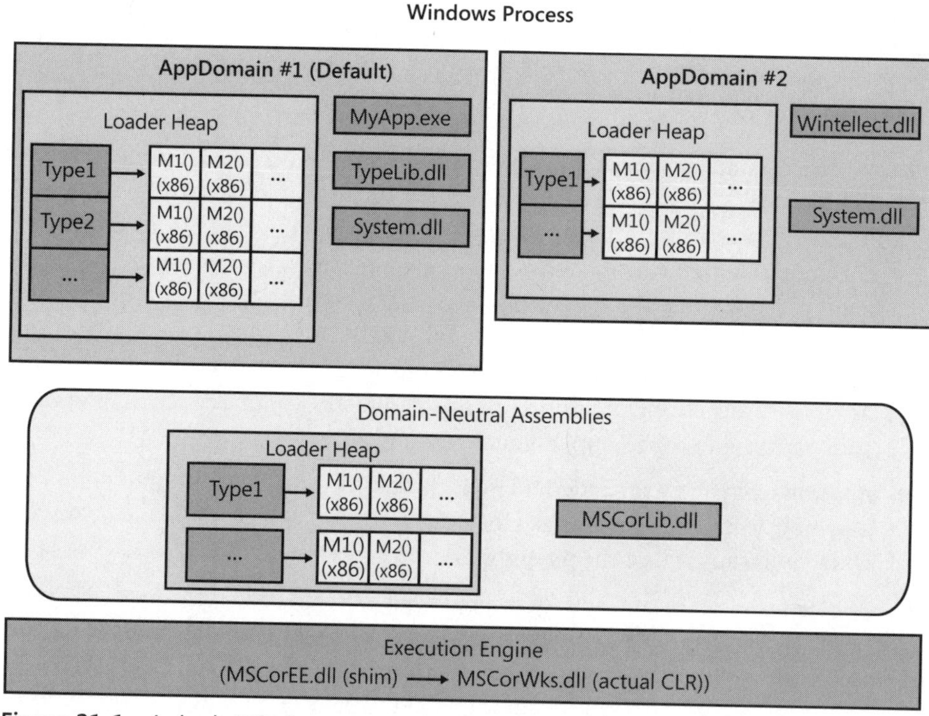

Figure 21-1   A single Windows process hosting the CLR and two AppDomains

In addition, each AppDomain has some assemblies loaded into it. AppDomain #1 (the default AppDomain) has three assemblies: MyApp.exe, TypeLib.dll, and System.dll. AppDomain #2 has two assemblies loaded into it: Wintellect.dll and System.dll.

You'll notice that the System.dll assembly has been loaded into both AppDomains. If both AppDomains are using a single type from System.dll, both AppDomains will have a type object for the same type allocated in each loader heap; the memory for the type object is not shared by all of the AppDomains. Furthermore, as code in an AppDomain calls methods defined by a type, the method's IL code is JIT-compiled, and the resulting native code is associated with each AppDomain; the code for the method is not shared by all AppDomains that call it.

Not sharing the memory for the type objects or native code is wasteful. However, the whole purpose of AppDomains is to provide isolation; the CLR needs to be able to unload an AppDomain and free up all of its resources without adversely affecting any other AppDomain. Replicating the CLR data structures ensures that this is possible.

Some assemblies are expected to be used by several AppDomains. The best example is MSCorLib.dll. This assembly contains **System.Object**, **System.Int32**, and all of the other types that are so integral to the .NET Framework. This assembly is automatically loaded when the CLR initializes, and all AppDomains share the types in this assembly. To reduce resource usage, MSCorLib.dll is loaded in an AppDomain-neutral fashion; that is, the CLR maintains a special loader heap for assemblies that are loaded in a domain-neutral fashion. All type objects in this loader heap and all native code for methods of these types are shared by all AppDomains in the process. Unfortunately, the benefit gained by sharing these resources does come with a price: assemblies that are loaded domain-neutral can never be unloaded. The only way to reclaim the resources used by them is to terminate the Windows process to cause Windows to reclaim the resources.

Accessing Objects Across AppDomain Boundaries

Code in one AppDomain can communicate with types and objects contained in another AppDomain. However, the access to these types and objects is allowed only through well-defined mechanisms. The AppDomainMarshalling sample application below demonstrates how to create a new AppDomain, load an assembly into it, and construct an instance of a type defined in that assembly. The code shows the different behaviors when constructing a type that is marshaled by reference, a type that is marshaled by value, and a type that can't be marshaled at all. The code also shows how these differently marshaled objects behave when the AppDomain that created them is unloaded. The AppDomainMarshalling sample application has very little code in it, but I have added a lot of comments. After the code listing, I'll walk through the code explaining what the CLR is doing.

```
using System;
using System.Reflection;
using System.Threading;
using System.Runtime.Remoting;

public static class Program {
    public static void Main() {
        // Get a reference to the AppDomain that the calling thread is executing in
        AppDomain adCallingThreadDomain = Thread.GetDomain();
```

```
// Every AppDomain is assigned a friendly string name, which is helpful
// for debugging. Get this AppDomain's friendly name and display it
String callingDomainName = adCallingThreadDomain.FriendlyName;
Console.WriteLine("Default AppDomain's friendly name={0}", callingDomainName);

// Get & display the assembly in our AppDomain that contains the 'Main' method
String exeAssembly = Assembly.GetEntryAssembly().FullName;
Console.WriteLine("Main assembly={0}", exeAssembly);

// Define a local variable that can refer to an AppDomain
AppDomain ad2 = null;


// DEMO 1: Cross-AppDomain Communication using Marshal-by-Reference
Console.WriteLine("{0}Demo #1: Marshal-by-Reference", Environment.NewLine);

// Create a new AppDomain (security & configuration match current AppDomain)
ad2 = AppDomain.CreateDomain("AD #2", null, null);

// Load our assembly into the new AppDomain, construct an object, marshal
// it back to our AD (we really get a reference to a proxy)
MarshalByRefType mbrt = (MarshalByRefType)
   ad2.CreateInstanceAndUnwrap(exeAssembly, "MarshalByRefType");
Type t = mbrt.GetType();

// Prove that we got a reference to a proxy object
Console.WriteLine("Is proxy={0}", RemotingServices.IsTransparentProxy(mbrt));

// This looks as if we're calling a method on a MarshalByRefType instance, but
// we're not. We're calling a method on an instance of a proxy type.
// The proxy transitions the thread to the AppDomain owning the object and
// calls this method on the real object
mbrt.SomeMethod(callingDomainName);

// Unload the new AppDomain
AppDomain.Unload(ad2);
// mbrt refers to a valid proxy object;
// this proxy refers to an invalid AppDomain now

try {
   // We're calling a method on the proxy type object.
   // The AD is invalid, an exception is thrown
   mbrt.SomeMethod(callingDomainName);
   Console.WriteLine("Successful call.");
}
catch (AppDomainUnloadedException) {
   Console.WriteLine("Failed call.");
}


// DEMO 2: Cross-AppDomain Communication using Marshal-by-Value
Console.WriteLine("{0}Demo #2: Marshal-by-Value", Environment.NewLine);

// Create a new AppDomain (security & configuration match current AppDomain)
ad2 = AppDomain.CreateDomain("AD #2", null, null);
```

```
         // Load our assembly into the new AppDomain, construct an object, marshal
         // it back to our AD (we really get a copy of the object with the same state)
         MarshalByValType mbvt = (MarshalByValType)
             ad2.CreateInstanceAndUnwrap(exeAssembly, "MarshalByValType");

         // Prove that we did NOT get a reference to a proxy object
         Console.WriteLine("Is proxy={0}", RemotingServices.IsTransparentProxy(mbvt));

         // This looks as if we're calling a method on a MarshalByValType object, and we are
         mbvt.SomeMethod(callingDomainName);

         // Unload the new AppDomain
         AppDomain.Unload(ad2);
         // mbvt refers to valid object; unloading the AppDomain has no impact.

         try {
             // We're calling a method on an object; no exception is thrown
             mbvt.SomeMethod(callingDomainName);
             Console.WriteLine("Successful call.");
         }
         catch (AppDomainUnloadedException) {
             Console.WriteLine("Failed call.");
         }


         // DEMO 3: Cross-AppDomain Communication using non-marshalable type
         Console.WriteLine("{0}Demo #3: Non-Marshalable Type", Environment.NewLine);

         // Create a new AppDomain (security & configuration match current AppDomain)
         ad2 = AppDomain.CreateDomain("AD #2", null, null);

         // Load our assembly into the new AppDomain, construct an object, try
         // to marshal it back to our AD (exception is thrown)
         NotMarshalableType nmt = (NotMarshalableType)
             ad2.CreateInstanceAndUnwrap(exeAssembly, "NotMarshalableType");
         // We won't get here...
     }
}


// Instances can be marshaled by reference across AppDomain boundaries
public class MarshalByRefType : MarshalByRefObject {
    DateTime creation = DateTime.Now;

    public MarshalByRefType() {
        Console.WriteLine("{0} ctor running in {1}",
            this.GetType().ToString(), Thread.GetDomain().FriendlyName);
    }

    public void SomeMethod(String callingDomainName) {
        Console.WriteLine("Calling from '{0}' to '{1}'.",
            callingDomainName, Thread.GetDomain().FriendlyName);
    }
}
```

```
// Instances can be marshaled by value across AppDomain boundaries
[Serializable]
public class MarshalByValType : Object {
   DateTime creation = DateTime.Now;

   public MarshalByValType() {
      Console.WriteLine("{0} ctor running in {1}",
         this.GetType().ToString(), Thread.GetDomain().FriendlyName);
   }

   public void SomeMethod(String callingDomainName) {
      Console.WriteLine("Calling from '{0}' to '{1}'.",
         callingDomainName, Thread.GetDomain().FriendlyName);
   }
}


// Instances cannot be marshaled across AppDomain boundaries
// [Serializable]
public class NotMarshalableType : Object {
   DateTime creation = DateTime.Now;

   public NotMarshalableType() {
      Console.WriteLine("{0} ctor running in {1}",
         this.GetType().ToString(), Thread.GetDomain().FriendlyName);
   }

   public void SomeMethod(String callingDomainName) {
      Console.WriteLine("Calling from '{0}' to '{1}'.",
         callingDomainName, Thread.GetDomain().FriendlyName);
   }
}
```

If you build and run the AppDomainMarshalling application, you get the following output:

```
Default AppDomain's friendly name=AppDomainMarshalling.exe
Main assembly=AppDomainMarshalling, Version=0.0.0.0, Culture=neutral, PublicKeyToken=null

Demo #1: Marshal-by-Reference
MarshalByRefType ctor running in AD #2
Is proxy=True
Calling from 'AppDomainMarshalling.exe' to 'AD #2'.
Failed call.

Demo #2: Marshal-by-Value
MarshalByValType ctor running in AD #2
Is proxy=False
Calling from 'AppDomainMarshalling.exe' to 'AppDomainMarshalling.exe'.
Calling from 'AppDomainMarshalling.exe' to 'AppDomainMarshalling.exe'.
Successful call.

Demo #3: Non-Marshalable Type
NotMarshalableType ctor running in AD #2
```

```
Unhandled Exception: System.Runtime.Serialization.SerializationException:
Type 'NotMarshalableType' in assembly 'AppDomainMarshalling, Version=0.0.0.0,
Culture=neutral, PublicKeyToken=null' is not marked as serializable.
   at System.AppDomain.CreateInstanceAndUnwrap(String assemblyName, String typeName)
   at Program.Main() in C:\AppDomainMarshalling.cs:line 97
```

Now, I will discuss what this code and the CLR are doing.

Inside the **Main** method, I first get a reference to an **AppDomain** object that identifies the App-Domain the calling thread is currently executing in. In Windows, a thread is always created in the context of one process, and the thread lives its entire lifetime in that process. However, a one-to-one correspondence doesn't exist between threads and AppDomains. AppDomains are a CLR feature; Windows knows nothing about AppDomains. Since multiple AppDomains can be in a single Windows process, a thread can execute code in one AppDomain and then execute code in another AppDomain. From the CLR's perspective, a thread is executing code in one AppDomain at a time. A thread can ask the CLR what AppDomain it is currently executing in by calling **System.Threading.Thread**'s static **GetDomain** method. The thread could also query **System.AppDomain**'s static, read-only **CurrentDomain** property to get the same information.

When an AppDomain is created, it can be assigned a *friendly name*. A friendly name is just a **String** that you can use to identify an AppDomain. This is typically useful in debugging scenarios. Since the CLR creates the default AppDomain before any of our code can run, the CLR uses the executable file's file name as the default AppDomain's friendly name. My **Main** method queries the default AppDomain's friendly name by using **System.AppDomain**'s read-only **FriendlyName** property.

Next, my **Main** method queries the strong-name identity of the assembly (loaded into the default AppDomain) that defines the entry point method, **Main**. This assembly defines several types: **Program**, **MarshalByRefType**, **MarshalByValType**, and **NonMarshalableType**. At this point, we're ready to look at the three demos that are all pretty similar to each other.

Demo #1: Cross-AppDomain Communication that Uses Marshal-by-Reference

In Demo #1, **System.AppDomain**'s static **CreateDomain** method is called instructing the CLR to create a new AppDomain in the same Windows process. The **AppDomain** type actually offers several overloads of the **CreateDomain** method; I encourage you to study them and select the version that is most appropriate when you are writing code to create a new AppDomain. The version of **CreateDomain** that I call accepts three arguments:

- A **string** identifying the friendly name I want assigned to the new AppDomain. I'm passing in "AD #2" here.

- A **System.Security.Policy.Evidence** identifying the evidence that the CLR should use to calculate the AppDomain's permission set. I'm passing **null** here so that the new AppDomain will inherit the same permission set as the AppDomain creating it. Usually, if you want to create a security boundary around code in an AppDomain, you'd construct a `System.Security.PermissionSet` object, add the desired permission objects to it (instances of types that implement the `IPermission` interface), and then pass the resulting `PermissionSet` object reference to the overloaded version of the `CreateDomain` method that accepts a `PermissionSet`.

■ A `System.AppDomainSetup` identifying the configuration settings the CLR should use for the new AppDomain. Again, I'm passing `null` here so that the new AppDomain will inherit the same configuration settings as the AppDomain creating it. If you want the AppDomain to have a special configuration, construct an `AppDomainSetup` object, set its various properties to whatever you desire such as the name of the configuration file for example, and then pass the resulting `AppDomainSetup` object reference to the `CreateDomain` method.

Internally, the `CreateDomain` method creates a new AppDomain in the process. This AppDomain will be assigned the specified friendly name, security, and configuration settings. The new AppDomain will have its very own loader heap, which will be empty because there are currently no assemblies loading into the new AppDomain. When you create an AppDomain, the CLR does not create any threads in this AppDomain; no code runs in the AppDomain unless you explicitly have a thread call code in the AppDomain.

Now to create an instance of an object in the new AppDomain, we must first load an assembly into the new AppDomain and then construct an instance of a type defined in this assembly. This is precisely what the call to `AppDomain`'s public, instance `CreateInstanceAndUnwrap` method does. When calling `CreateInstanceAndUnwrap`, I pass two arguments: a `String` identifying the assembly I want loaded into the new AppDomain (referenced by the `ad2` variable) and another `String` identifying the name of the type that I want to construct an instance of. Internally, `CreateInstanceAndUnwrap` causes the calling thread to transition from the current AppDomain into the new AppDomain. Now, the thread (which is inside the call to `CreateInstanceAndUnwrap`) loads the specified assembly into the new AppDomain and then scans the assembly's type definition metadata table, looking for the specified type ("MarshalByRefType"). After the type is found, the thread calls the `MarshalByRefType`'s parameterless constructor. Now the thread transitions back to the default AppDomain so that `CreateInstanceAndUnwrap` can return a reference to the new `MarshalByRefType` object.

Note   There are overloaded versions of `CreateInstanceAndUnwrap` that allow you to call a type's constructor passing in arguments.

While this sounds all fine and good, there is a problem: the CLR cannot allow a variable (root) living in one AppDomain to reference an object created in another AppDomain. If `CreateInstanceAndUnwrap` simply returned the reference to the object, isolation would be broken, and isolation is the whole purpose of AppDomains! So just before `CreateInstanceAndUnwrap` returns the object reference, it performs some additional logic.

You'll notice that the `MarshalByRefType` type is derived from a very special base class: `System.MarshalByRefObject`. When `CreateInstanceAndUnwrap` sees that it is marshalling an object whose type is derived from `MarshalByRefObject`, the CLR will marshal the object by reference across the AppDomain boundaries. Here is what it means to marshal an object by reference from one AppDomain (the source AppDomain where the object is really created) to another AppDomain (the destination AppDomain from where `CreateInstanceAndUnwrap` is called).

When a source AppDomain wants to send or return the reference of an object to a destination AppDomain, the CLR defines a proxy type in the destination AppDomain's loader heap. This proxy type is defined using the original type's metadata, and therefore, it looks exactly like the original type; it has all of the same instance members (properties, events, and methods). The instance fields are not part of the type, but I'll talk more about this in a moment. This new type does have some instance fields defined inside of it, but these fields are not identical to that of the original data type. Instead, these fields indicate which AppDomain "owns" the real object and how to find the real object in the owning AppDomain. (Internally, the proxy object uses a `GCHandle` instance that refers to the real object. The `GCHandle` type is discussed in Chapter 20, "Automatic Memory Management (Garbage Collection).")

Once this type is defined in the destination AppDomain, `CreateInstanceAndUnwrap` creates an instance of this proxy type, initializes its fields to identify the source AppDomain and the real object, and returns a reference to this proxy object to the destination AppDomain. In my AppDomainMarshalling application, the `mbrt` variable will be set to refer to this proxy. Notice that the object returned from `CreateInstanceAndUnwrap` is actually not an instance of the `MarshalByRefType` type. The CLR will usually not allow you to cast an object of one type to an incompatible type. However, in this situation, the CLR does allow the cast because this new type has the same instance members as defined on the original type. In fact, if you use the proxy object to call `GetType`, it actually lies to you and says that it is a `MarshalByRefType` object.

However, it is possible to prove that the object returned from `CreateInstanceAndUnwrap` is actually a reference to a proxy object. To do this, my AppDomainMarshalling application calls `System.Runtime.Remoting.RemotingService`'s public, static `IsTransparentProxy` method passing in the reference returned from `CreateInstanceAndUnwrap`. As you can see from the output, `IsTransparentProxy` returns `true` indicating that the object is a proxy.

Now, my AppDomainMarshalling application uses the proxy to call the `SomeMethod` method. Since the `mbrt` variable refers to a proxy object, the proxy's implementation of this method is called. The proxy's implementation uses the information fields inside the proxy object to transition the calling thread from the default AppDomain to the new AppDomain. Any actions now performed by this thread run under the new AppDomain's security and configuration settings. Then, the thread uses the proxy object's `GCHandle` field to find the real object in the new AppDomain, and then it uses the real object to call the real `SomeMethod` method.

There are two ways to prove that the calling thread has transitioned from the default AppDomain to the new AppDomain. First, inside the **SomeMethod** method, I call **Thread.GetDomain()** **.FriendlyName**. This will return "AD #2" (as evidenced by the output) since the thread is now running in the new AppDomain created by using **AppDomain.CreateDomain** with "AD #2" as friendly name parameter. Second, if you step through the code in a debugger and display the Call Stack window, the [AppDomain Transition] line marks where a thread has transitioned across an AppDomain boundary. See the Call Stack window near the bottom of Figure 21-2.

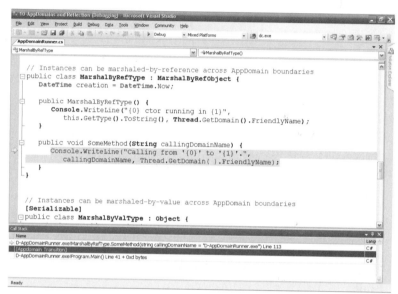

Figure 21-2 The Debugger's Call Stack window showing an AppDomain transition

When the real **SomeMethod** method returns, it returns to the proxy's **SomeMethod** method, which transitions the thread back to the default AppDomain, and then the thread continues executing code in the default AppDomain.

> **Note** When a thread in one AppDomain calls a method in another AppDomain, the thread transitions between the two AppDomains. This means that method calls across AppDomain boundaries are executed synchronously. However, at any given time, a thread is considered to be in just one AppDomain. If you want to execute code in multiple AppDomains concurrently, you should create additional threads and have them execute whatever code you desire in whatever AppDomains you desire.

The next thing that my AppDomainMarshalling application does is call **AppDomain**'s public, static **Unload** method to force the CLR to unload the specified AppDomain including all of the assemblies loaded into it, and a garbage collection is forced to free up any objects that were created by code in the unloading AppDomain. At this point, the default AppDomain's **mbrt** variable still refers to a valid proxy object; however, the proxy object no longer refers to a valid AppDomain (because it has been unloaded).

When the default AppDomain attempts to use the proxy object to call the `SomeMethod` method, the proxy's implementation of this method is called. The proxy's implementation determines that the AppDomain that contained the real object has been unloaded, and the proxy's `SomeMethod` method throws an `AppDomainUnloadedException` to let the caller know that the operation cannot complete.

Wow! The CLR team at Microsoft had to do a lot of work to ensure AppDomain isolation, but it is important work because these features are used heavily and are being used more and more by developers every day. Obviously, accessing objects across AppDomain boundaries by using marshal-by-reference semantics has some performance costs associated with it, so you typically want to keep the use of this feature to a minimum.

I promised you that I'd talk a little more about instance fields. A type derived from `MarshalBy-RefObject` can define instance fields. However, these instance fields are not defined as being part of the proxy type and are not contained inside a proxy object. When you write code that reads from or writes to an instance field of a type derived from `MarshalByRefObject`, the JIT compiler emits code that uses the proxy object (to find the real AppDomain/object) by calling `System.Object`'s `FieldGetter` or `FieldSetter` methods, respectively. These methods are private and undocumented; they are basically methods that use reflection to get and set the value in a field. So although you can access fields of a type derived from `MarshalByRefObject`, the performance is particularly bad because the CLR really ends up calling methods to perform the field access. In fact, the performance is bad even if the object that you are accessing is in your own AppDomain.

Finally, from a usability standpoint, a type derived from `MarshalByRefObject` should really avoid defining any static members. The reason is that static members are always accessed in the context of the calling AppDomain. No AppDomain transition can occur because a proxy object contains the information identifying which AppDomain to transition to, but there is no proxy object when calling a static member. Having a type's static members execute in one AppDomain while instance members execute in another AppDomain would make a very awkward programming model.

Demo #2: Cross-AppDomain Communication Using Marshal-by-Value

Demo #2 is very similar to Demo #1. Again, another AppDomain is created exactly as Demo #1 did it. Then, `CreateInstanceAndUnwrap` is called to load the same assembly into the new AppDomain and to create an instance of a type in this new AppDomain. This time, the type I want to create an instance of is `MarshalByValType`, which is not derived from `System .MarshalByRefObject`. As before, `CreateInstanceAndUnwrap` must preserve isolation, and therefore, it cannot simply return a reference to the object back to the default AppDomain. Since `MarshalByValType` is not derived from `System.MarshalByRefObject`, `CreateInstance-AndUnwrap` is not allowed to define a proxy type to create an instance from; the object can't be marshaled by reference.

However, since `MarshalByValType` is marked with the `[Serializable]` custom attribute, `CreateInstanceAndUnwrap` is allowed to marshal the object by value. The next paragraph describes what it means to marshal an object by value from one AppDomain (the source AppDomain) to another AppDomain (the destination AppDomain).

When a source AppDomain wants to send or return a reference to an object to a destination AppDomain, the CLR serializes the object's instance fields into a byte array. This byte array is copied from the source AppDomain to the destination AppDomain. Then, the CLR deserializes the byte array in the destination AppDomain. This forces the CLR to load the assembly that defines the type being deserialized into the destination AppDomain if it is not already loaded. Then, the CLR creates an instance of the type and uses the values in the byte array to initialize the object's fields so that they have values identical to those they had in the original object. In other words, the CLR makes an exact duplicate of the source object in the destination's AppDomain. `CreateInstanceAndUnwrap` then returns a reference to this copy; the object has been marshaled by value across the AppDomains boundary.

> **Important**   When loading the assembly, the CLR uses the destination AppDomain's policies and configuration settings (for example, the AppDomain can have a different AppBase directory or different version binding redirections). These policy differences might prevent the CLR from locating the assembly. If the assembly cannot be loaded, an exception will be thrown, and the destination will not receive a reference to the object.

At this point, the object in the source AppDomain and the object in the destination AppDomain live separate lifetimes, and their states can change independently of each other. If there are no roots in the source AppDomain keeping the original object alive (as in my AppDomain-Marshalling application), its memory will be reclaimed at the next garbage collection.

To prove that the object returned from `CreateInstanceAndUnwrap` is not a reference to a proxy object, my AppDomainMarshalling application calls `System.Runtime.Remoting.Remoting-Service`'s public, static `IsTrasparentProxy` method passing in the reference returned from `CreateInstanceAndUnwrap`. As you can see from the output, `IsTrasparentProxy` returns `false` indicating that the object is a real object, not a proxy.

Now, my program uses the real object to call the `SomeMethod` method. Since the `mbvt` variable refers to a real object, the real implementation of this method is called, and no AppDomain transition occurs. This can be evidenced by examining the output; inside the `SomeMethod` method, the call to `Thread.GetDomain().FriendlyName` returns "AppDomainMarshalling." In addition, the debugger's Call Stack window will not show an [AppDomain Transition] line.

To further prove that no proxy is involved, my AppDomainMarshalling application unloads the new AppDomain and then attempts to call the `SomeMethod` method again. Unlike in Demo #1, this time, the call succeeds because unloading the new AppDomain had no impact on objects "owned" by the default AppDomain, and this includes the object that was marshaled by value.

At this point, you may be wondering why you would ever want to create and marshal an object across an AppDomain by using marshal-by-value semantics. In my scenario, the `MarshalBy-ValType` constructor does run in the new AppDomain. This means that it will run using the permissions and configuration settings granted to this AppDomain, which is useful in some scenarios. But once the object is marshaled by value across the boundary, any future calls that use the object occur using the permissions and configuration settings of the default AppDomain. In the "Marshaling Arguments and Return Values Across AppDomain Boundaries" section, I'll explain the main reason why it is useful to marshal objects by value across an AppDomain boundary. In fact, most types are defined to be marshaled by value across AppDomain boundaries.

Demo #3: Cross-AppDomain Communication Using Non-Marshalable Types

Demo #3 starts out very similar to Demos #1 and #2. Again, another AppDomain is created exactly as in Demos #1 and #2. Then, `CreateInstanceAndUnwrap` is called to load the same assembly into the new AppDomain and to create an instance of a type in this new AppDomain. This time, the type I want to create an instance of is `NonMarshalableType`. As before, `Create-InstanceAndUnwrap` must preserve isolation, and it therefore cannot simply return a reference to the object back to the default AppDomain. Since `NonMarshalableType` is not derived from `System.MarshalByRefObject` and is also not marked with the `[Serializable]` custom attribute, `CreateInstanceAndUnwrap` is not allowed to marshal the object by reference or by value—the object cannot be marshaled across an AppDomain boundary at all! To report this, `CreateInstanceAndUnwrap` throws a `SerializationException` in the default AppDomain. Since my program doesn't catch this exception, the program just dies.

Marshaling Arguments and Return Values Across AppDomain Boundaries

In my code, you'll notice that the `SomeMethod` methods take a `string` argument. So in Demo #1, the `string` passed to the proxy's `SomeMethod` must ultimately be passed to the real object's `SomeMethod` method. But if the CLR just passed the reference to the object from one AppDomain to another, isolation would be broken. So when an argument is going to cross an AppDomain boundary, the CLR must check if the object's type is derived from `MarshalByRefObject`; if so, the object is marshaled by reference. If the object's type is not derived from `MarshalBy-RefObject`, the CLR checks if the type is marked with the `[Serializable]` custom attribute. If so, the object is marshaled by value. If the object's type is not derived from `MarshalByRefObject` and is not marked with the `[Serializable]` custom attribute, the CLR cannot marshal the object at all, and an exception is thrown.

If a method takes multiple arguments, the CLR must perform all of this marshalling for every argument. Similarly, when a method tries to return an object across an AppDomain boundary, the CLR must marshal it by reference or by value, or throw an exception. By the way, if the object being marshaled across is a complex type consisting of several fields, the CLR must walk the entire object graph and marshal each and every field by reference or by value depending on each field's type.

> **Note**   In my AppDomainMarshalling application, I am passing a `String` across an
> AppDomain boundary. Since `System.String` is not derived from `MarshalByRefObject`, it
> cannot be marshaled by reference. Fortunately, `System.String` is marked as `[Serializable]`,
> and this is what allows a `String` object to be marshaled by value. For `String` objects, the CLR
> performs a special optimization. When marshaling a `String` object across an AppDomain
> boundary, the CLR just passes the reference to the `String` object across the boundary; it does
> not make a copy of the `String` object. The CLR can offer this optimization because `String`
> objects are immutable, and therefore, it is impossible for code in one AppDomain to corrupt
> a `String` object's characters. For more about `String` immutability, see Chapter 11, "Chars,
> Strings, and Working with Text."

AppDomain Unloading

One of the great features of AppDomains is that you can unload them. Unloading an AppDomain
causes the CLR to unload all of the assemblies in the AppDomain, and the CLR frees the
AppDomain's loader heap as well. To unload an AppDomain, you call `AppDomain`'s `Unload`
static method (as the AppDomainMarshalling application does). This call causes the CLR to
perform a lot of actions to gracefully unload the specified AppDomain:

1. The CLR suspends all threads in the process that have ever executed managed code.

2. The CLR examines all of the threads' stacks to see which threads are currently executing
    code in the AppDomain being unloaded or which threads might return at some point
    to code in the AppDomain that is being unloaded. The CLR forces any threads that
    have the unloading AppDomain on their stack to throw a `ThreadAbortException`
    (resuming the thread's execution). This causes the threads to unwind, executing any
    `finally` blocks on their way out so that cleanup code executes. If no code catches the
    `ThreadAbortException`, it will eventually become an unhandled exception that the
    CLR swallows; the thread dies, but the process is allowed to continue running. This is
    unusual because for all other unhandled exceptions, the CLR kills the process.

> **Important**   The CLR will not immediately abort a thread that is currently executing
> code in a `finally` block, `catch` block, a class constructor, a critical execution region, or in
> unmanaged code. If the CLR allowed this, cleanup code, error recovery code, type initial-
> ization code, critical code, or arbitrary code that the CLR knows nothing about would not
> complete, resulting in the application behaving unpredictably and with potential security
> holes. An aborting thread is allowed to finish executing these code blocks and then, at the
> end of the code block, the CLR forces the thread to throw a `ThreadAbortException`.

3. After all threads discovered in step #2 have left the AppDomain, the CLR then walks the
    heap and sets a flag in each proxy object that referred to an object created by the
    unloaded AppDomain. These proxy objects now know that the real object they referred
    to is gone. If any code now calls a method on an invalid proxy object, the method will
    throw an `AppDomainUnloadedException`.

4. The CLR forces a garbage collection to occur, reclaiming the memory used by any objects that were created by the now unloaded AppDomain. The `Finalize` methods for these objects are called, giving the objects a chance to clean themselves up properly.

5. The CLR resumes all of the remaining threads. The thread that called `AppDomain.Unload` will now continue running; calls to `AppDomain.Unload` occur synchronously.

My AppDomainMarshalling application uses just one thread to do all of the work. Whenever my code calls `AppDomain.Unload`, there are no threads in the unloading AppDomain, and therefore, the CLR doesn't have to throw any `ThreadAbortException` exceptions. I'll talk more about `ThreadAbortException` later in this chapter.

By the way, when a thread calls `AppDomain.Unload`, the CLR waits 10 seconds (by default) for the threads in the unloading AppDomain to leave it. If after 10 seconds, the thread that called `AppDomain.Unload` doesn't return, it will throw a `CannotUnloadAppDomainException`, and the AppDomain may or may not be unloaded in the future.

> **Note**   If a thread calling `AppDomain.Unload` is in the AppDomain being unloaded, the CLR creates another thread, and this new thread attempts to unload the AppDomain. The first thread will forcibly throw the `ThreadAbortException` and unwind. The new thread will wait for the AppDomain to unload, and then the new thread terminates. If the AppDomain fails to unload, the new thread will process a `CannotUnloadAppDomainException`, but since you did not write the code that this new thread executes, you can't catch this exception.

How Hosts Use AppDomains

So far, I've talked about hosts and how they load the CLR. I've also talked about how the hosts tell the CLR to create and unload AppDomains. To make the discussion more concrete, I'll describe some common hosting and AppDomain scenarios. In particular, I'll explain how different application types host the CLR and how they manage AppDomains.

Console and Windows Forms Applications

When invoking a managed executable (console or Windows Forms application), the shim examines the CLR header information contained in the application's assembly. The header information indicates the version of the CLR that was used to build and test the application. The shim uses this information to determine which version of the CLR to load into the process. After the CLR loads and initializes, it again examines the assembly's CLR header to determine which method is the application's entry point (`Main`). The CLR invokes this method, and the application is now up and running.

As the code runs, it accesses other types. When referencing a type contained in another assembly, the CLR locates the necessary assembly and loads it into the same AppDomain. Any additionally referenced assemblies also load into the same AppDomain. When the application's `Main` method returns, the Windows process terminates (destroying the default AppDomain and all other AppDomains).

> **Note**   By the way, you can call **System.Environment**'s static **Exit** method if you want to shut down the Windows process including all of its AppDomains. **Exit** is the most graceful way of terminating a process because it first calls the **Finalize** methods of all of the objects on the managed heap and then releases all of the unmanaged COM objects held by the CLR. Finally, **Exit** calls the Win32 **ExitProcess** function.

It's possible for the application to tell the CLR to create additional AppDomains in the process's address space. In fact, this is what my AppDomainMarshalling application did.

Microsoft Internet Explorer

When you install the .NET Framework, it installs a MIME filter (MSCorIE.dll) that is hooked into Internet Explorer versions 5.01 and later. This MIME filter handles downloaded content marked with a MIME type of "application/octet-stream" or "application/x-msdownload". When the MIME filter detects a managed assembly being downloaded, it calls the **CorBindToRuntimeEx** function to load the CLR; this makes Internet Explorer's process a host.

The MIME filter is in control of the CLR and ensures that all assemblies from one Web site are loaded into their own AppDomain. Since an AppDomain can be secured, this gives an administrator the ability to grant different permission sets to code that was downloaded from different Web sites. Since AppDomains can be unloaded, the code downloaded and running from one Web site can be unloaded when the user surfs to a different Web site.

Microsoft ASP.NET Web Forms and XML Web Services Applications

ASP.NET is implemented as an ISAPI DLL (implemented in ASPNet_ISAPI.dll). The first time a client requests a URL handled by the ASP.NET ISAPI DLL, ASP.NET loads the CLR. When a client makes a request of a Web application, ASP.NET determines if this is the first time a request has been made. If it is, ASP.NET tells the CLR to create a new AppDomain for this Web application; each Web application is identified by its virtual root directory. ASP.NET then tells the CLR to load the assembly that contains the type exposed by the Web application into this new AppDomain, creates an instance of this type, and starts calling methods in it to satisfy the client's Web request. If the code references more types, the CLR will load the required assemblies into the Web application's AppDomain.

When future clients make requests of an already running Web application, ASP.NET doesn't create a new AppDomain; instead, it uses the existing AppDomain, creates a new instance of the Web application's type, and starts calling methods. The methods will already be JIT compiled into native code, so the performance of processing all subsequent client requests is excellent.

If a client makes a request of a different Web application, ASP.NET tells the CLR to create a new AppDomain. This new AppDomain is typically created inside the same worker process as the other AppDomains. This means that many Web applications run in a single Windows process, which improves the efficiency of the system overall. Again, the assemblies required by each Web application are loaded into an AppDomain created for the sole purpose of isolating that Web application's code and objects from other Web applications.

A fantastic feature of ASP.NET is that the code for a Web site can be changed on the fly without shutting down the Web server. When a Web site's file is changed on the hard disk, ASP.NET detects this, unloads the AppDomain that contains the old version of the files (when the last currently running request finishes), and then creates a new AppDomain, loading into it the new versions of the files. To make this happen, ASP.NET uses an AppDomain feature called *shadow copying*.

Microsoft SQL Server 2005

Microsoft SQL Server 2005 is an unmanaged application because most of its code is still written in unmanaged C++. SQL Server 2005 allows developers to create stored procedures by using managed code. The first time a request comes in to the database to run a stored procedure written in managed code, SQL Server loads the CLR. Stored procedures run in their own secured AppDomain, prohibiting the stored procedures from adversely affecting the database server.

This functionality is absolutely incredible! It means that developers will be able to write stored procedures in the programming language of their choice. The stored procedure can use strongly typed data objects in its code. The code will also be JIT compiled into native code when executed, instead of being interpreted. And developers can take advantage of any types defined in the Framework Class Library (FCL) or in any other assembly. The result is that our job becomes much easier and our applications perform much better. What more could a developer ask for?!

The Future and Your Own Imagination

In the future, productivity applications such as word processors and spreadsheets will also allow users to write macros in any programming language they choose. These macros will have access to all of the assemblies and types that work with the CLR. They will be compiled, so they will execute fast, and, most important, these macros will run in a secure AppDomain so that users don't get hit with any unwanted surprises.

Advanced Host Control

In this section, I'll mention some more advanced topics related to hosting the CLR. My intent is to give you a taste of what is possible, and this will help you to understand more of what the CLR is capable of. I encourage you to seek out other texts (especially Steven Pratschner's book, to which I referred at the beginning of this chapter) if you find this information particularly interesting.

Managing the CLR by Using Managed Code

The `System.AppDomainManager` class allows a host to override CLR default behavior by using managed code instead of using unmanaged code. Of course, using managed code makes implementing a host easier. All you need to do is define your class and derive it from the `System .AppDomainManager` class, overriding any virtual methods where you want to take over control. Your class should then be built into its very own assembly and installed into the GAC because the assembly needs to be granted full-trust, and all assemblies in the GAC are always granted full-trust.

Then, when the Windows process starts, you need to tell the CLR to use your `AppDomainManager`-derived class. A process can have one and only one `AppDomainManager`-derived class associated with it for the CLR to use. And each AppDomain that is created in this process will have one and only one instance of this class associated with it. There are three ways to associate an `AppDomainManager`-derived class with a Windows process:

- **Unmanaged hosting API (the best choice)**   In this case, the host must have a little bit of unmanaged code. Just after the host calls `CorBindToRuntimeEx`, the host should query the `ICLRControl` interface and call this interface's `SetAppDomainManagerType` function passing in the identity of the GAC-installed assembly and the name of the `AppDomainManager`-derived class.

- **Environment variables (the second-best choice)**   Before starting the CLR, the Windows process must set two environment variables. The APPDOMAIN_MANAGER_ASM variable must be set to the identity of the GAC-installed assembly, and the APPDOMAIN_MANAGER_TYPE variable must be set to the name of the `AppDomainManager`-derived class. Frequently, a small stub program is used to set these variables, and then the stub program can launch the managed executable file—this allows all of the code to be managed; no unmanaged code is necessary.

- **Registry keys (worst choice)**   Before starting the CLR, the HKEY_LOCAL_MACHINE (or HKEY_CURRENT_USER)\Software\Microsoft\.NETFramework\ registry key must have two values added to it. The APPDOMAIN_MANAGER_ASM value must be set to the identity of the GAC-installed assembly, and the APPDOMAIN_MANAGER_TYPE value must be set to the name of the `AppDomainManager`-derived class. This choice is the worst because it affects all managed applications running on the machine; all managed applications will use the same `AppDomainManager`-derived class. This is ridiculous. You should use this registry method only for testing on your own machine (assuming that you don't run any other managed applications). See why this is ridiculous?!

Now, let's talk about what an `AppDomainManager`-derived class can do. The purpose of the `AppDomainManager`-derived class is to allow a host to maintain control even when an add-in tries to create AppDomains of its own. When code in the process tries to create a new AppDomain, the `AppDomainManager`-derived object in that AppDomain can modify security and configuration settings. It can also decide to fail an AppDomain creation, or it can decide to return a reference to an existing AppDomain instead. When a new AppDomain is created, the CLR creates a new `AppDomainManager`-derived object in the AppDomain. This object can also modify configuration settings, how execution context is flowed between threads, and permissions granted to an assembly.

Writing a Robust Host Application

A host can tell the CLR what actions to take when a failure occurs in managed code. Here are some examples (listed from least severe to most severe):

- The CLR can abort a thread if the thread is taking too long to execute and return a response. (I'll discuss this more in the next section.)

- The CLR can unload an AppDomain. This aborts all of the threads that are in the AppDomain and causes the problematic code to be unloaded.

- The CLR can be disabled. This stops any more managed code from executing in the process, but unmanaged code is still allowed to run.

- The CLR can exit the Windows process. This aborts all of the threads and unloads all of the AppDomains first so that cleanup operations occur, and then the process terminates.

The CLR can abort a thread or AppDomain gracefully or rudely. A graceful abort means that cleanup code executes. In other words, code in `finally` blocks runs, and objects have their `Finalize` methods executed. A rude abort means that cleanup code does not execute. In other words, code in `finally` blocks may not run, and objects may not have their `Finalize` methods executed. A graceful abort cannot abort a thread that is in a `catch` or `finally` block. However, a rude abort will abort a thread that is in a `catch` or `finally` block. Unfortunately, a thread that is in unmanaged code or in a Critical Execution Region (CER) cannot be aborted at all.

A host can set what is called an *Escalation Policy* telling the CLR how to deal with managed code failures. For example, SQL Server 2005 tells the CLR what to do should an unhandled exception be thrown while the CLR is executing managed code. When a thread experiences an unhandled exception, the CLR first attempts to upgrade the exception to a graceful thread abort. If the thread does not abort in a specified time period, the CLR attempts to upgrade the graceful thread abort to a rude thread abort.

What I just described is what usually happens. However, if the thread experiencing the unhandled exception is in a *critical region*, the policy is different. A thread that is in a critical region is a thread that has entered a thread synchronization lock that must be released by the same thread, for example, a thread that has called `Monitor.Enter`, `Mutex`'s `WaitOne`, or one of **ReaderWriterLock**'s **AcquireReaderLock** or **AcquireWriterLock** methods. Successfully waiting for an **AutoResetEvent**, **ManualResetEvent**, or **Semaphore** doesn't cause the thread to be in a critical region because another thread can signal these synchronization objects. When a thread is in a critical region, the CLR believes that the thread is accessing data that is shared by multiple threads in the same AppDomain. After all, this is probably why the thread took the lock. If the thread is accessing shared data, just terminating the thread isn't good enough because other threads may then try to access the shared data that is now corrupt, causing the AppDomain to run unpredictably or with possible security vulnerabilities.

So when a thread in a critical region experiences an unhandled exception, the CLR first attempts to upgrade the exception to a graceful AppDomain unload in an effort to get rid of all of the threads and data objects that are currently in use. If the AppDomain doesn't unload in a specified amount of time, the CLR upgrades the graceful AppDomain unload to a rude AppDomain unload.

How a Host Gets its Thread Back

Normally, a host application wants to stay in control of its threads. Let's take a database server as an example. When a request comes into the database server, a thread picks up the request and then dispatches the request to another thread that is to perform the actual work. This other thread may need to execute code that wasn't created and tested by the team that produced the database server. For example, imagine a request coming into the database server to execute a stored procedure written in managed code by the company running the server. It's great that the database server can run the stored procedure code in its own AppDomain, which is locked down with security. This prevents the stored procedure from accessing any objects outside of its own AppDomain, and it also prevents the code from accessing resources that it is not allowed to access, such as disk files or the clipboard.

But what if the code in the stored procedure enters an infinite loop? In this case, the database server has dispatched one of its threads into the stored procedure code, and this thread is never coming back. This puts the server in a precarious position; the future behavior of the server is unknown. For example, the performance might be terrible now because a thread is in an infinite loop. Should the server create more threads? Doing so uses more resources (such as stack space), and these threads could also enter an infinite loop themselves.

To solve these problems, the host can take advantage of thread aborting. Figure 21-3 shows the typical architecture of a host application trying to solve the runaway thread problem. Here's how it works (the numbers correspond to the circled numbers in the figure):

1.   A client sends a request to the server.

2.   A server thread picks up this request and dispatches it to a thread pool thread to perform the actual work.

3.   A thread pool thread picks up the client request and executes trusted code written by the company that built and tested the host application.

4. This trusted code then enters a **try** block, and from within the **try** block, calls across an AppDomain boundary (via a type derived from **MarshalByRefObject**). This AppDomain contains the untrusted code (perhaps a stored procedure) that was not built and tested by the company that produced the host application. At this point, the server has given control of its thread to some untrusted code; the server is feeling nervous right now.

5. When the host originally received the client's request, it recorded the time. If the untrusted code doesn't respond to the client in some administrator-set amount of time, the host calls **Thread**'s **Abort** method asking the CLR to stop the thread pool thread, forcing it to throw a **ThreadAbortException**.

6. At this point, the thread pool thread starts unwinding, calling **finally** blocks so that cleanup code executes. Eventually, the thread pool thread crosses back over the AppDomain boundary. Since the host's stub code called the untrusted code from inside a **try** block, the host's stub code has a **catch** block that catches the **ThreadAbortException**.

7. In response to catching the **ThreadAbortException**, the host calls **Thread**'s **ResetAbort** method. I'll explain the purpose of this call shortly.

8. Now that the host's code has caught the **ThreadAbortException**, the host can return some sort of failure back to the client and allow the thread pool thread to return to the pool so that it can be used for a future client request.

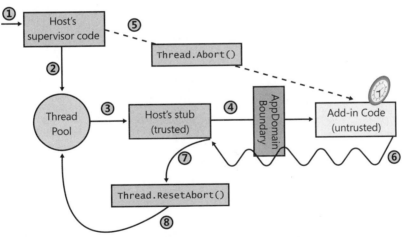

Figure 21-3 How a host application gets its thread back

Let me now clear up a few loose ends about this architecture. First, **Thread**'s **Abort** method is asynchronous. When **Abort** is called, it sets the target thread's **AbortRequested** flag and returns immediately. When the runtime detects that a thread is to be aborted, the runtime tries to get the thread to a *safe place*. A thread is in a safe place when the runtime feels that it can stop what the thread is doing without causing disastrous affects. A thread is in a safe place if it is performing a managed blocking operation such as sleeping or waiting. A thread can be corralled to a safe place by using hijacking (described in Chapter 20). A thread is not in a safe place if it is executing a type's class constructor, code in a **catch** or **finally** block, code in a critical execution region, or unmanaged code.

Once the thread reaches a safe place, the runtime will detect that the **AbortRequested** flag is set for the thread. This causes the thread to throw a **ThreadAbortException**. If this exception is not caught, the exception will be unhandled, all pending **finally** blocks will execute, and the thread will kill itself gracefully. Unlike all other exceptions, an unhandled **Thread-AbortException** does not cause the application to terminate. The runtime silently eats this exception and the thread dies, but the application and all of its remaining threads continue to run just fine.

In my example, the host catches the **ThreadAbortException**, allowing the host to regain control of the thread and return it to the pool. But there is a problem: What is to stop the untrusted code from catching the **ThreadAbortException** itself to keep control of the thread? The answer is that the CLR treats the **ThreadAbortException** in a very special manner. Even when code catches the **ThreadAbortException**, the CLR doesn't allow the exception to be swallowed. In other words, at the end of the **catch** block, the CLR automatically rethrows the **ThreadAbortException** exception.

This CLR feature raises another question: If the CLR rethrows the **ThreadAbortException** at the end of a **catch** block, how can the host catch it to regain control of the thread? Inside the host's **catch** block, there is a call to **Thread**'s **ResetAbort** method. Calling this method tells the CLR to stop rethrowing the **ThreadAbortException** at the end of each **catch** block.

This raises another question: What's to stop the untrusted code from catching the **Thread-AbortException** and calling **Thread**'s **ResetAbort** method itself to keep control of the thread? The answer is that **Thread**'s **ResetAbort** method requires the caller to have the **Security-Permission** with the **ControlThread** flag set to **true**. When the host creates the AppDomain for the untrusted code, the host will not grant this permission, and now, the untrusted code cannot keep control of the host's thread.

I should point out that there is still a potential hole in this story: While the thread is unwinding from its **ThreadAbortException**, the untrusted code can execute **catch** and **finally** blocks. Inside these blocks, the untrusted code could enter an infinite loop, preventing the host from regaining control of its thread. A host application fixes this problem by setting an escalation policy (discussed earlier). If an aborting thread doesn't finish in a reasonable amount of time, the CLR can upgrade the thread abort to a rude thread abort, a rude AppDomain unload, disabling of the CLR, or killing of the process. I should also note that the untrusted code could catch the **ThreadAbortException** and, inside the **catch** block, throw some other kind of exception. If this other exception is caught, at the end of the **catch** block, the CLR automatically rethrows the **ThreadAbortException**.

It should be noted, though, that most untrusted code is not actually intended to be malicious; it is just written in such a way so as to be taking too long by the host's standards. Usually, `catch` and `finally` blocks contain very little code, and this code usually executes quickly without any infinite loops or long-running tasks. And so it is very unlikely that the escalation policy will have to go into effect for the host to regain control of its thread.

By the way, the `Thread` class actually offers two `Abort` methods: One takes no parameters, and the other takes an `Object` parameter allowing you to pass anything. When code catches the `ThreadAbortException`, it can query its read-only `ExceptionState` property. This property returns the object that was passed to `Abort`. This allows the thread calling `Abort` to specify some additional information that can be examined by code catching the `ThreadAbortException`. The host can use this to let its own handling code know why it is aborting threads.

Chapter 22

Assembly Loading and Reflection

This chapter is all about discovering information about types, creating instances of them, and accessing their members when you didn't know anything about them at compile time. The information in this chapter is typically used to create a dynamically extensible application. This is the kind of application for which one company builds a host application and other companies create add-ins to extend the host application. The host can't be built or tested against the add-ins because the add-ins are created by different companies and are likely to be created after the host application has already shipped. This is why the host needs to discover the add-ins at run time.

A dynamically extensible application would take advantage of common language runtime (CLR) hosting and AppDomains as discussed in Chapter 21, "CLR Hosting and AppDomains." The host would run the add-in code in an AppDomain with its own security and configuration settings. The host could also unload the add-in code by unloading the AppDomain. At the end of this chapter, I'll talk a little about how to put all of this stuff together—CLR hosting, AppDomains, assembly loading, type discovery, type instance construction, and reflection—in order to build a robust, secure, dynamically extensible application.

Assembly Loading

As you know, when the JIT compiler compiles the IL for a method, it sees what types are referenced in the IL code. Then at run time, the JIT compiler uses the assembly's TypeRef and AssemblyRef metadata tables to determine what assembly defines the type being referenced. The AssemblyRef metadata table entry contains all of the parts that make up the strong name of the assembly. The JIT compiler grabs all of these parts—name (without extension or path), version, culture, and public key token—concatenates them into a string, and then attempts to load an assembly matching this identity into the AppDomain (assuming that it's not already loaded). If the assembly being loaded is weakly named, the identity is just the name of the assembly (no version, culture, or public key token information).

Internally, the CLR attempts to load this assembly by using the **System.Reflection.Assembly** class's static **Load** method. This method is publicly documented, and you can call it to explicitly load an assembly into your AppDomain. This method is the CLR equivalent of Win32's **LoadLibrary** function. There are actually several overloaded versions of **Assembly**'s **Load** method. Here are the prototypes of the more commonly used overloads:

```
public class Assembly {
    public static Assembly Load(AssemblyName assemblyRef);
    public static Assembly Load(String assemblyString);
    // Less commonly used overloads of Load are not shown
}
```

Internally, **Load** causes the CLR to apply a version-binding redirection policy to the assembly and looks for the assembly in the GAC, followed by the application's base directory, private path subdirectories, and codebase locations. If you call **Load** passing a weakly named assembly, **Load** doesn't apply a version-binding redirection policy to the assembly, and the CLR won't look in the GAC for the assembly. If **Load** finds the specified assembly, it returns a reference to an **Assembly** object that represents the loaded assembly. If **Load** fails to find the specified assembly, it throws a **System.IO.FileNotFoundException**.

Note   In some extremely rare situations, you may want to load an assembly that was built for a specific version of Microsoft Windows. In this case, when specifying an assembly's identity, you can also include a process architecture part. For example, if my global assembly cache (GAC) happened to have an IL-neutral and an x86-specific version of an assembly, the CLR would favor the CPU-specific version of the assembly (as discussed in Chapter 3, "Shared Assemblies and Strongly Named Assemblies"). However, I can force the CLR to load the IL-neutral version by passing the following string to **Assembly**'s **Load** method:

```
"SomeAssembly, Version=2.0.0.0, Culture=neutral,
PublicKeyToken=01234567890abcde, ProcessorArchitecture=MSIL"
```

Today, the CLR supports four possible values for ProcessorArchitecture: MSIL (Microsoft IL), x86, IA64, and AMD64.

> **Important**   Some developers notice that System.AppDomain offers a Load method. Unlike
> Assembly's static Load method, AppDomain's Load method is an instance method that allows
> you to load an assembly into the specified AppDomain. This method was designed to be called
> by unmanaged code, and it allows a host to inject an assembly into a specific AppDomain.
> Managed code developers generally shouldn't call this method because when AppDomain's
> Load method is called, you pass it a string that identifies an assembly. The method then applies
> policy and searches the normal places looking for the assembly. Recall that an AppDomain has
> settings associated with it that tell the CLR how to look for assemblies. To load this assembly,
> the CLR will use the settings associated with the specified AppDomain, not the calling
> AppDomain.
>
> However, AppDomain's Load method returns a reference to an assembly. Because the
> System.Assembly class isn't derived from System.MarshalByRefObject, the assembly object
> must be marshaled by value back to the calling AppDomain. But the CLR will now use the call-
> ing AppDomain's settings to locate the assembly and load it. If the assembly can't be found
> using the calling AppDomain's policy and search locations, a FileNotFoundException is
> thrown. This behavior is usually undesirable and is the reason that you should avoid AppDo-
> main's Load method.

In most dynamically extensible applications, Assembly's Load method is the preferred way of
loading an assembly into an AppDomain. However, it does require that you have all of the
pieces that make up an assembly's identity. Frequently, developers write tools or utilities
(such as ILDasm.exe, PEVerify.exe, CorFlags.exe, GACUtil.exe, SGen.exe, SN.exe, XSD.exe)
that perform some kind of processing on an assembly. All of these tools take a command-line
argument that refers to the pathname of an assembly file (including file extension). To load an
assembly specifying a pathname, you call Assembly's **LoadFrom** method:

```
public class Assembly {
    public static Assembly LoadFrom(String path);
    // Less commonly used overloads of LoadFrom are not shown
}
```

Internally, LoadFrom first calls System.Reflection.AssemblyName's static GetAssemblyName
method, which opens the specified file, finds the AssemblyDef metadata table's entry,
and extracts the assembly identity information and returns it in an System.Reflection
.AssemblyName object (the file is also closed). Then, LoadFrom internally calls Assembly's Load
method, passing it the AssemblyName object. At this point, the CLR applies version-binding
redirection policy and searches the various locations looking for a matching assembly. If Load
finds the assembly, it will load it, and an Assembly object that represents the loaded assembly
will be returned; LoadFrom returns this value. If Load fails to find an assembly, LoadFrom loads
the assembly at the pathname specified in LoadFrom's argument. Of course, if an assembly
with the same identity is already loaded, LoadFrom simply returns an Assembly object that
represents the already loaded assembly.

By the way, the `LoadFrom` method allows you to pass a URL as the argument. Here is an example:

```
private static void SomeMethod() {
    Assembly a = Assembly.LoadFrom(@"http://Wintellect.com/SomeAssembly.dll");
}
```

When you pass an Internet location, the CLR downloads the file, installs it into the user's download cache, and loads the file from there. Note that you must be online or an exception will be thrown. However, if the file has been downloaded previously, and if Microsoft Internet Explorer has been set to work offline (See Internet Explorer's Work Offline menu item in its File menu), the previously downloaded file will be used, and no exception will be thrown.

> **Important**   It is possible to have different assemblies on a single machine all with the same identity. Because `LoadFrom` calls `Load`, it is possible that the CLR will not load the specified file and instead will load a different file giving you unexpected behavior. It is highly recommended that each build of your assembly change the version number; this ensures that each version has its own identity, and because of this, `LoadFrom` will now work as expected. In the very rare situation when you really want to load an assembly from a specified path without the CLR applying any policies or searching, you can call `Assembly`'s `LoadFile` method.

If you are building a tool that simply analyzes an assembly's metadata via reflection (discussed later in this chapter), and you will not execute any of the code contained inside the assembly, the best way for you to load an assembly is to use `Assembly`'s `ReflectionOnlyLoadFrom` method, or in some rarer cases, `Assembly`'s `ReflectionOnlyLoad` method. Here are the prototypes of both methods:

```
public class Assembly {
    public static Assembly ReflectionOnlyLoadFrom(String assemblyFile);
    public static Assembly ReflectionOnlyLoad(String assemblyString);
    // Less commonly used overload of ReflectionOnlyLoad is not shown
}
```

The `ReflectionOnlyLoadFrom` method will load the file specified by the path; the strong name identity of the file is not obtained, and the file is not searched for in the GAC or elsewhere. The `ReflectionOnlyLoad` method will search for the specified assembly looking in the GAC, application base directory, private paths, and codebases. However, unlike the `Load` method, the `ReflectionOnlyLoad` method does not apply versioning policies, so you will get the exact version that you specify. If you want to apply versioning policy yourself to an assembly identity, you can pass the string into `AppDomain`'s `ApplyPolicy` method.

When an assembly is loaded with `ReflectionOnlyLoadFrom` or `ReflectionOnlyLoad`, the CLR forbids any code in the assembly from executing; any attempt to execute code in an assembly loaded with either of these methods causes the CLR to throw an `InvalidOperationException`. These methods allow a tool to load an assembly that is delay-signed, would normally require security permissions that prevent it from loading, or was created for a different CPU architecture.

Frequently when using reflection to analyze an assembly loaded with one of these two methods, the code will have to register a callback method with AppDomain's `ReflectionOnly-AssemblyResolve` event to manually load any referenced assemblies (calling AppDomain's `ApplyPolicy` method, if desired); the CLR doesn't do it automatically for you. When the callback method is invoked, it must call Assembly's `ReflectionOnlyLoadFrom` or `ReflectionOnlyLoad` method to explicitly load a referenced assembly and return a reference to this assembly.

> **Note**   People often ask about assembly unloading. Unfortunately, the CLR doesn't support the ability to unload individual assemblies. If the CLR allowed it, your application would crash if a thread returned back from a method to code in the unloaded assembly. The CLR is all about robustness and security, and allowing an application to crash in this way would be counterproductive to its goals. If you want to unload an assembly, you must unload the entire AppDomain that contains it. This was discussed in great detail in Chapter 21.
>
> It would seem that assemblies loaded with either the `ReflectionOnlyLoadFrom` or the `ReflectionOnlyLoad` method could be unloaded. After all, code in these assemblies is not allowed to execute. However, the CLR also doesn't allow assemblies loaded via either of these two methods to be unloaded. The reason is that once an assembly is loaded this way, you can still use reflection to create objects that refer to the metadata defined inside these assemblies. Unloading the assembly would require the objects to be invalidated somehow. Keeping track of this would be too expensive in terms of implementation and execution speed.

Using Reflection to Build a Dynamically Extensible Application

As you know, metadata is stored in a bunch of tables. When you build an assembly or a module, the compiler that you're using creates a type definition table, a field definition table, a method definition table, and so on. The `System.Reflection` namespace contains several types that allow you to write code that reflects over (or parses) these metadata tables. In effect, the types in this namespace offer an object model over the metadata contained in an assembly or a module.

Using these object model types, you can easily enumerate all of the types in a type definition metadata table. Then for each type, you can obtain its base type, the interfaces it implements, and the flags that are associated with the type. Additional types in the `System.Reflection` namespace allow you to query the type's fields, methods, properties, and events by parsing the corresponding metadata tables. You can also discover any custom attributes (covered in Chapter 17, "Custom Attributes") that have been applied to any of the metadata entities. There are even classes that let you determine referenced assemblies and methods that return the IL byte stream for a method. With all of this information, you could easily build a tool very similar to Microsoft's ILDasm.exe.

> **Note**   You should be aware that some of the reflection types and some of the members defined by these types are designed specifically for use by developers who are producing compilers for the CLR. Application developers don't typically use these types and members. The Framework Class Library (FCL) documentation doesn't explicitly point out which of these types and members are for compiler developers rather than application developers, but if you realize that not all reflection types and their members are for everyone, the documentation can be less confusing.

In reality, very few applications will have the need to use the reflection types. Reflection is typically used by class libraries that need to understand a type's definition in order to provide some rich functionality. For example, the FCL's serialization mechanism uses reflection to determine what fields a type defines. The serialization formatter can then obtain the values of these fields and write them into a byte stream that is used for sending across the Internet, saving to a file, or copying to the clipboard. Similarly, Microsoft Visual Studio's designers use reflection to determine which properties should be shown to developers when laying out controls on their Web Forms or Windows Forms at design time.

Reflection is also used when an application needs to load a specific type from a specific assembly at run time to accomplish some task. For example, an application might ask the user to provide the name of an assembly and a type. The application could then explicitly load the assembly, construct an instance of the type, and call methods defined in the type. This usage is conceptually similar to calling Win32's **LoadLibrary** and **GetProcAddress** functions. Binding to types and calling methods in this way is frequently referred to as *late binding*. (*Early binding* is when the types and methods used by an application are determined at compile time.)

Reflection Performance

Reflection is an extremely powerful mechanism because it allows you to discover and use types and members at run time that you did not know about at compile time. This power does come with two main drawbacks:

- Reflection prevents type safety at compile time. Since reflection uses strings heavily, you lose type safety at compile time. For example, if you call **Type.GetType("Jef");** to ask reflection to find a type called "Jef" in an assembly that has a type called "Jeff," the code compiles but produces an error at run time because you accidentally misspelled the type name passed as the argument.

- Reflection is slow. When using reflection, the names of types and their members are not known at compile time; you discover them at run time by using a string name to identify each type and member. This means that reflection is constantly performing string searches as the types in the `System.Reflection` namespace scan through an assembly's metadata. Often, the string searches are case-insensitive comparisons, which can slow this down even more.

Invoking a member by using reflection will also hurt performance. When using reflection to invoke a method, you must first package the arguments into an array; internally, reflection must unpack these on to the thread's stack. Also, the CLR must check that the arguments are of the correct data type before invoking a method. Finally, the CLR ensures that the caller has the proper security permission to access the member being invoked.

For all of these reasons, it's best to avoid using reflection to access a member. If you're writing an application that will dynamically discover and construct type instances, you should take one of the following approaches:

- Have the types derive from a base type that is known at compile time. At run time, construct an instance of the derived type, place the reference in a variable that is of the base type (by way of a cast), and call virtual methods defined by the base type.

- Have the type implement an interface that is known at compile time. At run time, construct an instance of the type, place the reference in a variable that is of the interface type (by way of a cast), and call the methods defined by the interface. I prefer this technique over the base type technique because the base type technique doesn't allow the developer to choose the base type that works best in a particular situation.

When you use any of these two techniques, I strongly suggest that the interface or base type be defined in its own assembly. This will reduce versioning issues. For more information about how to do this, see the section "Designing an Application That Supports Add-Ins" beginning on page 562 in this chapter.

Discovering Types Defined in an Assembly

Reflection is frequently used to determine what types an assembly defines. The FCL offers many methods to get this information. By far, the most commonly used method is `Assembly`'s `GetExportedTypes`. Here is an example of code that loads an assembly and shows the names of all of the publicly exported types defined in it:

```
using System;
using System.Reflection;

public static class Program {
   public static void Main() {
      String dataAssembly = "System.Data, version=2.0.0.0, " +
         "culture=neutral, PublicKeyToken=b77a5c561934e089";
      LoadAssemAndShowPublicTypes(dataAssembly);
   }

   private static void LoadAssemAndShowPublicTypes(String assemId) {
      // Explicitly load an assembly in to this AppDomain
      Assembly a = Assembly.Load(assemId);
```

```
        // Execute this loop once for each Type
        // publicly-exported from the loaded assembly
        foreach (Type t in a.GetExportedTypes()) {
            // Display the full name of the type
            Console.WriteLine(t.FullName);
        }
    }
}
```

What Exactly Is a Type Object?

Notice that the previous code iterates over an array of **System.Type** objects. The **System.Type** type is your starting point for doing type and object manipulations. **System.Type** is an abstract base type derived from **System.Reflection.MemberInfo** (because a **Type** can be a member of another type). The FCL provides a few types that are derived from **System.Type**: **System.RuntimeType**, **System.ReflectionOnlyType**, **System.Reflection.TypeDelegator**, and some types defined in the **System.Reflection.Emit** namespace (**EnumBuilder**, **GenericType-ParameterBuilder** and **TypeBuilder**).

> **Note**   The **TypeDelegator** class allows code to dynamically subclass a **Type** by encapsulating the **Type**, allowing you to override some of the functionality while having the original **Type** handle most of the work. This powerful mechanism allows you to override the way reflection works.

Of all of these types, the **System.RuntimeType** is by far the most interesting. **RuntimeType** is a type that is internal to the FCL, which means that you won't find it documented in the Framework Class Library documentation. The first time a type is accessed in an AppDomain, the CLR constructs an instance of a **RuntimeType** and initializes the object's fields to reflect (pun intended) information about the type.

Recall that **System.Object** defines a public, non-virtual instance method named **GetType**. When you call this method, the CLR determines the specified object's type and returns a reference to its **RuntimeType** object. Because there is only one **RuntimeType** object per type in an AppDomain, you can use equality and inequality operators to see whether two objects are of the same type:

```
private static Boolean AreObjectsTheSameType(Object o1, Object o2) {
    return o1.GetType() == o2.GetType();
}
```

In addition to calling **Object**'s **GetType** method, the FCL offers several more ways to obtain a **Type** object:

- The **System.Type** type offers several overloaded versions of the static **GetType** method. All versions of this method take a **String**. The string must specify the full name of the type (including its namespace). Note that the primitive type names supported by the compiler (such as C#'s **int**, **string**, **bool**, and so on) aren't allowed because these names mean nothing to the CLR. If the string is simply the name of a type, the method checks the calling assembly to see whether it defines a type of the specified name. If it does, a reference to the appropriate **RuntimeType** object is returned.

If the calling assembly doesn't define the specified type, the types defined by MSCorLib.dll are checked. If a type with a matching name still can't be found, **null** is returned or a **System.TypeLoadException** is thrown, depending on which overload of the **GetType** method you called and what parameters you passed to it. The FCL documentation fully explains this method.

You can pass an assembly-qualified type string, such as "System.Int32, mscorlib, Version=2.0.0.0, Culture=neutral, PublicKeyToken=b77a5c561934e089", to **GetType**. In this case, **GetType** will look for the type in the specified assembly (loading the assembly if necessary).

- The **System.Type** type offers a static **ReflectionOnlyGetType** method. This method behaves similarly to the **GetType** method mentioned in the previous bullet, except that the type is loaded so that it can be reflected over but cannot be executed.

- The **System.Type** type offers the following instance methods: **GetNestedType** and **GetNestedTypes**.

- The **System.Reflection.Assembly** type offers the following instance methods: **GetType**, **GetTypes**, and **GetExportedTypes**.

- The **System.Reflection.Module** type offers the following instance methods: **GetType**, **GetTypes**, and **FindTypes**.

> **Note**   Microsoft has defined a Backus-Naur Form grammar for type names and assembly-qualified type names that is used for constructing strings that will be passed to reflection methods. Knowledge of the grammar can come in quite handy when you are using reflection, specifically if you are working with nested types, generic types, generic methods, reference parameters, or arrays. For the complete grammar, see the FCL documentation or do a Web search for "Backus-Naur Form Grammar for Type Names."

Many programming languages also offer an operator that allows you to obtain a **Type** object from a type name. When possible, you should use this operator to obtain a reference to a **Type** instead of using any of the methods in the preceding list, because the operator generally produces faster code. In C#, the operator is called **typeof**, and you use this operator typically to compare late-bound type information with early-bound (known at compile-time) type information. The following code demonstrates an example of its use:

```
private static void SomeMethod(Object o) {
   // GetType returns the type of the object at run time (late-bound)
   // typeof returns the type of the specified class (early-bound)
   if (o.GetType() == typeof(FileInfo))      { ... }
   if (o.GetType() == typeof(DirectoryInfo)) { ... }
}
```

Note The first **if** statement in the code on the previous page checks if the variable **o** refers to an object of the **FileInfo** type; it does not check if **o** refers to an object that is derived from the **FileInfo** type. In other words, the code above tests for an exact match, not a compatible match, which is what you would get if you use a cast or C#'s **is** or **as** operators.

Once you have a reference to a **Type** object, you can query many of the type's properties to learn more about it. Most of the properties, such as **IsPublic**, **IsSealed**, **IsAbstract**, **IsClass**, **IsValueType**, and so on, indicate flags associated with the type. Other properties, such as **Assembly**, **AssemblyQualifiedName**, **FullName**, **Module**, and so on, return the name of the type's defining assembly or module and the full name of the type. You can also query the **BaseType** property to obtain the type's base type, and a slew of methods will give you even more information about the type.

The FCL documentation describes all of the methods and properties that **Type** exposes. Be aware that there are a lot of them. In fact, the **Type** type offers more than 50 public instance properties. This doesn't even include the methods and fields that **Type** also defines. I'll be covering some of these methods in the next section.

Building a Hierarchy of Exception-Derived Types

The ExceptionTree application (source code shown below) uses many of the concepts discussed already in this chapter to load a bunch of assemblies into the AppDomain and display all of the classes that are ultimately derived from **System.Exception**. By the way, this is the program I wrote to build the exception hierarchy displayed on page 430 in Chapter 19, "Exceptions."

```
using System;
using System.Text;
using System.Reflection;
using System.Collections.Generic;

public static class Program {
   public static void Main() {
      // Explicitly load the assemblies that we want to reflect over
      LoadAssemblies();

      // Initialize our counters and our exception type list
      Int32 totalPublicTypes = 0, totalExceptionTypes = 0;
      List<String> exceptionTree = new List<String>();

      // Iterate through all assemblies loaded in this AppDomain
      foreach (Assembly a in AppDomain.CurrentDomain.GetAssemblies()) {

         // Iterate through all types defined in this assembly
         foreach (Type t in a.GetExportedTypes()) {
            totalPublicTypes++;
```

```csharp
            // Ignore type if not a public class
            if (!t.IsClass || !t.IsPublic) continue;

            // Build a string of the type's derivation hierarchy
            StringBuilder typeHierarchy = new StringBuilder(t.FullName, 5000);

            // Assume that the type is not an Exception-derived type
            Boolean derivedFromException = false;

            // See if System.Exception is a base type of this type
            Type baseType = t.BaseType;
            while ((baseType != null) && !derivedFromException) {
                // Append the base type to the end of the string
                typeHierarchy.Append("-" + baseType);

                derivedFromException = (baseType == typeof(System.Exception));
                baseType = baseType.BaseType;
            }

            // No more bases and not Exception-derived, try next type
            if (!derivedFromException) continue;

            // We found an Exception-derived type
            totalExceptionTypes++;

            // For this Exception-derived type,
            // reverse the order of the types in the hierarchy
            String[] h = typeHierarchy.ToString().Split('-');
            Array.Reverse(h);

            // Build a new string with the hierarchy in order
            // from Exception -> Exception-derived type
            // Add the string to the list of Exception types
            exceptionTree.Add(String.Join("-", h, 1, h.Length - 1));
        }
    }

    // Sort the Exception types together in order of their hierarchy
    exceptionTree.Sort();

    // Display the Exception tree
    foreach (String s in exceptionTree) {
        // For this Exception type, split its base types apart
        String[] x = s.Split('-');

        // Indent based on the number of base types
        // and then show the most-derived type
        Console.WriteLine(new String(' ', 3 * x.Length) + x[x.Length - 1]);
    }

    // Show final status of the types considered
    Console.WriteLine("\n---> Of {0} types, {1} are " +
        "derived from System.Exception.",
        totalPublicTypes, totalExceptionTypes);
}
```

```
    private static void LoadAssemblies() {
        String[] assemblies = {
            "System,                   PublicKeyToken={0}",
            "System.Data,              PublicKeyToken={0}",
            "System.Design,            PublicKeyToken={1}",
            "System.DirectoryServices, PublicKeyToken={1}",
            "System.Drawing,           PublicKeyToken={1}",
            "System.Drawing.Design,    PublicKeyToken={1}",
            "System.Management,        PublicKeyToken={1}",
            "System.Messaging,         PublicKeyToken={1}",
            "System.Runtime.Remoting,  PublicKeyToken={0}",
            "System.Security,          PublicKeyToken={1}",
            "System.ServiceProcess,    PublicKeyToken={1}",
            "System.Web,               PublicKeyToken={1}",
            "System.Web.RegularExpressions, PublicKeyToken={1}",
            "System.Web.Services,      PublicKeyToken={1}",
            "System.Windows.Forms,     PublicKeyToken={0}",
            "System.Xml,               PublicKeyToken={0}",
        };

        String EcmaPublicKeyToken = "b77a5c561934e089";
        String MSPublicKeyToken   = "b03f5f7f11d50a3a";

        // Get the version of the assembly containing System.Object
        // We'll assume the same version for all the other assemblies
        Version version =
            typeof(System.Object).Assembly.GetName().Version;

        // Explicitly load the assemblies that we want to reflect over
        foreach (String a in assemblies) {
            String AssemblyIdentity =
                String.Format(a, EcmaPublicKeyToken, MSPublicKeyToken) +
                ", Culture=neutral, Version=" + version;

            Assembly.Load(AssemblyIdentity);
        }
    }
}
```

Constructing an Instance of a Type

Once you have a reference to a **Type**-derived object, you might want to construct an instance of this type. The FCL offers several mechanisms to accomplish this:

- **System.Activator**'s **CreateInstance methods** The **Activator** class offers several overloads of its static **CreateInstance** method. When you call this method, you can pass either a reference to a **Type** object or a **String** that identifies the type of object you want to create. The versions that take a type are simpler. You get to pass a set of arguments for the type's constructor, and the method returns a reference to the new object.

  The versions of this method in which you specify the desired type by using a string are a bit more complex. First, you must also specify a string identifying the assembly that defines the type. Second, these methods allow you to construct a remote object if you have remoting options configured properly. Third, these versions don't return a reference to the new object. Instead, they return a `System.Runtime.Remoting.ObjectHandle` (which is derived from `System.MarshalByRefObject`).

An `ObjectHandle` is a type that allows an object created in one AppDomain to be passed around to other AppDomains without forcing the object to materialize. When you're ready to materialize the object, you call `ObjectHandle`'s `Unwrap` method. This method loads the assembly that defines the type being materialized in the AppDomain where `Unwrap` is called. If the object is being marshaled by reference, the proxy type and object are created. If the object is being marshaled by value, the copy is deserialized.

- **`System.Activator`'s `CreateInstanceFrom` methods**   The `Activator` class also offers a set of static `CreateInstanceFrom` methods. These methods behave just as the `CreateInstance` method, except that you must always specify the type and its assembly via string parameters. The assembly is loaded into the calling AppDomain by using `Assembly`'s `LoadFrom` method (instead of `Load`). Because none of these methods takes a `Type` parameter, all of the `CreateInstanceFrom` methods return a reference to an `ObjectHandle`, which must be unwrapped.

- **`System.AppDomain`'s methods**   The `AppDomain` type offers four instance methods (each with several overloads) that construct an instance of a type: `CreateInstance`, `CreateInstanceAndUnwrap`, `CreateInstanceFrom`, and `CreateInstanceFromAndUnwrap`. These methods work just as `Activator`'s methods except that these methods are instance methods, allowing you to specify which AppDomain the object should be constructed in. The methods that end with `Unwrap` exist for convenience so that you don't have to make an additional method call.

- **`System.Type`'s `InvokeMember` instance method**   Using a reference to a `Type` object, you can call the `InvokeMember` method. This method locates a constructor matching the parameters you pass and constructs the type. The type is always created in the calling AppDomain, and a reference to the new object is returned. I'll discuss this method in more detail later in this chapter.

- **`System.Reflection.ConstructorInfo`'s `Invoke` instance method**   Using a reference to a `Type` object, you can bind to a particular constructor and obtain a reference to the constructor's `ConstructorInfo` object. Then you can use the reference to the `ConstructorInfo` object to call its `Invoke` method. The type is always created in the calling AppDomain, and a reference to the new object is returned. I'll also discuss this method in more detail later in this chapter.

> **Note**   The CLR doesn't require that value types define any constructors. However, this is a problem because all of the mechanisms in the preceding list construct an object by calling its constructor. However, `Activator`'s `CreateInstance` methods will allow you to create an instance of a value type without calling a constructor. If you want to create an instance of a value type without calling a constructor, you must call the version of the `CreateInstance` method that takes a single `Type` parameter or the version that takes `Type` and `Boolean` parameters.

The mechanisms just listed allow you to create an object for all types except for arrays (**System .Array**-derived types) and delegates (**System.MulticastDelegate**-derived types). To create an array, you should call **Array**'s static **CreateInstance** method (several overloaded versions exist). The first parameter to all versions of **CreateInstance** is a reference to the **Type** of elements you want in the array. **CreateInstance**'s other parameters allow you to specify various combinations of dimensions and bounds. To create a delegate, you should call **Delegate**'s static **CreateDelegate** method (several overloads exist). The first parameter to all versions of **CreateDelegate** is a reference to the **Type** of delegate you want to create. **CreateDelegate**'s other parameters allow you to specify which instance method of an object or which static method of a type the delegate should wrap.

To construct an instance for a generic type, first get a reference to the open type, then call **Type**'s public, instance **MakeGenericType** method passing in an array of types that you want to use as the type arguments. Then, take the returned **Type** object and pass it into one of the various methods listed above. Here is an example:

```
using System;
using System.Reflection;

internal sealed class Dictionary<TKey, TValue> { }

public static class Program {
   public static void Main() {

      // Get a reference to the generic type's type object
      Type openType = typeof(Dictionary<,>);

      // Close the generic type by using TKey=String, TValue=Int32
      Type closedType = openType.MakeGenericType(
         new Type[] { typeof(String), typeof(Int32) });

      // Construct an instance of the closed type
      Object o = Activator.CreateInstance(closedType);

      // Prove it worked
      Console.WriteLine(o.GetType());
   }
}
```

If you compile the code shown above and run it, you get the following output:

```
Dictionary`2[System.String,System.Int32]
```

Designing an Application That Supports Add-Ins

When you're building extensible applications, interfaces should be the centerpiece. You could use a base class instead of an interface, but in general, an interface is preferred because it allows add-in developers to choose their own base class. Suppose, for example, that you're writing an application and you want others to be able to create types that your application can load and use seamlessly. Here's the way to design this application:

- Create a "Host SDK" assembly that defines an interface whose methods are used as the communication mechanism between the host application and the add-in components. When defining the parameters and return values for the interface methods, try to use other interfaces or types defined in MSCorLib.dll. If you want to pass and return your own data types, define them in this "Host SDK" assembly too. Once you settle on your interface definitions, give this assembly a strong name (discussed in Chapter 3), and then package and deploy it to your partners and users. Once "published," you should really avoid making any kind of breaking changes to the types in this assembly. For example, do not change the interface in any way. However, if you define any data types, it is OK to add new members. If you make any modifications to the assembly, you'll probably want to deploy it with a publisher policy file (also discussed in Chapter 3).

> **Note**   You can use types defined in MSCorLib.dll because the CLR always loads the version of MSCorLib.dll that matches the version of the CLR itself. Also, only a single version of MSCorLib.dll is ever loaded into a process. In other words, different versions of MSCorLib.dll never load side by side (as described in Chapter 3). As a result, you won't have any type version mismatches, and your application will require less memory.

- The add-in developers will, of course, define their own types in their own "Add-In" assembly. Their "Add-In" assembly will reference the types in your "Host SDK" assembly. The add-in developers are able to put out a new version of their assembly as often as they'd like, and the host application will be able to consume the add-in types without any problem whatsoever.

- Create a separate "Host Application" assembly containing your application's types. This assembly will obviously reference the "Host SDK" assembly and use the types defined in it. Feel free to modify the code in the "Host Application" assembly to your heart's desire. Because the add-in developers don't reference the "Host Application" assembly, you can put out a new version of it every hour if you want to and not affect any of the add-in developers.

This section contains some very important information. When using types across assemblies, you need to be concerned with assembly-versioning issues. Take your time to architect this cleanly by isolating the types that you use for communication across assembly boundaries into their own assembly. Avoid mutating or changing these type definitions. However, if you really need to modify the type definitions, make sure that you change the assembly's version number and create a publisher policy file for the new version.

I'll now walk through a very simple scenario that puts all of this together. First, here is the code for the HostSDK.dll assembly:

```
using System;

namespace Wintellect.HostSDK {
    public interface IAddIn {
        String DoSomething(Int32 x);
    }
}
```

Second, here is the code for an AddInTypes.dll assembly defining two public types that implement the HostSDK's interface. To build this assembly, the HostSDK.dll assembly must be referenced:

```
using System;
using Wintellect.HostSDK;

public sealed class AddIn_A : IAddIn {
    public AddIn_A() {
    }
    public String DoSomething(Int32 x) {
        return "AddIn_A: " + x.ToString();
    }
}

public sealed class AddIn_B : IAddIn {
    public AddIn_B() {
    }
    public String DoSomething(Int32 x) {
        return "AddIn_B: " + (x * 2).ToString();
    }
}
```

Third, here is the code for a simple Host.exe assembly (a console application). To build this assembly, the HostSDK.dll assembly must be referenced. To discover usable add-in types, this host code assumes that the types are defined in assemblies ending with a .dll file extension and that these assemblies are deployed into the same directory as the host's EXE file. Today, the CLR has no common add-in registration and discovery mechanism. Microsoft is considering adding these mechanisms to future versions of the CLR. Unfortunately, every host application must devise its own registration/discovery mechanism.

```
using System;
using System.IO;
using System.Reflection;
using System.Collections.Generic;
using Wintellect.HostSDK;

public static class Program {
    public static void Main() {
```

```
// Find the directory that contains the Host exe
String AddInDir = Path.GetDirectoryName(
   Assembly.GetEntryAssembly().Location);

// Assume AddIn assemblies are in same directory as host's EXE file
String[] AddInAssemblies = Directory.GetFiles(AddInDir, "*.dll");

// Create a collection of usable add-in Types
List<Type> AddInTypes = new List<Type>();

// Load add-in assemblies; discover which types are usable by the host
foreach (String file in AddInAssemblies) {
   Assembly AddInAssembly = Assembly.LoadFrom(file);

   // Examine each publicly exported type
   foreach (Type t in AddInAssembly.GetExportedTypes()) {
      // If the type is a class that implements the IAddIn
      // interface, then the type is usable by the host
      if (t.IsClass && typeof(IAddIn).IsAssignableFrom(t)) {
         AddInTypes.Add(t);
      }
   }
}

// Initialization complete: the host has discovered the usable add-ins

// Here's how the host can construct add-in objects and use them
foreach (Type t in AddInTypes) {
   IAddIn ai = (IAddIn) Activator.CreateInstance(t);
   Console.WriteLine(ai.DoSomething(5));
}
   }
}
```

The simple host/add-in scenario just shown doesn't use AppDomains. However, in a real-life scenario, you will certainly create each add-in in its own AppDomain with its own security and configuration settings. And of course, each AppDomain could be unloaded if you wanted to remove an add-in from memory. To communicate across the AppDomain boundary, you'd either tell the add-in developers to derive their add-in types from **MarshalByRefObject** or, more likely, have the host application define its own internal type that is derived from **MarshalByRefObject**. As each AppDomain is created, the host would create an instance of its own **MarshalByRefObject**-derived type in the new AppDomain. The host's code (in the default AppDomain) would communicate with its own type (in the other AppDomains) to have it load add-in assemblies and create and use instances of the add-in types.

Using Reflection to Discover a Type's Members

So far, this chapter has focused on the parts of reflection—assembly loading, type discovery, and object construction—necessary to build a dynamically extensible application. In order to have good performance and compile-time type safety, you want to avoid using reflection as much as possible. In the dynamically extensible application scenario, once an object is constructed, the host code typically casts the object to an interface type (preferred) or a base class known at compile time; this allows the object's members to be accessed in a high-performance and compile-time type-safe way.

In the remainder of this chapter, I'm going to focus on some other aspects of reflection that you can use to discover and then invoke a type's members. The ability to discover and invoke a type's members is typically used to create developer tools and utilities that analyze an assembly by looking for certain programming patterns or uses of certain members. Examples of tools/utilities that do this are ILDasm, FxCop, and Visual Studio's Windows Forms and Web Forms designers. In addition, some class libraries use the ability to discover and invoke a type's members in order to offer rich functionality as a convenience to developers. Examples of class libraries that do so are serialization/deserialization and simple data binding.

Discovering a Type's Members

Fields, constructors, methods, properties, events, and nested types can all be defined as members within a type. The FCL contains a type called **System.Reflection.MemberInfo**. This class is an abstract base class that encapsulates a bunch of properties common to all type members. Derived from **MemberInfo** are a bunch of classes; each class encapsulates some more properties related to a specific type member. Figure 22-1 shows the hierarchy of these types.

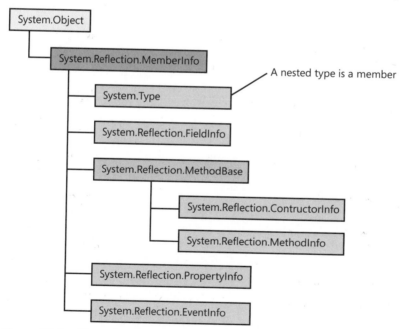

Figure 22-1   Hierarchy of the reflection types that encapsulate information about a type's member

The following program demonstrates how to query a type's members and display some information about them. This code processes all of the public types defined in all assemblies loaded in the calling AppDomain. For each type, the `GetMembers` method is called and returns an array of `MemberInfo`-derived objects; each object refers to a single member defined within the type. The `BindingFlags` variable, `bf`, passed to the `GetMembers` method tells the method which kinds of members to return. I'll talk about `BindingFlags` later in this chapter. Then, for each member, its kind (field, constructor, method, property, etc.) and its string value is shown.

```
using System;
using System.Reflection;

public static class Program {
   public static void Main() {
      // Loop through all assemblies loaded in this AppDomain
      Assembly[] assemblies = AppDomain.CurrentDomain.GetAssemblies();
      foreach (Assembly a in assemblies) {
         WriteLine(0, "Assembly: {0}", a);

         // Find Types in the assembly
         foreach (Type t in a.GetExportedTypes()) {
            WriteLine(1, "Type: {0}", t);

            // Discover the type's members
            const BindingFlags bf = BindingFlags.DeclaredOnly |
               BindingFlags.NonPublic | BindingFlags.Public |
               BindingFlags.Instance | BindingFlags.Static;

            foreach (MemberInfo mi in t.GetMembers(bf)) {
               String typeName = String.Empty;
               if (mi is Type)                  typeName = "(Nested) Type";
               else if (mi is FieldInfo)        typeName = "FieldInfo";
               else if (mi is MethodInfo)       typeName = "MethodInfo";
               else if (mi is ConstructorInfo)  typeName = "ConstructoInfo";
               else if (mi is PropertyInfo)     typeName = "PropertyInfo";
               else if (mi is EventInfo)        typeName = "EventInfo";

               WriteLine(2, "{0}: {1}", typeName, mi);
            }
         }
      }
   }
   private static void WriteLine(Int32 indent, String format,
      params Object[] args) {
      Console.WriteLine(new String(' ', 3 * indent) + format, args);
   }
}
```

When you compile and run this code, a ton of output is produced. Here is a small sampling of what it looks like:

```
Assembly: mscorlib, Version=2.0.0.0, Culture=neutral, PublicKeyToken=b77a5c561934e089
   Type: System.Object
      MethodInfo: Boolean InternalEquals(System.Object, System.Object)
      MethodInfo: Int32 InternalGetHashCode(System.Object)
      MethodInfo: System.Type GetType()
```

```
      MethodInfo: System.Object MemberwiseClone()
      MethodInfo: System.String ToString()
      MethodInfo: Boolean Equals(System.Object)
      MethodInfo: Boolean Equals(System.Object, System.Object)
      MethodInfo: Boolean ReferenceEquals(System.Object, System.Object)
      MethodInfo: Int32 GetHashCode()
      MethodInfo: Void Finalize()
      MethodInfo: Void FieldSetter(System.String, System.String, System.Object)
      MethodInfo: Void FieldGetter(System.String, System.String, System.Object ByRef)
      MethodInfo: System.Reflection.FieldInfo GetFieldInfo(System.String,
                    System.String)
      ConstructoInfo: Void .ctor()
  Type: System.Collections.IEnumerable
    MethodInfo: System.Collections.IEnumerator GetEnumerator()
  Type: System.Collections.Generic.IComparer`1[T]
    MethodInfo: Int32 Compare(T, T)
  Type: System.ValueType
    MethodInfo: Int32 GetHashCode()
    MethodInfo: Boolean CanCompareBits(System.Object)
    MethodInfo: Boolean FastEqualsCheck(System.Object, System.Object)
    MethodInfo: Boolean Equals(System.Object)
    MethodInfo: System.String ToString()
    ConstructoInfo: Void .ctor()
  Type: System.IDisposable
    MethodInfo: Void Dispose()
  Type: System.Collections.Generic.IEnumerator`1[T]
    MethodInfo: T get_Current()
    PropertyInfo: T Current
  Type: System.ArraySegment`1[T])
    MethodInfo: T[] get_Array()
    MethodInfo: Int32 get_Offset()
    MethodInfo: Int32 get_Count()
    MethodInfo: Int32 GetHashCode()
    MethodInfo: Boolean Equals(System.Object)
    MethodInfo: Boolean Equals(System.ArraySegment`1[T])
    MethodInfo: Boolean op_Equality(System.ArraySegment`1[T],
                    System.ArraySegment`1[T])
    MethodInfo: Boolean op_Inequality(System.ArraySegment`1[T],
                    System.ArraySegment`1[T])
    ConstructoInfo: Void .ctor(T[])
    ConstructoInfo: Void .ctor(T[], Int32, Int32)
    PropertyInfo: T[] Array
    PropertyInfo: Int32 Offset
    PropertyInfo: Int32 Count
    FieldInfo: T[] _array
    FieldInfo: Int32 _offset
    FieldInfo: Int32 _count
```

Since **MemberInfo** is the root of the member hierarchy, it makes sense for us to discuss it a bit more. Table 22-1 shows several read-only properties and methods offered by the **MemberInfo** class. These properties and methods are common to all members of a type. Don't forget that **System.Type** is derived from **MemberInfo**, and therefore, **Type** also offers all of the properties shown in Table 22-1.

Table 22-1   **Properties and Methods Common to All `MemberInfo`-Derived Types**

Member Name	Member Type	Description
Name	String property	Returns the name of the member. In the case of nested type, **Name** returns the concatenation of the name of the containing type, followed by '+', followed by the name of the nested type.
MemberType	MemberTypes (enum) property	Returns the kind of member (field, constructor, method, property, event, type (non-nested type or nested type).
DeclaringType	Type property	Returns the **Type** that declares the member.
ReflectedType	Type property	Returns the **Type** used to obtain this member.
Module	Module property	Returns the **Module** that declares the member.
MetadataToken	Int32 property	Returns the metadata token (within the module) that identifies the member.
GetCustom-Attributes	Method returning Object[]	Returns an array in which each element identifies an instance of a custom attribute applied to this member. Custom attributes can be applied to any member.
IsDefined	Method returning Boolean	Returns **true** if at least one instance of the specified custom attribute is applied to the member.

Most of the properties mentioned in Table 22-1 are self-explanatory. However, developers frequently confuse the **DeclaringType** and **ReflectedType** properties. To fully understand these properties, let's define the following type:

```
public sealed class MyType {
    public override String ToString() { return null; }
}
```

What would happen if the following line of code executed?

```
MemberInfo[] members = typeof(MyType).GetMembers();
```

The **members** variable is a reference to an array in which each element identifies a public member defined by **MyType** and any of its base types, such as **System.Object**. If you were to query the **DeclaringType** property for the **MemberInfo** element identifying the **ToString** method, you'd see **MyType** returned because **MyType** declares a **ToString** method. On the other hand, if you were to query the **DeclaringType** property for the **MemberInfo** element identifying the **Equals** method, you'd see **System.Object** returned because **Equals** is declared by **System .Object**, not by **MyType**. The **ReflectedType** property always returns **MyType** because this was the type specified when **GetMembers** was called to perform the reflection.

Each element of the array returned by calling **GetMembers** is a reference to one of the concrete types in the hierarchy (unless the **BindingFlags.DeclaredOnly** flag is specified). Although **Type**'s **GetMembers** method returns all of the type's members, **Type** also offers methods that return specific member types. For example, **Type** offers **GetNestedTypes**, **GetFields**, **GetCon-structors**, **GetMethods**, **GetProperties**, and **GetEvents**. These methods all return arrays in which each element is a reference to a **Type** object, **FieldInfo** object, **ConstructorInfo** object, **MethodInfo** object, **PropertyInfo** object, or **EventInfo** object, respectively.

Figure 22-2 summarizes the types used by an application to walk reflection's object model. From an AppDomain, you can discover the assemblies loaded into it. From an assembly, you can discover the modules that make it up. From an assembly or a module, you can discover the types that it defines. From a type, you can discover its nested types, fields, constructors, methods, properties, and events. Namespaces are not part of this hierarchy because they are simply syntactical gatherings of types. If you want to list all of the namespaces defined in an assembly, you need to enumerate all of the types in this assembly and take a look at their **Namespace** property.

From a type, it is also possible to discover the interfaces it implements. (I'll show how to do this a little later.) And from a constructor, method, property accessor method, or event add/remove method, you can call the **GetParameters** method to obtain an array of **ParameterInfo** objects, which tells you the types of the member's parameters. You can also query the read-only **ReturnParameter** property to get a **ParameterInfo** object for detailed information about a member's return value. For a generic type or method, you can call the **GetGenericArguments** method to get the set of type parameters. Finally, for any of these items, you can call the **GetCustomAttributes** method to obtain the set of custom attributes applied to them.

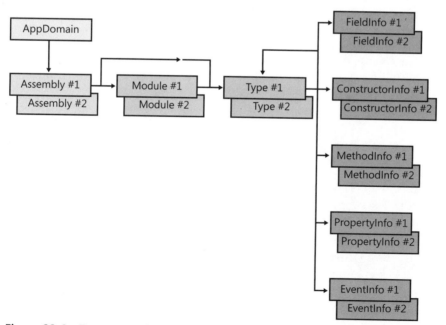

Figure 22-2 Types an application uses to walk reflection's object model

BindingFlags: Filtering the Kinds of Members that Are Returned

You query a type's members by calling Type's GetMembers, GetNestedTypes, GetFields, GetConstructors, GetMethods, GetProperties, or GetEvents methods. When you call any of these methods, you can pass in an instance of a System.Reflection.BindingFlags enumerated type. The enumerated type identifies a set of bit flags OR'd together to help you filter the members that are returned from these methods. Table 22-2 shows the relevant symbols defined by the BindingFlags enumerated type.

All of the methods that return a set of members have an overload that takes no arguments at all. When you don't pass a BindingFlags argument, all of these methods return only the public members. In other words, the default is BindingFlags.Public | BindingFlags.Instance | BindingFlags.Static.

Note that Type also defines GetMember, GetNestedType, GetField, GetConstructor, GetMethod, GetProperty, and GetEvent methods. These methods allow you to pass in a String that identifies a member's name to look up. This is when BindingFlags's IgnoreCase flag comes in handy.

Table 22-2 Search Symbols Defined by the BindingFlags Enumerated Type

Symbol	Value	Description
Default	0x00	A placeholder for no flags specified. Use this flag when you don't want to specify any of the flags listed in the remainder of this table.
IgnoreCase	0x01	Return members matching specified string regardless of case.
DeclaredOnly	0x02	Return only members of the reflected type, ignoring inherited members.
Instance	0x04	Return instance members.
Static	0x08	Return static members.
Public	0x10	Return public members.
NonPublic	0x20	Return nonpublic members.
FlattenHierarchy	0x40	Return static members defined by base types.

Discovering a Type's Interfaces

To obtain the set of interfaces that a type inherits, you can call Type's FindInterfaces, GetInterface, or GetInterfaces method. All of these methods return Type objects that represent an interface. Note that these methods scan the type's inheritance hierarchy and return all of the interfaces defined on the specified type as well as all of its base types.

Determining which members of a type implement a particular interface is a little complicated because multiple interface definitions can all define the same method. For example, the IBookRetailer and IMusicRetailer interfaces might both define a method named Purchase.

To get the **MethodInfo** objects for a specific interface, you call **Type**'s **GetInterfaceMap** instance method passing the interface type as an argument. This method returns an instance of a **System .Reflection.InterfaceMapping** (a value type). The **InterfaceMapping** type defines the four public fields listed in Table 22-3.

Table 22-3   Public Fields Defined by the InterfaceMapping Type

Field Name	Data Type	Description
TargetType	Type	This is the type that was used to call GetInterfaceMapping.
InterfaceType	Type	This is the type of the interface passed to GetInterfaceMapping.
InterfaceMethods	MethodInfo[]	This is an array in which each element exposes information about an interface's method.
TargetMethods	MethodInfo[]	This is an array in which each element exposes information about the method that the type defines to implement the corresponding interface's method.

The **InterfaceMethods** and **TargetMethods** arrays run parallel to each other; that is, **InterfaceMethods[0]** identifies the interface's **MethodInfo**, and **TargetMethods[0]** identifies the method defined by the type that implements this interface method. Here is some code that shows how to discover the interfaces and interface methods defined by a type:

```
using System;
using System.Reflection;

// Define two interfaces for testing
internal interface IBookRetailer : IDisposable {
   void Purchase();
   void ApplyDiscount();
}

internal interface IMusicRetailer {
   void Purchase();
}


// This class implements 2 interfaces defined by this assembly
// and 1 interface defined by another assembly
internal sealed class MyRetailer : IBookRetailer, IMusicRetailer, IDisposable {
   // IBookRetailer methods
   void IBookRetailer.Purchase() { }
   public void ApplyDiscount() { }

   // IMusicRetailer method
   void IMusicRetailer.Purchase() { }

   // IDisposable method
   public void Dispose() { }
```

```
        // MyRetailer method (not an interface method)
        public void Purchase() { }
    }


public static class Program {
    public static void Main() {
        // Find interfaces implemented by MyRetailer where the
        // interface is defined in our own assembly. This is
        // accomplished using a delegate to a filter method
        // that we create and pass to FindInterfaces.
        Type t = typeof(MyRetailer);
        Type[] interfaces = t.FindInterfaces(TypeFilter,
            typeof(Program).Assembly);
        Console.WriteLine("MyRetailer implements the following " +
            "interfaces (defined in this assembly):");

        // Show information about each interface
        foreach (Type i in interfaces) {
            Console.WriteLine("\nInterface: " + i);

            // Get the type methods that map to the interface's methods
            InterfaceMapping map = t.GetInterfaceMap(i);

            for (Int32 m = 0; m < map.InterfaceMethods.Length; m++) {
                // Display the interface method name and which
                // type method implements the interface method.
                Console.WriteLine("    {0} is implemented by {1}",
                    map.InterfaceMethods[m], map.TargetMethods[m]);
            }
        }
    }


    // Returns true if type matches filter criteria
    private static Boolean TypeFilter(Type t, Object filterCriteria) {
        // Return true if the interface is defined in the same
        // assembly identified by filterCriteria
        return t.Assembly == filterCriteria;
    }
}
```

When you build and run the code above, you get the following output:

```
MyRetailer implements the following interfaces (defined in this assembly):

Interface: IBookRetailer
    Void Purchase() is implemented by Void IBookRetailer.Purchase()
    Void ApplyDiscount() is implemented by Void ApplyDiscount()

Interface: IMusicRetailer
    Void Purchase() is implemented by Void IMusicRetailer.Purchase()
```

Note that the **IDisposable** interface does not appear in the output because this interface is not declared in the EXE file's assembly.

Invoking a Type's Members

Now that you know how to discover the members defined by a type, you may want to invoke one of these members. What *invoke* means depends on the kind of member being invoked. Invoking a `FieldInfo` lets you get or set a field's value, invoking a `ConstructorInfo` lets you create an instance of the type passing arguments to a constructor, invoking a `MethodInfo` lets you call a method passing arguments and obtaining its return value, invoking a `PropertyInfo` lets you call the property's get or set accessor method, and invoking an `EventInfo` lets you add or remove an event handler.

Let's discuss how to invoke a method first because this is the most complex member you can invoke. Then we'll discuss how to invoke the other members. The `Type` class offers an `Invoke-Member` method that lets you invoke a member. There are several overloaded versions of `InvokeMember`. I'll discuss one of the more common overloads; the other overloads work similarly.

```
public abstract class Type : MemberInfo, ... {
   public Object InvokeMember(
      String name,              // Name of member
      BindingFlags invokeAttr,  // How to look up members
      Binder binder,            // How to match members and arguments
      Object target,            // Object to invoke member on
      Object[] args,            // Arguments to pass to method
      CultureInfo culture);     // Culture used by some binders
   ...
}
```

When you call `InvokeMember`, it searches the type's members for a match. If no match is found, a `System.MissingMethodException`, `System.MissingFieldException`, or `System.Missing-MemberException` exception is thrown. If a match is found, `InvokeMember` invokes the member. If the member returns something, `InvokeMember` returns it to you. If the member doesn't return anything, `InvokeMember` returns `null`. If the member you call throws an exception, `InvokeMember` catches the exception and throws a new `System.Reflection.Target-InvocationException`. The `TargetInvocationException` object's `InnerException` property will contain the actual exception that the invoked method threw. Personally, I don't like this behavior. I'd prefer it if `InvokeMember` didn't wrap the exception and just allowed it to come through.

Internally, `InvokeMember` performs two operations. First, it must select the appropriate member to be called—this is known as *binding*. Second, it must actually invoke the member—this is known as *invoking*. When you call `InvokeMember`, you pass a string as the `name` parameter, indicating the name of the member you want `InvokeMember` to bind to. However, the type might offer several members with the same name. After all, there might be several overloaded versions of a method, or a method and a field might have the same name. Of course, `InvokeMember` must bind to a single member before it can invoke it. All of the parameters passed to `InvokeMember` (except for the `target` parameter) are used to help `InvokeMember` decide which member to bind to. Let's take a closer look at these parameters.

The **binder** parameter identifies an object whose type is derived from the abstract **System** **.Reflection.Binder** type. A **Binder**-derived type is a type that encapsulates the rules for how **InvokeMember** should select a single member. The **Binder** base type defines abstract virtual methods such as **BindToField**, **BindToMethod**, **ChangeType**, **ReorderArgumentArray**, **Select-** **Method**, and **SelectProperty**. Internally, **InvokeMember** calls these methods by using the **Binder** object passed via **InvokeMember**'s **binder** parameter.

Microsoft has defined an internal (undocumented) concrete type, called **System.Default-** **Binder**, which is derived from **Binder**. This **DefaultBinder** type ships with the FCL, and Microsoft expects that almost everyone will use this binder. Some compiler vendors will define their own **Binder**-derived type and ship it in a runtime library used by code emitted by their compiler. When you pass **null** to **InvokeMember**'s **binder** parameter, it will use a **DefaultBinder** object. **Type** offers a public, static, read-only property, **DefaultBinder**, that you can query to obtain a reference to a **DefaultBinder** object should you want one.

When a binder object has its methods called, the methods will be passed parameters to help the binder make a decision. Certainly, the binder is passed the name of the member that is being looked for. In addition, the binder's methods are passed the specified **BindingFlags** as well as the types of all of the parameters that need to be passed to the member being invoked.

Earlier in this chapter, I showed a table (Table 22-2) that described the following **Binding-** **Flags**: **Default**, **IgnoreCase**, **DeclaredOnly**, **Instance**, **Static**, **Public**, **NonPublic**, and **FlattenHierarchy**. The presence of these flags tells the binder which members to include in the search.

In addition to these flags, the binder examines the number of arguments passed via **Invoke-** **Member**'s **args** parameter. The number of arguments limits the set of possible matches even further. The binder then examines the types of the arguments to limit the set even more. However, when it comes to the argument's types, the binder applies some automatic type conversions to make things a bit more flexible. For example, a type can define a method that takes a single **Int64** parameter. If you call **InvokeMember**, and in the **args** parameter, pass a reference to an array containing an **Int32** value, the **DefaultBinder** considers this a match. When invoking the method, the **Int32** value will be converted to an **Int64** value. The **DefaultBinder** supports the conversions listed in Table 22-4.

Table 22-4 Conversions That DefaultBinder Supports

Source Type	Target Type
Any type	Its base type
Any type	The interfaces it implements
Char	UInt16, UInt32, Int32, UInt64, Int64, Single, Double
Byte	Char, UInt16, Int16, UInt32, Int32, UInt64, Int64, Single, Double
SByte	Int16, Int32, Int64, Single, Double
UInt16	UInt32, Int32, UInt64, Int64, Single, Double

Table 22-4   Conversions That DefaultBinder Supports

Source Type	Target Type
Int16	Int32, Int64, Single, Double
UInt32	UInt64, Int64, Single, Double
Int32	Int64, Single, Double
UInt64	Single, Double
Int64	Single, Double
Single	Double
A value type instance	A boxed version of the value type instance

There are two more BindingFlags that you can use to fine-tune the DefaultBinder's behavior. These are described in Table 22-5.

Table 22-5   BindingFlags Used with DefaultBinder

Symbol	Value	Description
ExactBinding	0x010000	The binder will look for a member whose formal parameters exactly match the types of the supplied arguments.
OptionalParamBinding	0x040000	The binder will consider any member whose count of parameters matches the number of arguments passed. This flag is useful when there are members whose parameters have default values and for methods that take a variable number of arguments. Only Type's InvokeMember method honors this flag.

InvokeMember's last parameter, culture, could also be used for binding. However, the DefaultBinder type completely ignores this parameter. If you define your own binder, you could use the culture parameter to help with argument type conversions. For example, the caller could pass a String argument with a value of "1,23". The binder could examine this string, parse it using the specified culture, and convert the argument's type to a Single (if the culture is "de-DE") or continue to consider the argument to be a String (if the culture is "en-US").

At this point, I've gone through all InvokeMember's parameters related to binding. The one parameter I haven't discussed yet is target. This parameter is a reference to the object whose member you want to call. If you want to call a type's static member, you should pass null for this parameter.

The InvokeMember method is a very powerful method. It allows you to call a method (as I've been discussing), construct an instance of a type (basically by calling a constructor method), get or set a field, or get or set a property. You tell InvokeMember which of these actions you want to perform by specifying one of the BindingFlags listed in Table 22-6.

For the most part, the flags in Table 22-6 are mutually exclusive—you must pick one and only one when calling `InvokeMember`. However, you can specify both `GetField` and `GetProperty`, in which case `InvokeMember` searches for a matching field first and then for a matching property if it doesn't find a matching field. Likewise, `SetField` and `SetProperty` can both be specified and are matched the same way. The binder uses these flags to narrow the set of possible matches. If you specify the `BindingFlags.CreateInstance` flag, the binder knows that it can select only a constructor method.

Table 22-6 `BindingFlags` Used with `InvokeMember`

Symbol	Value	Description
InvokeMethod	0x0100	Tells `InvokeMember` to call a method
CreateInstance	0x0200	Tells `InvokeMember` to create a new object and call its constructor
GetField	0x0400	Tells `InvokeMember` to get a field's value
SetField	0x0800	Tells `InvokeMember` to set a field's value
GetProperty	0x1000	Tells `InvokeMember` to call a property's get accessor method
SetProperty	0x2000	Tells `InvokeMember` to call a property's set accessor method

Important   With what I've told you so far, it would seem that reflection makes it easy to bind to a nonpublic member and invoke the member allowing application code a way to access private members that a compiler would normally prohibit the code from accessing. However, reflection uses code access security to ensure that its power isn't abused or exploited.

When you call a method to bind to a member, the CLR first checks to see whether the member you're trying to bind to would be visible to you at compile time. If it would be, the bind is successful. If the member wouldn't normally be accessible to you, the method demands the `System.Security.Permissions.ReflectionPermission` permission, checking to see whether the `System.Security.Permissions.ReflectionPermissionFlags`'s `TypeInformation` bit is set. If this flag is set, the method will bind to the member. If the demand fails, a `System.Security.SecurityException` is thrown.

When you call a method to invoke a member, the method performs the same kind of check that it would when binding to a member. But this time, it checks whether the `Reflection-Permission` has `ReflectionPermissionFlag`'s `MemberAccess` bit set. If the bit is set, the member is invoked; otherwise, a `SecurityException` is thrown.

Of course, if your assembly has full-trust, security checks are assumed to be successful allowing binding and invoking to just work. However, you should never, ever, use reflection to access any of a type's undocumented members because a future version of the assembly may easily break your code.

Bind Once, Invoke Multiple Times

`Type`'s `InvokeMember` method gives you access to all of a type's members (except for event members). However, you should be aware that every time you call `InvokeMember`, it must bind to a particular member and then invoke it. Having the binder select the right member each time you want to invoke a member is time-consuming, and if you do it a lot, your application's performance will suffer. So if you plan on accessing a member frequently, you're better off binding to the desired member once and then accessing that member as often as you want.

In this chapter, we've already discussed how to bind to a member by calling one of `Type`'s methods: `GetFields`, `GetConstructors`, `GetMethods`, `GetProperties`, `GetEvents`, or any similar method. All of these methods return references to objects whose type offers methods to access the specific member directly. Table 22-7 shows which method to call for each kind of member in order to invoke that member.

Table 22-7   How to Invoke a Member After Binding to It

Kind of Member Type	Method to Invoke Member
`FieldInfo`	Call `GetValue` to get a field's value.
	Call `SetValue` to set a field's value.
`ConstructorInfo`	Call `Invoke` to construct an instance of the type and call a constructor.
`MethodInfo`	Call `Invoke` to call a method of the type.
`PropertyInfo`	Call `GetValue` to call a property's get accessor method.
	Call `SetValue` to call a property's set accessor method.
`EventInfo`	Call `AddEventHandler` to call an event's add accessor method.
	Call `RemoveEventHandler` to call an event's remove accessor method.

The `PropertyInfo` type represents metadata information about a property (as discussed in Chapter 9, "Properties"); that is, `PropertyInfo` offers `CanRead`, `CanWrite`, and `PropertyType` read-only properties. These properties indicate whether a property is readable or writeable and what data type the property is. `PropertyInfo` has a `GetAccessors` method that returns an array of `MethodInfo` elements: one for the get accessor method (if it exists), and one for the set accessor method (if it exists). Of more value are `PropertyInfo`'s `GetGetMethod` and `GetSet-Method` methods, each of which returns just one `MethodInfo` object. `PropertyInfo`'s `GetValue` and `SetValue` methods exist for convenience; internally, they get the appropriate `MethodInfo` and call it. To support parameterful properties (C# indexers), the `GetValue` and `SetValue` methods offer an `index` parameter of `Object[]` type.

The `EventInfo` type represents metadata information about an event (as discussed in Chapter 10, "Events"). The `EventInfo` type offers an `EventHandlerType` read-only property that returns the `Type` of the event's underlying delegate. The `EventInfo` type also has `GetAddMethod` and `GetRemoveMethod` methods, which return the `MethodInfo` corresponding to the method that adds or removes a delegate to/from the event. To add or remove a delegate, you can invoke these **MethodInfo** objects, or you can call **EventInfo**'s more convenient **AddEventHandler** and **RemoveEventHandler** methods.

When you call one of the methods listed in the right column of Table 22-7, you're not binding to a member; you're just invoking the member. You can call any of these methods multiple times, and because binding isn't necessary, the performance will be pretty good.

You might notice that **ConstructorInfo**'s **Invoke**, **MethodInfo**'s **Invoke**, and **PropertyInfo**'s **GetValue** and **SetValue** methods offer overloaded versions that take a reference to a **Binder**-derived object and some **BindingFlags**. This would lead you to believe that these methods bind to a member. However, they don't.

When calling any of these methods, the **Binder**-derived object is used to perform type conversions on the supplied method parameters, such as converting an **Int32** argument to an **Int64**, so that the already selected method can be called. As for the **BindingFlags** parameter, the only flag that can be passed here is **BindingFlags.SuppressChangeType**. However, binders are free to ignore this flag. Fortunately, the **DefaultBinder** class heeds this flag. When **DefaultBinder** sees this flag, it won't convert any arguments. If you use this flag and the arguments passed don't match the arguments expected by the method, an **ArgumentException** will be thrown.

Usually when you use the **BindingFlags.ExactBinding** flag to bind to a member, you'll specify the **BindingFlags.SuppressChangeType** flag to invoke the member. If you don't use these two flags in tandem, it's unlikely that invoking the member will be successful unless the arguments you pass happen to be exactly what the method expects. By the way, if you call **MemberInfo**'s **InvokeMethod** to bind and invoke a member, you'll probably want to specify both or neither of the two binding flags.

The following sample application demonstrates the various ways to use reflection to access a type's members. The code shows how to use **Type**'s **InvokeMember** to both bind and invoke a member. It also shows how to bind to a member, invoking it later.

```
using System;
using System.Reflection;


// This class is used to demonstrate reflection
// It has a field, constructor, method, property, and an event
internal sealed class SomeType {
   private Int32 m_someField;
   public SomeType(ref Int32 x) { x *= 2; }
   public override String ToString() { return m_someField.ToString(); }
   public Int32 SomeProp {
      get { return m_someField; }
      set {
         if (value < 1)
            throw new ArgumentOutOfRangeException(
               "value", "value must be > 0");
         m_someField = value;
```

```
        }
    }
    public event EventHandler SomeEvent;
    private void NoCompilerWarnings() {
        SomeEvent.ToString();
    }
}

public static class Program {
    private const BindingFlags c_bf = BindingFlags.DeclaredOnly |
        BindingFlags.Public | BindingFlags.NonPublic |
        BindingFlags.Instance;

    public static void Main() {
        Type t = typeof(SomeType);
        UsingInvokeMemberToBindAndInvokeTheMember(t);
        Console.WriteLine();
        BindingToMemberFirstAndThenInvokingTheMember(t);
    }

    private static void UsingInvokeMemberToBindAndInvokeTheMember(Type t) {
        Console.WriteLine("UsingInvokeMemberToBindAndInvokeTheMember");

        // Construct an instance of the Type
        Object[] args = new Object[] { 12 };  // Constructor arguments
        Console.WriteLine("x before constructor called: " + args[0]);
        Object obj = t.InvokeMember(null,
            c_bf | BindingFlags.CreateInstance, null, null, args);
        Console.WriteLine("Type: " + obj.GetType().ToString());
        Console.WriteLine("x after constructor returns: " + args[0]);

        // Read and write to a field
        t.InvokeMember("m_someField",
            c_bf | BindingFlags.SetField, null, obj, new Object[] { 5 });
        Int32 v = (Int32)t.InvokeMember("m_someField",
            c_bf | BindingFlags.GetField, null, obj, null);
        Console.WriteLine("someField: " + v);

        // Call a method
        String s = (String)t.InvokeMember("ToString",
            c_bf | BindingFlags.InvokeMethod, null, obj, null);
        Console.WriteLine("ToString: " + s);

        // Read and write a property
        try {
            t.InvokeMember("SomeProp",
                c_bf | BindingFlags.SetProperty, null, obj, new Object[] { 0 });
        }
        catch (TargetInvocationException e) {
            if (e.InnerException.GetType() !=
                typeof(ArgumentOutOfRangeException)) throw;
            Console.WriteLine("Property set catch.");
        }
        t.InvokeMember("SomeProp",
            c_bf | BindingFlags.SetProperty, null, obj, new Object[] { 2 });
        v = (Int32)t.InvokeMember("SomeProp",
```

```
        c_bf | BindingFlags.GetProperty, null, obj, null);
    Console.WriteLine("SomeProp: " + v);

    // NOTE: InvokeMember doesn't support events
}


private static void BindingToMemberFirstAndThenInvokingTheMember(Type t) {
    Console.WriteLine("BindingToMemberFirstAndThenInvokingTheMember");

    // Construct an instance
    ConstructorInfo ctor = t.GetConstructor(
        new Type[] { Type.GetType("System.Int32&") });
    Object[] args = new Object[] { 12 };  // Constructor arguments
    Console.WriteLine("x before constructor called: " + args[0]);
    Object obj = ctor.Invoke(args);
    Console.WriteLine("Type: " + obj.GetType().ToString());
    Console.WriteLine("x after constructor returns: " + args[0]);

    // Read and write to a field
    FieldInfo fi = obj.GetType().GetField("m_someField", c_bf);
    fi.SetValue(obj, 33);
    Console.WriteLine("someField: " + fi.GetValue(obj));

    // Call a method
    MethodInfo mi = obj.GetType().GetMethod("ToString", c_bf);
    String s = (String) mi.Invoke(obj, null);
    Console.WriteLine("ToString: " + s);

    // Read and write a property
    PropertyInfo pi =
        obj.GetType().GetProperty("SomeProp", typeof(Int32));
    foreach (MethodInfo m in pi.GetAccessors())
        Console.WriteLine(m);
    try {
        pi.SetValue(obj, 0, null);
    }
    catch (TargetInvocationException e) {
        if (e.InnerException.GetType() != typeof(ArgumentOutOfRangeException))
            throw;
        Console.WriteLine("Property set catch.");
    }
    pi.SetValue(obj, 2, null);
    Console.WriteLine("SomeProp: " + pi.GetValue(obj, null));

    // Add and remove a delegate from the event
    EventInfo ei = obj.GetType().GetEvent("SomeEvent", c_bf);
    Console.WriteLine("AddMethod: "       + ei.GetAddMethod());
    Console.WriteLine("RemoveMethod: "    + ei.GetRemoveMethod());
    Console.WriteLine("EventHandlerType: " + ei.EventHandlerType);

    EventHandler ts = new EventHandler(EventCallback);
    ei.AddEventHandler(obj, ts);
    ei.RemoveEventHandler(obj, ts);
}

private static void EventCallback(Object sender, EventArgs e) {}
}
```

If you build and run this code, you'll see the following output:

```
UsingInvokeMemberToBindAndInvokeTheMember
x before constructor called: 12
Type: SomeType
x after constructor returns: 24
someField: 5
ToString: 5
Property set catch.
SomeProp: 2

BindingToMemberFirstAndThenInvokingTheMember
x before constructor called: 12
Type: SomeType
x after constructor returns: 24
someField: 33
ToString: 33
Int32 get_SomeProp()
Void set_SomeProp(Int32)
Property set catch.
SomeProp: 2
AddMethod: Void add_SomeEvent(System.EventHandler)
RemoveMethod: Void remove_SomeEvent(System.EventHandler)
EventHandlerType: System.EventHandler
```

Notice that **SomeType**'s constructor takes an **Int32** by reference as its only parameter. The previous code shows how to call this constructor and how to examine the modified **Int32** value after the constructor returns. Furthermore, inside the **BindingToMemberFirstAndThen-InvokingTheMember** method near the top is a call to **Type**'s **GetType** method passing in a string of "**System.Int32&**". The ampersand (&) in the string allows me to identify a parameter passed by reference. This ampersand is part of the Backus-Naur Form Grammar for type names, which you can look up in the FCL documentation.

Using Binding Handles to Reduce Working Set

Many applications bind to a bunch of types (**Type** objects) or type members (**MemberInfo**-derived objects) and save these objects in a collection of some sort. Then later, the application searches the collection for a particular object and then invokes this object. This is a fine way of doing things except for one small issue: **Type** and **MemberInfo**-derived objects require a lot of memory. So if an application holds on to too many of these objects and invokes them occasionally, the application's working set increases dramatically, having an adverse affect on the application's performance.

Internally, the CLR has a more compact way of representing this information. The CLR creates these objects for our applications only to make things easier for developers. The CLR doesn't need these big objects itself in order to run. Developers who are saving/caching a lot of **Type** and **MemberInfo**-derived objects can reduce their working set by using runtime handles instead of objects. The FCL defines three runtime handle types (all defined in the System namespace): RuntimeTypeHandle, RuntimeFieldHandle, and RuntimeMethodHandle. All of these types are value types that contain just one field, an IntPtr; this makes instances of these types extremely cheap (memory-wise). The IntPtr field is a handle that refers to a type, field, or method in an AppDomain's loader heap. So what you need now is an easy and efficient way to convert a heavyweight Type/MemberInfo object to a lightweight runtime handle instance and vice versa. Fortunately, this is easy using the following conversion methods and properties:

- To convert a Type object to a RuntimeTypeHandle, call Type's static GetTypeHandle method passing in the reference to the Type object.

- To convert a RuntimeTypeHandle to a Type object, call Type's static GetTypeFromHandle method passing in the RuntimeTypeHandle.

- To convert a FieldInfo object to a RuntimeFieldHandle, query FieldInfo's instance read-only FieldHandle property.

- To convert a RuntimeFieldHandle to a FieldInfo object, call FieldInfo's static GetFieldFromHandle method.

- To convert a MethodInfo object to a RuntimeMethodHandle, query MethodInfo's instance read-only MethodHandle property.

- To convert a RuntimeMethodHandle to a MethodInfo object, call MethodInfo's static GetMethodFromHandle method.

The program sample below acquires a lot of MethodInfo objects, converts them to Runtime-MethodHandle instances, and shows the working set difference:

```
using System;
using System.Reflection;
using System.Collections.Generic;


public sealed class Program {
    private const BindingFlags c_bf = BindingFlags.FlattenHierarchy |
        BindingFlags.Instance | BindingFlags.Static |
        BindingFlags.Public | BindingFlags.NonPublic;

    public static void Main() {
        // Show size of heap before doing any reflection stuff
        Show("Before doing anything");

        // Build cache of MethodInfo objects for all methods in MSCorlib.dll
        List<MethodBase> methodInfos = new List<MethodBase>();
        foreach (Type t in typeof(Object).Assembly.GetExportedTypes()) {
            // Skip over any generic types
            if (t.IsGenericTypeDefinition) continue;

            MethodBase[] mb = t.GetMethods(c_bf);
            methodInfos.AddRange(mb);
        }
```

```
            // Show number of methods and size of heap after binding to all methods
            Console.WriteLine("# of methods={0:###,###}", methodInfos.Count);
            Show("After building cache of MethodInfo objects");


            // Build cache of RuntimeMethodHandles for all MethodInfo objects
            List<RuntimeMethodHandle> methodHandles =
                methodInfos.ConvertAll<RuntimeMethodHandle>(
                    delegate(MethodBase mb) { return mb.MethodHandle; });

            Show("Holding MethodInfo and RuntimeMethodHandle cache");
            GC.KeepAlive(methodInfos); // Prevent cache from being GC'd early

            methodInfos = null;         // Allow cache to be GC'd now
            Show("After freeing MethodInfo objects");

            methodInfos = methodHandles.ConvertAll<MethodBase>(
                delegate(RuntimeMethodHandle rmh) {
                    return MethodBase.GetMethodFromHandle(rmh); });
            Show("Size of heap after re-creating MethodInfo objects");
            GC.KeepAlive(methodHandles);  // Prevent cache from being GC'd early
            GC.KeepAlive(methodInfos);    // Prevent cache from being GC'd early

            methodHandles = null;          // Allow cache to be GC'd now
            methodInfos = null;            // Allow cache to be GC'd now
            Show("After freeing MethodInfos and RuntimeMethodHandles");
    }

    private static void Show(String s) {
        Console.WriteLine("Heap size={0,12:##,###,###} - {1}",
            GC.GetTotalMemory(true), s);
    }
}
```

When I compiled and executed this program, I got the following output:

```
Heap size=     150,756 - Before doing anything
# of methods=44,493
Heap size=   3,367,084 - After building cache of MethodInfo objects
Heap size=   3,545,124 - Holding MethodInfo and RuntimeMethodHandle cache
Heap size=     368,936 - After freeing MethodInfo objects
Heap size=   1,445,496 - Size of heap after re-creating MethodInfo objects
Heap size=     191,036 - After freeing MethodInfos and RuntimeMethodHandles
```

Chapter 23
Performing Asynchronous Operations

In this chapter, I'll talk about the various ways that you can perform operations asynchronously. When performing an asynchronous compute-bound operation, you execute it using other threads. When performing an asynchronous Input/Output-bound operation, you have a Microsoft Windows device driver doing the work for you, and no threads are required. In this chapter, I will focus on how to architect and implement an application that takes advantage of compute-bound as well as I/O-bound asynchronous operations in order to improve responsiveness and scalability.

Before I start, I'd like to point out that I have produced a library of classes to help make asynchronous programming and thread synchronization tasks easier. This library is called the Wintellect Power Threading library and is freely downloadable and freely usable. The library is offered "as-is" and can be downloaded from *http://Wintellect.com*.

How the CLR Uses Windows Threads

I'd like to start by saying a few words about threading and how it relates to the common language runtime (CLR). The CLR uses the threading capabilities of Windows, so this chapter is really focusing on how the threading capabilities of Windows are exposed to developers who write code by using the CLR. In other words, I am assuming that readers of this chapter are already familiar with threading concepts. If you are new to threading, I recommend reading some of my earlier writings on the topic, such as my book *Programming Applications for Microsoft Windows* (Microsoft Press, 1999).

However, the CLR reserves the right to divorce itself from Windows threads, and in certain hosting scenarios, a CLR thread does not map exactly to a Windows thread. For example, the host can tell the CLR to represent each CLR thread as a Windows fiber.[1] It's even possible that a future version of the CLR may just use an existing thread even if you ask it explicitly to create a new thread. In addition, a future version of the CLR could determine that one of your threads is in a wait state and reassign that thread to do a different task. The current versions of the CLR do not offer any of these performance enhancements. However, Microsoft has many ideas along these lines, and it is likely that future versions of the CLR will incorporate ideas like these with the goal of improving performance by reducing operating system resource usage. For you, this means that your code should make as few assumptions as possible when manipulating threads. For example, you should avoid calling native Windows functions since these functions have no knowledge of a CLR thread. By avoiding native Windows functions and sticking with Framework Class Library (FCL) types whenever possible, you're guaranteed that your code will easily take advantage of these performance enhancements as they become available in the future.

If your code is running under a host (such as Microsoft SQL Server 2005), a thread can tell the host that it would like to execute its code using the current physical operating system thread by calling `System.Threading.Thread`'s static `BeginThreadAffinity` method. When the thread no longer requires running by using the physical operating system thread, it can notify the host by calling `Thread`'s static `EndThreadAffinity` method.

Pontificating about Efficient Thread Usage

It has been my experience that developers use threads all too much in their applications. If you look back on the history of threads, you'll see that early operating systems didn't support threads. These systems had just one thread that executed a little code here and a little code there. The problem with single-threaded systems is that bad code affected the entire system.

---

[1] A fiber is a lightweight thread that consists of a stack and a context (set of CPU registers), which makes them lightweight. In addition, Windows doesn't know anything about fibers. A thread can consist of multiple fibers, but the thread can execute only one fiber at a time. A thread/fiber must call a method to schedule another fiber to run on the thread because Windows doesn't know anything about fibers or how to schedule them.

For example, 16-bit versions of Windows were single-threaded operating systems, and if one application went into an infinite loop or hung for some reason, the entire system froze forcing users to press the reset button to reboot the machine. Windows NT 3.1 was the first version of Windows to offer multi-threading capabilities, and the main reason that this capability was added to Windows was for robustness. Each process got its own thread, and if one process's thread entered an infinite loop or hung for some reason, that one thread was frozen; the other processes' threads and the system itself continued to run.

Strictly speaking, threads are overhead. Creating a thread is not cheap: a thread kernel object has to be allocated and initialized, each thread gets 1 MB of address space reserved (and committed on demand) for its user-mode stack, and another 12 KB (or so) is allocated for its kernel-mode stack. Then, just after creating a thread, Windows calls a function in every DLL in the process notifying each DLL that a new thread has been created. Destroying a thread is also not cheap—every DLL in the process receives a notification that the thread is about to die, and the kernel object and the stacks have to be freed as well.

If there is only one CPU in a computer, only one thread can run at any one time. Windows has to keep track of the thread objects, and every so often, Windows has to decide which thread to schedule next to go to the CPU. This is additional code that has to execute once every 20 milliseconds or so. When Windows makes a CPU stop executing one thread's code and start executing another thread's code, we call this a *context switch*. A context switch is fairly expensive because the operating system has to:

1. Enter kernel mode.

2. Save the CPU's registers into the currently executing thread's kernel object. By the way, the CPU registers occupy approximately 700 bytes on x86, 1240 bytes on x64, and 2500 bytes on IA64.

3. Acquire a spin lock, determine which thread to schedule next, and release the spin lock. If the next thread is owned by another process, this can get more expensive because the virtual address space has to be switched.

4. Load the CPU's registers with values from the about-to-be-running thread's kernel object.

5. Leave kernel mode.

All of this is pure overhead that makes Windows and our applications execute more slowly than if we were running on a single-threaded system. But all of this is necessary because Microsoft's goal is to produce a robust operating system that isn't subject to problems that might occur when executing application code.

So all of this adds up to the following: You should really limit your use of threads as much as possible. The more threads you create, the more overhead you introduce into the system, and the slower you make everything run. In addition, since each thread requires resources (memory for a kernel object and two stacks), each thread consumes memory that will not be available to the operating system or applications.

In addition to robustness improvements, threads do serve another useful purpose: scalability. When a computer has multiple CPUs, Windows is capable of scheduling multiple threads: one thread per CPU. So it does make sense to have multiple threads in order to make use of the processing power available on the machine. In fact, this is the trend we now see happening. It used to be that faster CPUs became available each and every year. This meant that the applications we wrote would get faster if the user just ran them on a computer with a faster CPU. However, CPU manufacturers, such as Intel and AMD, are now finding it more difficult to produce faster CPUs because current CPU architectures and hardware components are reaching the limits of current designs.

Due to physical space and distance limitations of current CPU-manufacturing techniques, CPU manufacturers are finding it much more cost effective to build single chips that incorporate multiple CPUs. These newer chips can help multi-threaded operating systems and applications perform better by running multiple threads simultaneously. There are two types of technologies being used by CPU chip makers today: *hyper-threading* and *multi-core*. Both of these technologies allow a single chip to appear as two (or more) CPUs to Windows and your applications. And in fact, some chips (such as the Intel Pentium Extreme) incorporate both hyper-threading and multi-core technologies. To Windows, a single Pentium Extreme chip looks like four CPUs!

Some chips, such as the Intel Xeon and Intel Pentium 4, offer hyper-threading. A hyper-threaded CPU has two logical CPUs on it. Each logical CPU has its own architectural state (CPU registers), but the logical CPUs share a single set of execution resources such as the CPU cache. When one logical CPU is paused (because of cache miss, branch misprediction, or waiting for the results of a previous instruction), the chip switches over to the other logical CPU and lets it run. Ideally, you'd hope to get a 100-percent performance improvement from a hyper-threaded CPU; after all, there are two CPUs running now instead of just one. However, since the two logical CPUs share execution resources, a hyper-threaded CPU doesn't give the kind of performance boost you'd like to see. In fact, Intel reports that hyper-threaded CPUs cause about a 10- to 30-percent improvement in execution performance.

Some chips, such as the Intel Pentium D and AMD Athlon 64 X2, take advantage of the multi-core technology. A multi-core chip has two physical CPUs on it. Each CPU has its own architectural state as well as its own execution resources. You can expect to see greater performance characteristics when using a multi-core chip as compared to a hyper-threaded chip. In fact, you could expect to get 100-percent improvement as long as the two CPUs are running independent tasks. Chip manufacturers have even announced that within the next few years, they will be able to create chips that have 4, 8, 16, or even 32 independent CPUs in them. Wow, this will be a lot of computing power!

So since CPU manufacturers can't currently make CPUs substantially faster, they're giving us more (slow) CPUs instead. Therefore, if you want your applications to run faster in the future, you must design them to take advantage of the additional CPUs. To do this, you need to have multiple threads, and yet threads are pure overhead and make things run slower and consume resources. There are many applications that perform well enough with today's CPU processing speeds but, if application performance is important for your application, this tension is something that you'll have to start wrestling with. I believe that issues surrounding this will become much more important as time goes on. This tension is what drives my thoughts in this chapter as well as the next one.

Introducing the CLR's Thread Pool

As stated earlier in this chapter, creating and destroying a thread is a fairly expensive operation in terms of time. In addition, having lots of threads wastes memory resources and also hurts performance due to the operating system having to schedule and context switch between the runnable threads. To improve this situation, the CLR contains code to manage its own thread pool. You can think of a thread pool as being a set of threads that are available for your application's own use. There is one thread pool per process; this thread pool is shared by all AppDomains in the process.

When the CLR initializes, the thread pool has no threads in it. Internally, the thread pool maintains a queue of operation requests. When your application wants to perform an asynchronous operation, you call some method that appends an entry into the thread pool's queue. The thread pool's code will extract entries from this queue and dispatch the entry to a thread pool thread. If there are no threads in the thread pool, a new thread will be created. Creating a thread has a performance hit associated with it (as already discussed). However, when a thread pool thread has completed its task, the thread is not destroyed; instead, the thread is returned to the thread pool, where it sits idle waiting to respond to another request. Since the thread doesn't destroy itself, there is no added performance hit.

If your application makes many requests of the thread pool, the thread pool will try to service all of the requests using just this one thread. However, if your application is queuing up several requests faster than the thread pool thread can handle them, additional threads will be created. Your application will eventually get to a point at which all of its requests can be handled by a small number of threads, so the thread pool should have no need to create a lot of threads.

If your application stops making requests of the thread pool, the pool may have a lot of threads in it that are doing nothing. This is wasteful of memory resources. So when a thread pool thread has been idle for approximately 2 minutes (time is subject to change with future versions of the CLR), the thread wakes itself up and kills itself in order to free up resources. As the thread is killing itself, there is a performance hit. However, this probably doesn't matter since the thread is killing itself because it has been idle, which means that your application isn't performing a lot of work.

The great thing about the thread pool is that it manages the tension between having a few threads so as to not waste resources and having more threads to take advantage of multiprocessors, hyper-threaded processors, and multi-core processors. And the thread pool is heuristic. If your application needs to perform many tasks, and CPUs are available, the thread pool creates more threads. If your application's workload decreases, the thread pool threads kill themselves.

Internally, the thread pool categorizes its threads as either *worker threads* or *I/O threads*. Worker threads are used when your application asks the thread pool to perform an asynchronous compute-bound operation (which can include initiating an I/O-bound operation). I/O threads are used to notify your code when an asynchronous I/O-bound operation has completed. Specifically, this means that you are using the Asynchronous Programming Model (APM) to make I/O requests such as accessing a file, networked server, database, Web service, or other hardware device. Later in this chapter, I'll discuss how to perform an asynchronous compute-bound operation as well as how to use the APM to perform an asynchronous I/O-bound operation.

Limiting the Number of Threads in the Thread Pool

The CLR's thread pool allows developers to set a maximum number of worker threads and I/O threads. The CLR promises never to create more threads than this setting. I have run into many developers who spend a phenomenal amount of time and energy thinking about how to best set these limits. To make life a little easier, I'd like to offer some guidance here.

A thread pool should never place an upper limit on the number of threads in the pool because starvation or deadlock might occur. Imagine queuing 1,000 work items that all block on an event that is signaled by the 1,001st item. If you've set a maximum of 1,000 threads, the 1,001st work item won't be executed, and all 1,000 threads will be blocked forever. Also, it is very unusual for developers to artificially limit the resources that they have available to their application. For example, would you ever start your application and tell the system you'd like to restrict the amount of memory that the application can use or limit the amount of network bandwidth that your application can use? Yet, for some reason, developers feel compelled to limit the number of threads that the thread pool can have.

It is actually quite unfortunate that the CLR even offers the ability to limit the number of threads because it has wasted programmers' time. In earlier versions of the CLR, the maximum number of worker threads and I/O threads had low defaults. And in fact, some developers have experienced deadlocks and starvation due to these low limits. Fortunately, Microsoft's CLR team has come around on this issue. With version 2.0 of the CLR, the maximum number of worker threads default to 25 per CPU in the machine[2] and the maximum number of I/O threads defaults to 1000. A limit of 1000 is effectively no limit at all. They can't remove the limits entirely because doing so might break applications that were originally written targeting

---

2. You can query the number of CPUs by calling **System.Environment**'s static **ProcessorCount** property. This returns the number of logical CPUs in the machine; a machine with a single hyper-threaded CPU will cause **Environment**'s **ProcessorCount** property to return a value of **2**.

an earlier version of the CLR. By the way, Windows does not offer a Win32 API to set a limit on the Windows thread pool for the exact reasons I mentioned.

The **System.Threading.ThreadPool** class offers several static methods that you can call to manipulate the number of threads in the thread pool. Here are the prototypes of these methods:

```
void GetMaxThreads(out Int32 workerThreads, out Int32 completionPortThreads);
Boolean SetMaxThreads(Int32 workerThreads, Int32 completionPortThreads);

void GetMinThreads(out Int32 workerThreads, out Int32 completionPortThreads);
Boolean SetMinThreads(Int32 workerThreads, Int32 completionPortThreads);

void GetAvailableThreads(out Int32 workerThreads, out Int32 completionPortThreads);
```

You can query the thread pool's maximum limits by calling the **GetMaxThreads** method. You can also change these maximums by calling the **SetMaxThreads** method. I highly recommend that you do not call these methods. Playing with thread pool limits usually results in making an application perform worse, not better. If you think that your application needs more than 25 threads per CPU, there is something seriously wrong with the architecture of your application and the way that it's using threads. I will address the proper way to use threads throughout this chapter.

On a related note, the CLR's thread pool tries to avoid creating additional threads too quickly. Specifically, the thread pool tries to avoid creating more than one thread per 500 milliseconds. This has caused problems for some developers because queued tasks do not get processed quickly. If this turns out to be a problem for your application, you can call the **SetMinThreads** method passing in the minimum number of threads that you're OK with having in the pool. The thread pool will quickly create up to this many threads, and if all of these threads are in use when more tasks get queued up, the thread pool will continue to create additional threads at a rate of no more than one per 500 milliseconds. By default, the minimum number of worker and I/O threads is set to 2. I obtained these numbers by calling the **GetMinThreads** method.

Finally, you can get the number of additional threads that the thread pool could add to the pool by calling the **GetAvailableThreads** method. This method returns the maximum number of threads minus the number of threads currently in the pool. The values returned from this method are valid for a moment in time; by the time the method returns, more threads could have been added to the pool, or some threads could have been destroyed. There should be no reason for an application to call this method except for doing diagnostics, monitoring, or performance tuning.

Using the Thread Pool to Perform an Asynchronous Compute-Bound Operation

A compute-bound operation is an operation that requires computation. Examples include recalculating cells in a spreadsheet application and spell-checking words or grammar-checking sentences in a word-processing application. Ideally, a compute-bound operation will not perform any synchronous I/O operation because all synchronous I/O operations suspend the calling thread while the underlying hardware (disk drive, network card, etc.) performs the work. You should always strive to keep your threads running. A suspended thread is a thread that is not running and is using system resources—something that should always be avoided when trying to write a high-performance, scalable application. Later in this chapter, I'll explain how to use the APM to perform asynchronous I/O operations efficiently.

To queue an asynchronous compute-bound operation to the thread pool, you typically call one of the following methods defined by the **ThreadPool** class:

```
static Boolean QueueUserWorkItem(WaitCallback callBack);
static Boolean QueueUserWorkItem(WaitCallback callBack, Object state);
static Boolean UnsafeQueueUserWorkItem(WaitCallback callBack, Object state);
```

These methods queue a "work item" (and optional state data) to the thread pool's queue, and then all of these methods return immediately. A work item is simply a method identified by the **callBack** parameter that will be called by a thread pool thread. The method can be passed a single parameter specified via the **state** (the state data) argument. The version of **QueueUserWorkItem** without the **state** parameter passes **null** to the callback method. Eventually, some thread in the pool will process the work item, causing your method to be called. The callback method you write must match the **System.Threading.WaitCallback** delegate type, which is defined as follows:

```
delegate void WaitCallback(Object state);
```

The following code demonstrates how to have a thread pool thread call a method asynchronously:

```
using System;
using System.Threading;

public static class Program {
   public static void Main() {
      Console.WriteLine("Main thread: queuing an asynchronous operation");
      ThreadPool.QueueUserWorkItem(ComputeBoundOp, 5);
      Console.WriteLine("Main thread: Doing other work here...");
      Thread.Sleep(10000);  // Simulating other work (10 seconds)
      Console.WriteLine("Hit <Enter> to end this program...");
      Console.ReadLine();
   }

   // This method's signature must match the WaitCallback delegate
```

```
private static void ComputeBoundOp(Object state) {
    // This method is executed by a thread pool thread

    Console.WriteLine("In ComputeBoundOp: state={0}", state);
    Thread.Sleep(1000);  // Simulates other work (1 second)

    // When this method returns, the thread goes back
    // to the pool and waits for another task
  }
}
```

When I compile and run this code, I get the following output:

```
Main thread: queuing an asynchronous operation
Main thread: Doing other work here...
In ComputeBoundOp: state=5
```

And, sometimes when I run this code, I get this output:

```
Main thread: queuing an asynchronous operation
In ComputeBoundOp: state=5
Main thread: Doing other work here...
```

The difference in the order of the lines in the output is attributed to the fact that the two methods are running asynchronously with respect to one another. The Windows scheduler determines which thread to schedule first, or it may schedule them both simultaneously if the application is running on a multi-CPU machine.

> **Note** If the callback method throws an exception that is unhandled, the CLR terminates the process (unless the host imposes its own policy). Unhandled exceptions were discussed in Chapter 19, "Exceptions."

The **ThreadPool** class has an **UnsafeQueueUserWorkItem** method. This method is very similar to the more commonly used **QueueUserWorkItem** method. Let me briefly explain the difference between these two methods: When attempting to access a restricted resource (such as opening a file), the CLR performs a Code Access Security (CAS) check. That is, the CLR checks if all of the assemblies in the calling thread's call stack have permission to access the resource. If any assembly doesn't have the required permission, the CLR throws a **SecurityException**. Imagine a thread that is executing code defined in an assembly that does not have the permission to open a file. If the thread attempted to open a file, the CLR would throw a **SecurityException**.

To work around this, the thread could queue a work item to the thread pool and have the thread pool thread execute code to open the file. Of course, this would have to be in an assembly that has the right permission. This "workaround" circumvents security and allows malicious code to wreak havoc with restricted resources. To prevent this security exploit, the **QueueUserWorkItem** method internally walks up the calling thread's stack and captures all of the granted security permissions. Then, when the thread pool thread starts to execute, these permissions are associated with the thread. So the thread pool thread ends up running with the same set of permissions as the thread that called QueueUserWorkItem.

Walking up the thread's stack and capturing all of the security permissions is costly in terms of performance. If you want to improve the performance of queuing an asynchronous compute-bound operation, you can call the UnsafeQueueUserWorkItem method instead. This method just queues an item to the thread pool without walking up the calling thread's stack. As a result, this method executes faster than QueueUserWorkItem, but it opens a potential security hole in the application. You should call UnsafeQueueUserWorkItem only if you are sure that the thread pool thread will be executing code that doesn't touch a restricted resource, or if, in your scenario, you know that it's OK to touch the resource. Also, be aware that code calling the UnsafeQueueUserWorkItem method is required to have a SecurityPermission with the ControlPolicy and ControlEvidence flags turned on; this prevents untrusted code from accidentally or maliciously elevating permissions.

The "Execution Contexts" section in this chapter will delve deeper into explaining how to migrate a thread's context (which includes the security permissions) to another thread.

Using a Dedicated Thread to Perform an Asynchronous Compute-Bound Operation

I highly recommend that you use the thread pool to execute asynchronous compute-bound operations whenever possible. However, there are some occasions when you might want to explicitly create a thread dedicated to executing a particular compute-bound operation. Typically, you'd want to create a dedicated thread if you're going to execute code that requires the thread to be in a particular state that is not normal for a thread pool thread. For example, I'd create a dedicated thread if I wanted the thread to run at a special priority (all thread pool threads run at normal priority, and you should not alter a thread pool thread's priority). I would also consider creating and using my own thread if I wanted to make the thread a foreground thread (all thread pool threads are background threads), thereby preventing the application from dying until my thread has completed its task. I'd also use a dedicated thread if the compute-bound task were extremely long running; this way, I would not be taxing the thread pool's logic as it tries to figure out whether to create an additional thread. Finally, I'd use a dedicated thread if I wanted to start a thread and possibly abort it prematurely by calling Thread's Abort method (discussed in Chapter 21, "CLR Hosting and AppDomains").

To create a dedicated thread, you construct an instance of the System.Threading.Thread class passing the name of a method into its constructor. Here is the prototype of the constructor:

```
public sealed class Thread : CriticalFinalizerObject, ... {
    public Thread(ParameterizedThreadStart start);
    // Less commonly used constructors are not shown here
}
```

The **start** parameter identifies the method that the dedicated thread will execute, and this method must match the signature of the **ParameterizedThreadStart** delegate:

```
delegate void ParameterizedThreadStart(Object obj);
```

As you can see, the **ParameterizedThreadStart** delegate's signature is identical to the **Wait-Callback** delegate's signature (discussed in the previous section). This means that the same method can be called using a thread pool thread or using a dedicated thread.

Constructing a **Thread** object is a fairly lightweight operation because it does not yet actually create an operating system thread. To actually create the operating system thread and have it start executing the callback method, you must call **Thread**'s **Start** method passing into it the object (state) that you want passed as the callback method's argument. The following code demonstrates how to create a dedicated thread and have it call a method asynchronously:

```
using System;
using System.Threading;

public static class Program {
    public static void Main() {
        Console.WriteLine("Main thread: starting a dedicated thread " +
            "to do an asynchronous operation");
        Thread dedicatedThread = new Thread(ComputeBoundOp);
        dedicatedThread.Start(5);

        Console.WriteLine("Main thread: Doing other work here...");
        Thread.Sleep(10000);      // Simulating other work (10 seconds)

        dedicatedThread.Join();   // Wait for thread to terminate
        Console.WriteLine("Hit <Enter> to end this program...");
        Console.ReadLine();
    }

    // This method's signature must match the ParameterizedThreadStart delegate
    private static void ComputeBoundOp(Object state) {
        // This method is executed by a dedicated thread

        Console.WriteLine("In ComputeBoundOp: state={0}", state);
        Thread.Sleep(1000);  // Simulates other work (1 second)

        // When this method returns, the dedicated thread dies
    }
}
```

When I compile and run this code, I get the following output:

```
Main thread: starting a dedicated thread to do an asynchronous operation
Main thread: Doing other work here...
In ComputeBoundOp: state=5
```

And sometimes when I run this code, I get the following output (as explained in the previous section):

```
Main thread: starting a dedicated thread to do an asynchronous operation
In ComputeBoundOp: state=5
Main thread: Doing other work here...
```

Notice that the **ComputeBoundOp** method shown in this example is identical to the version shown in the previous section. Also, notice that the **Main** method calls **Join**. The **Join** method causes the calling thread to stop executing any code until the thread identified by **dedicatedThread** has destroyed itself or been terminated. When using **ThreadPool**'s **QueueUserWorkItem** method to queue an asynchronous operation, the CLR offers no built-in way for you to determine when the operation has completed. The **Join** method gives us a way to accomplish this when using a dedicated thread. However, do not use a dedicated thread instead of calling **QueueUserWorkItem** if you need to know when the operation has completed. Instead, you should use the APM (discussed later in this chapter).

Periodically Performing an Asynchronous Compute-Bound Operation

The **System.Threading** namespace defines a **Timer** class, which you can use to have the CLR call a method periodically. When you construct an instance of the **Timer** class, you are telling the CLR that you want a method of yours called back at a future time that you specify. The **Timer** class offers several constructors all quite similar to each other:

```
public sealed class Timer : MarshalByRefObject, IDisposable {
    public Timer(TimerCallback callback, Object state,
        Int32 dueTime, Int32 period);

    public Timer(TimerCallback callback, Object state,
        UInt32 dueTime, UInt32 period);

    public Timer(TimerCallback callback, Object state,
        Int64 dueTime, Int64 period);

    public Timer(TimerCallback callback, Object state,
        Timespan dueTime, TimeSpan period);
}
```

All four constructors construct a **Timer** object identically. The **callback** parameter identifies the method that you want called back by a thread pool thread. Of course, the callback method that you write must match the **System.Threading.TimerCallback** delegate type, which is defined as follows:

```
delegate void TimerCallback(Object state);
```

The constructor's **state** parameter allows you to pass state data to the callback method; you can pass **null** if you have no state data to pass. You use the **dueTime** parameter to tell the CLR how many milliseconds to wait before calling your callback method for the very first time. You can specify the number of milliseconds by using a signed or unsigned 32-bit value, a signed 64-bit value, or a **TimeSpan** value. If you want the callback method called immediately, specify **0** for the **dueTime** parameter. The last parameter, **period**, allows you to specify how long, in milliseconds, to wait before each successive call to the callback method. If you pass **Timeout.Infinite** (**-1**) for this parameter, a thread pool thread will call the callback method just once.

Internally, the CLR has just one thread that it uses for all **Timer** objects. This thread knows when the next **Timer** object's time is due. When the next **Timer** object is due, the CLR's thread wakes up, and it internally calls **ThreadPool**'s **QueueUserWorkItem** to enter an entry into the thread pool's queue causing your callback method to get called. If your callback method takes a long time to execute, the timer could go off again. This would cause multiple thread pool threads to be executing your callback method simultaneously. Watch out for this; if your method accesses any shared data, you will probably need to add some thread synchronization locks to prevent the data from becoming corrupted.

.The **Timer** class offers some additional methods that allow you to communicate with the CLR to modify when (or if) the method should be called back. Specifically, the **Timer** class offers **Change** and **Dispose** methods (each has overloads):

```
public sealed class Timer : MarshalByRefObject, IDisposable {
    public Boolean Change(Int32    dueTime, Int32    period);
    public Boolean Change(UInt32   dueTime, UInt32   period);
    public Boolean Change(Int64    dueTime, Int64    period);
    public Boolean Change(TimeSpan dueTime, TimeSpan period);

    public Boolean Dispose();
    public Boolean Dispose(WaitHandle notifyObject);
}
```

The **Change** method allows you to change or reset the **Timer** object's due time and period. The **Dispose** method allows you to cancel the timer altogether and optionally signal the kernel object identified by the **notifyObject** parameter when all pending callbacks for the time have completed.

> **Important** When a **Timer** object is garbage collected, the CLR cancels the timer so that it no longer goes off. So when using a **Timer** object, make sure that a variable is keeping the object alive, or your callback method will stop getting called. This was discussed and demonstrated in the "Garbage Collections and Debugging" section in Chapter 20, "Automatic Memory Management (Garbage Collection)."

The following code demonstrates how to have a thread pool thread call a method starting immediately and then every 2 seconds thereafter:

```
using System;
using System.Threading;

public static class Program {
    public static void Main() {
        Console.WriteLine("Main thread: starting a timer");
        Timer t = new Timer(ComputeBoundOp, 5, 0, 2000);

        Console.WriteLine("Main thread: Doing other work here...");
        Thread.Sleep(10000);   // Simulating other work (10 seconds)
        t.Dispose();           // Cancel the timer now
    }

    // This method's signature must match the TimerCallback delegate
    private static void ComputeBoundOp(Object state) {
        // This method is executed by a thread pool thread

        Console.WriteLine("In ComputeBoundOp: state={0}", state);
        Thread.Sleep(1000);   // Simulates other work (1 second)

        // When this method returns, the thread goes back
        // to the pool and waits for another task
    }
}
```

A Tale of Three Timers

Unfortunately, the FCL actually ships with three timers, and it is not clear to most programmers what makes each timer unique. Let me attempt to explain:

- **System.Threading's Timer class**   This is the timer discussed in the previous section, and it is the best timer to use when you want to perform periodic background tasks on another thread.

- **System.Windows.Forms's Timer class.**   Constructing an instance of this class tells Windows to associate a timer with the calling thread (see the Win32 **SetTimer** function). When this timer goes off, Windows injects a timer message (**WM_TIMER**) into the thread's message queue. The thread must execute a message pump that extracts these messages and dispatches them to the desired callback method. Notice that all of the work is done by just one thread—the thread that sets the timer is guaranteed to be the thread that executes the callback method. This also means that your timer method will not be executed by multiple threads concurrently.

- **System.Timers' Timer class.**   This timer is basically a wrapper around **System.Threading**'s **Timer** class that causes the CLR to queue events into the thread pool when the timer comes due. The **System.Timers.Timer** class is derived from **System.ComponentModel**'s **Component** class, which allows these timer objects to be placed on a design surface in Microsoft Visual Studio. Also, its members are a little different. This class was added to the FCL years ago while Microsoft was still sorting out the threading and timer stuff. This class probably should have been removed so that everyone would be using the **System .Threading.Timer** class instead. In fact, I never use the **System.Timers.Timer** class, and I'd discourage you from using it, too, unless you really want a timer on a design surface.

Introducing the Asynchronous Programming Model

Performing asynchronous operations is the key to building high-performance, scalable applications that allow you to use very few threads to execute a lot of operations. And when coupled with the thread pool, asynchronous operations allow you to take advantage of all of the CPUs that are in the machine. Microsoft's CLR team realized the enormous potential here and went about designing a pattern that would make it easy for developers to take advantage of this capability. This pattern is called the Asynchronous Programming Model (APM).

Personally, I love the APM because it is a single pattern that can be used to asynchronously execute both compute-bound and I/O-bound operations. The APM is relatively easy to learn, simple to use, and is supported by many types in the FCL. Here are some examples:

- All **System.IO.Stream**-derived classes that communicate with hardware devices (including **FileStream** and **NetworkStream**) offer **BeginRead** and **BeginWrite** methods. Note that **Stream**-derived classes that do not communicate with hardware devices (including **BufferedStream**, **MemoryStream**, and **CryptoStream**) also offer **BeginRead** and **BeginWrite** methods to fit into the APM. However, the code in these methods performs compute-bound operations, not I/O-bound operations, and therefore a thread is required to execute these operations.

- The **System.Net.Dns** class offers **BeginGetHostAddresses**, **BeginGetHostByName**, **BeginGetHostEntry**, and **BeginResolve** methods.

- The **System.Net.Sockets.Socket** class offers **BeginAccept**, **BeginConnect**, **BeginDisconnect**, **BeginReceive**, **BeginReceiveFrom**, **BeginReceiveMessageFrom**, **BeginSend**, **BeginSendFile**, and **BeginSendTo** methods.

- All **System.Net.WebRequest**-derived classes (including **FileWebRequest**, **FtpWebRequest**, and **HttpWebRequest**) offer **BeginGetRequestStream** and **BeginGetResponse** methods.

- The **System.IO.Ports.SerialPort** class has a read-only **BaseStream** property that returns a **Stream**, which as you know, offers **BeginRead** and **BeginWrite** methods.

- The **System.Data.SqlClient.SqlCommand** class offers **BeginExecuteNonQuery**, **BeginExecuteReader**, and **BeginExecuteXmlReader** methods.

Furthermore, all delegate types define a **BeginInvoke** method for use with the APM. And finally, tools that produce Web service proxy types (such as WSDL.exe and SvcUtil.exe) also generate **Begin*Xxx*** methods for use with the APM. By the way, there is a corresponding **End*Xxx*** method for each and every **Begin*Xxx*** method. As you can see, support for the APM is pervasive throughout the FCL.

A great feature of the APM is that it offers three rendezvous techniques. You'll recall that when using the **ThreadPool**'s **QueueUserWorkItem** method, there was no built-in way for you to know when the asynchronous operation completed. In addition, there was no built-in way to discover the result of the asynchronous operation. For example, if you queued up an asynchronous operation to check the spelling of a word, there is no built-in way for the thread pool thread to report back if it determined whether the word was spelled correctly. Well, the APM offers three mechanisms for you to use to determine when an asynchronous operation is complete, and all three mechanisms will also let you know the result of the asynchronous operation.

Using the APM to Perform an Asynchronous I/O-Bound Operation

Let's say that you want to read some bytes from a file stream asynchronously using the APM. First, you'd construct a **System.IO.FileStream** object by calling one of its constructors that accepts a **System.IO.FileOptions** argument. For this argument, you'd pass in the **FileOptions.Asynchronous** flag; this tells the **FileStream** object that you intend to perform asynchronous read and write operations against the file.

To synchronously read bytes from a **FileStream**, you'd call its **Read** method, which is prototyped as follows:

```
public Int32 Read(Byte[] array, Int32 offset, Int32 count)
```

The **Read** method accepts a reference to a **Byte[]** that will have its bytes filled with the bytes from the file. The **count** argument indicates the maximum number of bytes that you want to read. The bytes will be placed in the **array** between **offset** and (**offset + count − 1**). The **Read** method returns the number of bytes actually read from the file. When you call this method, the read occurs synchronously. That is, the method does not return until the requested bytes have been read into the byte array. Synchronous I/O operations are very inefficient because the timing of all I/O operations is unpredictable, and while waiting for the I/O to complete, the calling thread is suspended, so it is not capable of doing any work, thereby wasting resources.

If Windows has cached the file's data, this method will return almost immediately. But the data might not be cached, and then Windows will have to communicate with the disk drive hardware in order to load the data off the disk. Windows might even have to communicate over the network to a server machine and have the server communicate with its disk drive hardware (or its cache) to return the data. It should be clear to you that when you call **Read**, you have no idea when this method will actually get the data and return back to your code. And if a network connection goes down, **Read** will have to eventually time out and throw an exception to report the failure.

To asynchronously read bytes from a file, you'd call **FileStream**'s **BeginRead** method:

```
IAsyncResult BeginRead(Byte[] array, Int32 offset, Int32 numBytes,
    AsyncCallback userCallback, Object stateObject)
```

Notice that **BeginRead**'s first three parameters are identical to those of **Read**. But there are two additional parameters: **userCallback** and **stateObject**. I'll discuss these two parameters later. When you call **BeginRead**, you are requesting that Windows read the bytes from the file into the byte array. Since you are performing I/O, **BeginRead** actually queues a request to a Windows device driver that knows how to talk to the correct hardware device. The hardware now takes over the operation, and *no threads* need to perform any actions or even wait for the outcome—this is extremely efficient!

> **Note** Even though this discussion has been focused on file I/O, it is important to remember that other types of I/O work similarly. For example, when using a NetworkStream, the I/O request is queued to the Windows network device driver, which waits for the response. Also, when talking about network I/O, abstractions built on top of it (such as the DNS lookups, Web service requests, and data base requests) ultimately queue asynchronous I/O operations to the network driver; they just parse the returned data in order to make it more usable by your application code.

The **BeginRead** method returns a reference to an object whose type implements the **System .IAsyncResult** interface. When you call **BeginRead**, it constructs an object that uniquely identifies your I/O request, it queues up the request to the Windows device driver, and then it returns the **IAsyncResult** object back to you. You can think of this object as your receipt. When **BeginRead** returns, the I/O operation has only been queued; it has not completed. So you should not try to manipulate the bytes in the byte array because the array does not contain the requested data.

Well, actually, the array might contain the requested data because I/O is being performed asynchronously, and so by the time **BeginRead** returns, the data may have actually been read. Or the data might come in from a server in a few seconds. Or the connection to the server might go down, and the data may never come in. Since all of these outcomes are possible, you need a way to discover which one of them has actually happened, and you need to know when the outcome was detected. I refer to this as *rendezvousing* with the asynchronous operation's result. As mentioned earlier, the APM offers three rendezvous techniques that you can use. We'll look at all of these in turn and compare them to each other.

> **Note** When you create a `FileStream` object, you get to specify whether you want to communicate using synchronous or asynchronous operations via the `FileOptions.Asynchronous` flag (which is equivalent to calling the Win32 `CreateFile` function and passing into it the `FILE_FLAG_OVERLAPPED` flag). If you do not specify this flag, Windows performs all operations against the file synchronously. Of course, you can still call `FileStream`'s `BeginRead` method, and to your application, it looks as if the operation is being performed asynchronously; but internally, the `FileStream` class uses another thread to emulate asynchronous behavior. This additional thread is wasteful and hurts performance.
>
> On the other hand, you can create a `FileStream` object by specifying the `FileOptions.Asynchronous` flag. Then you can call `FileStream`'s `Read` method to perform a synchronous operation. Internally, the `FileStream` class emulates this behavior by starting an asynchronous operation and then immediately puts the calling thread to sleep until the operation is complete. This is also inefficient, but it is not as inefficient as calling `BeginRead` by using a `FileStream` constructed without the `FileOptions.Asynchronous` flag.
>
> So, to summarize: When working with a `FileStream`, you should decide up front whether you intend to perform synchronous or asynchronous I/O against the file and indicate your choice by specifying the `FileOptions.Asynchronous` flag (or not). If you specify this flag, always call `BeginRead`. If you do not specify this flag, always call `Read`. This will give you the best performance. If you intend to make some synchronous and some asynchronous operations against the `FileStream`, it is more efficient to construct it using the `FileOptions.Asynchronous` flag.

The APM's Three Rendezvous Techniques

The APM supports three rendezvous techniques: *wait-until-done*, *polling*, and *method callback*. Let's discuss all of these starting with the wait-until-done technique.

The APM's Wait-Until-Done Rendezvous Technique

To start an asynchronous operation, you call some **Begin*Xxx*** method. All of these methods queue the desired operation and return an **IAsyncResult** object identifying the pending operation. To get the result of the operation, you simply call the corresponding **End*Xxx*** method passing into it the **IAsyncResult** object. For the record, all **End*Xxx*** methods accept an **IAsyncResult** object as an argument. Basically, when you call an **End*Xxx*** method, you are asking the CLR to give you back the result from the asynchronous operation identified by the **IAsyncResult** object (your receipt from calling the **Begin*Xxx*** method).

Now, if the asynchronous operation has completed, when you call the **End*Xxx*** method, it will return immediately with the result. On the other hand, if the asynchronous operation has not yet completed, the **End*Xxx*** method will suspend the calling thread until the operation has completed, and then it will return the result.

Let's return to our example of reading bytes from a `FileStream` object. The `FileStream` class offers an **EndRead** method:

```
Int32 EndRead(IAsyncResult asyncResult)
```

Notice that **EndRead**'s only parameter is an **IAsyncResult**. But, more important, notice that **EndRead**'s return type, **Int32**, is identical to that of **Read**'s return type. When **EndRead** returns, it returns the number of bytes read from the **FileStream**.

So now, let's put all of this together into a sample application:

```
using System;
using System.IO;
using System.Threading;

public static class Program {
    public static void Main() {
        // Open the file indicating asynchronous I/O
        FileStream fs = new FileStream(@"C:\Boot.ini", FileMode.Open,
            FileAccess.Read, FileShare.Read, 1024,
            FileOptions.Asynchronous);

        Byte[] data = new Byte[100];

        // Initiate an asynchronous read operation against the FileStream
        IAsyncResult ar = fs.BeginRead(data, 0, data.Length, null, null);

        // Executing some other code here...

        // Suspend this thread until the asynchronous
        // operation completes and get the result
        Int32 bytesRead = fs.EndRead(ar);

        // No other operations to do, close the file
        fs.Close();

        // Now it is OK to access the byte array and show the result.
        Console.WriteLine("Number of bytes read={0}", bytesRead);
        Console.WriteLine(BitConverter.ToString(data, 0, bytesRead));
    }
}
```

When I compile and run this program on my machine, I get the following output (your results will probably be different, but similar):

```
Number of bytes read=100
5B-62-6F-6F-74-20-6C-6F-61-64-65-72-5D-0D-0A-74-69-6D-65-6F-
75-74-3D-33-30-0D-0A-64-65-66-61-75-6C-74-3D-6D-75-6C-74-69-
28-30-29-64-69-73-6B-28-30-29-72-64-69-73-6B-28-30-29-70-61-
72-74-69-74-69-6F-6E-28-31-29-5C-57-49-4E-44-4F-57-53-0D-0A-
5B-6F-70-65-72-61-74-69-6E-67-20-73-79-73-74-65-6D-73-5D-0D
```

As written, this program doesn't use the APM efficiently. It is silly to call a **Begin**Xxx method and then to immediately call an **End**Xxx method, because the calling thread just goes to sleep waiting for the operation to complete. If I want to execute the operation synchronously, I might was well have just made one call to the **Read** method instead; this would be more efficient.

However, if I put some code between the calls to **BeginRead** and **EndRead**, we see some of the APM's value because this other code would execute as the bytes are being read from the file. Here is a substantially revised version of the previous program. This new version reads data from multiple streams simultaneously. In this example, I'm using **FileStream** objects, but this code would work with all kinds of **Stream**-derived objects, so it can simultaneously read bytes from multiple files, sockets, and even serial ports. To support any of these, you'd just have to use my **AsyncStreamRead** class and pass specific arguments to **AsyncStreamRead**'s constructor.

```
private static void ReadMultipleFiles(params String[] pathnames) {
    AsyncStreamRead[] asrs = new AsyncStreamRead[pathnames.Length];

    for (Int32 n = 0; n < pathnames.Length; n++) {
        // Open the file indicating asynchronous I/O
        Stream stream = new FileStream(pathnames[n], FileMode.Open,
            FileAccess.Read, FileShare.Read, 1024,
            FileOptions.Asynchronous);

        // Initiate an asynchronous read operation against the Stream
        asrs[n] = new AsyncStreamRead(stream, 100);
    }

    // All streams have been opened and all read requests have been
    // queued; they are all executing concurrently!

    // Now, let's get and display the results
    for (Int32 n = 0; n < asrs.Length; n++) {
        Byte[] bytesRead = asrs[n].EndRead();

        // Now it is OK to access the byte array and show the result.
        Console.WriteLine("Number of bytes read={0}", bytesRead.Length);
        Console.WriteLine(BitConverter.ToString(bytesRead));
    }
}

private sealed class AsyncStreamRead {
    private Stream       m_stream;
    private IAsyncResult m_ar;
    private Byte[]       m_data;

    public AsyncStreamRead(Stream stream, Int32 numBytes) {
        m_stream = stream;
        m_data = new Byte[numBytes];

        // Initiate an asynchronous read operation against the Stream
        m_ar = stream.BeginRead(m_data, 0, numBytes, null, null);
    }

    public Byte[] EndRead() {
        // Suspend this thread until the asynchronous
        // operation completes and get the result
        Int32 numBytesRead = m_stream.EndRead(m_ar);
```

```
        // No other operations to do, close the stream
        m_stream.Close();

        // Resize the array to save space
        Array.Resize(ref m_data, numBytesRead);

        // Return the bytes
        return m_data;
    }
}
```

While this code now performs all reads simultaneously, which is very efficient, there is still inefficiency within this code. After queuing all of the read requests, the `ReadMultipleFiles` method enters a second loop where it ends up calling `EndRead` for each stream sequentially in the same order that the read requests were issued. This is inefficient because different streams will require different amounts of time to read the data. So it's possible for the data to come in from the second stream prior to the data coming in from the first stream. Ideally, if this happened, we'd like to process the data from the second stream first and then process the data from the first stream when it comes in. The APM does allow you to accomplish this but not by using the wait-until-done technique I showed here.

The APM's Polling Rendezvous Technique

The `IAsyncResult` interface defines a number of read-only properties:

```
public interface IAsyncResult {
    Object     AsyncState             { get; }
    WaitHandle AsyncWaitHandle        { get; }
    Boolean    IsCompleted            { get; }
    Boolean    CompletedSynchronously { get; }
}
```

By far, the most commonly used property is `AsyncState`. The `AsyncWaitHandle` and `IsCompleted` properties are used when you use the polling technique that I will explain in this section. The `CompletedSynchronously` property is sometimes queried by developers who are implementing `BeginXxx` and `EndXxx` methods (I've never seen anyone who needed to call these methods query the `CompletedSynchronously` property).

I don't like the polling rendezvous technique, and I'd discourage you from using it as much as possible because it is inefficient. When you write code to use the polling technique, you are making a thread periodically ask the CLR if the asynchronous request has finished running yet. So you are essentially wasting a thread's time; however, if you'd rather trade some efficiency for easier programming, the polling technique can be convenient to use in some scenarios. Here is some code that demonstrates the polling technique:

```
public static void PollingWithIsCompleted() {
    // Open the file indicating asynchronous I/O
    FileStream fs = new FileStream(@"C:\Boot.ini", FileMode.Open,
        FileAccess.Read, FileShare.Read, 1024,
        FileOptions.Asynchronous);
```

```
   Byte[] data = new Byte[100];

   // Initiate an asynchronous read operation against the FileStream
   IAsyncResult ar = fs.BeginRead(data, 0, data.Length, null, null);

   while (!ar.IsCompleted) {
      Console.WriteLine("Operation not completed; still waiting.");
      Thread.Sleep(10);
   }

   // Get the result. Note: EndRead will NOT suspend this thread
   Int32 bytesRead = fs.EndRead(ar);

   // No other operations to do, close the file
   fs.Close();

   // Now it is OK to access the byte array and show the result.
   Console.WriteLine("Number of bytes read={0}", bytesRead);
   Console.WriteLine(BitConverter.ToString(data, 0, bytesRead));
}
```

After the call to **BeginRead** is a loop that periodically queries **IAsyncResult**'s **IsCompleted** property. This property returns **false** if the asynchronous operation has not yet completed and **true** if it has. If it returns **false**, the loop where I display a message is entered. Then, I call **Thread**'s **Sleep** method in an effort to be good citizen and put the thread to sleep. Without the call to **Sleep**, the thread would just keep looping and CPU usage would go way up even though the thread is doing no useful work. It is possible for the asynchronous operation to complete before the loop queries the **IsCompleted** property for the first time. If this happens, the property will return **true**, and the loop will not be entered at all.

Eventually, the asynchronous operation will complete, the **IsCompleted** property will return **true**, and the loop will terminate. When this happens, I call **EndRead** to get the results. However, this time I know that **EndRead** will return immediately and will not put the calling thread to sleep since I know that the operation is complete.

Here is another example of the polling technique. This example queries **IAsyncResult**'s **AsyncWaitHandle** property:

```
public static void PollingWithAsyncWaitHandle() {
   // Open the file indicating asynchronous I/O
   FileStream fs = new FileStream(@"C:\Boot.ini", FileMode.Open,
      FileAccess.Read, FileShare.Read, 1024,
      FileOptions.Asynchronous);

   Byte[] data = new Byte[100];

   // Initiate an asynchronous read operation against the FileStream
   IAsyncResult ar = fs.BeginRead(data, 0, data.Length, null, null);

   while (!ar.AsyncWaitHandle.WaitOne(10, false)) {
      Console.WriteLine("Operation not completed; still waiting.");
```

```
    }

    // Get the result. Note: EndRead will NOT suspend this thread
    Int32 bytesRead = fs.EndRead(ar);

    // No other operations to do, close the file
    fs.Close();

    // Now it is OK to access the byte array and show the result.
    Console.WriteLine("Number of bytes read={0}", bytesRead);
    Console.WriteLine(BitConverter.ToString(data, 0, bytesRead));
}
```

IAsyncResult's **AsyncWaitHandle** property returns a reference to a **WaitHandle**-derived object, which is usually a **System.Threading.ManualResetEvent**. In Chapter 24, "Thread Synchronization," I describe the **WaitHandle** class and the types derived from it. This code has a loop that is similar to the previous example except that the call to **Thread**'s **Sleep** is not necessary because the 10-millisecond sleep value is passed as an argument to the **WaitOne** method.

The APM's Method Callback Rendezvous Technique

Of all of the APM rendezvous techniques, the method callback technique is by far the best one to use when architecting an application for high performance and scalability. The reason is that this technique never causes a thread to enter a wait state (unlike the wait-until-done technique) and because this technique never wastes CPU time by periodically checking to see if the asynchronous operation has completed (unlike the polling technique).

Here's the basic idea of how the method callback technique works: First, you queue up an asynchronous I/O request, and then your thread continues doing whatever it wants to do. Then, when the I/O request completes, Windows queues a work item into the CLR's thread pool. Eventually, a thread pool thread will dequeue the work item and call some method you have written; this is how you know that the asynchronous I/O operation has completed. Now, inside your callback method, you first call the **End***Xxx* method to obtain the result of the asynchronous operation, and then the method is free to continue processing the result. When the method returns, the thread pool thread goes back into the pool ready to service another queued work item (or it waits until one shows up).

Now that you understand the basic idea, let's look at how you accomplish it. Here again is the prototype for **FileStream**'s **BeginRead** method:

```
IAsyncResult BeginRead(Byte[] array, Int32 offset, Int32 numBytes,
    AsyncCallback userCallback, Object stateObject)
```

Like **BeginRead**, every **Begin***Xxx* method's last two parameters are the same: a **System .AsyncCallback** and an **Object**. **AsyncCallback** is a delegate type defined as follows:

```
delegate void AsyncCallback(IAsyncResult ar);
```

This delegate indicates the signature required by the callback method that you must implement. For the **Begin*Xxx*** method's **stateObject** argument, you can pass anything you want. This argument simply gives you a way to pass some data from the method that queues the operation to the callback method that will be processing the operation's completion. As you can see, your callback method will receive a reference to an **IAsyncResult** object, and your callback method can obtain the reference to the state object by querying **IAsyncResult**'s **AsyncState** property. Here is some code that demonstrates the method callback rendezvous technique:

```
using System;
using System.IO;
using System.Threading;

public static class Program {
    // The array is static so that it can be accessed by Main and ReadIsDone
    private static Byte[] s_data = new Byte[100];

    public static void Main() {
        // Show the ID of the thread executing Main
        Console.WriteLine("Main thread ID={0}",
            Thread.CurrentThread.ManagedThreadId);

        // Open the file indicating asynchronous I/O
        FileStream fs = new FileStream(@"C:\Boot.ini", FileMode.Open,
            FileAccess.Read, FileShare.Read, 1024,
            FileOptions.Asynchronous);

        // Initiate an asynchronous read operation against the FileStream
        // Pass the FileStream (fs) to the callback method (ReadIsDone)
        fs.BeginRead(s_data, 0, s_data.Length, ReadIsDone, fs);

        // Executing some other code here would be useful...

        // For this demo, I'll just suspend the primary thread
        Console.ReadLine();
    }

    private static void ReadIsDone(IAsyncResult ar) {
        // Show the ID of the thread executing ReadIsDone
        Console.WriteLine("ReadIsDone thread ID={0}",
            Thread.CurrentThread.ManagedThreadId);

        // Extract the FileStream (state) out of the IAsyncResult object
        FileStream fs = (FileStream) ar.AsyncState;

        // Get the result
        Int32 bytesRead = fs.EndRead(ar);

        // No other operations to do, close the file
        fs.Close();

        // Now it is OK to access the byte array and show the result.
        Console.WriteLine("Number of bytes read={0}", bytesRead);
        Console.WriteLine(BitConverter.ToString(s_data, 0, bytesRead));
    }
}
```

When I compile and run this program on my machine, I get the following output (your results will be different, but similar):

```
Main thread ID=1
ReadIsDone thread ID=4
Number of bytes read=100
5B-62-6F-6F-74-20-6C-6F-61-64-65-72-5D-0D-0A-74-69-6D-65-6F-
75-74-3D-33-30-0D-0A-64-65-66-61-75-6C-74-3D-6D-75-6C-74-69-
28-30-29-64-69-73-6B-28-30-29-72-64-69-73-6B-28-30-29-70-61-
72-74-69-74-69-6F-6E-28-31-29-5C-57-49-4E-44-4F-57-53-0D-0A-
5B-6F-70-65-72-61-74-69-6E-67-20-73-79-73-74-65-6D-73-5D-0D
```

First, notice that the **Main** method was executed by the primary thread with an ID of 1, while **ReadIsDone** was executed by a thread pool thread with an ID of 4. This proves that two different threads were involved in making this program work. Second, notice that the **IAsyncResult** object that is returned from **BeginRead** is not saved in a variable in **Main**. This is not required because the CLR will pass the **IAsyncResult** object to the callback method for us. Third, I pass the name of the callback method as the fourth argument to **BeginRead**. Fourth, notice that I'm passing **fs** as the last argument to **BeginRead**. This is how I get the **FileStream** into the callback method. The callback method obtains a reference to the **FileStream** by querying the passed **IAsyncResult** object's **AsyncState** property.

I'm pretty happy with the code above except for one thing: I made the **Byte[]** (named **s_data**) a static field so that it could be accessed from both the **Main** and **ReadIsDone** methods. This works fine in this example, but it is not an architecture that I would usually implement because it doesn't allow for future extensibility. Someday, I might want to initiate multiple I/O requests, and it would just be better to dynamically create a **Byte[]** for each request. There are two ways to improve this architecture:

- I could define another class that contains a **Byte[]** field and a **FileStream** field, create an instance of this class, initialize the fields, and pass the reference as **BeginRead**'s last argument. Now the callback method has access to both pieces of data and can use them both inside the method.

- I could use C#'s anonymous methods feature (discussed in Chapter 15, "Delegates") and let the C# compiler write this code for me automatically.

Here is a revised version of the code modified to take advantage of C#'s anonymous method feature:

```
public static void Main() {
    // Show the ID of the thread executing Main
    Console.WriteLine("Main thread ID={0}",
        Thread.CurrentThread.ManagedThreadId);

    // Open the file indicating asynchronous I/O
    FileStream fs = new FileStream(@"C:\Boot.ini", FileMode.Open,
        FileAccess.Read, FileShare.Read, 1024,
        FileOptions.Asynchronous);
```

```
    Byte[] data = new Byte[100];

    // Initiate an asynchronous read operation against the FileStream
    // Pass the FileStream (fs) to the callback method (ReadIsDone)
    fs.BeginRead(data, 0, data.Length,
        delegate(IAsyncResult ar)
        {
            // Show the ID of the thread executing ReadIsDone
            Console.WriteLine("ReadIsDone thread ID={0}",
                Thread.CurrentThread.ManagedThreadId);

            // Get the result
            Int32 bytesRead = fs.EndRead(ar);

            // No other operations to do, close the file
            fs.Close();

            // Now it is OK to access the byte array and show the result.
            Console.WriteLine("Number of bytes read={0}", bytesRead);
            Console.WriteLine(BitConverter.ToString(data, 0, bytesRead));

        }, null);

    // Executing some other code here would be useful...

    // For this demo, I'll just suspend the primary thread
    Console.ReadLine();
}
```

In this version of the code, I just pass **null** as the last argument to **BeginRead**; I can do this because the anonymous method has access to all of the local variables (including **data** and **fs**) defined inside **Main**. I'll leave it to you to decide whether you stylistically prefer this anonymous method version of the code or whether you'd prefer to explicitly implement the helper class and use the local variables as fields of this class.

Note   Many of the examples shown in this chapter initiate an asynchronous operation from inside the application's **Main** method. And in many of the examples, I've had to call **Console**'s **ReadLine** method in order to stop **Main** from returning, which would kill the entire process, the thread pool, and all outstanding asynchronous operations.

In many applications, you will actually initiate an asynchronous operation from a method being executed by a thread pool thread. Then, the method should return allowing the thread to return back to the pool. This thread can then be used to call a method when any asynchronous operation completes; it may be used to process the completion of the asynchronous operation that just got queued. And frequently, when a method is called to handle the completion of one asynchronous operation, the method initiates another asynchronous operation.

All of this is awesome! And this is the secret to how your application can use so few threads to accomplish so much work in so little time using so little resources.

In the "The APM's Wait-Until-Done Rendezvous Technique," section earlier in this chapter, I showed a method called **ReadMultipleFiles** that reads data from multiple streams. This method was not as efficient as it could be because it processed the data in the same order it was queued, whereas it would be more efficient to process the data as it arrived. I have revised that earlier version of the code to use the callback method technique. This new version fixes that inefficiency and is the best way to use the APM to get high performance and scalability:

```
private static void ReadMultipleFiles(params String[] pathnames) {
    for (Int32 n = 0; n < pathnames.Length; n++) {
        // Open the file indicating asynchronous I/O
        Stream stream = new FileStream(pathnames[n], FileMode.Open,
            FileAccess.Read, FileShare.Read, 1024,
            FileOptions.Asynchronous);

        // Initiate an asynchronous read operation against the Stream
        new AsyncStreamRead(stream, 100,
            delegate(Byte[] data)
            {
                // Process the data.
                Console.WriteLine("Number of bytes read={0}", data.Length);
                Console.WriteLine(BitConverter.ToString(data));
            });
    }

    // All streams have been opened and all read requests have been
    // queued; they are all executing concurrently and they will be
    // processed as they complete!

    // The primary thread could do other stuff here if it wants to...

    // For this demo, I'll just suspend the primary thread
    Console.WriteLine("Hit <Enter> to end this program...");
    Console.ReadLine();
}

private delegate void StreamBytesRead(Byte[] streamData);

private sealed class AsyncStreamRead {
    private Stream m_stream;
    private Byte[] m_data;
    StreamBytesRead m_callback;

    public AsyncStreamRead(Stream stream, Int32 numBytes,
        StreamBytesRead callback) {
        m_stream = stream;
        m_data = new Byte[numBytes];
        m_callback = callback;

        // Initiate an asynchronous read operation against the Stream
        stream.BeginRead(m_data, 0, numBytes, ReadIsDone, null);
    }
```

```
// Called when IO operation completes
private void ReadIsDone(IAsyncResult ar) {
   Int32 numBytesRead = m_stream.EndRead(ar);

   // No other operations to do, close the stream
   m_stream.Close();

   // Resize the array to save space
   Array.Resize(ref m_data, numBytesRead);

   // Call the application's callback method
   m_callback(m_data);
   }
}
```

Using the APM to Perform an Asynchronous Compute-Bound Operation

So far, all of the discussion about the APM has been directed toward using it to perform asynchronous I/O operations. And the great thing about this model is that no threads are running or waiting for the I/O to complete—the model is very efficient. What's even better is that the APM can also be used for compute-bound operations. However, to perform a compute-bound operation means that a thread must be running, and so compute-bound operations are not as efficient. But, what can you do? Computers can't just do I/O all day; they need to process the data too.

You can call any method by using the APM, but first, you need to define a delegate that has the same signature as the method you want to call. For example, let's say you want to call a method that sums up the numbers from 1 to **n**. This computationally intensive task (that performs no I/O) could take a long time to execute if **n** is a large value.[3] Here is the **Sum** method:

```
private static UInt64 Sum(UInt64 n) {
   UInt64 sum = 0;
   for (UInt64 i = 1; i <= n; i++) {
      checked {
         // I use checked code so that an OverflowException gets
         // thrown if the sum doesn't fit in a UInt64.
         sum += i;
      }
   }
   return sum;
}
```

[3.] Yes, I know that a sum can be calculated quickly for any value of **n** using this formula: $n(n+1)/2$. For this example, let's just forget that this formula exists and do it the old fashioned way by manually adding up the numbers so that it takes a long time.

If n is large, Sum could take a long time to execute. To keep the user-interface of my application responsive or to take advantage of other CPUs in the computer, I'd like to execute this method asynchronously. To do this, I first define a delegate that has the same signature as the method I want to call asynchronously (Sum):

```
internal delegate UInt64 SumDelegate(UInt64 n);
```

You'll recall from the delegate discussion in Chapter 15 that the C# compiler compiles this line of code into a class definition that logically looks like this:

```
internal sealed class SumDelegate : MulticastDelegate {
    public SumDelegate(Object object, IntPtr method);
    public UInt64 Invoke(UInt64 n);
    public IAsyncResult BeginInvoke(UInt64 n,
        AsyncCallback callback, Object object);
    public UInt64 EndInvoke(IAsyncResult result);
}
```

When you define a delegate in C# source code, the compiler always produces a class that has BeginInvoke and EndInvoke methods. The BeginInvoke method has the same parameters as the delegate definition with two additional parameters at the end: AsyncCallback and Object. All BeginInvoke methods return an IAsyncResult. The EndInvoke method has one parameter, an IAsyncResult, and the EndInvoke method returns whatever data type the delegate's signature returns.

Now that you understand all of this, using a delegate to execute a compute-bound operation is trivial because it follows the APM pattern we've been talking about. In fact, you can use the wait-until-done, the polling, or the method callback rendezvous technique when calling a method asynchronously via a delegate. Here is some code that shows how to call Sum asynchronously using the callback method rendezvous technique:

```
public static void Main() {
    // Initialize a delegate variable to refer
    // to the method we want to call asynchronously
    SumDelegate sumDelegate = Sum;

    // Call the method using a thread pool thread
    sumDelegate.BeginInvoke(1000000000, SumIsDone, sumDelegate);

    // Executing some other code here would be useful...

    // For this demo, I'll just suspend the primary thread
    Console.ReadLine();
}
```

The sumDelegate variable is first initialized to refer to the method you want to call asynchronously. Then BeginInvoke is called to initiate the asynchronous calling of the method. Internally, the CLR constructs an IAsyncResult object to identify the asynchronous operation. As you know, I/O operations are queued to a Windows device driver; however, a delegate's

BeginInvoke method queues compute-bound operations to the CLR's thread pool by internally calling **ThreadPool**'s **QueueUserWorkItem**. Finally, **BeginInvoke** returns the **IAsyncResult** object back to its caller. The caller can now use this object as it would when performing an asynchronous I/O operation.

Since **BeginInvoke** queued the operation to the CLR's thread pool, a thread pool thread will wake, dequeue the work item, and call the compute-bound method (**Sum** in this example). Normally, when a thread pool thread returns from executing a method, the thread returns back to the pool. However, in my example, **BeginInvoke** was called passing in the name of a method (**SumIsDone**) for the second-to-last parameter. Because of this, when **Sum** returns, the thread pool thread does not return back to the pool; instead, it now calls **SumIsDone**. In other words, the callback is called when the compute-bound operation has completed just as it would be called when an I/O-bound operation has completed. Here is what my **SumIsDone** method looks like:

```
private static void SumIsDone(IAsyncResult ar) {
    // Extract the SumDelegate (state) from the IAsyncResult object
    SumDelegate sumDelegate = (SumDelegate) ar.AsyncState;

    // Get the result
    UInt64 sum = sumDelegate.EndInvoke(ar);

    // Show the result
    Console.WriteLine("Sum={0}", sum);
}
```

The APM and Exceptions

Whenever you call a **Begin*Xxx*** method, it could, of course, throw an exception. If this happens, you can assume that the asynchronous operation has not been queued.

When a Windows device driver is processing an asynchronous I/O request, it is possible for something to go wrong, and Windows will need to inform your application of this. For example, while waiting for bytes to come in over the network, Windows will wait only as long as you have told it (by setting some time-out value). If the data does not come in time, Windows will want to tell you that the asynchronous operation completed with an error. To accomplish this, Windows posts a notification to the CLR's thread pool. Your code will rendezvous with the result of the operation by calling an **End*Xxx*** method. Normally, an **End*Xxx*** method returns the result of the operation back to your code, but if the operation failed, the **End*Xxx*** method will throw an exception. The exact exception object thrown depends on what caused the operation to fail.

Similarly, if you use the APM to perform an asynchronous compute-bound operation, the method (executed by using a thread pool thread) could execute some code that results in a thrown exception. If this exception is unhandled, the CLR catches it automatically. If you are using the method callback rendezvous technique, the thread pool thread calls the callback method. Inside the callback method, when you call **EndInvoke**, the previously caught exception is rethrown. If this exception is also unhandled, the CLR terminates the process (unless the host imposes its own policy). But you can catch and handle the exception any way you'd like and allow your application to gracefully recover.

Below is a modified version of the **SumIsDone** method (shown in the previous section) that catches the potential **OverflowException** and gracefully recovers:

```
private static void SumIsDone(IAsyncResult ar) {
    // Extract the SumDelegate (state) from the IAsyncResult object
    SumDelegate sumDelegate = (SumDelegate)ar.AsyncState;

    try {
        // Get the result; this could throw an OverflowException
        UInt64 sum = sumDelegate.EndInvoke(ar);

        // Show the result
        Console.WriteLine("Sum={0}", sum);
    }
    catch (OverflowException) {
        // EndInvoke threw an OverflowException; recover gracefully
        Console.WriteLine("Sum can't be shown: number is too big.");
    }
}
```

Important Notes about the APM

All in all, I am a huge fan of the APM, but I must admit that it does have some shortcomings, and it would be nice if Microsoft solved some of these or at least provided some guidance for developers. Let's discuss these issues:

You must call **End*Xxx*** or you will leak resources. Some developers have written code to call **Begin*Xxx*** to write some data to a device, and there is no processing that needs to be done after the data has been written, so they don't care about calling **End*Xxx***. However, calling **End*Xxx*** is required for two reasons. First, the CLR allocates some internal resources when you initiate an asynchronous operation. When the operation completes, the CLR will hold onto these resources until **End*Xxx*** is called. If **End*Xxx*** is never called, these resources remain allocated and will be reclaimed only when the process terminates. Second, when you initiate an asynchronous operation, you don't actually know if the operation eventually succeeded or failed. The only way you can discover this is by calling **End*Xxx*** and checking the return value or seeing if it throws an exception.

You should not call **End*Xxx*** more than once for any given asynchronous operation. When you call **End*Xxx***, it could access some internal resources and then release them. If you call **End*Xxx*** again, the resources will have been released already, and the results will be unpredictable. In reality, calling **End*Xxx*** multiple times for a single operation may or may not work; it depends on how the class that implements the **IAsyncResult** interface has been written. Since Microsoft never told developers how this should behave, different developers implemented in different ways. The only thing you can count on is that calling **End*Xxx*** just once will work.

Whatever object you use when calling **Begin*Xxx*** should be the same object that you use to call **End*Xxx*.** For example, don't construct a delegate and call its **BeginInvoke** method and then construct another delegate (of the same type referring to the same object/method) and use it to call its **EndInvoke** method. While this seems as if it should work (since both delegate objects are identical in every way), it doesn't work because the **IAsyncResult** object internally keeps a reference to the original object used when calling **BeginInvoke**, and if they don't match, **EndInvoke** throws an **InvalidOperationException** with a string message of "The IAsyncResult object provided does not match this delegate." Again, using one object to call **BeginInvoke** and another object to call **EndInvoke** may work for some object types depending on how they were implemented.

The parameters of **Begin*Xxx*** and **End*Xxx*** methods will deviate slightly from the patterns I've described in this chapter if the non-asynchronous version of the method uses any **out**/**ref** parameters or if it has a parameter marked with the **params** keyword. Since this is very rare, I won't show an example, but you should be aware of it. You'll easily figure out how to call the methods correctly when you need to.

There is currently no way to cancel an outstanding asynchronous operation. This is a feature that many developers would like, but it is actually quite hard to implement. After all, if you request 1000 bytes from a server and then you decide you don't want those bytes anymore, there really is no way to tell the server to forget about your request. The way to deal with this is just to let the bytes come back to you and then throw them away. In addition, there is a race condition here: your request to cancel the request could come just as the last byte is being read in. Now what should your application do? You'd need to handle this potential race condition occurring in your own code and decide whether to throw the data away or act on it. Some **Begin*Xxx*** methods might return an object that implements the **IAsyncResult** interface as well as offer some kind of cancel method. In this case, you could cancel the operation. You'd have to check the documentation for the **Begin*Xxx*** method or the class it returns to see whether cancellation is supported.

Whenever you call a **Begin*Xxx*** method, it constructs an instance of a type that implements the **IAsyncResult** interface. This means that an object is created for every asynchronous operation that you want to perform. This adds more overhead and creates more objects on the heap, which causes more garbage collections to occur. The result: poorer application performance. So if you know for a fact that your I/O operations are going to execute extremely quickly, it may make more sense to perform them synchronously. Many developers (including myself) wish that the APM returned value types instead or had some other lightweight way of identifying a queued asynchronous operation; maybe Microsoft will improve the CLR someday by supporting this.

The Win32 API offers many functions that execute I/O operations. Unfortunately, a good percentage of these methods do not let you perform the I/O asynchronously. For example, the Win32 **CreateFile** method (called by **FileStream**'s constructor) always executes synchronously. If you're trying to create/open a file on a network server, it could take several seconds before `CreateFile` returns—the calling thread is idle all the while. An application that cares about performance and scalability would ideally call a Win32 function that lets you create/ open a file asynchronously so that your thread is not sitting and waiting for the server to reply. Unfortunately, Win32 has no `CreateFile`-like function to let you do this, and therefore the FCL cannot offer an efficient way to open a file asynchronously.

You can always call any method asynchronously via a delegate's `BeginInvoke` method, but when you do this, you are using a thread, so you are losing some efficiency. And actually, you can't use a delegate to call a constructor. So the only way to new up a `FileStream` object asynchronously is to call some other method asynchronously and have this other method new up the `FileStream` object. Windows doesn't offer functions to asynchronously access the registry, access the event log, get a directory's files/subdirectories, or change a file's/ directory's attributes, to name just a few.

In Windows, a window is always created by a thread, and this thread must be used to process all actions for the window. One reason for this is because 16-bit Windows versions were single-threaded operating systems, and in order to maintain backward compatibility, 32-bit and 64-bit versions of Windows kept the single-threaded architecture for handling window operations such as `WM_MOVE`, `WM_SIZE`, `WM_PAINT`, `WM_CLOSE`, etc. It's common for a Windows Forms application to use the asynchronous techniques explained in this chapter. However, since Windows Forms is built on top of Windows, a thread pool thread is not allowed to directly manipulate a window; or more specifically, a class derived from `System.Windows.Forms.Control`.

Fortunately, the `System.Windows.Forms.Control` class offers three methods—`Invoke`, `BeginInvoke`, and `EndInvoke`—that you can call from any thread (including a thread pool thread) to marshal an operation from the calling thread to the thread that created the window. Internally, `Control`'s `Invoke` method calls the Win32 `SendMessage` method to have the window's thread execute a task synchronously. `Control`'s `BeginInvoke` method internally calls the Win32 `PostMessage` method to have the window's thread execute a task asynchronously. If the calling thread wants to know when the window's thread has completed executing the task, it can call `Control`'s `EndInvoke` method. If you don't care, this is one of the rare cases when you do not have to call an `EndInvoke` method.

Execution Contexts

Every thread has an *execution context* associated with it. The execution context includes things such as:

- Security settings (compressed permission stack of `IPermission` objects, `Thread`'s `Principal` property, and Windows thread token)

- Localization settings (`Thread`'s `CurrentCulture` and `CurrentUICulture` properties and Windows thread locale)

- Transaction settings (`System.Transactions.Transaction`'s static `Current` property)

When a thread executes code, some operations are affected by the values of the thread's execution context settings. Ideally, whenever a thread uses another (helper) thread to perform some tasks, the first thread's execution context should *flow* (be copied) to the helper thread. This ensures that any operations performed by helper thread(s) are executing with the same security, localization, and transaction settings as the first thread.

By default, the CLR automatically causes the first thread's execution context to flow to any helper threads. This provides for a better and more secure system, but it does come at a performance cost. The reason is because there is a lot of information in an execution context, and accumulating all of this information and then copying it for the helper threads takes a fair amount of time. In particular, it can be costly for the CLR to walk up the first thread's stack to compress all of the security permission objects.

In the **System.Threading** namespace, there is an **ExecutionContext** class that allows you to control how a thread's execution context flows from one thread to another. Using this class to suppress the flowing of an execution context is a dangerous thing to do because you are effectively elevating the privileges of the helper thread. For this reason, many of the **ExecutionContext** class's methods require that the calling assembly be granted **SecurityPermission** with the **SecurityPermissionFlag.Infrastructure** flag turned on. Furthermore, when an execution context does not flow to a helper thread, the helper thread will execute using whatever execution context it had last. So if you suppress the flowing of an execution context, the thread really shouldn't execute any code that relies on execution context state (such as security, culture, or transaction state).

In addition to suppressing the flow of a thread's execution context, the **ExecutionContext** class allows you to capture a thread's execution context at an arbitrary execution point. You can later call a method at another execution point by using the previously captured execution context. Here is some code that demonstrates how to control how the CLR flows an execution context. The code shows how to modify a thread's context, how to suppress the flowing of a thread's execution context to another thread (improving performance), how to capture a thread's execution context, and how to use the captured context to call another method. (This program requires a file named "ReadMe.txt" to exist in the C:\ directory in order to run successfully).

```
using System;
using System.IO;
using System.Security;
using System.Threading;
using System.Security.Permissions;

public static class Program {
    public static void Main() {
        // Show that the method works just fine
        AttemptAccess("Default context");
```

```
    // Change the thread's execution context
    // to disallow all file access
    new FileIOPermission(PermissionState.Unrestricted).Deny();

    // Show that the method no longer works due
    // to a change in the execution context
    AttemptAccess("No file permissions");

    ECFlowing();
    ECFlowingSuppressed();

    // Capture this thread's current execution context
    ExecutionContext ec = ExecutionContext.Capture();

    // Change the thread's execution context
    // to allow file access
    SecurityPermission.RevertDeny();

    // Show that the method works just fine
    AttemptAccess("Default context again");

    ECCaptureAndRun(ec);
}

private static void ECFlowing() {
    // Initialize a delegate variable to refer
    // to the method we want to call asynchronously
    WaitCallback wc = AttemptAccess;

    // Use a thread pool thread to attempt access
    // EndInvoke returns when thread pool thread returns to pool
    wc.EndInvoke(wc.BeginInvoke("ECFlowing", null, null));
}

private static void ECFlowingSuppressed() {
    // Initialize a delegate variable to refer
    // to the method we want to call asynchronously
    WaitCallback wc = AttemptAccess;

    // Temporarily tell the CLR not to flow this
    // thread's execution context to helper threads
    using (AsyncFlowControl afc = ExecutionContext.SuppressFlow()) {
        wc.EndInvoke(wc.BeginInvoke("ECFlowingSuppressed", null, null));
    }
}

private static void ECCaptureAndRun(ExecutionContext ec) {
    // Call AttemptAccess by using the
    // previously captured execution context
    ExecutionContext.Run(ec, AttemptAccess,
        "ECCaptureAndRun with Run");
}

private static void AttemptAccess(Object test) {
    // Assume this method fails
    Boolean success = false;
    try {
```

```
        // Try to get the file's attributes
        File.GetAttributes(@"C:\ReadMe.txt");

        // If we got the attributes, method succeeded
        success = true;
    }
    catch (SecurityException) {
        // Method failed due to insufficient security
        // on thread's execution context
    }

    // Show whether the attempted access succeeded or failed
    Console.WriteLine("{0}: {1}", test, success);
    }
}
```

When I build and run this program, I get the following output:

```
Default context: True
No file permissions: False
ECFlowing: False
ECFlowingSuppressed: True
Default context again: True
ECCaptureAndRun with Run: False
```

Chapter 24
Thread Synchronization

As explained in Chapter 23, "Performing Asynchronous Operations," applications will achieve the highest performance when the application's threads are not waiting for operations to complete. So it is best to implement methods that operate on their own data and avoid writing methods that access any kind of shared data. However, it is rare for a thread to execute entirely on its own without accessing any kind of shared data.

All threads in the system must have access to system resources such as heaps, serial ports, files, windows, and countless others. If one thread requests exclusive access to a resource, other threads that need that resource cannot get their work done. On the flip side, you can't just let any thread touch any resource at any time. Imagine a thread writing to a memory block while another thread reads from the same memory block. This would be analogous to reading a book while someone is changing the text on the page. The thoughts on the page are all jumbled, and nothing useful comes of it.

To prevent a shared resource from being corrupted by multiple threads, programmers must use thread synchronization constructs in their code. Microsoft Windows and the common language runtime (CLR) offer many thread synchronization constructs, each with its pros and cons. These constructs are the focus of this chapter. In this chapter, I will not be explaining how these thread synchronization constructs are implemented internally because most programmers do not care. However, if you are interested in understanding how these constructs are implemented, I'd like to refer you to my MSDN Concurrent Affairs columns (for example, *http://msdn.microsoft.com/msdnmag/issues/05/10/ConcurrentAffairs/*). Also, my Power Threading Library (available for download from *http://Wintellect.com*) includes many thread synchronization constructs of my own devising. The source code for these constructs is included in the library.

Many of the CLR's thread synchronization constructs are really just object-oriented class wrappers around Win32 thread synchronization constructs. After all, CLR threads are Windows threads; which means that Windows schedules and controls the synchronization of threads. Windows thread-synchronization constructs have been around since 1992, and a ton of material has been written about them.[1] Therefore, I give them only cursory treatment in this chapter.

> **Note**   If you are building a reusable class library, you should make sure that all of the types' static methods are thread safe to ensure that if multiple threads call a type's static methods concurrently, there is no way for the type's static state to get corrupted. To accomplish this, you will use some of the thread synchronization constructs discussed in this chapter. The reason why you must ensure that static methods are thread safe is because it's impossible for users of a class to write the proper code to accomplish this.
>
> For example, imagine that some code in a library assembly wants to call Assembly's static Load method, and some code in an executable assembly also wants to call Assembly's Load method. The code in these two assemblies would have to agree on a thread synchronization construct up front, and they'd both have to be able to discover it as well. In fact, all assemblies in the AppDomain would have to agree to use the same construct and have a way to discover it. Since the CLR provides no built-in mechanism to help here, the solution is for the Assembly type to perform its own thread synchronization (which it can easily discover since it must create it itself).
>
> On the other hand, a reusable class library does not have to make sure that all of the types' instance methods are thread safe. The reason is that adding thread safety to methods makes them slower, and most objects are used by a single thread; adding thread safety would hurt performance too much. In addition, when code creates an object, no other code has access to the object unless a reference to the object is somehow passed around to the other code. Any code that hands out a reference to an object could also hand out a thread synchronization construct as well so that code executed by other threads could access the object in a thread-safe way.
>
> Certainly, Microsoft follows these rules. Microsoft guarantees all Framework Class Library types' static methods to be thread safe and makes no guarantees about a type's instance methods being thread safe.

Memory Consistency, Volatile Memory Access, and Volatile Fields

To improve the performance of repeatedly accessing memory, today's CPUs have on-chip cache memory. Accessing this memory is extremely fast, especially when compared to the speed of the CPU accessing motherboard memory. The first time that a thread reads some value in memory, the CPU fetches the desired value from the motherboard's memory and stores it in the CPU's on-chip cache. In fact, to improve performance more, the CPU actually fetches several surrounding bytes (called a *cache line*) at one time because applications typically read bytes that are near each other in memory. When one of the surrounding bytes is

---

[1]   In fact, my own book, *Programming Applications for Microsoft Windows* (Microsoft Press, 2000), has several chapters devoted this subject.

read, it may already be in the cache, and if so, motherboard memory will not be accessed, and performance will be high. When a thread writes to memory, the CPU actually modifies the byte in its cache and does not write the modified value to motherboard memory; again, this improves performance. Eventually, the CPU does flush any values in its cache out to memory, but this happens at some unpredictable time in the future.

When an application runs on a single-CPU machine (which can have a hyper-threaded CPU), the programmer of that application doesn't have to be aware of any of this because the program can't experience any impact by it. But the application does get the benefit of improved performance. If a computer has a single hyper-threaded CPU, there is also no visible impact because the two logical CPUs share a single CPU cache. However, when your application runs on a multi-CPU machine or a machine with dual-core CPUs, the impact of the CPU cache can be quite apparent, and developers do have to take it into account when writing their code. Of course, even on these processors, the impact is apparent only if multiple threads are trying to access the same bytes in memory. If they are accessing different bytes, there is no apparent impact.

Take the following program as an example:

```
internal sealed class CacheCoherencyProblem {
    private Byte  m_initialized = 0;
    private Int32 m_value = 0;

    // This method is executed by one thread
    public void Thread1() {
        m_value = 5;
        m_initialized = 1;
    }

    // This method is executed by another thread
    public void Thread2() {
        if (m_initialized == 1) {
            // This may execute and display 0
            Console.WriteLine(m_value);
        }
    }
}
```

Now, let's say that an instance of this class is created on a machine with multiple CPUs; CPU1 is executing the **Thread1** method while CPU2 is executing the **Thread2** method. Imagine that execution goes as follows:

- CPU2's thread reads a byte from memory, and this byte is immediately before the object's **m_value** field's bytes. In this case, a whole cache line is read in, and so the bytes for **m_value** are in CPU2's cache. From a programmer's perspective, it appears that the CPU has read the value of this field before your code actually requested that the field be read.

- CPU1's thread executes **Thread1**, which changes **m_value** to **5**, but this change could happen in CPU1's cache; the change will eventually be written out to motherboard memory. From a programmer's perspective, it appears that the CPU is writing the value of this field out to memory long after your code actually requested that the field be written.

- CPU1's thread continues executing **Thread1** and changes **m_initialized** to **1**. This change also occurs in CPU1's cache, but for whatever reason, the bytes for the **m_initialized** field are in a different cache line, and therefore, these bytes could be flushed from the CPU1's cache to the motherboard memory.

- CPU2's thread starts executing the **Thread2** method, which first queries the value of the object's **m_initialized** field. Since the bytes for this value are not in CPU2's cache, it reads the bytes from motherboard memory. The **m_initialized** field will contain **1**, so the **if** statement will be entered.

- CPU2's thread continues executing **Thread2**, which then reads the value of the object's **m_value** field. Since the bytes for this field are already in CPU2's cache, it reads the bytes out of the cache (not out of motherboard memory), so the **m_value** field has the value of **0**!

Hopefully, you see the problem here. To summarize: CPU caches improve performance, but caches can make multiple threads think that a field has different values at the same time. This cache coherency problem is significant, and there are various things that you can do in your application code to force cache coherency, but they all hurt performance significantly. The best way to avoid cache coherency problems is to avoid writing code that could access shared data from multiple threads. For example, try to implement methods that access only parameters and local variables, since other threads cannot possibly access these variables. Of course, if the variable is of a reference type, the variable itself is thread safe, but the object it refers to is not because multiple threads can each have a reference to the same object. Furthermore, if multiple threads access shared data in a read-only fashion, there is no problem. The cache coherency problem exists only for shared data that some thread might write to.

To make matters worse, when the C# or JIT compiler compiles your code, it can reorder the instructions so that they execute in a different order than written. In fact, the CPU itself can execute CPU instructions out of order. Even though the instructions can execute out of *program order*, the C# compiler, JIT Compiler, and CPU ensure that your code executes as you would expect from the perspective of a single thread. However, the executing of instructions out of program order can be noticed when multiple threads are accessing shared memory (as shown in the earlier example).

Now you may be thinking that you've never actually seen any program that you've written experience a problem with unordered program execution, and this may very well be true. It is certainly true if you've done all of your testing on a single-CPU or even a hyperthreaded machine today. So it is more likely that you'd notice the problem on a multi-CPU or dual-core machine. Also, different CPUs treat cache coherency differently. For example, x86 CPUs work very hard at keeping the CPU caches coherent. Since the x64 architecture is backward compatible with the x86 architecture, x64 CPUs also maintain cache coherency. So if the `CacheCoherencyProblem` class's methods execute on a machine with x86 or x64 CPUs, you'll never notice the problem. That is, `Thread2` will either not display anything, or it will display a **5**.

But newer CPU architectures (such as the IA64) are designed to really exploit the fact that each CPU has its own cache, and to improve performance, these chips try to avoid cache coherency as much as possible. The IA64 offers the normal CPU instructions to read a value from memory into a register and to write a register's value out to memory. But the IA64 also offers a modified version of the read instruction, which reads bytes from memory and then invalidates the CPU's cache, forcing future reads to come from main memory. This is called a *volatile read* or *read with acquire semantics*. The IA64 also offers a modified version of the write instruction, which writes bytes in a register out to memory and flushes the CPU's cache to main memory so that other threads reading from main memory will see the freshest data. This is called a *volatile write* or *write with release semantics*. In addition, the IA64 offers a *memory fence* instruction, which flushes the CPU's cache to main memory and then invalidates the cache.

Volatile Reads and Writes

OK, so now you know that CPU caches affect your application's behavior. You also know that some CPUs offer special instructions to allow a programmer to have some control over cache coherency. The next step is to learn how the CLR exposes these special instructions so that you can take advantage of them in your code. Obviously, one of the big goals of the CLR is to provide a virtual machine for which programmers don't write code specific to any particular kind of CPU architecture. The most common way to abstract a CPU-specific implementation is to provide a method. The `System.Threading.Thread` class offers several static methods that look like this:

```
static Object  VolatileRead(ref Object address);
static Byte    VolatileRead(ref Byte address);
static SByte   VolatileRead(ref SBbyte address);
static Int16   VolatileRead(ref Int16 address);
static UInt16  VolatileRead(ref UInt16 address);
static Int32   VolatileRead(ref Int32 address);
static UInt32  VolatileRead(ref UInt32 address);
static Int64   VolatileRead(ref Int64 address);
static UInt64  VolatileRead(ref UInt64 address);
static IntPtr  VolatileRead(ref IntPtr address);
static UIntPtr VolatileRead(ref UIntPtr address);
static Single  VolatileRead(ref Single address);
static Double  VolatileRead(ref Double address);

static void VolatileWrite(ref Object address, Object value);
static void VolatileWrite(ref Byte address, Byte value);
static void VolatileWrite(ref SByte address, SByte value);
static void VolatileWrite(ref Int16 address, Int16 value);
static void VolatileWrite(ref UInt16 address, UInt16 value);
static void VolatileWrite(ref Int32 address, Int32 value);
static void VolatileWrite(ref UInt32 address, UInt32 value);
```

```
static void VolatileWrite(ref Int64 address, Int64 value);
static void VolatileWrite(ref UInt64 address, UInt64 value);
static void VolatileWrite(ref IntPtr address, IntPtr value);
static void VolatileWrite(ref UIntPtr address, UIntPtr value);
static void VolatileWrite(ref Single address, float value);
static void VolatileWrite(ref Double address, Double value);

static void MemoryBarrier();
```

All of the **VolatileRead** methods perform a read with acquire semantics; they read the value referred to by the **address** argument and then invalidate the CPU's cache. All of the **Volatile-Write** methods perform a write with release semantics; they flush the CPU's cache to main memory and then they modify the value referred to by the **address** argument with the value in the **value** argument. The **MemoryBarrier** method performs a memory fence; it flushes the CPU's cache to main memory and then invalidates the CPUs cache.

So now we can modify the code in the **CacheCoherencyProblem** class to produce the **VolatileMethod** class:

```
internal sealed class VolatileMethod {
    private Byte  m_initialized = 0;
    private Int32 m_value = 0;

    // This method is executed by one thread
    public void Thread1() {
        m_value = 5;
        Thread.VolatileWrite(ref m_initialized, 1);
    }

    // This method is executed by another thread
    public void Thread2() {
        if (Thread.VolatileRead(ref m_initialized) == 1) {
            // If we get here, 5 will be displayed
            Console.WriteLine(m_value);
        }
    }
}
```

Important   When threads are using shared memory to communicate with each other, the last byte written to the shared memory should be done using a volatile write. And the first byte read should be done using a volatile read. The code above demonstrates this.

C#'s Support for Volatile Fields

Making sure that programmers call the **VolatileRead** and **VolatileWrite** methods correctly is a lot to ask. It's hard for programmers to keep all of this in their minds and to start imagining what other threads might be doing to shared data in the background. The C# compiler offers the **volatile** keyword, which can be applied to static or instance fields of any of these types: **Byte**, **SByte**, **Int16**, **UInt16**, **Int32**, **UInt32**, **Char**, **Single**, or **Boolean**. You can also apply the

volatile keyword to reference types and any enum field as long as the enumerated type has an underlying type of **Byte**, **SByte**, **Int16**, **UInt16**, **Int32**, **UInt32**, **Single**, or **Boolean**. The JIT compiler ensures that all accesses to a volatile field are performed as volatile reads and writes so that it is not necessary to explicitly call any of **Thread**'s static **volatile***Xxx* methods. Furthermore, the **volatile** keyword tells the C# and JIT compilers not to cache the field in a CPU register, ensuring that all reads to and from the field actually cause the value to be read from memory.[2]

Using the **volatile** keyword, we can modify the code in the **VolatileMethod** class to produce the **VolatileField** class:

```
internal sealed class VolatileField {
   private volatile Byte m_initialized = 0;
   private Int32 m_value = 0;

   // This method is executed by one thread
   public void Thread1() {
      m_value = 5;
      m_initialized = 1;
   }

   // This method is executed by another thread
   public void Thread2() {
      if (m_initialized == 1) {
         // If we get here, 5 will be displayed
         Console.WriteLine(m_value);
      }
   }
}
```

There are some developers (and I am one of them) who do not like C#'s **volatile** keyword, and they think that the language should not provide it. Our thinking is that most algorithms require few volatile read or write accesses to a field, and that most other accesses to the field can occur normally, improving performance; seldom is it required that all accesses to a field be volatile. For example, it is difficult to interpret how to apply volatile read operations to algorithms like these:

```
m_amount = m_amount + m_amount; // m_amount is a field defined in a class
m_amount *= m_amount
```

Furthermore, C# does not support passing a volatile field by reference to a method. For example, if **m_amount** is defined as a **volatile Int32**, attempting to call **Int32**'s **TryParse** method causes the compiler to generate a warning as shown here:

```
Boolean success = Int32.TryParse("123", out m_amount);
// The above line causes the C# compiler to generate a warning:
// CS0420: a reference to a volatile field will not be treated as volatile
```

---

2   Historically, this is what the volatile keyword meant in unmanaged C/C++.

While Microsoft's CLR team was building a JIT compiler for the IA64 architecture, they realized that many developers (including themselves) had written code that would not work correctly if executed with non-volatile (*unordered*) read and write memory accesses. So they thought about making the IA64 JIT compiler always produce read instructions that include acquire semantics and write instructions that always include release semantics. This would allow already-written applications that work on the x86 to continue to work just fine on the IA64. Unfortunately, this would hurt performance significantly, and so a compromise was struck. Microsoft's IA64 JIT compiler ensures that all writes are always performed with release semantics, but reads are allowed to be unordered; programmers still must call `Thread`'s `VolatileRead` method or apply C#'s `volatile` keyword to a field so that it is read with acquire semantics.

This produces a much more sane memory model for programmers to rationalize in their heads. In fact, Microsoft now promises that all of its JIT compilers that exist today or are created in the future will adhere to this memory model in which reads can be unordered but writes always occur with release semantics. To be more precise, the memory access rules are a bit more complicated than what I discussed in this section. The other memory access rules would be expected by most programmers anyway.

> **Note**   As mentioned in Chapter 1, "The CLR's Execution Model," ECMA has defined a standard version of the CLR called the Common Language Infrastructure (CLI). The ECMA documents describe the memory model that all CLI-compliant runtime engines must follow. In the ECMA version of the memory model, all reads and writes are unordered unless a programmer specifically calls a `VolatileRead`/`VolatileWrite` method or uses C#'s `volatile` keyword. This also explains why the FCL still includes the `Thread`'s `VolatileWrite` methods even though they offer no value when an application is running on Microsoft's CLR.
>
> Microsoft felt that the ECMA model was too weak for programmers to rationalize, and so Microsoft's implementation of the CLI (the CLR) uses the stronger memory model in which all writes are performed with release semantics. This change allows Microsoft's CLR to still be considered compatible with the standard since any application written adhering to the ECMA memory model will run just fine on top of Microsoft's CLR.
>
> However, there is the potential problem that someone will write an application and test it running on top of Microsoft's CLR. This application may run perfectly, but if the application is then run on another CLI implementation that has the weaker memory model, the application may fail. It would be better for everyone if the ECMA standard and all implementations of the ECMA standard followed a single memory model. It is Microsoft's hope that future versions of the ECMA standard will adopt the stronger memory model currently employed by the CLR.

Finally, I should point out that whenever a thread calls an interlocked method (discussed in the next section), the CPU forces cache coherency. So if you are manipulating variables via interlocked methods, you do not have to worry about all of this memory model stuff. Furthermore, all thread synchronization locks (`Monitor`, `ReaderWriterLock`, `Mutex`, `Semaphore`, `AutoResetEvent`, `ManualRsesetEvent`, etc.) call interlocked methods internally, so you also don't have to worry about memory models when you are using thread synchronization locks.

> **Important**   In general, I highly recommend that you avoid calling Thread's VolatileRead/ VolatileWrite methods, and I also recommend that you avoid using C#'s volatile keyword. Instead, I recommend you use the interlocked methods or other higher-level thread synchronization constructs. These methods will always work regardless of the memory model and CPU platform.

The Interlocked Methods

When multiple threads access shared data, that data must be accessed in a thread-safe way. By far, the fastest way to manipulate data in a thread-safe way is to use the interlocked family of methods. These methods are extremely fast (as compared to other thread synchronization constructs), and these methods are easy to use. The downside is that they are very limited in what they can accomplish. The System.Threading.Interlocked class defines a bunch of static methods that can atomically modify a variable in a thread-safe way. The methods that operate on **Int32** variables are by far the most commonly used methods. I show them here:

```
public static class Interlocked {
    // Atomically performs (location++)
    public static Int32 Increment(ref Int32 location);

    // Atomically performs (location--)
    public static Int32 Decrement(ref Int32 location);

    // Atomically performs (location1 += value)
    // Note: value can be a negative number allowing subtraction
    public static Int32 Add(ref Int32 location1, Int32 value);

    // Atomically performs (location1 = value)
    public static Int32 Exchange(ref Int32 location1, Int32 value);

    // Atomically performs the following:
    // if (location1 == comparand) location1 = value
    public static Int32 CompareExchange(ref Int32 location1,
        Int32 value, Int32 comparand);
    ...
}
```

In addition to these methods, the **Interlocked** class offers Exchange and CompareExchange methods that take **Object**, **IntPtr**, **Single**, **Double**, and there is also a generic version in which the type is constrained to **class** (any reference type). All of the interlocked methods require that the variable address you pass is properly aligned, or they might throw a DataMisaligned-Exception. Fortunately, the CLR ensures that a type's fields are properly aligned automatically unless the type has the [**StructLayout(LayoutKind.Explicit)**] attribute applied to it and [**FieldOffset(...)**] attributes applied to individual fields, forcing the field to be misaligned.

> **Important** The **Interlocked** class also offers methods that operate on **Int64** variables. However, you should never call these methods because the CLR doesn't guarantee that **Int64** variables are properly aligned.

My MSDN Concurrent Affairs columns show several examples of how to properly use the various interlocked methods. For one such column, visit *http://MSDN.Microsoft.com/ MSDNMag/Issues/05/10/ConcurrentAffairs/Default.aspx*.

The **Monitor** Class and Sync Blocks

In the Win32 API, the **CRITICAL_SECTION** structure and its associated functions offer the fastest and most efficient way to synchronize threads for mutual exclusive access to a shared resource when the threads are all running in a single process. Mutual exclusive access to a shared resource by multiple threads is probably the most common form of thread synchronization. The CLR doesn't expose a **CRITICAL_SECTION** structure, but it does offer a similar mechanism allowing mutual exclusive access to a resource among a set of threads running in the same process. This mechanism is made possible by way of the **System.Threading.Monitor** class and sync blocks.

In this section, I'm going to explain how this common form of thread synchronization is exposed by the CLR. Specifically, I'm going to explain the motivation for how the **Monitor** class and sync blocks were designed as they are and how they work. Then, at the end of this section, I'm going to explain why this design has problems and show you how to use this mechanism in a good and safe fashion to work around these problems.

The "Great" Idea

The CLR offers an object-oriented platform. This means that developers construct objects and then call the type's members in order to manipulate the objects. Occasionally, these objects are manipulated by multiple threads, and to ensure that the objects' state will not become corrupted, thread synchronization must be performed. While designing the CLR, Microsoft's developers decided to create a mechanism that makes synchronizing access to an object's state easy for developers.

Here's the basic idea: every object in the heap has a data structure associated with it (similar to a Win32 **CRITICAL_SECTION** structure) that can be used as a thread synchronization lock. Then the Framework Class Library (FCL) provides methods that accept a reference to an object, and these methods will use the object's data structure to take and release the thread synchronization lock.

In Win32, an unmanaged C++ class with this design would look like this:

```
class SomeType {
private:
    // The private CRITICAL_SECTION field associated with each object
    CRITICAL_SECTION m_csObject;

public:
    SomeType() {
        // The constructor initialize the object's CRITICAL_SECTION field
        InitializeCriticalSection(&m_csObject);
    }

    ~SomeType() {
        // The destructor deletes the object's CRITICAL_SECTION field
        DeleteCriticalSection(&m_csObject);
    }

    void SomeMethod() {
        // We use the object's CRITICAL_SECTION field to synchronize
        // access to the object by multiple threads.
        EnterCriticalSection(&m_csObject);
        // Execute thread-safe code here...
        LeaveCriticalSection(&m_csObject);
    }

    void AnotherMethod() {
        // We use the object's CRITICAL_SECTION field to synchronize
        // access to the object by multiple threads.
        EnterCriticalSection(&m_csObject);
        // Execute thread-safe code here...
        LeaveCriticalSection(&m_csObject);
    }
};
```

In essence, the CLR provides every object with its own **CRITICAL_SECTION**-like field, and the CLR takes over the responsibility of initializing and deleting this field. All the developer has to do is write code to enter and leave the field as necessary in each method that requires thread synchronization.

Implementing the "Great" Idea

Now obviously, associating a **CRITICAL_SECTION** field (which is approximately 24 bytes on a 32-bit system and about 40 bytes on a 64-bit system) with every object in the heap is quite wasteful, especially since most objects never require thread-safe access to them. To reduce memory usage, the CLR team uses a more efficient way to offer the functionality just described. Here's how it works: When the CLR initializes, it allocates an array of sync blocks. A *sync block* is a chunk of memory that can be associated with an object. Each sync block contains the same fields that you would find in a Win32 **CRITICAL_SECTION** structure.

As discussed elsewhere in this book, whenever an object is created in the heap, it will get two additional overhead fields associated with it. The first overhead field, the type object pointer, contains the memory address of the type's type object. The second overhead field, the sync block index, contains an integer index into the array of sync blocks.

When an object is constructed, the object's sync block index is initialized to a negative value indicating that it doesn't refer to any sync block. Then, when a method is called to enter the object's sync block, the CLR finds a free sync block in the array and sets the object's sync block index to refer to the sync block that was found. In other words, sync blocks are associated with an object on the fly. When all threads have released an object's sync block, the object's sync block index is reset back to a negative number, and the sync block is considered to be free again and may be associated with another object in the future. See Figure 24-1 to help you visualize this more concretely.

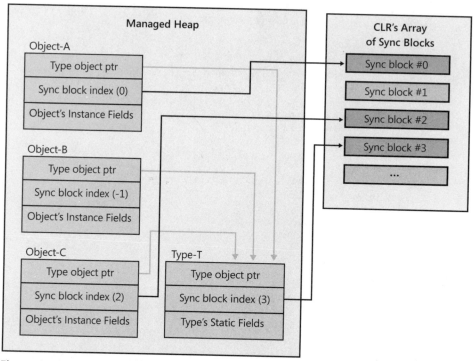

Figure 24-1   Objects in the heap (including type objects) can have their sync block index refer to an entry in the CLR's sync block array

So logically, every object in the heap has a sync block associated with it that can be used for fast, exclusive thread synchronization. Physically, however, the sync block structures are associated with an object only when they are needed and are disassociated from an object when they are no longer needed. This means that memory usage will be efficient. By the way, the sync block array is able to create more sync blocks if necessary, so you shouldn't worry about the system running out of sync blocks if many objects are being synchronized on simultaneously.

Using the `Monitor` Class to Manipulate a Sync Block

So now that you understand the sync block infrastructure, we can examine how to take and release an object's lock. To lock/unlock an object's sync block, we call static methods defined by the `System.Threading.Monitor` class. Here is the method that you call to lock an object's sync block:

```
static void Enter(Object obj);
```

When you call this method, it first checks to see if the specified object's sync block index is negative, and if it is, the method finds a free sync block and records the index of it in the object's sync block index. By the way, the CLR has a thread-safe way of finding a free sync block and associating it with an object. Once a sync block is associated with the object, `Monitor.Enter` examines the specified object's sync block to see if another thread currently owns the sync block. If the sync block is currently unowned, the calling thread becomes the owner of the sync block. If, on the other hand, another thread owns the sync block when `Monitor.Enter` is called, the calling thread is suspended until the thread that currently owns the sync block releases ownership of it.

If you want to code more defensively, instead of calling `Monitor.Enter`, you can call the `Monitor.TryEnter` method (three overloads of this method exist):

```
static Boolean TryEnter(Object obj);
static Boolean TryEnter(object obj, Int32 millisecondsTimeout);
static Boolean TryEnter(Object obj, TimeSpan timeout);
```

The first version simply checks if the calling thread can gain ownership of the object's sync block and returns **true** if it is successful. The other two overloads allow you to specify a timeout value indicating how long you'll allow the calling thread to wait for ownership. All of the methods return **false** if ownership cannot be obtained.

Once ownership is obtained, the code can access whatever data the object's sync block is being used to protect. When finished, the thread should release the sync block by calling `Monitor.Exit`:

```
static void Exit(Object obj);
```

If the thread calling `Monitor.Exit` doesn't own the specified object's sync block, a `SynchronizationLockException` is thrown. Also note that a thread can own a sync block recursively: every successful call to `Monitor.Enter` or `Monitor.TryEnter` must be matched by a corresponding call to `Monitor.Exit` before the sync block can be considered as unowned.

Synchronizing the Way Microsoft Intended

Now let's look at some example code that shows how Microsoft originally intended developers to use the `Monitor` class and the sync block:

```
internal sealed class Transaction {

    // Field indicating the time of the last transaction performed
    private DateTime timeOfLastTransaction;
```

```
    public void PerformTransaction() {
        Monitor.Enter(this); // Enter this object's lock
        // Perform the transaction...

        // Record time of the most recent transaction
        timeOfLastTransaction = DateTime.Now;

        Monitor.Exit(this);  // Exit this object's lock
    }

    // Read-only property returning the time of the last transaction
    public DateTime LastTransaction {
        get {
            Monitor.Enter(this); // Enter this object's lock

            // Save the time of the last transaction
            // in a temporary variable
            DateTime dt = timeOfLastTransaction;

            Monitor.Exit(this);  // Exit this object's lock
            return dt; // Return the saved date/time
        }
    }
}
```

This code sample shows how to use **Monitor**'s **Enter** and **Exit** methods to lock and unlock an object's sync block. Note that the implementation of the property requires calls to **Enter**, **Exit**, and a temporary variable, **dt**. This is important in order to prevent returning a possibly corrupt value. This could happen if a thread calls **PerformTransaction** at the same time another thread accesses the property.

> **Important**   The code above demonstrates how Microsoft originally thought developers would use an object's sync block. However, there is something severely wrong with the code just shown, and you should not mimic this code in your own projects. A little later on, I'll explain what is wrong with this code and how you should write code to prevent the problem.

Simplifying the Code with C#'s lock Statement

Because this pattern of calling **Monitor.Enter**, accessing the protected resource, and then calling **Monitor.Exit** is so common, the C# language offers a special syntax to simplify the code. The following two C# code fragments are identical:

```
private void SomeMethod() {
    lock (this) {


        // Access object here...
    }


}
```

```
private void SomeMethod() {
    Object temp = this;
    Monitor.Enter(temp);
    try {
        // Access object here...
    }
    finally {
        Monitor.Exit(temp);
    }
}
```

Using C#'s **lock** statement, we can simplify the **Transaction** class substantially (see the following code). In particular, look at the new, improved **LastTransaction** property; the temporary variable is no longer necessary.

```
internal sealed class Transaction {

   // Field indicating the time of the last transaction performed
   private DateTime timeOfLastTransaction;

   public void PerformTransaction() {
      lock (this) {  // Enter this object's lock
         // Perform the transaction...

         // Record time of the most recent transaction
         timeOfLastTransaction = DateTime.Now;
      } // Exit this object's lock
   }

   // Read-only property returning the time of the last transaction
   public DateTime LastTransaction {
      get {
         lock (this) {  // Enter this object's lock
            return timeOfLastTransaction; // Return the date/time
         }  // Exit this object's lock
      }
   }
}
```

In addition to shortening and simplifying the code, the **lock** statement ensures that **Monitor.Exit** is called, thereby releasing the sync block even if an exception occurs inside the **lock** block. You should always use exception handling with thread synchronization mechanisms to ensure that locks are released properly. If you use C#'s **lock** statement, the compiler writes the proper code for you automatically.

> **Important**   Again, the code above demonstrates how Microsoft originally thought developers would use an object's sync block. However, there is still something severely wrong with the code just shown and you should not mimic this code in your own projects.

Synchronizing Static Members the Way Microsoft Intended

The **Transaction** class demonstrates how to synchronize access to an object's instance fields. But what if your type defines a number of static fields and static methods that access these fields? In this case, you don't have an instance of the type in the heap, and therefore, there is no sync block that can be used, and there is no object reference to pass to **Monitor**'s **Enter** and **Exit** methods.

Figure 24-1 shows that Object-A, Object-B, and Object-C all have their type object pointer member set to refer to Type-T (a type object). This means that all three objects are of the same type. As discussed in Chapter 4, "Type Fundamentals," a type object is also an object in the heap, and like all other objects, a type object has the two overhead members: a sync block index and a type object pointer. This means that a sync block can be associated with a type object and a reference to a type object can be passed to **Monitor**'s **Enter**, **TryEnter**, and **Exit** methods. In the version of the **Transaction** class shown below, all of the members have been changed to static members, and the **PerformTransaction** method and **LastTransaction** property have been modified to show how Microsoft originally intended developers to synchronize access to static members.

```
internal static class Transaction {

   // Field indicating the time of the last transaction performed
   private static DateTime timeOfLastTransaction;

   public static void PerformTransaction() {
      lock (typeof(Transaction)) {  // Enter the type object's lock
         // Perform the transaction...

         // Record time of the most recent transaction
         timeOfLastTransaction = DateTime.Now;
      }  // Exit the type object's lock
   }

   // Read-only property returning the time of the last transaction
   public static DateTime LastTransaction {
      get {
         lock (typeof(Transaction)) {  // Enter the type object's lock
            return timeOfLastTransaction; // Return the date/time
         }  // Exit the type object's lock
      }
   }
}
```

In this code, the static method and property get accessor cannot refer to **this** since it is not available in static members. Instead, to the **lock** statement, I pass a reference to the type's type object (obtained using C#'s **typeof** operator).

Important   Once again, the code above demonstrates how Microsoft originally thought developers would use a type object's sync block. However, there is still something severely wrong with the code just shown, and you should not mimic this code in your own projects. Finally, in the next section, I will explain what is wrong with the previous three code samples, and I'll also explain how to fix them.

Why the "Great" Idea Isn't So Great After All

The idea of having a synchronization data structure logically associated with every object in the heap sounds like a great idea, and it is. But Microsoft made a big mistake when they implemented this feature into the CLR. Let me explain why: Remember, the unmanaged C++ code shown in the "The 'Great' Idea" section in this chapter? If you were coding this yourself, would you ever make the **CRITICAL_SECTION** field public? Of course not—this would be ridiculous!

Making this field public allows any code in the application to manipulate the CRITICAL_SECTION structure. It would now be trivially simple for malicious code to deadlock threads that use instances of this type.

Well, guess what—the sync block is just like having a public synchronization data structure associated with every object in the heap! Any code that has a reference to an object can pass the reference to Monitor's Enter and Exit methods at any time, thereby taking this lock. What's worse is that any code could also pass a reference to any type object in to Monitor's Enter and Exit methods at any time thereby taking a lock on a type. There is also a problem if you pass a String object that has been interned because now there are multiple strings sharing a single lock. And, if you pass a reference to an object whose type is derived from MarshalByRefObject, you may be locking the actual object, or you may be locking a proxy object and not affecting the actual object at all. As you can see, Microsoft did not think all of this through, and there are many potential pitfalls.

The code below demonstrates how horrible this situation can be. In the code below, Main constructs a SomeType object and then enters this object's lock. At some point, a garbage collection occurs (in this code, the GC is forced for demonstration purposes), and when SomeType's Finalize method is called, it attempts to enter the object's lock. Sadly, the CLR's finalizer thread can't acquire the object's lock because the application's primary thread owns the object's lock. This causes the CLR's finalizer thread to stop—no more objects in the process (which includes all AppDomains in the process) can be finalized, and no more finalizable objects will ever have their memory reclaimed from within the managed heap!

```
using System;
using System.Threading;

public sealed class SomeType {
    // This is SomeType's Finalize method
    ~SomeType() {
        // For demonstration purposes, have the CLR's
        // finalizer thread attempt to enter the object's lock.
        // NOTE: Since the Main thread owns the object's lock,
        // the finalizer thread is deadlocked!
        Monitor.Enter(this);
    }
}

public static class Program {
    public static void Main() {
        // Construct a SomeType object
        SomeType st = new SomeType();

        // This malicious code enters the object's lock
        // but never exits the object's lock
        Monitor.Enter(st);

        // For demonstration purposes, force a GC and
        // wait for Finalize methods to finish executing
        st = null;
```

```
    GC.Collect();
    GC.WaitForPendingFinalizers();

    Console.WriteLine("We never get here, both threads are deadlocked!");
    }
}
```

Unfortunately, the CLR, the FCL, and the compilers offer a lot of functionality based on the fact that every object can be locked. I already mentioned the potential problems with events in the "Events and Thread Safety" section of Chapter 10, "Events." The CLR also uses the type object's public lock when calling a type's class constructor.

In the `System.Runtime.CompilerServices` namespace, there is a custom attribute class called `MethodImplAttribute`. You can apply this attribute to a method specifying the `Method-ImplOptions.Synchronized` flag. When you do this, the JIT compiler surrounds all of the code in the method with a `lock(this)` if the method is an instance method. If the method is a static method, all of the code is surrounded with a `lock(typeof(TypeName))` where *TypeName* is the name of the type itself. For all of the reasons already mentioned, this is bad, and you should never use the `MethodImplAttribute` with the `MethodImplOptions.Synchronized` flag.

You can't fix the CLR, the FCL, or the C# compiler, but when you are writing your own code, you can code defensively and implement your code to work around the public lock problem. All that you need to do is to define a private `System.Object` field as a member of your type, construct the object, and then use C#'s `lock` statement passing in a reference to the private `Object`. Here is the modified version of the `Transaction` class that uses a private lock object and is therefore coded more defensively:

```
internal sealed class TransactionWithLockObject {
    // Allocate a 'private' object used for locking
    private Object m_lock = new Object();

    // Field indicating the time of the last transaction performed
    private DateTime timeOfLastTransaction;

    public void PerformTransaction() {
        lock (m_lock) {  // Enter the private field object's lock
            // Perform the transaction...

            // Record time of the most recent transaction
            timeOfLastTransaction = DateTime.Now;
        } // Exit the private field object's lock
    }

    // Read-only property returning the time of the last transaction
    public DateTime LastTransaction {
        get {
            lock (m_lock) {  // Enter the private field object's lock
                return timeOfLastTransaction; // Return the date/time
            } // Exit the private field object's lock
        }
    }
}
```

Important   This code shows how to fix the problems discussed in the previous code examples. The most important feature of this code sample is that the thread synchronization lock is now a private field; this prevents any arbitrary code from accessing it. Because of this, arbitrary code cannot interfere with your type's code to introduce a deadlock situation.

It seems odd to construct a `System.Object` object just for synchronization with the `Monitor` class. When you get right down to it, Microsoft designed the `Monitor` class improperly. It should have been designed so that you construct an instance of the `Monitor` type to create a thread synchronization lock. Then, the static methods would have been instance methods that operate on the lock object itself, and therefore, you wouldn't need to pass a `System.Object` argument to any of `Monitor`'s methods. This would have solved all of the problems and would have simplified the programming model for all developers. By the way, the code above is trivially modified to synchronize static methods; just change all of the members to `static`, and everything just works.

If your type already defines some private data fields, you can use one of these fields as the lock object that you pass to `Monitor`'s methods. This can save you a little memory because you can avoid allocating a `System.Object` object. However, I'd be wary of doing this just to reduce a tiny bit of memory usage; the private fields' type might internally call `lock(this)`. If this were to happen, your code would be interfering with the lock, and you might have unwittingly introduced a deadlock situation.

Important   Never pass a variable of a value type to `Monitor.Enter` or C#'s `lock` statement. The reason is because unboxed value type instances do not have a sync block index member, and therefore, they cannot be used for synchronization. When you pass an unboxed value type instance to `Monitor.Enter`, the C# compiler automatically generates code to box the instance. If you pass the same value type instance to `Monitor.Exit`, it gets boxed again. The result is that your code ends up locking one object and unlocking a completely different object—you end up with no thread safety whatsoever. If you pass an unboxed value type instance to C#'s `lock` statement, the compiler can detect this, and it will issue the following: error CS0185: '*valuetype*' is not a reference type as required by the lock statement. However, the compiler issues no warning or error if you pass a value type instance to `Monitor.Enter` or `Monitor.Exit`.

The Famous Double-Check Locking Technique

There is a famous technique called the *double-check locking* technique. This technique is used by developers who want to defer constructing a singleton object until an application first requests it (sometimes called *lazy initialization*). If the application never requests the object, it never gets constructed, saving time and memory. A potential problem occurs when multiple threads request the singleton object simultaneously. In this case, some form of thread synchronization must be used to ensure that the singleton object gets constructed just once.

This technique is not famous because it is particularly interesting or useful. It is famous because there has been much written about it. This technique was used heavily in Java, and it was later discovered that Java couldn't guarantee that it would work everywhere. The famous document that describes the problem can be found on this Web page: www.cs.umd.edu/ ~pugh/java/memoryModel/DoubleCheckedLocking.html.

Anyway, the CLR exhibited the same problem as Java, and Microsoft put forth a great effort to solve the problem in Microsoft's CLR. The result is that Microsoft decisively arrived at the memory model that the CLR would use and clearly documented it for everyone. This is what I describe in the "Memory Consistency, Volatile Memory Access, and Volatile Fields" section in this chapter. Because of the arrived-at memory model employed by the CLR, the double-check locking technique is not a problem on the CLR at all. Here is code that demonstrates how to implement the double-check locking technique in C#:

```csharp
public sealed class Singleton {
    // s_lock is required for thread safety and having this object assumes that creating
    // the singleton object is more expensive than creating a System.Object object and that
    // creating the singleton object may not be necessary at all. Otherwise, it is more
    // efficient and easier to just create the singleton object in a class constructor
    private static Object s_lock = new Object();

    // Volatile is not required for the CLR's memory model, but it is
    // required for ECMA's memory model. To be conservative, I include it here.
    private static volatile Singleton s_value;

    // Private constructor prevents any code outside
    // this class from creating an instance
    private Singleton() { }

    // Public, static property that returns the
    // singleton object (creating it if necessary)
    public static Singleton Value {
        get {
            // Has the singleton object already been created?
            if (s_value == null) {
                // No, only one thread should create it
                lock (s_lock) {
                    // Did another thread create it?
                    if (s_value == null) {
                        // No, OK, this thread will create it.

                        // Volatile ensures that all of singleton object's fields
                        // (initialied by the constructor) are flushed before
                        // other threads see the reference to the Singleton object
                        s_value = new Singleton();
                    }
                }
            }

            // Return a reference to the single object
            return s_value;
        }
    }
}
```

The idea behind the double-check locking technique is that a call to the get accessor method quickly checks the **s_value** field to see if the object has already been created, and if it has, the method returns a reference to it. The beautiful thing here is that no thread synchronization is required once the object has been constructed; the application will run very fast. On the other hand, if the first thread that calls the **value** property's get accessor method sees that the object hasn't been created, it takes a thread synchronization lock to ensure that only one thread constructs the single object. This means that a performance hit occurs only the first time a thread queries the singleton object.

By the way, it is theoretically possible for the JIT compiler to read the value of the **s_value** field into a CPU register at the beginning of the get accessor property method and then just query the register when evaluating the second **if** statement. If the JIT compiler produced the code this way, the second **if** statement would always evaluate to **true**, and multiple threads could end up creating **Singleton** objects. This is certainly not the behavior we want. However, the JIT compiler knows not to cache a field if that field is marked with C#'s **volatile** keyword. Also, the JIT compiler always re-reads a field accessed after a call to a method when that method includes a volatile read or write operation (e.g., **Monitor.Enter** or **Monitor.Exit**).[3]

In the beginning of this section, I mentioned that the double-check locking technique is not that interesting. In my opinion, developers think this is cool, and they use it far more often then they should. In most scenarios, this technique actually hurts efficiency. Here is a much simpler version of the **Singleton** class that behaves the same as the previous version. This version does not use the double-check locking technique:

```
public sealed class Singleton {
    private static Singleton s_value = new Singleton();

    // Private constructor prevents any code outside
    // this class from creating an instance
    private Singleton() { }


    // Public, static property that returns the singleton object
    public static Singleton Value {
        get {
            return s_value;  // Return a reference to the single object
        }
    }
}
```

---

[3] In reality, the JIT compiler doesn't actually know that **Monitor.Enter** (or any other method for that matter) performs a volatile read or write operation inside it. To know this, the JIT compiler would have to examine the code in this method and all of the methods it calls. First, this would be time consuming, and second, some methods are written in unmanaged code, which the JIT compiler can't parse. So the JIT compiler just assumes that all methods perform a volatile read or write operation, and therefore, the JIT compiler always re-reads a field's value after a method call. A future version of the CLR's JIT compilers could get more advanced and somehow recognize that a method internally performs a volatile read or write operation, and therefore, you should not write any code that relies on today's behavior. The only guarantee you have is that the JIT compiler will not cache a value across a call to a method that internally performs a volatile read or write operation.

Since the CLR automatically calls a type's class constructor the first time code attempts to access a member of the class, the first time a thread queries `Singleton`'s `Value` get accessor property method, the CLR will automatically call the class constructor, which creates an instance of the object. Furthermore, the CLR already ensures that calls to a class constructor are thread safe. I explained all of this in Chapter 8, "Methods: Constructors, Operators, Conversions, and Parameters."

The double-check locking technique is less efficient than the class constructor technique because you need to construct your own lock object (in the class constructor) and write all of the additional locking code yourself. The double-check locking technique is interesting only if a class has a lot of members and you want to construct the singleton object only when one of the members is called. Also, creating the singleton object must be far more expensive than creating the object you use for locking in order to gain any benefit.

The `ReaderWriterLock` Class

There is a very common thread synchronization problem known as the *multiple-reader/ single-writer* problem. The problem involves an arbitrary number of threads that attempt to access a shared resource. Some of these threads (the writers) need to modify the contents of the data, and some of the threads (the readers) need only to read the data. Synchronization is necessary because of the following four rules:

- When one thread is writing to the data, no other thread can write to the data.

- When one thread is writing to the data, no other thread can read from the data.

- When one thread is reading from the data, no other thread can write to the data.

- When one thread is reading from the data, other threads can also read from the data.

The FCL provides a `ReaderWriterLock` class that encapsulates these rules. You can construct an instance of this class and call methods to acquire and release its lock. The `ReaderWriter-Lock` class has no static members, but it has several instance methods and properties. Normally, at this point in the book, I'd describe how to use this lock in your own applications; however, I just can't do that here because I don't recommend that anyone *ever* use it. As you will see, this class has many problems with its implementation:

First, the performance of just entering and leaving the lock is awfully slow. It is even slow when there is no contention on the lock. My own performance testing shows that the `ReaderWriterLock` is about five times slower than entering and exiting a `Monitor`.

Second, when a thread completes writing with reader and writer threads waiting, this lock gives priority to the reader threads, which causes processing of waiting writer threads to occur very slowly. You typically use a `ReaderWriterLock` when you know that a resource will have few writers and many readers. After all, if the resource had all readers, you wouldn't need a lock at all, and if a resource had only writers, you'd use a mutually exclusive lock such as a sync block (which you manipulate by using the **Monitor** class). So when using a **Reader-WriterLock**, if you have writers waiting, you want to give them higher priority than the readers. I know several people who have tried to use the **ReaderWriterLock**, but due to its policy of favoring readers over writers, writers get starved for time and do not complete their work in a timely fashion.

Third, the **ReaderWriterLock** supports recursion. That is, the thread that enters the lock must be the thread to exit the lock. While many developers will consider this to be a feature, I consider it a bug. It is becoming much more commonplace for one thread to enter a lock and start an operation to access some data and then have another thread eventually complete the operation on the data and exit the lock. This is especially likely if you use the asynchronous programming model as described in Chapter 23. Locks that support recursion such as **ReaderWriterLock** and **Monitor** do not support this programming architecture.

If you want to use a reader/writer lock in your own application, I'd recommend that you implement your own, or you can use the one that is included in my Power Threading library (available from *http://Wintellect.com*). My reader/writer lock class is called **OneManyResourceLock**, and my lock is almost as fast as the **Monitor**. My lock favors writers over readers, and it does not support recursion.

Using Windows Kernel Objects from Managed Code

Windows offers several kernel objects for the sole purpose of thread synchronization: mutexes, semaphores, and events. In this section, we'll look at how the CLR exposes these kernel objects. I will not fully describe how these Windows kernel objects work and when to use them because this information has been around for many years and is well documented in many places, including my own book: *Programming Applications for Microsoft Windows, 4th Edition* (Microsoft Press, 1999).

Whereas the **Monitor** and **ReaderWriterLock** methods allow synchronization of threads running only in a single AppDomain, kernel objects can be used to synchronize threads that are running in different AppDomains or in different processes. Because of this, when you create a kernel object, you can associate security rights with it indicating who can do what with the kernel object. Whenever a thread waits on a kernel object, the thread must always transition from user mode to kernel mode, causing the thread to incur a performance hit. For this reason, synchronizing threads by using kernel objects is the slowest mechanism that you can use to synchronize threads. Using kernel objects is substantially slower than using the **ReaderWriterLock**. In my performance testing, using kernel objects is about 33 times slower than using the **Monitor** class's methods.

The **System.Threading** namespace offers an abstract base class called **WaitHandle**. The **WaitHandle** class is a simple class whose sole purpose is to wrap a Windows kernel object handle. The FCL provides several classes derived from **WaitHandle**. All classes are defined in the `System.Threading` namespace, and all classes are implemented in MSCorLib.dll except for `Semaphore`, which is implemented in System.dll. The class hierarchy looks like this:

```
WaitHandle
    Mutex
    Semaphore
    EventWaitHandle
        AutoResetEvent
        ManualResetEvent
```

Internally, the `WaitHandle` base class has a field that holds a Win32 kernel object handle. This field is initialized when a concrete `WaitHandle`-derived class is constructed. Additionally, the `WaitHandle` class publicly exposes methods that are common to all of the concrete derived classes. The pseudo-class definition below summarizes `WaitHandle`'s interesting public methods (some overloads for some methods are not shown):

```
public abstract class WaitHandle : MarshalByRefObject, IDisposable {
    // Close internally calls the Win32 CloseHandle function.
    public virtual void Close();

    // WaitOne internally calls the Win32 WaitForSingleObjectEx function.
    public virtual Boolean WaitOne();
    public virtual Boolean WaitOne(
        Int32 millisecondsTimeout, Boolean exitContext);

    // WaitAny internally calls the Win32 WaitForMultipleObjectsEx function
    public static Int32 WaitAny(WaitHandle[] waitHandles);
    public static Int32 WaitAny(WaitHandle[] waitHandles,
        Int32 millisecondsTimeout, Boolean exitContext);

    // WaitAll internally calls the Win32 WaitForMultipleObjectsEx function
    public static Boolean WaitAll(WaitHandle[] waitHandles);
    public static Boolean WaitAll(WaitHandle[] waitHandles,
        Int32 millisecondsTimeout, Boolean exitContext);

    // SignalAndWait internally calls the Win32 SignalObjectAndWait function
    public static Boolean SignalAndWait(WaitHandle toSignal,
        WaitHandle toWaitOn);
    public static Boolean SignalAndWait(WaitHandle toSignal,
        WaitHandle toWaitOn, Int32 millisecondsTimeout, Boolean exitContext);

    public const Int32 WaitTimeout = 0x102;
}
```

There are a few things to note about these methods:

■ You call `WaitHandle`'s `Close` (or `IDisposable`'s parameterless `Dispose` method) to close the underlying kernel object handle. Internally, these methods call the Win32 `CloseHandle` function.

■ You call **WaitHandle**'s **WaitOne** method to have the calling thread wait for the underlying kernel object to become signaled. Internally, this method calls the Win32 **WaitFor-SingleObjectEx** function. The returned **Boolean** is **true** if the object became signaled or **false** if a time out occurs.

■ You call **WaitHandle**'s static **WaitAny** method to have the calling thread wait for any one of the kernel objects specified in the **WaitHandle[]** to become signaled. The returned **Int32** is the index of the array element corresponding to the kernel object that became signaled or **WaitHandle.WaitTimeout** if no object became signaled while waiting. Internally, this method calls the Win32 **WaitForMultipleObjectsEx** function passing **FALSE** for the **bWaitAll** parameter.

■ You call **WaitHandle**'s static **WaitAll** method to have the calling thread wait for all of the kernel objects specified in the **WaitHandle[]** to become signaled. The returned **Boolean** is **true** if all of the objects became signaled or **false** if a time out occurs. Internally, this method calls the Win32 **WaitForMultipleObjectsEx** function passing **TRUE** for the **bWaitAll** parameter.

■ You call **WaitHandle**'s static **SignalAndWait** method to atomically signal one kernel object and wait for another kernel object to become signaled. The returned **Boolean** is **true** if the object became signaled or **false** if a time out occurs. Internally, this method calls the Win32 **SignalObjectAndWait** function.

The versions of the **WaitOne**, **WaitAll**, and **SignalAndWait** that do not accept a time-out parameter should be prototyped as having a **void** return type, not **Boolean**. The reason is because these methods will return only **true** because the implied time out is infinite (**System.Threading.Timeout.Infinite**). When you call any of these methods, you do not need to check their return value.

The versions of the **WaitOne**, **WaitAll**, **WaitAny**, and **SignalAndWait** that do not accept an **exitContext** parameter assume **false** for this argument. The CLR offers the ability to place an object in its own context by applying the **System.Runtime.Remoting.Contexts.Context-Attribute** or the **System.Runtime.Remoting.Contexts.SynchronizationAttribute** to a class. A context is like a mini-AppDomain or a mini-environment for instances of the class. Anyway, as you can see, these attributes have to do with remoting, and use of these features is now discouraged. If you call one of **WaitHandle**'s methods that accept an **exitContext** parameter, you should usually pass **false**.

As already mentioned, the **Mutex**, **Semaphore**, **AutoResetEvent**, and **ManualResetEvent** classes are all derived from **WaitHandle**, and so they inherit **WaitHandle**'s behavior. These classes introduce some additional methods, and I'll address them now.

First, the constructors for all of these classes internally call the Win32 **CreateMutex**, **Create-Semaphore**, **CreateEvent** (passing **FALSE** for the **bManualReset** parameter), or **CreateEvent** (passing **TRUE** for the **bManualReset** parameter) functions. The handle value returned from all of these calls is saved in a private field defined by the **WaitHandle** base class.

Second, the `Mutex`, `Semaphore`, and `EventWaitHandle` classes all offer static `OpenExisting` methods, which internally call the Win32 `OpenMutex`, `OpenSemaphore`, or `OpenEvent` functions passing a `String` argument that identifies an existing named kernel object. The handle value returned from all of these calls is saved in a newly constructed object that is returned from the `OpenExisting` method. If no kernel object exists with the specified name, a `WaitHandle-CannotBeOpenedException` is thrown.

Third, to release a mutex or semaphore kernel object, you call `Mutex`'s `ReleaseMutex` method or `Semaphore`'s `Release` method. To set or reset an auto-reset event or a manual-reset event kernel object, you call `AutoResetEvent`'s or `ManualResetEvent`'s `Set` or `Reset` methods (inherited from `EventWaitHandle`). Note that `EventWaitHandle`'s `Set` and `Reset` methods are prototyped as returning a `Boolean`, but they will always return `true`; there is no need to write code to check the value returned by either of these methods.

Calling a Method When a Single Kernel Object Becomes Signaled

While doing performance research, Microsoft discovered that many applications spawn threads simply to wait for a single kernel object to become signaled. Once the object is signaled, the thread posts some sort of notification to another thread and then loops back, waiting for the object to signal again. Some developers even write code in which several threads each wait for a single object. This is incredibly wasteful of system resources. So if you currently have threads in your application that wait for single kernel objects to become signaled, the thread pool is, again, the perfect tool for you to improve your application's performance.

To have a thread pool thread call your callback method when a kernel object becomes signaled, you call the `System.Threading.ThreadPool` class's static `RegisterWaitForSingleObject` method. There are several overloads of this method, but they are all very similar. Here is the prototype for one of the more commonly used overloads:

```
public static RegisterWaitHandle RegisterWaitForSingleObject(
    WaitHandle waitObject, WaitOrTimerCallback callback, Object state,
    Int32 millisecondsTimeoutInterval, Boolean executeOnlyOnce);
```

When you call this method, the `waitObject` argument identifies the kernel object that you want the thread pool to wait on. Since this parameter is of the abstract base class `WaitHandle`, you can specify any class derived from this base class. Specifically, you can pass a reference to a `Semaphore`, `Mutex`, `AutoResetEvent`, or `ManualResetEvent` object. The second parameter, `callback`, identifies the method that you want the thread pool thread to call. The callback method that you write must match the `System.Threading.WaitOrTimerCallback` delegate, which is defined as follows:

```
public delegate void WaitOrTimerCallback(Object state, Boolean timedOut);
```

`RegisterWaitForSingleObject`'s third parameter, `state`, allows you to specify some state data that should be passed to the callback method when the thread pool thread calls it; pass `null` if you have no special state data to pass. The fourth parameter, `millisecondsTimeoutInterval`, allows you to tell the thread pool how long it should wait for the kernel object to become signaled. It is common to pass `Timeout.Infinite` or `-1` here to indicate an infinite time out. If the last parameter, `executeOnlyOnce`, is `true`, a thread pool thread will execute the callback method just once. But if `executeOnlyOnce` is `false`, a thread pool thread will execute the callback method every time the kernel object becomes signaled. This is most useful when waiting on an `AutoResetEvent` object.

When the callback method is called, it is passed state data and a `Boolean` value, `timedOut`. If `timedOut` is `false`, the method knows that it is being called because the kernel object became signaled. If `timedOut` is `true`, the method knows that it is being called because the kernel object did not become signaled in the time specified. The callback method can perform whatever action it desires based on the value that it receives in the `timedOut` argument.

You'll notice that the `RegisterWaitForSingleObject` method returns a reference to a `RegisteredWaitHandle` object. This object identifies the kernel object that the thread pool is waiting on. If, for some reason, your application wants to tell the thread pool to stop watching the registered wait handle, your application can call `RegisteredWaitHandle`'s `Unregister` method:

```
public Boolean Unregister(WaitHandle waitObject);
```

The `waitObject` parameter indicates how you want to be notified when all queued work items for the registered wait have executed. You should pass `null` for this parameter if you don't want a notification. If you pass a valid reference to a `WaitHandle`-derived object, the thread pool will signal the object when all pending work items for the registered wait handle have executed.

The code below demonstrates how to have a thread pool thread call a method whenever an `AutoResetEvent` object becomes signaled:

```
using System;
using System.Threading;

public static class Program {
    public static void Main() {
        // Construct an AutoResetEvent (initially not signaled)
        AutoResetEvent are = new AutoResetEvent(false);

        // Tell the thread pool to wait on the AutoResetEvent
        RegisteredWaitHandle rwh = ThreadPool.RegisterWaitForSingleObject(
            are,               // Wait on this AutoResetEvent
            EventOperation,    // Call back this method
            null,              // Pass null to EventOperation
            5000,              // Wait 5 seconds for the event to become signaled
            false);            // Call EventOperation every time the event is signaled
```

```csharp
      // Start our loop
      Char operation;
      do {
         Console.WriteLine("S=Signal, Q=Quit?");
         operation = Char.ToUpper(Console.ReadKey(true).KeyChar);
         if (operation == 'S') {
            // User wants to signal the event, set it
            are.Set();
         }
      } while (operation != 'Q');

      // Tell the thread pool to stop waiting on the event
      rwh.Unregister(null);
   }


   // This method is called whenever the event is signaled or
   // when 5 seconds have elapsed since the last signaling/timeout
   private static void EventOperation(Object state, Boolean timedOut) {
      if (timedOut) {
         Console.WriteLine("Timedout while waiting for the AutoResetEvent.");
      } else {
         Console.WriteLine("The AutoResetEvent became signaled.");
      }
   }
}
```

Index

Symbol

& (ampersand), 582
@ symbol for verbatim strings, 246
[] (brackets) indicating custom attributes, 389
+= (delegate combine overload), 345
?? (null-coalescing operator), 413
+ operator (concatenating strings), 246
[] operator, overloading. *See* indexers
!= operator, 146
== operator, 146, 412
!= operator, 412
+ symbol, 195
\~ (tilde) indicator for Finalize methods, 468
64-bit Windows
   32-bit applications, running, 9–10
   assembly references, 81
   cache coherency of, 624–625
   IA64 (Itanium). *See* IA64 Windows
   loading CLR for, 8–10
   MSCorEE.dll file versions installed, 522
   multi-core CPUs with, 588
   PE32+ headers, 5
   platform switches, 8–10
   selection for with ProcessorArchitecture string, 550
   WoW64, 9–10

A

aborting threads, 544–547
abstract class constructors, 184
abstract type version effects, 164
abstraction technologies
   historical examples of, xxi
   .NET Framework goal for, xxi
   purpose of, xxi
   superiority of .NET, xxii
accessibility
   accessor methods, of, 224
   constructors, rule for, 184
   design guidelines, 171–172
   modifiers, 158–160

accessor methods
   accessibility issues, 224
   defined, 214
   generic, 224
   get methods of. *See* get methods
   indexers with, 218–222
   performance issues, 223–224
   PropertyInfo class for finding associations with, 223
   set methods of. *See* set methods
Activator class
   CreatInstance methods, 560–561
   CreatInstanceFrom methods, 561
Active Template Library (ATL), xxi
add-ins
   AppDomains, controlling, 542–543
   AppDomains with, 565
   application design for, 562–565
   assembly versioning issues, 563
   discovery for, 549, 564
   Host Application assemblies, 563
   Host SDK assembly creation, 563
   interfaces use in, 562–563
   MSCorLib.dll types for, 563
   sample code console applications, 564
   sample code for, 564
   sample code for hosts, 564
add instruction overflow checking, 121
Add method of Interlocked, 629–630
addition, overflow checking for, 121
AddMemoryPressure method, 507–510
/addmodule switch, 48
address spaces for applications, 17
administrative control configuration
   advanced, 88–93
   advantages of, 90
   assemblyIdentity elements, 89–90
   bindingRedirect elements, 89–90
   codeBase elements, 89, 90
   dependentAssembly elements, 89–90

P

Jeffrey Richter

Jeffrey Richter is a co-founder of Wintellect (*http://www.Wintellect.com/*), a training, design, and debugging company dedicated to helping companies produce better software faster. Jeff has written many books, including *Applied Microsoft .NET Framework Programming* (Microsoft Press, 2002), *Programming Applications for Microsoft Windows* (Microsoft Press, 1999) and *Programming Server-Side Applications for Microsoft Windows 2000* (Microsoft Press, 2000). Jeff is also a contributing editor for *MSDN Magazine*, where he has written several feature articles and is a columnist. Jeff also speaks at various trade conferences worldwide, including VSLive!, WinSummit, and Microsoft's TechEd and PDC.

Jeff has consulted for many companies, including AT&T, DreamWorks, General Electric, Hewlett-Packard, IBM, and Intel. Jeff's code has shipped in many Microsoft products, among them Microsoft Visual Studio, Microsoft Golf, Windows Sound System, and various versions of Microsoft Windows, from Windows 95 to Windows Vista and the Windows Server Family. Since October 1999, Jeff has consulted with the .NET Framework team and has used the .NET Framework to produce the XML Web service front end to Microsoft's very popular TerraServer Web property (*http://www.TerraService.net*).

On the personal front, Jeff holds both airplane and helicopter pilot licenses, though he never gets to fly as often as he'd like. He is also a member of the International Brotherhood of Magicians and enjoys showing friends sleight-of-hand card tricks from time to time. Jeff's other hobbies include music, drumming, and model railroading. He also enjoys traveling and the theater. He lives in Kirkland, Washington, with his wife, Kristin, and his son, Aidan.

Additional Resources for Web Developers

Published and Forthcoming Titles from Microsoft Press

Microsoft® Visual Web Developer™ 2005 Express Edition: Build a Web Site Now!
Jim Buyens ● ISBN 0-7356-2212-4

With this lively, eye-opening, and hands-on book, all you need is a computer and the desire to learn how to create Web pages now using Visual Web Developer Express Edition! Featuring a full working edition of the software, this fun and highly visual guide walks you through a complete Web page project from set-up to launch. You'll get an introduction to the Microsoft Visual Studio® environment and learn how to put the lightweight, easy-to-use tools in Visual Web Developer Express to work right away—building your first, dynamic Web pages with Microsoft ASP.NET 2.0. You'll get expert tips, coaching, and visual examples at each step of the way, along with pointers to additional learning resources.

Microsoft ASP.NET 2.0 Programming
Step by Step
George Shepherd ● ISBN 0-7356-2201-9

With dramatic improvements in performance, productivity, and security features, Visual Studio 2005 and ASP.NET 2.0 deliver a simplified, high-performance, and powerful Web development experience. ASP.NET 2.0 features a new set of controls and infrastructure that simplify Web-based data access and include functionality that facilitates code reuse, visual consistency, and aesthetic appeal. Now you can teach yourself the essentials of working with ASP.NET 2.0 in the Visual Studio environment— one step at a time. With *Step by Step*, you work at your own pace through hands-on, learn-by-doing exercises. Whether you're a beginning programmer or new to this version of the technology, you'll understand the core capabilities and fundamental techniques for ASP.NET 2.0. Each chapter puts you to work, showing you how, when, and why to use specific features of the ASP.NET 2.0 rapid application development environment and guiding you as you create actual components and working applications for the Web, including advanced features such as personalization.

Programming Microsoft ASP.NET 2.0
Core Reference
Dino Esposito ● ISBN 0-7356-2176-4

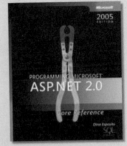

Delve into the core topics for ASP.NET 2.0 programming, mastering the essential skills and capabilities needed to build high-performance Web applications successfully. Well-known ASP.NET author Dino Esposito deftly builds your expertise with Web forms, Visual Studio, core controls, master pages, data access, data binding, state management, security services, and other must-know topics—combining definitive reference with practical, hands-on programming instruction. Packed with expert guidance and pragmatic examples, this *Core Reference* delivers the key resources that you need to develop professional-level Web programming skills.

Programming Microsoft ASP.NET 2.0
Applications: *Advanced Topics*
Dino Esposito ● ISBN 0-7356-2177-2

Master advanced topics in ASP.NET 2.0 programming—gaining the essential insights and in-depth understanding that you need to build sophisticated, highly functional Web applications successfully. Topics include Web forms, Visual Studio 2005, core controls, master pages, data access, data binding, state management, and security considerations. Developers often discover that the more they use ASP.NET, the more they need to know. With expert guidance from ASP.NET authority Dino Esposito, you get the in-depth, comprehensive information that leads to full mastery of the technology.

Programming Microsoft Windows® Forms
Charles Petzold ● ISBN 0-7356-2153-5

Programming Microsoft Web Forms
Douglas J. Reilly ● ISBN 0-7356-2179-9

CLR via C++
Jeffrey Richter with Stanley B. Lippman
ISBN 0-7356-2248-5

Debugging, Tuning, and Testing Microsoft .NET 2.0 Applications
John Robbins ● ISBN 0-7356-2202-7

CLR via C#, Second Edition
Jeffrey Richter ● ISBN 0-7356-2163-2

For more information about Microsoft Press® books and other learning products,
visit: **www.microsoft.com/books** *and* **www.microsoft.com/learning**

Additional Resources for Developers: Advanced Topics and Best Practices

Published and Forthcoming Titles from Microsoft Press

Code Complete, Second Edition
Steve McConnell • ISBN 0-7356-1967-0

For more than a decade, Steve McConnell, one of the premier authors and voices in the software community, has helped change the way developers write code—and produce better software. Now his classic book, *Code Complete*, has been fully updated and revised with best practices in the art and science of constructing software. Topics include design, applying good techniques to construction, eliminating errors, planning, managing construction activities, and relating personal character to superior software. This new edition features fully updated information on programming techniques, including the emergence of Web-style programming, and integrated coverage of object-oriented design. You'll also find new code examples—both good and bad—in C++, Microsoft® Visual Basic®, C#, and Java, although the focus is squarely on techniques and practices.

More About Software Requirements: Thorny Issues and Practical Advice
Karl E. Wiegers • ISBN 0-7356-2267-1

Have you ever delivered software that satisfied all of the project specifications, but failed to meet any of the customers expectations? Without formal, verifiable requirements—and a system for managing them—the result is often a gap between what developers think they're supposed to build and what customers think they're going to get. Too often, lessons about software requirements engi-neering processes are formal or academic, and not of value to real-world, professional development teams. In this follow-up guide to *Software Requirements*, Second Edition, you will discover even more practical techniques for gathering and managing software requirements that help you deliver software that meets project and customer specifications. Succinct and immediately useful, this book is a must-have for developers and architects.

Software Estimation: Demystifying the Black Art
Steve McConnell • ISBN 0-7356-0535-1

Often referred to as the "black art" because of its complexity and uncertainty, software estimation is not as hard or mysterious as people think. However, the art of how to create effective cost and schedule estimates has not been very well publicized. *Software Estimation* provides a proven set of procedures and heuristics that software developers, technical leads, and project managers can apply to their projects. Instead of arcane treatises and rigid modeling techniques, award-winning author Steve McConnell gives practical guidance to help organizations achieve basic estimation proficiency and lay the groundwork to continue improving project cost estimates. This book does not avoid the more complex mathematical estimation approaches, but the non-mathematical reader will find plenty of useful guidelines without getting bogged down in complex formulas.

Debugging, Tuning, and Testing Microsoft .NET 2.0 Applications
John Robbins • ISBN 0-7356-2202-7

Making an application the best it can be has long been a time-consuming task best accomplished with specialized and costly tools. With Microsoft Visual Studio® 2005, developers have available a new range of built-in functionality that enables them to debug their code quickly and efficiently, tune it to op-timum performance, and test applications to ensure compat-ibility and trouble-free operation. In this accessible and hands-on book, debugging expert John Robbins shows developers how to use the tools and functions in Visual Studio to their full advantage to ensure high-quality applications.

The Security Development Lifecycle
Michael Howard and Steve Lipner • ISBN 0-7356-2214-0

Adapted from Microsoft's standard development process, the Security Development Lifecycle (SDL) is a methodology that helps reduce the number of security defects in code at every stage of the development process, from design to release. This book details each stage of the SDL methodology and discusses its implementation across a range of Microsoft software, including Microsoft Windows Server™ 2003, Microsoft SQL Server™ 2000 Service Pack 3, and Microsoft Exchange Server 2003 Service Pack 1, to help measurably improve security features. You get direct access to insights from Microsoft's security team and lessons that are applicable to software development processes worldwide, whether on a small-scale or a large-scale. This book includes a CD featuring videos of developer training classes.

Software Requirements, Second Edition
Karl E. Wiegers • ISBN 0-7356-1879-8

Writing Secure Code, Second Edition
Michael Howard and David LeBlanc • ISBN 0-7356-1722-8

CLR via C#, Second Edition
Jeffrey Richter • ISBN 0-7356-2163-2

For more information about Microsoft Press® books and other learning products, visit: **www.microsoft.com/mspress** *and* **www.microsoft.com/learning**

Microsoft®
Press

Additional Resources for C# Developers

Published and Forthcoming Titles from Microsoft Press

Microsoft® Visual C#® 2005 Express Edition: Build a Program Now!
Patrice Pelland • ISBN 0-7356-2229-9

In this lively, eye-opening, and hands-on book, all you need is a computer and the desire to learn how to program with Visual C# 2005 Express Edition. Featuring a full working edition of the software, this fun and highly visual guide walks you through a complete programming project—a desktop weather-reporting application—from start to finish. You'll get an unintimidating introduction to the Microsoft Visual Studio® development environment and learn how to put the lightweight, easy-to-use tools in Visual C# Express to work right away—creating, compiling, testing, and delivering your first, ready-to-use program. You'll get expert tips, coaching, and visual examples at each step of the way, along with pointers to additional learning resources.

Microsoft Visual C# 2005 *Step by Step*
John Sharp • ISBN 0-7356-2129-2

Visual C#, a feature of Visual Studio 2005, is a modern programming language designed to deliver a productive environment for creating business frameworks and reusable object-oriented components. Now you can teach yourself essential techniques with Visual C#—and start building components and Microsoft Windows®–based applications—one step at a time. With *Step by Step*, you work at your own pace through hands-on, learn-by-doing exercises. Whether you're a beginning programmer or new to this particular language, you'll learn how, when, and why to use specific features of Visual C# 2005. Each chapter puts you to work, building your knowledge of core capabilities and guiding you as you create your first C#-based applications for Windows, data management, and the Web.

Programming Microsoft Visual C# 2005 Framework Reference
Francesco Balena • ISBN 0-7356-2182-9

Complementing *Programming Microsoft Visual C# 2005 Core Reference*, this book covers a wide range of additional topics and information critical to Visual C# developers, including Windows Forms, working with Microsoft ADO.NET 2.0 and Microsoft ASP.NET 2.0, Web services, security, remoting, and much more. Packed with sample code and real-world examples, this book will help developers move from understanding to mastery.

Programming Microsoft Visual C# 2005 *Core Reference*
Donis Marshall • ISBN 0-7356-2181-0

Get the in-depth reference and pragmatic, real-world insights you need to exploit the enhanced language features and core capabilities in Visual C# 2005. Programming expert Donis Marshall deftly builds your proficiency with classes, structs, and other fundamentals, and advances your expertise with more advanced topics such as debugging, threading, and memory management. Combining incisive reference with hands-on coding examples and best practices, this *Core Reference* focuses on mastering the C# skills you need to build innovative solutions for smart clients and the Web.

CLR via C#, Second Edition
Jeffrey Richter • ISBN 0-7356-2163-2

In this new edition of Jeffrey Richter's popular book, you get focused, pragmatic guidance on how to exploit the common language runtime (CLR) functionality in Microsoft .NET Framework 2.0 for applications of all types—from Web Forms, Windows Forms, and Web services to solutions for Microsoft SQL Server™, Microsoft code names "Avalon" and "Indigo," consoles, Microsoft Windows NT® Service, and more. Targeted to advanced developers and software designers, this book takes you under the covers of .NET for an in-depth understanding of its structure, functions, and operational components, demonstrating the most practical ways to apply this knowledge to your own development efforts. You'll master fundamental design tenets for .NET and get hands-on insights for creating high-performance applications more easily and efficiently. The book features extensive code examples in Visual C# 2005.

Programming Microsoft Windows Forms
Charles Petzold • ISBN 0-7356-2153-5

CLR via C++
Jeffrey Richter with Stanley B. Lippman
ISBN 0-7356-2248-5

Programming Microsoft Web Forms
Douglas J. Reilly • ISBN 0-7356-2179-9

Debugging, Tuning, and Testing Microsoft .NET 2.0 Applications
John Robbins • ISBN 0-7356-2202-7

For more information about Microsoft Press® books and other learning products, visit: **www.microsoft.com/books** *and* **www.microsoft.com/learning**

Additional SQL Server Resources for Developers

Published and Forthcoming Titles from Microsoft Press

Microsoft® SQL Server™ 2005 Express Edition
Step by Step
Jackie Goldstein • ISBN 0-7356-2184-5

Teach yourself how to get database projects up and running quickly with SQL Server Express Edition—a free, easy-to-use database product that is based on SQL Server 2005 technology. It's designed for building simple, dynamic applications, with all the rich functionality of the SQL Server database engine and using the same data access APIs, such as Microsoft ADO.NET, SQL Native Client, and T-SQL. Whether you're new to database programming or new to SQL Server, you'll learn how, when, and why to use specific features of this simple but powerful database development environment. Each chapter puts you to work, building your knowledge of core capabilities and guiding you as you create actual components and working applications.

Microsoft SQL Server 2005 Programming
Step by Step
Fernando Guerrero • ISBN 0-7356-2207-8

SQL Server 2005 is Microsoft's next-generation data management and analysis solution that delivers enhanced scalability, availability, and security features to enterprise data and analytical applications while making them easier to create, deploy, and manage. Now you can teach yourself how to design, build, test, deploy, and maintain SQL Server databases—one step at a time. Instead of merely focusing on describing new features, this book shows new database programmers and administrators how to use specific features within typical business scenarios. Each chapter provides a highly practical learning experience that demonstrates how to build database solutions to solve common business problems.

Microsoft SQL Server 2005 Analysis Services
Step by Step
Hitachi Consulting Services • ISBN 0-7356-2199-3

One of the key features of SQL Server 2005 is SQL Server Analysis Services—Microsoft's customizable analysis solution for business data modeling and interpretation. Just compare SQL Server Analysis Services to its competition to understand the great value of its enhanced features. One of the keys to harnessing the full functionality of SQL Server will be leveraging Analysis Services for the powerful tool that it is—including creating a cube, and deploying, customizing, and extending the basic calculations. This step-by-step tutorial discusses how to get started, how to build scalable analytical applications, and how to use and administer advanced features. Interactivity (enhanced in SQL Server 2005), data translation, and security are also covered in detail.

Microsoft SQL Server 2005 Reporting Services
Step by Step
Hitachi Consulting Services • ISBN 0-7356-2250-7

SQL Server Reporting Services (SRS) is Microsoft's customizable reporting solution for business data analysis. It is one of the key value features of SQL Server 2005: functionality more advanced and much less expensive than its competition. SRS is powerful, so an understanding of how to architect a report, as well as how to install and program SRS, is key to harnessing the full functionality of SQL Server. This procedural tutorial shows how to use the Report Project Wizard, how to think about and access data, and how to build queries. It also walks through the creation of charts and visual layouts for maximum visual understanding of data analysis. Interactivity (enhanced in SQL Server 2005) and security are also covered in detail.

Programming Microsoft SQL Server 2005
Andrew J. Brust, Stephen Forte, and William H. Zack
ISBN 0-7356-1923-9

This thorough, hands-on reference for developers and database administrators teaches the basics of programming custom applications with SQL Server 2005. You will learn the fundamentals of creating database applications—including coverage of T-SQL, Microsoft .NET Framework, and Microsoft ADO.NET. In addition to practical guidance on database architecture and design, application development, and reporting and data analysis, this essential reference guide covers performance, tuning, and availability of SQL Server 2005.

Inside Microsoft SQL Server 2005:
The Storage Engine
Kalen Delaney • ISBN 0-7356-2105-5

Inside Microsoft SQL Server 2005:
T-SQL Programming
Itzik Ben-Gan • ISBN 0-7356-2197-7

Inside Microsoft SQL Server 2005:
Query Processing and Optimization
Kalen Delaney • ISBN 0-7356-2196-9

Programming Microsoft ADO.NET 2.0 Core Reference
David Sceppa • ISBN 0-7356-2206-X

For more information about Microsoft Press® books and other learning products,
visit: **www.microsoft.com/mspress** *and* **www.microsoft.com/learning**

Microsoft®
Press

Additional Resources for Visual Basic Developers

Published and Forthcoming Titles from Microsoft Press

Microsoft® Visual Basic® 2005 Express Edition: Build a Program Now!
Patrice Pelland ● ISBN 0-7356-2213-2

Featuring a full working edition of the software, this fun and highly visual guide walks you through a complete programming project—a desktop weather-reporting application—from start to finish. You'll get an introduction to the Microsoft Visual Studio® development environment and learn how to put the lightweight, easy-to-use tools in Visual Basic Express to work right away—creating, compiling, testing, and delivering your first ready-to-use program. You'll get expert tips, coaching, and visual examples each step of the way, along with pointers to additional learning resources.

Microsoft Visual Basic 2005 *Step by Step*
Michael Halvorson ● ISBN 0-7356-2131-4

With enhancements across its visual designers, code editor, language, and debugger that help accelerate the development and deployment of robust, elegant applications across the Web, a business group, or an enterprise, Visual Basic 2005 focuses on enabling developers to rapidly build applications. Now you can teach yourself the essentials of working with Visual Studio 2005 and the new features of the Visual Basic language—one step at a time. Each chapter puts you to work, showing you how, when, and why to use specific features of Visual Basic and guiding as you create actual components and working applications for Microsoft Windows®. You'll also explore data management and Web-based development topics.

Programming Microsoft Visual Basic 2005 *Core Reference*
Francesco Balena ● ISBN 0-7356-2183-7

Get the expert insights, indispensable reference, and practical instruction needed to exploit the core language features and capabilities in Visual Basic 2005. Well-known Visual Basic programming author Francesco Balena expertly guides you through the fundamentals, including modules, keywords, and inheritance, and builds your mastery of more advanced topics such as delegates, assemblies, and My Namespace. Combining in-depth reference with extensive, hands-on code examples and best-practices advice, this *Core Reference* delivers the key resources that you need to develop professional-level programming skills for smart clients and the Web.

Programming Microsoft Visual Basic 2005 Framework Reference
Francesco Balena ● ISBN 0-7356-2175-6

Complementing *Programming Microsoft Visual Basic 2005 Core Reference*, this book covers a wide range of additional topics and information critical to Visual Basic developers, including Windows Forms, working with Microsoft ADO.NET 2.0 and ASP.NET 2.0, Web services, security, remoting, and much more. Packed with sample code and real-world examples, this book will help developers move from understanding to mastery.

Programming Microsoft Windows Forms
Charles Petzold ● ISBN 0-7356-2153-5

Programming Microsoft Web Forms
Douglas J. Reilly ● ISBN 0-7356-2179-9

Debugging, Tuning, and Testing Microsoft .NET 2.0 Applications
John Robbins ● ISBN 0-7356-2202-7

Microsoft ASP.NET 2.0 *Step by Step*
George Shepherd ● ISBN 0-7356-2201-9

Microsoft ADO.NET 2.0 *Step by Step*
Rebecca Riordan ● ISBN 0-7356-2164-0

Programming Microsoft ASP.NET 2.0 *Core Reference*
Dino Esposito ● ISBN 0-7356-2176-4

For more information about Microsoft Press® books and other learning products,
visit: **www.microsoft.com/books** *and* **www.microsoft.com/learning**

Prepare for Certification with Self-Paced Training Kits

Official Exam Prep Guides—
Plus Practice Tests

Ace your preparation for the skills measured by the MCP exams—and on the job. With official *Self-Paced Training Kits* from Microsoft, you'll work at your own pace through a system of lessons, hands-on exercises, troubleshooting labs, and review questions. Then test yourself with the Readiness Review Suite on CD, which provides hundreds of challenging questions for in-depth self-assessment and practice.

- **MCSE Self-Paced Training Kit (Exams 70-290, 70-291, 70-293, 70-294): Microsoft® Windows Server™ 2003 Core Requirements.** 4-Volume Boxed Set. ISBN: 0-7356-1953-0. (Individual volumes are available separately.)

- **MCSA/MCSE Self-Paced Training Kit (Exam 70-270): Installing, Configuring, and Administering Microsoft Windows® XP Professional, Second Edition.** ISBN: 0-7356-2152-7.

- **MCSE Self-Paced Training Kit (Exam 70-298): Designing Security for a Microsoft Windows Server 2003 Network.** ISBN: 0-7356-1969-7.

- **MCSA/MCSE Self-Paced Training Kit (Exam 70-350): Implementing Microsoft Internet Security and Acceleration Server 2004.** ISBN: 0-7356-2169-1.

- **MCSA/MCSE Self-Paced Training Kit (Exam 70-284): Implementing and Managing Microsoft Exchange Server 2003.** ISBN: 0-7356-1899-2.

For more information about Microsoft Press® books, visit: **www.microsoft.com/mspress**

For more information about learning tools such as online assessments, e-learning, and certification, visit: **www.microsoft.com/mspress** *and* **www.microsoft.com/learning**

Microsoft Windows Server 2003 Resource Kit

The *definitive* resource

for Windows Server 2003!

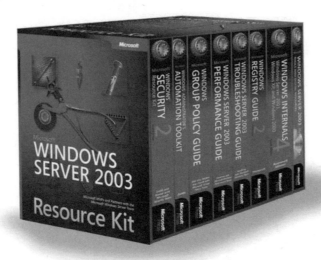

Get the in-depth technical information and tools you need to manage and optimize Microsoft® Windows Server™ 2003—with expert guidance and best practices from Microsoft MVPs, leading industry consultants, and the Microsoft Windows Server team. This official *Resource Kit* delivers seven comprehensive volumes, including:

- **Microsoft Windows® Security Resource Kit, Second Edition**
- **Microsoft Windows Administrator's Automation Toolkit**
- **Microsoft Windows Group Policy Guide**
- **Microsoft Windows Server 2003 Performance Guide**
- **Microsoft Windows Server 2003 Troubleshooting Guide**
- **Microsoft Windows Registry Guide, Second Edition**
- **Microsoft Windows Internals, Fourth Edition**

You'll find 300+ timesaving tools and scripts, an eBook of the entire *Resource Kit*, plus five bonus eBooks. It's everything you need to help maximize system performance and reliability—and help reduce ownership and support costs.

Microsoft Windows Server 2003 Resource Kit
Microsoft MVPs and Partners with the Microsoft Windows Server Team
ISBN: 0-7356-2232-9

For more information about Microsoft Press® books, visit: **www.microsoft.com/mspress**

For more information about learning tools such as online assessments, e-learning, and certification, visit: **www.microsoft.com/learning**

Microsoft®
Press

Additional Windows (R2) Resources for Administrators

Published and Forthcoming Titles from Microsoft Press

Microsoft® Windows Server™ 2003 Administrator's Pocket Consultant, Second Edition

William R. Stanek • ISBN 0-7356-2245-0

Here's the practical, pocket-sized reference for IT professionals supporting Microsoft Windows Server 2003—fully updated for Service Pack 1 and Release 2. Designed for quick referencing, this portable guide covers all the essentials for performing everyday system administration tasks. Topics include managing workstations and servers, using Active Directory® directory service, creating and administering user and group accounts, managing files and directories, performing data security and auditing tasks, handling data back-up and recovery, and administering networks using TCP/IP, WINS, and DNS, and more.

MCSE Self-Paced Training Kit (Exams 70-290, 70-291, 70-293, 70-294): Microsoft Windows Server 2003 Core Requirements, Second Edition

Holme, Thomas, Mackin, McLean, Zacker, Spealman, Hudson, and Craft • ISBN 0-7356-2290-6

The Microsoft Certified Systems Engineer (MCSE) credential is the premier certification for professionals who analyze the business requirements and design and implement the infrastructure for business solutions based on the Microsoft Windows Server 2003 platform and Microsoft Windows Server System—now updated for Windows Server 2003 Service Pack 1 and R2. This all-in-one set provides in-depth preparation for the four required networking system exams. Work at your own pace through the lessons, hands-on exercises, troubleshooting labs, and review questions. You get expert exam tips plus a full review section covering all objectives and sub-objectives in each study guide. Then use the Microsoft Practice Tests on the CD to challenge yourself with more than 1500 questions for self-assessment and practice!

Microsoft Windows® Small Business Server 2003 R2 Administrator's Companion

Charlie Russel, Sharon Crawford, and Jason Gerend • ISBN 0-7356-2280-9

Get your small-business network, messaging, and collaboration systems up and running quickly with the essential guide to administering Windows Small Business Server 2003 R2. This reference details the features, capabilities, and technologies for both the standard and premium editions—including Microsoft Windows Server 2003 R2, Exchange Server 2003 with Service Pack 1, Windows SharePoint® Services, SQL Server™ 2005 Workgroup

Edition, and Internet Information Services. Discover how to install, upgrade, or migrate to Windows Small Business Server 2003 R2; plan and implement your network, Internet access, and security services; customize Microsoft Exchange Server for your e-mail needs; and administer user rights, shares, permissions, and Group Policy.

Microsoft Windows Small Business Server 2003 R2 Administrator's Companion

Charlie Russel, Sharon Crawford, and Jason Gerend • ISBN 0-7356-2280-9

Here's the ideal one-volume guide for the IT professional administering Windows Server 2003. Now fully updated for Windows Server 2003 Service Pack 1 and R2, this *Administrator's Companion* offers up-to-date information on core system administration topics for Microsoft Windows, including Active Directory services, security, scripting, disaster planning and recovery, and interoperability with UNIX. It also includes all-new sections on Service Pack 1 security updates and new features for R2. Featuring easy-to-use procedures and handy work-arounds, this book provides ready answers for on-the-job results.

MCSA/MCSE Self-Paced Training Kit (Exam 70-290): Managing and Maintaining a Microsoft Windows Server 2003 Environment, Second Edition

Dan Holme and Orin Thomas • ISBN 0-7356-2289-2

MCSA/MCSE Self-Paced Training Kit (Exam 70-291): Implementing, Managing, and Maintaining a Microsoft Windows Server 2003 Network Infrastructure, Second Edition

J.C. Mackin and Ian McLean • ISBN 0-7356-2288-4

MCSE Self-Paced Training Kit (Exam 70-293): Planning and Maintaining a Microsoft Windows Server 2003 Network Infrastructure, Second Edition

Craig Zacker • ISBN 0-7356-2287-6

MCSE Self-Paced Training Kit (Exam 70-294): Planning, Implementing, and Maintaining a Microsoft Windows Server 2003 Active Directory® Infrastructure, Second Ed.

Jill Spealman, Kurt Hudson, and Melissa Craft • ISBN 0-7356-2286-8

For more information about Microsoft Press® books and other learning products, visit: **www.microsoft.com/mspress** *and* **www.microsoft.com/learning**

Microsoft® Press

Additional SQL Server Resources for Administrators

Published and Forthcoming Titles from Microsoft Press

Microsoft® SQL Server™ 2005 Reporting Services *Step by Step*

Hitachi Consulting Services ● ISBN 0-7356-2250-7

SQL Server Reporting Services (SRS) is Microsoft's customizable reporting solution for business data analysis. It is one of the key value features of SQL Server 2005: functionality more advanced and much less expensive than its competition. SRS is powerful, so an understanding of how to architect a report, as well as how to install and program SRS, is key to harnessing the full functionality of SQL

Server. This procedural tutorial shows how to use the Report Project Wizard, how to think about and access data, and how to build queries. It also walks the reader through the creation of charts and visual layouts to enable maximum visual understanding of the data analysis. Interactivity (enhanced in SQL Server 2005) and security are also covered in detail.

Microsoft SQL Server 2005 Administrator's Pocket Consultant

William R. Stanek ● ISBN 0-7356-2107-1

Here's the utterly practical, pocket-sized reference for IT professionals who need to administer, optimize, and maintain SQL Server 2005 in their organizations. This unique guide provides essential details for using SQL Server 2005 to help protect and manage your company's data—whether automating tasks; creating indexes and views; performing backups and recovery; replicating transactions; tuning performance; managing server

activity; importing and exporting data; or performing other key tasks. Featuring quick-reference tables, lists, and step-by-step instructions, this handy, one-stop guide provides fast, accurate answers on the spot, whether you're at your desk or in the field!

Microsoft SQL Server 2005 Administrator's Companion

Marci Frohock Garcia, Edward Whalen, and Mitchell Schroeter ● ISBN 0-7356-2198-5

Microsoft SQL Server 2005 Administrator's Companion is the comprehensive, in-depth guide that saves time by providing all the technical information you need to deploy, administer, optimize, and support SQL Server 2005. Using a hands-on, example-rich approach, this authoritative, one-volume reference book provides expert advice, product information, detailed solutions, procedures, and real-world troubleshooting tips from experienced SQL Server 2005 professionals. This expert guide shows you how to design high-availability database systems, prepare for installation, install and configure SQL Server 2005, administer services and features, and maintain and troubleshoot your database system. It covers how to configure your system for your I/O system and model and optimize system capacity. The expert authors provide details on how to create and use defaults, constraints, rules, indexes, views, functions, stored procedures, and triggers. This guide shows you how to administer reporting services, analysis services, notification services, and integration services. It also provides a wealth of information on replication and the specifics of snapshot, transactional, and merge replication. Finally, there is expansive coverage of how to manage and tune your SQL Server system, including automating tasks, backup and restoration of databases, and management of users and security.

Microsoft SQL Server 2005 Analysis Services *Step by Step*

Hitachi Consulting Services ● ISBN 0-7356-2199-3

One of the key features of SQL Server 2005 is SQL Server Analysis Services—Microsoft's customizable analysis solution for business data modeling and interpretation. Just compare SQL Server Analysis Services to its competition to understand/grasp the great value of its enhanced features. One of the keys to harnessing the full functionality of SQL Server will be leveraging Analysis Services for the powerful tool that it is—including creating a cube, and deploying, customizing, and extending the basic calculations. This step-by-step tutorial discusses how to get started, how to build scalable analytical applications, and how to use and administer advanced features. Interactivity (which is enhanced in SQL Server 2005), data translation, and security are also covered in detail.

Microsoft SQL Server 2005 Express Edition
Step by Step
Jackie Goldstein ● ISBN 0-7356-2184-5

Inside Microsoft SQL Server 2005:
The Storage Engine
Kalen Delaney ● ISBN 0-7356-2105-5

Inside Microsoft SQL Server 2005:
T-SQL Programming
Itzik Ben-Gan ● ISBN 0-7356-2197-7

Inside Microsoft SQL Server 2005:
Query Processing and Optimization
Kalen Delaney ● ISBN 0-7356-2196-9

For more information about Microsoft Press® books and other learning products,
visit: **www.microsoft.com/mspress** *and* **www.microsoft.com/learning**

Microsoft Press products are available worldwide wherever quality computer books are sold. For more information, contact your book or computer retailer, software reseller, or local Microsoft Sales Office, or visit our Web site at **www.microsoft.com/mspress**. To locate your nearest source for Microsoft Press products, or to order directly, call 1-800-MSPRESS in the United States. (In Canada, call **1-800-268-2222**.)

Additional Resources for Business and Home Users

Published and Forthcoming Titles from Microsoft Press

Beyond Bullet Points: Using Microsoft® PowerPoint® to Create Presentations That Inform, Motivate, and Inspire
Cliff Atkinson • ISBN 0-7356-2052-0

Improve your presentations—and increase your impact—with 50 powerful, practical, and easy-to-apply techniques for Microsoft PowerPoint. With *Beyond Bullet Points*, you'll take your presentation skills to the next level—learning innovative ways to design and deliver your message. Organized into five sections, including Distill Your Ideas, Structure Your Story, Visualize Your Message, Create a Conversation, and Maintain Engagement—the book uses clear, concise language and just the right visuals to help you understand concepts and start getting better results.

Take Back Your Life! Special Edition: Using Microsoft Outlook® to Get Organized and Stay Organized
Sally McGhee • ISBN 0-7356-2215-9

Unrelenting e-mail. Conflicting commitments. Endless interruptions. In this book, productivity expert Sally McGhee shows you how to take control and reclaim something that you thought you'd lost forever—your work-life balance. Now you can benefit from Sally's popular and highly regarded corporate education programs, learning simple but powerful techniques for rebalancing your personal and professional commitments using the productivity features in Outlook. When you change your approach, you can change your results. So learn what thousands of Sally's clients worldwide have discovered about taking control of their everyday productivity—and start transforming your own life today!

On Time! On Track! On Target! Managing Your Projects Successfully with Microsoft Project
Bonnie Biafore • ISBN 0-7356-2256-6

This book focuses on the core skills you need to successfully manage any project, giving you a practical education in project management and how-to instruction for using Microsoft Office Project Professional 2003 and other Microsoft Office Professional Edition 2003 programs, such as Excel® 2003, Outlook 2003, and Word 2003. Learn the essentials of project management, including creating successful project plans, tracking and evaluating performance, and controlling project costs. Whether you're a beginner just learning how to manage projects or a project manager already working on a project, this book has something for you. Includes a companion CD with sample Project templates.

Design to Sell: Using Microsoft Publisher to Inform, Motivate, and Persuade
Roger C. Parker • ISBN 0-7356-2260-4

Design to Sell relates the basics of effective message creation and formatting to the specific capabilities built into Microsoft Publisher—the powerful page layout program found on hundreds of thousands of computers around the world. Many Microsoft Office users already have Publisher on their computers but don't use it because they don't think of themselves as writers or designers. Here is a one-stop guide to marketing that even those without big budgets or previous design or writing experience can use to create compelling, easy-to-read marketing materials. Each chapter has an interactive exercise as well as questions with answers on the author's Web site. Also on the Web site are downloadable worksheets and templates, book updates, more illustrations of the projects in the book, and additional before-and-after project makeovers.

Microsoft Windows® XP Networking and Security Inside Out: Also Covers Windows 2000
Ed Bott and Carl Siechert • ISBN 0-7356-2042-3

Configure and manage your PC network—and help combat privacy and security threats—from the inside out! Written by the authors of the immensely popular *Microsoft Windows XP Inside Out*, this book packs hundreds of timesaving solutions, troubleshooting tips, and work-arounds for networking and security topics—all in concise, fast-answer format.

Dig into the tools and techniques for configuring workgroup, domain, Internet, and remote networking, and all the network components and features in between. Get the answers you need to use Windows XP Service Pack 2 and other tools, tactics, and features to help defend your personal computer and network against spyware, pop-up ads, viruses, hackers, spam, denial-of-service attacks, and other threats. Learn how to help secure your Virtual Private Networks (VPNs), remote access, and wireless networking services, and take ultimate control with advanced solutions such as file encryption, port blocking, IPSec, group policies, and tamper-proofing tactics for the registry. Get up to date on hot topics such as peer-to-peer networks, public wireless access points, smart cards, handheld computers, wireless LANs, and more. Plus, the CD includes bonus resources that make it easy for you to share your new security and networking expertise with your colleagues, friends, and family.
